FOUNDATIONS,
RETAINING
AND
EARTH STRUCTURES

FOUNDATIONS, RETAINING AND EARTH STRUCTURES

The Art of Design and Construction and Its Scientific Basis in Soil Mechanics

GREGORY P. TSCHEBOTARIOFF
Consulting Engineer, P.E.
Dipl.Ing.   Dr.Ing.   Dr.h.c.

Second Edition
of SOIL MECHANICS, FOUNDATIONS, and EARTH STRUCTURES
INTERNATIONAL STUDENT EDITION

McGRAW-HILL KOGAKUSHA, LTD.

Tokyo   Düsseldorf   Johannesburg   London   Mexico
New Delhi   Panama   Rio de Janeiro   Singapore   Sydney

Library of Congress Cataloging in Publication Data

Tschebotarioff, Gregory Porphyriewitch, date.
  Foundations, retaining and earth structures.

  First ed. published in 1951 under title: Soil
mechanics, foundations, and earth structures.
  Bibliography: p.
  1. Foundations.   2. Soil mechanics.   3. Earthwork.
I. Title.
TA775.T78   1973   624'.15   72-11824
ISBN 0-07-065377-1

*The editors for this book were William G. Salo, Jr., and
Ross J. Kepler, the designer was Naomi Auerbach, and its production
was supervised by Stephen J. Boldish.   It was set in Baskerville
by Santype Limited.*

TOSHO PRINTING COMPANY, LTD. TOKYO

CONTENTS

PREFACE TO THE SECOND EDITION

The title of this book, *Foundations, Retaining and Earth Structures,* reflects a change of emphasis when it is compared with the title of the first edition, *Soil Mechanics, Foundations, and Earth Structures,* which appeared in 1951.

The overall objective of both editions remains the same, namely, to illustrate by practical examples (1) the strong element of art in all soil and foundation work, (2) the limitations imposed on the validity of rigorous mathematical solutions by the extremely complex interrelationship between the relevant soil properties and the structural design and the construction procedures used, and (3) the numerous factors which must be considered and weighed in order to arrive at safe and economical solutions.

Perhaps as a consequence of some modern aberrations in painting and sculpture, the word *art* may imply something esoteric to nonengineers. A definition of its use in this book is therefore indicated.

The terms *art* and *science* are frequently and loosely interchanged in common usage. This can be seen, for instance, by comparing some of the seven definitions of the word *art* in the *American Heritage Dictionary of the English Language* (1969) with some of the six definitions of the word *science* in the same dictionary.

An examination of the definition given there first for each of these two terms, however, shows that, although both deal with the forces and phenomena of nature, *science* is primarily concerned with the determination of the characteristics of these phenomena, whereas *art* is concerned with putting these established characteristics to human use by evolving a system of procedures to do so.   It is therefore not by chance that the phrase *art of building* is used by this dictionary as an illustration of one of the meanings of the word *art*.

In the Russian-language translation of the first edition, edited by Professor N. N. Maslov of Moscow, my words *art in engineering* were freely translated as *the creative element in engineering*.   This expresses very well the meaning I attach to the term.

I do not use the term *applied science* instead of *art* in this book.   This is partly because of its misuse at some universities to promote mathematically rigorous analyses of engineering problems without proper consideration of the physical validity of assumptions made and of the results obtained (see my relevant comments in Art. 1-10).   But I avoid using the term *applied science* mainly because the exercise of "art" or of "the creative element" in engineering requires much more than just the ability to supply scientific facts to an isolated engineering problem.   In addition, it requires the ability to coordinate these scientific facts with the practical requirements of other problems on which the success of the overall project depends and which can only be estimated—such as possible construction procedures, available equipment, costs, and environmental effects.   The relative importance of all these and of other factors has to be weighed, and this requires the exercise of common sense in its broadest meaning.   The analysis of performance case histories of past engineering projects is a good way to develop a feeling for the mental processes required for a successful handling of real-life projects at all levels.   This is much more exacting than can or should be expected from "applied scientists," accustomed to deal with rigorous solutions of isolated problems, or from "technicians" trained in details of trade skills and technology.

During the past twenty years the writer, as a consultant for different clients, has had an opportunity to study and analyze many kinds of difficulties and problems encountered in soil and foundation engineering practice.   The performance case histories thus obtained are incorporated in this edition and serve to develop further the relevant aspects of the first edition which primarily account for its long success and that of its translations into Japanese, Russian, and Spanish.

The number of illustrations in this edition is about 4 per cent greater than that of the first edition, and only about 47 per cent of the total were taken from the first edition.   Approximately the same proportions apply to the text.

Some cuts have been made to compensate for the new material added, but their nature is such that they do not impair the objectives and the effectiveness of the book.   Many of the data concerning details of the writer's anchored-bulkhead and other related large-scale model research have been omitted because these results, obtained in the late 1940s, have since been confirmed elsewhere and are no longer questioned by the profession at large. Therefore only a summary of the findings and of their practical significance, which is still valid, are now given. Much of the detailed presentation of the elementary theory of soil mechanics and nearly all relevant derivations (which were contained in Chaps. 3 to 10 of the first edition) have been eliminated. The essentials of soil testing have been condensed into Chap. 3, which is cross-referenced to summaries of relevant theoretical highlights in other chapters.

A great number of elementary soil-mechanics books have appeared in recent years, and it would be an unproductive waste of effort to try to include their scope in a book like this one. However, to facilitate more detailed refresher reading on theoretical topics, references to appropriate recent and past publications are made throughout the book, and the extensive list of references of the first edition has been completely revised and brought up to date. The total number of references has been reduced only slightly, from 448 to 416. Of these 268, or 64 per cent, are new. Some of the old references have not been eliminated either because they represent milestones in the development of the field or because they describe certain important facts better than this was done in later publications. Many of the detailed presentations in the first edition, which are now omitted to economize space, nevertheless have not lost their validity. Therefore references to the relevant articles of the first edition are made where this is advisable.

Since it was assumed in the first edition that the reader would be familiar with the details of reinforced-concrete design, the determination of the depth of concrete and of the steel reinforcement was not included. This approach has been maintained in the present edition and, as explained above, is extended to details of introductory soil-mechanics theory and laboratory soil testing, which are now more widely known than they were two decades ago.

Therefore the present edition is not recommended for an introductory undergraduate course, as the first half of the first edition occasionally was used. The present edition is primarily oriented toward the categories of engineers who responded most favorably to the first edition, namely, engineers in active practice and instructors and students of graduate-level foundation-engineering courses.

To enhance the book's usefulness in such professionally oriented university or continuing-education courses, I have made arrangements to reproduce in sets some 215 slides from my collection. One third are in color. All are of the standard 2 in. by 2 in. (5 cm by 5 cm) size and are consecutively numbered. These selected slides illustrate 19 of the performance case histories briefly described in the text of the book, where only 41 illustrations could be used because of space limitations. Interested lecturers should write to me, through the publisher, for a free 25-page typewritten descriptive list of these 215 slides which connects them to relevant passages in the book. I will then supply on request slide sets on a nonprofit basis at a cost which will be indicated on the list and which will cover only reproduction and handling expenses.

Various tests and methods of analysis are not merely outlined, but are critically evaluated. Specific recommendations are made concerning the limits of their use and applications. Throughout the book emphasis is on differentiation between what is definitely known and what is only surmised, requiring greater caution and higher factors of safety in the latter case.

Some new topics—the inclined bracing of the lining of wide cuts in soft ground, the lateral pressures of clay layers against piles supporting bridge abutments with high adjoining embankment fills, and the dowel action of piles intersecting shearing slip planes—are examined on the basis of experimental data. A theoretical approach to the practical treatment of relevant design problems is suggested.

The results of full-scale field measurements are often referred to in the book. The extension of their use is advocated by outlining new improvements in the techniques of such measurements. The role of new analytical tools, such as stress-path, finite-element, and wave-equation methods, is also briefly examined.

The expected adoption of metric units in the United States has been recognized by giving the metric equivalents in parentheses after values expressed in the foot-pound system. As explained below under Notation, this has been complicated by the fact that the metric designations of force are in a state of imprecise transition. Since the new unit of force, the newton, is not yet universally recognized and another unit of force, the pond, serves the same purpose in some countries, neither is used in the present book, although conversion factors are given below under Notation to facilitate the study of some foreign references. Instead, grams and kilograms are used in this book with the subscript f added to indicate that they refer to units of force.

In general, the book attempts to develop a broad picture of the subject which would be useful not only to soil-engineering specialists, but also at the interfaces of the specialties involved in relevant decision making, namely soil engineers, structural engineers, and architect-engineer administrators. In performing postmortems of various failures, the writer has found that in the vast majority of serious cases the basic cause of the trouble was a lack of broad understanding of their border fields by representatives of these three specialties.

Material for this revised edition has been accumulated over the past two decades. However, the start of detailed work thereon coincided with my decision to retire from 16 years of exclusive part-time association with the firm of King and Gavaris, consulting engineers of New York City. In this connection I wish to express my appreciation to Philip King and to Peter Gavaris for several dispensations they gave me to investigate directly for other consulting engineers, construction firms, and federal and state agencies some specially interesting soil and foundation problems encountered by them, including failures. This was in addition to my participation in the regular highway and harbor engineering work of their firm on three continents. Important field measurements on full-scale structures were also performed by their firm under the writer's guidance.

A great many individuals have helped me obtain data referred to in this book. I am particularly indebted to Professor John F. Kennedy, Director, Institute Hydraulic Research, University of Iowa, for reviewing Chap. 12 on Cofferdams; to Professor José A. Jiménez-Salas, Chairman of the Organizing Committee, Fifth European Conference on Soil Mechanics and Foundation Engineering (Madrid, April 1972) for sending me microfilm copies of the conference papers for advance study; and to Professor G. A. Leonards, Chairman, ASCE Soil Mechanics and Foundation Engineering Division Task Committee on Specialty Conferences, for providing me with advance information on relevant papers submitted for publication by the ASCE Specialty Conference on Performance of Earth and Earth Supported Structures at Purdue University in June 1972. Professor Ernest T. Selig of the State University of New York at Buffalo has reviewed the entire manuscript and has made valuable suggestions.

Finally, I should mention with gratitude that I first had the opportunity to outline the planned scope of this revised edition in connection with the evening course CE825, Advanced Foundations and Substructures, which I gave as a visiting professor at the University of Delaware in the spring term of 1969 for practicing engineers and graduate students in the Civil Engineering Department, of which Professor Eugene Chesson, Jr., is chairman.

My wife, Florence B. Tschebotarioff, as usual, has helped me by editing the text. Willard Starks did most of the supporting photographic work. Geraldine DiCicco typed the manuscript.

GREGORY P. TSCHEBOTARIOFF

LAWRENCEVILLE, NEW JERSEY
January, 1973

FOREWORD TO FIRST EDITION

This book has characteristics which will, I believe, lead to its recognition as a publication of real importance. It should, first of all, be of great value to the student as a text. Secondly, its clarity and readability commend it to the engineer who wishes to improve and broaden his knowledge of soil mechanics and allied subjects. Finally, it should prove an invaluable reference to the practicing engineer who handles foundation work and the engineering of earth structures. This is because it not only describes the way in which the techniques of soil mechanics can lead to sound solutions of many problems in these fields but it also acknowledges the limitations of these techniques, and, indeed, of our present-day knowledge of many soil phenomena.

Over a quarter of a century has passed since Dr. Karl Terzaghi coined the German term "Erdbaumechanik" which, freely translated, gave to English-speaking engineers the term "soil mechanics." Since then many books, papers, and publications on soil mechanics have appeared in English. Many of these possess great merit and practically all contain information of value either to the student, the teacher, or the practicing engineer.

The great value of this new book by Professor Tschebotarioff stems, I believe, from the unusually broad and firm foundation of practical experience upon which it rests. Its author is firstly an engineer of wide experience both in America and abroad. Teaching has enabled him to develop, to an unusual degree, his native gift for imparting knowledge to others. Finally, his teaching career has been carried on simultaneously with consulting and research work which have not merely kept him abreast of the times, but made him an outstanding pioneer in the investigation of such important phenomena as earth pressures.   The results of his extensive research in this field are given in this book and should alone make it invaluable to practicing engineers.   In addition it is a general text of outstanding merit on *Soil Mechanics, Foundations, and Earth Structures.*

W. MACK ANGAS
Vice Admiral, Civil Engineer Corps
United States Navy, Retired

PREFACE TO FIRST EDITION

This book has been developed from lecture notes for courses which the author has given at Princeton University since 1937, when undergraduate instruction in soil mechanics was started in the Department of Civil Engineering.   Instruction at a graduate level followed a few years later.†

In this work the author was guided by the following thoughts.   Every civil engineer should be prepared to deal with soil engineering and foundation problems and should therefore have a general knowledge of the fundamentals involved.   However, the first thing to be learned about soils is that they differ in several important aspects from other materials which civil engineers have to handle.   An essentially different approach to their study is therefore indicated.   The strength and the deformation characteristics and other engineering properties are not constant for a given soil but may be altered appreciably with time and by the manner in which construction operations are carried out.   Stress analyses in soil masses are much more complex than in other civil engineering structures.   Rigorous solutions are therefore often based on oversimplified assumptions and hence have only a limited value.   By contrast, experimental procedures, which include measurements on full-scale structures, often yield information of decisive importance.   Previously accepted theories frequently have to be modified or even rejected on the basis of new experimental data.   Such data are

† See first edition, Refs. 376 and 394.

far from easy to obtain and at present are rather limited, so that some latitude is still left for the exercise of judgment as to the proper use of existing theories.   Hence the strong element of art in all soil and foundation engineering work should not be overlooked.   The acknowledgment of its existence is necessary for the understanding of the present status of this field of knowledge and endeavor, as well as of the methods of approach which are essential for its further advancement.   This requires the cooperation of the entire civil engineering profession.

These facts lead to the conclusion that an introductory presentation of the theories of soil mechanics should be closely linked to a brief description of the related design and construction practices of soil and foundation engineering.   This principle has been followed in this book, which is intended for use at undergraduate and graduate levels and as a general reference.

The past quarter of a century has seen an exceptionally rapid growth of our knowledge concerning the engineering properties of soils.   Many time-honored concepts have been proved invalid by the new semiempirical techniques of correlated field observations, laboratory testing, and theoretical analyses.   New concepts have been introduced.   Many of these concepts have successfully withstood the test of repeated checks in the field.   The understandable pressure from practicing engineers for the accelerated development of new simplified guiding rules, combined with the incomplete data as yet available concerning many essential points, however, has led in some instances to the premature acceptance of generalizations which later were shown to be unwarranted.   This has been the case in a number of special fields of considerable practical importance; for instance, in problems concerned with the effects of sensitivity of different types of clay to remolding; with the effects of plastic flow on the shearing strength and on the lateral pressures of clay; with the natural frequency of soils subjected to vibrations; and with the effects of so-called "arching" on the lateral pressures of sands.   An uninterrupted continuation of this process of reexamination and reevaluation is necessary for the further healthy development of soil engineering.   A constructively critical attitude is a prerequisite to that end; to be effective, it has to be combined with a thorough knowledge of the factual basis on which our modern concepts have been erected.

Considerable space in this book has therefore been devoted to records of failures, of field measurements and to other experimental evidence.   Emphasis has been placed on differentiation between hypotheses and proven facts.   The importance of understanding by civil engineers of allied geotechnical sciences, especially geology and soil physics, is demonstrated by examples.   The effect on the soil engineering practice in different countries of varied geological, climatic, and economic conditions have been stressed.

Whenever possible, theoretical concepts have been developed from first principles along lines most familiar to American engineers. For instance, the equations of the so-called "classical" earth-pressure theories, instead of being explained by references to conjugate stresses, have been derived from the equilibrium conditions of a small prism, as is done in most undergraduate textbooks on mechanics of materials when developing the concept of principal stresses. Evaluations have been made of the limits of practical application of theories and of points of view, especially when some of them are in conflict with each other.

The wide field covered by the book compelled numerous cross references and a very condensed presentation, which was facilitated by the provision of a large number of diagrams (approximately 400) and of other illustrations. Case problems and their numerical solutions have been used for the same purpose. Repetition of material available in regularly used textbooks on other subjects has been avoided. For instance, the determination of the depth of concrete and of the steel reinforcement of footings and of retaining walls has not been included in the book. A few selected references are given at the end of each chapter to permit a more detailed study of the subject matter treated in that chapter. In addition, an extensive list of more than 440 references has been provided at the end of the book in support of statements made and to facilitate further advanced studies, including work of a research character.

Our present knowledge of the engineering properties of soils is the result of work by many men in different countries all over the world, and every effort has been made to give in the text of the book proper credit to the pioneers in this field, as well as to their successors.

The author acknowledges the valuable experience he gained on the banks of the Nile while in the service of the Egyptian Government (1929 to 1936) and the splendid opportunities for further research which arose for him at Princeton University from projects in the field of applied soil mechanics sponsored by the Technical Development Service of the Civil Aeronautics Administration (1943 to 1946) and, especially by the Bureau of Yards and Docks of the United States Navy (1943 to 1949) and the Earth Sciences Division of the Office of Naval Research in Washington, D.C. Very valuable data concerning lateral earth pressure measurements in the approach cuts to the Rotterdam subaqueous tunnel became available through the courtesy of Mr. J. P. van Bruggen, Chief Director of Public Works, Rotterdam, The Netherlands. Private consulting work also served to provide a substantial amount of material for this book. The author is particularly indebted to Spencer, White and Prentis, Inc., of New York City, who not only released data obtained by him when serving as their consultant, but supplied further valuable and so far unpublished information. The cooperation in research work by Sprague and Henwood, Inc., of Scranton, Pennsylvania, is much appreciated, as well as the preparation by that firm of several drawings for this book. Other acknowledgments are made in the text.

The author wishes to express his thanks to Dean Kenneth H. Condit for the provision of funds by the Princeton School of Engineering for the typing of this manuscript, to Vice Admiral W. Mack Angas (CEC), USN, Ret., Chairman of the Princeton Civil Engineering Department, for the review of the entire manuscript and for many valuable suggestions, and to his colleague Dr. Hans F. Winterkorn for the review of the articles on soil physics in Chap. 3 and on soil stabilization in Chap. 11; also to Yasamaru Ishii for reading the manuscript and pointing out some insufficiently clear passages. The manuscript was typed by Mrs. W. Brickley.

GREGORY P. TSCHEBOTARIOFF

PRINCETON, N.J.
June, 1951

NOTATION

The recommendations of the International Society of Soil Mechanics and Foundation Engineering (ISSMFE), Ref. 140, concerning nomenclature have been closely observed in this book. In general, these recommendations agree with those of the ASTM (American Society for Testing and Materials), Ref. 18. The exceptions are few. Symbols of secondary importance, including most subscripts, are not listed below but are defined in the text.

In the first edition of this book the metric system was employed in connection with laboratory work whereas the foot-pound system was used mainly in connection with field tests and design problems. In the present revised edition such values are still given in the foot-pound system but as a rule are supplemented by their metric equivalents.

But this conversion could not follow in every detail the Metric Practice Guide issued by the ASTM (Ref. 17). That guide is based entirely on the SI, the International System of Units, which is being promoted by the ASTM in anticipation that "metrication" will soon become a reality in the United States as it already has in the United Kingdom.

The SI reflects a trend which seems to be a by-product of the space age. Starting from the fundamental relationship that force = mass × acceleration and because of the difference in the accelerations of gravity on the earth and on the moon, it is shown† than an old-fashioned 1-kg

† Ref. 17, p. 33.

weight suspended from a spring-scale would register 9.8 newtons (the new SI unit of force) at sea level on earth but only 1.6 newtons at Tranquility Base on the moon. Therefore the SI requires the use of kilogram units only to designate mass and the use of newtons (abbreviation N) for units of force. One newton is approximately equal to one-tenth of the old kilogram force.

However, this recommendation has not yet been generally adopted even in countries which have been using the metric system for years. Some Central European countries use a new term *pond* (abbreviated p) to designate a force exerted at sea level by the weight of a mass of 1 g.

An examination of papers for the Proceedings of the Fifth European Conference on Soil Mechanics and Foundation Engineering (Madrid, 1972) shows that, in addition to the old units of kilograms per square centimeter to express unit pressure or stress, the following four different designations of relevant units have been used in important papers:

1. $\mathrm{kg}_f/\mathrm{m}^2$
2. kN/m^2
3. Mp/m^2
4. bar

where g_f = gram force
$$\mathrm{p} = \mathrm{pond} = g_f$$
$$\mathrm{k} = \mathrm{kilo} = 10^3$$
$$\mathrm{M} = \mathrm{mega} = 10^6$$
$$\mathrm{kp} = \mathrm{kg}_f = 9.806\ \mathrm{N}$$
$$\mathrm{Mp} = 9.806\ \mathrm{kN}$$
$$\mathrm{N} = \mathrm{newton} = 1/9.806\ \mathrm{kg}_f$$
$$1\ \mathrm{m}^2 = 10^4\ \mathrm{cm}^2$$
$$\mathrm{bar} = 10^5\ \mathrm{N}/\mathrm{m}^2$$

Therefore

$$1\ \mathrm{kg}_f/\mathrm{m}^2 = 10^{-4}\ \mathrm{kg}_f/\mathrm{cm}^2 = 1\ \mathrm{kp}/\mathrm{m}^2 = 10^{-3}\ \mathrm{Mp}/\mathrm{m}^2$$
$$= 10\ \mathrm{Mp}/\mathrm{cm}^2 = 9.806\ \mathrm{N}/\mathrm{m}^2 = 10^{-5} \times 9.806\ \mathrm{bar}$$

Thus 1 bar approximately equals a pressure of $1.02\ \mathrm{kg}_f/\mathrm{m}^2$.

The above information should be of help in comparing data in European publications, which often are quite important.

The term *newton* will not be used in this book. Even after its use is coordinated with the competing term *pond* for units of force, it may take up to a generation until force values expressed in newtons can be visualized by practicing engineers as easily as they can now visualize pounds (lb) or kilograms (kg).

However, to emphasize that the gram and kilogram units in this book refer to force and not to mass, the letter f will be subscripted throughout the text to the abbreviations g and kg, reading g_f and kg_f respectively.

Some authors now add the letter f even to the lb abbreviation for pounds, but this will not be done in this book since it should be obvious that lb too refers here to force and not to mass.

The procedure adopted in this respect appears to be essentially the same as that of the American National Standards Institute (*Letter Symbols for Units Used in Science and Technology,* 1969, sponsored by the American Society of Mechanical Engineers).

ISSMFE Symbols (Ref. 140) Used in This Book

1. General
     t = time
     g = acceleration due to gravity
     V = volume
     W = weight
     M = moment
     F = factor of safety
2. Stress and strain
     u = pore pressure [see Eq. (3-21)]
     σ = normal stress [see Eq. (3-21)]
     $\bar{\sigma}$ = effective normal stress [see Eq. (3-21)]
     τ = shear stress
     ϵ = linear strain
     ν = Poisson ratio
3. Soil properties
     a. Unit weight
          γ = unit weight of soil [see Eq. (3-9)]
          γ_w = unit weight of water = 62.4 lb/ft^3 = 1 g$_f$/cm^3
          γ_d = unit weight of dry soil [see Eq. (3-7)]
          γ' = unit weight of submerged soil [see Eq. (3-10)]
          G = specific gravity of solid particles [see Eq. (3-1a)]
          e = void ratio [see Eq. (3-3)]
          n = porosity [see Eq. (3-2)]
          w = water content [see Eq. (3-5)]
          S_r = degree of saturation [see Eq. (3-6a)]
     b. Consistency
          w_L = liquid limit
          w_P = plastic limit
          I_P = plasticity index [see Eq. (3-13)]
          w_s = shrinkage limit
          I_L = liquidity index [see Eq. (3-17)]
          I_C = consistency index [see Eq. (3-16)]
          D_r = relative density or density index [see Eq. (3-13)]

   c. Permeability
     v = velocity of flow
     i = hydraulic gradient
     k = coefficient of permeability [see Eq. (8-3)]
     j = seepage force [see Eq. (8-14)]
   d. Consolidation (one-dimensional)
     m_v = coefficient (or modulus) of volume change [see Eq. (3-31)]
     C_c = compression index [see Eq. (3-34)]
     c_v = coefficient of consolidation [see Eq. (3-38)]
     t = consolidation time [see Eq. (4-22)]
     T_v = time factor [see Eq. (3-39)]
     U = degree of consolidation [see Eq. (3-39a)]
   e. Shearing strength
     ϕ_u = apparent angle of internal friction (*Note:* ϕ is used in the sense of
       ϕ_u in this book)
     ϕ' = effective angle of internal friction [see Eq. (3-54)]
     c_u = apparent cohesion intercept [see Eq. (3-19)] (*Note:* c is used in the
       sense of c_u in this book)
     c' = effective cohesion intercept [see Eq. (3-54)]
     S_t = sensitivity [see Eq. (3-20)]
4. Earth pressure
    δ = angle of wall friction
    K = earth-pressure coefficient
    K_0 = coefficient of earth pressure at rest
5. Foundations
    N = bearing-capacity factor [see Eq. (4-11)]
    k_s = modulus of subgrade reaction [see Art. 14-4C]
    B = breadth of foundation
    L = length of foundation
    D = depth of foundation beneath ground

A number of other symbols are used throughout the book and are defined in the text.

Conversion of Foot-Pound to Metric Units

The following conversion factors were used with slide-rule accuracy in the book in relating numerical values of the two systems:

1 in. = 2.54 cm = 25.4 mm
1 ft = 12 in. = 0.305 m = 30.5 cm
1 yd = 3 ft = 0.914 m
1 mile = 1,760 yd = 5,280 ft = 1,609 m = 1.609 km
1 in.^{2} = 6.45 cm^2
1 ft^2 = 144 in.^{2} = 929 cm^2 = 0.093 m^2

$1 \text{ yd}^2 = 9 \text{ ft}^2 = 0.836 \text{ m}^2$

$1 \text{ acre} = 4,840 \text{ yd}^2 = 43,560 \text{ ft}^2 = 4,050 \text{ m}^2 = 0.405 \text{ hectare}$

$1 \text{ in.}^3 = 16.4 \text{ cm}^3$

$1 \text{ in.}^3/\text{ft} = 53.8 \text{ cm}^3/\text{m}$

$1 \text{ oz} = 1 \text{ fluid ounce} = 1.804 \text{ in.}^3 = 29.6 \text{ cm}^3$

$1 \text{ ft}^3 = 1,728 \text{ in.}^3 = 0.0283 \text{ m}^3 = 28,300 \text{ cm}^3$

$1 \text{ yd}^3 = 27 \text{ ft}^3 = 0.765 \text{ m}^3$

$1 \text{ in.}^4 = 41.6 \text{ cm}^4$

$1 \text{ lb} = 0.454 \text{ kg}_f = 454 \text{ g}_f$

$1 \text{ kip} = 1,000 \text{ lb} = 0.5 \text{ ton} = 0.454 \text{ metric ton} = 454 \text{ kg}_f$

$1 \text{ ton} = 2,000 \text{ lb} = 0.907 \text{ metric ton} = 907 \text{ kg}_f$

$1 \text{ in.-lb} = 1.153 \text{ cm-kg}_f$

$1 \text{ ft-lb} = 13.85 \text{ cm-kg}_f = 0.1385 \text{ m-kg}_f$

$1 \text{ ft-kip} = 138.5 \text{ m-kg}_f = 0.1385 \text{ meter-metric ton}$

$1 \text{ lb/in.} = 0.179 \text{ kg}_f/\text{cm}$

$1 \text{ kip/ft} = 14.9 \text{ kg}_f/\text{cm}$

$1 \text{ lb/in.}^2 = 0.0703 \text{ kg}_f/\text{cm}^2$

$1 \text{ ton/ft} = 29.8 \text{ kg}_f/\text{cm}$

$1 \text{ ft-ton/ft} = 9.07 \text{ m-kg}_f/\text{cm} = 907 \text{ m-kg}_f/\text{m}$

$1 \text{ ft-lb/ft}^3 = 4.88 \text{ m-kg}_f/\text{m}^3$

$1 \text{ kip/in.}^2 = 70.2 \text{ kg}_f/\text{cm}^2$

$1 \text{ lb/ft}^2 = 4.89 \text{ kg}_f/\text{m}^2$

$1 \text{ kip/ft}^2 = 4,880 \text{ kg}_f/\text{m}^2$

$1 \text{ ton/ft}^2 = 9,760 \text{ kg}_f/\text{m}^2 = 0.976 \text{ kg}_f/\text{cm}^2 \approx 1 \text{ kg}_f/\text{cm}^2$
$\approx 0.1 \text{ metric ton/m}^2$

$1 \text{ lb/in.}^3 = 2.77 \text{ g}_f/\text{cm}^3$

$1 \text{ lb/ft}^3 = 0.016 \text{ g}_f/\text{cm}^3$

CHAPTER 1

SPECIAL FEATURES OF FOUNDATION AND SOIL ENGINEERING

1-1. The Purpose and Importance of a Foundation. The term *foundation* is used to designate the part of a structure which serves to transmit to the soil beneath it its own weight, the weight of the superstructure above it, and any forces which may act upon them. A foundation is therefore the connecting link between the superstructure and the soil.

The function of a properly designed foundation is to support the loads resting on it and to distribute them in a satisfactory manner over the contact surfaces of the soil layer on which it rests. In order to be satisfactory, this distribution must not produce excessive stresses within the soil mass at any depth beneath the foundation. One must obviously consider as excessive stresses which would cause a complete rupture within the supporting soil mass and a noticeable tilting and sinking of the structure as a whole. This is not a frequent occurrence where buildings are concerned, but, as may be seen from Fig. 4-9, it is far from being unknown. Damage to roadbeds or earth dams due to rupture failures and slides of the soil or supporting embankments also happens occasionally (Figs. 7-3 and 7-13).

Stresses are also to be rated as excessive if the cumulative action of the strains they produce causes a settlement of the supporting soil surface so uneven that the structure above it would be cracked or otherwise damaged while undergoing deformations required to adapt it to this uneven settlement. Extreme cases of this type of damage due to unsatisfactory foundations are illustrated by Figs. 4-24(II) and 6-19. The importance of foundations is self-evident, since no structure can endure without an adequate foundation.

When the surface soil layers are too weak, the foundation has to be carried down to more resisting layers if such are present within easy reach. According to circumstances, this can be done by open excavation, by driving piles, or by sinking caissons to the desired depth. But, whatever may be the type of foundation or the depth below the soil surface to which the foundation reaches, the loads that it will transmit to these layers will always cause stresses and therefore strains in the supporting soil mass. As in all other materials, the magnitude of the unit strains will depend on the magnitude of the corresponding unit stresses and on the elastic and plastic properties of the supporting soil. These strains will always be present, and their sum will always produce some deformation and settlement of the contact surfaces between the foundation and the supporting soil.

1-2. The Interaction between Superstructure, Foundation, and Soil. A foundation will naturally tend to follow any settlement of the soil on which it rests. In turn, the superstructure will follow the settlement of the foundation which supports it. Both will tend to equalize uneven settlements by resisting deformation and thereby transmitting more load to those parts of the soil surface which have settled least. No deformation of the soil surface beneath a structure can take place without a corresponding deformation of both the foundation and the superstructure above it. This remains true for any type of structure—building, bridge, road, or dam.

The supporting soil, the foundation, and the superstructure form one single unit and should therefore always be considered as a whole. The interaction between them is very complicated and will be discussed in greater detail later (Art. 4-4). However, it is most important to bear in mind the fact of such interaction from the very start of studies in this field. It has been too often disregarded in the past, largely because of the complexity of the problem, analysis of which was not even attempted with the more limited knowledge available in earlier periods in the history of engineering. As a result of this complexity of foundation problems the scientific development of foundation engineering has remained far behind that of structural engineering proper. For the same reason even present-day foundation work requires methods of approach which differ from those usual in structural engineering.

1-3. Causes of the Past Lag in the Scientific Development of Foundation Engineering. As compared with the structural engineer, the foundation engineer was, and still is, in a much less favorable position.

The analysis of stress distribution in soil masses is a complicated problem of a highly indeterminate nature requiring a thorough knowledge of advanced higher mathematics and of the theories of elasticity and plasticity. For new problems the help of specialists in these fields must be resorted to. Their solutions for idealized conditions then have to be critically examined by the engineer in order to be adapted as closely as possible to the actual and generally much more complicated field conditions. Such adaptations often reduce the value of the mathematically exact solution to that of a simple estimation.   Frequently no direct use of the solution can be made, although it generally retains the value of an indication of likely limit conditions.

The main difficulty lies in the much more complicated engineering properties of soils as compared with other building materials.   Most soils are three-phase systems; i.e., they are composed of solid matter, of water, and of air.   Their behavior under stress is strongly affected by their density and by the relative proportions of water and of air filling their voids.   These properties may vary with time and depend to a limited extent on a number of other factors.   The time element becomes very important in the study of the stress-strain relationships of soils.

Other factors which are relatively negligible in the study of these relationships for other building materials, such as the rate and the manner of application of loads, may become of cardinal importance where some soils are concerned.   Changes in the moisture content of most soils may greatly alter many of their important engineering properties.   These properties may also be strongly affected by vibrations and by changes in the condition of lateral confinement of the soil.   All the above is true both for undisturbed natural soil deposits supporting foundations and for artificially selected and compacted soils used as a construction material for earth structures such as dams and embankments.

In the case of undisturbed natural soil deposits which support structures erected on them, the difficulties of determining their engineering properties are still further increased by their frequent lack of uniformity due to the erratic processes of their formation by nature.   It is therefore not always possible to proceed in a manner identical with that used for other building materials and to judge accurately the average engineering properties of a large soil mass on the strength of tests on a few samples.   Further, it is extremely difficult to extract for testing small samples from the depth of a natural deposit without changing their properties.   Under the circumstances it is not surprising that the scientific development of foundation engineering lagged far behind that of structural engineering.

The present major problems in the further development of soil and foundation engineering are outlined in Art. 1-10.

1-4. Nonengineering and Early Engineering Soil Studies.   Many soil studies have been made for other than civil engineering purposes but their results could not be directly applied to foundation work.   Very extensive soil studies have been carried out by agricultural soil scientists and by geologists, naturally for purposes of their own specialty.

Agricultural soil scientists are concerned mainly with the properties of a few upper feet of the soil crust which are of importance to the growth of plants.   Nevertheless, some of their work is valuable for understanding the properties of all soil materials.   For instance, the chemical processes of soil deterioration and leaching, the effect of the prevailing climate on the nature of the chemical changes accompanying such decomposition, and some drainage and various other problems have been extensively treated by agricultural soil scientists. These investigations have a special character, but the study of their development is, nevertheless, recommended to civil engineers specializing in laboratory soil research or in highway or airport soil stabilization. The same may be said concerning some interesting aspects of research on clays performed by ceramic engineers and chemists.

The approach of geologists to soil problems naturally differs from that of engineers. A geologist will call *rock* any material of which the earth is composed, no matter whether it is hard or soft, and is mainly interested in its origin and manner of formation. The systematic study of the behavior of soils under stress, with which engineers are mainly concerned, has not been undertaken by geologists. Nevertheless, in other respects they can provide assistance of an indispensable nature to engineers. Cooperation between geologists and engineers is therefore essential.†

Civil engineers were thus compelled to solve their own soil problems. One of the earliest efforts on record in this field was made by Coulomb (1776) and was connected with the determination of earth pressures on retaining walls. Although true for granular soils and rigid walls only, it is particularly notable because with some restrictions its results are valid to this day.

Other early attempts consisted mainly of field load tests on small footings and single piles and of the measurement of the resistance of piles to driving. Their interpretation was purely empirical in view of the general lack of basic knowledge concerning the stress-strain relationship and other important physical properties of soils as well as of the laws governing the stress distribution within them. A number of fallacious conceptions resulted.

1-5. Scientific Soil Studies by Civil Engineers; Appearance of the Term Soil Mechanics. A better understanding of the limitations of small-scale field load tests was reached after a series of laboratory-model tests in several countries, involving the actual measurement of pressures within sand fills. The similarity under certain conditions of the pressure distribution thus obtained and of the pressure distribution derived from a purely mathematical analysis of homogeneous elastic bodies led to cooperation between foundation engineers and the specialists in the field of the theory of elasticity.

The understanding of the basic physical properties of soils in general and of the plasticity of clay in particular was advanced at the beginning of this century by the Swedish scientist Atterberg and through studies of landslides by the Geotechnical Commission of the Swedish State Railways. The systematic study of the shearing characteristics of soils was begun at about the same time by Krey in Germany.

A particularly important advance was made through the work of Terzaghi, who in 1923 published a mathematically rigorous solution of the rate of

† *Glossary of Geologic Terms for Engineers* (Ref. 324) can be useful in this connection.

consolidation of clays under applied pressures. This theory was confirmed experimentally and explained the strong time lag of settlements on fully waterlogged clay deposits. Terzaghi was a rare example of a practicing civil engineer combining extensive field experience with advanced scientific training and an aggressive pioneer spirit. Apart from his theory of consolidation and other original research, the engineering profession is indebted to him for the first attempts to coordinate and systematically apply to foundation practice the results of engineering research on soils and to correlate their field performance to their numerically defined engineering properties. The term *soil mechanics* was coined by him in 1925 when one of his books appeared under the equivalent German title *Erdbaumechanik*. Although written in German, this book was dedicated to the American Robert College in Istanbul. In the same year Terzaghi came to the United States to serve as a research consultant to the U.S. Bureau of Public Roads. Since that time his further work and the work of many men he helped to initiate to the new science of soil mechanics in different countries have exercised a great influence on foundation-engineering practice all over the world.

At present most of the important engineering schools are equipped with soil-mechanics laboratories. Many important organizations, for instance, the U.S. Army Engineers, the U.S. Bureau of Reclamation, and state highway departments, maintain numerous soil laboratories both for research and for field control testing. The principles of soil mechanics are applied to their engineering design work as a matter of routine.

Nevertheless, civil engineers with little practical experience with soils often expect too much at first from the new science and sometimes are disappointed when they find that the results of mathematical derivations contained in its theory or the results of its laboratory soil tests cannot always be directly applied to actual practice in a manner similar to that to which they are accustomed in structural engineering. Many mistakes by practicing engineers in the past may be traced to an insufficient understanding of the special nature of soil mechanics. Also, it is much too often believed that scientific engineering and a rigorous treatment of a design problem are synonymous.

A common fallacy is to attempt to assume simplified conditions different from those actually existing, in order to permit a mathematically rigorous treatment, and to forget afterward that the result refers to idealized conditions only. Actually mathematics should be considered by engineers as only *one* of the tools designed to help them. The scrutiny of *all* factors affecting a foundation problem is essential and must be followed by an approximate estimation of their combined action on the basis of known facts concerning these factors and by an exercise of sound judgment as to their relative importance. This method involves a strong element of experience and personal skill and therefore of art.

The following chapters of this book will attempt to outline how this desirable approach to soil and foundation problems can be realized in actual present-day practice. The present stage of development is far from complete. Much further development is yet to be expected in this field as a result of continued research. But it is well to understand its special features and to realize that there should be a basically different approach to the problems of earth structures and to the problems of foundations.

1-6. Difference in the Advisable Approach to the Study of Foundations and Earth Structures. The erection of earth structures, such as earth dams, embankments, airports, roads, and other fills, involves the artificial removal of soil from its natural deposit, the selection of suitable material, and the placing of this material in the new structure in a definite, controlled manner. The average nature, the composition, and other properties of the soil in the structure can be known to the engineers, as well as the extent of likely variation from this average. It is therefore possible to reproduce fairly closely in the laboratory conditions approximating the ones which will prevail in the finished structure and to test under these conditions the same types of soil material as the ones of which it will be composed. It is therefore further possible to approach the study of earth structures in a manner not very different from the one used in branches of structural engineering which work with ordinary man-made building materials.

The approach to foundation engineering proper should be entirely different. Here one has to deal with natural soil deposits performing the engineering function of supporting the foundation and the superstructure above it. Nature has erected most of these deposits in an extremely erratic manner, producing an infinite variety of possible combinations of factors affecting the choice and the execution of foundations. In many cases foundation engineers do not have the option of selecting a more suitable site for a structure, but have to meet soil conditions as they find them on sites selected for geographical, traffic, commercial, and other considerations.

The most modern methods of soil exploration and testing cannot at present provide completely accurate information concerning the actual average engineering properties of the whole undisturbed, naturally deposited soil mass under the structure, and probably will never be able to do so. All they can do is to give indications as to what these properties are likely to be. This is already a very great step forward compared to previous pure guesswork in this field. The foundation engineer has to weigh these indications in the light of recorded experiences with similar structures under similar conditions and then act on the basis of his judgment. Recording foundation experiences in a suitable manner thus assumes a very important function. Foundation engineering is likely always to retain features of an art, with soil mechanics maintaining the position of its most important auxiliary science. The solutions provided by soil mechanics necessarily refer to idealized conditions. These idealized conditions should be so selected as to provide solutions for *limit* conditions likely to be met in the field. Determination of such limits becomes very important, since the designs should then take into account possible variations within the limits.

1-7. Rupture and Deformation Problems in Foundation and Soil Engineering. It is further important to differentiate between problems involving complete rupture of a soil mass and problems involving only its deformation. The maximum bearing capacity of a spread foundation and the maximum unsupported height of a vertical cut or of a slope in clay soils are examples of rupture problems, governed by the shear strength of the soil. The latest methods of determining the ultimate shearing strength of soils, including field sampling and laboratory testing procedures, have been found fairly reliable.

On the other hand, deformation problems, such as the settlement of a structure, are much more difficult to handle in practice. Experience has shown that in many cases laboratory tests may give not entirely accurate values, especially in the case of natural undisturbed soils. Any slight disturbance or swelling of such soils during or after sampling strongly affects the numerical values of coefficients by which the deformation characteristics of soils are defined. Corrections based on full-scale observations of the performance of actual structures in the field become essential. Because of the great variety of soil types, such studies have to be performed on a regional basis. A semiempirical approach of this kind has actually been tried in several localities with satisfactory results.

A number of problems, such as the lateral pressures exerted by different types of soils against the timbering of cuts or against other earth-retaining structures, may involve both rupture and deformation characteristics of soils.

It should be noted that soil-deformation problems may have great practical importance. Thus excessive differential settlements of the soil surface under a building may not involve any rupture of the soil itself but may cause cracking and other types of failure in the superstructure unless it is specially designed to resist such differential settlements.

Problems involving gravitational and nongravitational flow of water through soils are also in a separate class, since such water movements may affect both the rupture and the deformation of soils.

1-8. Special Need for Construction Quality Control. In foundation work this need is much greater than in any other branch of civil engineering. The erection methods of a superstructure can seldom damage any of its elements without this becoming immediately apparent. This is not so in the case of a foundation, as illustrated by Fig. 1-1 (Ref. 3).

A change in the design layout of a harbor during its construction required the removal of an already built bulkhead with its timber-pile anchorage. The photograph in Fig. 1-1A shows that the originally unplanned excavation revealed serious damage to the timber piles, presumably due to overdriving (Art. 6-1). This was unsuspected and seriously impaired the usefulness of the anchorage as intended by the designers (see Fig. 1-1B).

Once a foundation element is installed in the ground and the superstructure built over it, it is usually impossible, or at least very difficult, to
remove it for inspection.   The point is illustrated by Fig. 1-2.   Timber
piles, 25 ft (7.65 m) long, had to be driven in three shifts for the urgent
construction of a concrete wall to retain new fill along the bank of a river.
The job was almost completed when it was discovered, accidentally, that
due to lax inspection during the night shift the contractor's men drove the
piles only 10 ft or so, cutting off and carting away the rest.   When had they
begun doing so?   Part of the wall was already concreted.   By ministerial
order the contractor, at his own expense, had to make three cuts in the
concrete wall where night shifts had worked, of the type shown in Fig. 1-2.

Then, with the help of jacks, all the piles within the area of the cut were
pulled and two new piles were driven for each one pulled.   In addition, the
contractor was blacklisted for several years on government projects.

Timber piles are not the only type that can be damaged or improperly
installed.   For instance, many cases are known of trouble resulting from
discontinuities in the concrete of cast-in-the-ground piles (Art. 6-7).

Constant attention to every detail of construction procedures is therefore a
must in all foundation work.   Above all, continuous competent on-the-site
inspection is essential, supplemented in special cases by various types of field
measurements

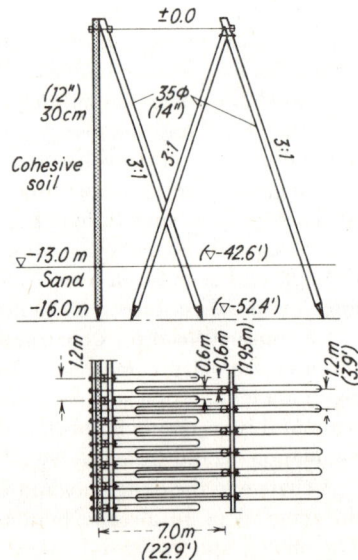

(*A*)   (*B*)

Fig. 1-1.   (*A*) Unsuspected condition of an overdriven timber pile anchorage compared to
the intent of the designers (*B*).   (*Ref.* 3.)

Fig. 1-2. Cut in new concrete retaining wall had to be ordered to permit extraction of some timber piles for a check of their length after fraudulent cutting was accidentally discovered. (*Photo by Tschebotarioff, 1930.*)

1-9. Field Performance Measurements for Control and Research. Special cases requiring field measurements usually arise where deposits of soft clays are involved. It is then often difficult to draw a clear distinction between field "control" and "research" measurements. The two often blend, especially when a design-as-you-go approach was selected. This approach is possible in some types of structures, such as the bracing of a long cut (see Art. 11-3).

A brief outline of presently available observational techniques for various purposes will now be given.

The earliest and simplest kind of field performance measurements was the determination of settlements of structures by means of *leveling* (Art. 4-5). Unobtrusive permanent benchmarks were developed for buildings, as well as a water level permitting work in crowded basements (Ref. 337, pp. 1434†, 1487). See Soil Test Catalog M-202 (Ref. 307).

† The units in fig. 42, p. 1434, should be millimeters (mm), not inches.

The determination of the start of potentially dangerous sliding (by means of *transit sighting along* a row of *displacement stakes* at the toe of an embankment built on soft clay) is another early and simple control procedure still useful to this day (Art. 5-2).

Settlement platforms are regularly used in highway embankment work. They usually consist of a rigid 3-ft-square (91-cm) steel or timber plate which is laid on the surface of the natural soil. A vertical steel pipe is welded to the center of the plate and the elevation of the latter established by leveling. The pipe is extended upward as the height of the fill increases. Markings on the pipe permit repeated levelings to determine the settlement of the plate and of the soft soil beneath it.

The U.S. Bureau of Reclamation developed a multiple-level settlement platform which permits determination of the relative settlement of various successive layers in a high rolled-fill earth dam. At the elevations of the surface of these layers steel plates resting on them were welded to vertical pipe sections which could slide past each other. A specially designed cylindrical " torpedo " attached to a tape could be lowered into the pipe and successively latch on to each pipe joint, thus establishing their elevation changes in respect to the known elevation of the dam surface and the bottom plate (see Ref. 307, item C-300).

Suggestions have been made that the relative compression of natural deposits could be determined by placing *underground bench marks* at the bottom of boreholes of varying depth. The writer used half a dozen underground bench marks of the type suggested in Ref. 337, fig. 52, p. 1446, but with little success. Apparently drilling the hole relieved the stress in the high-plasticity clay around its bottom, resulting in irregular swelling of the clay and heaving of the bench mark.

One of the more sophisticated early measuring operations which required special equipment was the *earth-pressure cells* operated by remote control. Their use within a mass of soil has now been almost entirely discontinued, even when it is sand, because it was realized that accurate results could be expected only if the cell had exactly the same compressibility characteristics as the surrounding soil. This is something impossible to achieve in practice. But such cells can be and are very successfully used when mounted with their face flush against a rigid surface—to measure soil reactions against the bottom of a foundation slab or lateral earth pressures against the back of a retaining wall. In either case best results are achieved by mounting the cells in a group of three to four cells to support a rigid steel plate flush with the concrete surface. This averages out, over the larger contact area of the plate, local discontinuities in the soil, which for small individual cells can become very pronounced and obscure the overall picture (see the end of Art. 14-10).

Figure 1-4 shows two stages in the installation of such a group of four *Carlson* earth-pressure cells or *stress meters*.

Strut loads in braced cuts have been measured in a number of ways. One is to insert hydraulic jacks on both sides of a strut (Ref. 338, pp. 75–76), relieve the pressure in the strut, and use a graphical procedure to determine the original load. Another is to measure directly the strains in the strut when it is made of steel.

Kérisel et al. (Ref. 159) have reported a new type of strut the length of which can be changed at will after it is already in place. Forty-two pairs of such struts were successfully used for research purposes on an advance section of the Lyon subway.

Several experimental methods exist to investigate the performance of structural *foundation units subjected to bending* such as piles or sheet-pile bulkheads. The diagram in Fig. 1-3 illustrates the discussion which follows. The theoretical relationship between the pressure p on the structural member, the shear V at the same point, the bending moment M, the slope θ of the deflection curve, and the deflection y is given by Eq. (1-1) in Fig. 1-3.

The direct mounting of pressure cells on piles usually is not possible, unless the piles are of a specially designed large cross section (Ref. 193). Pressure cells actually have been successfully mounted and used on steel sheet piling (Ref. 89, pp. 1141, 1162).

Strain gages and inclinometers are the most frequently employed methods to study flexural problems in foundations.

In view of the uncertain and time-dependent elastic properties of concrete, *strain gages* can reliably be used only on steel piles. The stress at a given point

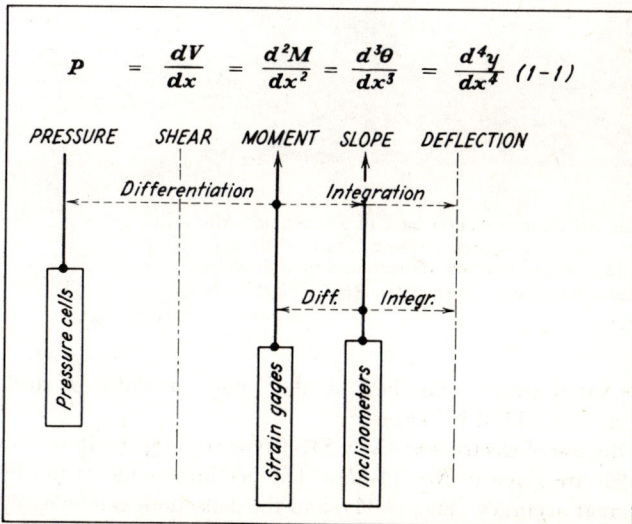

$$P = \frac{dV}{dx} = \frac{d^2M}{dx^2} = \frac{d^3\theta}{dx^3} = \frac{d^4y}{dx^4} \quad (1\text{-}1)$$

PRESSURE   SHEAR   MOMENT   SLOPE   DEFLECTION

Differentiation   *Integration*

Diff.   *Integr.*

Pressure cells   Strain gages   Inclinometers

Fig. 1-3. Theoretical basis for various experimental techniques used in studies of interaction between soil and a deflected structural element.

(A)

(B)

Fig. 1-4. Four Carlson stress meters on back of a retaining wall: (A) wiring before concrete was poured around them; (B) after removal of plywood formwork but before suspension of the 1 by 30 by 48 in. (2.5 by 76 by 124 cm) steel cover plate. (*Ref. 170, photos by Antes.*)

is then the measured strain multiplied by the Young modulus of steel, $E_s = 3 \times 10^7$ lb/in.$^2 = 2.11 \times 10^6$ kg$_f$/cm^2.

Examples of the use of electric resistivity SR-4 type strain gages in testing large-scale models are given in Art. 14-3B. The bending moments can be obtained with great accuracy (Fig. 14-11), and the deflections can be easily computed from them by conventional strength-of-materials methods.   The determination of the pressure distribution, however, requires double differentiation (see Fig. 1-3). Therefore a large number of points of measurement are required to obtain smooth curves and permit the computation and check procedures outlined in Art. 14-3*B*.

Attempts have been made to use SR-4 type gages on full-scale structures. Considerable difficulties are then encountered in waterproofing them and ensuring that no creep of the bonding cement develops over long periods of time. The vibrating-wire type of magnetic strain gage favored in Europe appears to have a better performance record in this respect. However, neither type stands up well to shocks sustained during driving of the piles on which they are mounted.

Nor does the *Carlson strain meter;* but it is quite stable over long periods of time under static conditions. Figure 1-5 shows one such strain meter mounted on the corner of an H-pile flange by means of two steel brackets welded to the pile after it was driven. The meter operates on the same electric-resistivity principle as the SR-4 strain gages; very thin wires stretched on porcelain supports within the meter follow the elongation of the steel-pile surface between the brackets supporting the meter. The elongation or contraction of the wire changes its cross section and hence its resistance, which can be measured and related to the strain, giving for a 10-in. (25.4-cm) gage length a sensitivity of 4×10^{-7} in./in. or 12.0 lb/in.^{2} = 0.84 kg$_f$/cm^2 in steel. Since the strained wires are submerged in oil within a sealed container, the readings have been known to remain stable over periods of years. Four

Fig. 1-5. The first of the four Carlson strain meters at each corner of an H-pile shown mounted just below the bottom of the future footing. (*Ref. 170, photo by Tschebotarioff.*)

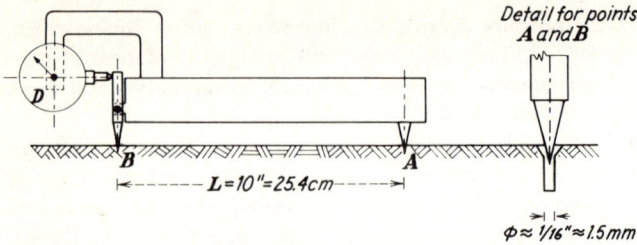

Fig. 1-6.   Sketch of the Whittemore mechanical strain gage.

such Carlson strain meters, mounted at the four corners on each of several H-piles of the Allamuchy project just below the concrete footing of the abutment, permitted determination of the fixation moment M_B of the pile (see Fig. 10-29).   The cable conduits from the strain meters are protected in the same manner as those of the stress meters (Fig. 1-4A) and are carried through the concrete of the abutment to switches inside a massive lockable control box on the exposed face of the abutment (Ref. 170).

Carlson strain meters can be provided with special fittings permitting their substitution for an equivalent length of $1\frac{1}{4}$-in.-diameter (32-mm) steel reinforcing rods for concrete.

All such remote-control measurements require elaborate and expensive installation work which is not always justified in the case of temporary structural elements, such as the bracing of cuts (Art. 11-3).   All the more so since electric cables are apt to be accidentally damaged during heavy construction work in excavations.   The use of a portable mechanical strain gage, developed over 40 years ago, is then of advantage.   In Europe it was known as the Huggenberger Deformeter and in the United States as the *Whittemore strain gage*.   Its operation is illustrated in Fig. 1-6.   Shallow holes are drilled into the metal surface for the gage supports A and B.   Support A is rigidly attached to the body of the gage.   Total strains along the gage length AB are registered by the dial gage D, reading to $1/10,000$ in. (0.00254 mm).   With a gage length AB of 10 in. (25.4 cm) this means that unit strains of 1×10^{-5} can be recorded, or stress changes of 300 lb/in.$^2 = 21$ kg$_f$/cm^2 in steel.   This type of gage was successfully used for the measurements summarized by Fig. 11-16.   It is still commercially available in the United States (Ref. 307, item CT-171).

Whittemore type strain gages can also be conveniently used for repeated accurate measurements of *changes in the width of masonry cracks* (Art. 4-5). Special rock bolts are then made which are cemented into the masonry on both sides of the crack at a 10-in. (25.4-cm) distance between holes in the heads of the bolts which are identical to the holes shown on the right-hand side of Fig. 1-6.

Inclinometer measurements have found extensive application in the field control of embankment slides (Chap. 7).   Several types of instruments have been developed which employ some form of pendulum within a waterproof jacket and varying techniques to record the slope changes indicated by the pendulum as the instrument slides down along a special light flexible casing and then, as a check, as it is pulled back to the soil surface.   One instrument, plus an emergency spare, can be used to make repeated measurements in a large number of guide casings installed in as many boreholes on a single job. Readings can be taken at any desired interval both on the way down and on the way up.   Deflections can be easily computed from the slope readings [see Eq. (1-1) in Fig. 1-3].   A plot of deflection changes with depth, compared to the initial curve, will then indicate whether and in what layer plastic deformations are threatening to develop into a general slide as the embankment is built up.   To permit timely countermeasures it is essential to have immediate on-the-spot evaluation of the inclinometer readings by plotting data in a manner similar to Fig. 3-29.   A case is known where inclinometer readings indicated a developing slide 3 days before it occurred, but the relevant evaluation took 4 days to reach the engineer in charge of the embankment construction job—1 day too late.

Figure 1-7 shows an inclinometer of the Slope Indicator Company (Seattle) about to be lowered into a guide casing for determining both the deflection and the bending moments of an H-pile (see Art. 10-9).   The type shown is quite satisfactory for control measurements of potential slides in the

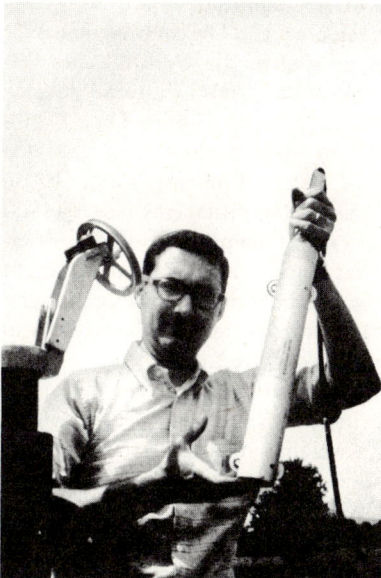

Fig. 1-7.   A   removable   Wilson inclinometer about to be lowered into its guide casing.   (*Ref. 170, photo by Tschebotarioff.*)

soil, but more miniaturized models are now available (e.g., Ref. 307, slope meter C-350) and should be used with piles, to which their casings have to be attached (Ref. 170).

An important method for the field control of the degree of consolidation of a soft clay layer is provided by *pore-pressure measurements* using *piezometers*. Several types are commercially available (e.g., Ref. 307, items K-650A, K-652, K-1052, and K-1057) but all are very sensitive to the manner of their installation.   They all have a porous tip, similar to that of well points (see Fig. 9-7), except that now the tip, enclosed in sand, must be completely isolated from the overlying and underlying layers by about 2 ft of very impervious bentonitic slurry at each end.   Unless this slurry forms effectively impervious barriers, the piezometer cannot fulfill its purpose of registering variations in the water pressure within the pores of the consolidating clay at the elevation of the piezometer tip only.   Often two plastic tubes lead from the piezometer tip to a pressure gage to permit periodic flushing of air bubbles from the circuit.

Figure 2-22 and its description illustrate the practical value of piezometers when properly installed by specialized personnel.

Experience shows that the performance of most of the field control measurements described above and certainly of all measurements made for research purposes should not be assigned to the regular construction supervisory personnel at the site, who are always too busy with their main duties—rapid completion of the contruction job.   All such measurements should be made and evaluated by specialized personnel with no other duties to distract them.

1-10. Problems of Soil-engineering Development.   The continued healthy development of soil and foundation engineering in the United States was threatened for a while in the late 1950s and in the 1960s by a trend at some prestigious private universities which aimed at the elimination of professional or "know-how" courses from both undergraduate and graduate engineering curricula (see Refs. 54, 55, 77, 372).   Emphasis was to be on "science" or the "know-why," whereby science was mistakenly (see Art. 1-3) equated with rigorous mathematical solutions.   One prominent administrator of engineering education even urged that if design as such "is to be taught successfully outside of industry, it should be taught at the post-doctoral level." The writer's comment was that "such an approach ignores the realities of civil engineering work and its educational needs" (Ref. 370).

Unfortunately, civil engineering students usually are a small minority in the engineering schools of private universities, with the result that the voices of their faculty carry correspondingly little weight with administrators.   The trend to teach only "science" at a university may perhaps have some justification in the aerospace, chemical, and electrical fields of engineering but, as explained in the preceding articles, certainly none whatsoever in the soil and foundation branches of civil engineering.   As a result of administrative pressures some civil engineering departments have in reality become little more than departments of engineering mechanics whose narrow approach widens rather than closes the undesirable gap between theory and practice within the profession.

In his General Report to the Third Pan-American Conference on Soil Mechanics and Foundation Engineering (Ref. 373, p. 305), the writer pointed out the absurdity of some practical conclusions reached by authors of two purely theoretical papers, one of them rheological, and stated

> my criticism . . . of abstract theoretical papers is not meant as a reflection on their authors, but rather is directed at the recent administrative climate of some educational institutions which has encouraged and made fashionable complex mathematical studies as an objective per se, without due consideration whether their assumptions and results are compatible with physical and engineering realities.

There appears to be a growing recognition within the civil engineering profession of the harmful fallacies inherent in this " climate," and opposition to it is increasing.   Full-scale experimental studies related to design problems are again beginning to be recognized as a prerequisite for further progress in the field of foundation engineering.   This is illustrated by the outstanding success of the ASCE Specialty Conference on the Performance of Earth and Earth Supported Structures held in June 1972 at Purdue University (Ref. 8a).

A notable exception to the all too frequent disregard of known physical properties of soils by rheologists in their theoretical " creep " studies is the investigations of overconsolidated varved clays in the Seattle area by Sherif (Refs. 289 to 292).   His studies combined a sound theoretical analysis with a laboratory and full-scale experimental approach which took into account the relevant physical and geological factors.   The resulting findings were of considerable practical importance for the stability of future highway cuts in the area (see Art. 7-6).

In the past there has been too little rather than too much correlated teaching at universities of the theory and practice in various interconnected branches of civil engineering.   About 80 percent of all soil and foundation failures the writer had to study over the past quarter of a century were primarily caused by one or more of the following factors: either the structural engineers involved in the design and construction had no proper understanding of the relevant soil-engineering problems; or the soil engineers did not appreciate the structural problems; or the engineering administrators had no real grasp of either field.

A change of emphasis in the professional education of civil engineers and the broadening thereof is therefore essential.   A change in the overall methods of research is also long overdue.   The present haphazard nature and lack of continuity of disconnected research efforts at many small universities can no longer alone assure a continued healthy development of our knowledge in the field.   The writer therefore fully endorses the following excerpts from the published Report (Ref. 16) of the distinguished Research Committee, Soil Mechanics and Foundations Division, American Society of Civil Engineers.†

> There is a need for creation of several institutions which can attract the best research workers and engineers and provide the climate, facilities and access to major projects to permit a broad attack on complex problems involving (1) the best possible analytical procedures, (2) the use of the most advanced testing procedures, and (3) the direct measurement of performance of structures, for the purpose of conducting major research studies and evaluating design approaches.
>   There are many ways in which such agencies might be established but it seems doubtful that they could be developed within the present framework of any one Federal, state, or university operation.   Perhaps the best means would be cooperative endeavours between state design organizations, state universities, and Federal agencies in strategic locations throughout the country. . . . 100 small to medium-sized laboratories could contribute significantly to the overall effort.

Another problem which requires correction is the delay in the availability for professional public discussion of information obtained from soil and foundation failures.   Such discussion is essential for the advancement of our professional knowledge, yet it is often delayed for years, or even prevented entirely, by the efforts of lawyers of opposing sides who seem to aim at keeping control of all phases of relevant controversies solely in their own hands.

1-11. New Analytical Tools.   As in all other fields of engineering, the use of *electronic computers* has greatly simplified many soil-engineering design computations, for instance, the location of the most unfavorable center of rotation when investigating the stability of slopes (see Art. 7-2).   This leads to considerable savings in the time of engineers.   But the errors which may result from less accurate and more time-consuming methods of computation are quite small by comparison with the inevitable errors in the estimation of the actual shearing strength and consolidation characteristics of the supporting soft cohesive soils.

This limitation on the practical accuracy of all purely analytical procedures, irrespective of whether they are computerized or not, i.e., the uncertainty as to the accuracy of the assumed soil strength and consolidation coefficients unless their values have been checked by full-scale field observations, also applies to a new potentially very powerful analytical tool, the *finite-element* method.   Fortunately, in some cases it is possible to make a preliminary field check (see Art. 14-10) of these assumptions.   As illustrated by Fig. 14-55, the finite-element method then permits a verifiably correct procedure for analyzing problems which could not be tackled by any other method of computation.   In its application to plain strain problems the

---

† Chairmen: G. A. Leonards and W. G. Holtz; members: H. B. Seed, R. V. Whitman, and F. E. Richart.

method consists in separating an actually continuous mass of soil into *finite elements*, usually of rectangular shape, but composed of triangles, which are considered to be interconnected only at their corners, or *nodal points*. Equilibrium of the entire mass is considered in respect to forces applied at the nodal points, the displacements of which points are related to these forces by a *general stiffness matrix*, or an assemblage of stiffnesses of the individual finite elements. Determining the nodal-point displacements involves the solution of a large number of simultaneous equations by means of high-speed computers. The whole operation requires a high degree of specialization on the part of the analysts who undertake it.

For the basic theory of the finite-element method see Zienkewicz and Cheung (Ref. 414) and for an example of its application to a river-lock design analysis see Duncan and Clough (Ref. 90).

The method can also be used for research into the theoretical influence of factors which cannot be taken into account by previously used simpler methods. An example of this is provided by the comparison of conventionally computed distribution of lateral earth pressures against a retaining wall with the effect thereon of variations in the depth of underlying compressible soil and in the smoothness of the base (see Morgenstern and Eisenstein in Ref. 15, pp. 66–69).

Another recent analytical tool is the *wave equation* for pile-driving analysis (see Art. 6-3). It also requires the use of electronic computers.

Laboratory investigations have been helped by the *stress-path concept* advanced by Lambe (see Art. 3-5*A* and Ref. 181).

CHAPTER 2

SITE EXPLORATION

2-1. Methods of Soil Exploration. There are two main subdivisions. *Surface surveys* form the first group. They include the study of geological maps and of available records of previous borings in the general vicinity of the proposed new construction site, from which a general idea can be formed about the subsurface conditions likely to be encountered. Air photos can be of great help in selecting tentative locations for proposed new highways or airfields. Geophysical methods of soil exploration from the surface, namely, the seismic and the electric-resistivity methods, can give valuable data when it is important to ascertain the depth at which rock is located.

All surface surveys can give only approximate indications of the probable soil conditions at a site. Therefore they should be relied upon for preliminary investigations only, although it should be recognized that they provide very valuable data, especially for the rational planning of the necessarily slower and more expensive *subsurface exploration*. No important engineering structure should be designed without adequate data concerning the nature of the underlying soil. Such data can be obtained only by the appropriate subsoil-sampling and -testing procedures. The samples can be obtained either from boreholes or from test pits; soundings provide additional, and sometimes essential, information.

These methods will be discussed in the subsequent articles of this chapter. The selection for a particular job of any one procedure should be based not only on the soil conditions and the technical merits of the procedure itself but also on the relative costs of the procedure as compared with the cost of the proposed structure.   Thus an expensive method of subsoil exploration may be justified when used for the study of a site for a large new dam, both because its cost will form only a small fraction of the cost of the dam and because the failure of a dam may have particularly disastrous consequences.   The use of the same method may be unjustified, however, for some smaller and less vulnerable type of structure.   The method to be employed should be the least expensive of the procedures which will provide the desired information.   Thus there is no point in taking large-sized undisturbed samples of clay if the structure is so heavy that its foundation will obviously have to be carried down through the clay to sand or to rock.

2-2. Surface Surveys.   These include studies of the geology of a proposed site, air-photo soil surveys, and electrical and seismic methods of soil exploration.

Geological studies of a new site are always advisable; failure to undertake them at the right time may lead to considerable trouble later.   Figure 2-10 illustrates such a case.

The foundation of the Ward Island tower of the Hell Gate Bridge in New York (Ref. 6) originally was to have consisted of a number of separate caissons sunk by open dredging to rock.   At the time the final location of the bridge was selected, the presence of a deep clay-filled fissure right under the bridge tower (see Fig. 2-10) had not been observed.   Apparently it was missed by the preliminary borings.   They were all vertical; a few inclined boreholes would have revealed its presence.   Such inclined holes are always advisable in areas where the geology indicates that the presence of deep fissures is possible. Since the discovery of the fissure was a surprise, it became necessary to sink the caissons with the help of compressed air (Art. 6-10) and to span the clay-filled fissure by means of an underground concrete arch on which the caissons then came to rest.   The complicated sequence of the operations which thus became unavoidable is illustrated by Fig. 2-10.   The bedding planes of the faulted rock were almost vertical at this location, and the fissure filled with clay had developed along the vertical plane of contact between two different types of rock—solid gneiss and dolomite limestone.   During the construction of the new Croton aqueduct in New York a similar fissured zone, filled with decayed rock, at a junction of schist and limestone was ascertained by means of an experimental tunnel and was then underpassed by means of an inverted siphon which carried the aqueduct tunnel some 300 ft (91 m) below its original surface (Ref. 258).

Other cases of trouble resulting from inadequate preliminary geological studies of a site are given in Arts. 4-8F and 8-10 (see also 1st ed., Figs. 12-2 and 12-3, showing a concrete dam which could not be put into service because all the water behind it leaked out through sinkholes).

Geological advice can therefore be invaluable in the selection and exploration of sites of dams, tunnels, and other similar structures, and during their construction as well.   Geological information, however, cannot be a substitute for soil tests.   For instance, the geological age of a clay is not necessarily an indication of its probable stiffness.   Clays of ancient Devonian age may still be fairly compressible.

But knowing the geological classification of the soils in a given area by origin—whether glacial, wind-deposited (loess), marine, or residual—is a good guide to advisable methods of soil exploration and testing.

A number of state highway departments have cooperated with the Bureau of Public Roads in Washington by jointly sponsoring the preparation of engineering soil maps for their states on the basis of available geological and agricultural soil data and supplementary identification testing and research. An example is the Engineering Soil Survey of New Jersey (Ref. 276), a series of 22 published separate reports for every county of the state.   It provides information on the engineering properties of surface soil deposits which is very useful for preliminary planning.

Air-photo surveys are of great help in engineering surface evaluation of soils, especially in areas where no adequate soil-engineering maps are available. A series of overlapping photographs taken from the air can be of considerable help in the preliminary selection of a route for a proposed highway or of the site for a new airport.   The nature of eroded soil surfaces, the type of vegetation which grows on the soil, and many other features can be recognized from air photos by a specially trained and experienced observer and can then be interpreted for identification of the underlying soil.   A thorough knowledge of geology, geomorphology (the study of land forms), pedology (the maturing of surface soils as governed by climate), and soil engineering and experience in the art of such identifications are needed for successful interpretations of this kind.

Two *geophysical methods,* the *electric* and the *seismic,* are possible from the ground surface without any borings.   The first of these two methods of exploration consists in measuring changes in the electric resistance of the soil. These measurements are performed with the help of electrodes placed at the ground surface.   Dense rock has a very high electric resistivity.   In other rocks and soils the resistivity decreases with the amount of salts contained in solution.   Therefore, when the general nature of the underlying soil is known, for instance, from a few borings, the limits of certain soil layers close to the surface can be established with the help of electric-resistivity measurements.   The electric method does not seem to be used as frequently as the seismic method.

The seismic method of soil exploration is employed for the purpose of determining the limits of soils of different density and, especially, the limits between soil and rock.   The method is based on the fact that the velocity of compression-wave propagation increases with the density of the material. In soils it can vary between 500 and 8,000 ft/sec (150 and 2,400 m/sec), whereas in most unweathered and sound rocks it exceeds 6,000 ft/sec (1,800 m/sec) and may reach values of 25,000 ft/sec (7,700 m/sec) (see Hvorslev, Ref. 139).   Since the velocity of wave propagation through water is 4,700 ft/sec (1,435 m/sec), it follows that the seismic method can be successfully employed for the determination of the depth to sound rock even when the rock surface is located below the groundwater level.   The waves are usually induced by the explosion of a dynamite cartridge at the ground surface. They are picked up by several detectors placed at varying distances from the point of the shot and are all simultaneously recorded on the same film of an oscillograph.   Studies of this kind should be carried out only by men with special training.   They have been successfully used for the selection of possibly suitable dam sites by determining the depth of overburden to sound rock and the extent of rock weathering.   Of course, borings are invariably performed later on the sites selected.

Light portable engineering seismographs (e.g., Ref. 307, item MD-5, and Ref. 29a), which can be operated in conjunction with a tamper and do not require explosives, are available for seismic surveys (see also Art 5-3).

2-3. Soil Sampling.   *(A). Sampling from Test Pits.*   Exploration of this type usually is performed to shallow depths only—10 to 20 ft (3 to 6 m).   In pervious soils it is necessarily limited by the elevation of the groundwater table.   Well points (Art 9-6) have to be used in such soils to lower the groundwater table if a test pit is to be carried below its natural elevation. The use of well points is an expensive procedure, which is justified for soil surveys only in special cases, e.g., for exploration problems of a semiresearch character in connection with the design of important structures.

Shallow test pits, however, are frequently dug " in the dry " in connection with highway and airport work when it is desired to obtain a large " chunk " of undisturbed soil and, in general, when one wishes to get, by direct visual examination, a better idea of the exact soil profile than is possible from the study of borehole records.

A method of obtaining such a chunk sample of cohesive soil is illustrated by Fig. 2-1.   A trench is first dug around the chunk at the bottom of the pit, and the chunk is trimmed down to the desired size with a knife, 8 to 12 in. (20 to 30 mm) length of sides of cube.   It is then cut off with a large knife at the plane *ABC* and covered with $\frac{1}{8}$ in. (3 mm) of paraffin to prevent loss

Fig. 2-1. Method of obtaining a chunk sample. (*After Bertram, Ref. 27.*)

of moisture by evaporation, if it is to be tested in the field laboratory on the site.   When shipment of the sample is contemplated, a better protection is needed.   This can be provided as follows.   A solid wooden box, with its two ends removed, is placed over the sample after it has been trimmed down on its sides but before it has been cut off at the plane *ABC*.   The sample should be trimmed to provide approximately $\frac{1}{2}$ in. (12.3 mm) free space between the soil and the walls of the box.   Hot paraffin is poured into that space and allowed to cool and harden before the sample is cut off at the plane *ABC* and removed together with the box.   Some of the exposed soil at the two free ends is then scraped off.   Paraffin is poured into the space thus formed, and the lids of the box are screwed down.   The entire box is then placed, with a layer of sawdust all around it, inside a larger wooden box, to prevent damage to the sample from shocks during shipment.   One may obtain a chunk sample from the wall of a test pit by digging a small cavern into the wall, large enough to permit trimming of the chunk on all four vertical faces.

In the case of clean sands it is seldom attempted to take chunk samples as described above.   Instead one usually determines the natural density of the sand by one of the procedures described in Art. 5-5.   The material removed is weighed on the spot and is then shipped in a disturbed state to the laboratory for the determination of its densest and loosest states, the knowledge of which is necessary for the computation of its relative density (see Art. 3-2*E*).

(B). Disturbed and Undisturbed Sampling from Boreholes.   Shallow borings for highway and airport work are frequently performed by means of hand-operated *screw-type augers*.   Dry, clean sands excepted, most soils above the water table will permit the advancement of boreholes to 15 or 20 ft (4 to 6 m) depth without any casing to support the walls of the hole and prevent their caving in.   The screw auger is used both for advancing the hole and for bringing up to the surface for examination disturbed specimens of the soil layers encountered.†

For greater depths, or for work at any depth below the groundwater level, it is necessary to provide support for the walls of the hole.   This is usually done by means of steel tubes, or casings (see Fig. 2-2), which are driven into the ground with the help of a tripod, motor winch, drive hammer, and other accessories.   The casing comes in lengths varying from 5 to 10 ft (1.5 to 3 m). It is driven into the ground up to 3 ft (0.9 m) at a time, whereupon the soil within the casing is cleaned out before driving is resumed or dry sampling is undertaken.   In countries where manual labor is very cheap and mechanical appliances are scarce, the cleaning of the casing frequently is done by means of weighted screw-type augers which are manually rotated by a team of laborers.   Similarly, a team of laborers is often substituted for a motor winch

---

† Augers and all accessories can be obtained in a box suitable for transportation in a car, for instance, from the Acker Drill Co., Inc.

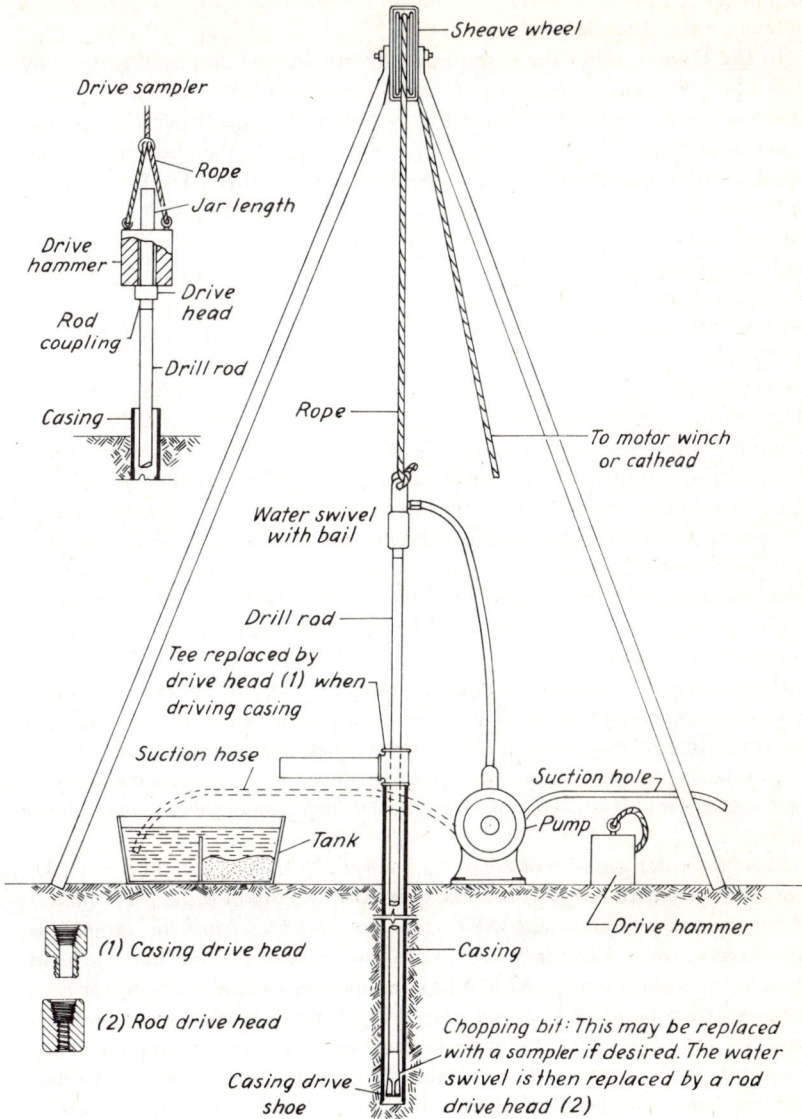

Drive sampler

Rope

Jar length

Drive hammer

Drive head

Rod coupling

Drill rod

Casing

Sheave wheel

Rope

To motor winch or cathead

Water swivel with bail

Drill rod

Tee replaced by drive head (1) when driving casing

Suction hose

Tank

Suction hole

Pump

Drive hammer

(1) Casing drive head

(2) Rod drive head

Casing

Casing drive shoe

Chopping bit: This may be replaced with a sampler if desired. The water swivel is then replaced by a rod drive head (2)

Fig. 2-2.   The advancement of a cased hole by washing; driving split-barrel samplers [Fig. 2-3(1)] for disturbed dry sampling.   (*Sprague & Henwood, Inc.*)

to pull the drill rods with their augers or attachments up to the surface and
to operate the drive hammer.

In the United States the casings usually are washed out, as illustrated by
Fig. 2-2. A pump continuously forces water through the hollow drill rods
and the openings of the chopping bit, which at the same time is repeatedly
raised and dropped with the help of the motor winch, thereby churning up
the soil inside the casing. The water then rises in the space between the
drill rods and the casing and flows out through a tee into a tank on the soil
surface. Particles of the churned-up soil are carried upward with the water
and are partially deposited in the tank. Careful observation of the wash
water, as it comes up to the surface, can provide an experienced foreman with
many useful indications concerning any changes in the soil layers he is piercing.
In the past, such observations of the wash water were sometimes extended to
the preservation of soil samples periodically taken from the settling tank; this
is known as *wash sampling*. Such samples can be extremely misleading, since
most of the fines are carried away from the tank with the water which over-
flows its rim, and since there occurs considerable mixing of soils from different
layers before the wash water reaches the soil surface. The past practice of
wash-sample borings, therefore, cannot be considered sound and should be
abandoned entirely. Boreholes can and should be advanced with the help
of wash water, where care should be exercised not to wash below the bottom
of the casing, but soil samples should be taken by so-called dry-sampling or
undisturbed-sampling procedures.

Dry sampling is somewhat of a misnomer, since the soil samples are taken
from the ground approximately at their natural water content. The term is
used to distinguish such samples from the samples taken from the wash water.
A split-barrel sampler of the type shown in Fig. 2-3 (1) is usually employed
for the purpose. The flap valve is removed for all soils except cohesionless
sands.

This particular sampler of 2.0 in. (5.1 cm) O.D. and $1\frac{1}{2}$ in. (3.81 cm) I.D.
is of the type which has now become generally accepted for the performance
of the *standard penetration test* (SPT) (see Art. 2-4A). After the sampler is
pulled out of the soil and is brought up to the surface, the shoe and the head
are unscrewed and the barrel is split open along its seam. The soil it contains can then be examined and placed in properly labeled wide-mouthed
glass jars with watertight and airtight screw tops, so that the sample will not
dry out before it reaches the laboratory or the designing office for further
examination. The jars should have a capacity of at least 8 oz. (236 cm³).
The samples obtained by this procedure give a good idea of the general
nature and stratification of the soil layers penetrated. They permit general
identification and classification tests (Arts. 3-2A to 3-2D), but their structure
is much too disturbed to permit determination of their strength or consolidation characteristics. If the knowledge of the latter properties is required,
then so-called undisturbed sampling has to be undertaken.

The determination of the *groundwater levels* is a very important part of all soil investigations. The use of wash water for the purpose of advancing cased boreholes complicates the recording of the necessary data in cohesive soils. The casing is usually filled with water to its top, and it may take a long time for the excess water in the casing to seep out through its bottom and adjust itself to the natural water level in the surrounding soil. Special standpipes or piezometers should then be employed to observe the ground-water-level variations (see Art. 2-5).

Heavy *drilling mud* is sometimes used instead of steel casings to prevent the walls of the borehole from collapsing. The practice appears to have originated in the oil-well industry and is used for foundation exploration mainly in the southern regions of the United States.

There is no such thing as a completely undisturbed soil sample extracted from a borehole. Some deformations of the soil layers are unavoidable, even

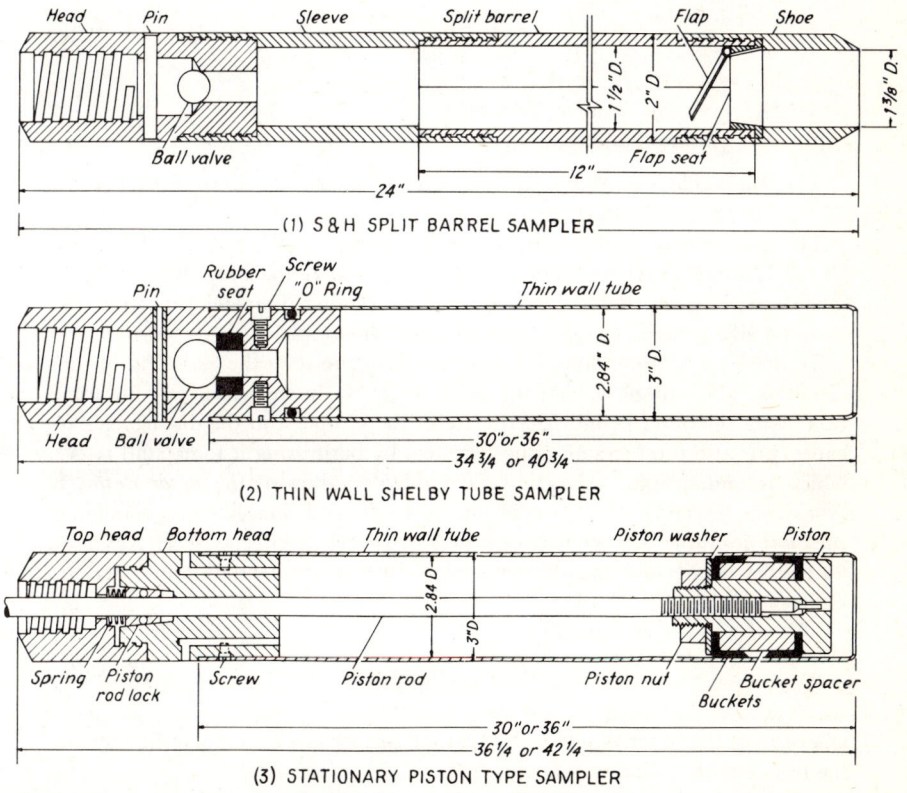

Fig. 2-3. Samplers: (1) for disturbed dry sampling of all soils; (2) and (3) for undisturbed sampling of cohesive soils. (*Sprague & Henwood, Inc.*)

with the most carefully conducted sampling operations. The removal of a sample from the surrounding soil mass changes the stresses which had been originally acting at the boundaries of the sample, and this, in turn, may also cause its subsequent deformation unless special precautions are taken. Therefore the term *undisturbed soil sample* is intended to mean a sample which has been disturbed so little that it can be used for the laboratory determination of the strength and consolidation characteristics of the natural soil in situ without any practically important errors.

An extensive 10-year study (1938 to 1948) of the problem of undisturbed sampling by Hvorslev (Ref. 139) led to the wide adoption of thin-walled samplers of the type shown in Fig. 2-3 (2) and (3). Hvorslev's classic studies indicated that the best results were obtained when the samplers were pressed (Fig. 2-4) and not driven into the soil and when their so-called *area ratio* C_a, that is, the ratio of the area of the displaced soil to the area of soil sample, was reduced to a minimum.

$$C_a = \frac{D_w^2 - D_e^2}{D_e^2} \tag{2-1}$$

where D_w = outside diameter of tube
D_e = inside diameter of orifice

The thin-walled, or *Shelby*, tube samplers [Fig. 2-3(2)] were developed as a result of Hvorslev's studies.

These samplers usually come in three tube sizes, I.D. 2.0, 2.8, and 3.37 in. (5.1, 7.1, and 8.5 cm), and in lengths varying from 18 to 30 in. (46 to 76 cm). The shorter length should be used with the smaller-diameter tube; for the medium size a length of 24 in. (61 cm) appears ample.

To decrease friction along the inner walls of the tube the lower tip of the sampling tube is slightly bent in. This relieves, during sampling, the friction along the outer cylindrical surface of the sample and the disturbance it causes but also produces an opposite effect by permitting it to expand later, which is undesirable. Hvorslev recommends values of the *inside clearance ratio* C_i not exceeding 1.5 percent for most soils and samplers, as producing the most desirable balance between these two opposite effects. (See Ref. 139 for further details and possible variations of this recommendation in different kinds of soil.)

$$C_i = \frac{D_s - D_e}{D_e} \tag{2-2}$$

where D_s is the inner diameter of the tube proper above the bent-in edge of the orifice with a diameter D_e.

As the sample tube is pushed a distance H into the ground, some of the soil may be displaced laterally and upward. As a result, the length L of soil

— Single pole
derrick

— Drill rod

— Hydraulic
head

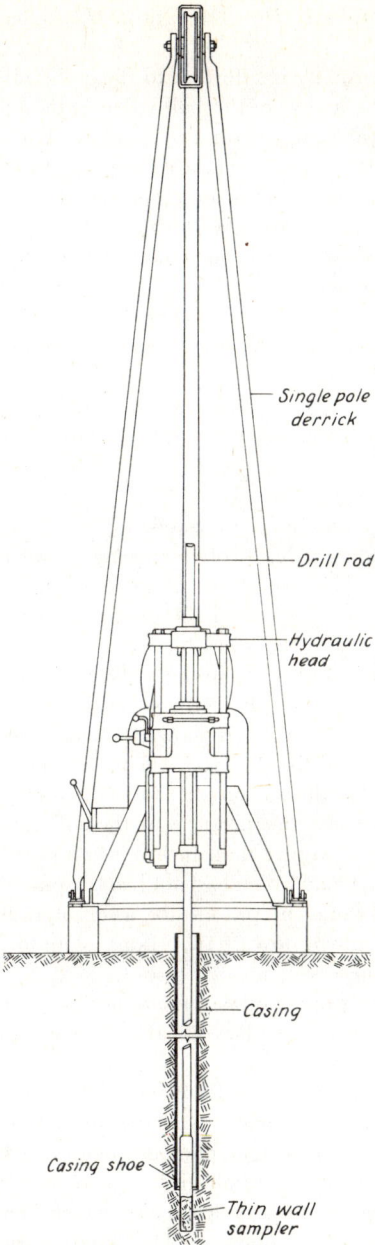

Fig. 2-4. For undisturbed sampling the samplers should be pressed, not driven, into the soil. (*Sprague & Henwood, Inc.*)

— Casing

Casing shoe

— Thin wall
sampler

in the sampler may be smaller than the distance H. The ratio L/H is called the *recovery ratio* (see Fig. 2-5).

A twist of the drill rod through 360° usually is sufficient to shear the soil off at the lower tip of the sampler. The action of the ball valve at its top [Fig. 2-3(2)] will then help to prevent the sample from dropping out while it is raised to the surface. The samples almost invariably expand fairly rapidly, at least over part of their length, so that they adhere to the walls of the tube. This also helps to retain them in the tube during withdrawal.

In some cases this is not sufficient, and samplers of the *stationary-piston type* have to be resorted to [see Fig. 2-3(3), in which the piston is shown in the position it occupies before the start of the sampling]. After the assembly, as shown, is lowered to the bottom of the borehole and comes to rest on the soil, the piston rod is clamped at the soil surface, where it protrudes from the drill rod. The sampler tube is then pushed into the soil by means of the drill rod, past the piston, which remains stationary in space (see Fig. 2-4). During the withdrawal any relative movement of the piston and tube is prevented by a conical piston-rod lock.

Stationary-piston-type samplers were first used in Sweden. The clay there frequently is very soft, its shear strength $(q_u/2)$ often varying between 0.1 and 0.2 ton/ft² (0.1 and 0.2 kg$_f$/cm²). The use of steel casing of the borehole is inadequate in such soft clays, since they are liable to be squeezed upward into the casing by the weight of the overlying soil. A stationary-piston-type sampler, however, can be pushed down from the surface through the soft clay to the elevation where one wishes to take the sample. The clay is allowed to close over the sampler around the drill rod. The piston rod is then clamped at the soil surface, and the sampler tube is pushed past the piston into the soil to a depth sufficient to ensure that the lower half of the tube is filled with clay which had not been displaced and disturbed while the piston-tube assembly was being pushed down toward it. Long sampling tubes may be necessary in such cases.

A hydraulically operated piston sampler has been developed by Osterberg (Ref. 238a). It does not require a separate piston rod.

Hvorslev's studies of the effectiveness of different types of samplers frequently were performed on varved clays of glacial origin, photographs of which in a partially dried condition give a good record of the nature of the disturbance, if any, which they underwent during sampling. The photograph should be taken after the coarser-grained silt (summer) varves have dried out sufficiently to

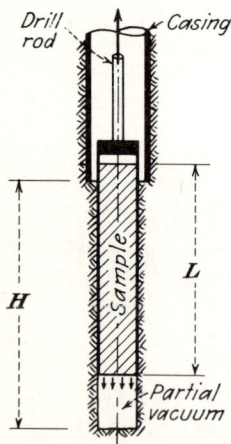

Fig. 2-5. Sketch illustrating the term *recovery ratio* L/H of a soil sample and the cause of suction forces on the bottom of the sample. (*After Hvorslev, Ref. 139.*)

VERTICAL SLICE

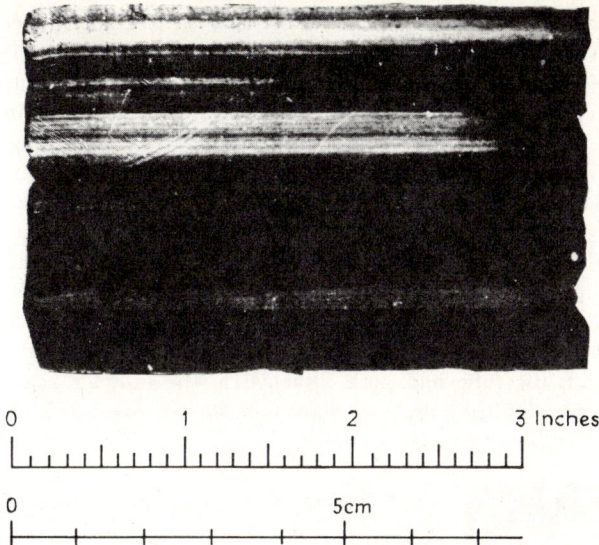

0   1   2   3 Inches

0   5cm

Fig. 2-6. Horizontally stratified, varved-clay sample in perfect condition. (*From Tschebotarioff and Bayliss, Ref. 378.*)

change their original dark color to a light one but before this has happened to the finer-grained clay (winter) varves.

This technique should be employed with all finely stratified soils as a routine laboratory control for the selection of suitable samples for strength and consolidation testing. It is fortunate that the varved clays, which are extremely sensitive to remolding, also photograph best.

Figure 2-6 shows a sample in perfect condition, which was taken with a thin-walled sampler. The stratification is horizontal, and a photograph of a vertical slice is therefore sufficient. Horizontal slices would all pass through the same varve and would therefore all be of the same color. A naturally inclined stratification would show up as parallel lines both on a vertical and on a horizontal slice of a really undisturbed sample. On the other hand, any disturbance due to sampling operations will show up in the form of curved lines both on the vertical and the horizontal slice (see Fig. 2-7 and compare with the data given by Prob. 2-1).

The following precautions are advisable when taking undisturbed samples. Prior to sampling, all loose and disturbed material should be removed from the casing down to the level of its cutting edge. A specially designed clean-out auger may be used for this purpose. Nevertheless, as an additional precaution, it is advisable to make laboratory strength and consolidation tests only on the lower half of the sample.   After the sampler is brought up to the surface, the soil-filled tube is disconnected from its head.   The tube will serve as a container.   All loose material should be removed from the upper end, and the soil at the lower end should be cut $\frac{1}{4}$ in. (6 mm) deep.   The space between the ends of the sampling tube and the surface of the soil inside the tube is then filled with hot paraffin.   This is done first at the lower end of the tube.   After the paraffin has cooled somewhat, it will generally be found that a slight shrinkage crack has formed between the edge of the paraffin and the wall of the tube.   A notch of triangular cross section, some $\frac{3}{16}$ in. (5 mm) deep, is then cut all around the edge of the paraffin and is immediately resealed with hot paraffin to fill up the shrinkage crack.   To that end, it is important to wipe away carefully any wet soil which may have adhered to the inside wall of the tube before the paraffining.   The paraffin is to fill the entire upper end of the tube, down to $\frac{1}{2}$ in. (12 mm) past the lowest of the screw holes by which the tube had been attached to the sampler head. Specially prepared, snugly fitting brass caps are then slipped over the ends

VERTICAL
SLICE

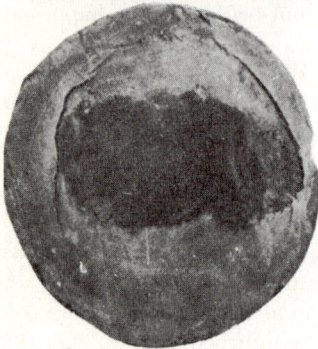

HORIZONTAL
SLICE

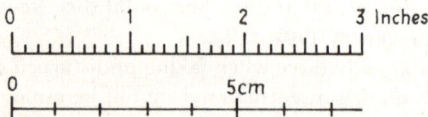

0   1   2   3 Inches

0   5cm

Fig. 2-7. The deflection of the natural horizontal stratification of a varved-clay sample caused by using a sampler with walls somewhat too thick.   (*From Tschebotarioff and Bayliss, Ref. 378.*)

of the tube.   The joints between these caps and the tubes, as well as the screw holes, should be sealed by overlapping layers of friction tape.   The tape should be brushed over with varnish or lacquer, extending over the surface of the adjoining metal.   In this condition the clay sample can be expected not to lose any of its moisture for several weeks and even months.

The *sampling of sands* presents special problems.   The provision of various types of valves at the bottom of the sampler has sometimes been undertaken for the purpose of retaining the sand sample in the tube during the withdrawal of the latter through water to the surface; otherwise the sand would trickle out of the tube.   The natural stratification of the sand may be partially preserved in such sampling, but there are no truly reliable methods for preserving for later testing its natural density in the tube.   For that reason penetration testing of sands (Art. 2-4*A*) is still the most reliable method for the estimation of the natural density of sands in situ.

Coming into increased use are devices which utilize *nuclear energy* for determining the in situ density of soils.   They appear to have been found reliable in practice for the *density-moisture control of compacted fills* (see Refs. 347, 189, and 307, item NIC-5).

(C). Layout of Boreholes and Presentation of Data.   A decision as to the exploration procedure to be selected can frequently be made on the strength of data obtained during previous constructions in the immediate vicinity.   When dealing with an entirely new location, however, it is advisable to make from the very start arrangements for a flexible program of exploration, which could be expanded or curtailed, depending on the nature of the first data obtained.

For instance, if one had to make a soil investigation for a rectangular building on a site about which nothing whatsoever is known, it would be advisable to start with five preliminary borings of $2\frac{1}{2}$ in. (6.35 cm) diameter at the four corners and at the center of the building, carried down to a depth equal to $1\frac{1}{2}$ times the length of the building, unless rock is encountered first.   Disturbed dry samples (Art. 2-3*B*) and driving records of the dry-sampling spoon (Art. 2-4*A*) would be taken in all soil layers; 2-in. (5.1-cm) undisturbed samples (Art. 2-3*B*) would be taken in layers of soft to stiff clay.   All samples would be shipped to a soil-testing laboratory as they are extracted. The natural water contents w_n (Art. 3-2*C*), the liquid limits w_L, the plastic limits w_P (Art. 3-2*F*), the unconfined compressive strengths q_u in the undisturbed and in the remolded conditions, and the corresponding strains at failure (Art. 3-2*G*) would be determined and plotted for the cohesive samples of each borehole, in a manner similar to that shown in Fig. 2-8.   The essential properties of all soil layers encountered can then be seen at a glance. If the weight of the building is such that there are doubts whether it is necessary to carry the foundation down to the sand layer at 65 ft. (20 m) depth, then a more careful study of the upper clay layer would be necessary, including a settlement analysis (Art. 4-6).   Supplementary boreholes of at least 4 in. diameter for undisturbed samples would then be required.

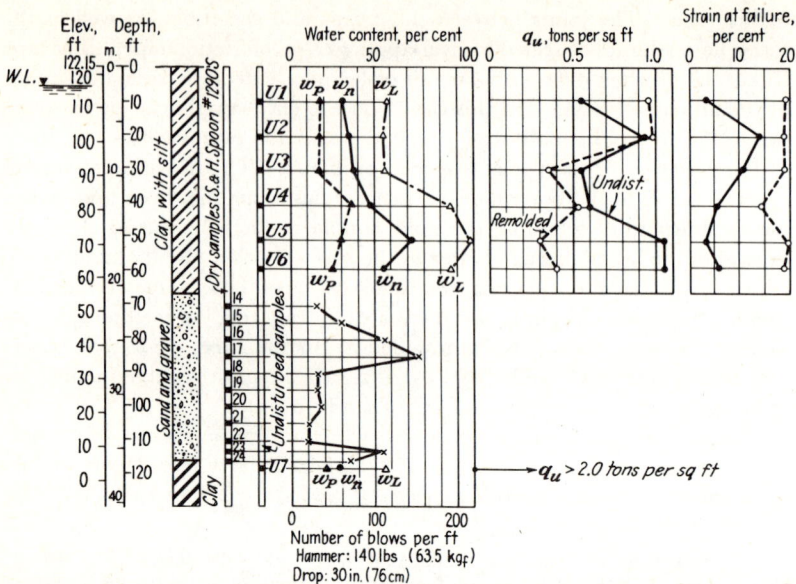

Fig. 2-8. Graphical presentation of the most essential properties of soil samples from one borehole.

Frequently, variations in soil conditions along horizontal planes make it necessary to locate borings in such a manner that a complete soil profile can be obtained. For instance, if preliminary borings 1 to 4, performed as shown in Fig. 2-9 in connection with the proposed construction of an airport, disclosed the presence of a layer of soft clay of varying thickness, then the supplementary borings 5 to 9 would be needed to complete the profile and to permit a comprehensive settlement analysis (see Prob. 4-4).

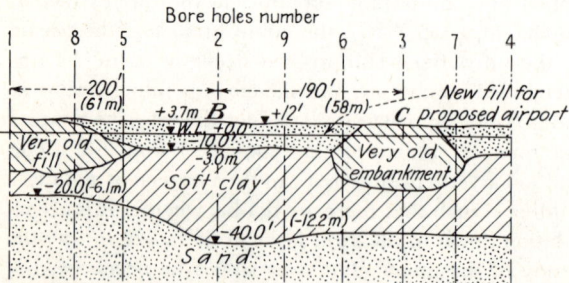

Fig. 2-9. The possible sequence of boreholes located so as to establish a comprehensive soil profile.

Figure 2-10 illustrates the need for *inclined boreholes* in geological areas where the presence of *clay-filled fissures in rock* is possible.   A grid of vertical holes missed the fissure; the problems which resulted are outlined in Art. 2-2. A similarly missed fissure caused construction problems for a concrete dam in South America.

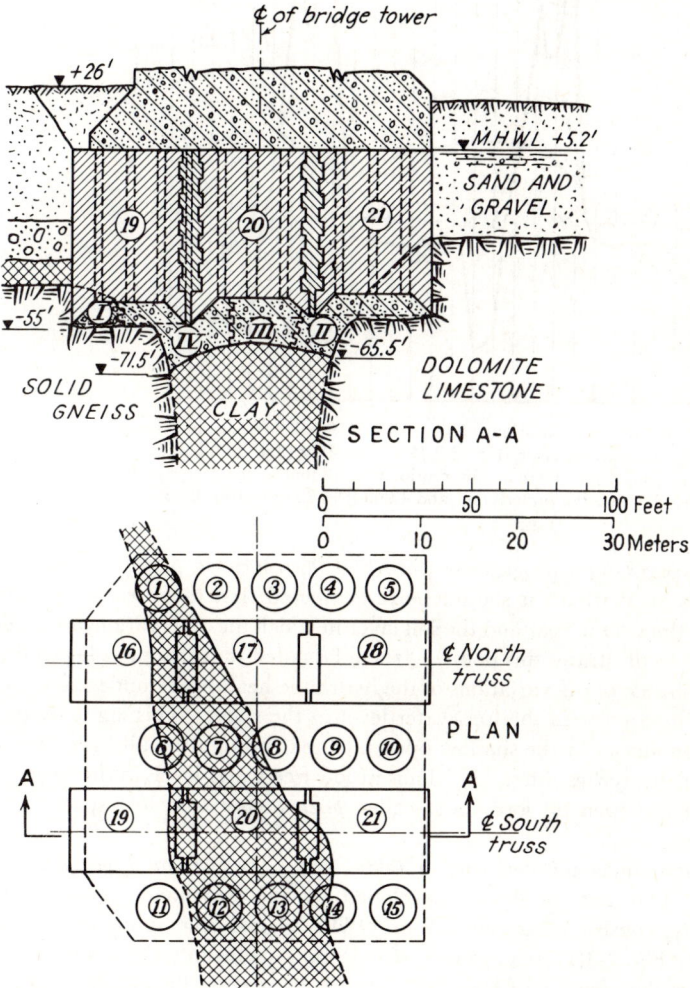

Fig. 2-10. An underground arch had to be concreted in the sequence (I), (II), (III), (IV) to bridge a clay-filled crevasse in rock beneath the compressed-air caissons of the Ward Island tower for the Hell Gate Bridge, New York. (*After Ammann, Ref. 6.*)

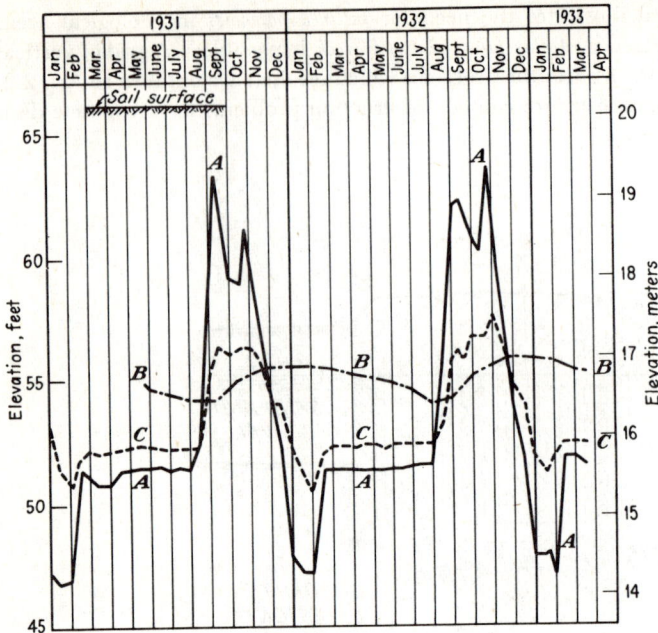

Fig. 2-11. Water-level variations: (*A*) in the river Nile; (*B*) in an open pit 3,000 ft (915 m) from the river, dug 13 ft (4 m) into 10 ft (3 m) of fill and a clay layer 25 ft (7.6 m) deep; (*C*) in an observation pipe 43 ft (13.2 m) deep reaching through the clay into the underlying sand 4,000 ft (1,225 m) from the river.

When planning a program of *water-level observations* to permit the rational design of excavations, it should be remembered that these levels can vary with the time of the year and the soil layer in which the observations are made. Figure 2-11 illustrates this point. It will be noted that there is a lag in time and amplitude of the variations of the hydraulic head in the underlying sand layer, compared with the free-water level in the river. This lag is particularly pronounced in the shallow open pit sunk through the fill into the clay layer which overlies the sand. Thus at low free-water levels in the river, the water in the open pit forms a so-called *perched water table* in respect to the underlying sand.

2-4. Soundings and Penetration Tests. *(A).* *The Standard Penetration Test* *(SPT)*. This test, originally developed by the Raymond Concrete Pile Company, consists in driving a 2-in.-O.D. (5.1-cm) split spoon of the type shown by Fig. 2-3(I) to a distance $H = 18$ in. (46 cm) into the soil below the bottom of the casing (see Figs. 2-2 and 2-5) by means of a 140-lb (63.5-kg$_f$) hammer dropped from a height of 30 in. (76 cm). The number of blows for each of the 6-in. (15.2-cm) penetrations is recorded. The first 6 in. (15.2 cm) of soil below the bottom of the casing are considered to be disturbed, and the hammer blows corresponding to that penetration are ignored.   The blows corresponding to the second and third 6-in. (15.2-cm) penetrations are then added to give the SPT value N in blows per foot.   This value originally was considered to directly reflect the density of the soil.

However, large-scale laboratory tests conducted in the early 1950s by the U.S. Bureau of Reclamation demonstrated the considerable influence of the overburden pressure on the value of N.   During these tests a large steel cylinder was filled with sand at a specified controlled density to a depth approximately equal to the cylinder's diameter.   The surface of the sand was subjected to the pressure of compressed air through a thin rubber membrane.   In the center of the membrane was a hole for a casing through which a split-spoon sampler was driven in the same manner as in the field.

The four full-line curves on Fig. 2-12 summarize the results obtained in this way for different intensities of surcharge pressure and values of the relative density D_r [Eq. (3-13)] of the sand.   The same Fig. 2-12 gives in broken-line curves the results obtained later by Bazaraa at the University of Illinois (Refs. 25 and 248).   The full circles in Fig. 2-12 refer to the average of the N values below el. -40 ft (-12.2 m) of the six boreholes shown in Fig. 2-14 with reference to the Gibbs and Holtz results, whereas the open circles refer the same average N values to the Bazaraa results.   It can be

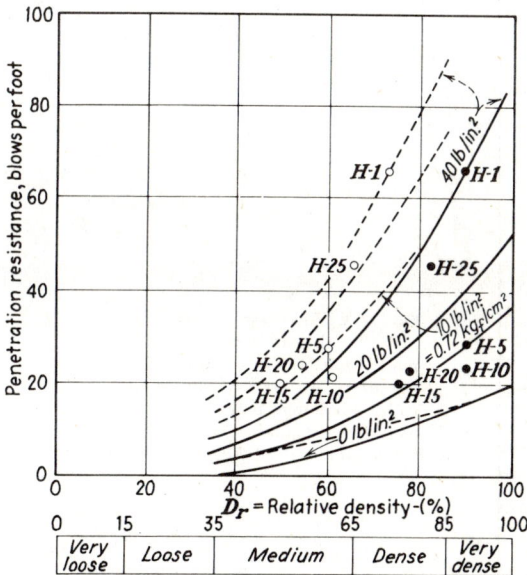

Fig. 2-12.   Effect of the overburden pressure and the relative sand density D_r on the SPT resistance N.   Full-line curves give results of Gibbs and Holtz (*Ref. 106*); the broken-line curves give the results by Bazaraa (*Ref. 134*).

seen that the fine sand at the site illustrated by Fig. 2-14 would be classified as "dense" to "very dense" according to Gibbs and Holtz but only "medium" to "dense" according to Bazaraa.

Full-scale field observations have confirmed the dependence of the N penetration-resistance values on the magnitude of the overburden pressure.

Figure 2-13 illustrates the considerable difference between the N values obtained by the SPT in two boreholes which were close to each other in plan. The first hole, PT-1, was made from the original ground surface before excavation was begun. The second hole, PT-1A, was made from the bottom

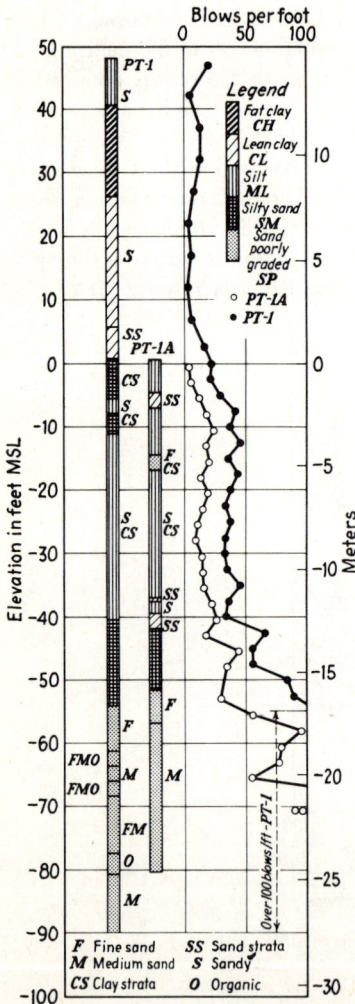

Fig. 2-13. Decrease of SPT N blows/ft values in borehole PT-1A made from bottom of 50 ft (15.3 m) deep excavation compared with adjoining borehole PT-1 made from original ground surface. (*From Mansur and Kaufman, Ref. 208.*)

Boring No.

H-1   H-5   H-10   H-15   H-20   H-25

	200'	200'	300'	200'	280'	
	(61m)	(61m)	(91.5m)	(61m)	(85.5m)	

+40'

+30'   +10m

+20'

+10'   +5m

Sand fill   ▽ W.L.   Sand fill

+0.0'   N=8 to 48 bl/ft.   ±0.0

-10'

-20'   -5m

Very soft grey clay   N = 0 to 3 bl/ft.

-30'

-40'   50   15   27   20   13.   26   -10m
                                                        18

-50'   53   16   15   11   12   41   -15m
                 30   22   14   15   44
         54   33   23   17   30   47
-60'   65   36   27   22   31   66
         79   41   30   33   33   45
-70'   90   28   30   46   69   -20m
         N   46   N(bl/ft.) 30   39   67
                 N   52   65   -25m
-80'   74   N

Fine red sand and rock flour silt   N

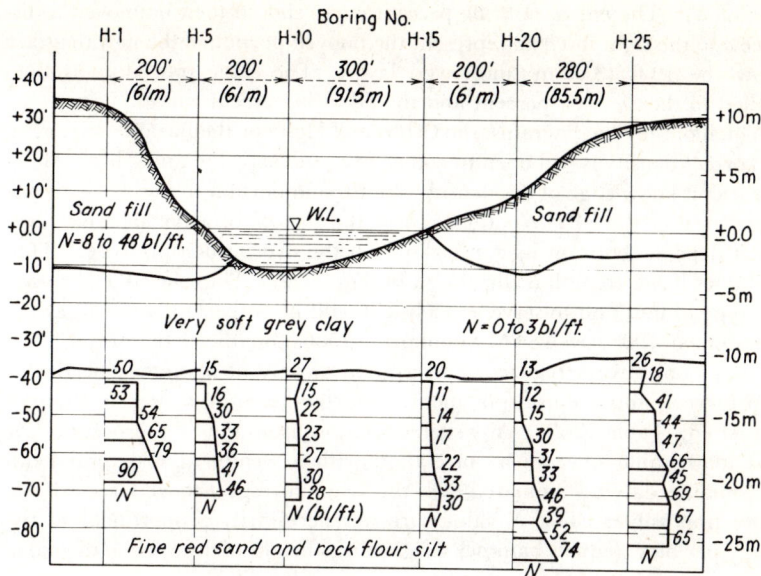

Fig. 2-14. Soil profile at the site of the highway bridge in Fig. 10-34. (*From Tschebotarioff, Ref. 374.*)

of the 50-ft-deep (15-m) excavation after the 100 by 150 ft (30.5 by 46.7 m) area in plan was fully excavated. This excavation was equivalent to the removal (Ref. 208) of some 2,500 lb/ft^2 = 17.35 lb/in.^{2} = 1.23 kg$_f$/cm^2 overburden pressure. It can be seen from Fig. 2-13 that as a result the N values decreased everywhere to about half their original values.

Another field example of the influence of overburden pressure on the N values is given by Figs. 2-14 and 2-15. The deep layer of fine red sand and rock-flour silt is of glacial origin. It will be noted from Figs. 2-14 and 2-15 that the N values in that deep layer increased with the height of fill at the location of each borehole.

Figure 2-16 shows how the N blow-count values in a boring can be related to the sand density, using the curves of Fig. 2-12. The scale on the left-hand side of each of the two diagrams refers to a fully submerged buoyed overburden weighing $\gamma' = 60$ lb/ft^3 = 0.960 g$_f$/cm^3. The scale on the right-hand side of the diagrams refers to a nonbuoyed overburden weighing $\gamma = 100$ lb/ft^3 = 1.60 g$_f$/cm^3. Diagrams corresponding to any combination of these two conditions can be constructed, point by point, as shown in Fig. 2-16A. Let us suppose that there are 10 ft (3.05 m) of unbuoyed overburden above the free-water table. A horizontal line is then drawn through the 10-ft (3.05-m) point on the right-hand scale until it intersects the $D_r = 85$ percent curve, from where it is then projected upward to the zero depth scale of N.   The entire $D_r = 85$ percent curve should then be moved a distance a to the right if it is to represent the buoyed portion of the new diagram below the 10-ft (3.05-m) unbuoyed layer.   The same procedure is then applied to the $D_r = 65$ percent and the $D_r = 35$ percent curves.

Which of the two diagrams, the Gibbs and Holtz or the Bazaraa one, gives the correct density is still open to conjecture (see Refs. 134 and 248).   However, exact knowledge of the density is not too important in most cases if one considers that the SPT N values reflect the *strength* of a noncohesive layer which depends both on its density and on the overburden pressure.   That sand does have strength is illustrated by Fig. 3-22.   Thus the SPT is a *yardstick* type of test, and to serve as such it should be truly standardized, as has been done in 1966 (see ASTM Standard D-1586, also discussions of Ref. 142). This was not always realized, and a great variety of hammers, heights of drop thereof, and even of split-spoon diameters have been used in the past (see 1st ed., Table 12-2).   Any such deviations from the SPT procedure are most inadvisable since then correlation with a wealth of structural field-performance data accumulated over the years in respect to SPT records becomes impossible.   The N values are not necessarily proportional to the energy per blow (equals hammer weight times height of drop) or to the cross-sectional areas of the spoon.

The effect of overburden pressure on the N values of cohesive soils has not yet been ascertained.   However, in contrast to sandy soils, this is not important since the essential strength and consolidation characteristics of clays can be obtained by undisturbed sampling and subsequent laboratory testing. The SPT serves only as a rough preliminary indication of the clay consistency (see Art. 3-7D).

(B). Soundings and Cone-penetration Tests.   The simplest type of sounding consists in driving a steel rod into the soil for the purpose of determining the

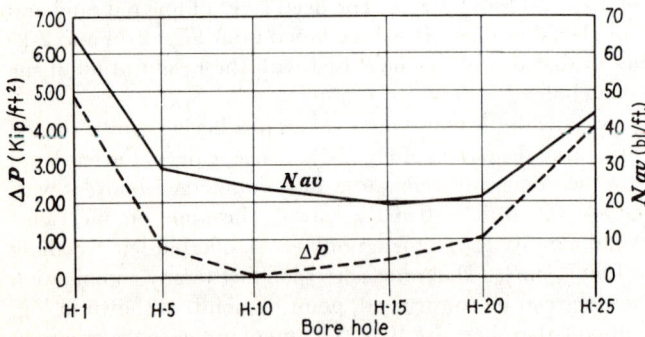

Fig. 2-15. Increase of average SPT N values in the six boreholes shown on Fig. 2-14 with the increment of overburden pressure Δp, compared with the pressure at borehole H-10. *(From Tschebotarioff, Ref. 374.)*

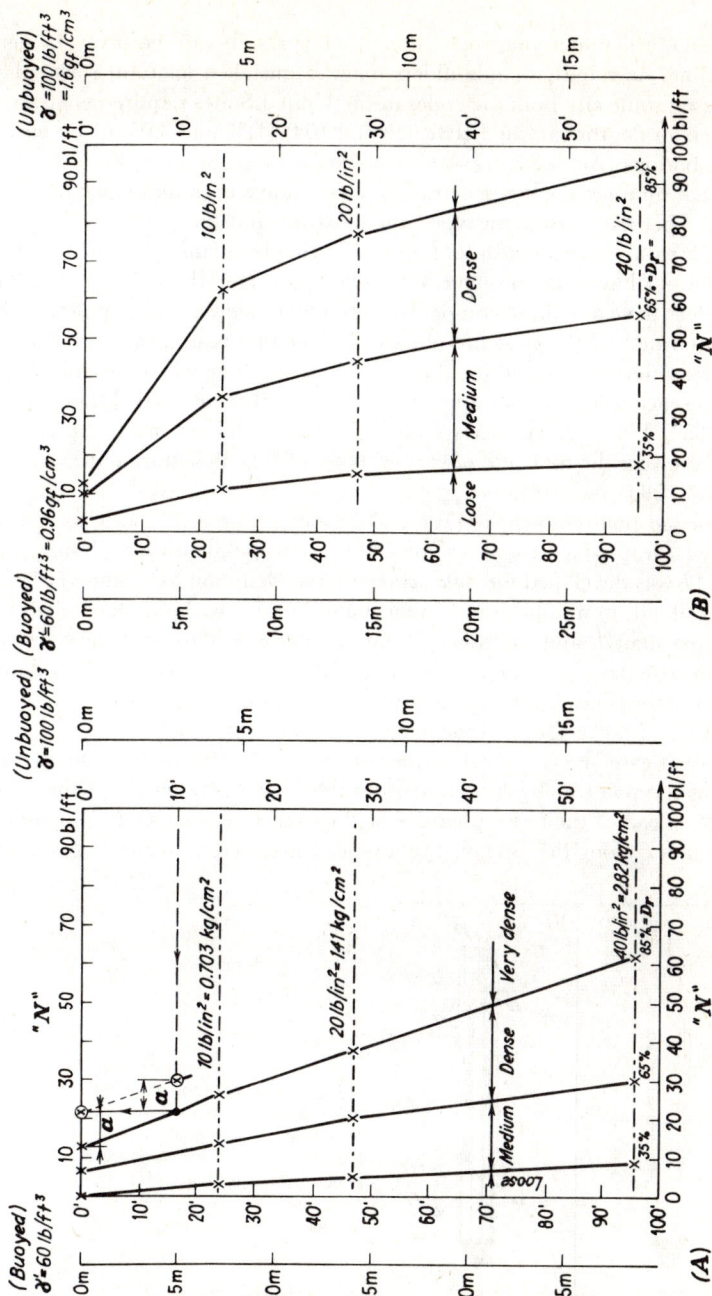

Fig. 2-16. Relationship between the relative sand density D_r and the SPT N values in a borehole after (A) Gibbs and Holtz and (B) Bazaraa.

elevation of the underlying rock surface. The results can, however, be very misleading, since individual boulders may be mistaken for solid rock. For this reason some city building codes in the United States require penetration into rock for depths varying between 5 and 10 ft (1.52 and 3.05 m) by means of core borings (Art. 2-6).

A great number of cone-penetration devices have been developed over the years. There are two main types, the dynamic and the static.

The *dynamic cone-penetration test* requires driving by a falling weight and does not seem to have any pronounced advantages over the split-spoon SPT. But it does have a definite comparative disadvantage since no samples of the soil penetrated by the cone are obtained. For that reason the U.S. Bureau of Reclamation abandoned the use of the dynamic cone method in mid-1955, and reference to it does not appear in any issue of their Earth Manual after 1956 (Ref. 135). Nevertheless, various attempts have been made to correlate results of the SPT and of various types of cone penetration devices (see Refs. 282, 283, and 246).

The cone point shown in Fig. 2-17(I) can be used for both static and dynamic (drop-penetration) testing. The cone point of type II shown in Fig. 2-17 was developed for *static testing* by the Delft Soil Mechanics Laboratory, Holland, to minimize the danger of soil grains wedging themselves between the shaft R and the tube T when the latter is pushed down. In the position shown in Fig. 2-17(II) the shaft R has been pushed down the amount b ahead of the tube T. It can be pushed down only the distance a before the maximum distance L of its independent movement is reached.

In either case one can obtain either the resistance P of the cone point—by pressing the point or by driving it from the surface, by means of the inner shaft R, ahead of the outer pipe T—or the total resistance $P + F$, including the friction F along the pipe T, if that pipe is used to force the cone point into

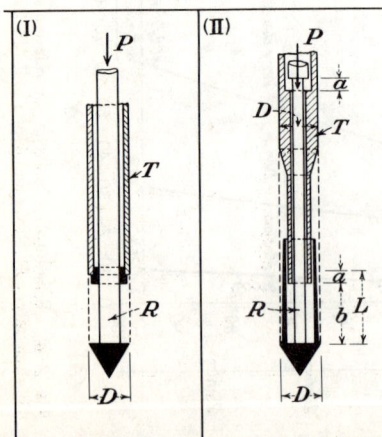

Fig. 2-17. Two of the many types of conical points used for deep soundings: (I) simple type used both for static and dynamic (drop-penetration) testing; (II) Delft type used for static penetration testing.

the soil.   Usually one alternates the two methods every foot or so.   In some recent models electric pressure gages register simultaneously but separately the point P and the frictional F resistances.

Cone-penetration tests are performed as a matter of routine in Holland and in Belgium, where the soil conditions are particularly favorable for this type of investigation.   Peat or soft clays frequently are found there down to depths of some 60 ft (18.3 m) and are followed by sands of varying density. The cone points can then be easily pushed right down to and into the sand, to determine in advance of construction the elevation to which pile points should reach.   Correlations have been obtained between the resistance of the cone point and the bearing capacity of the end-bearing piles (Ref. 391).

Two comparative studies illustrated by Figs. 2-18 and 2-19 showed that the Delft type [Fig. 2-17(II)] of cone-penetration test could be a very useful auxiliary to the SPT in medium to dense sands since it is more sensitive to strength variations of very thin layers (see Fig. 2-18).   However, it could not be used to penetrate very dense layers with $N > 70$ blows/ft (see Fig. 2-19).

In these studies a 300-lb (136-kg$_f$) hammer dropped from a height of 12 in. (30.5 cm) was used on the spoon shown by Fig. 2-3(I).   Thus the sampler was identical to the SPT, but the energy per blow was 3,600 in.-lb (4,150 cm-kg$_f$), or somewhat smaller than the 4,200 in.-lb (4,840 cm-kg$_f$) in the SPT.   The hydraulic swivelhead of a core-drilling machine of the type shown in Fig. 2-23 was adapted to press the cone points into the soil and to measure their resistance by gages which recorded the pressure in the oil of the swivelhead press.

The first study was made possible, by the cooperation of Spencer, White & Prentis, Inc., and of G. Lutz of the Turner Construction Co., on the site of a heavy structure founded on a deep bed of loose sand which was known to have settled approximately 3.5 in. (9 cm).   Other records referring to that structure are given in Fig. 4-21 and Prob. 4-1.   Three cone-penetration soundings were performed at a distance of 4 ft (1.2 m) from each other.   It can be seen from Fig. 2-18 that they all gave results which agreed fairly closely with each other, as well as with the results of the S. & H. dry-sampling spoon-driving record.   The static cone-point records appeared to be somewhat more sensitive to changes in soil density than the dynamic driving records of the spoon, but both showed the same trends.   Immediately under the old footing foundation the sand was found to be somewhat compacted by the weight of the building which had rested on it in the past.   Deeper down the sand was found to be of a loose to medium density (compare the spoon-driving record with Fig. 2-16).   The sand gradually increased in density with depth.   The spoon was driven 18 in. (45 cm).   Note that the number of blows between 0- and 12-in. (30-cm) penetration is practically identical with the number recorded between 6- and 18-in. (15- and 45-cm) penetration. The loosening of the sand after the driving and the withdrawal of the S. & H.

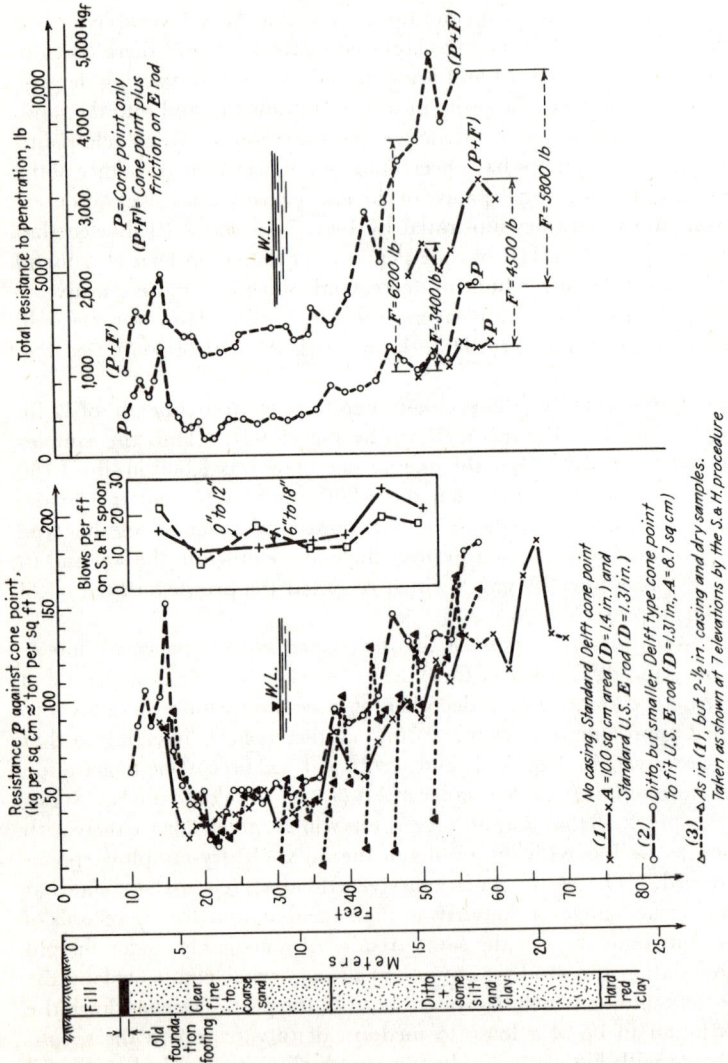

Fig. 2-18. Comparison between S. & H. dry-sampling spoon-driving record in *loose sand* and the penetration resistance of Delft type cones. *(Tests performed by Sprague & Henwood, Inc.; supervised by Tschebotarioff.)*

44

sampler every 5 ft (1.5 m) or so is clearly shown by the cone-point record of the corresponding test 3 in Fig. 2-18.   The disturbance, however, did not reach down more than a couple of feet.   The use of a rod T for test 1, which had a diameter 0.1 in. (2.5 mm) smaller than the diameter of the cone, decreased the total friction F along the rod by some 25 to 45 percent compared with test 2, where the diameters of the rod and of the cone were identical.

The second study was made on the site of a building in Philadelphia founded on a layer of very compact sand and gravel (Fig. 2-19).   The building had settled only between $\frac{1}{8}$ and $\frac{1}{4}$ in. (3.2 and 6.4 mm).   The settlement occurred very rapidly and ceased soon after application of the loads.   It can be seen from Fig. 2-19 that it proved possible to drive the S. & H. spoon at all elevations and to obtain a driving record which indicated the very dense nature of the soil (compare with Fig. 2-16).   On the other hand, it did not prove possible in many cases to press the Delft cone even a fraction of an inch into the soil at the bottom of the $2\frac{1}{2}$-in. (6.4-cm) casing without bending the rod R [see Fig. 2-17(II)].   This location is marked by the infinity sign (∞) in the resistance chart (Fig. 2-19).   It can thus be concluded that the present Delft cone point cannot penetrate dense granular materials in which more than 50 to 70 blows/ft were required to drive a 2-in.-O.D. (5-cm) sampler.

Therefore the cone-penetration test could not be expected to find general use in the United States as an independent means of investigation, i.e., in the way it is employed in Holland, where it is sometimes used prior to the performance of borings.   It is necessary to anchor the entire rig to the soil, in order to provide an effective reaction to the $P + F$ resistance of cone and tube, which may frequently exceed 11,000 lb (5,000 kg$_f$) (see Fig. 2-18).   The rig has to be reanchored at each location of a sounding, a matter of no great importance in countries with low wage rates, but in the United States it may increase the total cost appreciably and offset economic advantages derived from the rapid performance of the sounding itself.

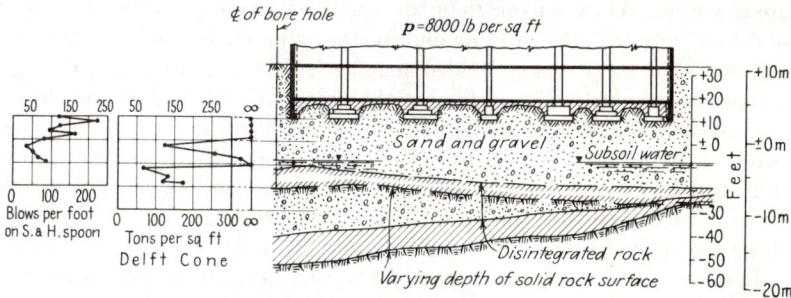

Fig. 2-19.   Comparison between S. & H. dry-sampling spoon-driving record in *dense sand* and the penetration resistance of a Delft type cone.   (*Tests performed by Sprague & Henwood, Inc.; supervised by Tschebotarioff; sponsored by Foundation Committee, Philadelphia Section, ASCE.*)

A comprehensive review of the uses of various types of penetrometers in soil exploration work and of the interpretation of the data obtained has been given by G. Sanglerat (Ref. 278a).

A book by Schultze and Muhs (Ref. 283) provides information on methods of soil exploration customary in Germany.

2-5. Soil Tests in Boreholes.   Attempts to perform *vertical load tests* in boreholes have been made.   Nevertheless, later correlations with the performance of actual structures indicated the complete unreliability of the results of such load tests, especially below groundwater level, since the soil of the bottom of the borehole has inevitably been disturbed or has expanded somewhat, so that its compressibility is much greater than in the natural state.

The same criticism applies to most models of the so-called *pressiometer,* an expanding device first developed by Koegler (Ref. 172) for the purpose of testing the horizontal resistance to such expansion of the borehole walls. The revival of relevant attempts in the 1960s brought about a desirable miniaturization of the instruments and the development of evaluation theories, especially in France (Ref. 179).   However, in the writer's opinion, many claims of what the instrument can achieve in practice have not been substantiated so far.   For instance, it does not appear possible to reconstruct the deformation characteristics of an undisturbed sensitive clay by any method of analysis once it has been remolded, any more than this is possible, say, in a laboratory triaxial test.   And remolding of a sensitive clay is inevitable once the borehole casing is pulled while the pressiometer is expanded to replace the casing's contact with the soil.   This objection appears to have been at least partially met by a modified device *(sonde autoforeuse, Ponts et Chaussées)* which incorporated the pressiometer in the walls of the casing itself (see fig. 30, pp. 20–21 of Ref. 179, and Baguelin et al., Ref. 21).

The generally accepted and frequently used types of soil tests in boreholes are the vane shear tests and the piezometer pore-pressure measurements in plastic clay layers.

The *vane shear tests* were first developed in Sweden, where some of the clays are so soft that they are liable to be squeezed up into the casing by the weight of the soil outside it, thus making undisturbed sampling impossible.   A vane, i.e., two thin metal plates welded together to form a cross in horizontal section, is protected by a sturdier metal housing which is pushed down from the soil surface to slightly above the elevation where the shear test is to be made.   Then the vane is thrust out of the housing and down into the undisturbed clay mass by means of an inner rod reaching to the surface.   A measured torque is then slowly applied to that rod to produce a cylindrical shear failure in the clay.

In some cases it has been found advantageous to use such vanes below the bottom of regular borehole casings, especially when the clay was so soft that the handling of undisturbed samples for laboratory unconfined compression tests became difficult.   Figures 2-20 and 2-21 show one such vane model.

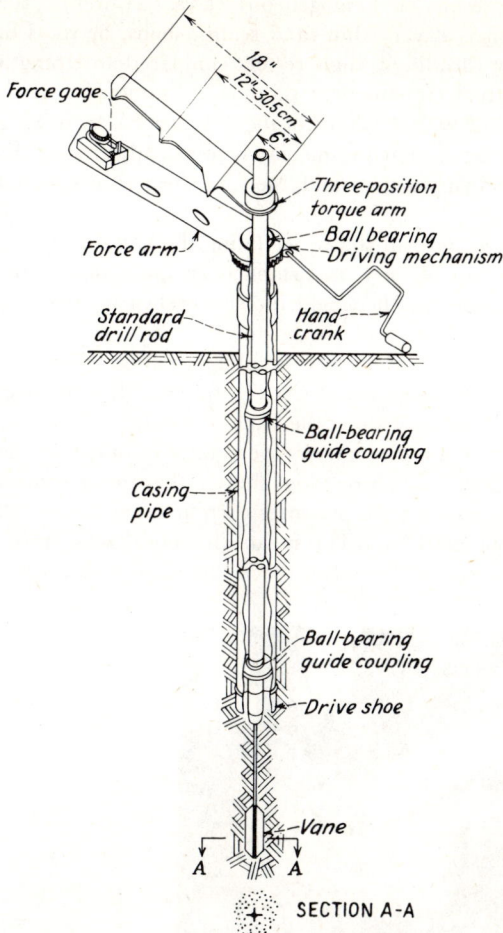

Fig. 2-20. Vertical section through a vane shear-test assembly. (*Acker Drill Co.*)

The vanes for this particular model come in three different sizes for use in casings with diameters of $2\frac{1}{2}$, 3, or 4 in. (6.35, 7.6, or 10.2 cm).   By varying the position of the force gage on the torque arm the sensitivity of the readings can be varied: the 6-in. (15.3-cm) position is for soft clays, the 12-in. (30.5-cm) position for medium clays, and the 18-in. (45.6-cm) position for stiff clays. Charts indicating the shearing strength of the clay for the measured torque and a given vane size are available.   The initial readings give the undisturbed peak strength.   Continued rotation of the vane can be made to indicate the remolded strength.

The vanes give reliable results in homogeneous clays. However, the writer found that the presence of very thin sand seams, shells, or roots in organic deposits will give misleadingly high results compared to strength values obtained from an actual embankment slide at the same site. It is therefore advisable to take a disturbed sample of the soil sheared, by driving a split-spoon sampler to the depth tested immediately after withdrawing the vane. If roots, shells, or sand varves are found, the vane shear values should be suspected of being too high.

The measurement of *pore pressures* in the water filling the voids of a consolidating plastic clay layer can be very important as an indication of the actual rate at which consolidation and hence the increase of shearing strength has progressed (see Arts. 3-5A, 3-5D, and 5-2).

Figure 2-22 illustrates the kind of practically useful information which can be obtained by properly installed *piezometers* (Art. 1-9). As fill was being placed over a deep deposit of soft clay along the bank of a large river, a surface mud wave developed. Four piezometers were then installed at the elevations indicated in Fig. 2-22. Their readings showed that in the central portion of the clay layer the excess pore pressures corresponded to the full effective weight of the newly placed fill. This meant that no increase in the shearing strength of the clay had as yet taken place there and that a deep

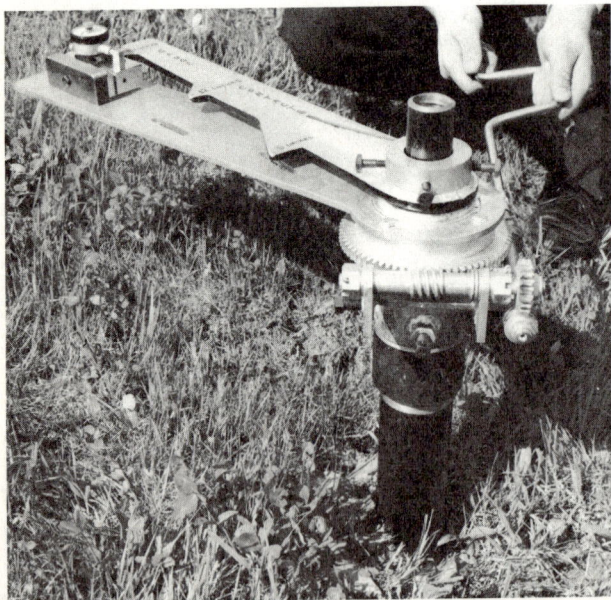

Fig. 2-21. Upper portion of vane shear-test assembly in Fig. 2-20. (*Acker Drill Co.*)

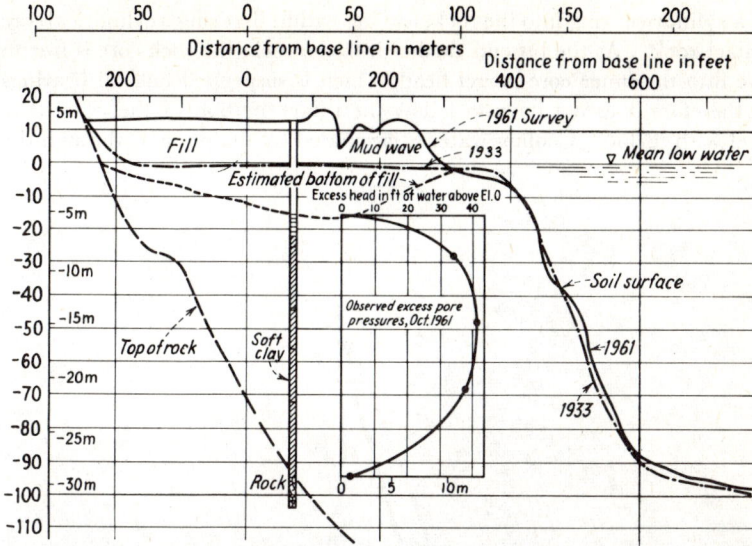

Fig. 2-22. Example of useful pore-pressure data provided by properly installed piezometers; 1 : 10 ratio of vertical to horizontal scales. (*From a U.S. Waterways Experiment Station report.*)

slide was on the point of developing. Further placement of the fill was therefore postponed.

In this case the piezometers were installed by·expert personnel of the U.S. Waterways Experiment Station. It should be emphasized in this connection that piezometer installation (Art. 1-9) is far from being a foolproof procedure. The writer had an unpleasant experience when piezometers installed on his recommendation by a reputable drilling contractor reflected tidal variations in a nearby river estuary. This meant that the bentonitic slurry in the borehole (Art. 1-9) did not properly isolate the piezometers within the clay layer from the overlying sand layers, thereby making all their readings useless for the desired estimation of the actual rate of consolidation of the clay.

2-6. Core Borings. This type of boring is used when one wishes to penetrate into rock and to obtain a continuous core sample thereof. The type of equipment which is employed for this purpose is illustrated by Fig. 2-23. The machine operates on principles somewhat similar to those of the drill presses found in most machine shops.

The engine *A*, by means of a bevel-gear drive and drill-rod chuck, rotates the drill rod, to the end of which is attached a coring device. The outer barrel of this device rotates with the drill rod. It is pressed down against the rock by means of the hydraulic swivelhead *B*. A special bit, studded with industrial diamonds for use in hard rock, or a sawtooth bit tipped with carbide for use in soft rock is mounted at the end of the outer-core barrel and cuts a cylindrical ring into the rock, leaving within that ring a cylindrical core of intact rock. As the bit cuts further into the rock, the rock core is free to move into the inner core-barrel head, which is suspended on ball bearings and therefore does not have to follow the rotary motion of the outer-core barrel with its bit. Cooling water is circulated by the pump C through the

Fig. 2-23. A core-boring machine in operation. (*Sprague & Henwood, Inc.*)

TABLE 2-1

Nominal size	EX	AX	2 in. (5.1 cm)	BX	NX
Core diameter, in.	$\frac{7}{8}$	$1\frac{1}{8}$	$1\frac{3}{8}$	$1\frac{5}{8}$	$2\frac{1}{8}$
mm	24.4	29.6	35.0	41.2	54.0

hose D and hollow drill rod.   A length of several feet of rock core can be obtained in this manner.   As the withdrawal is begun, a split conical ring, the so-called core lifter, wedges itself around the bottom of the rock core and thus permits it to be torn from the underlying rock.   Cores as small as 1 in. (2.54 cm) in diameter can be obtained.   Customary bit sizes and their designations in the United States are given in Table 2-1.

To obtain satisfactory cores of soft rocks, such as shales, bit sizes smaller than $NX = 2\frac{1}{8}$ in. (54.0 mm) in diameter should be avoided.

The time of coring should be recorded, as an indication of the rock hardness and, especially, the recovery (L/H; see Fig. 2-5) in percent.

The drill rig shown in Fig. 2-23, in addition to coring, can be used for advancing the casing of a borehole (Fig. 2-2) and for all types of sampling (Figs. 2-3 and 2-4).   The sheave wheel E on Fig. 2-23 is then used to operate the 300-lb (136-kg$_f$) hammer F to drive the casing and the 140-lb (63.5-kg$_f$) hammer G for the SPT.   Heavier machines than the ones shown in Fig. 2-23 have to be used if cores of more than a few inches in diameter are to be obtained.   For the exploration of the sites of some important dams very large cores have been taken, leaving holes of 30 in. (76 cm) diameter into which geologists could be lowered for visual examination of the rock formation along the entire depth of the hole.   Steel shot is customarily used instead of diamond-studded bits for holes larger than those listed in Table 2-1.

Attempts have been made to apply the procedures of core boring to the undistorted sampling of clays.   Notable is the Denison sampler, developed during the construction of the Denison (Texoma) Dam.   Its inner stationary barrel has a diameter of 6 in. (15.3 cm) and provides satisfactory cores of stiff clays and soft rocks (see Fig. 2-24).   It should not be used, however, in soft or only partially cohesive soils, especially below the water table (see Fig. 2-25).

2-7. Rigs for Water Borings.   One of the simplest methods is illustrated by Fig. 2-26.   The drilling rig is mounted on a platform which bridges the space between two boats, forming a catamaran type of vessel.   It is not convenient to work from except in very calm water.

Driving timber piles in shallow water for the stable support of temporary platforms represents a slow and, in most cases, uneconomical procedure.

Steel lattice towers shaped like a truncated pyramid have been used in the Far East, especially in harbors where floating cranes are available to move

Fig. 2-24. A satisfactory core of soft chalk obtained by the Denison sampler.   (*Photo by Tschebotarioff.*)

Fig. 2-25. Misuse of Denison sampler in a saturated layer of medium-stiff sandy clay. (*Photo by Tschebotarioff.*)

Fig. 2-26. Drilling from a platform supported by two boats. (*Photo by Tschebotarioff.*)

Fig. 2-27. Drilling from a truncated steel lattice pyramid lifted by hoist of small steamer for transportation from one location to another.   (*Photo by Tschebotarioff.*)

them from one drilling location to another. Where this is not the case, small steamers have to be rented for the purpose, as shown in Fig. 2-27, a photograph taken from such a steamer in Thailand. Some tower models have hollow steel cylinders attached to each of the four legs to provide temporary flotation to the tower when compressed air expels water from the cylinders. Small tugs can then move the tower. However, no type of tower can well be used on underwater slopes since they are apt to tilt.

A level, fully stable, easily movable but expensive support for drilling in water depths of 100 ft (30.5 m) and more can be provided by De Long type platforms (see Fig. 6-29).

A simpler unit with three hand-operated winches has been used by Tecnosolo of Brazil (see Fig. 2-28). A floatable hollow metal box in the shape of an approximately 25-ft (7.6-m) equilateral triangle in plan, with an opening for borehole casings at its center, is supported at its corners by a total of three piles, fabricated of welded U-shaped steel sheet piles, which are capable of sliding along guide openings in the box. A cable, anchored to

Fig. 2-28. Drilling in Brazil from a Tecnosolo hollow steel platform, capable of floating and lifting itself along three special supporting piles. (*Courtesy of A. J. Da Costa Nunes.*)

the deck, strung over a pulley on top of each pile P and connected to one of the winches via another pulley on the deck, makes it possible to exert a downward force on the pile. Once all three piles have been pushed down to refusal into the soil, further operation of the winches will lift the box out of the water above the expected wave-crest height, when it can be firmly wedged against the piles. After work is completed at one location, the piles are pulled out of the soil with the help of the winches and of the derrick at the center of the box, whereupon the entire contraption can be towed to a new borehole location.

Figure 2-28 shows the platform operating in 90 ft (27.5 m) of water well above the crest of waves 4 ft (1.23 m) high.

REVIEW PROBLEMS

2-1. The sample illustrated in Fig. 2-6 is in perfect condition. It was extracted by a thin-walled sampler of the type shown in Fig. 2-3(II) with $D_w = 3.00$ in. (7.6 cm) and $D_e = 2.8$ in. (7.1 cm) [see Eq. (2-1)]. On the other hand, the strongly distorted sample shown in Fig. 2-7 was extracted by a sampler with an inner lining tube, outer split cylinder, and a somewhat thicker shoe to hold the assembly together, $D_w = 3.625$ in. (9.2 cm), and $D_e = 2.93$ in. (7.45 cm). What are the area ratios of C_a of the two samplers?

Answer. According to Eq. (2-1), the thin-walled sampler will have a low value of the area ratio

$$C_a = \frac{3.00^2 - 2.80^2}{2.80^2} = 0.147$$

The second sampler, which had walls of medium thickness and produced unsatisfactory results, has a value about 4 times higher,

$$C_a = \frac{3.625^2 - 2.930^2}{2.930^2} = 0.530$$

2-2. In view of the results of Prob. 2-1, would there be much point in performing strength tests on clay samples extracted by means of the dry-sampling technique and samplers of the type illustrated in Fig. 2-3(I)?

Answer. No; the area ratio of such samplers is much too high:

$$C_a = \frac{2.00^2 - 1.437^2}{1.437^2} = 0.94$$

If one is compelled for reasons of economy to use $2\frac{1}{2}$-in. (6.35-cm)-diameter casing, then a 2-in. (5.1-cm) thin-walled Shelby tube sampler, of the type shown in Fig. 2-3(II), should be employed [$D_w = 2.00$ in. (5.1 cm); $D_e = 1.80$ in. (4.6 cm)] for strength tests. It has

$$C_a = \frac{2.0^2 - 1.8^2}{1.8^2} = 0.23$$

This is satisfactory for strength tests of a preliminary nature but is too high for accurate consolidation testing.

2-3. A 4-in. (10.2-cm) casing was sunk on a riverbank through a layer of clay and reached sand at a depth of 60 ft (18.3 m) from the soil surface. The groundwater level, before the hole reached the sand, was at a depth of 15 ft (4.6 m) below the soil surface but rose by 10 ft

(3 m) after the clay layer was pierced. The bottom of the casing was washed out by a chopping bit (Fig. 2-2), which was then withdrawn, and a dry sampler [Fig. 2-5(I)] was lowered to obtain a driving record for the purpose of estimating the density of the sand. It was, however, found that the sand had risen 2 ft (0.6 m) into the casing. How would you meet the situation?

Answer. The rise of the water in the casing after the clay layer was pierced indicates some artesian pressure in the sand layer. It is therefore particularly important to keep the casing continuously filled with water to its top at all stages of the work. This includes the time during which the chopping bit is withdrawn. The volume of the bit and of 60 ft (18.3 m) of drill rod above it is sufficient to cause a drop of several feet of the water level in the casing unless water is continuously added to keep the casing full to the top. A drop of the water level in the casing, even if it occurs for a very short time only, may be sufficient to produce a quick condition (Art. 8-3) in the sand at its bottom and upward flow of the liquefied sand into the casing. Of course, the sand below the casing is also loosened thereby for a foot or two.

CHAPTER 3

SOIL IDENTIFICATION AND TESTING

3-1. Properties of Solid Soil Particles and Adsorbed Water. *(A). Specific Gravity of Solid Particles.* The specific gravity of solid particles is determined as follows:

$$G = \frac{W_s}{V_s} \tag{3-1}$$

where G = specific gravity of the solid particles

W_s = weight of the solid particles, g$_f$

V_s = volume of the solid particles, cm³

Thus with metric units the specific gravity represents the weight per unit of volume γ_s of the solid substance. Another definition of the specific gravity reads: the ratio of the weight in air of a given volume of a material at a stated temperature to the weight in air of an equal volume of distilled water at a stated temperature, i.e.,

$$G = \frac{W_s}{V_s \gamma_w} \tag{3-1a}$$

This expression corresponds to Eq. (3-1) at 4°C since then $\gamma_w = 1.00$.

The specific gravity of the solid particles of most inorganic soils varies between 2.60 and 2.80. Sand particles composed of quartz have a specific gravity around 2.65. Clays can have values as high as 2.90.

Most minerals of which the solid matter of soil particles is composed will have a specific gravity greater than 2.60.   Therefore values of specific gravity smaller than that figure are an indication of the possible presence of *organic matter* in the soil in appreciable quantity and show that caution is required.   Soils with considerable organic content are very compressible, for instance peat, which is composed almost entirely of vegetable matter, with the result that it may burn when dry.   Apart from the high compressibility which results from their structure, soils with high organic content are undesirable in engineering work because of the possibilities of decay of the organic matter.   They are also undesirable in soil-stabilization work.

The organic content of soils is sometimes assumed to equal the loss in weight suffered by a soil held over a flame until the soil particles are red hot, i.e., the so-called *ignition loss*.   This method is liable to give too high values, since, in addition to the destruction of the organic matter, chemically bound and adsorbed water may be liberated and removed at temperatures exceeding 105°C.

The specific gravity of soils is generally determined through the measurement of the volume of water displaced by the solid soil particles.   The adsorbed water films (Art. 3-1C) are included in the volume of the solid particles.   However, these films are so thin that their presence does not appreciably change the values of the specific gravity of solids which have adsorbed them.

For techniques of testing, see Ref. 18, item D-854.

This test is not very important by itself; it is performed in connection with computations required for other tests.

(B). Clay Minerals; Shape and Hardness of Grains.   X-ray studies of clays have shown that they are composed of extremely small crystals, in spite of the amorphous appearance of the whole clay mass.   In this manner the existence of at least two definite *clay minerals* of extreme types, *kaolinite* and *montmorillonite*, and of some intermediate types has been established.   Kaolinite was found to have a very rigid crystal structure, whereas montmorillonite can expand by admitting water between its crystal planes.   Its crystal structure thus has an accordionlike nature which explains the swelling tendencies of bentonite clays largely composed of the montmorillonite type of clay minerals.

The shape of the soil grains has been found to be of considerable importance for the explanation of many phenomena.   It was suspected for some time that the plasticity and also the considerable compressibility of clays might be due to the scalelike shape of their particles.   The Swedish scientist Atterberg proved this by pulverizing various minerals and separating the particles of colloid size.   Only the minerals which were apt to split along parallel planes into scale-shaped fragments gave particles of colloid size possessing plasticity.   Similar quartz particles were not plastic.   By *plasticity* one generally understands the ability of a substance easily to undergo considerable shearing deformations without rupture.

This consideration leads to a limiting definition of clay, i.e., that it is plastic. According to this definition, quartz powder particles of 1 μm diameter should not be classified as clay but as silt (see Art. 3-7 for soil-classification terms).

Numerous experiments have shown that most clays are composed of scale-shaped particles. Electron-microscope photographs (see 1st ed., Art. 3-8) show that in dickite clay mineral crystals the axial ratio of width to thickness is approximately 10 : 1 but that this ratio for unit plates of Wyoming bentonite is of the order of 250 : 1. The penetration of water between these thin plates is believed to cause the pronounced swelling properties of Wyoming bentonite and other montmorillonite mineral clays.

In most cases the *hardness of individual soil grains* is of little importance. Most sands are composed of very hard quartz grains with rounded edges. The foundation pressures normally considered permissible on such deposits are not sufficient to crush or to split any grains.

If in some exceptional cases the sand is composed of some other mineral, softer than quartz and with sharp edges, the effects on these grains of the unit pressures which are planned to be applied to the sand deposit may be investigated as follows. The granular composition of a sand sample is first accurately determined by sieving, and its grain-size-distribution curve is plotted. Then the same sample is compressed by unit pressures equal to the pressures planned for design use or some 50 percent larger. After this test the sample is sieved again. If the comparison of the grain-size-distri-bution curves before and after the compression test shows an appreciable increase in the percentage of smaller grains and dust, this is an indication that grain crushing has occurred and that the design pressures should be reduced accordingly. Considerations of the above kind impose a limit on the height of rock-fill dams.

The presence in some sand deposits of *hollow shells* sometimes causes considerable compression of the deposit when loaded, with resulting founda-tion trouble, because of the ease with which such shells are crushed. Their presence should therefore be carefully noted during all preliminary soil investigations for foundation purposes. Shell fragments or clam-shaped shells filled with sand do not present an additional hazard.

Chemists call particles larger than 1 nm but smaller than 0.2 μm (or 200 nm) *colloids* and their solutions *colloidal solutions*. The upper limit represents the resolving power of the best possible optical microscope.

In engineering soil work, particles smaller than 1 μm (0.001 mm) have been defined as colloidal clay. Particles smaller than this diameter cannot be accurately determined by sedimentation methods. The reason is that below this size the speed of sedimentation is extremely slow and ceases completely for particles smaller than 0.2 μm (0.0002 mm). Such colloidal particles remain in suspension indefinitely.

The particles of colloidal solutions (or *sols*) are therefore too small to be seen by the naked eye and execute rapid movements in all directions, called *brownian movements*. These movements are caused by the impacts of the molecules of the liquid in which the colloidal particles are dispersed. The velocities thus gained by the particles are sufficient to prevent their sedimentation. Another characteristic of colloids is that all particles carry a like electric charge. This like electric charge prevents the particles from attracting each other. The charge of most soil dispersions is negative.

By adding to the colloidal solutions an electrolyte, i.e., a chemical solution some of the ions of which have opposite charges to that of the colloid particles, the charges of the colloid particles can be neutralized. These particles then *flocculate,* or *coagulate,* and cling to each other, forming much larger grains which then sediment rapidly.

This circumstance has some practical applications. Thus, electrolytes are added to the water in settling tanks of waterworks to accelerate the clarification of muddy water.

Exactly the same thing can happen during a sedimentation test in a laboratory if the soil tested contains salts liable to form an electrolyte. This effect is most undesirable, as the grain diameter obtained from the test is then not that of the real particles but the diameter of the much larger honeycombed bunches of coagulated particles. Other chemical solutions of opposite action, so-called dispersers or stabilizers, then have to be used.

The presence of dissolved salts in seawater is responsible for its clarity. The presence or absence of such salts in appreciable quantities in the water of rivers generally explains why some rivers are perfectly clear and others very muddy.

(C). Adsorbed Moisture Films; Base Exchange. Chemically combined atoms form *molecules,* which represent the smallest indivisible particle of the new compound. The atoms of the molecule are firmly held together by the electrochemical bonds formed through the exchange or the sharing of electrons. Some molecules are *dipoles;* i.e., they act as if they had opposite electric charges at their opposite ends. Water is a *dipole;* paraffin oil is not.

Investigations of the chemical composition and crystal structure of soils show that individual ions of different minerals may be attached (adsorbed) to the surface of a soil crystal.

Univalent ions, like Na^+, are loosely bound to the soil crystal. The bivalent ions Ca^{++} and Mg^{++} are attached to it somewhat more firmly. The slightly dissociated H ion and the trivalent cations of Al^{+++} and Fe^{+++} can be bound very strongly.

At the same time water molecules, being dipoles, are attached (adsorbed) both to the surface of the crystal lattice and to the cations. Some water molecules may even penetrate into the interior of the lattice.

The number of water molecules adsorbed by a cation increases with an increase of its charge and is also a function of the ionic radius. Therefore the Na^+ cations will have a thicker layer of adsorbed water around them, which together with the cation may form a particularly thick *film of adsorbed water* around the soil crystal.

This adsorbed water film has properties different from those of ordinary water because of the great pressure to which it is subjected by the electrostatic forces of adsorption.

Winterkorn and Baver (Ref. 408) computed the average adsorption pressure of water to be of the order of 20,000 tons/ft². Winterkorn (Ref. 406) concluded that close to the surface of soil particles of clay size adsorbed water films must have the properties of solid ice. Observed volume changes of clays during freezing and thawing are explained by the above hypothesis.

When chemists speak of hydrogen, calcium, or sodium clays, they do not refer to the composition of the soil particles but only to the kind of cations (H, Ca, or Na) adsorbed on their surfaces. *Sodium clays* in nature are a product either of the deposition of clays in seawater or of their saturation by saltwater flooding or capillary action. *Calcium clays* are formed essentially by freshwater sediments. *Hydrogen clays* are a result of prolonged leaching of a clay by pure or acid water, with the resulting removal of all other exchangeable bases. In most natural clays the soil particles may have different cations adsorbed on their surfaces.

By *base exchange* is meant the capacity of colloidal particles to change the cations adsorbed on their surface. Thus a hydrogen clay (colloid with adsorbed H cations) can be changed to a sodium clay (colloid with adsorbed Na cations) by a constant percolation of water containing dissolved Na salts. Such changes can be used to decrease the permeability of a soil. Not all adsorbed cations are exchangeable. The quantity of exchangeable cations in a soil is termed *exchange capacity*.

The rate at which the base exchange takes place will increase with the concentration of the solution of the base and with the velocity at which this solution will percolate through the soil. The nature of the changes in the physical properties of a soil as caused by base exchange depends on the nature both of the soil and of the exchangeable bases.

Exchange capacity increases with the *acidity* of the soil crystals, as expressed by higher values of the *silica-sesquioxide ratio* SiO_2/R_2O_3. Another measure for the acidity of a soil, if considered as a suspension, is its *pH value*, which, however, refers mainly to the acidity of the soluble particles.

Acid solutions have a pH value smaller than 7, and basic or alkaline solutions have a pH value greater than 7.

The *corrosion of iron and of steel* embedded in soils is also possible only in the presence of soil moisture. It increases with the acidity (small pH value) of the soil because acid solutions facilitate the formation on the iron surface of electric couples between the iron and some impurities it may contain. Electrolytic action results, and the liberated oxygen combines with the iron, progressively forming what is known as rust. Electric currents of external origin can have a similar but much stronger effect, for instance, on water mains. This circumstance sometimes forms the source of litigation between electric-streetcar and water-supply companies. The use of water pipes made of different metals such as iron, brass, and lead embedded close to each other in a moist acid soil can also facilitate strong corrosion by the formation of electric couples.

A phenomenon of engineering importance caused by adsorbed water films of a different kind is the bulking of sand. Bulking should not be confused with swelling, which may cause an increase of volume of a clay even if it absorbs water in situ. Swelling is not reversible when the clay is submerged, whereas the bulking of sands disappears entirely when the sand is submerged. *Bulking* represents an increase of volume of moist sand, compared with dry sand, but will take place only if moist sand is loosely reshoveled. The moisture films are sufficiently viscously rigid to prevent the sand grains from touching each other once the films are formed, but they cannot push them apart during the process of their formation, as is the case in the *swelling of clays*. The amount of bulking increases with the fineness of sand particles because of the increase in the total surface area of the particles per unit of volume. Its effects can be considerable and are the main reason why in all important modern concrete work the aggregates are measured by weight and not by volume. The films are comparatively thick and readily evaporate at room temperature. Since bulking disappears when the sand is fully saturated, surface tension of the water is probably responsible for the phenomenon. It should be noted that bulking is present only in loosely dumped sand. Moist sand can be compacted by high pressures just as well as dry sand. This is an indication that the thick water films which produce bulking can offer only a relatively small amount of resistance to pressure.

3-2. Laboratory Soil-identification Tests. *(A). Grain-size Determination.* According to their grain size, soil particles are classified as sand, silt, and clay, subject to limitations indicated in Arts. 3-2A and 3-7A. The metric system is used in this classification. Metric measures are currently employed by soil laboratories in the United States, just as these measures are generally used in chemistry and physics.

The ASTM (American Society for Testing Materials) classifies soil particles according to their size as indicated in Fig. 3-1 (see Ref. 18, item D-422-63).

It should be noted that the ASTM *definitions of clay, silt, and sand,* although used in several other countries, do not represent an international standard. In European engineering practice a definition is often used according to which particles smaller than 2 μm (instead of 5 as defined by the ASTM) are considered as clay, and particles between 0.02 and 0.002 mm as silt. The latter definition of clay and silt sizes is also internationally used in agricultural soil work (see Fig. 3-1).

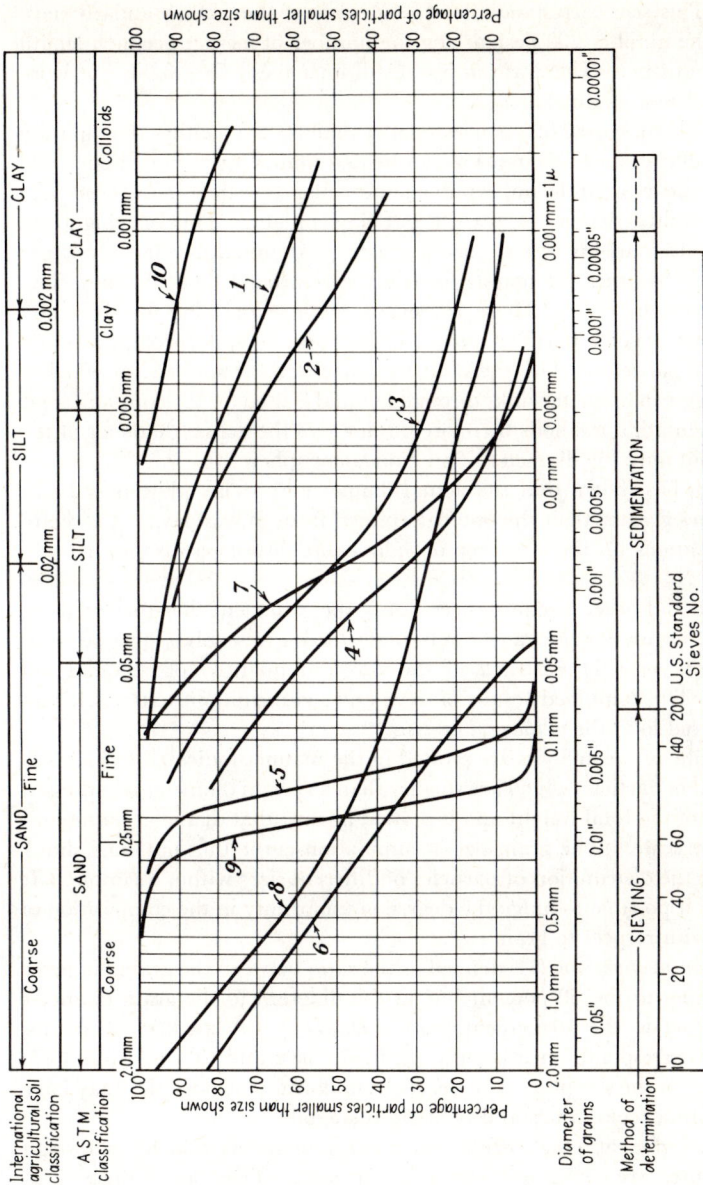

Fig. 3-1. Some grain-size-accumulation curves. 1, 2: clay soils of the Nile delta; 3, 4: silts from the Nile delta; 5: Port Said beach sand; 6: sand artificially graded for maximum density; 7: Vicksburg loess; 8: New Mexico adobe brick; 9: Daytona Beach sand; 10: Wyoming bentonite. Soils 1 to 9 were tested by G. P. Tschebotarioff.

The size of particles larger than 0.074 mm (74 μm) can be determined by sieving. This size corresponds to the opening of the U.S. Standard sieve No. 200, the number 200 designating the number of meshes per inch length of the sieve tissue. There are sieves of still finer mesh (No. 325), but work with them becomes difficult.

Since silt is composed of particles smaller than 50 μm, neither the quantity of silt nor of clay particles in a soil can be determined by sieving alone. At the same time, most of the important engineering properties of soils, especially the permeability, depend on the silt and clay content. Thus, sieving alone is an entirely inadequate test except where predominantly sandy soils are concerned. Sedimentation tests have to be resorted to for silt- and clay-content determinations. There are several methods of doing this, based on the fact that smaller particles take a longer time to sink through a liquid than larger particles. The equation by Stokes for the speed with which a sphere of a given diameter sinks through a liquid is used for the computations. The sedimentation methods therefore do not give the actual diameter of the particles but only the diameter of an equivalent sphere.

Research has shown that the actual diameter of a clay plate may be at least 5 times greater than the one determined from Stokes' law. There are other limitations on the accuracy of sedimentation-test results (see 1st ed., Art. 3-6).

All these and other circumstances justify the statement that the sedimentation test, no matter how accurately performed, gives only a general indication of the *order of magnitude* of the size and quantity of colloidal soil particles. The combined results of sieve and sedimentation tests are sometimes referred to as the *mechanical analysis*.

The results of the analysis are plotted in the manner indicated in Fig. 3-1. The weight of particles which are smaller than a certain diameter is expressed in percent of the total weight and is plotted against that diameter on a semi-logarithmic scale. The grain-size-accumulation curve thus obtained shows at a glance the distribution of particles of different sizes within a sample. It also makes it possible to judge the degree of uniformity in the composition of a sample with respect to grain size.

The *coefficient of uniformity* is defined as the ratio between the grain diameter corresponding to the 60 percent line in the diagram to the grain diameter corresponding to the 10 percent line ($=D_{60}/D_{10}$). A small value of this coefficient corresponds to a steeply inclined curve and to a more uniform composition of the sample. The degree of uniformity of grain size may have a certain influence on the stability of granular soils.

Figure 3-1 gives also the corresponding grain diameters in inches, although inch measures are never used for this purpose. They are indicated in Fig. 3-1 merely to help those unfamiliar with metric measures to visualize them.

For the techniques of testing see Ref. 18, items D-422 and D-1140.

(B). Porosity and Void Ratio.   The volume of voids is generally expressed in percent of the total volume and is termed *porosity.*

$$n = \frac{V_v}{V} \times 100 \tag{3-2}$$

where n = volume of voids, percent of total volume

V_v = volume of voids

V = total volume

The porosity of sands can vary between 30 and 50 percent.   The lower values are generally met in deposits formed in slow-flowing water, as on lake bottoms.   Natural clays can have a porosity as high as 89 percent (Fig. 3-6).

Another expression, the void ratio e, is used for most computations.   It is defined as the ratio of the volume of voids to the volume of solids (Fig. 3-2).

$$e = \frac{V_v}{V_s} = \frac{n}{100 - n} \tag{3-3}$$

$$n = \frac{e}{1 + e} \times 100 \tag{3-4}$$

The use of the void ratio e is more convenient for computation purposes than the porosity n because e gives the ratio of voids in respect to a constant value, that of the volume of solids, whereas the total volume, in respect to which the ratio n is given, undergoes change with every alteration in the volume of voids following changes of pressure.   On the other hand, values of the porosity n are easier to visualize.   This accounts for the existence and parallel use of both expressions n and e which define the same soil characteristic—the volume of its voids or pore space.

The values required for the determination of n and e are obtained as follows.   The total volume V is measured directly, i.e., either by immersion in mercury or, if the sample is sufficiently large and of a regular shape, by direct measurement or by measurement of the volume of the hole from which the sample has been extracted (Art. 5-5).   The volume of solids V_s is computed from Eq. (3-1).   The weight of solids W_s is obtained by direct weighing before and after drying in an electric oven.   The specific gravity of the solid substance G is determined by a separate test (Art. 3-1).

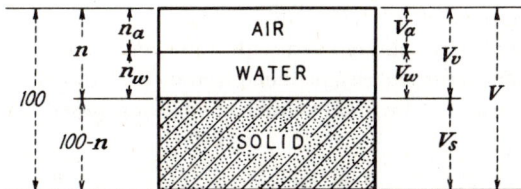

Fig. 3-2.   Diagram illustrating the terms porosity n and void ratio e.

(C). Water Content and Degree of Saturation.   The *water or moisture content w* is generally expressed as a ratio of the weight of water to the weight of solids, and not to the total weight, the latter not having a constant value under varying conditions.

$$w = \frac{W_w}{W_s} \times 100 \qquad (3\text{-}5)$$

where w = water content, percent of weight of solids
   W_w = weight of water
   W_s = weight of solids

Both W_w and W_s are obtained by direct weighing before and after drying in an electric oven at 105 to 110°C.

Therefore, the water content thus obtained includes the gravitational, the capillary, and the hygroscopic moisture, but not the film moisture (Art. 3-1*C*).

Hygroscopic moisture is defined as the moisture which is still contained in an air-dried soil but which evaporates if the soil is dried at over 100°C, i.e., over the boiling point.

Provided all the voids are filled with water, i.e., when the soil is *saturated (waterlogged)*, the void ratio is equal to

$$e = \frac{w}{100} G \qquad (3\text{-}6)$$

The relationship expressed by Eq. (3-6) is presented graphically in Fig. 3-3.

For fully waterlogged conditions the water content of sands may vary only from about 12 to 36 percent, but that of clays may vary from 12 to 325 percent (Fig. 3-6).   The value of 325 percent water content should not be surprising, since it is to be found only in freshly deposited clay or in particularly loosely sedimented, very fine volcanic ash, such as is found beneath Mexico City, and since it is given in respect to the weight of solids and not to the total weight.   The reason for this now generally accepted method of expressing the water content is similar to the reason for the use of the void ratio e instead of the porosity n.   The total weight of a clay sample changes as the sample dries out or is otherwise compressed, whereas the weight of solids remains unchanged.   It is therefore preferable to determine the water content in respect to this constant value.

For techniques of testing see Ref. 18, item D-2216.

Sometimes not all the voids of a soil are filled with water, but some air is present (Fig. 3-2).   The *degree of saturation S_r* is then given by the ratio of the volume of voids filled with water to the total volume of voids, expressed as a percentage.

$$S_r = \frac{V_w}{V_v} \times 100 = \frac{n_w}{n} \times 100 \qquad (3\text{-}6a)$$

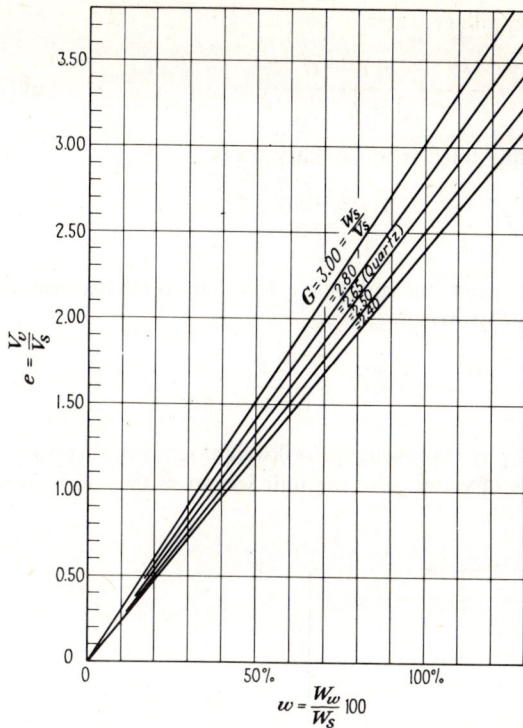

Fig. 3-3. Relationship between the void ratio e and the water content w for full saturation and for limit values of the specific gravity G.

The *air content* a_c is given by the ratio of the volume of voids filled with air to the total volume of voids expressed as a percentage (see Fig. 3-2).

$$a_c = \frac{V_a}{V_v} \times 100 = \frac{n_a}{n} \times 100 = 100 - S_r \qquad (3\text{-}6b)$$

(D). Unit Weight. The *unit weight of soil above the groundwater table* is given by the ratio of the total weight of the soil in air to the total volume of the soil, all voids included.   It expresses the ratio of the weight of the solid and liquid phases of a soil to the weight of a volume of water equal to the sum of the volumes of the solid, liquid, and gas phases of the same soil.

If no moisture is present, or if only the unit weight of dry soil γ_d has to be determined,

$$\gamma_d = \frac{W_s}{V} = \frac{G}{1+e} \qquad (3\text{-}7)$$

If all voids are filled with capillary water,

$$\gamma = \frac{G}{1+e} + \frac{\gamma_w e}{1+e} = \frac{G+e}{1+e} \tag{3-8}$$

If the voids are only partially filled with capillary water,

$$\gamma = \frac{W}{V} = \frac{G(1+w/100)}{1+e} \tag{3-9}$$

When entirely *submerged* in water, the soil weighs less than in air because of the effects of buoyancy (law of Archimedes).

$$\gamma' = \frac{W_s - (V_s \gamma_w)}{V} = \frac{G-1}{1+e} \tag{3-10}$$

Equations (3-7) to (3-10), by expressing the soil weight as a ratio in respect to a corresponding volume of water, give the unit weight of the soil in the

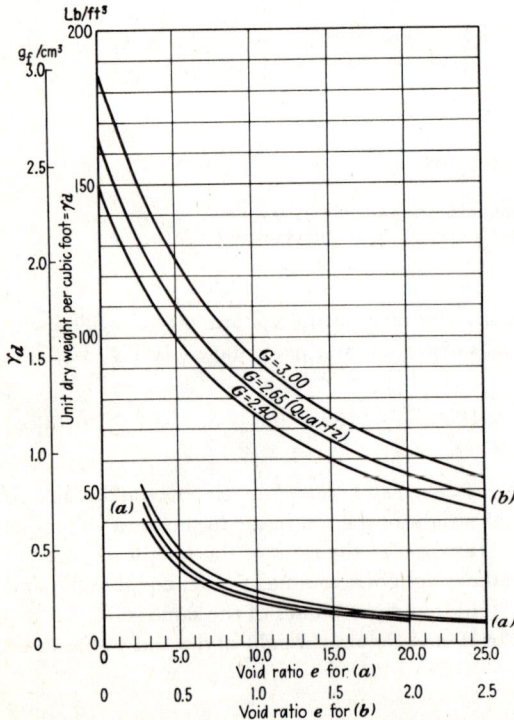

Fig. 3-4. Relationship between the void ratio e and the unit dry weight γ_d for limit values of the specific gravity G.

metric system in grams per cubic centimeter, since 1 cm³ of water weighs 1 g_f. To express the unit weight γ in the foot-pound system the ratios given by the preceding four equations should be multiplied by the weight of a cubic foot of water, 62.5 lb.

In Eqs. (3-8) and (3-10) $\gamma_w = 1.00$ is the specific gravity of water in grams per cubic centimeter.

The expression $1/(1 + e)$ which appears in all the above equations will occur later in some other equations. It is therefore advisable to understand its physical significance. The derivation of the preceding equations will then become apparent. This expression can be transformed as follows:

$$\frac{1}{1 + e} = \frac{1}{1 + V_v/V_s} = \frac{V_s}{V_v + V_v} = \frac{V_s}{V} \tag{3-11}$$

The absolute specific gravity G, which appears in Eqs. (3-7) to (3-10), when multiplied by V_s gives the weight of the solids W_s, and the division by V reduces it in proportion to the total volume, thus giving γ, the unit weight of the whole mass (voids + solids). Similarly, the multiplication of γ_w by V_s expresses the effects of buoyancy in accordance with the law of Archimedes. Also

$$\frac{e}{1 + e} = \frac{V_v/V_s}{1 + V_v/V_s} = \frac{V_v}{V_s + V_v} = \frac{V_v}{V} = \frac{n}{100} \tag{3-12}$$

This expression appears in Eqs. (3-8) and (3-10). The multiplication of $\gamma_w = 1.00$ by V_v gives the weight of water W_w when the soil is fully saturated.

The charts in Figs. 3-4 and 3-5 show the relationship between the values γ_d, G, e, n, γ, and w.

(E). Relative Density of Sands. The relative density of sands is expressed by a relation between the void ratios in the loosest possible state, in the densest possible state, and in the actual state in nature of the particular sand specimen.

$$D_r = \frac{e_{\max} - e}{e_{\max} - e_{\min}} \tag{3-13}$$

where D_r = relative density
  $e_{\max}$ = void ratio of the sand in loosest possible state
  e = void ratio of the sand in actual state in nature
  $e_{\min}$ = void ratio of the sand in densest possible state
The term *density index* I_D is also used instead of relative density D_r.

The relative density D_r expresses the ratio of the decrease of the voids from the loosest possible state to the actual state in nature to the maximum possible decrease through compaction from the loosest to the densest state. Usually it is expressed as a percentage (see Figs. 2-12 and 2-16 and the discussions thereof). Often the void ratio e is not actually determined in some field

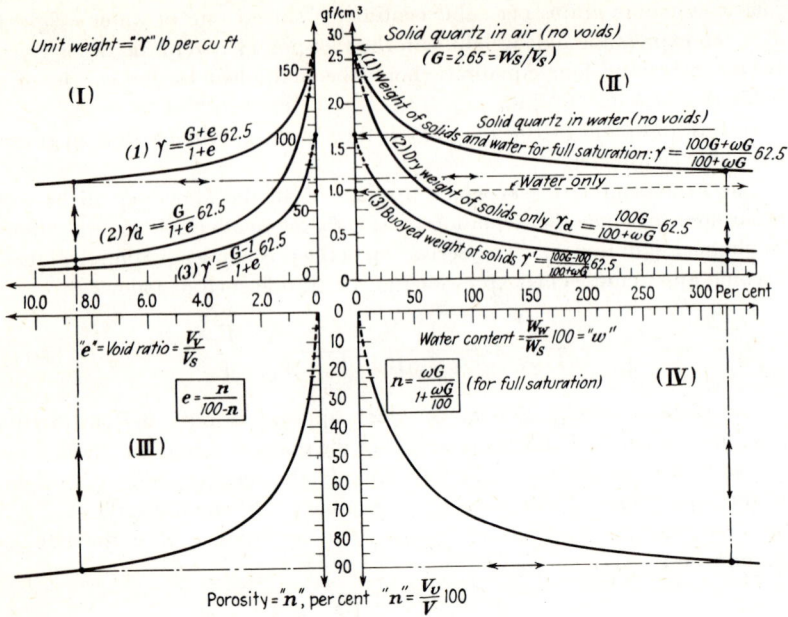

Fig. 3-5. The relationship between the porosity n, the void ratio e, the water content w, and the unit weight γ for a value of the specific gravity $G = 2.65$. Full lines refer to the limits which these values may assume for the whole range of densities of various known soils in their natural state.

investigations, and only the dry density of the soil γ_d, expressed in pounds per cubic foot, is available.

It is shown (1st ed., Art. 4-6) that since $\gamma_{d(min)}$ corresponds to e_{max}, Eq. (3-13) can be transformed to read

$$D_r = \frac{\gamma_d - \gamma_{d(min)}}{\gamma_{d(max)} - \gamma_{d(min)}} \frac{\gamma_{d(max)}}{\gamma_d} \qquad (3\text{-}14)$$

For sands of different granulometric composition, e_{max} and e_{min} can assume different values. In the case of spheres of equal size, the following values are obtained:

$$e_{max} = 0.91 \qquad n_{max} = 48\%$$

$$e_{min} = 0.35 \qquad n_{min} = 26\%$$

The more *uniform* a sand is (sieve curve 5 in Fig. 3-1) the nearer its e_{max} and e_{min} will approach the above values for equal spheres. Less uniform, i.e., *better-graded*, sands (for instance, curve 6 in Fig. 3-1) will have smaller values for both e_{max} and e_{min}. This would also be the case for an idealized soil composed of spheres if a sufficient number of smaller spheres were present to fill the voids between the larger ones.

In actual sands the effect of the presence of smaller particles is offset by the more angular shape of sand grains.   The result is that the observed approximate density limits of actual sands, as given in Art. 3-2B ($n_{max} = 50$ percent and $n_{min} = 30$ percent), correspond very closely to the same limits of spheres of equal size, as given above.

The determination of both e_{max} and e_{min} can be made in a laboratory (see Ref. 18, item D-2049), but the reproduction of e, that is, of the actual natural state of a deposit, is not possible in a laboratory.   The determination of e in the field is difficult because of the difficulty of extracting really undisturbed samples of sand.   It requires great care and is possible only for the upper layers which are accessible by open excavation.   No fully reliable methods have been devised so far for the really undisturbed extraction of sand samples from below the water level or from boreholes.

Correlations have been established, however, between the relative density D_r of sands and the SPT (standard penetration test) values N of natural sand deposits (see Art. 2-4A and Fig. 2-12).   The relative density D_r of sands indicates the extent to which the natural soil is capable of further increasing its density as a result of heavy loads, shocks, vibration, and other external influences.   Thus, the value of D_r gives direct data concerning the stability of the sand in its natural state.   The knowledge of this value therefore is of direct practical importance.

(F). Limits of Consistency of Clays; Capillary Phenomena.   A clay deposit in the process of formation, i.e., during sedimentation at the bottom of a lake, of a pond, or of other slow-flowing waters, has at first the consistency of *liquid* mud.   In this state, if removed from the deposit, it will not keep its shape by itself and will easily flow.

As the volume of voids of the deposit decreases (either as a result of the applied weight of newly deposited upper layers or as a consequence of water evaporation if the deposit has become exposed to the air), the clay becomes more compact and loses its capacity to flow.   However, it is still fairly soft and *plastic*, i.e., a laterally unrestrained clay has the capacity of altering its shape under the effect of an applied force without any appreciable change of volume and of subsequently retaining the newly acquired shape.

Under further compression or drying a clay loses its plastic properties and is apt to crumble if remolded; it has reached the *semisolid* state.

After still further drying the clay finally reaches a state when it will not reduce its volume any further; i.e., it will stop *shrinking*.   This corresponds to a change in color; the clay takes on a lighter shade.   It has then reached the *solid* state.

The limits between the liquid, the plastic, the semisolid, and the solid states of a fine-grained soil are respectively termed the liquid, the plastic, and the shrinkage limits.

They have a collective name of *consistency limits* and are sometimes referred to as *Atterberg limits*, from the name of the Swedish scientist who first introduced them.   These limits are generally expressed by the water content w of a given soil at a particular limit or by the corresponding void ratio e. Table 3-1 illustrates the relationship between the state of a fine-grained soil and the consistency limits.   By *consistency* is meant the degree of resistance of a fine-grained soil to flow or to deformation in general.

The difference between the water contents at the liquid and at the plastic limit indicates the range of plasticity of a given soil and is sometimes termed the *plasticity index I_p* (or PI).

$$I_p = w_L - w_p \qquad\qquad (3\text{-}15)$$

where I_p = plasticity index, percent

$\qquad w_L$ = water content at liquid limit, percent of weight of solids

$\qquad w_p$ = water content at plastic limit, percent of weight of solids

For instance, if a clay has $w_L = 63$ percent and $w_p = 22$ percent, its plasticity index I_p will be equal to 41 percent.   The higher the plasticity index, the greater the plasticity of that soil.

The International Society of Soil Mechanics and Foundation Engineering (Ref. 140) recommends the use of the symbols w_L, w_P, and I_p, whereas the ASTM (Ref. 18, item D-653) in addition permits the abbreviations LL, PL, and PI, which are customary in highway engineering practice in the United States.

A further limit, the so-called *sticky limit*, is used in agricultural soil science to determine the water content at which a soil ceases to stick to metal.   The liquid and plastic limits have a certain physical significance, as already explained, but their exact values are determined by an arbitrary agreement between research workers to provide a common basis of comparison.

The *shrinkage limit w_s* of a soil is, however, directly defined in its exact value by changes in the physical characteristics which depend on *capillary phenomena*.   These will therefore be discussed first.

Water has a certain surface tension, which has been found to equal 75 dynes ($=0.0764$ g) across a width of 1 cm.   In very narrow tubes, termed

TABLE 3-1.   Consistency Limits of Cohesive Soils

State of soil (consistency)	Lower limit of consistency
Liquid	Liquid limit w_L (or LL)
Plastic	Plastic limit w_p (or PL)
Semisolid	Shrinkage limit w_s
Solid	

capillary tubes, the water will rise by itself, whereby a meniscus is formed. The thinner a tube, the higher the water will rise. When equilibrium is reached, the meniscus takes the shape of a semisphere of a diameter equal to that of the capillary tube.

This phenomenon is caused by the surface tension of the water and its molecular attraction to the walls of the tube. A prerequisite for this attraction and for all the ensuing phenomena of capillary rise is a greater *affinity* between the liquid and the material which it wets than would exist between that material and air.

Such greater affinity exists between water and glass, metals, rocks, and soils. Some other materials, e.g., paraffin oil, have greater affinity for air than for water. A coating of oil covering all soil grains may therefore prevent capillary phenomena.

Equilibrium requires that the weight of water pulled up by the force of surface water tension should equal the vertical component of that force (see 1st ed., Art. 4-5).

The force which pulls up the water in a capillary tube is balanced by a force which compresses the walls of such a tube. The existence and the action of this force may be visualized by considering the behavior of compressible capillary tubes under the effect of the evaporation of water within them. Suppose such a tube had been entirely filled with water by submerging it and was then exposed to drying. Just after the evaporation has started, causing the appearance of a slightly curved meniscus, a slight shortening of the column of water and of the tube will occur. Under the effect of continued evaporation the meniscus gets more and more curved as the water column gets shorter. The component of the force exerted by the surface tension of the water in the direction of the walls of the tube is correspondingly increased, causing these walls to shorten too, if they are compressible. No further shortening will occur when the increasing resistance of the tube equals the maximum possible value of the compressive force. After that, with further evaporation, the meniscus will withdraw within the tube. If the tube is submerged again, the force acting on the tube disappears, so that if the material of the tube is perfectly elastic, it will expand back to its original length.

The knowledge of the height of active capillary rise in a soil is important in many practical cases; for instance, when determining whether a soil beneath a road pavement is likely to heave during frost by drawing up water from an underlying subsoil water table and thus allowing the growth of ice crystals.

The height of capillary rise is measured either by direct observation of soil filling a glass tube—*active capillarity*—or by measuring in a special apparatus the suction required to overcome the capillary forces in the voids of the soil—*passive capillarity.* The latter comes into play in nature during lowering of the groundwater table by drainage.

The theoretical heights of capillary rise indicated in Table 3-2, when of the active type, seldom occur in nature, sometimes because of the formation of shrinkage cracks, but mainly because of the decrease of the free diameter of the voids by the adsorbed water films.   There are, however, indications that the theoretical values of H_{max} for passive capillarity and the values of maximum capillary pressures are not estimated too high (Art. 3-4C).

The decrease of volume, or *shrinkage*, of a fine-grained soil during drying is caused by the capillary forces.   It ceases at the so-called *shrinkage limit* w_s, and the menisci of the water in the voids then recede into the interior of the sample.   This induces a change of color from a dark to a light shade.   Very great pressures can be exerted in particularly fine-grained soils by capillary forces at this stage.   A characteristic pattern of shrinkage cracks is formed on the surface of an originally liquid clay layer after it dries out.   The pattern is induced by the resistance to shrinkage offered along the lower restrained surface of the new layer as it dries out.

If the soil is again submerged, the capillary forces cease to act and the soil expands; it *swells*.   Generally, being imperfectly elastic, the clay does not reach its full original volume, especially if it had a high water content prior to drying.

The *plastic limit* is defined and determined as the lowest water content at which a soil can still be rolled into threads of $\frac{1}{8}$ in. (3.2 mm) diameter without the threads breaking into pieces, i.e., without crumbling.   A small piece of plastic soil is rolled by hand on a glass plate; the threads of the soil are folded and rolled again; some moisture is lost as a result.   The process is repeated until the threads cannot be rolled without crumbling.   The water content is then determined by weighing the soil threads, drying them in an oven, and weighing again.   This water content is considered to represent the plastic limit w_p of the soil tested (Ref. 18, item D-424).

The *liquid limit* w_L is defined as the water content at which a soil will just begin to flow if slightly jarred several times.   Atterberg (1912) originally determined it by jarring a pat of soil in a porcelain dish by hand.   The personal factor involved in such a determination is now almost entirely

TABLE 3-2.   Theoretical Effects of Capillarity

Soil	Size of particles and of openings, mm	H_{max}		p'	
		cm	in.	kg/cm²	lb/in.²
Sand, coarse....	2.00–0.025	1.5–12	$\frac{5}{8}$–5	0.0015–0.012	0.021–0.171
Fine	0.025–0.05	12–61	5–24	0.012–0.061	0.171–0.87
Silt	0.05–0.005	61–610	24–240	0.061–0.610	0.87–8.7
Clay	0.005–0.001	610–3,050	240–1,200	0.610–3.05	8.7–43.5
Colloids	0.001 and finer	3,050 and more	1,200 and more	3.05 and more	43.5 and more

eliminated by the general use of the mechanical device developed by Casagrande (see 1st ed., Art. 4-9, and Ref. 18, item D-423).

The ASTM standards have been rightly criticized for requiring the drying of the soil *before* the performance of the liquid limit test. This is of no particular importance in highway engineering work dealing with disturbed soils, but it lowers appreciably the w_L value of samples from natural clay deposits taken in connection with foundation work, impairing thereby the comparative identification value of the test. The timing of the drying, i.e., before or after the test, should therefore be stated when reporting w_L values. Many European laboratories dry their samples *after* the test.

The *consistency index* I_c is expressed as a percentage and defines the consistency of the soil in its natural state, as expressed by its natural water content w, in respect to its plastic and liquid limits.

$$I_c = \frac{w_L - w}{w_L - w_p} \times 100 = \frac{w_L - w}{I_p} \times 100 \qquad (3\text{-}16)$$

The physical significance of the consistency index I_c for clays is similar to that of the relative density D_r for sands (Art. 3-2E). If the water content of the soil in its natural state corresponds to the plastic limit, a very dense state, the value of I_c will be 100 percent. Water contents below the plastic limit will give I_c values higher than 100 percent. A natural water content corresponding to the liquid limit will give an I_c value of 0 percent, and a still higher natural water content will give negative I_c values.

A reverse relationship is given by the *liquidity index* I_L.

$$I_L = \frac{w - w_p}{I_p} \times 100 \qquad (3\text{-}17)$$

When $w = w_p$, $I_L = 0$ percent; when $w = w_L$, $I_L = 100$ percent.

The consistency index I_c or the liquidity index I_L of clays can be easily determined. However, this is not usually done as a matter of routine since, taken alone, their values are insufficient to express the actual consistency of the soil in its natural state because the liquid limit is determined for the completely remolded state of the soil. It can therefore happen that in the case of highly sensitive clays (Art. 3-2G) the natural water content of a clay corresponds to its liquid limit, although that clay in its natural state safely carries multistoried buildings.

The liquid and plastic limits are, however, generally determined for all cohesive soils, since they are easily and quickly obtained and are very helpful in the classification of the potential properties of the soil material, which they define better than the grain-size determinations (Art. 3-2A). They belong to the so-called *index*, or *classification*, *tests*.

The liquid limit gives a measure of the shearing resistance which a soil has when mixed with water. In other words, it measures the potential true cohesion of a material, which, in turn, depends on the total size of the contact areas, i.e., on the fineness and shape of the grains. The finer and flatter the grains of a clay, i.e., the "richer" or "fatter" a clay is, the greater the total contact area between grains and the higher the amount of water required to coat the grains. The liquid limit of the clay will therefore also be higher. In other words, one will have to add more water to it to make it flow.

With the admixture of sand or silt, the clay will become leaner and its liquid limit will have a lower value. The plastic limit will decrease at the same time but not so rapidly as the liquid limit, so that the admixture of coarser particles causes a simultaneous decrease of the plasticity index I_p. For sands I_p equals zero.

The plastic limit is strongly affected by organic content, which raises its value without simultaneously raising the liquid limit. Therefore soils with organic content have low plasticity indices corresponding to comparatively high liquid limits. This circumstance is used in some classifications of soils (Art. 3-7C).

Figure 3-6 illustrates the density variations of some types of soils. It should be understood that the figures of that diagram give only the order of magnitude of the corresponding values (to help in visualizing their significance) and that minor deviations from these figures are entirely possible. It will be noted from Fig. 3-6 that the range of density variations of sands is relatively small and of the same order of magnitude as that of lean clays ($I_p < 10$ percent) but that both the range of density variations and the porosity of possible structures for fat clays increase with increasing values of the plasticity index I_p of a clay. *Diatomaceous earth* and Mexico City clay represent special and not too frequent types of soils. The low unit weight, the high porosity, and the absence of plasticity of diatomaceous earth are accounted for by the round shape of the *hollow* silica shells of which it is composed. *Mexico City clay* is of volcanic origin. Its high plasticity and porosity are caused by the special properties of the clay minerals of which it is formed. These appear to have an accordionlike structure of scale-shaped particles, somewhat similar to that of bentonites. [The sodium bentonites from Wyoming have liquid-limit values up to 700 percent. In contact with water they swell and increase their dry volume more than 10 times. They are used commercially as an admixture to granular soils to decrease the permeability (Art. 8-10).]

The natural water content and the consistency limits of cohesive soils can be easily and quickly determined by weighing, drying, and again weighing a soil sample. The dry unit weight γ_d of a cohesive soil can also be easily determined in the field. Here, in addition to the dry weight of a soil specimen, the volume of the space originally occupied by the specimen in the ground has to be determined by one of the methods described in Art. 5-5. On the other hand, calculation of the porosity n and the void ratio e requires

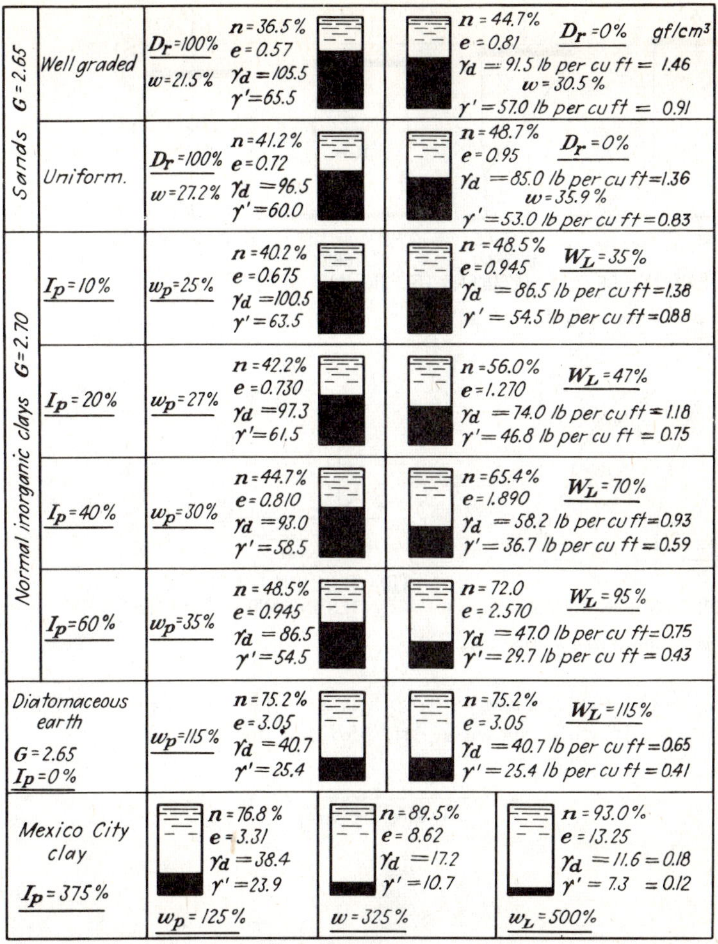

	Type		Dense state	Loose state
Sands $G = 2.65$	Well graded	$D_r = 100\%$, $w = 21.5\%$	$n = 36.5\%$, $e = 0.57$, $\gamma_d = 105.5$, $\gamma' = 65.5$	$n = 44.7\%$, $e = 0.81$, $D_r = 0\%$ gf/cm³, $\gamma_d = 91.5$ lb per cu ft $= 1.46$, $w = 30.5\%$, $\gamma' = 57.0$ lb per cu ft $= 0.91$
	Uniform	$D_r = 100\%$, $w = 27.2\%$	$n = 41.2\%$, $e = 0.72$, $\gamma_d = 96.5$, $\gamma' = 60.0$	$n = 48.7\%$, $e = 0.95$, $D_r = 0\%$, $\gamma_d = 85.0$ lb per cu ft $= 1.36$, $w = 35.9\%$, $\gamma' = 53.0$ lb per cu ft $= 0.83$
Normal inorganic clays $G = 2.70$	$I_p = 10\%$	$w_p = 25\%$	$n = 40.2\%$, $e = 0.675$, $\gamma_d = 100.5$, $\gamma' = 63.5$	$n = 48.5\%$, $e = 0.945$, $W_L = 35\%$, $\gamma_d = 86.5$ lb per cu ft $= 1.38$, $\gamma' = 54.5$ lb per cu ft $= 0.88$
	$I_p = 20\%$	$w_p = 27\%$	$n = 42.2\%$, $e = 0.730$, $\gamma_d = 97.3$, $\gamma' = 61.5$	$n = 56.0\%$, $e = 1.270$, $W_L = 47\%$, $\gamma_d = 74.0$ lb per cu ft $= 1.18$, $\gamma' = 46.8$ lb per cu ft $= 0.75$
	$I_p = 40\%$	$w_p = 30\%$	$n = 44.7\%$, $e = 0.810$, $\gamma_d = 93.0$, $\gamma' = 58.5$	$n = 65.4\%$, $e = 1.890$, $W_L = 70\%$, $\gamma_d = 58.2$ lb per cu ft $= 0.93$, $\gamma' = 36.7$ lb per cu ft $= 0.59$
	$I_p = 60\%$	$w_p = 35\%$	$n = 48.5\%$, $e = 0.945$, $\gamma_d = 86.5$, $\gamma' = 54.5$	$n = 72.0$, $e = 2.570$, $W_L = 95\%$, $\gamma_d = 47.0$ lb per cu ft $= 0.75$, $\gamma' = 29.7$ lb per cu ft $= 0.43$
Diatomaceous earth $G = 2.65$ $I_p = 0\%$		$w_p = 115\%$	$n = 75.2\%$, $e = 3.05$, $\gamma_d = 40.7$, $\gamma' = 25.4$	$n = 75.2\%$, $e = 3.05$, $W_L = 115\%$, $\gamma_d = 40.7$ lb per cu ft $= 0.65$, $\gamma' = 25.4$ lb per cu ft $= 0.41$
Mexico City clay $I_p = 375\%$		$n = 76.8\%$, $e = 3.31$, $\gamma_d = 38.4$, $\gamma' = 23.9$, $w_p = 125\%$	$n = 89.5\%$, $e = 8.62$, $\gamma_d = 17.2$, $\gamma' = 10.7$, $w = 325\%$	$n = 93.0\%$, $e = 13.25$, $\gamma_d = 11.6 = 0.18$, $\gamma' = 7.3 = 0.12$, $w_L = 500\%$

Fig. 3-6. Density variations for some types of soil.

knowledge of the volume of solids of a sample, which can be obtained from its weight once the specific gravity G is known.   The determination of G must be performed in a laboratory and requires considerable care.   For that reason the porosity n and the void ratio e are used to define the consistency of soils mainly in connection with laboratory investigations, whereas the *dry unit weight* γ_d is more generally used for field reports of the density of soils.

(*G*). *Unconfined Compressive Strength and Sensitivity of Clays.*   Triaxial tests performed with no lateral confining pressure ($\sigma_3 = 0$) are known as *unconfined compression tests*.   Standard-type compression tests on concrete cylinders fall into this category.   The value of σ_1 at failure is known in soil

(A)-BEFORE TESTING   (B)- BRITTLE   (C)-SEMI-BRITTLE   (D)-PLASTIC MATERIAL
                              MATERIAL   MATERIAL
(I)-APPEARANCE OF CLAY SPECIMENS. (BEFORE AND AFTER TESTING)

(II)-STRESS-STRAIN DIAGRAM

(III)-TRIMMING SAMPLE FOR
TESTING AND PHOTOGRAPHY

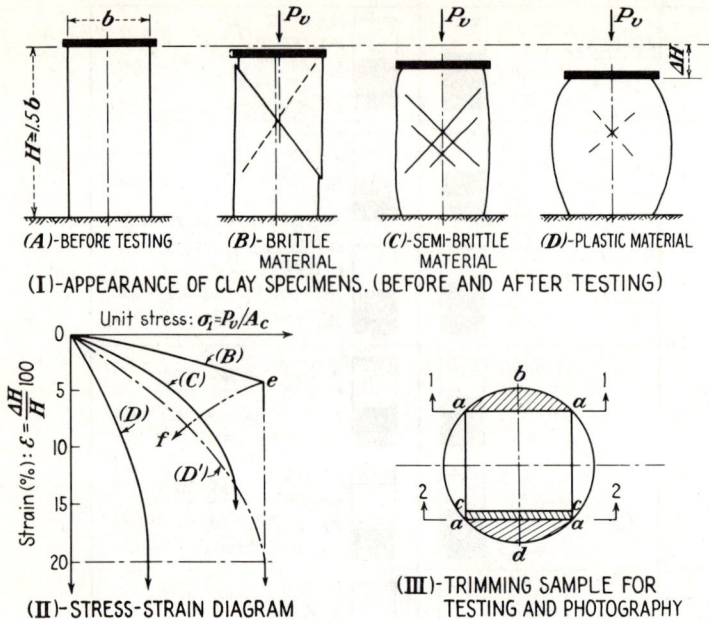

Fig. 3-7. Unconfined compression tests.

mechanics as the *unconfined compressive strength* q_u. The subscript u stands for "undrained." It will be shown in Art. 3-5B that the cohesion c_u is

$$c_u = \frac{q_u}{2 \tan(45° + \phi/2)} \tag{3-18}$$

and if $\phi = 0$,

$$c_u = \frac{q_u}{2} \tag{3-19}$$

The Mohr diagram of an unconfined compression test becomes a circle tangent to the point of origin O. $\tau_{\max}$ is equal to the cohesion c_u in accordance with Eq. (3-19), and this value remains unchanged during triaxial tests if no change of water content is permitted. Therefore, under such conditions the unconfined compression test has considerable advantages over the triaxial test because of its simplicity. As shown in Fig. 3-7(I) and (II) and Tables 3-6 and 3-7, the unconfined compression test can be used as a classification test (Art. 3-7D) not only in respect to the ultimate strength of a clay soil but also in respect to its deformation characteristics, as expressed by the strain at failure. The value of the strain at failure may be strongly influenced by large differences in the rate of loading. However, within the customary limit of approximately 10 min for the duration of a test, which can easily be achieved through adjustment of the rate of loading, there is not much variation to be expected in the values of the strain at failure ϵ_f.

The stress-strain diagrams shown in Fig. 3-7(II) refer to the *controlled-stress* type of tests.   In the *controlled-strain* type of tests the curve B would be likely to approximate the line *ef*, in which case the point e giving the *peak stress* would have to be taken in determining the value of ϵ_f for classification purposes.   (Compare with Fig. 3-27.)

In some cases plastic clays have a high strength (curve D'), but usually it is much lower (curve D) than that of brittle clays.   This circumstance can be utilized for determining the sensitivity of clays to remolding.   Some clays develop fracture planes even after remolding (see 1st ed., fig. 7-15).

Figure 3-7(III) shows how, for testing, a cylindrical sample is usually trimmed down to a prism, marked by the letters a at the corners.   One of the segments, for instance *aba*, can then be photographed before testing (Fig. 3-8).   After the end of the test, a slice *acca* can be cut for photographing

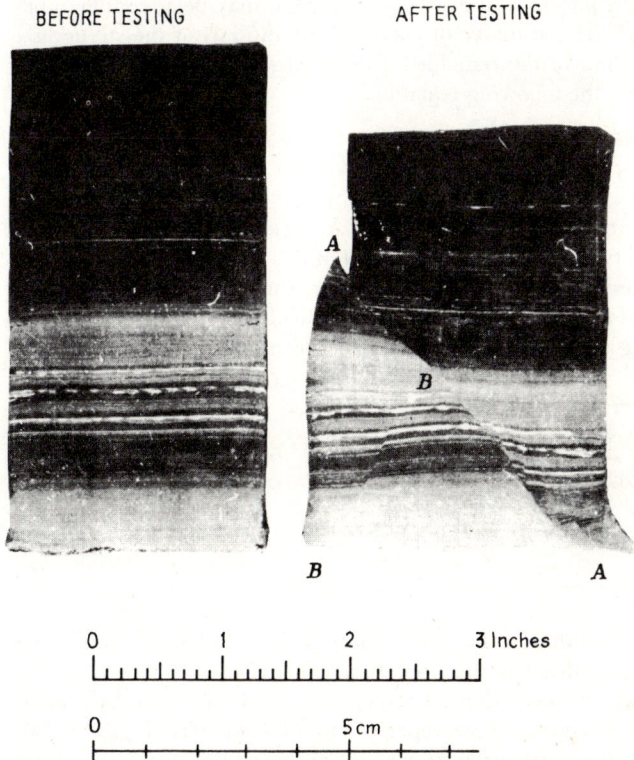

Fig. 3-8. Unconfined compression test. Brittle failure of a varved-clay specimen from Albany, New York (see Art. 2-3B). (*Tschebotarioff and Bayliss, Ref. 378.*)

the deformations which accompanied failure.   When the same specimen is remolded for a repeated test to determine its sensitivity, the loss of the material of slice *acca* can be made up from one of the remaining three segments, for instance *ada*.

An important practical routine application of this test is its use for the determination of the so-called *sensitivity of a clay*, by which is meant the degree of its weakening as a result of a breakdown of its structure by remolding. The sensitivity S_t of a clay is defined as the ratio of the unconfined compressive strengths in the undisturbed and in the remolded conditions.

$$S_t = \frac{q_u}{q_{ur}} \tag{3-20}$$

Most naturally deposited and really undisturbed clays exhibit brittle types of failure at relatively small strains.   Remolding usually increases the strain at failure of sensitive clays up to the ultimate value of 20 percent, which characterizes fully plastic failure.   In some cases it may be advisable to base the definition of the sensitivity of clays on the ratio S'_t of the strengths of the undisturbed and of the remolded samples *at equal strains,* in accordance with Fig. 3-9 and the following equation:

$$S'_t = \frac{q_u}{q'_{ur}} \tag{3-21}$$

The direct use of Eq. (3-21) is predicated on the construction of stress-strain diagrams of the type illustrated by Fig. 3-9 and is therefore more time-consuming than the use of Eq. (3-20).   However, the approximate value of S'_t can be estimated from Eq. (3-20) and the following data, based on the strain ϵ_f corresponding to failure in the undisturbed condition:

ϵ_f, %	S'_t
5	$2.50S_t$–$3.00S_t$
10	$1.30S_t$–$2.00S_t$
15	$1.05S_t$–$1.30S_t$
20	S_t

It should be noted that in the case of controlled-strain tests q_u should refer to the peak value and not to the strength at final failure.

It was originally believed that all clays are strongly weakened by remolding.   Tests on Egyptian clays reported by Tschebotarioff (Ref. 350), however, showed some clays are even strengthened by remolding.   Similar data were obtained elsewhere.   Clays exposed to drying after their deposition usually have low sensitivities.

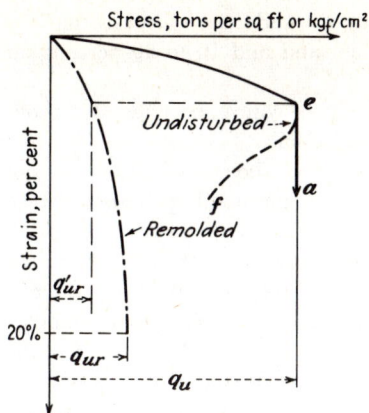

Fig. 3-9. Determination of the sensitivity of a clay by means of an undisturbed and a remolded unconfined compression test on the same specimen. Curve *a*: controlled stress; curve *b*: controlled strain type of test. (*After Tschebotarioff and Bayliss, Ref. 378.*)

Marine clays, especially if they have been partially leached of their salt content, have very high sensitivities (>4; see Table 4-2).   Some such clays, like the Norwegian "quick clays," flow like a liquid after remolding so that an unconfined compression test is impossible to perform. A comparative laboratory cone-penetration test is used instead in Scandinavia.   Or an in situ vane test (Art. 2-5) can be used to determine both the *peak and the remolded strengths*.   The significance of these two terms is illustrated by Fig. 3-27.

3-3. Field Soil-identification Tests. *(A). Visual Inspection.*   Visual inspection is, as a rule, sufficient to permit proper field identification of the gradation and of the shape and size of the grains of coarse-grained soils, i.e., sands and gravels.   A pocket magnifying glass may be of help.

When soil samples are described, the first word indicates the type of grain (sand, silt, or clay) which predominates, i.e., is estimated to represent more than 50 percent of the sample.   This is followed by one of the terms "and," "some," "little," or "trace" to designate the approximate percentage of the next most prevalent grain-size type, estimated according to Table 3-3, as originally proposed by Burmister.

The letters *c* and *f* can be used to designate *coarse* and *fine* sands, respectively (Fig. 3-1); sometimes *m* is used for *medium*.

TABLE 3-3

Term	Percentage of sample
and	50–35
some	35–20
little	20–10
trace	<10

Thus the description "sand, c to f, little silt and clay" suggests that the sample has 90 to 80 percent coarse to fine sand and 10 to 20 percent silt and clay.

Some laboratory training and practice are, of course, necessary for proficiency in the field identification of all types of soils.

Differentiation among fine-grained soils, and their subdivisions, is not possible by visual inspection alone. A few simple auxiliary tests must be employed.

In the *moist condition* one can *differentiate between the silts and the clays* with the help of the *shaking test,* which gives a measure of the mobility of the water in the voids. A remolded pat of moist soil is placed in the palm of the hand or in a rubber cup formed by cutting a tennis ball in two. The surface of the soil is smoothed out with a knife, and the soil pat is shaken by tapping the back of one hand on the palm of the other. If the soil is a silt e.g., a loess or a soil of the rock-flour type, its surface will begin to glisten with the moisture which is pressed out of the voids of the soil as the soil grains with little cohesion slip past each other into a denser position as a result of the shaking. If one then squeezes the soil pat, the moisture will disappear from the surface, since the shearing stresses induced by the squeezing will cause the slightly cohesive or noncohesive soil to expand in very much the same manner as a saturated dense sand (see Fig. 3-21 and Art. 3-5A). A highly cohesive clay soil will not exhibit such changes in the appearance of its surface when shaken or squeezed, since its grains will not slip past each other with the same ease.

The sensitivity of a plastic clay soil to *remolding* can be estimated by taking a 1-in. cube of undisturbed material in its natural state and gently feeling its resistance to finger pressure before and after completely remolding it by hand.

The *plasticity* of a cohesive soil can be estimated by *rolling* it into *threads* in the manner used for the determination of the plastic limit. The feel of the threads after they start crumbling provides indications of the nature of the material.

In a *dry state* the strength of the soil is an indication of its cohesion and hence of its nature. It can be estimated by *crushing* some dried soil by finger pressure. A silt will crumble easily, whereas a rich clay will feel very hard. The surface of a rich dry clay rubbed with a knife will appear shiny.

For further details and supplementary procedures see ASTM Designation D-2488 (Ref. 18).

(B). Pocket Penetrometer Test. This test is based on the fact that the shear strength at failure of a cohesive soil under a footing is independent of the area of a footing [see Fig. 4-2(III), Eq. (4-7), and Art. 4-2]. Tests performed by the writer have shown that this is true for the pocket penetrometer so long as the plasticity index of the cohesive soil is greater than approximately 12. Lower I_p values indicate an appreciable sand content, the frictional properties of which will increase the shear-failure resistance of the soil to values well in excess of its purely cohesive strength.

Subject to this limitation the pocket penetrometer shown in Fig. 3-10 is a very useful tool for approximate on-the-spot estimation of the shearing strength of cohesive soils, e.g., in excavation pits or by pressing the penetrometer point into the bottom of a Shelby tube sample before the tube is sealed for shipping to a laboratory.

Fig. 3-10. Pocket penetrometer indicates the unconfined compressive strength of clays having an $I_p > 12$ percent within the limits of $0.25 < q_u < 4.50$ tons/ft². (*Soiltest, Inc., Ref. 307, CL-700.*)

The penetrometer is designed along the lines of the larger Proctor needle (Art. 5-5) and is graduated in 0.25 ton/ft² (0.25 kg$_f$/cm²) to permit reading directly the unconfined compressive strength up to values of 4.5 tons/ft².

A *pocket shear vane* has become available in England (Ref. 287).

3-4. Consolidation Tests. *(A). General Concepts.* The compression of a soil occurs mainly as a function of a decrease in the volume of the voids. By comparison, the component of compression produced by a decrease in the volume of the grains of the solid skeleton is quite negligible. Therefore, if the voids of a soil are entirely filled with water, measurable compression can occur only as a result of the escape of excess water from the voids. Gradual compression of a soil under such conditions, when induced by static forces of gravity, such as the weight of the soil itself or of structures erected upon it, is termed *consolidation*. It is *not* synonymous with *compaction* (Art. 5-1), which is the artificial compression of a soil by mechanical means.

If a saturated soil is quite pervious, e.g., a clean sand, its consolidation under newly applied static loads will be almost instantaneous, since excess water has no difficulty in escaping from the voids. On the other hand, if the saturated soil is a clay with low permeability, its consolidation will be quite slow, since any excess water in the voids will take time to be squeezed out toward pervious boundaries of the clay layer.

When a load is applied to a fully saturated cohesive soil in its plastic range of consistency (Art. 3-2F), the entire compressive stress σ created by the load is at first carried by the water in the voids. It is then said that $\sigma = u$, where u is the stress in the water which resulted from the application of the pressure σ. The stress u is termed *neutral stress*. Other terms frequently used to designate the stress u are *hydrostatic excess pressure* or *excess pore pressure*.

As time goes by, some water is squeezed out of the clay and escapes through the pervious boundaries of the clay mass where such pervious boundaries are available. The decrease of the volume of the voids in a fully saturated clay corresponds to the amount of water squeezed out. As a result of this process, the solid grains of the soil skeleton are brought into closer contact with each other and consequently take up some of the newly applied load.   The stresses thus created in the soil skeleton are termed *effective stresses* $\bar{\sigma}$.   Any decrease of the neutral stresses of the water in the voids must correspond to an equal increase of the effective stresses in the solid skeleton, and vice versa.   The sum of the effective stresses $\bar{\sigma}$ and the neutral stresses u at any point and at all times must remain constant and equal to the applied stress σ.

$$\sigma = u + \bar{\sigma} \qquad (3\text{-}21a)$$

When all the stress σ has been transferred to the soil skeleton so that $\sigma = \bar{\sigma}$, the neutral stress or excess pore pressure u becomes equal to zero.   Further expulsion of water from the voids and, hence, further compression of the clay will then cease.   The consolidation has reached 100 percent of its final value.   Intermediate stages in this process can be defined by the *percentage of consolidation*

$$U = \frac{S}{S_2} \times 100 \qquad (3\text{-}22)$$

where S = linear change of length of a soil specimen or settlement of layer during one-dimensional vertical consolidation at consolidation stage to be defined

S_2 = linear compression or settlement at final stage of consolidation

The process of consolidation can be visualized better with the help of the model shown in Fig. 3-11, which Terzaghi used in the 1920s to explain his theory.   The sketch shows a cylinder filled with a liquid.   A piston fits into the cylinder and is supported by a system of springs which simulates the action of the solid soil skeleton.   The piston is provided with a number of small

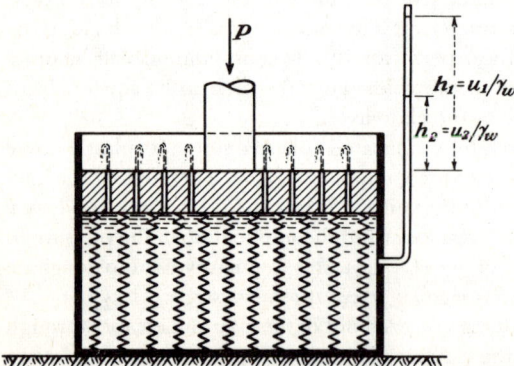

Fig. 3-11.   Model of the type used by Terzaghi to explain by analogy the process of consolidation of a saturated clay.

openings through which the liquid can escape if a load P is applied to the piston. The amount of resistance offered to the load P by the liquid and the rate of the decrease of that resistance are functions of the rate at which the water can escape through the openings and hence are also functions of the diameter of these openings. If the diameter of the openings is made smaller, the rate of the escape of water will decrease. (This principle has been applied for many years in hydraulic shock absorbers in artillery guns.) As the water escapes through the openings, the piston moves downward under the action of the external load P. The springs compress as a result and offer progressively increasing resistance as the downward movement continues. The pressure $u = \gamma_w h$ on the water decreases at the same time, and the level h of the water in the standpipe shown in Fig. 3-11 drops correspondingly. The downward movement and the expulsion of water will stop when the resistance of the compressed springs equals the external load P, and u and h will then be equal to zero.

A rigorous mathematical solution of the process of consolidation was first published by Terzaghi in 1923. He thus became the founder of the new science of *soil mechanics,* which differs from the conventional mechanics of solids by the predominant influence which is exercised on the mechanical properties of soils by the water in the voids of the soil. The time factor becomes all-important in this connection. The development of soil mechanics permitted insight into the causes of the long duration of the settlements of structures erected on deep saturated clay deposits, which sometimes last for many years. In addition, insight into the process of consolidation permitted the improved understanding of the variable shearing strength of soils, which was found to increase with the pressures transmitted from grain to grain of the solid soil skeleton, i.e., with the so-called intergranular pressures or effective stresses. On the other hand, pressures carried by the water in the voids did not contribute to the increase of the shearing strength of a soil—hence the name *neutral stresses.*

(B). Laboratory Testing. Consolidation tests are performed on clay samples carefully fitted into brass rings of 2.5 to 3.0 in. (6.4 to 7.6 cm) diameter (see 1st ed., Art. 6-2). Therefore the consolidation test is sometimes termed a *compression test with confined lateral expansion.* The height of the test sample should be kept small in respect to its diameter so as to decrease the effect of friction between the clay and the sides of the enclosing metal ring. The load is applied to a clay sample during a standard-type consolidation test in increments, where each increment is equal to the previous total load. Each increment of load is allowed to consolidate the clay sample for at least 24 hr. In that time most types of clay can be expected to consolidate fully when the sample thickness equals 1 in. (2.5 cm). A careful continuous record is kept of the compression of the sample during each increment. The final accumulated compression of the sample at the end of its consolidation period after each increment or decrement of loading is then plotted to a semilogarithmic

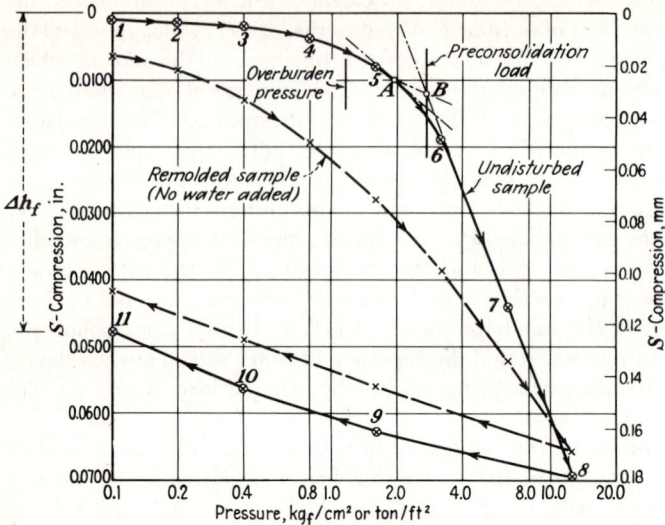

Fig. 3-12. Records of the total (accumulated) compression of clay samples during consolidation tests.

scale, as shown in Fig. 3-12. It should be noted that the clay sample should be allowed to expand for at least 24 hr after each decrement of load, since the expansion can fully develop only as a result of absorption of water, the rate of the absorption depending on factors similar to those which govern the rate of water expulsion during the compression of the sample.

(C). Evaluation of Compressibility. After unloading is completed, the clay sample is removed from the apparatus and its water content is determined by weighing, drying, and weighing again. The volumes of the solid matter and the water can then be expressed in terms of the corresponding fractions of the height of the sample. If the dry weight of the solid is found to be W_s in grams, its specific gravity is G, and the horizontal cross-sectional area of the clay sample within the consolidometer ring is A in square centimeters, then the height h_s in inches of the solid will be

$$h_s = \frac{W_s}{AG \times 2.54} \tag{3-23}$$

Similarly, the height h_{w2} in inches of the water in the sample at the end of the test will be

$$h_{w2} = \frac{W_{w2}}{A \times 1.00 \times 2.54} \tag{3-24}$$

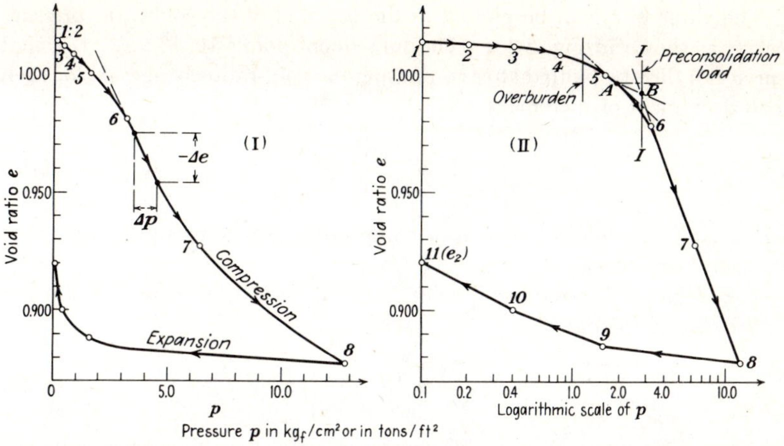

Fig. 3-13. Void-ratio-pressure curves of an undisturbed sample of clay (computed from the data given in Fig. 3-12).

The following relationship should hold for a fully saturated sample (see Fig. 3-14):

$$H_1 = h_s + h_{w2} + \Delta h_f \tag{3-25}$$

where H_1 = initial height of sample

Δh_f = residual compression at end of test (see Fig. 3-12)

The area A of the sample remains constant during all stages of the test. Therefore the void ratio can be expressed as a ratio of heights instead of volumes

$$e = \frac{V_v}{V_s} = \frac{h_v A}{h_s A} = \frac{h_v}{h_s} \tag{3-26}$$

and the void ratio at the end of the test is then

$$e_2 = \frac{h_{w2}}{h_s} \tag{3-27}$$

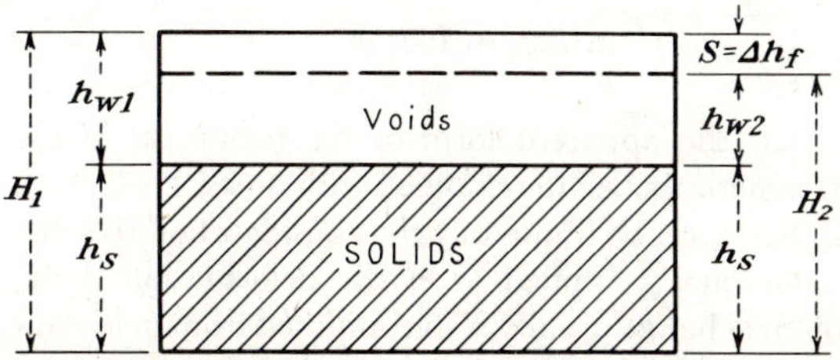

Fig. 3-14. Computation of the settlement S of a fully saturated clay subjected to compression.

The value of e_2 can be plotted as the point 11 of the void-ratio–pressure curve, as shown in Fig. 3-13. The subsequent points 10, 9, . . . , 1 of that curve can then be plotted after computing the void-ratio changes Δe for each load decrement or increment

$$\Delta e = \frac{\Delta h}{h_s} \qquad (3\text{-}28)$$

where Δh is the total expansion or compression registered by the dial gage for each load stage.

The degree of compressibility of a soil is sometimes expressed by the *compressibility coefficient* a_v

$$a_v = \frac{-\Delta e}{\Delta p} \times 10^{-3} \qquad cm^2/g_f \qquad (3\text{-}29)$$

In Eq. (3-29) Δp is given in kilograms per square centimeter $\approx$ tons per square foot. It will be seen from Fig. 3-13(I) that the coefficient a_v represents the slope of the void-ratio–pressure curve. It is given in square centimeters per gram for reasons explained in the discussion of Fig. 3-16.

With reference to Fig. 3-14, the total compression or *settlement* S is

$$S = h_{w1} - h_2 = \frac{h_{w1} - h_{w2}}{h_s + h_{w1}} H_1 = \frac{h_{w1}/h_s - h_{w2}/h_s}{1 + h_{w1}/h_s} H_1$$

$$= \frac{e_1 - e_2}{1 + e_1} H_1 = \frac{\Delta e}{1 + e_1} H_1 = \frac{a_v}{1 + e_1} \Delta p H_1 \times 10^3 \qquad (3\text{-}30)$$

Another coefficient, the *modulus of volume change* m_v, is frequently used.

$$m_v = \frac{a_v}{1 + e_1} \qquad cm^2/g_f \qquad (3\text{-}31)$$

For practical purposes, when estimating settlements, it is more convenient to take the modulus of volume change m_v in square centimeters per kilogram, so that

$$m_v' = m_v \times 10^3 \qquad (3\text{-}32)$$

and

$$m_v' = \frac{S}{\Delta p H_1} \qquad cm^2/kg_f \ or \ ft^2/ton \qquad (3\text{-}33)$$

Thus the coefficient m_v' has the apparent form of the reciprocal of the Young modulus E and can sometimes be interchanged with it (see Prob. 4-1). Such a substitution should, however, be limited by the consideration that the Young modulus E is conventionally applied to elastic deformations only, whereas the modulus of volume change usually is so computed from field data that it includes both elastic and plastic deformations in addition to the deformations induced by consolidation.

The modulus m'_v represents the final compression in meters of a layer 1 m thick under an average pressure throughout the depth of that layer 1 kg_f/cm^2. The numerical values of this coefficient remain unchanged if both S and H_1 are expressed in feet (or in inches) and Δp in tons per square foot (1 ton/ft^2 is approximately, within 3 percent, equal to 1 kg_f/cm^2). The use of this modulus (the symbol X was employed at the time, instead of m'_v) was proposed by Tschebotarioff (Ref. 350) in connection with settlement studies of buildings in Egypt, since it permits the *direct* comparison of compressibility values computed from individual laboratory consolidation tests to the average value computed from observed settlements of full-scale structures in the field. The use of this coefficient has the further practical advantage that it can be computed at any stage of the laboratory consolidation test, without waiting for the water-content and void-ratio determination at the end of the test, directly from the dial readings and Eq. (3-33). The original thickness of the sample H_1 has to be estimated, but the error caused by this approximation does not exceed some 5 percent. The gain in time achieved by this procedure, however, is by no means negligible for cases of rush design jobs when preliminary settlement estimations are needed in a hurry, since a consolidation test may take up to 2 weeks to complete.

The range of possible variations in the compressibility of different types of soils and the comparison between laboratory values of the coefficient m'_v and values obtained in the field are given in Art. 4-6.

If a clay sample is completely remolded under addition of water up to and above the liquid limit and is then subjected to a consolidation test, its void-ratio–pressure curve will be a straight line when plotted to a semilogarithmic scale (see the curve for the second specimen in Fig. 3-15). This

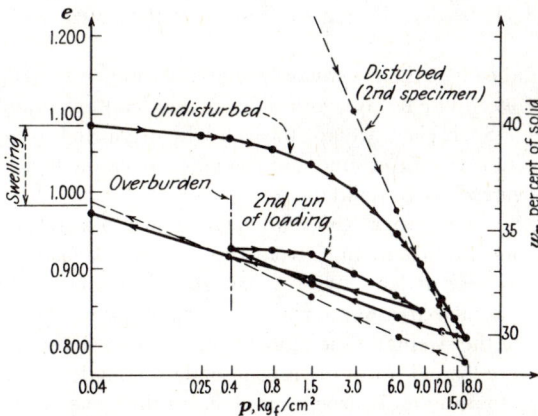

Fig. 3-15. The modulus of volume change m_v' of swelling clays tested in a submerged condition should be computed from the second run of loading in a consolidometer. (*From Tschebotarioff, Ref. 350.*)

branch of the curve is sometimes termed the *virgin compression curve*, since it presumably represents the compression of a naturally deposited clay mass under its own weight.

A dimensionless *compression index* C_c is used to define the tangent of the slope angle of the virgin compression curve plotted at a semilogarithmic scale

$$C_c = \frac{e_1 - e_2}{\log(p_1/p_2)} \tag{3-34}$$

where $e_1 - e_2$ is the decrease Δe in the void ratio due to an effective stress increase from p_1 to p_2 [Fig. 3-13(II)].

The compression index C_c is a constant for a given clay sample. It can be useful for the settlement estimation of clays consolidated only by the action of their own weight and of the still existing overlying soil layers, i.e., the so-called *naturally consolidated clays*. Any additional vertical stress applied to such clay layers by new construction is then likely to fall on the straight-line portion of the void-ratio–pressure semilogarithmic curve, for instance, 6-7-8 in Fig. 3-13(II).

The compression index C_c, however, should never be used for settlement computations of *overconsolidated clays*, i.e., clays which had been subjected in the past to the shrinkage forces of drying or to the weight of once existing glaciers or of presently eroded soil deposits. For such clays the preconsolidation load will be greater than the effective unit weight of the existing soil layers. Even some chemical action may have a similar effect on the void-ratio–pressure curve (see 1st ed., Art. 11-8, concerning effect of vivianite in marine clays).

The *preconsolidation load* of a clay sample can be determined from its void-ratio curve close to the point A of its greatest curvature by a graphical procedure shown in Fig. 3-13(II) (explained in greater detail in the 1st ed. with reference to its Fig. 6-7).

Particular caution is indicated when evaluating consolidation tests performed on strongly overconsolidated clays, especially if they contain some montmorillonite minerals. Such clays are apt to swell when removed from their natural confining pressures in the ground and brought into contact with water at initially low pressures in a consolidometer.

Studies in Egypt (see Tschebotarioff, Ref. 350) have shown that settlements computed in the conventional manner from the first run of loading during a consolidation test were at least twice as large as those observed. This was attributed to the initial expansion during sampling and after flooding in the consolidometer of the swelling type of local clays. To counteract this effect, such samples were loaded up to the preconsolidation load, which was first determined on a separate undisturbed sample from the same layer. Then the load was reduced to the value of the overburden at the elevation from which the sample was taken and was increased again. This second run of loading (see Fig. 3-15) was then used to compute the m'_v values, which were found to agree quite closely with the values computed from measurements of

full-scale structures.   Similar results were obtained through the application
of the same procedure to compact varved clays at Albany, New York, by
Tschebotarioff and Schuyler (Ref. 380), as shown in Fig. 4-33.   This diagram brings out the various other factors which have to be considered when
comparing the results of field settlement measurements and laboratory consolidation tests by means of the m_v' values.   The m_v' laboratory values of that
diagram refer to the range of pressure caused by an increment of 1 ton/ft² in
excess of the overburden pressure at the depth from which the soil sample
was extracted.

   (D). Rate of Consolidation.   The publication by Terzaghi in 1923 of a theory
which gave a rigorous solution of the problems concerned with the rate of
consolidation of clay layers permitted the development of the modern science
of soil mechanics, since the pore-water pressures treated by that theory influenced many other important phenomena, such as the shearing strength
of clays.   The general outline of Terzaghi's theory follows.

   Let us consider a clay layer of the thickness $2H$ (see Fig. 3-16) which is
sandwiched between two pervious sand layers and is stressed by a surface
unit load p.   Under the influence of this load the clay layer will begin to
compress as the excess of the water from its pores is squeezed out toward the

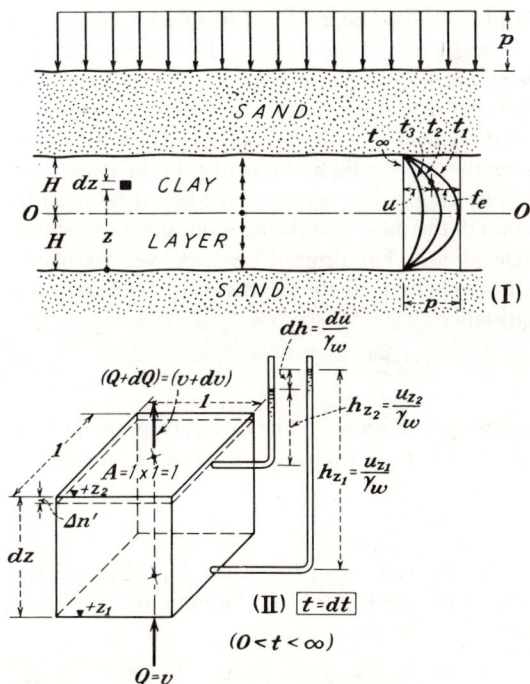

Fig. 3-16.   The one-dimensional consolidation of a clay layer and
some of the factors which affect its rate.

two pervious boundaries provided by the sand layers.   If the clay is homogeneous, excess pore water from the upper half of the layer, i.e., above its
center plane 0-0, will flow toward the upper sand layer, whereas the excess
pore water from the lower half of the layer will flow toward the lower sand
layer, as indicated by arrows in Fig. 3-16(I).

   Equation (3-21) ($p = \sigma = u + \bar{\sigma}$) must remain valid at all times and at all
points of the clay layer.   This is illustrated by the diagram in Fig. 3-16(I).
At the moment (t_0) the load is applied all the pressure p is carried by the pore
water, so that $p = u$.   This gives a straight line in the diagram.   A few in-
stants later, however, water will start escaping into the sand, so that the pore
pressures u at both pervious boundaries will equal zero at all times.   As time
goes by, the line of demarcation over the depth of the layer between the excess
pore pressures u and the effective stresses $\bar{\sigma}$ will be successively indicated by
the curves t_1, t_2, and t_3.   The slope of these curves at any point indicates the
rate of change of u with depth at a given time.   This change of u along the
depth of the layer represents the hydraulic gradient i upon which depends
the velocity v of the expulsion of the excess water from the voids.   After a
certain period of time t_∞ consolidation will be complete, and the excess pore
pressures will equal zero ($u = 0$; $p = \bar{\sigma}$), as indicated by the straight line in
the diagram.

   This process of consolidation will now be analyzed further in respect to a
small prism of clay from the upper half of the layer.   The prism has a horizontal cross-sectional area equal to unity and a height dz; it is drawn to a
large scale in Fig. 3-16(II).   Let us assume that two imaginary piezometer
tubes (standpipes) have been connected with the pores of the clay in the
prism, one of the standpipes at the upper edge and the other at the lower edge
of the prism.   Since water is flowing in the upward direction, there must be
a drop of head in the direction of the flow, and the water in the lower standpipe will rise to a higher elevation.   The drop of head dh over the height
of the prism is related at a given time to the decrease in the pore-water
pressure ∂u over the same distance.

$$dh = \frac{du}{\gamma_w} \tag{3-35}$$

   In Eq. (3-35) γ_w is the unit weight of water.   The hydraulic gradient i, by
definition [Eq. (8-1)], is the drop of head over a given distance, so that

$$i = \frac{\partial h}{\partial z} \tag{3-36}$$

   From these two equations, the law of Darcy [Eq. (8-1)], Eq. (3-31) for the
modulus of volume change m_v, and a number of transformations (see 1st ed.,
Art. 6-8), Terzaghi obtained the expression

$$\frac{\partial u}{\partial t} = c_v \frac{\partial^2 u}{\partial z^2} \tag{3-37}$$

This equation relates the rate of change of the excess pore pressure u in respect to time to the amount of water which is squeezed out of the voids of a clay prism during the same time interval.

c_v is the *coefficient of consolidation*.

$$c_v = \frac{k}{m_v \gamma_w} \qquad (3\text{-}38)$$

The units of c_v are square centimeters per minute if the coefficient of permeability k is given in centimeters per minute.

By deriving the differential equation (3-37) Terzaghi solved the problem, since that equation is analogous to the one which had already been studied in thermodynamics in connection with the rate of heat transfer from a flat plate. The solution of equations of this type is obtained by means of the Fourier series and takes the form expressed in Eq. (6-28) of the first edition for the pore pressure u.

In that equation z and H are the vertical distances shown in Fig. 3-16(I), and T_v is a dimensionless number called the *time factor*.

$$T_v = \frac{c_v t}{H^2} \qquad (3\text{-}39)$$

where $t =$ time which elapses until excess pore pressure u drops to value
  defined
  $c_v =$ coefficient of consolidation, as defined by Eq. (3-38).

For any given time t the variation with the depth z of the excess pore pressure u can be expressed as a fraction of the applied consolidation pressure p and then plotted as shown by the curves t_1, t_2, and t_3 of Fig. 3-16(I).

The percentage of consolidation U_z at a given depth z and time t will equal

$$U_z = \frac{p - u}{p} \times 100 = \left(1 - \frac{u}{p}\right)100 \qquad (3\text{-}39a)$$

The percentage of consolidation U for the entire layer at a given time t is taken as the average of the U_z values over the full depth $2H$. Since the terms *percentage of consolidation* and *percentage of settlement* are synonymous for the case illustrated by Fig. 3-16(I), the above definition of U is in agreement with Eq. (3-22).

The dimensionless time factor T_v [Eq. (3-39)] can be related to the average percentage of consolidation U of the entire layer. This relationship is presented graphically by curve T_v in Fig. 4-34. It should be noted that Eq. (3-39) corresponds only to the boundary and loading conditions illustrated in Fig. 3-16. Different boundary and loading conditions, for instance those for expulsion of surplus water in a horizontal direction toward vertical drains or the nonuniform distribution of the consolidation load with depth, give solutions of Eq. (3-37) which differ somewhat from each other and hence

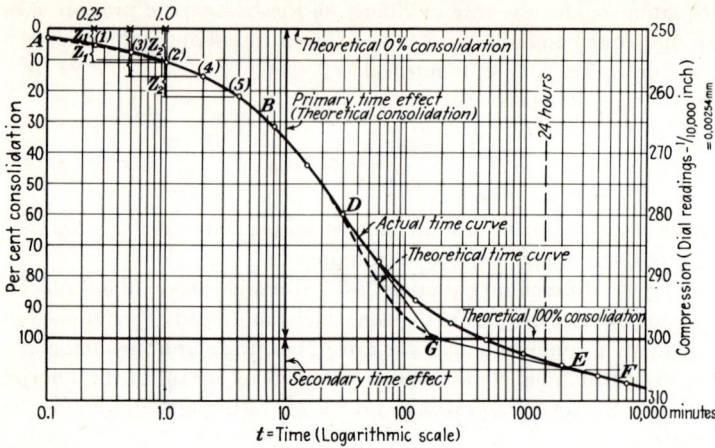

Fig. 3-17. Graphical analysis of a time-compression curve obtained from the dial readings of one load stage during a consolidation test.

produce a somewhat different relationship between the time factor T and the average percentage of consolidation U (see Fig. 4-34).

The *coefficient of permeability* k used in Eq. (3-38) is customarily determined by a graphical analysis of a time-compression record of each stage in a consolidation test. One such method, proposed by Casagrande and Fadum, is illustrated by Fig. 3-17, which gives a record, plotted to a semilogarithmic scale, of the dial readings obtained during one load stage. In this particular case the load increment was left unchanged for almost 5 days, i.e., for a longer period than the customary 24 hr. This was apparently done for the purpose of emphasizing the so-called *secondary* time effects.

A comparison of the actually recorded time curve (shown by the full line in Fig. 13-17) with the theoretical time curve (broken line in Fig. 3-17) shows that the shapes of the two curves agree fairly well over the first half AD of their length. In order to make a closer comparison between the recorded and the theoretical values, one first has to establish the theoretical lines of 0 and of 100 percent consolidation, as shown by Fig. 3-17 and explained in detail in the first edition, Art. 6-9.

The coefficients of permeability k and the coefficients of consolidation c_v can be computed from the theoretical percentages of consolidation as illustrated by the following example.

It can be seen from Fig. 3-17 that the actual and the theoretical time curves coincide in their central portion BD. It is therefore customary to compute the c_v and the k coefficients from Eqs. (3-38) and (3-39) by inserting the values of the time factor T_v and of the actual time t which correspond to a percentage of consolidation $U = 50$ percent. The T_v values for the boundary and loading conditions of a standard consolidation test are essentially the same as the conditions illustrated by Fig. 3-16. They are defined by curve T_v in Fig. 4-34; from that curve we find that for $U = 50$ percent, $T_v = 0.20$. Similarly, we find from Fig. 3-17 that until $U = 50$ percent was reached, the actual time which had elapsed during the particular laboratory test illustrated by that diagram was $t = 19.5$ min. The value of H for a 1-in.-thick laboratory sample is equal to $\frac{1}{2} \times 1.0 = 0.5$ in. $= 1.27$ cm. Hence, from Eq. (3-39) we obtain

$$c_v = \frac{T_v H^2}{t} = \frac{0.20 \times 1.27^2}{19.5} = 0.0166 \text{ cm}^2/\text{min} \qquad (3\text{-}40)$$

In order to compute the coefficient of permeability k from Eq. (3-38), we have to know the modulus of volume change m_v which must be given in square centimeters per gram, since the units of γ_w are grams per cubic centimeter. The units of k will then be

$$k = c_v m_v \gamma_w = \text{cm}^2/\text{min} \times \text{cm}^2/\text{g}_f \times \text{g}_f/\text{cm}^3 = \text{cm}/\text{min}$$

With reference to Art. 4-6 and Eq. (3-32), let us assume that the clay tested had a modulus of volume change $m_v' = 0.01$ ft^2/ton, or approximately 0.01 cm^2/kg$_f$. Thus the corresponding $m_v = m_v' \times 10^{-3} = 1 \times 10^{-5}$ cm^2/g$_f$, and with $\gamma_w = 1.0$ g$_f$/cm^3,

$$k = 0.0166 \times 1.0 \times 10^{-5} \times 1.0 = 1.66 \times 10^{-7} \text{ cm/min}$$
$$= 2.75 \times 10^{-9} \text{ cm/sec} \qquad (3\text{-}41)$$

This is a very impervious clay (see Fig. 8-2).

The computation of the permeability coefficient from the primary compression curve of a consolidation test gives accurate results only for comparatively impervious clays with permeability coefficients smaller than 1×10^{-7} cm/sec $= 6.0 \times 10^{-6}$ cm/min. For more permeable clays and silts, direct permeability tests of the falling-head type (1st ed., Art. 5-2) must be performed in order to determine the k values.

In certain types of clays and in peats the secondary time effects are very pronounced, to the extent that in some cases the entire time-compression curve has the shape of an almost straight sloping line when plotted to a semilogarithmic scale, instead of the typical inverted S shape of the curve (Fig. 3-17) of clays with pronounced primary consolidation effects. These so-called *secondary time effects* are a phenomenon somewhat analogous to the *creep* of other overstressed materials in a plastic state. A delayed progressive slippage of grain upon grain, or plate upon plate, as the particles adjust themselves to a denser condition, appears to be responsible for these secondary effects. Possibly some creep of the bent platelike clay particles themselves may also be a contributing factor. When the rate of such plastic deformations of the individual soil particles, or of their slippage on each other, is slower than the rate of the expulsion of the excess water from the decreasing volume of voids between the particles, secondary effects predominate and this is reflected by the shape of the time-compression curve. The factors

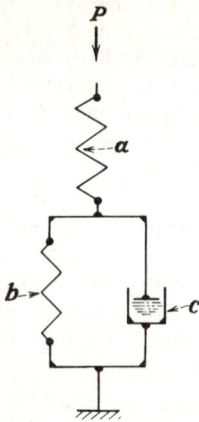

Fig. 3-18. A rheological model used by several authors to represent and analyze the compressibility of the skeleton of solid soil grains. (*After Christie, Ref. 58.*)

which affect the rate of the secondary compression of soils are not yet fully understood.

Many theoretical studies have been made on the rheology of soils. *Rheology* is a general term for the study of the deformation and flow of matter. To permit the mathematical analysis of the problem, models consisting of various combinations of springs and dashpots have been proposed by various investigators. The springs represent the component of instantaneous deformation under an applied load, whereas the dashpots represent the time-dependent component of deformation similar to the one shown in Fig. 3-11 for primary consolidation due to expulsion of water from the voids of the soil.

Figure 3-18 shows one such rheological model used for the theoretical study of *secondary consolidation*. In contrast to the Terzaghi model shown on Fig. 3-11, which refers to the process of consolidation of the entire soil mass, the model of Fig. 3-18 refers to the deformation of the skeleton of solid soil particles only. The spring a in Fig. 3-18 corresponds to the Terzaghi assumption of instantaneous elastic compression of the soil skeleton. The dashpot c is intended to represent the flow or viscous component of the soil-skeleton deformations. For a general outline of the theory involved see Scott, Ref. 284.

Many relevant mathematically complex solutions of theoretical importance have been published, but so far usable methods for the experimental determination of soil properties which would permit the direct application of these solutions to engineering design practice do not seem to have been developed.

See also the related discussion of Fig. 3-29 in Art. 3-5D.

3-5. Shear-strength Determination. *(A). General Concepts.* It is still customary to separate the shearing strength s of a soil into two components, one due to the *cohesion* between the soil particles and the other due to the *friction* between them, according to the following equation, which is based on the work of the French engineer Coulomb (Ref. 67):

$$s = c + \sigma \tan \phi \qquad (3\text{-}42)$$

This equation expresses the assumption that the cohesion c is independent of the normal pressure σ acting on the plane of failure, so that at zero normal pressure $s = c$. Thus, according to the Coulomb equation (3-42), the cohesion is defined as the shearing strength at zero normal pressure on the plane of failure. On the other hand, the frictional component of the shearing strength of a soil is defined as being directly proportional to the normal pressure σ, the value tan ϕ, where ϕ is the angle of internal friction, being taken as a constant for a given soil.

Equation (3-42) expresses the problem in a greatly oversimplified form. The shearing strength of a soil depends on a number of other factors not considered by that equation. Also, in actual practice, it is extremely difficult, if not impossible, to determine separately the quantitatively correct values of these two components of the shearing strength of an actual soil in situ. Alternative procedures will therefore be considered after an examination of the fundamentals involved.

Let us consider the behavior of a solid body resting on a plane surface 1-1, as shown in Fig. 3-19, and subjected to the action of two forces one of which, the force P_n, acts at right angles to the plane 1-1, whereas the other, the force P_t, acts tangentially to that plane. Let us further assume that P_n remains constant during the entire experiment whereas P_t gradually increases from zero to the value which will produce sliding. The angle formed by the resultant R of these two forces with the normal to the plane 1-1 is known as the *angle of obliquity*. The solid body will start sliding along the plane 1-1 when the force P_t reaches a value which will increase the angle of obliquity α to a certain maximum value ϕ. The angle ϕ is termed the *angle of friction*, and the value tan ϕ is termed the *coefficient of friction*. Experiments show that the critical value of P_t is proportional to P_n, that is,

$$P_t = P_n \tan \phi \qquad (3\text{-}43)$$

or since $P_t = sA$ and $P_n = \sigma A$, where A is the overall contact area,

$$s = \sigma \tan \phi \qquad (3\text{-}44)$$

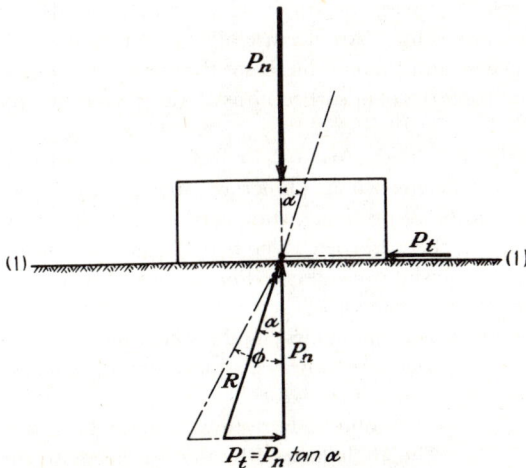

Fig. 3-19. Sketch illustrating the term *angle of friction*.

Equation (3-44) is identical with Eq. (3-42) when the cohesion c is equal to zero. It states that for $c = 0$ the maximum shearing resistance to sliding is directly proportional to the normal pressure on the plane of sliding.

The physical causes of this relationship are complex and not yet fully understood. For chemically clean surfaces the value of tan ϕ increases somewhat with the roughness of the surfaces. This indicates that in such cases the resistance to sliding is dependent on the interlocking of the protuberances of the two surfaces. Microscopic protuberances, however, are present even in the case of apparently polished surfaces. Therefore, when two surfaces are brought into contact over an area A, they will be actually touching each other only over a small fraction of that area and at the actual points of contact the material may be stressed up to its yield point by pressure normal to the plane of contact. Induced sliding will occur when the interlocks of the projections and their areas in direct plane contact with each other are sheared off. An increase of normal pressure presumably increases the percentage of the total overall area A of contact of the two surfaces which interlocks or which is in actual contact. As a result the total resistance to sliding is increased, since the total cross-sectional area of the material to be sheared off has also been increased.

Adsorbed films of liquid are also known to influence the frictional resistance strongly. Oil has been used for centuries to lubricate metal surfaces and decrease the friction between them. On the other hand the antilubricating action of water on some substances, for instance on steel or on glass, is less generally known. Since water is of paramount importance in soils, Terzaghi emphasized its antilubricating properties. According to the concept that the frictional resistance between soil grains is equal to the shearing strength of the actual contact layer between them, it was assumed that when a film of liquid separates the two solid surfaces, the frictional resistance equals the shearing strength of the adsorbed film. An increase of normal pressure presumably decreases the thickness and thereby increases the shearing strength of the film. The semisolid properties of adsorbed films of water have already been outlined (Art. 3-1C).

Tschebotarioff and Welch (see 1st ed., Art. 7-2, or Ref. 382) showed that *hydrophilic minerals,* quartz and calcite, when submerged, increase their frictional resistance 4.5 and 2.5 times, respectively, compared with the dry condition, indicating that water in the adsorbed layer had acquired semisolid characteristics. A reverse relationship was observed in the case of two *hydrophobic minerals* of the water-repellent talc variety.

The angle of internal friction ϕ of a cohesionless sand is sometimes assumed to equal the angle of repose α_R. There are, however, substantial differences, which will be outlined with reference to Fig. 3-20.

Let us consider the equilibrium of a solid body resting on an inclined surface, as illustrated in Fig. 3-20. The angle formed by that surface with the horizontal is designated by α. The weight of the body is W. Sliding is induced by its tangential component $W_t = W \sin \alpha$ and is resisted by its normal component multiplied by the friction coefficient $W \cos \alpha \tan \phi$. If we increase the angle α of the inclined slope, sliding will finally occur when it reaches a certain maximum value α_R. At that moment

$$W \sin \alpha_R = W \cos \alpha_R \tan \phi \qquad (3\text{-}45)$$

and $\qquad\qquad \tan \alpha_R = \tan \phi \quad$ or $\quad \alpha_R = \phi \qquad (3\text{-}46)$

A body of a spherical shape will start rolling down the slope at a much smaller angle α_r of the slope, since the coefficient of rolling friction of all materials is smaller than the coefficient of sliding friction.

Grains of sand or other granular materials may either *slide* or *roll* over each other when the slope is composed of the same material. In addition, they will *interlock* with each other, as illustrated in Fig. 3-20. The natural slope which a mass of soil will assume is termed the *angle of repose*. For granular materials, subject to certain reservations, the angle of repose α_R is frequently taken to equal the angle of internal friction ϕ, in accordance with Eq. (3-46). It should, however, be clearly understood that the resistance of sand to sliding along a plane is composed of sliding and rolling friction and the interlocking of the grains. A separate evaluation of all three components is not practicable for a mass of soil. All three components are directly proportional to the normal pressure. It should further be noted that a natural slope of sand, by its very nature, cannot restrict at its surface the expansion of sand, which is associated with the rolling of grains over each other, and which is restricted in the interior of a dense mass of sand by the interlocking of the individual grains.

Therefore the angle of repose reflects the frictional characteristics of a loose sloping-surface sand layer and will hardly be affected by the density of the underlying sand layers, whereas the angle of internal friction of such underlying and hence confined layers *is* affected by their density. Direct shear tests performed on a uniform sand of rounded grains (1st ed., Art 7-27)

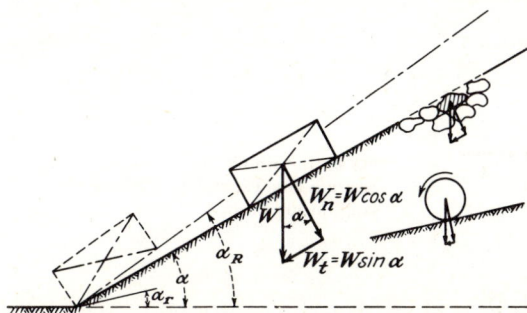

Fig. 3-20. Sketch illustrating the term *angle of repose.*

showed that the angle of internal friction increases with density from $\phi = 30°$ to $\phi = 39°$.

Unless drainage of water is prevented entirely, *volume changes during shear* will occur in all soils. Clays and *loose sands will contract* as their grains slide to assume a denser packing. This should not be difficult to vizualize. *Dense sands will expand during shear.* This can be demonstrated in the laboratory by means of a simple experiment illustrated by Fig. 3-21. A rubber cylinder *b* is filled with dense sand, which is then saturated with water, introduced through the stopcock *C* until it rises to the top of the capillary glass tube *a*. To prevent bulging and creep of the rubber as a result of the head of water thus developed, electricians' tape is wrapped around the cylinder. The sand is then thoroughly shaken down. If one exerts lateral pressure on the cylinder with two fingers, as indicated by arrows, the dense sand inside will have to bulge slightly, as shown by the broken lines in Fig. 3-21. Such bulging is essentially due to shearing deformations. A local increase of the total sand volume, and hence of the volume of its voids, will take place. This circumstance will be confirmed visually by a drop of the water level in the glass tube *a*, since some of the water in the tube will go to fill up the additional void space. The harder one presses on the rubber cylinder, the lower the water level will drop in the glass capillary tube above it. The original water level can be restored by shaking down the sand again.

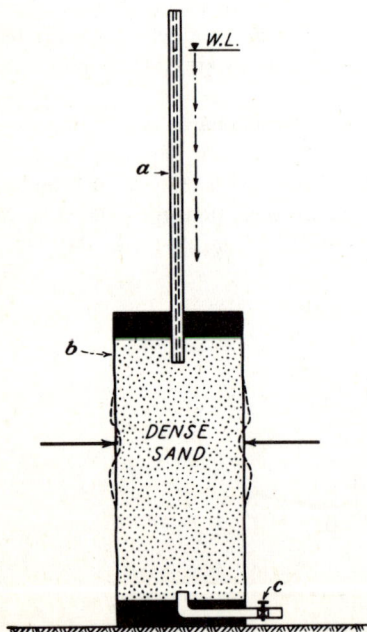

Fig. 3-21. Simple device to demonstrate the expansion of dense sand during shear.

(A)   (B)

Fig. 3-22. Simple experiment illustrating the properties of sand in a confined and loaded condition.

There is no evidence that under static conditions in the field the actual angle ϕ would be any different from the laboratory value. The lowest static values of ϕ to be recorded for any sand by triaxial or direct-box shear tests equal 28°, the highest 45°, depending on the absolute density of the sand. Values up to $\phi = 60°$ have been obtained by means of double-ring shear tests on sand, but this appears to indicate jamming of grains in this type of apparatus.

The angle of internal friction ϕ is essentially the same for a completely dry sand and for a fully submerged sand.

When the potential shearing strength of a sand is rendered effective by confining pressures, the sand will behave essentially like a solid body. Under such conditions sand has *beam strength* and will resist bending. This can be demonstrated in the laboratory by an experiment illustrated in the two photographs of Fig. 3-22. A football rubber bladder is filled with sand. When a suction pump is connected to the bladder, a partial vacuum is created inside. The unbalanced excess of external air pressure against the rubber of the bladder presses the sand grains together and makes the whole sand mass feel solid to the touch. In this condition, as shown in Fig. 3-22A, the sand-filled rubber bladder becomes a beam by virtue of the prestressing to which it is subjected and will support without visible deflection a concentrated 15-lb load at its center. However, as shown in Fig. 3-22B, the sand "beam" will immediately collapse under the loading applied, once the suction pump is disconnected from the football bladder. It should be noted that the beam strength illustrated by Fig. 3-22A was developed as a result of an all-round pressure not exceeding 1 atm, or approximately 1 ton/ft². Assuming 105 lb/ft³ (1.68 g$_f$/cm³) for the unbuoyed weight of a soil, and 62 lb/ft³ (0.99 g$_f$/cm³) for its buoyed weight, we find that an effective vertical pressure σ_1 approximately corresponding to 1 atm would be exerted by the weight of only 19 ft (5.8 m) of soil above the free-water level or by 33 ft (10.0 m) of submerged soil.

The corresponding lateral pressure σ_3 within a mass of sand at these depths, however, depends on a number of variables and will usually not exceed $0.4\sigma_1$ or $0.5\sigma_1$. Thus the conditions illustrated by Fig. 3-22 are hardly ever exactly reproduced in nature within a mass of sand. This experiment therefore serves only for a qualitative demonstration of the transformation of a confined sand into a solid body, and it cannot be used for any quantitative evaluations of beam strength.

There are two types of cohesion. The slight shearing strength of unconfined moist granular soils is usually referred to as *apparent cohesion,* since it disappears once the surface tension of the free-water menisci in the voids is removed either by renewed submergence or by complete drying. Thus caution is needed when one relies on apparent cohesion in engineering work. A case is on record where a cut was made through slightly moist clean sand on what was believed to be its natural angle of repose of 45°. The 1:1 slope was immediately paved. It proved too steep because the effect of the apparent cohesion was only temporary and disappeared after all the water dried out. The sand, including all its pavement, then slid out, adjusting itself to its true natural angle of repose.

True cohesion is produced by the actual bond which develops at the surfaces of contact of clay particles as a result of electrochemical forces of attraction. It is dependent on a great number of factors, the study of most of which falls within the provinces of soil physics and colloidal chemistry (see 1st ed., Art. 7-19). A detailed knowledge of these factors is essential in such branches of soil engineering as soil stabilization, where the cohesive properties of relatively small quantities of surface soils are altered and improved by appropriate chemical treatment. For the large masses of natural soils in situ with which foundation engineers or earth-dam builders are concerned, a general understanding of the effect which natural chemical factors may have on the shearing strength of soils will usually suffice. A detailed study of the controllable factors which affect the determination of the overall shearing strength of soils and its relation to the actual true values in the field is, however, essential for civil engineers of all fields of specialization.

True cohesion can sometimes develop even in sands if some cementing agent is present to bind the particles together in a dry, moist, or submerged state. For clays in a dry state, the true cohesion cannot be determined separately from the apparent cohesion. Submergence as such does not affect the true cohesion of clays, although, as will be shown later, any increase of volume reduces the shearing strength of clays, presumably by increasing the distance between particles and thereby decreasing the forces of attraction between them. The cohesion of a clay, however, can be gradually but completely destroyed as a result of submergence if it is accompanied by *slaking*. This is essentially a surface phenomenon. If the clay layer at the exposed surface swells first and therefore expands more than the adjoining inner layers, the induced relative displacements are liable to detach the surface layer and cause it to disintegrate and slough away. The process can then be repeated and gradually progress from the surface inward.

Clays increase their compressive strength in proportion to their preconsolidation pressure.

Skempton (Ref. 300) computed a ratio $(c/p)_n$ for naturally consolidated clays from several localities, where c is the cohesion, or shearing strength, taken as one-half of the compressive strength, and p is the effective weight of the overburden. When plotted against the liquid limit, this ratio was found to show a trend to increase from values of 0.18 for $w_L = 40$ percent to values of 0.38 for $w_L = 110$ percent. These field values are in approximate agreement with the s/p ratio computed from laboratory data (1st ed., Fig. 7-34). A high value of the liquid limit indicates a high percentage of very fine particles of colloidal size and therefore a very large total effective surface area of the particles per unit of volume of the soil. The electrostatic forces of attraction upon which the cohesion depends should therefore also increase somewhat with the value of the liquid limit.

Lambe has shown that the strength and consolidation characteristics of a soil depend on the sequence of all past pressure variations which it had undergone in the course of its geological history. The *stress-path method* proposed by Lambe (Ref. 181) is intended to permit a reconstruction in the laboratory of these variations. The loading and reloading of a clay sample in a Cairo (Egypt) consolidometer shown by Fig. 3-15 and discussed in Art. 3-4C seem to represent a practically valid but limited special case of the generalized stress-path approach suggested by Lambe.

(B). Equipment for Shear Testing. The first category of laboratory soil shear-testing devices performs *direct shear tests.*

Three main types of device fall into this category: the direct single-shear box apparatus, the direct double-shear ring apparatus, and the torsional-ring direct single-shear apparatus.

Figure 3-23 illustrates the main features of the *direct single-shear box apparatus.* This is the oldest and simplest type of soil shear-testing device. The soil specimen is fitted into the apparatus between two indented or grid plates a which help to distribute the tangential force P_t over the whole area of the specimen. The plates a can be made either pervious or impervious, depending on the conditions of drainage desired. The normal load P_n is maintained at a constant value during the test. The tangential force P_t is increased gradually until failure is produced along the plane ss. The lateral and vertical displacements are measured by sensitive dial gages not shown in Fig. 3-23. Usually the lower half of the apparatus is stationary and the upper half movable. Sometimes a reverse arrangement is used; this does not appear advisable, since it is apt to restrain somewhat the expansion of specimens which occurs during shear in the case of dense granular soils. Too high values of shearing resistance result.

Figure 3-24 illustrates the main features of the *direct double-shear ring apparatus.* The tangential force P_t is applied to the central, movable ring, so

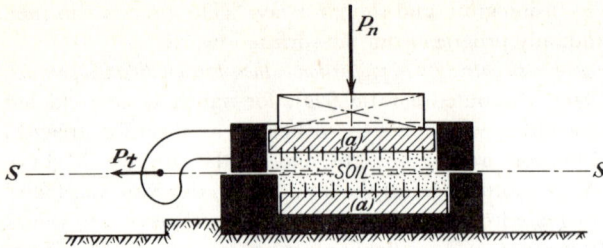

Fig. 3-23.   Main features of direct single-shear box apparatus.

as to produce shearing along two planes ss.   Frequently the two outer rings are made somewhat longer than the central one.   Not all of the normal force P_n would then be transmitted to the planes ss, part of it being taken up by friction along the walls of the outer rings; this would give too low values of shearing resistance.   On the other hand, expansion of dense sands might be partially prevented for the same reason; this would give too high values of shearing resistance.   Frequently the apparatus is so designed that the inner tube of a special sampler is formed by rings which will fit directly into the shearing device, without having to transfer the soil from them.   This procedure does not actually have the advantages which it appears to have at first glance.   It is sometimes claimed that the clay specimen does not have to be transferred in the laboratory from the sampling-tube liner to the testing device.   This is a somewhat questionable feature, since the use of special ring liners in a sampler necessarily increases the overall wall thickness of the sampler and its area ratio, thereby increasing the danger of remolding and weakening the clay sample.

The torsional-ring single-shear test (1st ed., Art. 7-5) is essentially an instrument for special types of research only.

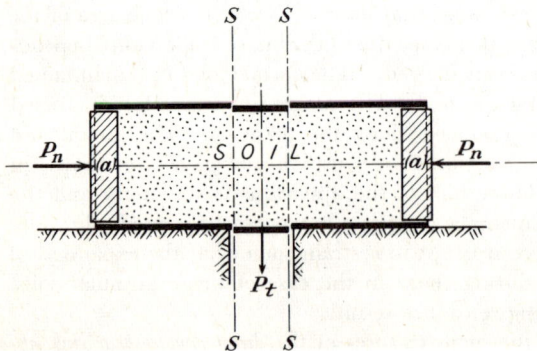

Fig. 3-24.   Main features of direct double-shear ring apparatus.

Shear testing of clays usually involves close control of water-content changes in the specimen during the test. The accurate control of such changes in the direct shear-type tests is much more difficult than in the triaxial tests.

The general setup for the so-called *confined compression tests,* the triaxial and cell tests, is illustrated in Fig. 3-25. A soil specimen is enclosed in a cylindrical rubber membrane and is placed in a pressure chamber formed by a cylinder of transparent material, usually Lucite, filled with liquid, usually glycerin. The vertical unit pressure σ_1 is applied through a piston with a sufficiently good fit to prevent leakage of the confining liquid from the chamber. Since a tight fit may decrease the normal load because of friction along the piston, for very precise measurements some recent apparatus interpose a load-measuring device, a proving ring, for instance, between the piston and the soil specimen by placing the device inside the pressure chamber (not shown in Fig. 3-25).

In the *triaxial* test stopcock 1 shown in Fig. 3-25 is open and thereby connects the pressure chamber with a compressor which in a standard-type test maintains the lateral pressure σ_3 in the chamber at a constant value throughout the duration of the test. The vertical pressure σ_1 is then gradually increased until failure occurs. Stopcock 2 may be either open or closed, depending on whether drainage of the specimen through the lower porous

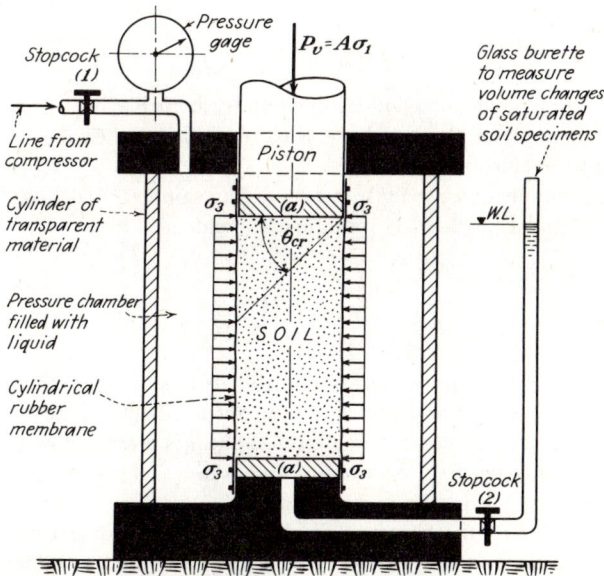

Fig. 3-25. Main features of the triaxial and cell types of cylindrical compression apparatus.

stone a is or is not desired.   In the case of a saturated specimen of granular soil the measurement of its volume changes can be conveniently performed by observing the fluctuations of the water level in a graduated glass burette connected to the open stopcock 2.

Failure will occur along a plane forming an angle θ_{cr} with the horizontal. An analysis of the equilibrium of a soil specimen subjected to a triaxial test is given in the first edition, Art. 7-8, where it is shown that the following relationships are valid:

$$\tau = \sin 2\theta(\sigma_1 - \sigma_3) \times \tfrac{1}{2} \tag{3-47}$$

$$\theta_{cr} = 45° + \frac{\phi}{2} \tag{3-48}$$

If $\phi = 0$,

$$\tau_{max} = \tfrac{1}{2}(\sigma_1 - \sigma_3) \tag{3-49}$$

$$\sigma_1 = \sigma_3 \tan^2\left(45° + \frac{\phi}{2}\right) + 2c \tan\left(45° + \frac{\phi}{2}\right) \tag{3-50}$$

If $c = 0$,

$$\sigma_1 = \sigma_3 \tan^2\left(45° + \frac{\phi}{2}\right) \tag{3-51}$$

If $\phi = 0$,

$$\sigma_1 = \sigma_3 + 2c \tag{3-52}$$

where τ = shearing stress along any plane inclined under angle θ to horizontal
    θ_{cr} = inclination angle of plane with the least resistance to shearing
The remaining symbols refer to Fig. 3-25.

In an unconfined compressive-strength test on a clay sample (Art. 3-2G) by definition $\sigma_3 = 0$, and Eq. (3-50) is simplified to read

$$\sigma_1 = q_u = 2c \tan\left(45° + \frac{\phi}{2}\right) \tag{3-53}$$

from which Eq. (3-18) of Art. 3-2G is obtained.

All types of shear test can be performed as controlled-stress or controlled-strain tests except for the cell test, which is of the controlled-stress type.

In the *controlled-stress tests* the load which induces shear is increased gradually until complete failure occurs.   Strains are then a function of the stress, giving a stress-strain curve of the shape *ab* in Fig. 3-27.

In the *controlled-strain tests* the shearing displacements are induced and controlled in such a manner that they occur at a constant predetermined rate.   This can be achieved by an electrically operated motor with appropriate gears.   The shearing resistance offered to this displacement by the soil specimen is measured by a proving ring or similar device.   The stress-strain curves of tests of this type have the shape ac in Fig. 3-27.   Nearly all compression and tension machines for testing such materials as steel and concrete are operated on the controlled-strain principle.

The controlled-strain type of test is easier to perform, although not to install, and has the advantage of readily recording not only the peak resistance (a in Fig. 3-27) but also the smaller resistances after greater deformations have broken down in part the structure of the soil.

The triaxial *cell* test derives its name from the fact that the liquid which provides lateral support to the soil specimen is sealed off in the pressure chamber as in a cell.   This is achieved by means of a setup which is essentially the same as in triaxial tests, except that the stopcock labeled 1, shown in Fig. 3-25, is closed during a cell test.   Thus in a triaxial test the lateral pressure σ_3 is maintained at a constant value during the test until failure occurs as a result of an increase of the vertical pressure σ_1.   In the cell test, however, the lateral pressure σ_3 is measured on the pressure gage not only at failure but at all intermediate stages of loading intensity σ_1.

The cell test therefore has an important advantage over the triaxial test in that it permits the direct determination of the ratio σ_3/σ_1 at all intermediate stages of loading.   This is of great importance in all research studies of lateral earth pressures against retaining walls and sheet-pile bulkheads, which frequently represent a problem of deformation and not of rupture. Another advantage of the cell test is that a test of only one specimen covers the entire range of possible pressures.   At least three to four specimens have to be tested in triaxial tests.

Failure conditions can be induced during any cell-test stage by bleeding a few drops of the supporting liquid (for instance by opening stopcock 1 shown in Fig. 3-25) and recording the corresponding minimum lateral pressure σ_3. This is taken to correspond to the limit equilibrium of pressures at failure.

A disadvantage of the cell test is the difficulty it presents in operation. First of all, a space with constant temperature control is required for any tests exceeding a few hours' duration.   Further, it is difficult to prevent any leakage whatsoever of the supporting liquid from the sealed pressure chamber during long-duration tests.   Finally, the models available at present appear to be too lightly built and to yield excessively under high internal pressures. This induces uncontrollable deformation of the soil specimen, which is particularly undesirable in the case of sensitive clays, since it may cause their partial remolding and may result in their weakening.   There also is some *spring action* of the entire apparatus during the reduction of the supporting pressures σ_3, for instance, during consolidation of a clay specimen.

(C). *Presentation and Analysis of Results.*   Figure 3-26 illustrates the conventional manner of graphical presentation and interpretation of the results of direct shear tests.   At least three tests on as many separate specimens from the same sample have to be performed under varying normal pressure p_n.

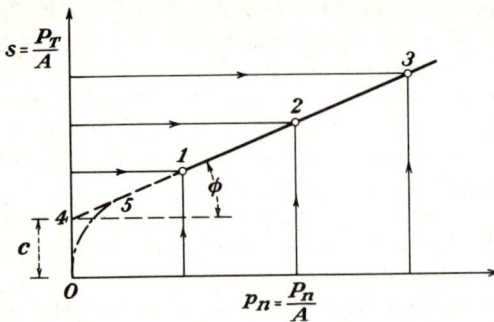

Fig. 3-26.   Conventional manner of interpreting the results of direct shear tests.

The shearing strengths $s = P_t/A$ obtained from each of the three tests are then plotted against the corresponding normal pressures p_n, giving three points such as 1, 2, and 3 in Fig. 3-26 corresponding to unit normal pressures of, say, 1.0, 2.0, and 3.0 tons/ft². These three points will usually lie on an approximately straight line, some scattering being sometimes caused by experimental errors or by slight variations in the properties of the three specimens tested. The slope of the line through the three points 1, 2, and 3 is $\tan \phi$, where ϕ is taken to represent the angle of internal friction. In the case of clean granular soils the extension of the line through the three points 1, 2, and 3 will pass through the origin O. This will also happen in the case of a clay soil which has been completely remolded under addition of water in the laboratory, placed in a semifluid condition into the shear device, and then reconsolidated under the normal pressures p_n, although the angle ϕ obtained in this case will vary greatly, depending on the subsequent manner of testing. In the case of a naturally undisturbed clay, as shown in Fig. 3-26, the extension of the line through points 1, 2, and 3 will cut the ordinate through the origin in point 4. The distance O-4 is then taken to represent the cohesion c of the sample. This does not mean, however, that this value will necessarily represent the shearing strength of the clay at zero normal pressure in the sense of Coulomb's equation (3-42). At normal pressures lower than the ones corresponding to point 5 in Fig. 3-26, the shearing strengths of some clays are apt to lie on the dash-dotted curve and to tend toward zero at zero normal pressure, because, as shown by the void-ratio–pressure diagram in Fig. 3-13, the expansion of a fully submerged specimen under decreasing pressure increases rapidly when low normal pressures are reached.

A plot of shearing deformations vs. shearing stress of the type shown in Fig. 3-27 demonstrates the *effect of the magnitude of deformations* on the variation in the shearing resistance of different soils.   The shearing resistance of undisturbed clay or dense sand rapidly reaches a *peak value* and then, as its structure is disturbed, drops off to merge with the curve of a remolded clay specimen or an originally dense sand, respectively.

The results of a triaxial test can be presented in graphical form by means of the so-called *Mohr circle,* as illustrated in Fig. 3-28 for a granular material with $c = 0$.   The distance O-1 is made equal to σ_3, and the distance O-1' to the value of σ_1 at which failure occurred.   A circle is then drawn through the points 1 and 1' with the point C_1, located midway between these two points, as center.   It will be noted that the ordinates of any point, for instance point A_1, located on the circumference of that circle give us the value of the shearing stress τ on the plane forming the corresponding angle θ with the plane on which the major principal stress σ_1 is acting, the latter plane being in the present case horizontal.   This is simply a graphical expression for Eq. (3-47).   Similarly, the abscissa of the same point A_1 represents the normal stress σ on the plane forming the same angle θ with the major principal plane.

Let us assume that three other triaxial tests have been performed with progressively increasing values of the lateral pressure σ_3, so that for the second test σ_3 will be equal to the distance O-2, for the third test to the distance O-3, and for the fourth test to the distance O-4, all as shown in Fig. 3-28.   Mohr circles will then be drawn for each of these tests.   If the

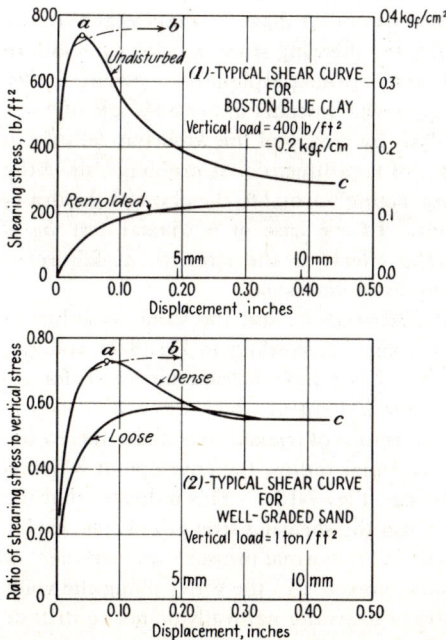

Fig. 3-27.   General shape of stress-strain curves.   Controlled strain direct-box shear tests.

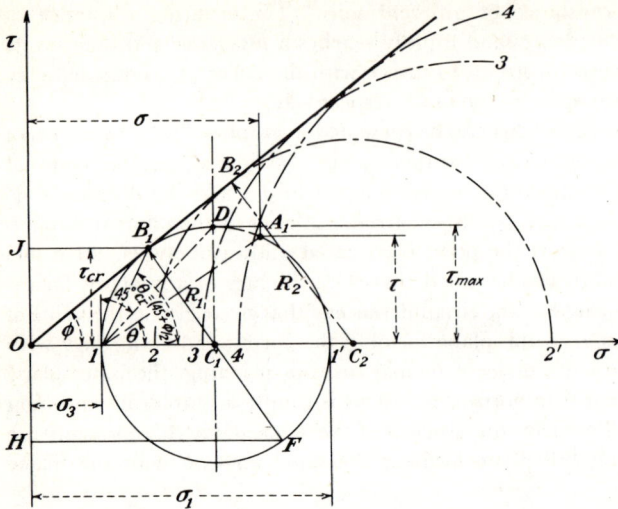

Fig. 3-28. Conventional presentation of the results of triaxial shear tests by means of the Mohr circle diagram (a noncohesive granular soil).

soil tested has no cohesion ($c = 0$), for instance if it is clean sand, then the envelope for all four tests will be found to be approximately a straight line forming the angle ϕ with the horizontal and passing through the origin O as shown in Fig. 3-28. It will be noted from that diagram that because of the relationship expressed by Eq. (3-47), the shearing stress τ_{cr} along the failure plane forming the angle θ_{cr} with the major principal plane is somewhat smaller than the greatest shearing stress τ_{max}, which occurs under an angle of 45°.

It should be noted that the analysis by means of the Mohr circle, strictly speaking, is possible only in respect of two-dimensional problems, since the effect of the third principal stress σ_2, acting normal to the plane of the drawing, cannot be taken into account. In the case of a triaxial test σ_2 is always equal to σ_3. However, the effect on the strength at failure of variations in the value of σ_2 is likely to be very small.

The value of $\sigma_1 - \sigma_3$ is termed *deviator stress*, and the value at failure is known as the *compressive strength* of a soil. According to Fig. 3-28 and Eq. (3-49), the latter is equal to $2\tau_{max}$. If we have a frictionless soil, for instance a fully saturated clay the water content of which has not been permitted to change during the tests, the results of triaxial tests under increasing values of σ_3 give a series of circles of equal radius, the envelope of which is horizontal ($\phi = 0$) (as shown in 1st ed., Fig. 7-13). This indicates that the compressive strength and therefore also the shearing strength of such a clay are constants which are independent of the normal pressure, an increment of the latter being carried by the neutral pressures in the water filling the voids of the clay. These neutral pressures in the water naturally do not contribute to an increase of the frictional component of the shearing strength of the soil, which depends only on the effective stresses $\sigma - u$, where u represents the neutral stresses or excess pore pressures (Art. 3-4A). Therefore, the Coulomb equation reads

$$s = c' + (\sigma - u)\tan \phi' \qquad (3\text{-}54)$$

where c' and ϕ' are *effective values* as compared to the *apparent values* c and ϕ in Eq. (3-42).

Attempts have been made to measure directly the pore pressure u within the clay sample subjected to a triaxial test to permit basing subsequent analyses and designs on the effective values of $\bar{\sigma} = \sigma - u$ and the corresponding ϕ'. These attempts have not been very successful. Measurement of pore pressures through the porous stones a at the top and at the bottom of the sample (see Fig. 3-25) did not correctly reflect the pore pressures within the interior of the sample, where most of the deformations take place. The insertion of hypodermic needles into the interior of the sample to measure the pore pressures there had a restraining effect on the deformations. Further, the field measurement of pore pressures within natural deposits also presented problems (see Art. 2-5).

(D). Effects of Drainage and Rate of Shearing. Some shear tests are performed under so-called *drained* conditions; i.e., the escape of water from the voids of the specimen, which tends to take place as a result of increased pressures during the test, is permitted at the boundaries of the soil specimen. This is achieved by making the plates a in Figs. 3-23 and 3-25 porous. Stopcock 2 shown in Fig. 3-25 is kept open.

The amount of drainage which can actually take place prior to failure will strongly affect the results. In the case of cohesive soils of low permeability the amount of drainage which can take place during a test largely depends on whether consolidation under normal load (or σ_3) was or was not permitted prior to shearing and on the rate at which the shearing force (or σ_1) was applied.

Any decrease in the water content of a plastic clay sample increases its shearing strength. Therefore, in the case of drained tests, the shearing strength of a cohesive soil increases with a decrease of the rate at which the shearing stresses are induced.

A reverse relationship is obtained in the case of *undrained* tests, where no decrease of water content, i.e., no consolidation, is permitted. In such cases the so-called *creep* or *plastic-flow* effects appear to exercise a predominant influence on the results of shear tests with undrained saturated cohesive soils. The resistance to a slowly applied shearing stress under the above conditions may therefore be found to be appreciably smaller than the resistance to a rapidly applied shearing stress.

Differentiation is essential between the following categories of triaxial tests on fully saturated plastic clays.

1. *Undrained tests, usually quickly performed in 10 to 20 min.*   No consolidation or drainage of water is permitted; stopcock 2 (Fig. 3-25) is kept closed. The apparent angle of internal friction on the Mohr diagram is then usually $\phi = 0$ (see 1st ed., fig. 7-13).   The symbol for the shearing strength is $s_u = c_u$.   A quickly performed direct shear test will give similar results.

2. *Unconfined compressive-strength* (q_u) *test.*   When conventionally carried out within 10 to 20 min, its results are essentially identical to those of the undrained triaxial test.   Symbol for the shearing strength is $s_u = c_u = q_u/2$.

3. *Consolidated quick tests.*   Full consolidation under the normal load, or σ_3 and $\sigma_1 = \sigma_3$, is allowed to take place prior to the start of the shear test proper, after which σ_1 is increased to produce a rapid failure.   The apparent angle of internal friction will then vary between $\phi = 12°$ and $\phi = 18°$.

4. *Slow tests.*   After complete consolidation, the shear test proper is conducted so slowly under drained conditions that any excess pore pressures u which may be induced by shearing deformations will have time to be completely dissipated under additional consolidation.   The apparent angle of internal friction will then be close to its effective value ϕ' and will vary between $\phi = 27°$ and $\phi = 30°$.

Therefore, since the angle of internal friction of a plastic clay may vary between $\phi = 0°$ and $\phi = 30°$ depending on the manner of testing, it is obviously essential to indicate the type of test on all relevant records and diagrams.

The most frequently used type of shear test is the unconfined compressive strength test (see Art. 3-2G).

The undrained triaxial test is of special advantage for specimens of over-consolidated stiff-fissured clays which are liable to fly apart in an unconfined compressive-strength test.   It is also useful as a check on the q_u values of low-plasticity clays with a high sand content for which the angle of internal friction ϕ may be greater than zero.

The consolidated quick tests are needed in all cases where the increase in the shearing strength due to the consolidation of the clay has to be estimated, for instance in the design of sand-drain installations (see Art. 5-2 and Prob. 5-2).

Slow shear tests usually are performed for research purposes only.

Figure 3-29 illustrates the *effects of the time of shear-stress application in undrained tests*.   Curves *a* refer to a low level of stress intensity not exceeding the yield point of the clay.   Curves *c* refer to a high level of stress intensity which produces failure within the conventional short (10 to 20 min) duration t_1 of a laboratory test.   Curves *b* refer to an intermediate stress intensity which produces *creep* ultimately culminating in failure.

This condition may occur in thick layers of sensitive clays where prolonged creep is likely to weaken their potentially unstable structure without an increase of density and strength due to consolidation.

Considerable attention has recently been given to this problem by theoreti-

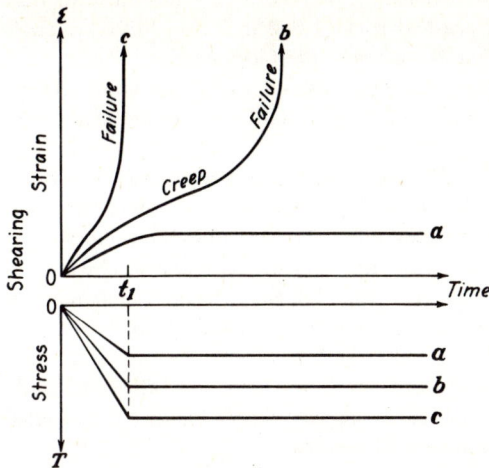

Fig. 3-29. Sketch illustrating effect of time and shearing-stress intensity on the deformations and ultimate failure of undrained plastic clays.

cal *rheological studies*.   However, simplified assumptions usually have to be made to permit mathematical treatment, whereby the actual physical properties of soils, as well as the reverse effects of consolidation, are frequently ignored, sometimes leading to absurd results (see Art. 1-10 and Ref. 373).

No reliable methods of accurately forecasting dangerous creep effects in the field appear to have been developed so far.

Therefore, on all field jobs where the yield point of clays is likely to be exceeded somewhat, it is advisable to make continuous on-the-spot shear-deformation–time plots on the type given by Fig. 3-29 to permit timely countermeasures. These deformations can be measured by inclinometers (Art. 1-9) or by transit measurements on displacement stakes (Art. 5-2).

3-6. Bearing-ratio (CBR) Test.   The test is used primarily for the design of highway and airport pavements as part of a purely empirical procedure with which experiments were begun in 1929 by the California State Highway Department; the letters CBR stand for "California bearing ratio."   The design procedure is based on the results of the CBR test, which is performed as follows.   A soil specimen is compacted in a 6-in.-diameter (15-cm) mold and tested in accordance with ASTM Designation D-1883-67 (Ref. 18).   After compaction a surcharge weight is placed on the soil surface, and the mold is submerged for 4 days.   The swelling of the soil is recorded.

After complete soaking the mold is placed in a testing machine or in a controlled-strain type of press.   A plunger of 3 in.² (19.35 cm²) area,

1.91 in. diameter (4.95 cm), is forced 0.1 in. (2.5 mm) into the soil, and the resistance encountered at that penetration is recorded. The ratio of that resistance to the resistance of crushed rock (1,000 lb/in.² = 70.31 kg$_f$/cm²) at the same penetration is taken to represent the CBR value.

A CBR value of 100 indicates excellent material with supporting properties as good as those of crushed rock. Low CBR values indicate poor material.

Observations were made on California highways having different base-course thicknesses and traveled by trucks. Correlation of the field data thus obtained to base-course and subgrade CBR values led to the development of design charts. Special test sections with varying base-course thicknesses were then built during World War II by the U.S. Engineering Department in several localities over which heavily loaded dump and carryall trucks with wheel loads reaching 70,000 lb (31,800 kg$_f$) traveled continuously. The design curves shown in Fig. 3-32 were developed from such *accelerated traffic tests;* they have since been extended to heavier wheel loads. Base-course material should be frost-resistant in cold regions.

The CBR pavement-design procedure is safe and even appears to be too conservative.

The CBR test can be performed on undisturbed subgrade soils in situ by jacking the plunger against a truck above it serving as a counterweight. This should never be done in a dry season since much too high CBR values will then be obtained compared to wet seasonal spells. A flexible pavement of a parking area for ship containers near a dock was underdesigned and subsequently failed for this reason.

3-7. Engineering Soil-classification Systems. *(A). Texture Expressed by Grain Size.* The classification of individual grains according to their size was outlined in Art. 3-2A. The terms *clay, silt,* and *sand* were applied there to grains of a specific size. The same terms are, however, often used for definite soil formations which do not consist exclusively of clay or of silt or of sand but which represent mixtures of all three types of grains in varying proportions. There is so far no generally recognized definition concerning the percentage of, for instance, clay particles that a soil must have to be classified as clay, etc.

In the first edition Fig. 3-4 gave a classification of the U.S. Bureau of Public Roads using a triangular diagram for the definition of the percentages of clay, silt, and sand particles in materials to be called *clays, loams, silty loams,* etc. A loam is a mixture of sand, silt, and clay particles in varying proportions. The term *loam* originated in agricultural soil work and was taken over by highway engineers who have to deal mainly with surface soil layers.

A recent trend is to eliminate the rather ambiguous term *loam* from foundation-engineering use. Figure 3-30 shows a similar triangular soil-classification chart of the Mississippi River Commission which does not use the term *loam* at all and replaces it by such terms as *silty clay, silty sand, sandy clay,* etc. This appears logical, since the whole classification is based only on the sand, silt, and clay content.

Figure 3-1 gives the grain-size-accumulation curves of 10 different soils. The same 10 soils are marked on the triangular chart in Fig. 3-30. The proper way to use these charts is indicated by a diagram in the upper right-hand corner of Fig. 3-30. The sand, silt, or clay content of a soil is expressed in percent of the total dry weight and is scaled off on the corresponding side of the diagram. Three lines are then drawn as shown in Fig. 3-30. They will always intersect in one point. Diagrams of this kind are used in granular-soil-stabilization work.

The classification of soils according to their grain size is the simplest possible, but it has the limitation that its relation to the main engineering properties of soils is of an indirect kind only. Generally speaking, all that the knowledge of the grain size of a soil conveys to us is a certain idea of some of the potential properties the material of the soil possesses.

The determination of the grain size is therefore done mainly in cases where one has to deal with soils to be used as an engineering material which must first be disturbed and then artificially recompacted (earth dams, roads, etc.).

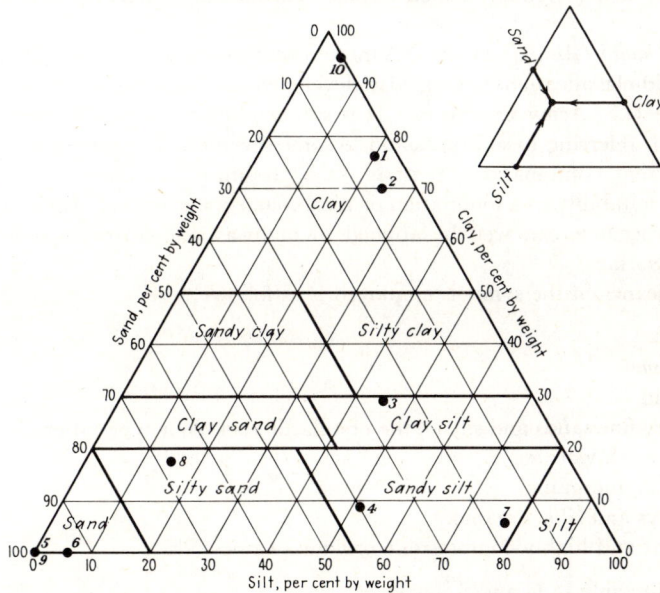

Fig. 3-30. Triangular soil-classification chart of the Mississippi River Commission. The term *loam* has been omitted. *Note:* The 10 soils of Fig. 3-1 have been marked with corresponding numbers in this chart. (*Courtesy of the President, Mississippi River Commission, Vicksburg, Mississippi.*)

In such cases the selection of the material possessing the potential properties required is facilitated by knowing its grain-size distribution.

(B). The AASHO (old PRA) Soil System. The PRA (Public Roads Administration) classification was originally developed in the 1920s to indicate the suitability of a given soil for the surfacing of low-cost secondary roads. The soils are divided into eight groups, designated by the symbols A-1 to A-8. The A-1 soils are sands with a slight amount of fines which is sufficient only to fill the voids around the sand grains partially and to cement the grains to each other but which is too slight to induce volume changes of the soil mass, i.e., swelling or shrinkage, as a result of alternating wetting or drying. The A-2 soils are similar to the A-1 soils, except that they are less favorably graded, so that they either are less well cemented or are more susceptible to volume changes with changes in their moisture content. A-3 soils are sands and gravels with no fines capable of cementing them. A-4 to A-7 soils are silts and clays of varying degrees of plasticity. A-8 soils are highly compressible peats and clays with a very high organic content. The PRA classification system has been amplified by the addition of subscripts and is now known as the AASHO (American Association of State Highway Officials) system. It is now seldom used in other than highway-engineering soil work. A graphical comparison between this system and the much more widespread unified (originally called airfield) classification system is given by Fig. 3-32.

(C). The Unified (Airfield) System. A more recent system, originally called AC or airfield-classification system, was developed by Casagrande (1942–1948) for the U.S. Army Engineers. It is summarized in Tables 3-4 and 3-5. Symbols referring to soil types and to some specific soil properties are used in different combinations to permit the classification of the soil in respect to its suitability as a foundation or a base-course material of airports. The same procedure can well be applied to highway and all other soil-engineering work.

The significance of the symbols employed is as follows:

Type of soil:
    G = gravel
    S = sand
    M = very fine sands and silts of the nonplastic rock-flour type (after the Swedish word *mo*)
    C = clays, inorganic
    O = clays and silts, organic
    Pt = peat and highly compressible organic swamp soils

Grading (applies only to G and S soils):
    W = well-graded clean material (Fig. 3-1)
    P = poorly graded clean material
    C = clay binder of well-graded G and S soils

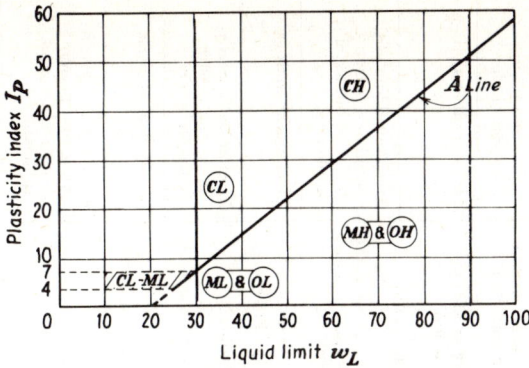

Fig. 3-31. Plasticity chart for classification of fine-grained soils and fine fraction of coarse-grained soils according to Unified soil classification system.   (Ref. 18, item D-2487-69.)

Compressibility [refers only to M, C, and O soils and to the potential compressibility of the material as defined by the virgin compression curve (see lines 6-7-8, Figs. 3-12 and 3-13)]:

> L = low potential compressibility, such as is encountered with clays having a liquid limit $w_L < 50$
>
> H = high potential compressibility, such as is encountered with clays having a liquid limit $w_L > 50$

The Unified soil classification is particularly useful in connection with preliminary surveys based on rapid field examination and identification of soils (Art. 3-3A).   In addition, as illustrated by Fig. 3-31, laboratory tests can provide a numerical basis for a more exact classification of borderline groups.   The equation of the A line in that diagram is

$$I_P = 0.73(w_L - 20) \tag{3-55}$$

Atterberg limits plotted in the hatched area are borderline classifications requiring use of dual symbols.

Figure 3-32 illustrates the engineering properties of various soil groups of the Unified classification in respect to the AASHO classification and the CBR method of flexible pavement design (Art. 3-6).

The practical advantages of the Unified soil classification were gradually recognized and it was adopted by a growing number of organizations, the U.S. Army Engineers, the U.S. Bureau of Reclamation, the ASTM (Ref. 18, item D-2487-69), the City of New York (Ref. 228), and others.

(D). Strength Classification of Clays.   The consistency classification of clays in respect to their shearing strength and to their SPT N values is given by

TABLE 3-4. The Soil Types of the Unified Classification (Airfield) System and Their Identification†

(1) Major divisions		(2) Soil groups and typical names	(3) Group symbol	(4) General identification (on disturbed samples)		(5) Observations and tests relating to material in place	(6) Principal classification tests (on disturbed samples)
				Dry strength‡	Other pertinent examinations		
Coarse-grained soils	Gravel and gravelly oils	Well-graded gravel and gravel-sand mixtures, little or no fines	GW	None			Mechanical analysis
		Well-graded gravel-sand mixtures with excellent clay binder	GC	Medium		Dry unit weight or void ratio	Mechanical analysis, liquid and plastic limits on binder
		Poorly graded gravel and gravel-sand mixtures, little or no fines	GP	None		Degree of compaction	Mechanical analysis
		Gravel with fines, silty gravel, clayey gravel, poorly graded gravel-sand-clay mixtures	GF	Very slight to high	Gradation; Grain shape; Examination of binder wet and dry	Cementation; Stratification and drainage characteristics	Mechanical analysis, liquid and plastic limits on binder, if applicable
	Sands and sandy soils	Well-graded sands and gravelly sands, little or no fines	SW	None		Groundwater conditions	Mechanical analysis
		Well-graded sand with excellent clay binder	SC	Medium to high	Durability of grains	Traffic tests; Large-scale load tests	Mechanical analysis, liquid and plastic limits on binder
		Poorly graded sands, little or no fines	SP	None		California bearing-ratio tests	Mechanical analysis
		Sand with fines, silty sands, clayey sands, poorly graded sand-clay mixtures	SF	Very slight to high			Mechanical analysis, liquid and plastic limits on binder, if applicable

Major divisions	Typical names	Group symbol[‡]	Degree of compressibility	Field identification procedures	Information required for describing soils	Laboratory classification criteria
Fine-grained soils containing little or no coarse-grained material — Fine-grained sands having low to medium compressibility; liquid limit <50	Silts (inorganic) and very fine sands, rock flour, silty or clayey fine sands with slight plasticity	ML	Very slight to medium	Shaking test and plasticity	Dry unit weight, water content, and void ratio	Mechanical analysis, liquid and plastic limits, if applicable
	Clays (inorganic) of low to medium plasticity, sandy clays, silty clays, lean clays	CL	Medium to high	Examination in plastic range	Consistency, undisturbed and remolded	Liquid and plastic limits
	Organic silts and organic silt-clays of low plasticity	OL	Slight to medium	Examination in plastic range, odor, color	Stratification, root holes, and fissures	Liquid and plastic limits from natural condition and after oven drying
Fine-grained soils having high-compressibility; liquid limit >50	Micaceous or diatomaceous fine sandy and silty soils, elastic silts	MH	Very slight to medium	Shaking test and plasticity	Drainage and groundwater conditions / Traffic tests	Mechanical analysis, liquid and plastic limits, if applicable
	Clays (inorganic) of high plasticity, fat clays	CH	High to very high	Examination in plastic range	Large-scale load tests / California bearing-ratio tests	Liquid and plastic limits
	Organic clays of medium to high plasticity	OH	Medium to high	Examination in plastic, range, odor, color	Compression tests	Liquid and plastic limits from natural condition and after oven drying
Fibrous organic soils with very high compressibility	Peat and other highly organic swamp soils	Pt	Readily identified		Consistency, texture, and natural water content	

† From Casagrande (Ref. 49). See also Table 3-5.
‡ For binder, fraction passing U.S. Standard mesh No. 40.

TABLE 3-5. Engineering Characteristics of Soils According to the Unified Classification (Airfield) System†

(3)	(7)	(8)		(9)	(10)	(11)	(12)	(13)	(14)	(15)
Group symbols	Value as foundation when not subject to frost action	Value as wearing surface for stage or emergency construction		Potential frost action	Compressibility and expansion	Drainage characteristics‡	Field compaction characteristics and equipment	Solids at optimum compaction, lb/ft³,§ and void ratio e	California bearing ratio for compacted and soaked specimen	Comparable groups in AASHO classification
		With dust palliative	With bituminous surface treatment							
GW	Excellent	Fair to poor	Excellent	None to very slight	Almost none	Excellent	Excellent; crawler tractor, rubber-tired equipment	>125 $e < 0.35$	>50	A-3
GC	Excellent	Excellent	Excellent	Medium	Very slight	Practically impervious	Excellent; tamping roller,¶ rubber-tired equipment	>130 $e < 0.30$	>40	A-1
GP	Excellent	Poor	Poor to fair	None to very slight	Almost none	Excellent	Good to excellent; crawler tractor, rubber-tired equipment	>115 $e < 0.45$	25-60	A-3
GF	Good to excellent	Poor to good	Fair to good	Slight to medium	Almost none to slight	Fair to practically impervious	Good to excellent; crawler tractor, rubber-tired equipment, tamping roller¶	>120 $e < 0.40$	>20	A-2
SW	Excellent	Poor	Good	None to very slight	Almost none	Excellent	Excellent; crawler tractor, rubber-tired equipment	>120 $e < 0.40$	20-60	A-3

Symbol						Compaction characteristics	Dry unit weight, pcf§	CBR	AASHO classification†
SC	Excellent	Excellent	Excellent	Medium	Very slight	Practically impervious	Excellent; tamping roller, rubber-tired equipment	>125 $e<0.35$	20–60	A-1
SP	Good	Poor	Poor	None to very slight	Almost none	Excellent	Good to excellent; crawler tractor, rubber-tired equipment	>100 $e<0.70$	10–30	A-3
ML	Fair to poor	Poor		Medium to very high	Slight to medium	Fair to poor	Good to poor; close control essential; rubber-tired roller	>100 $e<0.70$	6–25	A-4
CL	Fair to poor	Poor	Poor	Medium to high	Medium	Practically impervious	Fair to good; tamping roller¶	>100 $e<0.70$	4–15	A-4;A-6 A-7
OL	Poor	Very poor	Very poor	Medium to high	Medium to high	Poor	Fair to poor; tamping roller¶	>90 $e<0.90$	3–8	A-4 A-7
MH	Poor to very poor	Very poor	Very poor	Medium to very high	High	Fair to poor	Poor to very poor	>100 $e<0.70$	<7	A-5
CH	Poor to very poor	Very poor	Very poor	Medium	High	Practically impervious	Fair to poor; tamping roller¶	>90 $e<0.90$	<6	A-6 A-7
OH	Very poor	Useless	Useless	Medium	High	Practically impervious	Poor to very poor	<100 $e>0.70$	<4	A-7 A-8
Pt	Extremely poor	Useless	Useless	Slight	Very high	Fair to poor	Compaction not practical			A-8

† From Casagrande (Ref. 49). See also Table 3-4. ‡ These characteristics do not apply to undisturbed materials having fissures and root holes, such as most surface soils. § These weights apply only to soils having specific gravities from 2.65 to 2.75. ¶ Sheepsfoot roller.

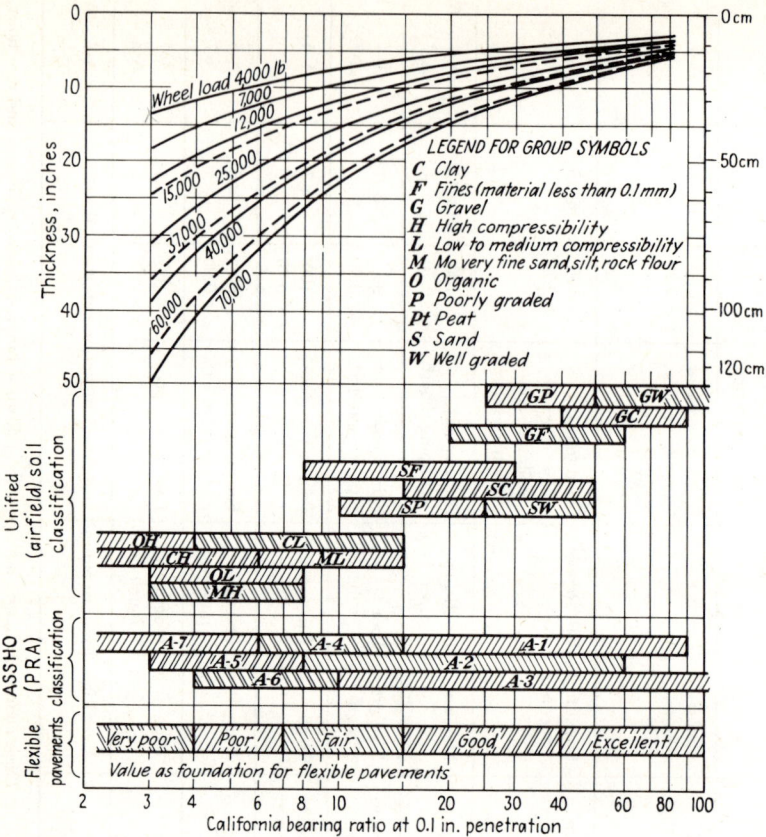

Fig. 3-32. Chart for the design of flexible pavements, giving combined thickness of pavement and base in respect to the CBR values of the underlying material. (*After Stratton, discussion of Ref. 49.*)

Table 3-6. Table 3-7 gives the strains at failure ϵ_f of an unconfined compressive strength test according to which a clay may be classified as brittle, semibrittle, or plastic.

For the classification of clays in respect to their *sensitivity*, see Table 4-2.

The *classification of sands according to their relative density* D_r (Art. 3-2E) on the basis of their N blows/ft SPT values is given by Figs. 2-12 and 2-16.

(E). Criteria for Collapsible and Expansive Soils. Loess soils, the structure of which is susceptible to collapse when wetted under additional load, can present serious foundation problems (see Arts. 4-8E and 5-4). Vast deposits of such windblown collapsible soils cover many of the southern regions of the Soviet Union.

The 1962 U.S.S.R. Building Code (Ref. 113) differentiates between two

TABLE 3-6.   Relationship between Consistency, Unconfined Compressive Strength of Clays, and N values of the SPT

Consistency	Unconfined compressive strength q_u, tons/ft² or kg$_f$/cm²	Shearing strength $c = \dfrac{q_u}{2}$	SPT N, blows/ft
Very soft.........	0.3	0.15	<2
Soft	0.3–0.6	0.15–0.30	2–4
Medium	0.6–1.2	0.30–0.60	4–8
Stiff...............	1.2–2.4	0.60–1.20	8–15
Very stiff.........	2.4	1.20	15–30
Hard	>4.5	>2.25	>30

types of collapsible loess soils.   Type I are loess soils the settlement of which under their own weight will not exceed 5 cm (2 in.) after wetting.   Type II are loess soils the settlement of which under their own weight will be greater than 5 cm (2 in.).

The estimation of the value of settlement under the weight of the natural overburden is made according to Eq. (4-25), whereby the *coefficient of natural relative collapsibility* $\delta_{n(col)}$ [Eq. (3-56)] appears to be then used in Eq. (4-25) instead of $\delta_{p(col)}$ [Eq. (3-57)]

$$\delta_{n(col)} = \frac{h_0 - h_0'}{h_0} \qquad (3-56)$$

where h_0 = height, in centimeters, of soil sample at its natural water content loaded in a confined condition by a pressure equal to the pressure of its natural overburden

h_0' = height, in centimeters, of same sample after percolation of water through it

According to Frolov (Ref. 103), the maximum recorded values of the coefficient of natural relative collapsibility $\delta_{n(col)}$ in the southern Ukraine are about 2 percent and occur at depths of 2 to 4 m (6.5 to 13 ft) from the surface, where the greatest porosity was found.   The same author points

TABLE 3-7.   Deformation Types of Natural Clays†

	ϵf_1 percent
Brittle clay (curve B)	3–8
Semibrittle clay (curve C)...........	8–14
Plastic clay (curve D).................	14–20

† Arranged according to their strains at failure during an unconfined compressive-strength test, as shown in Fig. 3-7(II).

TABLE 3-8†

Site No.	Relative collapsibility, %		
	$p = 0$ kg$_f$/cm² $\delta_{n(\text{col})}$	$p = 0.5$ kg$_f$/cm² $\delta_{p(\text{col})}$	$p = 2.0$ kg$_f$/cm² $\delta_{p(\text{col})}$
1	0.54	2.04	3.50
2	0.80	1.50	3.20
3	0.75	2.65	5.0

† After Frolov, Ref. 103.

out that some loesses with low values of that coefficient ($\delta_{n(\text{col})} = 0.1$ to 0.8 percent) nevertheless show considerable settlement increases when wetted under an additional pressure p in excess of the natural overburden weight. In this latter case the relevant coefficient $\delta_{p(\text{col})}$ is obtained (Ref. 113) from

$$\delta_{p(\text{col})} = \frac{h_p - h'_p}{h_0} \qquad (3\text{-}57)$$

where h_p = same as h_0 in Eq. (3-56) but sample loaded by overburden pressure *plus* pressure p due to weight of new structure

h'_p = height of same sample after percolation of water through it

h_0 = same as in Eq. (3-56)

Table 3-8 gives the variation in the average values of the relative collapsibility coefficient with an increase of p as reported by Frolov on the basis of laboratory tests on 186 samples from three sites in the southern Ukraine.

Earlier attempts to establish simple criteria for the susceptibility to collapse of loess soils on the basis of their liquid limit and natural water-content values (Refs. 236 and 112) do not appear to have been successful.

This also seems to have been the case (Ref. 20) of earlier attempts (Ref. 112) to establish simple criteria for the *swelling potential of expansive clays* on the basis of their liquid limit and natural water-content values.

Here too comparative swelling tests in a consolidometer appear necessary (see Art. 4-8D and Refs. 147 and 20).

REVIEW PROBLEMS

3-1. The settlement of a building resting on a 60-ft (18.3-m) deep layer of stiff clay was measured from the start of construction. It was found that after a number of years the settlement ceased after reaching a value of 2.07 in. (5.2 cm) at the center of the building. The average unit pressure on that layer, computed in the manner shown in Prob. 4-2, was found to be 0.7 ton/ft². Compute the average value of the modulus of volume change m'_v of the clay layer.

Answer. Since 1.0 ton/ft² is approximately equal to 1.0 kg$_f$/cm², we obtain from Eq. (3-33)

$$m'_v = \frac{2.07}{0.7 \times 60 \times 12} = 0.0041 \text{ cm}^2/\text{kg}_f$$

3-2. Let us assume that the void-ratio–pressure curve shown in Fig. 3-13 was plotted from a laboratory consolidation test of an undisturbed sample of stiff clay obtained 20 ft (6.1 m) below the surface of the ground. What will be the value of the modulus of volume change m'_v which will correspond to an increment of pressure on the sample of 0.7 ton/ft²?

Answer. Assuming that the unit weight of the soil is 120 lb/ft³ (1.92 g$_f$/cm²), we obtain the overburden pressure to which the sample is subjected in the soil.

$$p_1 = 120 \times 20 \, \frac{1}{2,000} = 1.20 \text{ tons/ft}^2$$

As a result of the application of the surcharge the pressure on the sample would be

$$p_2 = p_1 + 0.7 = 1.90 \text{ tons/ft}^2$$

From the curves of Fig. 3-13 we obtain the corresponding void ratios

$$
\begin{array}{r}
e_1 = 1.0050 \\
e_2 = 0.9970 \\
\hline
\Delta e = 0.0080
\end{array}
$$

From Eq. (3-29) we have

$$a_v = \frac{0.0080}{0.70} = 0.0114 \times 10^{-3} \text{ cm}^2/\text{g}_f$$

and from Eqs. (3-31) and (3-32),

$$m'_v = \frac{0.0114 \times 10^{-3}}{1 + 1.0050} \times 10^3 = 0.0057 \text{ cm}^2/\text{kg}_f$$

3-3. A structure has been erected on a 45-ft-thick (13.75-m) layer of very impervious clay, the time-compression curve of a sample of which is shown in Fig. 3-17. The boundary drainage conditions are as shown in Fig. 3-16(I). Compute the time which will elapse according to the Terzaghi theory of consolidation until 50 and 90 percent of the final settlement are reached.

Answer. Since drainage is possible both at the lower and the upper surfaces of the clay layer, as shown in Fig. 3-16(I), the value of $H = \frac{1}{2} \times 45 = 22.5$ ft = 686 cm.

The coefficient of consolidation of that clay sample was computed, as shown by Eq. (3-40), and found to be $c_v = 0.0166$ cm²/min. The time-factor values which correspond to the drainage conditions of the case are given by curve T_v in Fig. 4-34. It will be seen from that curve that the value which corresponds to $U = 50$ percent consolidation is $T_{50} = 0.20$, and to $U = 90$ percent consolidation, $T_{90} = 0.85$. Therefore, from Eq. (4-22) we obtain the time which will elapse until 50 percent of the final settlement, i.e., of the consolidation, is reached.

$$t_{50} = \frac{0.20 \times 686^2}{0.0166} = 5.68 \times 10^6 \text{ min} \times \frac{1 \text{ year}}{60 \times 24 \times 365 \text{ min}}$$

$$= 10.8 \text{ years}$$

The time which will elapse until 90 percent of the consolidation is reached is computed from

$$t_{90} = t_{50} \frac{T_{90}}{T_{50}} = 10.8 \frac{0.85}{0.20} = 46.0 \text{ years}$$

3-4. Assume that all conditions remain the same as in Prob. 3-3, except that the clay layer is underlain by sound rock, so that drainage is possible only at the upper surface of the clay. What effect will this have on the time which will elapse until a certain percentage of the final settlement is reached?

Answer. The value of H will now be 45 ft, instead of the 22.5 ft of Prob. 3-3. Therefore, according to Eq. (4-22), the time t will be increased in the proportion $45.0^2/22.5^2 = 4.0$. In other words, settlement will take four times longer to reach a certain value.

3-5. What will be the theoretical inclination of failure cracks in a mass of soil subjected to vertical loading if the angle of internal friction has the following values: (a) $\phi = 0$, (b) $\phi = 20°$, (c) $\phi = 30°$, (d) $\phi = 45°$?

Answer. According to Eq. (3-48), the angle formed by failure planes with the horizontal should be (a) $\theta_{cr} = 45°$, (b) $\theta_{cr} = 55°$, (c) $\theta_{cr} = 60°$, (d) $\theta_{cr} = 67.5°$.

3-6. Estimate the approximate shearing resistance at failure of a loose sand per unit of area at a depth of 20 ft (6.1 m) below the ground surface (water level 5 ft = 1.53 m below ground surface). The failure is to be induced by a gradual yielding of the lateral support of the sand and a corresponding reduction in the value of σ_3.

Answer. The effective unit weight of the loose sand above water level may be taken at 100 lb/ft³ (1.6 g$_f$/cm³) and below the water level at 60 lb/ft³ (0.96 g$_f$/cm³). Thus

$$\sigma_1 = 100 \times 5 + 60 \times 15 = 1,400 \text{ lb/ft}^2 \ (0.684 \text{ kg}_f/\text{cm}^2)$$

The value of $\phi = 30°$ may be selected for the loose sand and, according to Eq. (3-53), the minimum value of σ_3, that is, its value at failure, will be

$$\sigma_3 = \frac{\sigma_1}{\tan^2(45° + 30°/2)} = 0.333\sigma_1 = 467 \text{ lb/ft}^2 \ (0.227 \text{ kg}_f/\text{cm}^2)$$

The pressure normal to the failure plane ($\theta_{cr} = 60°$), will be

$$\sigma = 467 + \cos^2 60°(1400 - 467) = 700 \text{ lb/ft}^2 \ (0.342 \text{ kg}_f/\text{cm}^2)$$

The shearing resistance at failure will be, according to Eq. (3-42),

$$s = 700 \tan 30° = 404 \text{ lb/ft}^2 \ (0.196 \text{ kg}_f/\text{cm}^2)$$

3-7. What will be the value of the least shearing resistance at failure of a sand under the general conditions of Prob. 3-6, except that the sand is denser, and its angle of internal friction is found to be (a) $\phi = 35°$, (b) $\phi = 40°$, (c) $\phi = 45°$?

Answer. Substituting the above values in the computations of Prob. 3-6, we obtain:
(a) $\sigma_3 = 0.271\sigma_1 = 380 \text{ lb/ft}^2$; $\sigma = 597 \text{ lb/ft}^2$; $s = 417 \text{ lb/ft}^2$ (0.204 kg$_f$/cm²)
(b) $\sigma_3 = 0.217\sigma_1 = 304 \text{ lb/ft}^2$; $\sigma = 500 \text{ lb/ft}^2$; $s = 419 \text{ lb/ft}^2$ (0.205 kg$_f$/cm²)
(c) $\sigma_3 = 0.172\sigma_1 = 241 \text{ lb/ft}^2$; $\sigma = 410 \text{ lb/ft}^2$; $s = 410 \text{ lb/ft}^2$ (0.200 kg$_f$/cm²)

3-8. Three triaxial shear tests were performed with a certain type of sand. During the first test (a) the confining lateral pressure was $\sigma_3 = 0.20$ ton/ft², and failure occurred under a vertical pressure $\sigma_1 = 0.82$ ton/ft². During the second test (b) $\sigma_3 = 0.40$ ton/ft², and at failure $\sigma_1 = 1.60$ tons/ft². During the third test (c) $\sigma_3 = 0.60$ ton/ft², and failure occurred at $\sigma_1 = 2.44$ tons/ft². Draw the Mohr diagram for these three tests. Determine from that diagram the value of the angle of internal friction ϕ and the values of the shearing stresses τ_{cr} on the failure planes in each of these three tests.

Answer. A diagram similar to Fig. 3-28 is obtained. $\phi = 37°20'$.
(a) $\tau_{cr} = 0.24$ ton/ft² = 480 lb/ft² (0.234 kg$_f$/cm²)
(b) $\tau_{cr} = 0.48$ ton/ft²
(c) $\tau_{cr} = 0.72$ ton/ft²

3-9. Two soil samples were described as CL-SC and SF-ML, respectively. What do these symbols mean?

Answer. According to the Unified classification (Art. 3-6*C*), the first sample represents a borderline case between a low-potential-compressibility (lean) clay (CL) and a sand having some clay binder (SC). The second sample is also a borderline case, this time between sand with some fines (SF) and a nonplastic silt soil of low potential compressibility (ML).

RECOMMENDED FOR FURTHER STUDY

ASTM, Ref. 18.
Lambe and Whitman, Ref. 182.
Leonards, Ref. 192.

CHAPTER 4

SPREAD FOOTINGS AND MAT FOUNDATIONS

4-1. General Principles of Foundation Design. An adequate knowledge of the soil and of the groundwater conditions at the proposed site for a new structure is a prerequisite for any rational study of its foundation. In some cases it is even advisable to investigate the proposed construction site by means of a few borings before the land is purchased, since an excessive cost of the foundation might indicate the advisability of selecting a different location. The information which is to be obtained by a properly conducted soil investigation is outlined in Art. 2-1.

Simultaneously with the soil investigation a load plan for the proposed structure should be prepared. For a building, the plan should indicate the concentrated loads of individual columns in tons or in kips and the linearly distributed loads of bearing walls in tons per foot or in kips per foot. Each load plan should include sketches indicating the assumed nature, weight, and dimensions of all materials in the walls and in the floors, as well as the live loads which were used in the preparation of the load plan. This facilitates the necessary corrections and helps to prevent overloading the foundation in case of later revisions of design.

With the data on the subsoil conditions and the load plan, the selection of a foundation type can be undertaken. The following main points must be considered:

1. The loads of the structure must be transferred to soil layers capable of supporting them without failing in shear (see Arts. 4-2 and 6-2).

2. The deformations of the soil layers underlying the foundation should be compatible with the deformations which the foundation itself and its superstructure, as well as adjoining structures, can safely undergo (see Arts. 4-4 and 4-5).

3. The construction operations should not endanger adjoining existing structures (see Arts. 6-8, 7-1, and 9-7).

A study of the building codes and regulations of the city where the structure is to be built is essential, so that the foundation design and its execution will conform with any special local rules.

The 1968 *Building Code of the City of New York* (Ref. 228) follows the concepts of soil mechanics in its stipulations, many of which will be referred to by article and page number in this book (see Arts. 4-2 and 4-7).

Several different safe solutions are often technically feasible for the design of a proposed foundation. Naturally, preference should then be given to the solution which achieves the desired objective at least cost. Sometimes a rough estimation will be sufficient to clarify this point, but frequently several alternative projects have to be worked out in some detail before their relative costs can be properly evaluated.

All estimates and plans should include provisions for adequate supervision of construction operations. The competence and integrity of field inspectors are of the utmost importance in all foundation work (Art. 1-8). Usually it is a simple matter to check at any later time the nature of the materials and the quality of the workmanship employed in the superstructure. It is, however, extremely expensive and sometimes impossible to do so in respect to a foundation unit once it is embedded in the ground.

Estimates and specifications should also include provisions for the control of the performance of the foundation, both during its construction and after completion of the entire structure. It should be realized that the state of our present soil-engineering knowledge is incomplete in many respects. Properly conducted measurements of the actual performance of a structure therefore provide at very little extra cost a necessary insurance against the unchecked development of an unforeseen situation and permit adequate countermeasures in time (see Art. 4-5). In all cases the foundation should be carried down below the depth h [see Fig. 4-1(I)] of seasonal variations in the upper soil layer, i.e., through the so-called *active soil layer*, which may be affected by frost action and other similar influences such as summer thawing in permafrost areas or alternating swelling and shrinking in areas of seasonal rainfall (see Art. 4-8).

Three hypothetical soil layers, A, B, and C, are shown in Fig. 4-1. The thickness of each layer may be assumed to vary from 10 to 40 ft (3 to 12 m), and the foundation may be supported by any of these three layers, depending on the following considerations. Whenever possible, deep foundations should be avoided, since their cost increases rapidly with depth. A foundation resting on the upper layer A, as shown in Fig. 4-1(I), will be

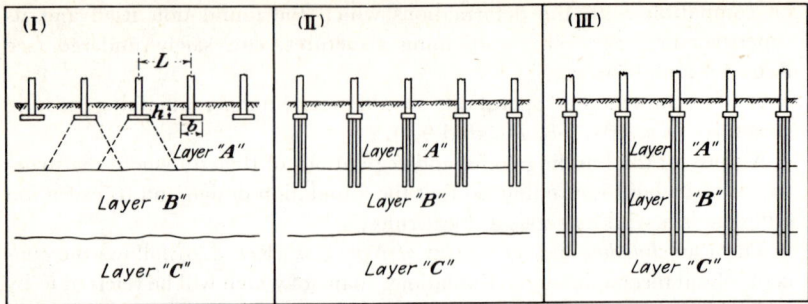

Fig. 4-1. Sketch illustrating the discussion of the depth to which foundations should reach.

acceptable for all types and weights of structures when all three layers A, B, and C have satisfactory supporting properties. If layer A is compact and stiff, whereas either or both of layers B and C are soft, then only light structures can be supported on layer A. The limit permissible weight of the structure can be determined by means of settlement analyses (Art. 4-6), under consideration of the special points discussed in Art. 4-4.

If layer A is soft, whereas layer B is stiff, the loads of the structure should be transferred to B by means of piles or caissons, as shown in Fig. 4-1(II). If the underlying layer C is soft to a great depth, the limit weight of the structure which can be supported on B is to be determined in a manner similar to the one just outlined for layer A.

When both layers A and B are too weak to support the loads of the proposed structure, whereas layer C is compact, the foundation should be carried down to layer C.

In any case, it is advisable to avoid founding different parts of the same structure on different soil layers, even if the loads vary greatly, since otherwise differential settlements may be accentuated. This point is illustrated by Fig. 14-5 and the description thereof in Art. 14-2.

The preceding discussion gives only a brief outline of the procedures to be followed under somewhat simplified limit conditions. It should be realized that in actual practice an innumerable number of combinations of other special conditions may arise in the field and that the selection of the solution best suited to meet all these conditions in the particular combination encountered is an *art* which can be developed only through experience in its practice, built up on a sound knowledge and understanding of the fundamentals involved.

The *main theoretical points* to be remembered in connection with spread-footing designs are illustrated by Fig. 4-2. First, in all uniform soils, the settlement S_1 of a full-sized footing of width b_1 in a structure will always be greater than the settlement of S_2 of a smaller test plate of width b_2. This is because the depth to which vertical pressures of the same intensity will penetrate is a function of the width b of a footing (see Art. 4-3).

Experiments show that in uniform soils the settlement increases with the square root of the area ratio of the footings:

$$S_1 = S_2 \sqrt{\frac{A_1}{A_2}} \tag{4-1a}$$

Second, as shown in Fig. 4-2(II), the shear failure load p_{max} of a footing resting on a uniform plastic clay layer is independent of the size of the

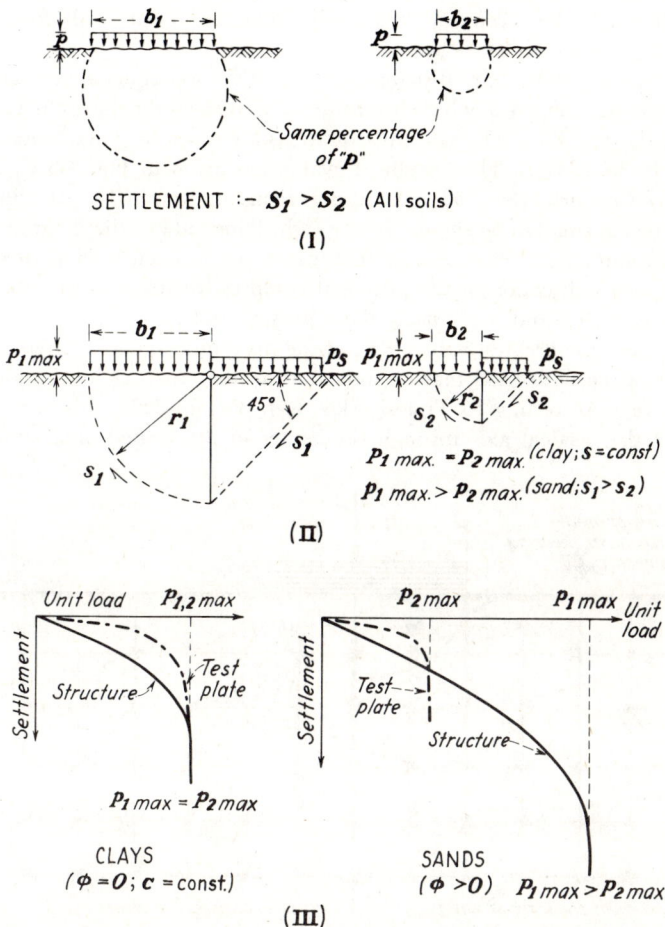

Fig. 4-2. Relationship between width b of footing, settlement S thereof, type of soil (sand or plastic clay), and ultimate load p_{max} leading to soil shear failure.

footing if its shearing strength $s = c$ is constant within the entire depth equal to the width b_1 of the larger footing. On sands the soil shearing strength will increase with depth, and therefore the ultimate failure load $p_{1(max)}$ for a footing in a structure will be greater than the ultimate load $p_{2(max)}$ of a smaller test footing.

These facts are summarized graphically by the qualitative load-settlement curves of Fig. 4-2(III). A more detailed discussion follows in the next articles.

4-2. Shear Stresses and Shear Failures in Soil under Footings. Numerous experimental studies have shown that mathematically rigorous theoretical solutions of stress distribution within a semi-infinite elastic solid can be applied with reasonable accuracy to cohesive soils and even, with some limitations, to granular soils, such as sands.

The way shearing stresses are distributed through the soil under a circular load area is shown in Fig. 4-3, where it is assumed that the soil behaves like a semi-infinite elastic solid. The relevant equations are given by Timoshenko (Ref. 346, pp. 333–337). The graphical evaluation given in Fig. 4-3 was performed by Converse (Ref. 63) (see also Jurgenson, Ref. 154). It will be noted from the small cube shown on the right-hand side of the diagram that the maximum shearing stress at that point, τ_{max}, occurs on planes inclined 45° to the direction of the principal compressive stress σ_1 (see the discussion of Fig. 10-5 and the *Winkler ellipse* in Art. 10-3).

The location of the greatest values τ'_{max} of the maximum shearing stresses at any point of the entire soil mass is indicated on the cross section by an elliptical curve. According to Timoshenko (Ref. 346, p. 337), this curve will intersect the vertical axis through the center of the loaded area at a

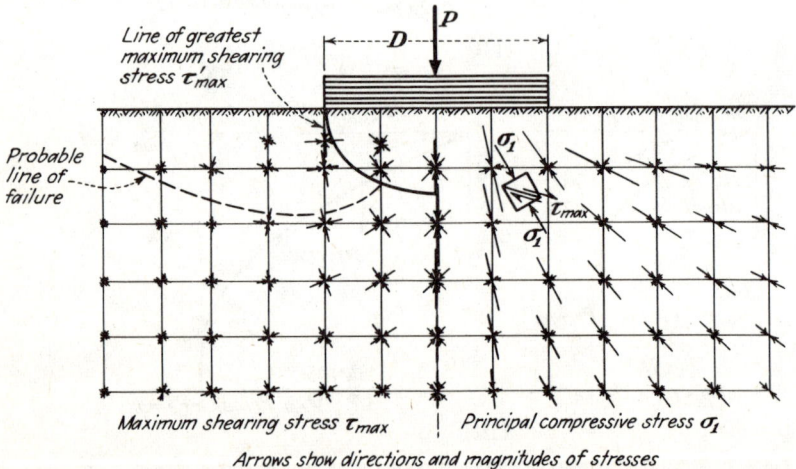

Fig. 4-3. Distribution of stresses under a circular loaded area. (*After Converse, Ref. 63.*)

depth $z = 0.638D/2$.   This will hold for a value of the Poisson ratio $\nu = 0.3$. The corresponding value of the greatest maximum shearing stress will then be

$$\tau'_{max} = 0.33p \qquad (4\text{-}1b)$$

where $p = P/A$ is the average unit load on the area of contact between the footing and the soil.   It should be noted that, whereas the shearing stress on vertical planes τ_{rz} due to a concentrated surface load is independent of the Poisson ratio, the value of the greatest maximum shearing stress under a loaded footing is dependent thereon, although only to a slight extent.   Thus it can be shown, by substituting the limit value of $\nu = 0.5$ in Eqs. (h) and (k) of Ref. 346, p. 337, that

$$\tau'_{max} = 0.29p \qquad (4\text{-}2)$$

and $z' = 0.692D/2$.   Thus the possible variation of τ'_{max} because of uncertainties in the value of the Poisson ratio of soils is negligible and does not exceed 15 percent.   The actual value of τ'_{max} is of practical importance since, once it is exceeded, plastic deformations will begin developing within the soil mass and the surface settlements will exceed values caused by normal consolidation (see discussions of Fig. 4-28 in Art. 4-5 and of Fig. 10-33 in Art. 10-9).

This undesirable situation will be reached within a purely cohesive ($\phi = 0$) soil once the surface load reaches the yield value p_y of the soil.   This will happen as soon as τ'_{max} anywhere within the soil mass exceeds its shearing strength $s = c$, where c is the cohesion.   It follows from Eq. (4-1b) that

$$p_y = \frac{\tau'_{max}}{0.33} = 3.0c \qquad (4\text{-}3)$$

The term *bearing capacity* of a soil, as used in this book, refers to the ultimate value of the average unit contact pressure between a foundation mat or footing and the soil which will produce a shear failure within the soil mass.

Many modern analyses of this problem are based on a solution by Prandtl (Ref. 252).   Prandtl investigated the plastic failures of metals.   A special case (horizontal surface) of his general solution is applicable to foundations and is illustrated by Fig. 4-4.   Since Prandtl was mainly concerned with the penetration of punches into metals, where movement of these punches was *guided*, a basic assumption of his solution is that a loaded footing of width b and a very great length L will sink vertically downward into the underlying material, thereby producing shear failures on both sides of the footings. The wedge-shaped soil zone I immediately beneath the footing is assumed to move downward without any deformation together with the footing.   Soil zones II are assumed to be in a plastic state and to push soil zones III upward as units.   The assumed displacements are shown by broken lines in Fig. 4-4.

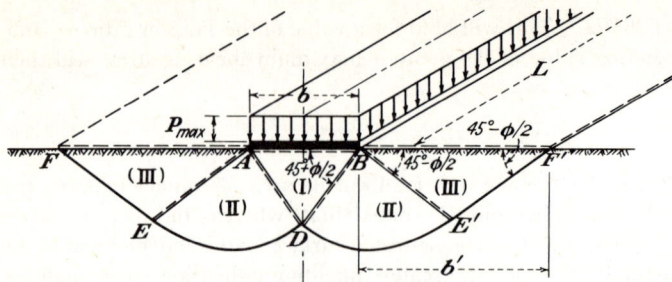

Fig. 4-4. Determination of the ultimate bearing capacity p_{max} of a very long footing ($L/B \to \infty$) under the assumption of simultaneous upward yielding of the soil on both sides of the footing. (*After Prandtl, Ref. 252.*)

Prandtl's analysis covered varying values of the angle of internal friction ϕ. For $\phi = 0$ his solution was

$$p_{max} = 2.571q \tag{4-4}$$

where q is the compressive strength of the soil. For $\phi > 0$, p_{max} increased rapidly with the value of ϕ, as shown by Table 4-1.

Of practical importance in actual foundation work are the values of p_{max} for $\phi = 0$, since experience shows that complete shear failures of the soil under overloaded foundations occur only on plastic clays, for which the angle of internal friction ϕ may be taken as zero or, at least, the shearing strength of which may be taken as one-half of the unconfined compressive strength [see Eq. (3-19)]. With this assumption, Eq. (4-4) becomes

$$p_{max} = 2.571q_u = 5.14c \tag{4-5}$$

In the above derivations Prandtl did not consider the effect of the weight of the soil in zones II and III (Fig. 4-4). However, in some publications, this effect is included in modifications of the original Prandtl equation. Further, Terzaghi (Ref. 341) restricted the validity of Eq. (4-5) to foundations with a perfectly smooth base in contact with the soil. Shearing stresses along a rough

TABLE 4-1. Values of p_{max} According to Prandtl†

ϕ	b'/b	p_{max}/q
0°	1.000	2.571
10°	1.572	3.499
20°	2.530	5.194
30°	4.290	8.701
40°	8.462	17.560

† Ref. 252.

base were believed to exert a restraining effect on the soil, and p_{max} was claimed to be increased thereby to a value of $5.7c$. The application to all foundation designs of the above suggestions to increase to this extent the original values obtained by Prandtl, however, appears questionable in the light of the following considerations.

In a great many cases the nature of the possible downward movement of a foundation is not restrained in any manner, so that the foundation is *free to rotate* about any one of its edges. Thus the basic assumption of the Prandtl solution, illustrated by Fig. 4-4, does not necessarily hold in all cases. Actual records of shear failures of the clay underlying large foundations usually indicate rotational displacements of the soil, as shown in Figs. 4-8 and 4-9. The clay deposit cannot always be absolutely homogeneous to such an extent that a shear failure would develop in it simultaneously on both sides of the foundation (Fig. 4-4). It is likely to be somewhat weaker on one side than on the other, so that a rotational failure would result, of the kind indicated in Fig. 4-2(II).

By taking moments around the center of rotation O, assumed to be at the edge of the foundation, we obtain

$$p_{max} - p_s = c(\pi + 2) = 5.14c \tag{4-6}$$

which is identical with the Prandtl solution [Eq. (4-5)] for $\phi = 0$ and no surcharge ($p_s = 0$) around the loaded area.

All the preceding equations of this article are valid for very long foundations for which the ratio L/b tends to approach infinity. The resistance to rotation of somewhat shorter foundations will be increased by the shearing strength of the soil on vertical planes beneath the two ends of the foundation strip. The increased bearing capacity of the entire foundation can then be roughly estimated, as illustrated by Fig. 4-5.

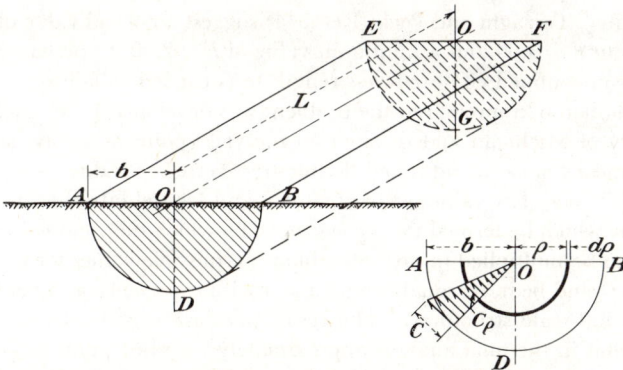

Fig. 4-5. Method of evaluating the end resistance to rotational sliding of cohesive soil beneath foundations with values of the ratio $b/L > 0$.

When the shearing resistance on the cylindrical surface *ADBGEF* of radius b reaches its maximum value of c, the conservative assumption can be made that at some smaller distance ρ from the axis of rotation OO the unit shearing resistance c on a vertical plane through the short ends *AB* or *EF* of the rectangular foundation will be reduced in direct proportion to the distance from O.

It is shown in the first edition, Art. 9-9, that this approximate method of estimating the end effects increases the ultimate values of Eqs. (4-5) and (4-6) by about $0.44b/L$, giving $p_{\max} = 7.95c$ for a *square footing* resting on the soil surface. Values obtained by other procedures for *circular footings* fall within the range

$$p_{\max} = 6.5c \text{ to } 7.95c \qquad (4\text{-}7)$$

As an extension of the analysis by Wilson (Ref. 403) it has been shown (1st ed., Art. 9-9) that the following general expression gives the approximate value of the ultimate failure load on clay soils of a foundation b wide, L long, and h deep:

$$p_{\max} = 5.52c\left(1 + 0.38\,\frac{h}{b} + 0.44\,\frac{b}{L}\right) \qquad (4\text{-}8)$$

The problem of *selecting an adequate factor of safety* is particularly important when dealing with clay soils. The low shearing strengths of such soils do not permit excessive values of safety factors which would include our "factors of ignorance," since in many cases this would make it impossible to build the proposed structure on the location otherwise most suited for it. At the same time, the accurate determination of the actual shearing strength of clays is difficult.

Two main lines of approach to this problem have been developed. In the first and most generally accepted line, the permissible bearing value is based on the shearing strength at failure as determined by quick laboratory tests. For instance, Terzaghi and Peck (Ref. 344) suggest a normal value of the factor of safety $F = 3.00$ and a minimum value of $F = 2.00$, to be based on the results of unconfined compressive-strength tests carried to failure.

The second method of approach to the problem was developed by Housel at the University of Michigan and is based on the yield point of a clay, as determined by means of slow undrained double-transverse-shear direct-ring tests (Art. 3-5B). Very low values were obtained, and Housel introduced a correction factor, which he termed the *overload ratio*, by which the yield value of the clay was to be multiplied in order to obtain permissible values for use in design which would be in reasonable agreement with experience and field observations on full-scale structures. The result (as shown in the 1st ed., Art. 14-2) was that in the final analysis approximately the same permissible bearing values were obtained by both the Terzaghi-Peck and the Housel methods.

The Housel overload-ratio method will not be discussed further now since it appears to be based on the assumption that a progressive failure of a clay may develop under constant loading over a period of years.   This assumption ignores the possibility of an increase of the shearing strength of a stressed clay over a period of years, caused by some additional consolidation when drainage is possible, as is frequently the case.   Additional consolidation under the action of stresses imposed by the foundation loads may be unimportant in the case of the compact type of clays of the Detroit region, studies of which appear to have formed the basis for the development of Housel's theories. Some of these clays are very soft ($q_u = 0.18$ ton/ft^2) ($= 0.18$ kg$_f$/cm^2) at natural water contents of only 20 percent.   This is a rather unusual relationship, which does not seem to be frequently encountered elsewhere.   In most clay deposits of other localities the favorable effect of additional consolidation over periods of years should not be ignored, since it may counterbalance detrimental effects of gradual plastic flow.

This favorable aspect, however, is still ignored by many *rheological studies* of soil *creep* (see Art. 3-5D).   Detrimental creep is not likely to develop if the yield point of the clay is not exceeded.   The factor of safety F_y corresponding to this condition can be obtained by dividing Eq. (4-7) by Eq. (4-3):

$$F_y = \frac{p_{max}}{p_y} = \frac{6.5}{3.0} \text{ to } \frac{7.95}{3.0} = 2.20 \text{ to } 2.65 \qquad (4\text{-}9)$$

An essential point, however, appears to have been disregarded so far in this connection, namely, the fact that the detrimental effect of plastic deformations of clay masses is dependent on the sensitivity of the clay to remolding (Art. 3-2G).   Table 4-2 attempts to take this into account by suggesting higher values of the factors of safety F for sensitive clays and for permanent structures.   In practice the F values for temporary structures would be used mainly in connection with excavation problems.   The permissible bearing value p_0 for a foundation would then be

$$p_0 = \frac{p_{max}}{F} \qquad (4\text{-}10)$$

TABLE 4-2.   Selection of Factors of Safety on the Basis of the Average Sensitivity of a Clay to Remolding

Degree of sensitivity	Sensitivity ratio S	Suggested factors of safety F	
		Permanent structures	Temporary structures
High	≥ 4	3.0	2.5
Medium	2–4	2.7	2.0
Slight.	1–2	2.5	1.8
Not sensitive	≤ 1	2.2	1.6

The procedure for the selection of minimum F values suggested in Table 4-2 should serve only as a general guide; other circumstances should also be considered before taking a decision, for instance, the degree of susceptibility of the clay to increasing its shearing strength by further consolidation (see Art. 3-5D) and the possible rate of further consolidation depending on the thickness of the clay layer and the nature of the available drainage boundaries (Art. 3-4D).

Figure 4-6 gives a graph for the preliminary estimation of the permissible bearing value of strip and square footings on clay soil once the unconfined compressive strength $q_u = 2c$ of the clay has been determined and the factor of safety F selected. The p_0 values of the chart are by some 7 percent higher than would follow from Eqs. (4-6), (4-7), and (4-10).

With reference to Fig. 4-2 it has already been explained that shear failures of the type shown in that sketch and in Fig. 4-4 do not present a problem for most full-sized structures if they are supported by noncohesive soils.

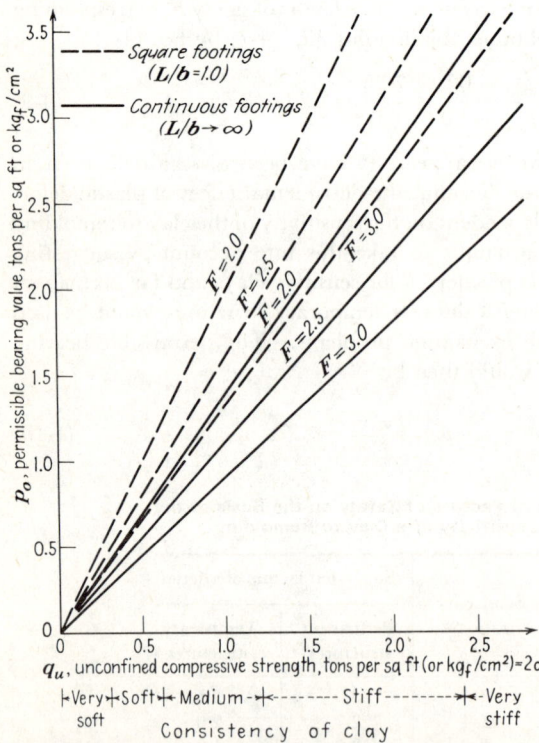

Fig. 4-6. The permissible bearing values of clays [based on Eqs. (4-6) and (4-7), for $h = 0$] (compare with Table 4-2).

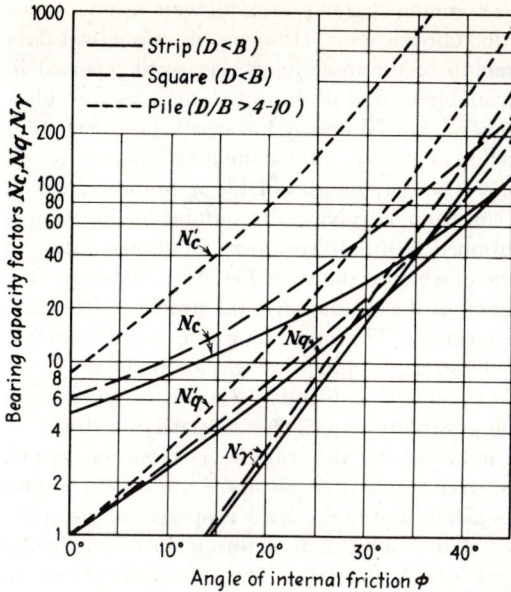

Fig. 4-7.   Bearing-capacity factors for spread and pile foundations. (*After Meyerhof, Ref. 215.*)

An equation for the ultimate failure load of a strip footing proposed by Terzaghi and Peck (in the first edition of Ref. 344) can be used to demonstrate this:

$$p_{max} = cN_c + \gamma h N_q + 0.5\gamma b N_\gamma \qquad (4\text{-}11)$$

The three coefficients N_c, N_q, and N_γ are dimensionless, are termed *bearing-capacity factors*, and depend largely on the value of the angle of internal friction ϕ of the soil (see Fig. 4-7, which is based on later studies by Meyerhof).

The first term in Eq. (4-11) represents the contribution of the cohesion of the soil under the footing; the second term gives the contribution of the surcharge $p_s = \gamma h$ around the footing, where h is the depth of embedment of the footing (see Fig. 4-1); the third term represents the contribution of the friction within the soil mass beneath the footing; it will be noted that it increases proportionately to the width b of the footing.   As shown in Fig. 4-7, all three bearing-capacity factors increase rapidly with the value of ϕ and are somewhat larger for a square footing than for a strip footing.

The bearing-capacity factors N_c' and N_q' of Fig. 4-7 refer to pile foundations (see Art. 6-2).

The type of *collapse of an actual structure due to shear failure of the clay soil beneath it* is illustrated by Figs. 4-8 and 4-9 and is by no means infrequent. For instance, Scheidig (Ref. 280) reproduced photographs of four other similar cases. They had one common characteristic; all were heavy silos or stockhouses erected on plastic cohesive soil. However, no numerical data concerning the shearing strength of the underlying clay were reported in these cases, nor were any available at first in respect to the structure illustrated in Fig. 4-8. The study of that failure by Lazarus White (Ref. 400) had to be limited to the selection of a more suitable site for the new structure to replace the one destroyed. The only data available were old records of borings made prior to the construction, giving the number of blows of a 360-lb (163-kg$_f$) hammer, dropped 18 in. (46 cm), per foot of penetration of a sampling spoon, the average of which is shown in Fig. 4-8. However, the diameter of the spoon, necessary for the evaluation of the strength of the clay, was not indicated in these records. The only thing one could therefore definitely conclude was that the strength of the clay was approximately constant between the depths of 15 and 60 ft (4.6 and 18.3 m) below the bottom of the foundation mat. The possibility of a higher strength of a dry crust above 15 ft was, however, indicated by the water-level elevation, which appeared to vary in depth between 7 and 15 ft (2.1 and 4.6 m). Permission was therefore obtained by Tschebotarioff to check the properties of the upper 20 ft (6.1 m) of that clay. Thin-walled 2-in.-diameter (5.1-cm) Shelby tubing was used for sampling (see Art. 2-3B). The results are shown in Fig. 4-8. The unconfined compressive strength dropped from $q_u = 2.0$ tons/ft^2 at the elevation of the foundation mat to $q_u = 1.0$ ton/ft^2 18 ft (5.5 m) below it. The corresponding water content increased with depth from 34

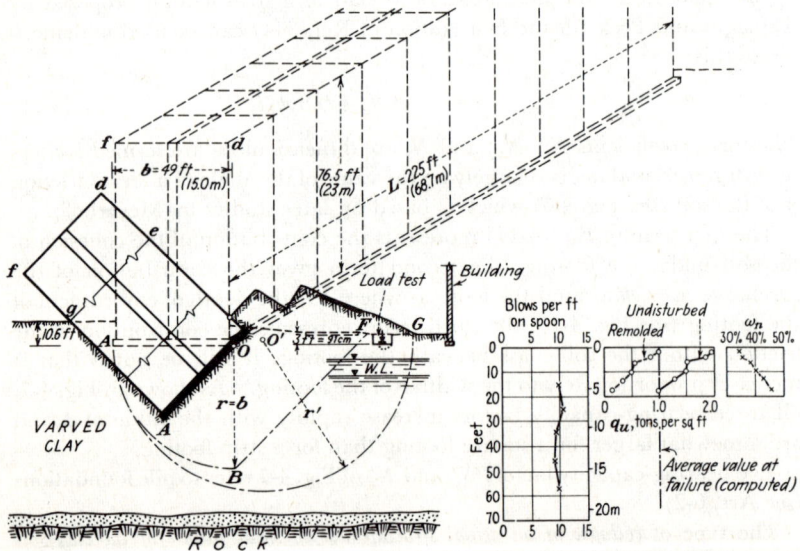

Fig. 4-8.   Profile before and after failure of the silos shown in Fig. 4-9.   (*After Lazarus White, Ref. 400.*)

to 46 percent.   The soil was a varved clay of glacial origin, of a mottled, brown-gray coloring, caused by oxidation, near the surface.   The brown-colored sections of the clay decreased with depth and disappeared entirely at a depth of 15 ft (4.6 m).   The sensitivity (see Art. 3-2G) increased with depth from $S = 2.0$ and $S' = 2.5$ to $S = 5.0$ and $S' = 10.0$.   This is therefore a clay which is sensitive to remolding.

A number of extensive laboratory investigations have been performed in recent years on varved clays of the general region where the structure illustrated by Fig. 4-8 is located.   The lowest average unconfined compressive strength of any layer found so far was $q_u = 0.8$ ton/ft².   This is therefore the minimum value which can be reasonably assigned to the layer below a depth of 20 ft (16.1 m).   Further, if we compare the q_u values with the blows-per-foot penetration of the spoon shown in Fig. 4-8, it does not appear likely that this value could be higher than $q_u = 1.0$ ton/ft² $= 1.0$ kg$_f$/cm².   The total depth affected by the failure is approximately 60 ft (18.3 m).   The average strength of the upper 20 ft has been shown to equal $q_u = 1.5$ tons/ft².   Therefore, if we assume $q_u = 1.0$ ton/ft² for the following 40 ft (12.2 m), we obtain $(1.5 \times 20 + 1.0 \times 40)\frac{1}{60} = 1.16$ tons/ft² as an average q_u value for the site. If we assume $q_u = 0.8$ ton/ft² for the lower 40 ft, the average value will be $q_u = 1.02$ tons/ft².   In accordance with Eq. (3-18), for $\phi = 0$ we then obtain the possible variation of the shearing strength $s = c = q_u/2$ within the limits of 0.58 and 0.52 ton/ft².

The actual value of $s = c$ at failure can then be computed from Eq. (4-8). Failure occurred when the unit load on the soil reached the value of $p_{max} = 3.05$ tons/ft².   With $h = 3$ ft (0.9 m), $b = 49$ ft (14.9 m), and $L = 225$ ft (68 m), we obtain

$$3.05 = 5.52c[1 + 0.38(\tfrac{3}{49}) + 0.44(\tfrac{49}{227})]$$
$$= 5.52c(1 + 0.023 + 0.096) = 6.20c$$

or
$$c = \frac{3.05}{6.20} = 0.49 \text{ ton/ft}^2 = 0.49 \text{ kg}_f/\text{cm}^2$$

This value is only 3 to 15 percent smaller than the one estimated from the laboratory tests.   The agreement can be considered quite good, since it appears probable that prior to failure this sensitive clay was somewhat weakened by the remolding which it underwent as a result of shearing deformations.   Evidence of such deformations is provided by the following observations (Ref. 400).

The pressures on the ground due to the weight of the silos proper, equal to approximately $p = 0.3p_{max}$, had produced a negligible settlement of $\frac{1}{8}$ in. at the side A and $\frac{1}{16}$ in. (1.6 mm) at the side O of the silos (see Fig. 4-8). The filling of the silo was then begun, so that within a month the pressure on the ground equaled $p = 0.82p_{max}$.   During that month the tilt of the structure reversed itself, the settlement reaching the values of 1.0 in. (2.5 m) at A

and $1\frac{5}{16}$ in. (3.3 cm) at O. For the following 6 months the silos remained partially filled, so that the pressure on the ground varied within the limits of $p = 0.82p_{max}$ and $p = 0.71p_{max}$. The settlement during the same period, however, increased rapidly and at a constant rate, so that at the end of that period the settlement at A was $8\frac{7}{8}$ in. (22.5 cm) and at O $10\frac{3}{4}$ in. (27.3 cm). This settlement could not have been caused by consolidation during that short time. The modulus of volume change (see Art. 3-4C) of varved clays in that region can be estimated from observations on other structures to be of the order of magnitude $m'_v = 0.005$ (see Fig. 4-33). If we consider that in Eq. (4-24) the value $1/E$ can be replaced by m'_v (see Art. 3-4C) and then substitute the relevant figures in that equation, we obtain the following estimate of the maximum possible value of settlement due to 100 percent consolidation:

$$S = 2.0pbm'_v \log\left(1 + 1.154\frac{H}{b}\right)$$

$$= 2.0 \times 0.82 \times 3.05 \times 49 \times 12 \times 0.005 \log[1 + 1.154(\tfrac{60}{49})]$$

$$= 4.8 \text{ in.} = 12.2 \text{ cm}$$

Therefore more than half of the settlement measured during that 6-month period must have been caused by shearing deformation which induced lateral and upward squeezing of the soil at the side O of the foundation. The constant rate of the settlement also indicated some form of plastic flow. An attempt was then made to complete the filling of the silos. During one more month the continued filling increased the pressure on the ground from $p = 0.71p_{max}$ to its final value. The rate of settlement increased, so that at the time of the failure the settlement had reached $11\frac{7}{16}$ in. (29.1 cm) at A and $13\frac{7}{8}$ in. (35.2 cm) at O. At the time of the failure the tilting first increased toward the side O to such an extent that attention was attracted by the noise produced by buckling members of a steel bridge (not shown in Fig. 4-8) which connected the silos to the building to the right of the side O. Then the direction of tilting suddenly changed and within approximately 2 min the silos assumed the position shown in the photographs of Fig. 4-9. The upper portion, marked *degf* in Fig. 4-8, broke off, thereby indicating that the silos may have come to rest with some impact.

This sequence of events suggests the following explanation. No important deformations of the clay occurred so long as the pressure p on the surface of the ground did not induce shearing stresses within the soil which exceeded its shearing strength at any point. For a circular footing the limit value of p_y which corresponds to such a condition can be estimated from Eq. (4-3) to read

$$p_y = 3.0c = 1.5q_u = 1.5 \times 1.16 = 1.74 \text{ tons/ft}^2 \ (1.74 \text{ kg}_f/\text{cm}^2)$$

Failure having occurred at $p_{max} = 3.05$ tons/ft² (3.05 kg$_f$/cm²), this means that $p_y = 0.58p_{max}$.

In the 6-month period during which the considerable settlement occurred the actual pressure exceeded this limit value, having varied between $0.71p_{max}$ and $0.82p_{max}$. Thus the shearing strength of the clay was exceeded in places, excessive deformations resulted, which weakened the sensitive clay further, especially on the side O of the foundation, where most of the preliminary lateral squeezing occurred. This weakening of the clay on that side then facilitated the development of the rotational failure, as shown in

(A)

(B)

Fig. 4-9. Collapse of heavy reinforced-concrete silos due to a shear failure of the underlying varved clay (see Fig. 4-8). (*From Lazarus White, Ref. 400.*)

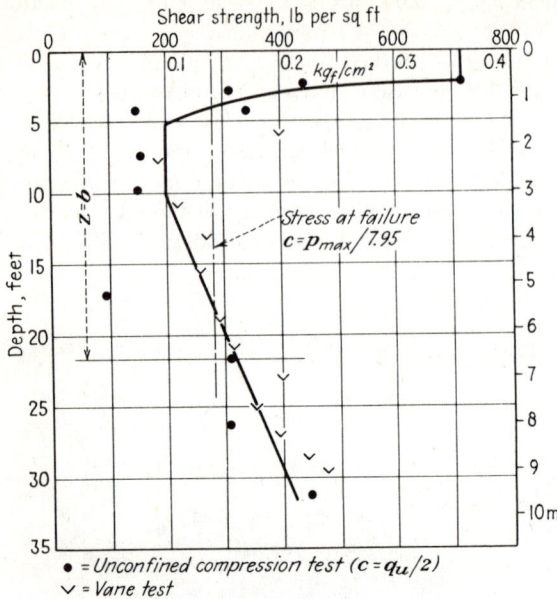

Fig. 4-10. Comparison of the actual shearing strength of the clay at Shellhaven to the average value computed from the failure load of a 22-ft-diameter (6.7-m) steel tank. (*After Nixon, Ref. 231.*)

Fig. 4-8. Increasing of the factors of safety for sensitive clays is therefore indicated.

The position of point G in Fig. 4-8 suggests that the first rotational movement may not have occurred around the edge O of the foundation. The location of the probable center of rotation O' and the final position of the silos shown in Fig. 4-8 may be a result of a combined secondary rotation and lateral and upward displacement of the silos which developed after the original rotational movement around the center O' was already underway and had destroyed part of the cohesion of the clay.

Another point is of interest with reference to Fig. 4-8. Prior to construction, a surface load test on a 1-ft (30.5-cm) square footing had been conducted for a short time with apparently satisfactory results. Since the unconfined compressive strength q_u of the clay close to the surface, which alone mattered in the case of such a small footing, was almost twice as large as the average value of the entire deposit, the satisfactory performance of the test footing is not surprising and illustrates how misleading the results of such tests can be, unless supplemented by other data and properly interpreted.

Two other collapses of large grain elevator silos due to shear failures of clays beneath them have been studied in postmortems (see Refs. 247 and 233).

The conclusions were similar to those arrived at concerning the cement silo of Figs. 4-8 and 4-9.

Nixon reported (Ref. 231) the results of an *experimental filling of a* 22 ft (6.7 m) *in diameter and* 30 ft (9.2 m) *high steel tank at Shellhaven.* The tank was placed on a layer of soft clay with a slightly stiffer upper crust as shown in Fig. 4-10. Both $q_u/2$ values and data from vane tests (see Art. 2-5) are given. The filling was continued over a period of 4 days until the clay failed and the tank overturned. The unit pressure on the surface of the ground at the moment of failure was $p_{max} = 2,230$ lb/ft² (1.1 kg$_f$/cm²).

With reference to the discussion preceding Eq. (4-7), the lowest average shearing strength of the clay at failure was $c = 2,230/7.95 = 280$ lb/ft² (0.14 kg$_f$/cm²). This value is plotted in Fig. 4-10. There was some discussion whether a distributing effect of the stiffer upper crust should be considered. It can be seen from Fig. 4-10 that the failure value $c = 280$ lb/ft² (0.14 kg$_f$/cm²) corresponds fairly closely to the average shearing strength of the entire layer down to the depth likely to be affected by a rotational failure, i.e., approximately, $r = b = 22$ ft (6.7 m). The cases discussed in this article show that modern methods of sampling, testing, and analysis permit a reasonably accurate forecast of the conditions under which failure of a heavy foundation is likely to occur when it is supported by a clay layer.

4-3. Vertical Stress Distribution in Soils and Soil Reactions against Foundations. Figure 4-11 illustrates in a simplified manner the fallacy of the assumption that pressures spread out through the soil under a footing at a well-defined angle will be uniformly distributed over underlying horizontal planes. Let us split up the width a of the footing into several sections of equal

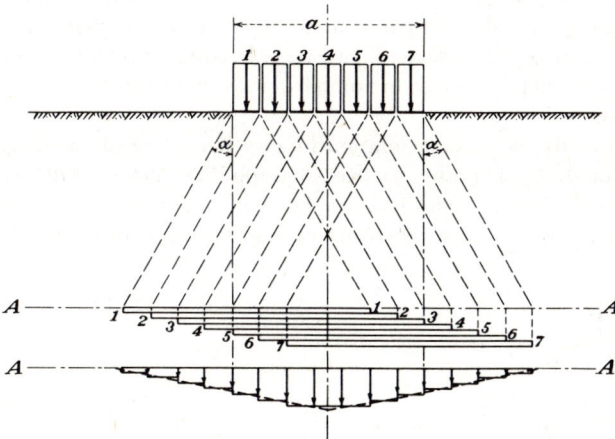

Fig. 4-11. Simplified proof of the fact that vertical pressures transmitted to the soil by a surface load cannot be distributed uniformly on deeper-lying horizontal planes. (*After Koegler and Scheidig, Ref. 174.*)

size and then assume that each of these sections spreads its load out through the soil under an angle $\alpha = 30°$ with the vertical, as shown by broken lines in Fig. 4-11. The truncated pyramids within which the soil is compressed by the load of each of the component sections of the footing will overlap. Therefore, if we add up the pressures transmitted to a plane AA by each of the overlapping pyramids, as shown in Fig. 4-11, greater pressures on the plane AA will be recorded beneath the center of the footing than beneath its edges. As a result, the center of the uniformly loaded footing will tend to settle more than its edges. This has been frequently observed on actual structures (see Figs. 4-29 and 6-20).

Another essential point revealed by an examination of Fig. 4-11 is that the vertical pressures on underlying soil layers spread out well beyond the vertical planes through the edges of the footing. Since a large part of the surface settlements can be represented by the summation of the compressive strains of all underlying soil layers, it follows that there will be no sharp differential settlement between the footing and the immediately adjoining surface of the ground; a gently curved so-called *settlement crater* will be formed around the footing.

The simplified treatment of the stress-distribution problems, which has been outlined in the preceding article, omitted to take into consideration the effect on the stress distribution of the lateral and shearing deformations of the soil load and of the soil properties which influence the magnitude of these deformations. A rigorous analysis of the problem was first carried out by the French mathematician Boussinesq (Ref. 35), in respect to a concentrated load applied to the surface of a so-called *semi-infinite elastic solid*, i.e., to a mass of elastic material limited on one side by a horizontal plane surface and extending an infinite distance in all directions below that plane. The soil beneath a horizontal surface may be considered to represent a semi-infinite solid when its depth is large in comparison to the dimensions of the loaded surface area.

A presentation of the Boussinesq solution in a modern English-language publication was made by Timoshenko (Ref. 346, pp. 328–333). With reference to the symbols shown in Fig. 4-12, the following values were obtained for stresses produced by a concentrated surface load P at a point within the

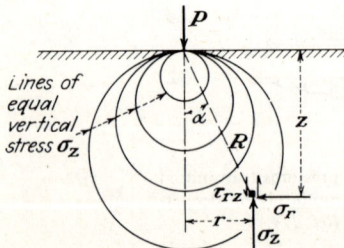

Fig. 4-12. The symbols of the Boussinesq solutions.

elastic soil mass located at a depth z and a horizontal distance r from the vertical line of action of the load P: Vertical stress:

$$\sigma_z = -\frac{3P}{2\pi} z^3 (r^2 + z^2)^{-5/2} \qquad (4\text{-}12)$$

Shearing stress:

$$\tau_{rz} = -\frac{3P}{2\pi} rz^2 (r^2 + z^2)^{-5/2} \qquad (4\text{-}13)$$

Horizontal radial stress:

$$\sigma_r = \frac{P}{2\pi} \left\{ (1 - 2\nu) \left[\frac{1}{r^2} - \frac{z}{r^2} (r^2 + z^2)^{-1/2} \right] - 3r^2 z (r^2 + z^2)^{-5/2} \right\} \qquad (4\text{-}14)$$

The expression for the horizontal tangential stress σ_θ may be found in Ref. 346.

The following facts are revealed by an examination of Fig. 4-12 and of Eqs. (4-12) to (4-14).   All stresses are independent of the value of the Young modulus E of the material.   The vertical stress σ_z and the shearing stress τ_{rz} in addition are independent of the value of the Poisson ratio ν.   Lines drawn through points of equal vertical stress σ_z have the approximate shape of circles; this is also true in the case of lines drawn through points of equal shearing stress τ_{rz}.   The horizontal radial stress σ_r, that is, the radial lateral pressure, however, *is* dependent on the value of the Poisson ratio ν.

Indirect evidence of the correctness of the Boussinesq solution for elastic materials has been provided by laboratory *photoelastic experiments*.   This type of study is based on the fact that the crystals of an elastic medium are re-oriented to an equal degree by shearing stresses of the same intensity, so that when polarized light is sent through stressed Bakelite, gelatine, or similar materials, points of equal shearing stress appear as lines of the same color. Under conditions of loading corresponding to Fig. 4-12, the lines of equal shear during a photoelastic experiment have the approximate shape of circles, as should be the case according to the Boussinesq solution.

Many *attempts to determine the stress distribution in sands experimentally* have been made during the past century with gradually improving instrumentation and testing techniques.   Sands were experimented with first, since it is comparatively easy to embed pressure-measuring devices in sand.

Particularly noteworthy are the *extensive tests with footings of different sizes* carried out by Koegler and Scheidig at the Mining Academy of Freiberg, Saxony, in 1927 (Ref. 173).   An improved method of vertical-pressure measurement was employed.   It consisted in using a very large number of pressure cells, which were placed so closely to each other that they formed continuous horizontal layers at several depths, thereby eliminating inaccuracies in the measurements due to differences in the compressibility of the pressure cells and of the surrounding sand.

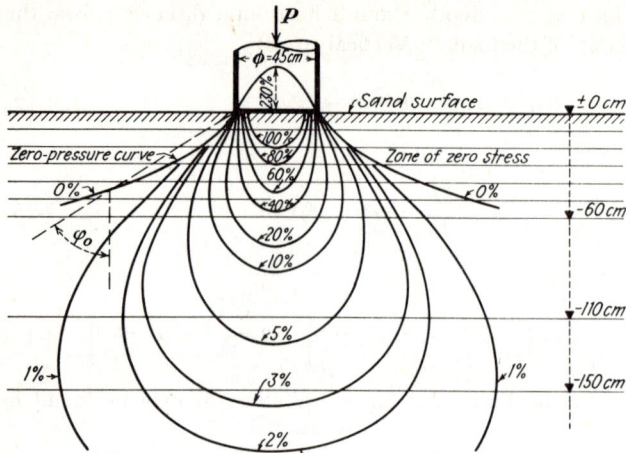

Fig. 4-13. Lines of equal vertical pressure in sand, as measured during the Freiberg tests. (*After Koegler and Scheidig, Ref. 173.*)

The results of one of the Freiberg tests are shown in Fig. 4-13. The curved, pear-shaped lines are drawn through points in the sand mass where vertical pressures of equal intensity were measured. These pressures are expressed in percent of the average unit surface pressure $p = P/A$ at the plane of contact between the test footing and the sand, where P is the total load applied, and A is the area of the footing.

It will be noted from Fig. 4-13 that the vertical pressures in the sand were somewhat more concentrated under the footing and were somewhat less spread out laterally than is indicated by the Boussinesq formulas (see Fig. 4-12). Near the sand surface there existed a zone of zero stress, limited by the curve of zero pressure, as shown in Fig. 4-13. The angle φ_0 between that curve and the vertical equaled 35° near the sand surface, then increased gradually till at a certain depth t is approached 90°. This depth t was found at Freiberg to be independent of the size of the footing and to vary between 3 and 4 ft (0.9 and 1.2 m) for surface-contact pressures in the range of 0.5 to 1.0 ton/ft² (0.5 to 1.0 kg$_f$/cm²) and sand of normal density. It did not exceed 6.5 ft (2 m) for very loose sand. It is reasonable to assume that the depth t will be greater for larger surface-contact pressures. The explanation of these observations follows.

The application of a load to the surface of a homogeneous body produces, as shown by Boussinesq, vertical and lateral pressures within that body. These pressures, together with the weight of the overlying layers of the soil, form a resultant pressure, which has a strong inclination in the upper layers. Here, outside of the surface loaded by the footing, the non-cohesive granular soils cannot resist its horizontal component. The resistance to shear of such soils depends only on intergranular friction, which is zero near the sand surface, since there is no overlying soil layer to produce, by its weight, pressures which would render the potential frictional resistance of the sand effective. Intergranular movements will occur there with little hindrance. Therefore the pressures from the footing cannot spread out laterally in the upper layers of the sand to the same extent as they would in a cohesive material. This produces in sand a greater concentration of vertical pressures below the loaded surface than is indicated by the Boussinesq formulas. Farther below the surface of the sand, conditions change. The inclination of the resultant pressure gradually decreases because of the added weight of the upper soil layers. For the same reason, the value of intergranular friction and therefore of the horizontal resistance of the soil is increased. At a depth t the sand can then behave like a homogeneous elastic body to which the Boussinesq equations may be applied.

The *distribution of the reactions of the soil* to the foundation loads *depends on the condition of the soil at the boundary* of the loaded footing. Sand with no surcharge around the footing, i.e., with no overlying layers of soil, will not have any shearing strength at the footing boundary for reasons just explained. The sand there will therefore yield readily, reducing the reactions against the footing at the boundary. Equilibrium will then require an increase of the intensity of the soil reactions at the center of the footing to values higher than the average uniformly distributed unit pressure $p = P/A$. For the test illustrated by Fig. 4-13 pressure-measuring cells were embedded in the lower face of the footing. The reaction pressure at the center was measured and found equal to 230 percent of P/A. The magnitude of this increase was found to be a function of the size of the footing. The length of the circumference of a footing increases linearly with an increase of the diameter or of the side length of the footing. It is therefore reasonable to expect that the influence of any boundary effects on the distribution of unit pressures will decrease with an increase of the size of a footing, since the unit pressures are dependent on its area, i.e., on the second power of the diameter or of the side length of the footing. It is even probable that for very large footings or for entire buildings founded on sand the boundary effects will affect only a small adjoining portion of the entire area, with a resulting distribution of soil-reaction pressures of the type shown in Fig. 4-14(I) and a tendency for a flexible superstructure to settle and to deflect as shown in Fig. 4-14(II).

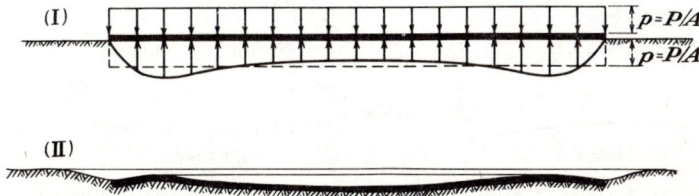

Fig. 4-14. (I) The probable distribution of the soil reactions and (II) the resulting deflection of a large flexible foundation on sand.

That the curvatures of a uniformly loaded, flexible footing may be reversed, depending on the nature of the soil reactions, is illustrated by Fig. 4-15. The type of curvature shown in Fig. 4-15(I) has actually been measured on sand (Ref. 174) but only for very small footings, where the effect of the yielding of the surface sand grains at the boundary of the footing overbalanced the effect of the greater compression beneath the center of the footing of the deeper-lying soil layers.   The curvature shown in Fig. 4-15(II) has been frequently measured on structures erected on clay soils (Fig. 6-20); it is the natural result of the stress-distribution pattern shown in Fig. 4-15(II). This pattern is in agreement with the rigorous Boussinesq solution and can be explained as follows.   In a *firm* cohesive soil the material immediately outside the boundary of the footing will receive some of the load, which will be transferred to it by shearing stresses which, in contrast to noncohesive sand, can be resisted by a clay at the ground surface irrespective of any surcharge pressures around the footing.   Thus the clay at the outer boundary of the footing will offer more resistance to the load of the footing than that at the center of the footing.   A concentration of reaction pressures at the perimeter of the footing will result, as shown in Fig. 4-15(II).   This concentration is a discontinuous localized phenomenon; deeper down below the contact surface between footing and soil the distribution of vertical pressures on a horizontal plane will be as shown in Fig. 4-11.   It will be noted that a greater deflection at the center of a flexible, uniformly loaded footing on clay is in agreement both with the soil-reaction diagram of Fig. 4-15(II) and with the vertical-pressure diagram of Fig. 4-11 if we consider that most of the surface settlements represent the sum of the vertical compressive strains of all underlying layers.

Nonuniformity of the soil may produce deviations from the computed stress distribution which cannot always be evaluated accurately.   For in-

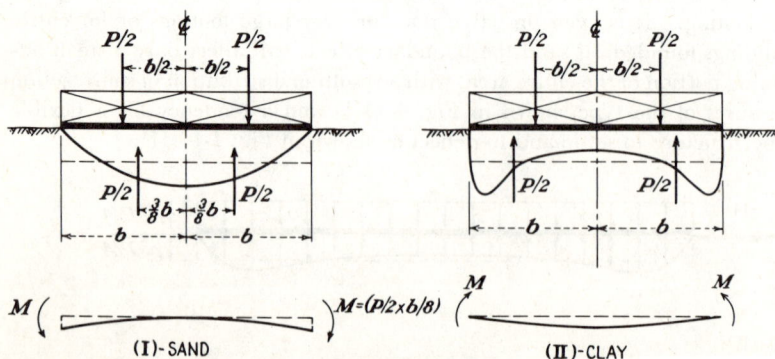

Fig. 4-15.   The relationship between the distribution of soil reactions and the curvature of small, uniformly loaded flexible footings on sand and on clay.

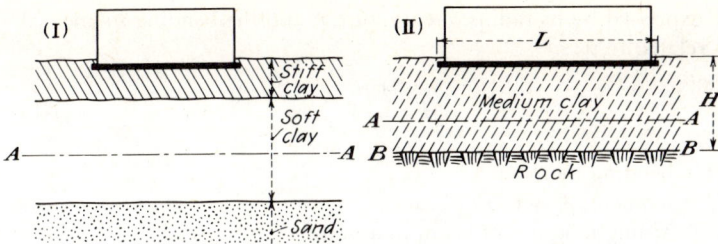

Fig. 4-16. (I) A stiff upper layer distributes pressures to a greater extent than indicated by the Boussinesq solution, whereas (II) a stiff underlying layer has a reverse effect on the stress distribution above it.

stance, as shown in Fig. 4-16(I), a stiff upper crust of clay may act as a foundation mat, so that the pressures on a plane AA of an underlying layer of soft clay will be distributed to a somewhat greater extent and will therefore be somewhat smaller than the values computed from charts based on the Boussinesq solution. A stiff layer, when underlying the foundation at a shallow depth, as shown in Fig. 4-16(II), will have a reverse effect on the stress distribution within the compressible layer above it. A rock surface BB will tend to restrain along that plane the lateral expansion of the overlying clay, so that a greater concentration of pressures will take place under the foundation on a plane AA than would be the case for a uniform layer of great depth. This concentration of pressures will increase with decreasing values of the ratio H/L.

4-4. Effect of Settlements on Different Types of Superstructure. The stress-distribution computations described in the preceding article assume that the foundation is perfectly flexible. This is true for such structures as steel tanks for the storage of oil and other liquids or of long brick buildings one to three stories high. On the other hand, such structures as bridge piers or reinforced concrete silos can be considered as entirely rigid. They are therefore unable to adapt themselves to the curvature of the settlement crater of the soil surface and will tend to span it, thereby increasing the pressures transmitted to the soil at the foundation perimeter to the extent necessary to enforce uniformity of settlement. There are a number of partially rigid types of superstructure which will deflect somewhat and yet redistribute pressures at the soil surface to a certain extent. Under such conditions considerable stresses are apt to be engendered in the superstructure.

Incompletely rigid structures may be overstressed and cracked if they are not strong enough to equalize the settlements by bridging the crater and thereby increasing the pressures at its periphery and, at the same time, are not flexible enough to adjust themselves to the surface of the crater. The following equations, the derivation of which can be found in most textbooks on mechanics of materials, give the relationship between the curvature of a beam, as expressed by its radius of curvature r, and the bending moment M which is related to it:

$$M = \frac{EI}{r} \qquad (4\text{-}15)$$

where M = bending moment
   I = moment of inertia of beam
   E = Young modulus of beam material
   r = radius of curvature.

For a beam of homogeneous material and thickness d the unit bending stress f is

$$f = \frac{Md/2}{I} = \frac{Ed}{2r} \qquad (4\text{-}16)$$

By assuming that the elastic line is a circle, the radius of curvature r can be roughly estimated from the differential settlement y_d at the center of the span L:

$$r = \frac{L^2}{8y_d} \qquad (4\text{-}17)$$

Substituting Eq. (4-17) into Eq. (4-16), we obtain

$$f = 4 \frac{Edy_d}{L^2} \qquad (4\text{-}18)$$

These equations, as well as Fig. 4-18, illustrate why it is now customary to build storage steel tanks of the type illustrated in Fig. 4-17 by placing the

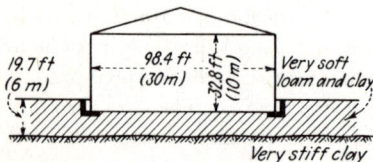

Fig. 4-17. A steel tank placed directly on the ground safely underwent differential settlements because of its flexible bottom. *(From ASCE Foundation Committee, Ref. 318.)*

steel bottom of the tank directly on the soil surface, which is covered with only a thin layer of sand and asphalt to protect the steel from corrosion. Studies by Terzaghi (Ref. 318) indicated that this type of construction could be successfully employed under the same conditions where a steel storage tank founded on a 1-ft-thick (30.5-cm) reinforced-concrete inverted T-beam mat had failed. A mat of this type and thickness would not be strong enough to equalize a differential settlement y_d greater than some 2 or 3 in.

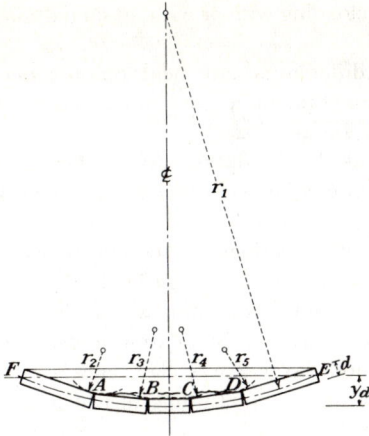

Fig. 4-18. Why a tank like that in Fig. 4-17 failed under similar soil conditions when it was founded on a reinforced-concrete mat 1 ft (30 cm) thick of the inverted T-beam type.

(5.1 to 7.6 cm).   Once the mat failed, say, at the points A, B, C, and D, indicated in cross section in Fig. 4-18, the elastic line of the bottom of the steel tank would have to adapt itself to the surface of the concrete mat, i.e., to the straight lines between these four points.   The steel plate of the tank would be bent sharply, with very small resulting values r_2, r_3, r_4, and r_5 of the radius of curvature at these points, much smaller than indicated in the sketch, which is not drawn to scale.   Failure of the steel plate would result, followed by leakage of the fluid stored in the tank.   On the other hand, the thin steel plate of the bottom of the tank, when resting directly on the ground, could safely adjust itself to the large radius of curvature r_1 without being in any way overstressed.   Steel tanks of this type have been known to safely undergo differential settlements of 2 to 3 ft (60 to 90 cm).   The exact permissible value should be obtained from the manufacturers of the steel tanks. It must be clearly understood, however, that large differential settlements can be safely withstood *only* if they are symmetrical in respect to a vertical axis through the center of the tank floor.   Otherwise they may cause the walls of the tank to buckle, as actually happened in a case illustrated by Fig. 4-19.   Either this tank should have been placed on piles, or the soft clay

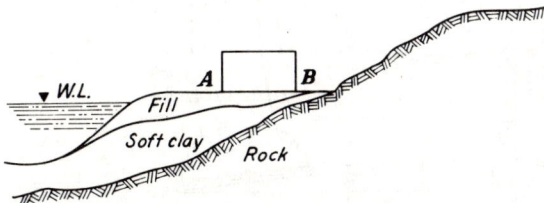

Fig. 4-19. Walls of cylindrical steel oil tank buckled because settlements at A were much larger than at B.

should have been first consolidated by preloading with or without sand drains (see Art. 5-2).

Of course, irrespective of the effects of differential settlements on the super-structure, the safety against a shear failure of the underlying soil, if it consists of clay, should be investigated (see Arts. 4-2 and 7-2).

This applies not only to individual tanks but to the stability of the entire mass of soil beneath groups thereof; a case is known where an entire tank farm slid out to sea.

Statically determinate bridges can undergo considerable settlements without damage (see Fig. 4-20). The simply supported steel-girder bridge was continuously jacked up to keep it at its original elevation while the pier masonry and the approach fill were built up as their foundation settled to a total of 19 ft. (5.7 m). Layer 1 was mud, layer 2 was clay, and layer 3 consisted of fine sand with many hollow shells, the crushing of which may have accounted for much of the settlement.

See also the three-hinged arch bridge in Fig. 6-21.

The opposite extreme type of rigid superstructure is illustrated in Fig. 4-21. A five-story storage building for a costly liquid was separated into small units which were perfectly rigid, since all the longitudinal and cross walls, as well as the slabs, were of reinforced concrete and formed a rigid monolith, capable of withstanding appreciable secondary stresses. The old structure, shown on the left of the diagram, is split up into four such units, and the new structure, shown at the center of the diagram, has six such units. The profile of the measured settlements in Fig. 4-21 shows that none of the units deflected at all and that all units of each structure even settled to a slight uniform tilt. This indicates that the expansion joints (1 in. = 2.5 cm wide) functioned only partially and that the combined action of tensile forces in the continuous foundation mat, plus compressive forces between adjoining units at the top of each joint, shown by arrows in Fig. 4-21, prevented any break in the uniformly inclined settlement surface, such as is sketched in Fig. 4-18. A

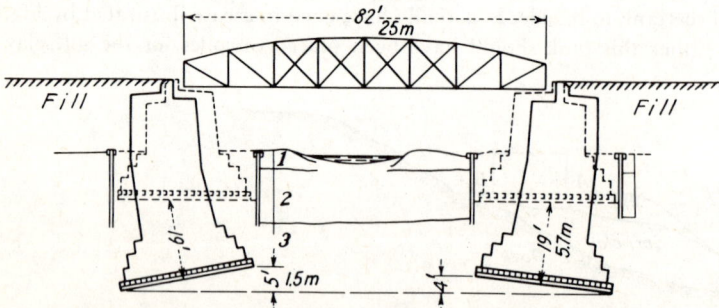

Fig. 4-20. Railroad service was maintained over this simply supported girder bridge in spite of a 19-ft (5.8-m) settlement. (*From Wochenschr. Ost. Ing. Arch. Ver., 1888, p. 342.*)

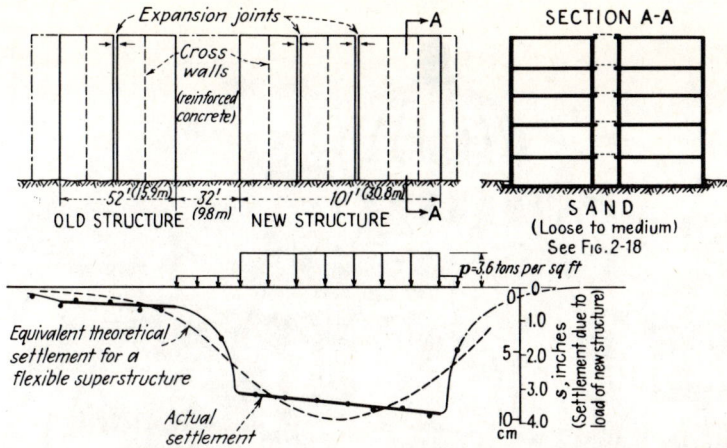

Fig. 4-21. Heavy structures can undergo differential settlements without damage when separated into small rigid units.

slightly smaller settlement of the new structure occurred at the end closest to the old structure, presumably because the soil (a loose to medium sand, see Fig. 2-18) was already somewhat compacted there by pressures from the old structure.

The method of splitting up new buildings into small, very rigid, and strong units is frequently followed in mining areas where unforeseen but large motions of the soil surface may occur, with time, owing to the collapse of old shafts and tunnels, which often are at best only partially backfilled after completion of the mining.   Such structural units are sometimes even given three-point support.

Figure 4-22 shows the National Theater at Mexico City, erected on a rigid foundation mat which stiffened the superstructure.   This prevented serious damage in spite of the considerable settlement, in part caused by the excessive weight of the 8-ft-thick (2.45 m) massive reinforced-concrete foundation mat, which alone weighed almost as much as the entire superstructure.   A cellular type of raft of a greater depth could have achieved the same degree of strength with much less weight.

It became necessary to excavate ramps around the building to permit access to what was originally the ground floor but became almost a subbasement after over 6 ft (1.8 m) of settlement.   Mexico City is founded on what was once an ancient lake.   It is filled to a great depth by clay interbedded with sand lenses.   The upper 100 ft (30 m) of the clay is very soft.   This location presents what are probably the most difficult foundation conditions in the world.   The clay was formed by particles of fine and sometimes decomposed volcanic ash deposited by the combined action of water flowing into the lake and of wind blowing over it.   An unusually loose structure of the

(A)

(B)

Fig. 4-22. The National Theater at Mexico City, which has settled over 6 ft (1.83 m) since its construction in 1909. (*A*) General view. (*B*) Approach ramp excavated to permit access to stage entrance from street level. Drive-in was originally at elevation where lined-up buses are shown. (*Photos by Boris Ashurkoff.*)

clay resulted.   When dried, it will shrink to one-tenth of its original volume (see also Figs. 3-6 and 9-4).

The great majority of buildings are of a type which occupies an inter-mediate position between the two extremes which have just been discussed; i.e., most buildings are of a semirigid type.   A rigorous analysis of the amount of deflection they can safely undergo is not possible, since very few numerical data are available concerning the strength and the elastic properties of entire masonry walls, especially when they are weakened by windows or doors.   It therefore becomes necessary to base oneself on observations and measurements of full-scale structures in the field (Art. 4-5).

So long as the total settlement does not exceed 2 or 3 in. (5 or 7.5 cm), no damage is to be expected with most buildings.   The differential settlement then does not exceed an inch or so, and it would appear that the masonry superstructure of most buildings can safely deflect by the necessary amount. Figure 4-29 illustrates this point.   It will be noted that the lines of equal measured settlements follow the same pattern in respect to the magnitude and distribution of the settlements as do the lines of equal vertical pressure on the underlying clay layer.   Since the vertical pressures were computed on the assumption of a perfectly flexible superstructure, the similarity of their distribution to the settlement distribution indicates that the three-story masonry building 50 ft (15.3 m) high and 280 ft (86 m) long actually behaved up to that point as if it were almost perfectly flexible and that the clay layer

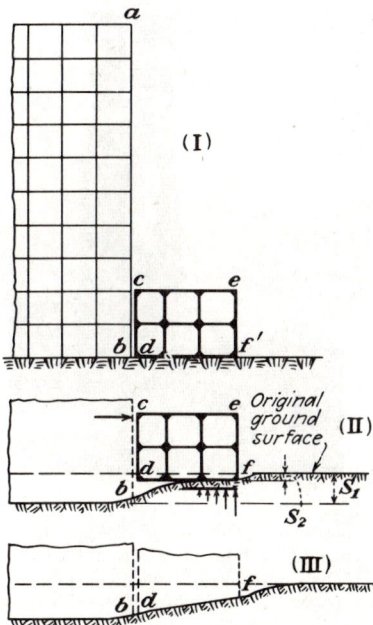

Fig. 4-23.   Sketch illustrating dis-cussion of measures necessary to prevent damage to light parts of a building by the settlement crater around adjoining heavy parts of the structure.

was fairly homogeneous horizontally in respect to its compressibility. No cracks whatsoever could be noticed in the building. As time went by and the settlements increased, the equalizing effect of the semiflexible super-structure became more apparent (see Hanna, Ref. 120).

Figure 4-23 illustrates the effects of the larger settlements of a heavy build-ing on an adjoining lower separate building or on a wing of the original struc-ture. The settlement crater of the heavier part will extend well beyond its limits, so that points b and d of the two structures will tend to settle equally, as shown in Fig. 4-23(III). If the total settlement is large, the resultant deformations of the lower building are likely to crack the masonry and plaster-work unless its structural framework is designed as a rigid Vierendeel type girder, as shown in Fig. 4-23(I) and (II). The provision of an expansion joint between the two structures is inadequate, since the joint cannot be extended down through the soil to limit the settlement crater laterally.

(I)   (II)

Fig. 4-24. Tilting of the foundation may or may not induce failure of the superstructure, depending on the design of the latter. (I) The campanile at Pisa still stands, although it is out of plumb by 9.7 percent of its height. (II) The campanile at Venice collapsed in 1902 as a result of being out of plumb by only 0.8 percent of its height. [*Photo (II) from Sandick, Ref. 228.*]

Damages to old small structures are known to have been caused by the settlements of new heavier ones in spite of a 10-ft-wide (3-m) open alleyway between them.

The amount of *tilting* which a tower or a factory chimney can undergo depends on its structural strength.   The point is illustrated by Fig. 4-24. The leaning tower of Pisa [Fig. 4-24(I)] began tilting from the very start of its construction; its foundation is underlain by alternating sand and clay layers (Ref. 295).   The average unit contact pressure on the soil is 5 tons/ft²; in high wind the pressure at the edge is 10 tons/ft² (10 kg$_f$/cm²).   The tower is 150 ft (46 m) high.   Early tilting of the tower provided danger signals, and a carefully conducted strengthening of the masonry was undertaken, so that it has to date successfully withstood stresses induced by its being 14.7 ft (4.5 m) out of plumb, i.e., 9.7 percent of its height.   A completely different situation developed at Venice, where the 330-ft (101-m) ancient campanile (bell tower) collapsed in 1902, as shown in Fig. 4-24(II).   The foundation was supported by closely spaced timber piles, the points of which were underlain by alternating layers of sand and clay (Ref. 295).   The average unit contact pressure at foundation level was 6.4 tons/ft² (6.4 kg$_f$/cm²), and during wind pressures of 62.5 lb/ft² (306 kg$_f$/m²) it reached a value of 8.6 tons/ft² (8.6 kg$_f$/cm²) at the edge of the foundation.   The tower was 2.6 ft, or 0.8 percent, of its height out of plumb.   It was safe until some structural modifications weakened the superstructure and caused its sudden collapse. The new tower, still standing, was built the exact architectural shape of the old one but on a much larger foundation.

4-5. Field Observations of Deformations and Settlements of Structures. A study of the condition of existing buildings near the proposed construction site can frequently provide valuable indications concerning the loading which the underlying soil layers can safely carry.   The inclination of cracks provides clues regarding the differential settlements which produced them. Thus the cracks shown in Fig. 4-25(I) indicate that the wall *AB* must have moved downward in respect to *CD* from its original position *A'B'*.   This elongated the diagonal *CB'* to *CB* produced tension in the direction of that diagonal and formed the cracks, as shown, at right angles to it.   Of course, the same effect could be obtained if the wall *A'B'* stayed in its original position and the wall *CD* moved upward, for instance, because dry clay under the foundation swelled most under the corner during a rainy season and lifted it (Ref. 410).   Similarly, the pattern of cracks shown in Fig. 4-25(II) can be produced either by the greater settlement of the center of a wall due to the natural compression of underlying soft clay layers (see Fig. 6-18) or by the greater swelling and lifting power of dry clay near the edges of a foundation, as will happen during rainy seasons in countries where such seasons occur periodically.   This is the case, for instance, of some regions in Burma, as described by Wooltorton (Ref. 410).   Thermoosmosis (Art. 4-8*D*) produces a reversed trend.

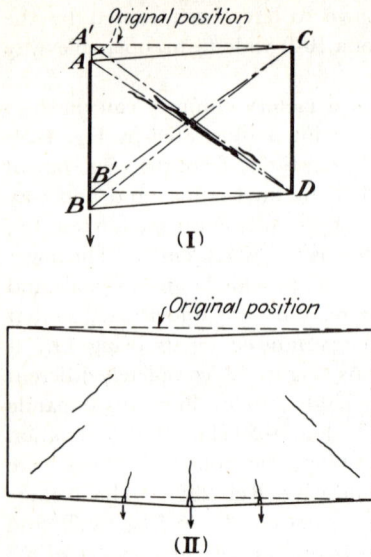

Fig. 4-25. Possible manner of estimating the direction of differential settlements of a building from the inclination of cracks in its walls. (I) Cracks in a cross wall, caused by the settlement of one of its ends from $A'B'$ to AB. (II) Cracks caused by the deflection of the central part of a front wall.

Levels taken along parapets or cornices sometimes indicate the deformations which a building has undergone (see Fig. 6-18).

Observations of cracks in masonry can also provide indications of whether settlements are continuing. It should be remembered, however, that, once a crack has been formed because of excessive structural deformations, it immediately becomes a temperature expansion joint. Therefore, if plaster telltales are placed across a masonry crack and also crack slightly, this may be due to temperature deformations only. Repeated extensometer measurements of the Whittemore strain-gage type (Art. 1-9) may become necessary to get a true idea as to the actual cause of crack-width changes.

The possibility of *temperature deformations* should also be remembered when evaluating transit measurements of the changes in tilt of nonuniformly settling high factory chimneys. Figures 4-26 and 4-27 illustrate this point.

Specially machined supporting plates, permitting measurements in two directions at right angles to each other by means of Huggenberger Klinometers, were cemented into the minaret masonry at six elevations shown on Fig. 4-26. This *Klinometer* is a very sensitive horizontal level, adjustable by a micrometer screw and capable of reading changes of inclination of 1 second of arc. The general purpose of the measurements was not related to any foundation problem and consisted in the control of minaret inclinations during the demolition and reconstruction in reinforced concrete of all inner domes, arches, and columns. Only the original outer walls and the two minarets were left intact. To establish normal minaret movements, continuous measurements were performed at all six levels during a 14-hr daylight period on Sept. 21, 1934, before the reconstruction work was begun. The results are shown in Figs. 4-26 and 4-27.   The normal lateral movement in plan of the top of the 128-ft-high (39-m) minaret had the shape of a loop due to the shifting position of the sun.   The maximum lateral displacement was about $\frac{1}{2}$ in. (12.9 mm) (Fig. 4-27).   In elevation the deflection curve of the minaret at any moment in time had the shape of a parabola.   Since there are very few cloudy days in Cairo, later control measurements during the reconstruction work had to be performed around midnight to eliminate the effects of one-sided heating.

Observations of the type shown by Fig. 4-28 helped determine whether the yield point of the silty soil at a site located on the floodplain of a large river had been exceeded.   In the center of the picture, immediately behind the small light-colored pile of sand, is a rainwater filled settlement crater of an earlier stockpile of iron ore, similar to the one still in place behind it.   The inclination of the telephone poles opposite both the earlier and the existing stockpiles indicates that the yield point of the underlying silt and clay deposit had been exceeded [Eq. (4-3)] and that shearing deformations had begun.   This was also shown by the closing at the same locations of a ditch running along the other side of the road.

To get a clear picture of the nature of the settlements of a new structure it is essential to know the distribution of settlements in plan and their variation

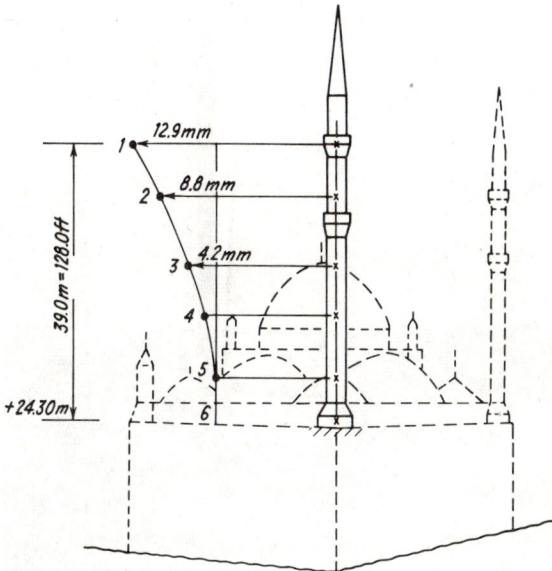

Fig. 4-26.   Maximum deflection due to one-sided heating by the sun of a minaret of the Mohammed Ali Mosque in Cairo at time C in Fig. 4-27.   (Measurements by Tschebotarioff, Ref. 326.)

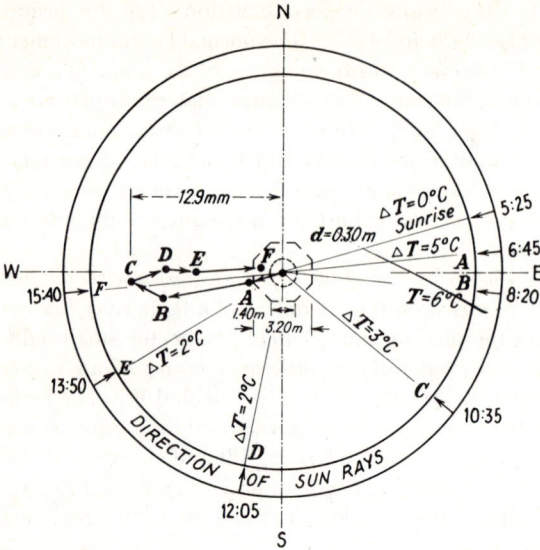

Fig. 4-27.   A daily lateral movement of point 1 at the upper balcony of the minaret shown on Fig. 4-26.   (*Measurements by Tschebotarioff, Ref. 326.*)

Fig. 4-28.   Inclination of telephone poles opposite an iron-ore stockpile and a water-filled settlement crater of an earlier stockpile in front of it show that the yield point of the soil has been exceeded in both cases.   (*Photo by Tschebotarioff.*)

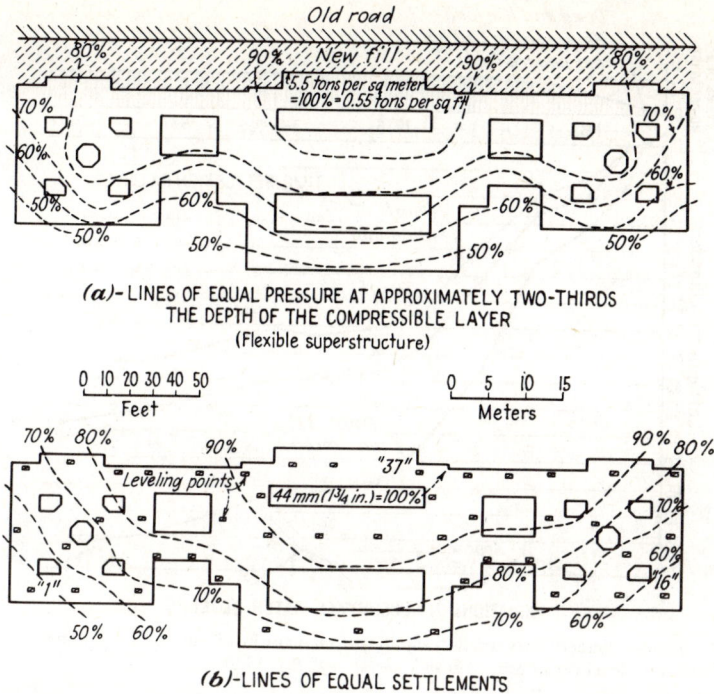

(a)- LINES OF EQUAL PRESSURE AT APPROXIMATELY TWO-THIRDS
THE DEPTH OF THE COMPRESSIBLE LAYER
(Flexible superstructure)

(b)-LINES OF EQUAL SETTLEMENTS

Fig. 4-29. The deflection of a long three-story masonry building indicates its great flexibility under the effect of small differential settlements (see Fig. 4-30). (*From Tschebotarioff, Refs. 351 and 352.*)

with time (see Figs. 4-29 and 4-30). These illustrations refer to a three-story masonry building in Upper Egypt along the Nile River. Its mat foundation rested on a layer of compact oxidized silt and clay, which at a depth of 7 to 10 m (23 to 33 ft) was underlain by a layer 3 m (10 ft) thick of softer dark clay (see building IV, Ref. 352). This layer appears to have been the *seat of settlements*† since it can be seen from Fig. 4-29 that the lines of equal pressure within that layer closely correspond to the lines of measured equal settlements. Over 40 permanent brass bench marks were embedded as leveling points in the masonry of the basement to permit repeated measurements from the very start of construction.

Properly kept records of the performance of a structure should permit the presentation of their summary in graphical form. In addition to the distribution of settlements in plan, as shown in Fig. 4-29, time-settlement curves should be plotted, as shown in Fig. 4-30, in conjunction with any other relevant data, for instance, water-level variations (compare with Prob. 4-5).

† Defined as the layer within which 70 percent of the surface settlements originate.

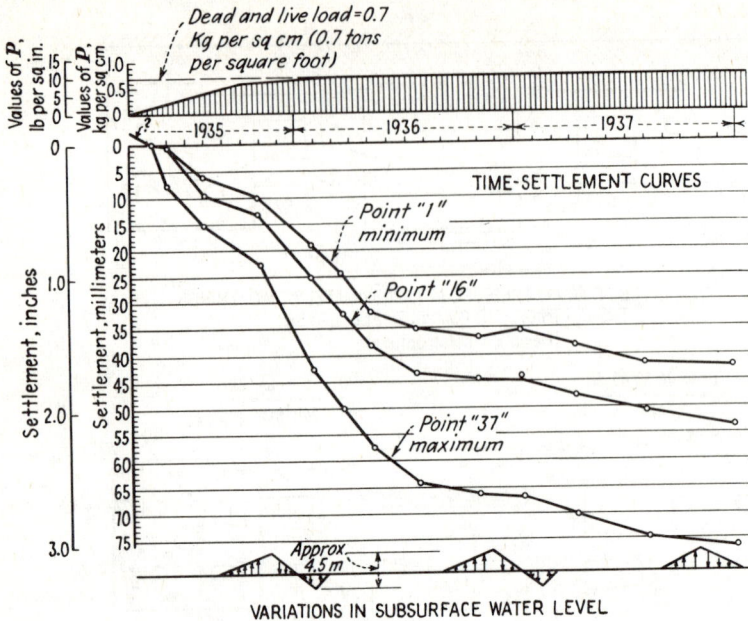

Fig. 4-30. Time-settlement curves reflect significant changes in the subsoil conditions e.g., groundwater-level variations.   *(From Tschebotarioff, Ref. 352.)*

Loading, foundation, soil, and settlement profiles should also be drawn, for example, as shown for a different building in Fig. 6-20.

There are *three main types of time-settlement curves of actual structures*. In the first type most of the settlement will occur during construction; this will be the case of foundations resting on compact pervious soils. For structures supported by clay and silt soils the shape of the time-settlement curve may vary, depending on whether primary or secondary time effects predominate (Art. 3-4D). If the soil follows the laws of Terzaghi's theory of consolidation, the settlements will decrease progressively and will stop entirely after a certain period of time, following the end of construction. The time-settlement curve will have a parabolic shape; this is the second type of curve. In the third type, the time-settlement curve may have the shape of a straight line, either from the very start or as a tangent to the initial parabola. This may indicate one of two things: either the settlements are caused by possible dangerous shearing deformations of the entire soil mass (see Art. 4-2), or the structure of the soil is such that the slippage of grain upon grain delays the consolidation. Such so-called secondary time effects will, however, also show up during a laboratory consolidation test (Art. 3-4D). They may happen in peat and in some other soils. This point is of importance in connection with the use of sand drains (Art. 5-2).

4-6. Settlement Analyses and Forecasts.   The first step of a settlement analysis or forecast consists in the *computation of vertical pressures* at different depths below the center, the corners, and other characteristic points of a structure.   Auxiliary charts have been developed for the purpose.   They are based on the integration of the Boussinesq formula for a concentrated load [Eq. (4-12)] over the entire loaded area.   Thus they cannot take into account the rigidity of the superstructure, and the results obtained correspond to one which is entirely flexible.   There are two main types of such charts.

The first type is illustrated by Fig. 4-31.   It permits the determination of the vertical stress σ_z at a depth z below the corner A of a rectangular footing of width b and length a uniformly loaded by a unit pressure p.   (The derivation of the equation on which this chart is based is given in the 1st ed., Art. 9-6.)   It also serves to illustrate the influence of the ratio a/b of the lengths of the sides of the loaded rectangle (see Prob. 4-2).

The chart of Fig. 4-31 is well suited for the computation of pressures in cases where the loaded areas are continuous, such as foundation mats or rafts, and are composed of only a few rectangular areas.   When the foundation consists of a large number of individual footings, a chart developed by Newmark (Ref. 227) is more practical.   It is based on the following

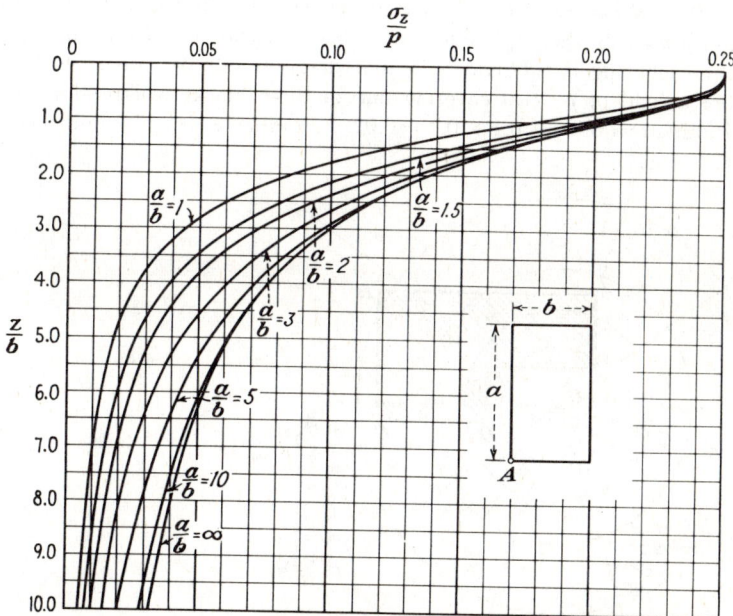

Fig. 4-31.   Chart for the computation of vertical stresses in the soil under the corner of a mat foundation.   (*After Steinbrenner in Ref. 34.*)

procedure.   The vertical stress σ_z at a depth z beneath the center of a circular, uniformly loaded area of radius r is equal to

$$\sigma_z = p\left[-1 + \frac{z^3}{(r^2 + z^2)^{3/2}}\right] \tag{4-19}$$

where p is the unit load on the circular area.   For the derivation of this equation see Timoshenko (Ref. 346).   It can be transformed to read

$$\frac{\sigma_z}{-p} = 1 - \left[\frac{1}{1 + (r/z)^2}\right]^{3/2} \tag{4-20}$$

It will be noted that when $r = \infty$, $\sigma_z/p = -1.0$, that is, $\sigma_z = -p$.   It is possible to determine from Eq. (4-20) the ratios r/z for which the ratio $\sigma_z/p = -0.8$ [Eq. (4-20)] gives $r/z = 1.387$.   By selecting some definite scale, for instance, the length OQ, as shown in Fig. 4-32, to represent the depth z, we obtain the length of the radius $r_{0.8}$ which corresponds to $\sigma_z/p = 0.8$ by multiplying the distance OQ by 1.387 and drawing a circle with that radius. This procedure can then be repeated for other values of σ_z/p, for instance, for $\sigma_z/p = 0.6$ and 0.4, as shown in Fig. 4-32.   The diagram thus obtained represents an influence chart for a surface unit load of unity $(p = 1.0)$. Thus the vertical stress σ_z will equal 0.8 if the entire circular area of radius $r_{0.8}$ is loaded by $p = 1.0$.   If only a ring between the radii $r_{0.8}$ and $r_{0.6}$ is loaded with $p = 1.0$, then $\sigma_z = 0.8 - 0.6 = 0.2$.   It will be noted from Fig. 4-32 that each ring is subdivided in that diagram into 10 equal blocks. Therefore a load of $p = 1.0$ covering one of these blocks will produce a vertical unit stress of $\sigma_z = 0.1 \times 0.2 = 0.02$.   In other words, the influence

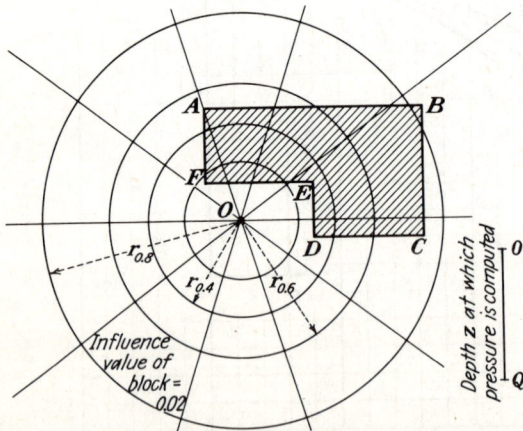

Fig. 4-32.   Use of the Newmark chart for the computation of vertical stresses in soils.   (*After Newmark, Ref. 237.*)

value of each loaded block is 0.02.   For values of p other than unity, the influence value of 0.02 of each loaded block should be multiplied by the actual value of p.

The computation procedure is as follows.   A plan of the foundation is drawn on tracing paper to such a scale that the distance OQ of the chart corresponds to the depth z at which the stress σ_z is to be computed (a different tracing has to be made for each different depth z).   The tracing of the foundation plan is then laid over the chart in such a way that the surface point, at a depth z beneath which the stress σ_z is to be computed, coincides with the center O of the chart.   The number of blocks covered by the foundation area $ABCDEF$ (see Fig. 4-32) is then counted.   This number is multiplied by the influence value of the blocks and by p.   The product thus obtained gives the value of σ_z for that particular point.   The charts used for actual computations have a much larger number of subdivisions than are shown in Fig. 4-32.   The influence values of the resulting blocks are correspondingly smaller, so that the evaluation of the areas covered by irregular-shaped foundation surfaces becomes easier.   Such charts, both for vertical and for horizontal stresses, are joined to Ref. 227.

The second step in the analysis of settlements on plastic clays is the laboratory *determination of* its compressibility, specifically of its *modulus of volume change m_v'* [see Eq. (3-32)].   Then the increment of vertical pressure caused by the foundation loads at several elevations of the underlying compressible layers is computed, as shown in Prob. 4-2.   The corresponding values of the moduli of volume change m_v' are determined from laboratory consolidation tests on undisturbed samples, as shown in Prob. 3-2.

The modulus of volume change m_v' can also be determined from available settlement records of structures in the same area by using Eq. (4-21).

It should be realized that soil samples are subject to many types of disturbance and that the verification of settlement forecasts by systematic regional field observations on actual structures is essential, as outlined in Art. 4-5.   Most observations carried out so far indicate that the observed settlements, as a rule, are somewhat smaller than the ones forecast on the strength of laboratory consolidation tests provided the yield point of the clay has not been exceeded.

Studies in Egypt (Ref. 350) have shown that settlements computed in the conventional manner from the first run of loading during a consolidation test were at least twice as large as those observed.   This was attributed to the initial expansion during sampling and after flooding in the consolidometer of the swelling type of local clays.   To counteract this effect, such samples were loaded up to the preconsolidation load (Art. 3-4C), which was first determined on a separate sample from the same layer.   Then the load was reduced to the value of the overburden at the elevation from which the sample was taken and was increased again.   This second run of loading (see Fig. 3-15) was then used to compute the m_v' values, which were found to agree quite

Computed from laboratory test results

Undisturbed. Not-flooded.	1st run	(1)
	2nd run	(2)
Undisturbed. Flooded.	1st run	(3)
	2nd run	(4)
Remolded.	1st run	(5)

$$m'_v = \frac{a'}{1+e_1} = \frac{e_1-e_2}{\Delta p(1+e_1)}$$

$m'_v = 0.001$ 0.002   0.004   0.006   0.010   0.020   0.040

$m'_v = 0.001$ 0.003   0.005   0.010   0.030 $\dfrac{s}{\Delta p H}$

Computed from observed settlements of buildings

Building "A"

Load reduced by weight of excavation	H_1	(6)
	H_2	(7)
Load not reduced by weight of excavation	H_1	(8)
	H_2	(9)

BUILDING "A"

Building "B"

Load reduced by weight of excavation	H	(10)
Load reduced by weight of excavation	H	(11)

BUILDING "B"

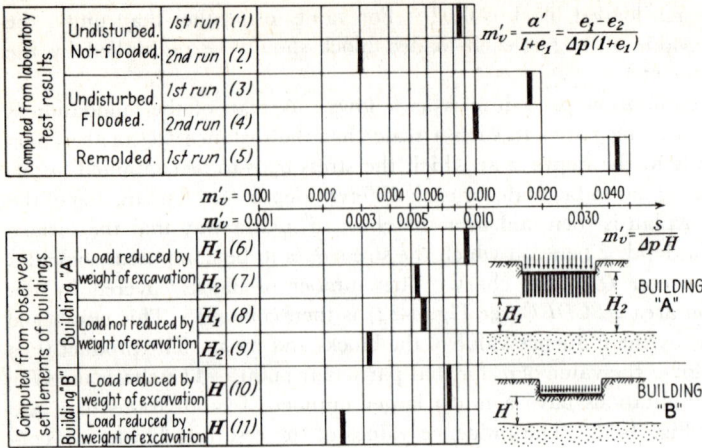

Fig. 4-33. Comparison of values of the modulus of volume change m'_v computed from the average results of different laboratory consolidation-test procedures and from settlement observations of two buildings, A and B. (*From Tschebotarioff and Schuyler, Ref. 380.*)

closely with the values computed from measurements of full-scale structures. Similar results were obtained through the application of the same procedure to compact varved clays at Albany, New York (Ref. 380), as shown in Fig. 4-33. This diagram brings out the various other factors which have to be considered when comparing the results of field settlement measurements and laboratory consolidation tests by means of the m'_v values. The m'_v laboratory values of that diagram refer to the range of pressure caused by an increment of 1 ton/ft² (1 kg$_f$/cm²) in excess of the overburden pressure at the depth from which the soil sample was extracted.

The compressibility of saturated clays can vary appreciably. Thus observations of structures show that naturally consolidated soft clays and silts may have m'_v values varying from 0.010 to 0.060 ft²/ton, whereas stiffer, overconsolidated clays (which acquired these characteristics, for instance, by past drying) will have m'_v values varying between 0.003 and 0.010 ft²/ton and recent marsh deposits up to 0.130 ft²/ton = 0.130 cm²/kg$_f$.

Once the thickness h of a compressible clay layer, the average increment of pressure Δp on that layer, and its modulus of volume change m'_v are known, *the final value of its* total compression or *settlement S* can be computed from

$$S = m'_v \, \Delta p \, h \qquad (4\text{-}21)$$

Both Δp and m'_v are taken in respect to an initial point on the log scale of pressures corresponding to the existing overburden weight (see Prob. 3-2). The settlements for each layer are then computed and added up to give the final value of the surface settlement, as shown in Prob. 4-4.

The last step in the settlement analysis of a structure resting on plastic clay is the *determination of the rate of settlement*. Let us assume that borings in the field have revealed the thickness of the deposit and the nature of the drainage conditions at its boundaries. In this connection it should be remembered that if these conditions are as shown in Fig. 3-16(I)—except that drainage is possible toward one boundary only, for instance when the clay deposit is underlain by sound, unfissured, and therefore impervious rock—then the centerline *OO* in Fig. 3-16(I) should be moved down to the bottom of the clay layer, so that the value H in Eqs. (3-39) and (4-22) should refer to the entire thickness of the clay stratum instead of just one half.

Let us further consider that the necessary laboratory tests have been performed, so that the values of the permeability coefficient k (Art. 8-1), of the modulus of volume change m_v (Art. 3-4C), and hence of the coefficient of consolidation c_v [Eq. (3-38)] are known. The subsequent steps for the computation of the time which will elapse until a certain percentage of consolidation is reached are as follows:

1. Select the TU curve in Fig. 4-34 which most closely corresponds to the actual boundary conditions of the case being studied.

2. Read off from the selected curve in Fig. 4-34 the value of T_v which corresponds to the percentage of consolidation U for which we want to find the time t.

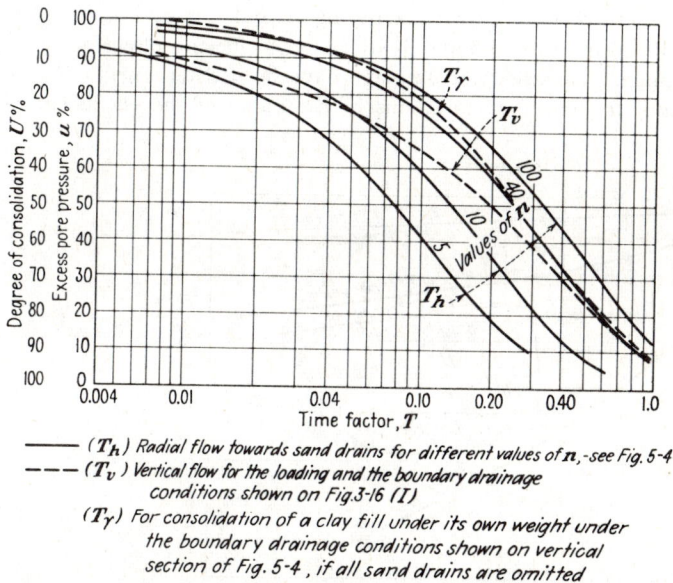

——— (T_h) *Radial flow towards sand drains for different values of n,-see Fig. 5-4*
- - - (T_v) *Vertical flow for the loading and the boundary drainage conditions shown on Fig.3-16 (I)*
    (T_γ) *For consolidation of a clay fill under its own weight under the boundary drainage conditions shown on vertical section of Fig. 5-4 , if all sand drains are omitted*

Fig. 4-34. Some time factors T for different conditions of loading and drainage. (*After Ref. 24.*)

3. Insert the value of T_v found under 2 into the modified equation (3-39)—for water $\gamma_w = 1.00$—from which equation the desired value of t can be computed.

$$t = \frac{m_v}{k} H^2 T_v = \frac{1}{c_v} H^2 T_v \qquad (4\text{-}22)$$

It will be noted that the time which elapses until a certain percentage of consolidation is reached is independent of the intensity of the applied pressure p which causes the consolidation. The reasons are as follows. A higher value of p produces more total compression of the clay and hence, as compared to a lower value of p, will have to expel from the voids a larger amount of excess water. But, simultaneously, the higher value of p will cause a larger hydraulic gradient S along the depth of the clay layer and hence also a higher velocity of outward flow. The two effects counterbalance each other, and the rate of consolidation theoretically remains unchanged by differences in the intensity of the pressure p.

The two most important factors which influence the rate of consolidation are the permeability coefficient k and the thickness H of the layer, i.e., the maximum distance which the excess water has to travel until it reaches a pervious boundary.

The application of this principle and of the relevant T values of Fig. 4-34 to settlement acceleration by means of sand drains is given in Art. 5-2.

The rate of settlement of a structure resting on a clay layer can be determined as outlined in Probs. 3-3 and 3-4 once the coefficients of permeability and the boundary conditions of drainage have been determined. Figure 4-35 illustrates the effect of variations in the value of the coefficient of

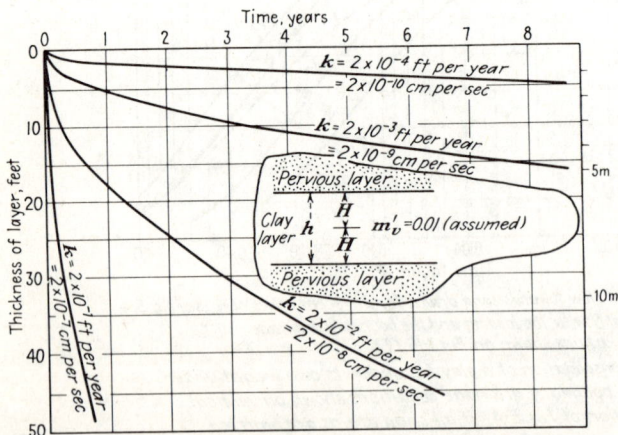

Fig. 4-35. Time required to reach 90 percent consolidation of homogeneous clay layer (based on Terzaghi's theory of consolidation).

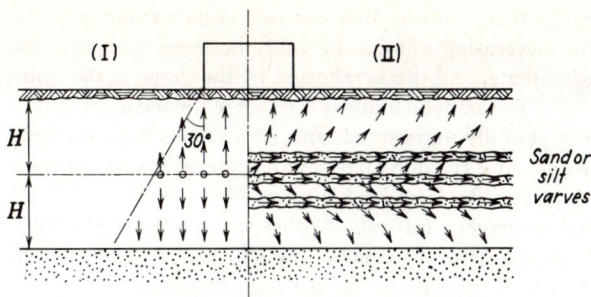

Fig. 4-36. Why structures on varved clays (II) settle much faster than on homogeneous clays (I). Arrows indicate direction of excess-water flow.

permeability and of a uniform layer thickness on the time which will elapse until 90 percent of the final settlements will occur. This diagram refers to the simplest type of boundary conditions, as shown, and to an assumed value of its modulus of volume change $m'_v = 0.01$ ft²/ton (0.01 cm²/kg$_f$). A higher value of m'_v will mean that more excess water will have to be expelled from the voids, so that settlements will take somewhat longer.

When the horizontal permeability of a clay layer is greater than the vertical one ($k_h > k_v$), this can greatly accelerate its consolidation for reasons shown by the sketch in Fig. 4-36.

The *settlements* of structures erected *on varved-clay layers* (Fig. 6-20 gives an example) have been found to *develop much more rapidly* than could be expected from a conventional analysis based on the vertical permeability and on escape of excess water in a vertical direction only. This is because the excess water expelled from the voids can travel laterally along the more pervious silt varves [Fig. 4-36(II)] and then upward over a much greater horizontal area than in a homogeneous clay mass [Fig. 4-36(I)].

The rate of settlements determined from Eq. (4-22) refers to the component thereof due to primary consolidation only (see Art. 3-4D and last paragraph of Art. 4-5).

In certain types of clays the *secondary time effects* are very pronounced, to the extent that in some cases the entire time-compression curve has the shape of an almost straight sloping line when plotted to a semilogarithmic scale, instead of the typical inverted S shape of the curve of clays with pronounced primary consolidation effects. These so-called *secondary time effects* are a phenomenon somewhat analogous to the *creep* of other overstressed materials in a plastic state. A delayed progressive slippage of grain upon grain, or plate upon plate, as the particles adjust themselves to a denser condition, appears to be responsible for these secondary effects. Possibly some creep of the bent platelike clay particles themselves may also be a contributing factor. When the rate of such plastic deformations of the individual soil particles, or of their slippage on each other, is slower than the rate of the expulsion of the excess water from the decreasing volume of voids between the particles, secondary effects predominate, and this is reflected by the shape of the time-compression curve.   The factors which affect the rate of the secondary compression of soils are not yet fully understood, and no methods have yet been developed for the rigorous and reliable analyses and forecasts of the magnitude of these effects (see Arts. 3-4D and 3-5D).

Here again regional settlement records of other structures are the most reliable guide to the magnitude of secondary time effects to be expected on local types of soils when their yield point has not been exceeded.

A simplified method of settlement analysis is illustrated by Fig. 4-37.   It can be useful for footings resting on sand or other noncohesive soils, undisturbed samples of which cannot be obtained for laboratory testing.   This method, as applied to a square footing, consists in assuming that the surface load $P = pb^2$ is carried by a truncated pyramid.   The surface settlement S will then equal the compression of the entire pyramid of height H.   This will be the sum of the compressive strains ϵ of all of the successive horizontal layers dH of the pyramid.   Each of these successive layers occupies a horizontal area $A = (b + 2H \tan \alpha)^2$.   If the Young modulus of the material of the pyramid is E, it has been shown (1st ed., Art. 9-1) that for $\alpha = 30°$ and a square footing

$$S = 0.867 \frac{pb}{E} C_s \qquad (4\text{-}23)$$

This value is only 39 percent smaller than that given by the rigorous solution of Timoshenko [Ref. 346, eq. (206)] for a square footing and $\nu = 0.5$.

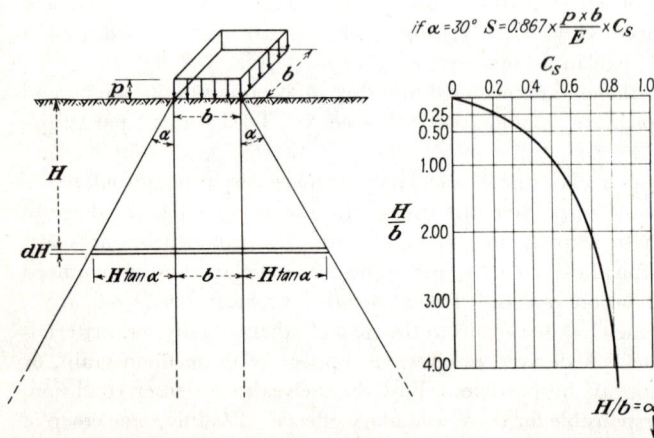

Fig. 4-37.   Compression S of a truncated pyramid of elastic material uniformly loaded over its top surface.

For values of $H < \infty$ the value of the compression S, as given by Eq. (4-23), must be multiplied by a coefficient $C_s < 1$. Values of this coefficient are given in graphical form on the right-hand side of Fig. 4-37. Problem 4-1 illustrates the practical application of this procedure.

Equation (4-23) holds for a square footing. For a footing of width b and an infinite length we can obtain in a similar manner, for $\alpha = 30°$,

$$S = 2.0 \frac{pb}{E} \log\left(1 + \frac{1.154H}{b}\right) \tag{4-24}$$

4-7. Design for Permissible Settlements. It is no longer customary to attempt the estimation of the settlements of structures from the results of load tests on small footings. The theoretical reasons for this have been outlined in Art. 4-1 and have been confirmed by numerous field observations and records (see, for instance, the discussion of Fig. 4-8 at the end of Art. 4-2 and Prob. 4-1).

General indications of allowable soil pressures can be obtained from building codes, e.g., from the 1968 Building Code of New York City (Ref. 228). Table 4-3 summarizes the main recommendations of Art. C26-1103.4 of the code. The symbols SW, CL, etc., are those of the Unified soil classification (see Art. 3-7C). It will be noted from Table 4-3 that the N value—the number of blows per foot obtained from the SPT (Art. 2-4A)—serves as a basis for determining the permissible bearing value of sands. The value of N is obtained by averaging the resistances measured within a depth of soil below the proposed footing level equal to the width b of the footing. A number of detailed supplementary provisions are given in Ref. 228.

It can be seen from Fig. 4-38 that the New York City code recommendation setting the permissible loading in tons per square foot as equal to $0.1N$ blows/ft corresponds fairly closely to an earlier semiempirical recommendation by Terzaghi and Peck (Ref. 344) for the design of footings on dry or moist sand if the maximum settlement is not to exceed 1 in. For saturated sands Terzaghi and Peck recommended the decrease of pressures to one-half or two-thirds of the values obtained from a chart on which Fig. 4-38 is based. This distinction between saturated sands and dry or moist ones does not appear to have been retained by the 1968 New York City code. It had been criticized as too conservative by Meyerhof (Ref. 216). In addition, on the strength of analyses of field observations, Meyerhof recommended increasing by 50 percent the original Terzaghi and Peck values. These increased values are also shown on Fig. 4-38.

None of the values given by Fig. 4-38 apply to *loose sands* ($N = 10$ blows/ft or less) when such sands may be subjected to *vibrations*. Such sands should be first compacted (see Chap. 5) if spread footings are to be used. Otherwise piles should be resorted to.

Other procedures for determining settlements of spread footings on sands have been tried with varying degrees of success. They include settlement

TABLE 4-3.   **Some Allowable Soil Pressures†**

Class of material	Description	Allowable bearing values, tons/ft^2 (or kg$_f$/cm^2)
1-65	Hard sound rock	60
2-65	Medium hard rock	40
3-65	Intermediate rock	20
4-65	Soft rock	8
5-65	Hardpan, Well cemented	12
	Poorly cemented	8
6-65	Gravel and gravel soils (groups GW, GP, GM, GC):	
	compact, well graded	10
	loose, poorly graded	6
	(Groups SW, SP, SM, more than 10% ret. No. 4 sieve):	
	compact, well graded	8
	loose, poorly graded	4
7-65	Sands, other than fine (groups SW, SP, SM, less than 10% ret. No. 4 sieve), $0.1N$ within limits	6-3
8-65	Fine sand, $0.1N$ within the limits	4-2
9-65	Clays and clay soils (groups SC, CL, CH):	
	Hard (strength tests and $F > 2$ required)	5
	Medium (strength tests and $F > 2$ required)	2
	Soft (stability and settlement analysis required)	
10-65	Silt and silt soils (groups ML, MH):	
	Dense	2
	Medium	1.5
	Loose (stability and settlement analysis required)	
11-65	Nominally unsatisfactory materials—fills, peat, organic, or varved silts—see special provisions	

† After New York City Building Code, Ref. 228.

predictions from plate load tests and from laboratory oedometer and triaxial tests, using the stress-path method (Art. 1-11). A comparison of these and of the customary SPT method with the results of extensive field measurements at a site on the south shore of Lake Michigan was made by D'Appolonia et al. (Ref. 10). Plate load tests were found to be the least reliable; laboratory tests, combined with the stress-path method, gave good results. However, forecasts on the basis of such tests are very difficult to perform and require special knowledge. Meyerhof's modification of the Terzaghi and Peck SPT procedure (see Fig. 4-38) came closest to reality but even so was somewhat conservative.

The comparisons of Ref. 10 also showed that differential settlements between adjacent footings of similar size and bearing pressure rarely exceed 50 percent of the total settlement, confirming the suggestion of Terzaghi and Peck in Ref. 344.

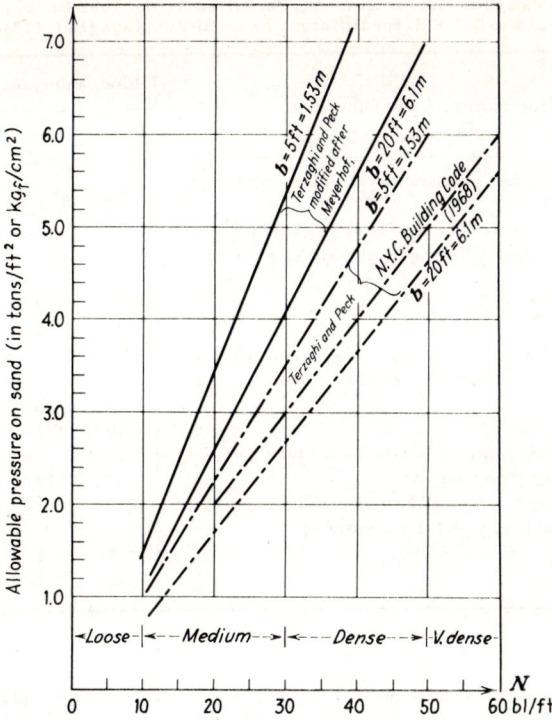

Fig. 4-38. Suggested relationships between permissible spread-footing loads on sand and the resistance of the sand to SPT.

An attempt to relate the maximum permissible average settlement to the type of superstructure employed was made in the 1962 Building Code of the Soviet Union (Ref. 113) (see Table 4-4). For sandy soils and *non*collapsible (Art. 3-7E) hard clay soils with a liquidity index [Eq. (3-17)] $I_L < 0$, according to art. 5-24 of Ref. 113, settlements may be considered as having ended during the period of construction if the rate of load increase on the foundation base does not exceed 1 kg_f/cm^2 (1 ton/ft²) per month.

For plastic clay soils structural foundation designs should be accompanied by settlement forecasts (see Art. 4-6). The yield point of the clay [Eq. (4-3)] should never be exceeded. The *provision of a basement has a beneficial effect,* in the sense that the excavation of the soil for the basement increases the ultimate load that the soil can carry by decreasing the danger of a shear failure under a mat covering the entire area. However, the ultimate or yield load on separate spread footings, when such are used, remains unaffected by basement excavation in a soil whose properties do not change with depth.

TABLE 4-4.   Limit Values of Settlements S_{lim} Permitted by the 1962 Building
Code of the U.S.S.R. for Different Types of Buildings (Ref. 113)

Type of superstructure and foundation	Limit value, S_{lim}	
	cm	in.
1. Buildings of large precast panels or blocks without a structural frame	8	3.15
2. Buildings with nonreinforced brick or large-block walls on strip or isolated spread footings for ratios of wall length L to its height H:		
$L/H \geq 2.5$	8	3.15
$L/H \leq 1.5$	10	4.00
3. Buildings with brick or large-block walls strengthened by reinforced-concrete or armored brick belts (irrespective of the ratio L/H)	15	6.00
4. Fully framed buildings	10	4.00
5. Monolithic reinforced concrete foundations of blast furnaces, smokestacks, silos, water towers, etc.	30	12.00
6. Foundations of one-story-high industrial buildings and similarly structured buildings with column spans of:		
6 m (19.7 ft)	8†	3.15
12 m (39.4 ft)	12†	4.72

† Total settlements.

Subject to some important limitations, an excavation for a basement may serve to decrease the settlements of the building.   These limitations were not realized at first (see 1st ed., Art. 13-6).   First, the clay bottom must not be allowed to swell due to expansion caused by the absorption of water after removal of the weight of the excavation.   Rapid construction is therefore important.   Second, the bottom of the excavation should not be allowed to heave due to shearing deformations in the underlying clay (see Arts. 9-3 and 11-4).   Otherwise, not only will this heaving be reversed once load is reapplied, but the clay, if sensitive, will be remolded and its compressibility increased by such deformations.

4-8. Measures for Special Conditions.   *(A). Permafrost.*   A basic rule of construction in temperate climates is never to found structures on frozen ground.   This means in effect that foundations should be carried down below the depth of frost penetration, since volume changes of the ground during freezing and thawing would otherwise produce uncontrollable motions of the foundations.   The depth of frost penetration, and hence the minimum depth of the foundations, varies in different localities.

The principle that foundations should rest on soil layers not subject to seasonal volume changes, i.e., *not* on the so-called *active layers*, is valid everywhere.   The methods for the implementation of this principle, however, are reversed in the so-called *permafrost* regions of the far north.   In a large part of Siberia and in certain areas of Alaska and of Canada the ground remains eternally frozen below a certain depth.   Above this layer of permanent frost, *permafrost,* the active layer thaws out in the summer and freezes again in the winter.   This poses numerous problems in highway design and construction (1st ed., Art. 19-7).   As in temperate zones, the depth of the active layer varies with the locality and with its climate.   Buildings founded on the active layer of the permafrost zones invariably suffer heavy damage because heat will flow from a building into the permafrost, as sketched on Fig. 4-39. The permafrost will thaw and lose its supporting capacity.

Structures are therefore founded on the eternally frozen ground which is not subject to volume changes so long as it *stays* frozen.   Properly designed foundations should prevent the transmission of heat to the ground from the building, since this might lower the elevation of the permafrost surface under the building.   Some measures to that effect, as employed for small structures in Siberia, are illustrated by Fig. 4-40.   A timber grillage is interposed between the concrete or masonry footing and the permanently frozen ground; timber is a fairly good thermic insulator and will not decay when frozen.   The faces of footings within the active layer are sloped as shown in the sketch and are coated with smooth cement-plaster finish and asphalt. These measures are intended to facilitate the separation of the soil from the footing when the active layer freezes and heaves in the winter.   The lower floor of the building is thoroughly insulated, but an air space connected to the outside is left between the floor and the ground.   Piles jetted into the permafrost zone by means of a steam jet are sometimes used in Alaska instead of footings.   Fiber glass is used there for insulation.   A comprehensive description of various relevant problems is given in the Proceedings of the 1963 International Conference on Permafrost (Ref. 45).

(B). Refrigerator Foundations.   Refrigerator plants have been frequently damaged by uneven heaving of the ground which froze beneath them. Apparently the most elaborate insulation could not prevent such freezing over a long period of time.   These conclusions were substantiated by

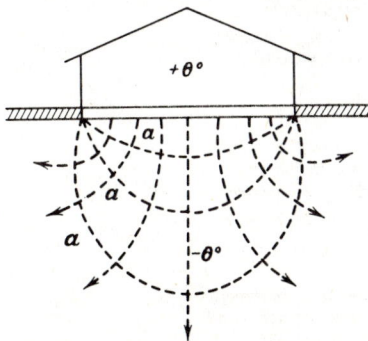

Fig. 4-39. Flow of heat from a building resting on permafrost and the resulting isothermal lines *a.* (*After Tsytovich, Ref. 386.*)

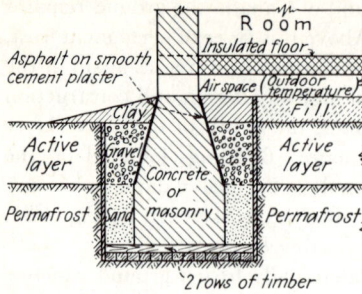

Fig. 4-40. Insulation of the wall footings of a building in the permafrost zone of Siberia. (*After Vassilieff, Ref. 390.*)

British measurements, reported by Cooling and Ward (Ref. 64). The provision of warm air vents between a thoroughly insulated floor of the refrigerator and the top of the foundation mat, as illustrated by Fig. 4-41, was tried out in the U.S.S.R. and was reported by Steuerman (Ref. 323) to have been successful.

Failure to realize the need for such measures can have unpleasant consequences even in subtropical regions when erecting refrigerator sheds. Figure 4-42 illustrates such a case investigated by the writer. A refrigerator shed built over saturated fine sand in central Florida in the 1950s developed a heave of some 18 in. (46 cm) at its center after a decade of operation. At the edges the heave was negligible. The resulting slope of the ice-covered asphaltic floor caused merchandise-moving forklift trucks to skid dangerously.

Three boreholes were then put down. At the center of the shed ice lenses (see Fig. 8-11, Art. 8-6) were found to reach some 23 ft (7 m) down, but they reached only a few feet at the edges. Apparently the " flow of cold " in this case followed the flow of heat according to Fig. 4-39. Later refrigerator sheds in the area were built with a grid of pipes under the floor filled with

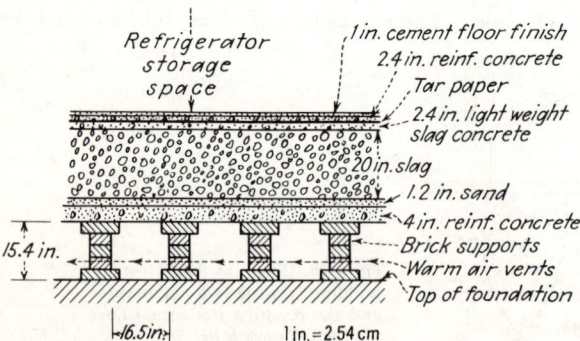

Fig. 4-41. Warm-air vents installed under an insulated basement floor of a U.S.S.R. refrigerator warehouse prevented freezing and heaving of the soil under the foundation. (*After Steuerman, Ref. 323.*)

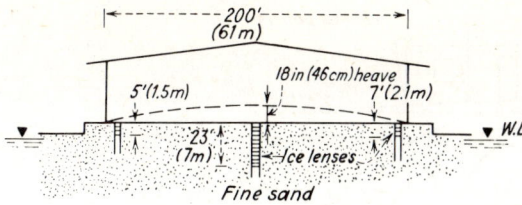

Fig. 4-42. Heaving (not to scale) of refrigerator storage shed floor in central Florida after a decade of operation.

a hot antifreeze-type liquid which was kept in constant motion by special pumps and reheated in the process.

(C). Furnace Foundations. A method of air-vent insulation similar to the one of Fig. 4-41 is proposed by Ward and Sewell (Ref. 396) for the insulation of furnaces. Numerical solutions of the effect of different insulation thicknesses are given in that paper. Several cases are on record where in the absence of such precautions the heat transmitted from furnaces through their foundation to underlying plastic clay caused uneven drying and shrinking. Serious damage to the whole structure resulted.

(D). Expansive (Swelling) Soils. In regions of heavy seasonal rainfall, for instance Burma (Ref. 410), some clay soils expand during the rainy season. This occurs mainly around the periphery of the building, so that the outer walls are frequently raised somewhat, mainly at the corners, with severe cracking resulting. Unit bearing pressures on the ground are therefore increased under such walls to the limit consistent with safety against shear failure. This is, however, only a partial remedy, since swelling pressures of some clays are extremely high. Proper drainage of the water away from the outer walls of a building by suitable slopes and by impervious coating of the soil surface is therefore necessary, as well as other similar measures. In cases of heavy buildings caissons are sometimes (Art. 6-10) carried down through the active (swelling) layer of clay, belled out in the inactive zone for anchorage, and suitably reinforced to resist tension.

The pattern of wall-crack inclinations which results from such heaving of the periphery of a building is similar to the one which follows larger settlements at its center [Fig. 4-25(II)], due to normal consolidation of deeper-lying layers.

A reverse situation may arise in regions of moderate rainfall when the center of a building founded on a clay prone to swelling may heave during dry spells. There are two possible explanations for this. The first is illustrated by Fig. 4-43.

Theoretical and experimental studies in the field of soil physics indicate that moisture has a tendency to migrate from warmer to colder soil zones, a phenomenon known as *thermoosmosis*. In hot climates a building shades the soil surface area which it occupies and thereby cools the layers beneath it.

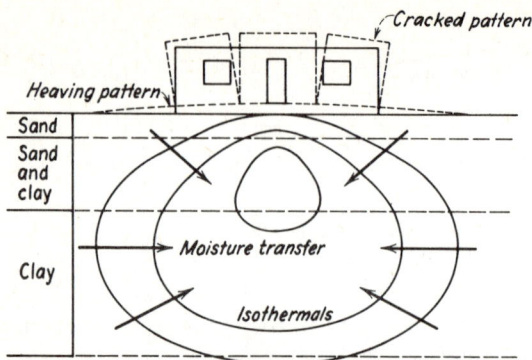

Fig. 4-43. Diagrammatic sketch of thermoosmotic heaving of building on desiccated clay foundation. (*After Jennings, Ref. 146.*)

The result is the migration of water, swelling of the desiccated clay, and heaving of the soil surface under the building, as shown by Fig. 4-43.

Another explanation is that a *building* resting directly on the surface of the ground *prevents normal evaporation* from beneath it, especially if its tiled floors are waxed, as they were in the case illustrated by Figs. 4-44 to 4-46. This case is illustrative of the severe cracking of a number of one-story houses at the Nicaro nickel mines in the Oriente province of Cuba, investigated by the writer in 1951 (Ref. 360). The houses were built on spread footings which rested on a mantle of surface clay, the predominent mineral of which was found to be montmorillonite (see Art. 3-1B), which has particularly high swelling properties. The plasticity indices of that clay varied from $I_p = 40$ percent to $I_p = 50$ percent ($w_L = 70$ to 90 percent; $w_p = 20$ to 30 percent). Outside the building the natural water content was just above the plastic

Fig. 4-44. Cracks in walls of a house shown in plan in Fig. 4-45. (*Photo 1 by Tschebotarioff.*)

limit, $w = 25$ to 35 percent. The clay mantle was underlain by soft rock, limestones and marls, locally known as "coco." Their surface was very irregular, with some deep clay-filled potholes and gullies.

To permit better ventilation of the rooms, the louvered window openings were carried right up to the roof, with no structural connections between the walls above the openings (Fig. 4-44). Further, because of World War II steel shortages when most of these houses were erected, no other reinforcing belts of any kind were provided in the masonry or in its strip footings.

The plan of the most badly damaged house is given in Fig. 4-45. Several closely spaced borings and pits showed that it was located over the edge of a more than 20-ft-deep (6.1-m) clay-filled gully in the coco, the side of which sloped away from the approximate line AA, in the direction shown by arrows. Elsewhere under the building the coco was found at a depth of only 4 to 5 ft (1.2 to 1.5 m).

It can be seen from Fig. 4-45 that the heaving was particularly pronounced in the part of the house beneath which the potentially swelling clay was deepest. The cracks in the walls shown by Figs. 4-44 and 4-46 correspond to the pattern of swelling indicated by the contour lines of the floor heave which were determined by leveling (Fig. 4-45).

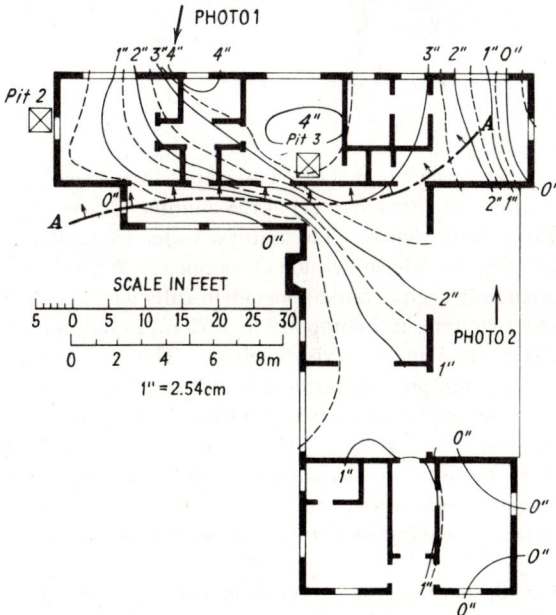

Fig. 4-45. Heaving of floors of house resting on a swelling clay, 5 ft (1.5 m) deep, except beyond line AA, where it was over 20 ft (6.1 m) deep. (*From Tschebotarioff, Ref. 360.*)

Fig. 4-46. Cracks in walls of a house shown in plan in Fig. 4-45. (*Photo 2 by Tschebotarioff, Ref. 360.*)

Block samples were taken at every 6 in. (15.2 cm) depth in the two pits, pit 2 (outside) and pit 3 (inside the heaved area) of the building, down to the water level at some 18 ft (5.5 m) depth. The natural water contents and the liquid and plastic limits were determined for all samples. Whereas the w_L and the w_p values varied only slightly and almost identically with depth in both pits, the natural water content in the upper 9 ft (2.75 m) of the interior pit 3 was markedly higher than in the outside pit 2. This total excess amount of water in the samples of pit 3 corresponded well to the 4-in. (10.2-cm) heave of the floor adjoining the location of that pit, as well as to the results of laboratory swell tests in a standard type of consolidometer.

A reverse direction of cracks to the one shown on Figs. 4-44 and 4-46 could be noted on some houses next to rainwater spouts with no grading drainage provisions. This indicated a heaving of the outside wall near the spout during rainy periods.

The walls of some later houses of the same general type were strengthened by continuous belts of reinforced concrete at the lintel, the windowsill, and the strip foundation levels. The rooms were made somewhat smaller. Some floors were found to have heaved up to 3 in. (7.6 cm) at their centers, but no cracks whatsoever developed in the reinforced walls. Therefore provision of reinforcing belts in the walls of houses erected on swell-prone (expansive) clay soils is always advisable.

Clays of high plasticity (CH group) with $w_L \geq 50$ percent and having a natural water content close to their plastic limit are particularly liable to swell during rainfall periods in semiarid regions. In the United States such conditions arise in some areas of Texas.

Seed, Woodward, and Lundgren discuss the swelling potential of compacted clays in Ref. 286a.

The provision of air-ventilation channels under floors, similar to the one shown on Fig. 4-41 for refrigerator plants but without thermal insulation, permits normal evaporation from beneath a building and hence inhibits swelling at its center. This method, combined with measures to carry away from the walls occasional runoff rainwater, has been successfully tried in some instances.

Two-story houses are less susceptible to damage, partly because of their greater weight and partly because of the greater structural strength of their walls.

A comprehensive description of *heave problems* in some areas of South Africa and of damage-prevention measures there is given by Jennings and Kerrich (Ref. 147). Depending on the range of the estimated heave, soil profiles in the area are divided into five groups:

Group	Amount of heave
Very good	$0-\frac{1}{4}$ in. (0–6.3 mm)
Good	$\frac{1}{4}-\frac{1}{2}$ in. (6.3–12.7 mm)
Fair	$\frac{1}{2}-2$ in. (12.7–51.0 mm)
Bad	2–4 in. (5.1–10.2 cm)
Very bad	>4 in. (>10.2 cm)

The heave is estimated on the basis of two oedometer, i.e., consolidometer, tests (Art. 3-4), and the thickness of expansive strata for each of the five categories is related to the thickness of the overlying nonexpansive soil cover.

Starting with the "fair" soil-profile category a *split-construction* building technique is recommended. It consists in splitting all walls by construction joints at wall intersections and at doors to permit seasonal opening and closing movements; in reinforcing the brickwork between the wall joints; and in suspending all floors. In addition to these measures, piles should be provided for houses on "bad" or "very bad" soil profiles.

(E). Collapsible (Loess) Soils. Loess soils on their original site of deposition are liable to cause trouble during the first rainy season following a new construction. The thin vertical channels left in the loess by decayed grass

roots are then likely to collapse under the combined action of the foundation loads and of percolating moisture. Considerable settlements of new structures are apt to result.

According to the 1962 U.S.S.R. Building Code the settlements $S_{p(col)}$ due to the collapse of the loess structure when wetted are to be estimated as follows:

$$S_{p(col)} = \sum_1^n \delta_{p(col)} H_{col} m \qquad (4\text{-}25)$$

where $\delta_{p(col)}$ = coefficient of relative collapsibility defined by Eq. (3-57)

H_{col} = thickness of soil layer to which $\delta_{p(col)}$ refers, cm

n = number of layers

m = coefficient, taken to a depth of $1.5b$ as $m = 2.0$ when smallest foundation dimension in plan is $b = 0.5$ to 2.0 m (1.6 to 6.6 ft)

$m = 1.0$ when $b > 2.0$ m (6.6 ft)

    1.0   for all soil layers below a depth of $1.5b$, irrespective of the value of b

The $S_{p(col)}$ values computed for Eq. (4-25) should not exceed the permissible limit settlement values S_{lim} given by Table 4-4 for different types of structures. Otherwise compaction of the active layer of such primary loess deposits becomes essential if spread footings are to be used. Such compaction can be accomplished by several methods, described in Art. 5-4. Otherwise, piles carried down into the inactive layer should be used (Fig. 6-11). The active layers h_1 are not relied on for support.

In all cases, graded slopes with bituminous cover should drain surface water away from the structure.

(F). Sinkhole Areas. The way in which a *sinkhole* is formed is illustrated by Fig. 4-47. Water flowing through soil toward fissures in the underlying surface of cavernous limestone gradually washes some of the soil through the rock fissures into the caverns below. An upper cavern then gradually develops in the soil and grows in size upward from the rock surface. When the roof of that second cavern becomes fairly thin, it collapses under its own weight, forming a so-called sinkhole. A case where a footing of a factory shed over a newly formed sinkhole remained hanging by its column from the reinforced-concrete roof, which cracked and was deflected to form a catenary, as shown in Fig. 4-47, has actually occurred.

Seepage into the soil of industrial waste from defective, leaking sewers may accelerate the formation of sinkholes, especially if the underlying limestone is fissured by a fault. Carlton Proctor (Ref. 256) cites a case where an industrial plant in Tennessee was by chance located right over such a faulted and fissured zone of limestone and suffered considerable and recurring damage because of the formation of sinkholes beneath it. Expensive cap grouting

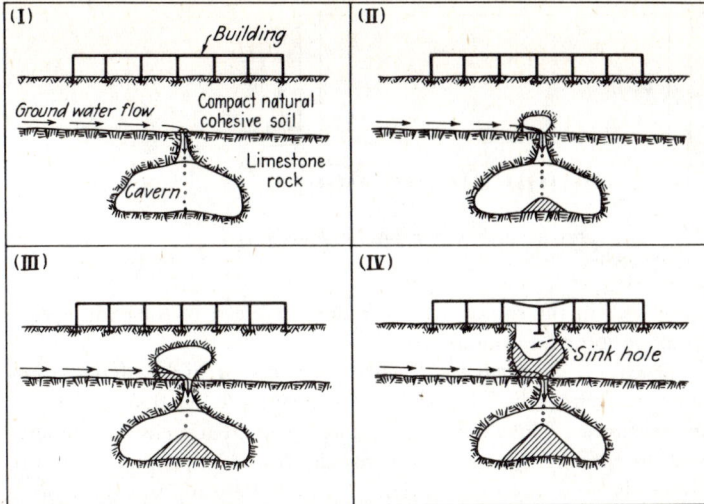

Fig. 4-47. Steps in the formation of sinkholes in cavernous limestone regions.

by a 1 : 1 : 8 mixture of cement, bentonite, and fine sand had to be resorted to, in order to seal off the surface of the fissured rock. A similar plant, located only a couple of miles away, did not have any sinkhole trouble. It was found that it lay outside the fissured zone of the fault and that an intact cover of shale protected the surface of the limestone there.

Drainage of not only surface water but subsurface water as well away from the area to be occupied by a new structure is an essential precaution in sink-hole-prone areas. Continuous mat foundations for the floors may help to some extent in bridging smaller sinkholes that may develop between columns supported on piles reaching into sound limestone rock. However, any construction in such areas involves inevitable hazards since the probable location of sinkholes cannot be accurately predicted without exorbitantly costly numerous deep borings.

(G). Antiuplift Measures. Some foundations, of the type shown on Fig. 4-48, have to be made in the shape of a hollow box to house sewage-treatment machinery or similar equipment. Their construction will frequently require temporary groundwater lowering (Art. 9-6). When built on pervious sand deposits located in low-lying areas subject to flooding, they can be endangered by uplift forces $h\gamma_w$ if a sudden flood raises the high-water level almost to their brim while they are still empty. Cantilevering the base slab to a distance L' beyond the outer perimeter of the walls can then help prevent the box from floating by adding to the dead weight of the box the weight $V\gamma'$ of buoyed soil, where V is the volume of the soil above the cantilevered rim and γ' is the buoyed unit weight of the soil [Eq. (3-10)].

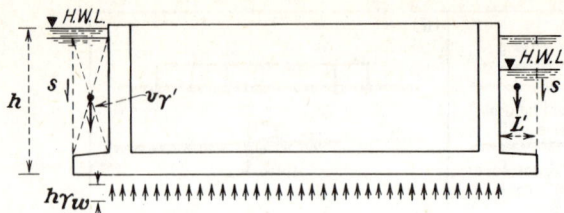

Fig. 4-48. Measures to prevent flotation of hollow box foundation in pervious sand due to high floodwater levels.

Shearing stresses s in the soil above the outer perimeter of the cantilevered slab will provide some additional safety.

(H). Anchorages of Transmission Towers. Towers of high-voltage transmission lines are frequently subjected to overturning forces due to wind or uneven line tensions. These overturning forces can create tension in one or more legs of the tower. This tension is usually resisted by footings with an enlarged base placed at a sufficient depth so that the weight of the footing and the soil above it can resist the uplift forces applied to it (see pullout tests reported by Killer, Ref. 162).

This procedure, however, leads to very large and uneconomical footing dimensions when uplift loads reach values of 600 to 800 kips (270 to 370 metric tons) per leg, as happens in towers which form part of a river span or where the lines turn at a large angle in plan (see Robinson, Ref. 214, pp. 126–130, and Adams and Klym, Ref. 2). Grouted anchors are then used in sand, gravel, stiff clay, glacial till, or rock. Holes 6 in. (15.3 cm) in diameter for approximately $1\frac{1}{2}$-in.-diameter (3.8-cm) steel anchors are drilled into the soil to depths of 10 to 50 ft (3 to 15 m), and the space around the rods is filled with sand-cement grout. In medium to stiff clays or in loose sands multihelix anchors are screwed into the soil to appreciable depths, up to 130 ft (40 m) in soft-clay areas.

REVIEW PROBLEMS

4-1. Prior to the construction of the heavy stockhouse illustrated by Figs. 2-18 and 4-21 a load test was performed on a 2 by 2 ft (61 by 61 cm) footing which rested on the surface of the sand layer, which was 70 ft (21 m) deep. The settlement of the footing under a unit load of 3.7 tons/ft² was 0.36 in. (9.1 mm). What will be the probable settlement of the 90 by 100 ft (27 by 30 m) structure under the same unit loading if we assume that the coefficient of compressibility of the sand has the same value throughout its depth?

Answer. With reference to Fig. 4-37, the ratio H/b of the footing is $\frac{7.0}{2} = 35$ and hence approaches infinity in respect to its influence on the coefficient C_s, which can therefore be taken as $C_s = 1.0$. Substituting the relevant values in Eq. (4-23), we obtain

$$0.36 = 0.867 \times 3.7 \times 2.0 \times 12 \times 1.0 \frac{1}{E} = 77.0 \frac{1}{E}$$

or

$$\frac{1}{E} = 0.0047 \, (= m_v')$$

For the building itself, $H/b = \frac{70}{90} = 0.78$ and, from Fig. 4-37, $C_s = 0.45$. Substituting these values in Eq. (4-23), we obtain

$$S = 0.867 \times 3.7 \times 90 \times 12 \times 0.78 \times 0.0047 = 7.3 \text{ in.}$$

It will be noted from Fig. 4-21 that the final settlement of the structure proved to be approximately 3.5 in. (8.9 cm). The actually measured value is thus approximately half of that to be expected from the surface test. The explanation of this discrepancy lies in the fact that the density of the sand layer increased with depth, as evidenced by its increased resistance with depth to penetration testing (see Fig. 2-18).

4-2. A 50 by 30 ft (15 by 9 m) foundation mat is uniformly loaded to an average intensity of $p = 1.7$ tons/ft² over its entire area. Compute the resulting unit vertical pressure σ_z on a plane $z = 45$ ft (13.7 m) below the bottom of the mat under points A, F, K, and N in Fig. 4-49.

Answer:

1. Point A (also points B, D, and E). With reference to Fig. 4-31, we obtain the ratios $z/b = \frac{45}{30} = 1.5$ and $a/b = \frac{50}{30} = 1.67$, with which we find from the chart $\sigma_z/p = 0.15$, so that $\sigma_z = 0.15 \times 1.7 = 0.255$ ton/ft² $= 0.250$ kg$_f$/cm².

2. Point F at the center of the mat. We have to find the effect of one-quarter of the area of the mat (rectangle $ATFQ$) and multiply it by 4. For the area $ATFQ$ $z/b = \frac{45}{15} = 3.0$ and $a/b = \frac{25}{15} = 1.67$, so that, from the chart in Fig. 4-31, $\sigma_z/p = 0.067$ and $\sigma_z = 4 \times 0.067 \times 1.7 = 0.455$ ton/ft² $= 0.446$ kg$_f$/cm².

3. Point K outside the area of the mat. We have to find the effect of the rectangle $GBMK$, subtract from it the effects of $ASKG$ and $HKME$, and add the effect of $HDSK$.

Rectangle $GBMK$: $\dfrac{z}{b} = \dfrac{45}{40} = 1.12 \qquad \dfrac{a}{b} = \dfrac{60}{40} = 1.5 \qquad$ from chart $\dfrac{\sigma_z}{p} = 0.185$

Rectangle $ASKG$: $\dfrac{z}{b} = \dfrac{45}{10} = 4.5 \qquad \dfrac{a}{b} = \dfrac{40}{10} = 4.0 \qquad$ from chart $\dfrac{\sigma_z}{p} = 0.055$

Rectangle $HKME$: $\dfrac{z}{b} = \dfrac{45}{10} = 4.5 \qquad \dfrac{a}{b} = \dfrac{60}{10} = 6.0 \qquad$ from chart $\dfrac{\sigma_z}{p} = 0.065$

Rectangle $HDSK$: $\dfrac{z}{b} = \dfrac{45}{10} = 4.5 \qquad \dfrac{a}{b} = \dfrac{10}{10} = 1.0 \qquad$ from chart $\dfrac{\sigma_z}{p} = 0.022$

The total effect is

$$\sigma_z = (0.185 - 0.055 - 0.065 + 0.022) \times 1.7 = 0.148 \text{ ton/ft}^2 = 0.145 \text{ kg}_f/\text{cm}^2$$

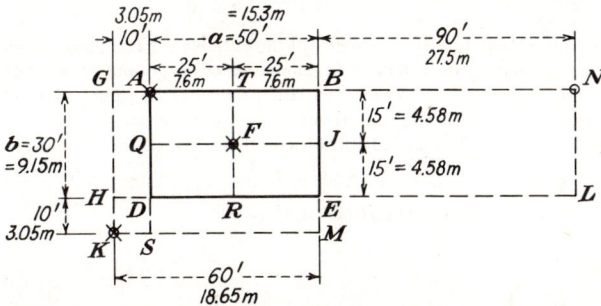

Fig. 4-49. Diagram illustrating Prob. 4-2.

This last computation illustrates the circumstance that in order to compute the effect of a number of isolated footings, the use of the chart in Fig. 4-32 is more convenient.

4. Point N outside the area of the mat. We would have to take the effect of the rectangle $ANLD$ and subtract from it the effect of $BNLE$; for the latter $z/b = \frac{45}{30} = 1.5$ and $a/b = \frac{90}{30} = 3.0$. From the chart in Fig. 4-31 we find that the curve $a/b = 3.0$ almost merges with the curve $a/b = \infty$ for the ratio $z/b = 1.5$. Therefore, even if the loaded area extended from BE well beyond AD to infinity, no measurable increase of σ_z would be produced at a depth $z = 45$ ft (13.8 m) below the point N.

4-3. A 16-story building is erected on a 70 by 100 ft (21 by 30 m) mat resting on a 120-ft-deep (36.6-m) layer of clay with an average unconfined compressive strength $q_u = 1.1$ tons/ft² (1.1 kg$_f$/cm²). The unit pressure on the clay is $p = 2.0$ tons/ft². What is the factor of safety against a shear failure of the clay if the bottom of the mat is 3 ft (91 cm) below the ground surface? Compare the result with Table 4-1.

Answer. From $c = q_u/2 = 0.55$ ton/ft² and Eq. (4-8)

$$p_{max} = 5.52 \times 0.55(1 + 0.38\tfrac{3}{70} + 0.44\tfrac{70}{120}) = 3.87 \text{ tons/ft}^2$$
$$= 3.80 \text{ kg}_f/\text{cm}^2$$

The factor of safety is

$$F_s = \frac{p_{max}}{p} = \frac{3.87}{2.00} = 1.93 \qquad \text{(too low)}$$

4-4. Estimate the final value of the settlement which will be caused by the consolidation under the weight of the new fill of the soft clay layer shown in Fig. 2-9. Assume for the first estimation that the full weight of the fill will be effective throughout the depth of the layer at the location of borehole 2, that the fill weighs 125 lb/ft³ (2.0 g$_f$/cm³) above the water level (el. ± 0.0 ft) and 65 lb/ft³ (1.04 g$_f$/cm³) below that level, and that the average value of the modulus of volume change of the soft clay is $m_v' = 0.060$ ft²/ton (0.060 cm²/kg$_f$) between the elevations -10 and -20 ft (-3.05 and -6.1 m) and $m_v' = 0.040$ ft²/ton (0.040 cm²/kg$_f$) between the elevations -20 and -40 ft (-61 and -12.2 m).

Answer. The fill weighs

$$12 \times 125 = 1{,}500 \text{ lb/ft}^2$$
$$10 \times 65 = 650 \text{ lb/ft}^2$$
$$\overline{2{,}150 \text{ lb/ft}^2} = 1.075 \text{ tons/ft}^2 \ (1.055 \text{ kg}_f/\text{cm}^2)$$

With reference to Eq. (3-33), the final settlement is found to be

$$S_1 = 10 \times 0.060 \times 1.075 \times 12 = 7.75 \text{ in.}$$
$$S_2 = 20 \times 0.040 \times 1.075 \times 12 = 10.35 \text{ in.}$$
$$S = \overline{18.10 \text{ in.}} \ (46.0 \text{ cm})$$

4-5. With reference to Fig. 4-30, by what amount will the effective vertical pressures on the underlying layers be changed by a 4.5-m (14.7-ft) fluctuation of the groundwater level? Assume that the soil within the range of water-level variation remains fully saturated at all times, that its specific gravity is $G = 2.7$, and that its void ratio is $e = 1.00$.

Answer. With reference to Eqs. (3-8) and (3-10), we find that when saturated by capillarity the soil weighs

$$\frac{2.7 + 1.0}{1 + 1.0} \times 62.4 = 115.5 \text{ lb/ft}^3 \ (1.85 \text{ g}_f/\text{cm}^3)$$

When buoyed, it weighs

$$\frac{2.7 - 1}{1 + 1.0} \times 62.4 = 53.1 \text{ lb/ft}^3 \ (0.84 \text{ g}_f/\text{cm}^3)$$

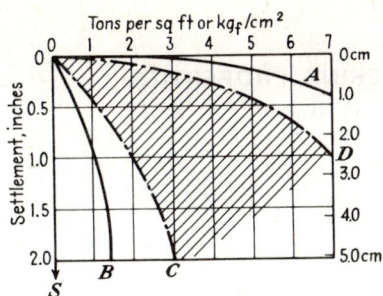

Tons per sq ft or kg_f/cm^2

Fig. 4-50. Results of load tests on natural sand deposits with 1-ft² (935-cm²) test footings. Curves A and B correspond to tests of the densest and loosest states of sands from different localities, reported by Terzaghi and Peck (Ref. 344). The shaded area between curves C and D gives the wide limits of variation of the curves for tests performed at a depth of 5 ft (1.5 m) over the area of a single factory shed in Iowa, studied by Tschebotarioff.

The difference per foot depth is $115.5 - 53.1 = 62.4$ lb/ft³ (1.0 g_f/cm^3). Thus full buoyancy is effective, and a rise of the water level shown in Fig. 4-30 will decrease the effective pressures on the underlying layers by $62.4 \times 14.7 = 908$ lb/ft² $= 0.45$ ton/ft² (0.45 kg_f/cm^2).

4-6. See parts (c) and (d) of Prob. 11-2.

4-7. The proposal was made to determine the permissible unit contact pressure with the soil (sand) of the footings for a new 200 by 300 ft (61 by 92 m) four-story building from the results of two surface load tests on 1-ft-square (30.5-cm) test footings. Was the proposal reasonable?

Answer. No, it was not. As shown in Fig. 4-50, the density of sand may vary within wide limits over the area of a single structure. Two load tests of the type suggested would provide insufficient information concerning the density of the sand at the elevation where the tests were performed and no information at all concerning its density at depths in excess of 2 ft (61 cm) below that elevation. A larger number of penetration tests (Art. 2-4A), in connection with a few borings, would give a much better idea of the limit and average values of the density of the entire soil mass which will have to support the new building.

CHAPTER 5

IMPROVEMENT OF SOIL-ENGINEERING PROPERTIES

5-1. Terminology. The term *compaction* is used in this book to designate the artificial increase of the density of a natural soil by mechanical means, i.e., the *densification*. The natural soil may be compacted either in situ (Art. 5-3) or, after transportation, in a new fill (Art. 5-5). By *consolidation* (Art. 3-4*A*) is meant the gradual increase in the density of a soil under the natural action of forces of gravity, such as the weight of the soil itself or of structures erected upon it. By *stabilization* is meant any artificial method employed for the purpose of improving by suitable regrading or by special admixtures such properties of a soil as are important for the maintenance of the shearing strength and of the volume and shape of the soil. The loading and climatic conditions which may obtain while the soil is serving as a foundation or construction material should be considered in this respect.

Thus reference will be made in this book to "acceleration of consolidation by means of sand drains" (Art. 5-2), to "compaction of a soil by means of sand piles" (Art. 5-3), and to "stabilization of sand by means of chemicals" (Art. 5-6). These distinctions are emphasized, since in the past all the above terms have been frequently and erratically interchanged in general usage. In addition, there are several schools of thought as to what the proper use of these terms should be. For instance, the term soil *solidification* is sometimes employed to designate soil stabilization, as defined above in a limited sense of the word. In its broadest interpretation, the term *stabilization* is sometimes used to cover any kind of action which improves the stability of a soil mass.

5-2. Preloading of Plastic Clay Deposits; Sand Drains. Displacement of very soft clays and muds (Art. 9-1) can hardly ever be successfully performed if the troublesome layer exceeds 50 to 60 ft (15 to 18 m) in depth; it is not always possible even at shallower depths when the clay is of a low to medium strength. Special measures then become necessary to improve the properties of the clay.

During the construction of the 1939 World's Fair at New York on a 70-ft-deep (21-m) layer of soft organic silt, so-called mud waves were apt to occur when the fill was placed in layers exceeding 4 ft (1.2 m) in height. A *mud wave* is essentially a slide along a cylindrical surface (see Fig. 7-4) which produces lateral and upward displacements of the underlying soft clay. Such displacements are liable to remold the clay and to lower its shearing strength still further (Art. 3-2G), thus facilitating further slides during continued filling. It therefore proved necessary to place the fill in layers extending over the entire area, not exceeding 4 ft (1.2 m) in depth and at a maximum grade of 3 percent. This ensured stability by preventing shear failures of the mud-wave type. However, settlements continuing for many years, owing to consolidation of the clay under the weight of the fill, could not be prevented by such measures.

For railroad embankments this is not particularly troublesome since broken-stone ballast is comparatively inexpensive and can easily be packed under the ties to raise them when needed. This is not so for concrete or asphalt pavements of highways.

Continued settlements of the soil under an embankment fill may damage concrete pavements and create undesirable dips in highways and airport runways, especially when the depth of soft underlying soil varies. It then becomes necessary to accelerate the consolidation of the clay so that it is largely completed before the concrete pavement is laid. *Sand drains* are used for this purpose; the theory on which their use is based is as follows. It will be noted from Eq. (4-22) that the time which elapses until a certain percentage of consolidation is reached changes with the square of the thickness of the layer H, that is, with the square of the maximum distance which a particle of water may have to travel until it reaches the pervious boundary. This circumstance permitted the development of practical methods for accelerating the consolidation of deep layers of clay under applied surcharges or of hydraulic clay fills under their own weight.

Vertical sand drains are driven into the clay in the manner illustrated in Fig. 5-1. If their spacing s is appreciably smaller than the thickness of the layer H, the rate of consolidation will be greatly accelerated, since now the excess pore water can escape in a radial direction toward the sand drains along a much shorter distance than was previously the case (see Prob. 5-2).

The main stages of construction are as follows. First, a number of settlement platforms (step 1) are installed on the original soil surface and their elevations are determined by leveling. They consist of a steel or timber

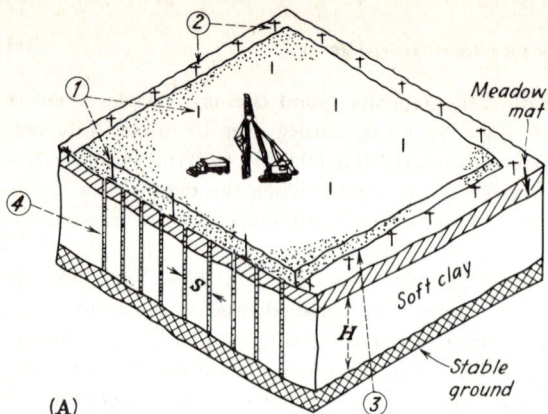

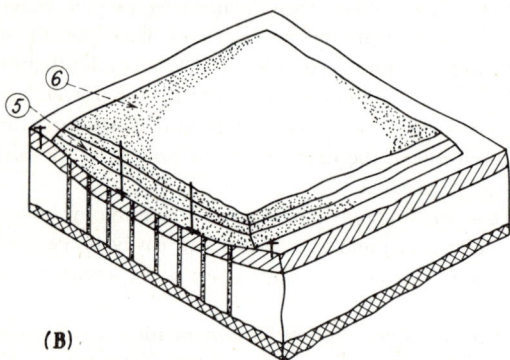

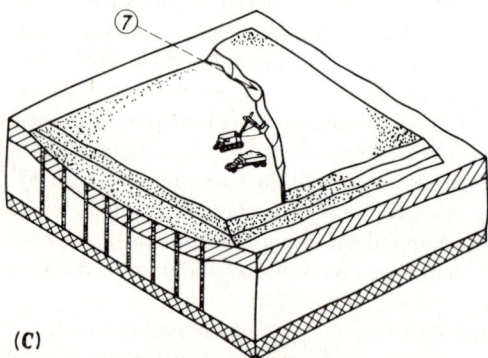

Fig. 5-1. Preloading of soft-clay deposit to eliminate later settlements of Port Newark warehouse floors. Sequence of operations: 1, installing settlement observation platforms on surface of meadow mat; 2, installing displacement observation stakes around periphery of loaded area; 3, placing first sand layer to permit work of heavy equipment and later drainage; 4, driving sand drains; 5, placing successive layers of permanent fill and 6 temporary surcharge; 7, removing excess surcharge. (*After Kyle, Ref. 176.*)

plate, at least 3 ft (90 cm) square in plan, to which is firmly attached a vertical steel pipe which can be extended upward as height of the fill is increased.

The second step is to install stakes around the periphery of the toe of the future fill lines of displacement (step 2) and to take transit readings on them in respect to reference stakes on the same lines extended beyond the area to be loaded.   These stakes are usually made of 2 by 4 in. (5 by 10 cm) wood, are driven some 7 ft (2.1 m) into the ground, and have a cross bar at their top with a horizontal scale painted on it.

The third step consists in placing a working mat of select clean sand to permit operation of heavy equipment if the surface is swampy as well as later escape of water from the sand drains.

It is essential to specify for the first fill layer (step 3) clean sand that is just as pervious as that in the sand drains and to ensure its connection to outside drainage ditches if the vertical sand drains are to perform their function satisfactorily.   The sand drains are then driven (step 4 in Fig. 5-1A).

A hollow mandrel, a heavy 16- to 20-in.-diameter (41- to 51-cm) steel pipe, is driven into the clay in very much the same manner as is done for cast-in-the-ground concrete piles of the Simplex type (Art. 6-7).   A metal plug closes the bottom of the pipe and, in some types of mandrel, is left in the ground when the mandrel is pulled out.   Prior to pulling, the mandrel is filled with clean sand (not more than 3 percent passing the 200-mesh sieve). One of the several possible techniques employs compressed-air pressure (up to 7 tons/ft$^2 \approx 97$ lb/in.^{2}) to force the sand down and to ensure the essential continuity of the sand shaft.   The air pressure against the top lid of the mandrel also helps somewhat to reduce the effort necessary to pull the mandrel out of the ground.   In some mandrels a permanent hinged plate is used to provide a plug at its bottom.

The next step (5) (see Fig. 5-1B) consists in placing the fill to the approximate elevation it will have in the permanent structure, and step 6 extends the fill to provide a temporary surcharge, under the assumption that the settlement due to, say, 60 percent consolidation under a high temporary overload may be greater than the settlement corresponding to 90 or 95 percent consolidation under the final smaller load of the permanent embankment. This procedure, however, does not take into account the possibility of secondary consolidation (Art. 3-4D), whose effects may be important in peat and some other soils.   In most inorganic soils, however, overloading can help reduce the time of preloading since (as can be seen from the time-consolidation curve of Fig. 3-17) the rate of settlement beyond the $U = 80$ percent consolidation value is extremely slow.

Figure 5-1 refers to the preloading of limited rectangular areas to be occupied by warehouses at Port Newark.   The same procedure applies to the accelerated construction of highway embankments on soft clays, except that there the permanent fill, as in step 5, will be higher and the temporary surcharge, steps 6 and 7, will be lower than in the case illustrated by Fig. 5-1.

Fill placement should proceed at a carefully controlled rate to make sure that no shear failure of the mud-wave type is about to develop owing to excessive weight of the surcharge. Such mud waves would be liable to sever the continuity of the individual sand drains and thereby render them useless (see Fig. 5-2 and discussion thereof which follows).

A preliminary estimate of the permissible rate at which fill may be placed can be made on the basis of laboratory unconfined compression and triaxial consolidated quick shear tests, as shown in part (a) of Prob. 5-3. This involves some uncertainties because of the unknown degree of remolding of the clay by the displacements thereof due to the customary method of sand-drain installation by driving a closed-end mandrel.† It is therefore essential to continue to make repeated control transit measurements on the displacement stakes at the toe of the fill and to plot any movements recorded against time. If such a plot reveals an accelerating or even a steady rate of outward movement of the soil surface at the toe of the fill, this will mean that the yield point of the underlying clay has been exceeded. Further placing of the fill should be stopped immediately and not resumed until further consolidation of the clay has sufficiently increased its shearing strength, as evidenced by a cessation of lateral movement of the displacement stakes. Such controls are most important since once even a small slide has developed, it is apt to shear off the vertical sand drains, rendering them useless.

Failure to realize this and the resulting undue haste of improperly supervised contractors has been responsible for some trouble of the type illustrated by Fig. 5-2. Borings made before and after construction showed no change in the water content in a deposit of very soft silt and clay 50 to 60 ft (15 to 18 m) deep, which prompted Housel (Ref. 137) to express doubts about the validity of the theory of consolidation. In his discussion of Ref. 137 Palmer correctly pointed out that no accelerated consolidation could take place once the sand drains had been sheared off by a slide induced by too rapid or uneven placing of the fill. In a later study Sowers (Ref. 310) showed that the observed settlements were entirely compatible with the theory of consolidation.

---

† The amount of displacement of the clay can be reduced by using a long hollow auger (proposed by Landau, Refs. 185 and 186) screwed into the soil to the full depth of the drain. Sand is forced in through a hollow shaft at the center of the auger as it is pulled out. Another method consists in using thin cardboard "wicks" instead of sand. This was first tried by Kjellman in Sweden and developed by the Franki Pile Company (Ref. 81). Several methods of jetting the clay out of the space to be occupied by the sand drain have also been developed.

An extensive study of the effectiveness of such augered or jetted sand drains in very sensitive clay of the state of Maine, as compared to conventionally driven closed-end mandrels, was reported by Ladd, Rixner, and Gifford in Ref. 180. The cost of individual drains of the augered or jetted type was found to be somewhat higher than the cost of the conventional type, but their effectiveness was greater, making a greater drain spacing possible and hence permitting some overall economies.

Fig. 5-2. Mud waves on paved airport taxiway caused by continued rapid placing of adjoining fill over sand drains which had been sheared off by earlier slide. (*After Housel and Palmer, Ref. 137.*)

Since then a number of records of properly handled and successful sand-drain installations have been published, indicating effective consolidation as evidenced by a marked decrease in the initial water content. The example given by Fig. 5-3 illustrates this point, as well as the generally stabilizing effect of sand drains. In this case they were used to permit the construction of a levee around La Guardia Airport (Ref. 177); first attempts to build such a levee failed because of slides toward the adjoining bay. The use of sand drains permitted the rapid increase of the shearing strength of the underlying soft clay as the levee was built up. The levee was required to prevent high tides from flooding the airport, which had settled 3 to 6 ft (0.9 to 1.8 m) as a result of the consolidation of the clay beneath the runways.

The last step (7) in the sequence of sand-drain installation (Fig. 5-1*C*) consists in the removal of the excess surcharge once the desired degree of consolidation of the underlying clay has been reached. After this is done, the paving for highway embankments can be placed or for buildings piles can be driven to firm ground through the fill and the underlying clay to support columns. Of course, nondisplacement piles, e.g., H-piles, should be used (Art. 6-1).

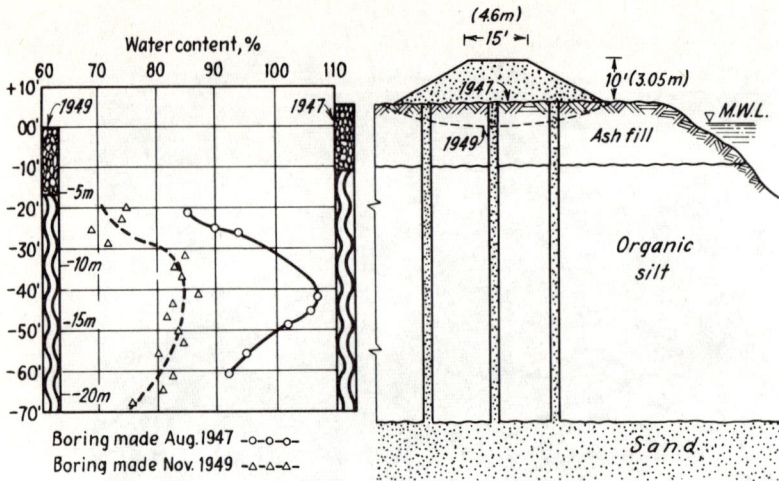

Fig. 5-3. Three rows of sand drains permitted the gradual construction of an antiflood dike at La Guardia Airport by rapidly consolidating the silt and thereby increasing its shearing strength. (*After Kyle and Kapp, Ref. 177.*)

A preliminary estimate of the time required to reach this desired degree of consolidation can be made using Eq. (4-22) and Fig. 4-34, which gives curves of the time factor T_h for radial drainage in a horizontal direction and varying values of the ratio

$$n = \frac{d_e}{d_w} \tag{5-1}$$

where d_e = effective diameter of soil cylinder within which water will flow toward drain well

d_w = actual diameter of drain well (see Fig. 5-4)

Equation (4-22) can be used for the solution of such problems if d_e is substituted for H.

As explained in the discussion of Fig. 4-36, the stratification of clay deposits can greatly accelerate consolidation, compared with theoretical values obtained on the assumption of a homogeneous layer. Control measurements on settlement platforms (step 1 in Fig. 5-1A) are therefore essential. Within a few months after the full height of the fill is in place a time-settlement plot of the platform readings should show the rate at which consolidation is progressing.

Pore-pressure measurements are also frequently used for this purpose, but they are less reliable for reasons explained in Arts. 1-9 and 2-5.

When planning this type of work in a new locality it is advisable to construct some test sections with different spacing of the sand drains and different heights of surcharge fill in order to decide on the procedure to be followed during later construction.   Careful settlement and lateral-displacement control measurements should be performed both during such preliminary studies and during all actual construction.

The spacing of sand drains customarily varies between 8 and 15 ft (2.4 and 4.6 m).

When the compressible soft clay and silt deposits are shallow—25 ft (7.6 m) thick or less—the use of sand drains ceases to be economical since the preloading of the soil surface without sand drains can often provide the desired degree of consolidation within a year.

The preloading can be done by sand surcharges, which are economical when the development of a large new marginal-value land area is planned to occur gradually over a period of years.   Then the sand can be repeatedly reused to successively preload adjoining sections.   Toward the end of such a development preloading by means of water surcharges can be of advantage.

Figure 5-5 illustrates the start of filling one of two such temporary artificial lakes at Port Elizabeth, New Jersey.   The first of these lakes covered an area of 18 acres (73,000 m² = 7.3 hectares) and the second 43 acres (17.5 hectares).

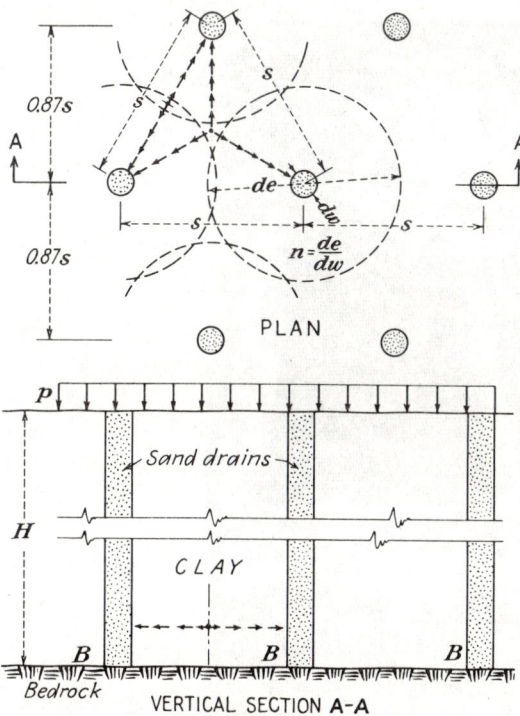

Fig. 5-4. Vertical sand drains accelerate consolidation of a clay layer when their spacing s is smaller than the thickness H of the layer.

Fig. 5-5. Start of filling one of the temporary artificial lakes for preloading by 22-ft (6.7-m) water surcharge the underlying shallow compressible deposits at Port Elizabeth, New Jersey. (*Photo courtesy of Port of New York Authority.*)

Fig. 5-6. Aerial view of start of filling two temporary artificial lakes, detail of one of which is shown in Fig. 5-5. (*Photo courtesy of Port of New York Authority.*)

A general view of both lakes is given by Fig. 5-6.   Both provided a surcharge of 22 ft (6.7 m) of water to compress some 10 ft (3 m) of hydraulic fill with a high clay content underlain by some 15 ft (4.6 m) of swamp deposits.   Earth dikes were built around the area to be flooded and a thin (10-mil† $= \frac{1}{4}$-mm) polyvinyl chloride membrane lined the bottom and the slopes of the lake. A system of drains was provided in the sand under the bottom membrane to prevent the development of localized uplift pressures if surcharge water leaked through accidental holes in the membrane.

5-3. In Situ Compaction of Loose Sands.   The compaction of deep layers of natural soil can be successfully accomplished by means of sand piles so long as the natural soil is of a fairly granular and permeable type.   One such method is based on a French cast-in-the-ground concrete pile of the Compressol type.   It is now seldom used for its original purpose but can be successfully employed for the compaction of granular soils with some slight cohesion, as may be caused by capillary saturation and a slight silt or clay content.   Only soils which will stand up when a heavy (2- to 3-ton) paraboloidal or conical steel weight is repeatedly dropped, so that it perforates a cylindrical hole to the desired depth, can be compacted in this manner. This has an overall compactive effect, since much of the soil is displaced laterally.   The hole is then backfilled in layers under continuous tamping.

In dry, clean sands or below the groundwater table, casings have to be employed.   The Franki type of cast-in-the-ground pile (see Fig. 6-22) has been successfully tried out in such cases (Ref. 199).   Sand instead of concrete is used, so that the objections raised against this type of concrete pile (see Art. 6-7) are no longer valid.

Experiments have shown that only noncohesive soils are strongly affected by vibrations and can therefore be efficiently compacted in this manner. Field experience substantiates this.

The compaction of deep layers of sand can be accomplished by means of the *vibroflotation* procedure of Steuerman.   A device is employed which is similar to a gigantic spud vibrator of the type used for vibratory compaction of mass concrete.   It consists of a 15-in.-diameter (38-cm) and 82-in.-long (208-cm) cylinder, inside of which an electric 1,800-rev/min motor drives a smaller inner cylinder mounted slightly off center.   This eccentricity produces the vibrations.   Hoses attached to the outer cylinder permit the operation of water jets at its upper and lower ends.   The entire device is lowered into the ground from a lead-carrying crane.   As it sinks into the ground, the water jets loosen up the sand around the cylinder and the vibrations shake it down.   The resulting compaction is evidenced by the formation of a crater at the ground surface.   Sand is added to fill up this crater.   This procedure is repeated as the "vibroflot" is withdrawn to the surface.   A very dense sand core with dense sand all around it results.   The

---

† 1 mil = 1/1,000 in. = 0.0254 mm.

Fig. 5-7. Compaction of a 35-ft-deep (10.7-m) underwater granular fill by a Terra-Probe 45 ft (13.7 m) long and 30 in. (76 cm) in diameter. The fill was to support the floor of a dock at Sparrows Point, Maryland. (*L. B. Foster Co.*)

satisfactory operation of this device has been checked in relatively clean sands (Ref. 199). It does not appear to be effective in silty sands, possibly because the reconsolidation by vibrations of the less permeable soil, after it is loosened up by the water jets, cannot occur rapidly enough. Better results can therefore be expected in silty sands from sand piles which are molded by impact, as described above.

The *Terra-Probe* method has been successfully used for the compaction of underwater sand fills or deep natural deposits of loose sand below the free-water table. In contrast to the vibroflotation method, no jetting has to be used, nor is any sand added at the surface around the 30-in.-diameter (76-cm) closed-end steel pipe, which is sunk into the sand as shown in Fig. 5-7. A low-frequency Foster vibro-driver is used, which can also serve as an extractor (see Art. 15-6). When the pipe is withdrawn, the saturated cohesionless sand is shaken down as it slips into the void left by the pipe. The operation is repeated 4 to 5 ft (1.2 to 1.5 m) on centers (Ref. 86). Borings with standard penetration tests were made before and after the operation, and an appreciable increase in the blows/per foot count was found.

During the construction of the Aswan high dam in Egypt (Ref. 1) dune sand placed underwater was compacted by deep vibrators, six of which were mounted on each of three floating rigs.

Some moderately successful attempts have been made to compact fully saturated deposits of natural sand by the detonation of explosives in boreholes (Refs. 201 and 118).

Vibratory rollers can be more effective than ordinary rollers in compacting shallow layers of submerged sand 5 to 10 ft (1.5 to 3.0 m) deep (see discussion of Fig. 5-14 in Art. 5-5).

Once the nature of a soil material has been established by borings, it is possible to check later appreciable changes in its overall density by comparing the changed velocity of wave propagation to the one measured originally. This procedure was employed in Germany during the preliminary studies of different possible methods of compaction of a natural loose deposit of clean sand (see Loos, Ref. 199).   Prior to compaction of the deposit the wave-propagation velocity was 490 ft/sec (150 m/sec); after its compaction by Franki type sand piles it increased to 1,410 ft/sec (430 m/sec).   Compaction of the clean sand by use of the vibro-flotation method increased the wave-propagation velocity to 1,540 ft/sec (470 m/sec).   According to a later personal communication (1949) to the writer from Lorenz, for the study of profiles less than 325 ft (100 m) long the waves were induced by dropping a 45-lb (20.4-kg_f) weight to the ground surface from a height of 6 ft (1.83 m).   Explosives were used only for the study of soil profiles exceeding 325 ft (100 m) in length at the ground surface.   It was found possible to study very short distances, approximately 100 ft (31 m) by using very sensitive recording instruments and inducing the shock waves by means of sledge hammer blows on a 4 by 4 in. (10 by 10 cm) steel plate laid on the soil surface (see also Art. 2-2).

5-4. In Situ Treatment of Collapsible Loess Soils.   Windblown loess soils on their original site of deposition are liable to cause trouble during the first rainy season following a new construction.   The thin vertical channels left in the loess by decayed grass roots are then likely to collapse under the combined action of the foundation loads and percolating moisture.   Considerable settlements of new structures are apt to result.   Load tests, with and without flooding of the soil surface, can be used to detect possible danger of this kind in advance of construction.   Sand piles (Art. 5-3) have been successfully used to compact the loess before construction and to close its open channels.

Other methods of treating loess soils are preflooding of the construction site (Fig. 5-8), in situ baking of the loess to a bricklike strength (Fig. 5-9), and prebored situ-cast piles reaching down into layers below the soil zone which can be affected by surface moisture after construction (see Fig. 6-22 and Art. 6-7).

These methods have been extensively used on primary loess deposits in the southern regions of the Soviet Union.   The conventional flooding procedure used there is shown on the left-hand side of Fig. 5-8.   A number of vertical boreholes H are filled with coarse sand and are kept filled with water for a period of time until the resulting consolidation due to a collapse of the loess structure is evidenced by the appearance of surface cracks which accompany the formation of a settlement crater.   Of course this method cannot be used next to existing structures.   An improved method, authored by Litvinov, is shown on the right-hand side of Fig. 5-8.   A narrow trench is cut around the periphery of the area to be consolidated, and light explosive charges are detonated in special boreholes after the loess soil has been saturated through the holes *H*.   It is claimed that this procedure accelerates the consolidation and reduces the limits of lateral saturation and hence of the settlement crater (see Ref. 195; Ref. 306, SM2-1966, SM6-1967, SM6-1968, and SM6-1970, which contains a review of Litvinov's book; and Ref. 196).† See also Ref. 197.

Saturation from the surface only, without any holes of the type *H*, may have a detrimental effect by transforming the upper layers into a soggy mush, especially if the loess is not on its primary site of deposition by wind, so that its natural vertical channels have been destroyed in the process of re-deposition.

† In addition to these issues containing articles by Litvinov, the following issues of Ref. 306 contain other articles on loess foundation problems, also in English translation, by N. N. Goldstein, A. A. Grigorian, and others: SM3-1967; SM2 and SM4-1968; SM3, SM4, SM6-1969; SM4, SM6-1970; SM2-1971.

PLAN

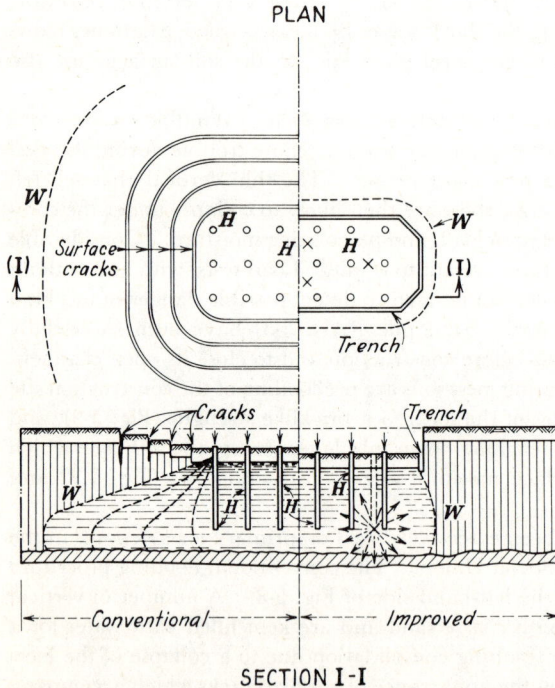

SECTION I-I

Fig. 5-8.   Procedures for compaction of loess soils by localized in situ flooding and use of explosive charges.   (*After Litvinov, Refs. 195 and 306.*)

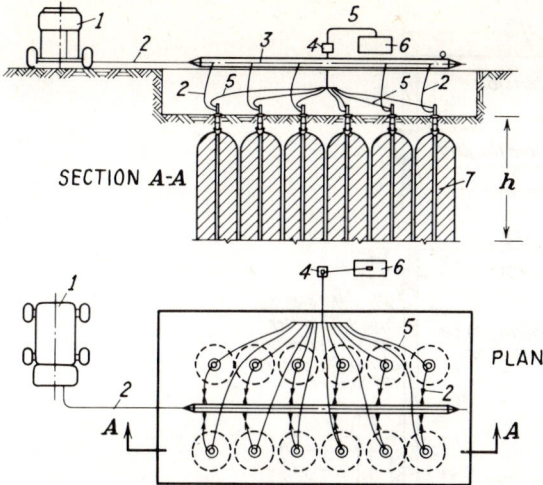

Fig. 5-9. Sketch of equipment for simultaneous burning of 12 holes for in situ thermal solidification of loess. 1 = compressor, 2 = pipe for compressed cold air, 3 = receiver, 4 = pump for delivery under pressure of fuel to borehole, 5 = pipes for fuel, 6 = fuel container, 7 = holes. (*After Litvinov, Refs. 160 and 194.*)

Figure 5-9 illustrates the thermal treatment of loess soils. The method involves burning various types of fuels in sealed boreholes under controlled temperature, then forcing the heated air under pressure through the pores of the soil. The temperature of the products of combustion must not exceed the fusion temperature of the soil, otherwise an impervious klinkerlike membrane would be created along the surface of the holes, preventing further lateral penetration of the hot air and gases. The method has been successfully used to depths of 30 to 45 ft (9 to 14 m) below foundation level. Under proper precautions 6- to 9-ft-diameter (1.8- to 2.7-m) cylinders of thermally stabilized soil can be successfully formed around each hole.

5-5. Moisture–Density–Compaction-energy Relationships of Earth Fills. The following experiments will demonstrate the relationship between the various factors involved. Let us take some silty sand, the general properties of which are indicated for soil 1 in Table 5-2, and let us compact it in the mold (Fig. 5-10) by means of the type of hammer shown in Fig. 5-11, employing procedure B from Table 5-1. That is, the hammer will weigh 5.5 lb (2.5 kg_f), and the guide cylinder around it will have such a height that the height of drop will be $H = 12$ in. (30.5 cm). To that end, the cylinder is set on the surface of the soil with one hand of the operator and the hammer is raised with the other hand as far as it will go and then released. The soil will be filled into the mold in increments so selected that the compaction can take place in three layers; 25 blows of the hammer will be applied to

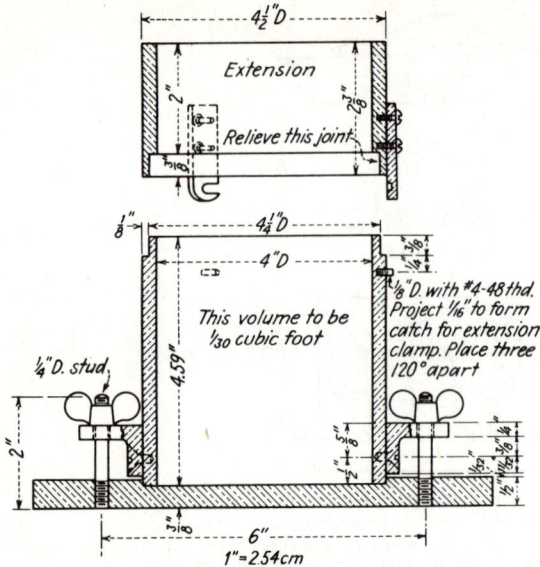

Fig. 5-10. Standard Proctor type (also ASTM and AASHO) mold for soil compaction.

each layer. The extension piece shown in Fig. 5-10 is then removed, the soil along the surface of the lower mold, the volume of which is $\frac{1}{30}$ ft^3 (950 cm^3), is leveled off with a straightedge, the soil and mold are weighed, and the moist unit weight of the soil is computed. Let us assume that the value obtained was 124.5 lb/ft^3 (1.99 g$_f$/cm^3) and that the natural water content of that soil was found to be $w = 4.8$ percent. This will give us point a in Fig. 5-12.

If we add some water to increase the water content to $w = 6.0$ percent and repeat the same compaction procedure, point b in Fig. 5-12 will be obtained.

TABLE 5-1. Data on Laboratory Compaction Procedures

Type	Weight of hammer		Height of drop		Number of blows per layer	Number of layers	Compaction energy	
	lb	kg$_f$	in.	cm			ft-lb/ft^3	m-kg$_f$/m^3
(A) modified Proctor (or AASHO)†	10.0	4.54	18	46.7	25	5	56,200	272,000
(B) standard Proctor (or AASHO)†	5.5	2.50	12	30.5	25	3	12,300	59,600
(C) 15-blow Proctor	5.5	2.50	12	30.5	15	3	7,400	38,800

† American Association of State Highway Officials.

By increasing the water content in small increments and repeating the same compaction procedure each time, points c, d, e, and f can be plotted. These points represent the moist density, i.e., the unit weight of the soil solids plus the weight of the water in the voids. The dry density, i.e., the unit weight of the soil solids only, can then be computed from Eqs. (3-7) and (3-9), giving the corresponding points a', b', c', d', e', and f' and curve B_1 (Table 5-1) applied to soil 1 (Table 5-2) at different moisture contents.

By applying compaction procedures A and C in the same manner to soil 1, curves A_1 and C_1 are obtained, as shown in Fig. 5-12. The three compaction procedures applied to soil 2 give curves A_2, B_2, and C_2, and applied to soil 3 give curves A_3, B_3, and C_3. It will be noted from Fig. 5-12 that in the case of soils 1 and 3 the *greatest dry density* $\gamma_{d(max)}$ is reached at a definite moisture content, which is termed the *optimum moisture content* w_{opt} (see Table 5-3).

The explanation of the recorded facts is as follows. At a low moisture content cohesive soils form lumps which cannot be broken up easily. They therefore hamper compaction. Addition of water at first helps to soften up these lumps and break them down, so that with the expenditure of the same compactive effort a greater density is obtained. The addition of water, however, is beneficial only up to a certain point. Theoretically this point is reached when the amount of water present is sufficient to fill all the voids of the soil, after having coated the individual particles, so that any further water added will only serve to keep the solid particles apart from each other and thereby will decrease the dry density. In other words, the experimental curves should at the optimum moisture content reach the zero-air-voids curve, which corresponds to the value of the specific gravity G of the soil tested, and follow that curve if any more water is added. Three such theoretical zero-air-voids (100 percent saturation) curves have been plotted in Fig. 5-12 for values of $G = 2.8$, $G = 2.7$, and $G = 2.6$. Equations (3-6) and (3-7) were used for the computations. It will be noted from Fig. 5-12 and Table 5-2 that at moisture contents greater than the optimum, the experimental curves do not quite reach their theoretical zero-air-voids curve but run parallel to it. This is an indication that saturation is not complete but that some air is unavoidably trapped in the voids of the soil during its compaction.

Other conditions being equal, an increase of the compactive effort produces an increased density of the soil, but only at moisture contents smaller than

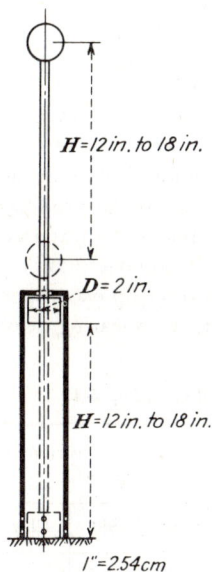

Fig. 5-11. Type of hammer employed for the field-laboratory compaction of soil in the mold shown in Fig. 5-10.

$H = 12\,in.\,to\,18\,in.$

$D = 2\,in.$

$H = 12\,in.\,to\,18\,in.$

$1'' = 2.54\,cm$

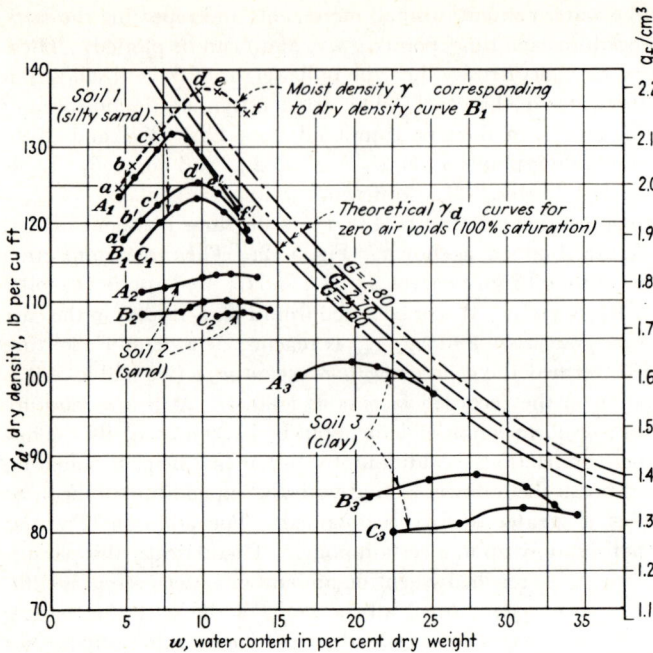

Fig. 5-12. The moisture-density relationship of three limit types of soils and the effect thereon of the energy expended on the compaction (see Tables 5-1, 5-2, and 5-3).

the optimum content which corresponds to the greater effort. At moisture contents higher than the optimum no further compaction can be produced by an increased effort, since instantaneous expulsion of the excess water entrapped in the voids is not possible. As a result, increased compactive efforts at water contents higher than the optimum only serve to set up excess pore pressures in the water filling the voids, which then facilitate shearing defor-

TABLE 5-2.   Characteristics of the Three Soils Referred to in Fig. 5-12

Soil type	Specific gravity G	Consistency limits, percent			Grain-size distribution, percent		
		w_L	w_P	I_p	Sand	Silt	Clay
No. 1, silty sand...	2.67	17	16	1	80	15	5
No. 2, sand	2.67	†	†	0	92	5	3
No. 3, clay	2.73	68	21	47	10	28	62

† Nonplastic

Table 5-3. Summary of Data Given in Fig. 5-12

Soil type	Optimum moisture, percent			Maximum dry density					
				lb/ft³			g_f/cm^3		
	A	B	C	A	B	C	A	B	C
No. 1, silty sand	8	10	10	132	125	123	2.11	2.00	1.98
No. 2, sand....	†	†	†	113	110	108	1.81	1.76	1.73
No. 3, clay	20	28	31	102	88	83	1.63	1.41	1.33

† Indefinite

mations of the entire soil mass. This fact has considerable practical importance for the selection of the water content at which field compaction should be undertaken and explains why it is usually preferable to make that selection "on the dry side" of the optimum.

The following additional important facts will be noted from Fig. 5-12 and Table 5-3. The water content of a relatively clean sand (soil type 2) has practically no influence on its dry density, as produced by the same compactive effort. A slight addition of silt or of clay to sand improves its grading and permits the development of a greater density for the same compactive effort. The effect of moisture during molding is then considerable. So long as the amount of silt and clay added is only small and no greater than is needed to partially fill the voids of the sand, the maximum density will increase and the optimum moisture content will decrease, compared with cleaner sand and the same compactive effort. A larger amount of clay reverses this trend; the maximum density decreases, and the optimum moisture content increases. Because of the greater surface area of fine particles, more water is required to coat them and part of the water is adsorbed.

Most of the above facts were first ascertained experimentally and reported by R. R. Proctor (Ref. 257). His original method is listed as method B in Table 5-1. As the weight of field-compaction equipment increased, it was found necessary to increase the compaction energy if laboratory results were to correspond to those obtained in the field. Method A of Table 5-1 was developed to meet this requirement. Method C, which is seldom used, was designed to duplicate conditions produced in the field by lightweight compaction equipment.

There are a number of devices used for the mechanical operation in the laboratory of the hammer illustrated in Fig. 5-11. Also, a different type of the so-called CBR mold, which is larger, 6-in. (15.3-cm) diameter, is frequently used (see Art. 3-6). As compared to Table 5-1, the number of hammer blows is then increased in proportion to the volume of the molded specimens.

R. R. Proctor also used an auxiliary device, known as the *plasticity needle,* to check the moisture content and density of a compacted soil.   The device consists of a small plunger which is placed on the surface of the soil and pressed a specified distance into it by manual pressure applied by means of a handle and a calibrated spring which can measure loads up to 100 lb (45.4 kg_f). The compression of the spring indicates the resistance offered by the soil. Several interchangeable plunger sizes are available, varying from 1.0 to 0.05 in.² (6.45 to 0.32 cm²) in area.   The device can be operated only on screened soil, since the presence of small gravel is liable to produce erratic results.   Individual operator characteristics also appear to be of importance. For the above reasons this device is not used universally.

Proper compaction of fills is of the greatest importance, since upon it depends the shearing strength of the fill and hence the stability of earth dams, embankments, and road and airport base courses.   It has been shown that the shearing strength of a fill increases with its density but, in addition, depends on the initial water content which was used for the molding of the specimen.   For the same density the highest strengths were frequently obtained by the use of higher compactive efforts and of molding water contents somewhat below the optimum.

Soil compaction in the field by rolling is the most effective compaction procedure when large masses of earth fill are to be handled.   For the compaction of clay fills, a so-called *sheepsfoot roller* is usually employed; a close-up view of one of the existing models is given in Fig. 5-13.   It is sometimes called a *tamping roller*.   A steel drum has welded to its surface a number of steel studs, the shape of which resembles somewhat that of a sheep's foot; hence the name.

Fig. 5-13.   Close-up view of a sheepsfoot roller.

The drum is empty for transportation but is filled with sand and water on the site where it is to be used. The entire weight of the drum comes to bear on only a few of the sheepsfoot studs at the same time. So-called *footprint* pressures are thereby developed which are sufficient to crush and to compact any lumps of clay they come to bear on. Individual drums can then be attached side by side or tandem and drawn all together by one tractor.

The first known sheepsfoot roller was built in 1906 in California. In the 1920s this type of equipment came into general use in the United States. The present light standard sheepsfoot roller has a 43-in.-diameter (110-cm) drum, a loaded weight varying from 6,000 to 15,000 lb (2,700 to 6,800 kg_f) per 8-ft (2.44-m) drum width, and footprint pressures varying from 60 to 300 lb/in.² (4.21 to 21.1 kg_f/cm^2). The heavy standard sheepsfoot roller has a 60-in.-diameter (152-cm) drum and footprint pressures from 300 to 600 lb/in.² (21.1 to 42.2 kg_f/cm^2). Some experimental giant sheepsfoot rollers have been built with 96-in.-diameter (244-cm) drums and 400 to 1,000 lb/in.² (28.1 to 70.2 kg_f/cm^2), i.e., up to 72 tons/ft², footprint pressures. These extra heavy rollers frequently are employed for a follow-up of the preliminary compaction of a layer by lighter rollers.

For sandy soils with little cohesion better results are obtained with *pneumatic-tire rollers,* which are being employed more and more for such soils instead of the sheepsfoot type. Since no lumps requiring crushing by very high concentrated pressures are present in sandy soils, a pressure more uniformly distributed over a greater area avoids the danger of localized shear failures or churning of the soil by the individual sheepsfoot studs. Rubber-tired rollers of this type have been built up to a total weight of 200 tons and produce efficient compaction. The air pressure of the tires can be used to regulate the area of their footprints. Heavy rubber-tired earth-moving equipment also can materially assist in the fill compaction during the deposition of the successive layers.

The thickness of layers to be compacted varies between 3 and 12 in. (7.6 and 30.5 cm); 6 in. (15 cm) is the customary value. The number of passes required by a roller to achieve a certain amount of compaction also varies. The rolling of experimental sections is sometimes advisable for important construction work, in order to decide on the thickness of fill layers and on the corresponding number of passes to be used in later work.

Vibratory rollers are most useful in the compaction of clean cohesionless sands, permitting some increase in the thickness of fill layers to be compacted. For fully saturated hydraulic fills or natural deposits of loose sands below the free-water table it has been found that the compactive action of a vibratory roller reaches to a greater depth than nonvibrating rollers of the same weight. This is because vibrations destroy the friction and hence the shearing strength of a clean, fully saturated sand. The weight of the roller can therefore no longer be effectively distributed laterally to greater areas with depth, and most of it is transmitted directly downward.

Reference 219 gives data on the compaction of a layer of sand fill 10 ft (3 m) thick, 7 ft (2.1 m) of which was below the free-water level. Eight coverages with a DynaPac model CT-60 vibratory compactor produced an appreciable increase of density from a depth of 1.5 ft to 5.5 ft (46 to 168 cm) and had some effect to a depth of 10 ft (3 m). The upper 1.5 ft (46 cm) were loosened. The vibratory drum assembly of the Vibro-Plus CT-60 compactor weighs 25 kips (11,000 kg$_f$), and a centrifugal force of 60 kips (27,200 kg$_f$) is obtained at an operating frequency of 25 Hz $=$ 25 cycles/sec.

Figure 5-14 shows a somewhat lighter model, the CH-43, the vibrating drum assembly of which weighs 10 kips (4,450 kg$_f$) and develops a centrifugal force of 23 kips (10.420 kg$_f$) at an operating frequency of 26.7 Hz (1,600 cycles/min). A considerable variety of models is now available in different sizes, some of them self-propelled.

The effectiveness of compaction depends upon vibrator weight and the centrifugal force (see Arts. 15-1 and 15-2). The vibration destroys the shearing strength of the sand, but the application of an external force is needed to move the grains past each other into a denser position. Brumund and Leonards (Ref. 43) have concluded from their laboratory-model tests that the ultimate densification of a granular sand mass under a vibrating footing resting on its surface depends on the logarithm of transmitted energy, which is influenced by the static weight applied, the impressed dynamic force, the acceleration, and the frequency of vibration. (See Ref. 11 for further relevant points obtained in the field by D'Appolonia et al.)

A method of rating compactors has been proposed by Selig, Ref. 286b. A general review of the art of soil compaction is given in Ref. 148a.

Moisture control during field compaction is very important. It is no accident that the methods of soil compaction in relation to proper moisture control were developed in the semiarid regions of the western United States. It is comparatively easy to add water to a fill, but it is very difficult rapidly to dry

Fig. 5-14. DynaPac model CH-43. (*Vibro-Plus Products, Inc.*)

out soil which is too wet, e.g., as a result of rain. No rolling can be done during protracted rainy spells. This is one reason why hydraulic fills are sometimes selected instead of rolled fills for earth dams in regions with high precipitation. Where compaction by rolling is essential, e.g., in the construction of highway and airport base courses, the sequence of the work should be planned to permit at all times the easy runoff of rainwater from the surfaces where compaction is to be continued. Only a small depth of a few inches of soil will then get mushy on such surfaces after a heavy rainfall, and it can be quickly scraped off by a bulldozer before compaction is resumed.

An *impact soil-compaction* device initially developed in Germany (see 1st ed., Art. 11-4) has been modified by the Barco Mfg. Company of Chicago. A gasoline motor is incorporated in the head of the device, which has two inner pistons. An explosion of the mixture between the two pistons lifts the heavy head of the device into the air, past the lower piston, which is attached to the foot of the device, thereby compressing a spring below that piston. This spring pulls up the foot of the device while the rest of it is still in the air. The entire rammer then falls to the soil surface before the next explosion in the gasoline motor occurs. It weighs 210 lb (95.5 kg$_f$). The diameter of its foot is 9.5 in. (24.2 cm) ($A = 0.492$ ft² $= 457$ cm²). The device rises approximately 14 in. (35.6 cm) into the air, and the compaction energy developed by it is thus 240 ft-lb (33.3 m-kg$_f$) per blow. The device is particularly well suited for the compaction of backfill in trenches dug for sewer or water pipes, or quite close to concrete structures, where there is no space for rollers to operate. In such cases it may have advantages over the smaller pneumatic tampers connected to jackhammer-type devices operated by compressed air. Tampers of the latter type have been conventionally used so far for compaction in cramped space, but to be effective, because of their small foot area, they appear to require the fill to be placed in very thin layers.

Control checks of the fill density achieved in the field should be performed as a matter of routine. The usual procedure consists in removing the loose surface layer of a fill and then making a hole in the fill with a hand-operated auger. The soil extracted from the hole is carefully collected, sometimes in a special tray which is laid on the planed-off surface of the ground and which is provided with a hole in its center for the passage of the auger. The soil thus extracted is weighed both before and after drying in a field laboratory. The volume of the hole is measured to determine the volume which the soil originally occupied in the ground. From these data the dry density of the soil is computed (see Prob. 5-1).

There are three methods for determining the volume of the hole. In the first, heavy oil is poured from a measuring cylinder into the hole. This procedure is quite simple but can be safely used only in fills with some clay content. In more pervious soils one has to use either a rubber balloon filled with water or uniform dry sand poured into the hole from a specified height from a calibrated receptacle, usually a gallon jar provided with a metal funnel.

5-6. Soil Stabilization by Admixtures.   One way to improve the properties of a soil fill is to mix it with some other locally available soil in order to obtain a desirable gradation.   In the United States it is frequently desirable to obtain an A-1 or an A-2 type of soil (see Art. 3-7*B*).   In such a soil the skeleton is provided by the sand—addition of gravel is also beneficial—but there is just enough silt or clay to fill the voids and to bind the sand and gravel particles together.   Swelling during wetting or shrinkage during drying is then reduced to a minimum.   Soils of this type are good for the construction of rammed-earth houses.

In arid regions of the world conditions may be quite different.   For instance, Mayer (Ref. 212) reported that in the French zones of the Sahara well-graded soil surfaces of desert roads were gradually worn down by traffic. The loosened particles of dry clay and silt were carried away by the wind, leaving only coarse sand and gravel at the surface, which then formed objectionable corrugations under continued traffic.   Much better results were obtained by surfacing such low-cost roads with wetted-down and rolled silty clay.

Mixing clay soils with granular material requires breaking down the clay lumps, in order to permit the effective mixing of the two soils.   The same requirement holds for all other forms of stabilization of fills by admixtures of any kind.   Machines for crushing and pulverizing dry soils have been developed, but their effectiveness is limited to friable soil types.

Most soils can be effectively and economically stabilized by mixing them with cement.   Thus soil-cement roads frequently have been constructed for light-duty service.   The amounts of cement employed usually vary from 8 to 12 percent of the soil by volume.   Preliminary tests are frequently needed to determine the amount of cement which should be added.   These tests include determination of the optimum moisture content and the maximum density of the soil-cement mixture, as well as its compressive strength and durability.

The Portland Cement Association (Chicago, Ill.) has issued a number of instructive publications on soil-cement stabilization.   Repetitional wetting-drying and freezing-thawing tests are employed in the laboratory to test the durability, in accordance with standards set up by the ASTM and the AASHO.

Cement stabilization is ineffective in soils with a high organic content or in soils containing substances, such as sulfur, which may produce a disintegration of concrete.   Such subtances may be strongly detrimental even when they are present only in the subgrade on which the soil-cement or concrete pavement is placed, since they can be accumulated in the pavement during dry seasons by the upward capillary movement of moisture from the subgrade and its subsequent evaporation near the pavement surface.   The concrete pavement of an airport built on a sulfur-containing subgrade is known to have disintegrated.

Bituminous-soil stabilization can be substituted under such conditions, since one of its effects is to waterproof the soil and maintain the low water content essential for continued stability of cohesive soils. Cold-mixed asphalts in soils, however, are liable to be attacked by bacteria and in time may be completely eaten up. To prevent this, Winterkorn (Ref. 405) recommended the addition to bitumen of aniline furfural as a bactericidal agent.

Lime, fly ash, and a number of chemicals have been used for soil stabilization and described in publications of the Highway Research Board.

A general characteristic of modern chemical soil-stabilization methods is the need for partial drying of the chemically treated soil before the treatment becomes effective.

An unusual case of accidental *underwater stabilization* of a natural clay deposit, presumably by the action of a phosphate-rich mineral *vivianite*, is described in the first edition, Art. 11-8.

5-7. Grouting. The injection of cement or chemicals into the soil is known as *grouting*. Cement or chemicals can be successfully injected into a soil only if it is sufficiently pervious to permit the easy passage of the solution or if it contains cracks which require filling.

Cracks may form during prolonged drought seasons in recent embankments for which rich clay was used. Cement injections into such cracks may prevent later instability resulting from the filling of such cracks with water during a subsequent rainy season. Proper initial compaction, however, should render such expensive remedial measures unnecessary in most cases.

Cement grouting of cracks to render them impervious to the passage of water is used as a matter of routine in the treatment of rock under and around the foundations of dams, especially when the rock is composed of limestone or dolomite and is therefore liable to have large open seams. Techniques of this kind have been successfully applied to the dams of the Tennessee Valley Authority.

The injection of chemicals for the improvement of the mechanical properties of a soil can be successfully performed only in pervious soils, such as sands. Even so, a very close spacing of the injection pipes is required—approximately 12 in. on centers—if the entire mass of the soil is to be impregnated. Otherwise the injected fluid is liable to follow the paths of least resistance to flow, i.e., more pervious seams, which are not necessarily the least resistant parts of the soil mass in respect to compression or to shear. Such chemical treatment of a soil is therefore rather expensive and is seldom used on a large scale for routine construction purposes. It does, however, have advantages in some special cases where local treatment of sand seams is desired to simplify excavation operations or, in lieu of underpinning (Fig. 15-11), for the widening of the bases of foundations. Another example is provided by a case where a layer of completely dry sand was unexpectedly encountered during the driving of a tunnel. The dry sand trickled through the smallest openings in the timbering, thereby greatly increasing the pressures thereon, since the sand movements destroyed all relieving effects of arching. Stabilization of the dry sand by chemical injections through pipes driven ahead of the tunnel face was then successfully undertaken (Ref. 411).

Two types of chemical injections may be performed. In the first type, of which the Joosten process is representative, two solutions of chemicals, usually sodium silicate and calcium chloride, which form a gel when brought into contact with each other, are employed. The first chemical is pressed into the ground as the injection pipe is driven in, and the second chemical while the pipe is pulled out. In the second type only one solution is employed, which is designed to begin hardening after a given period of time.

A further discussion of complex grouting techniques is beyond the scope of this book (see two Symposiums on Grouting, Refs. 115 and 116).

Impregnation of a soil from its surface may be successfully resorted to when it is desired to improve the properties of a relatively thin upper layer. For instance, the 10-in.-thick lining of a calcium type of clay originally used in an artificial lagoon during the San Francisco International Exposition (1939) was found to permit seepage losses of the fresh water in the lagoon of 1.00 in. (25 mm) per day. By allowing salt water to percolate for a while through the lining, the calcium clay was changed into a sodium clay, and the seepage dropped to 0.10 in. (2.5 mm) per day. This happened because the thicker films of adsorbed water on sodium ions, compared with calcium ions (Art. 3-1C), filled the voids and blocked the passage of free water.

REVIEW PROBLEMS

5-1. During a field density test the volume of the hole made in a moist sand prior to its compaction was found by one of the methods outlined in Art. 5-5 to be $V = 0.072$ ft^3. Before drying the weight of the sand extracted was $W = 7.25$ lb, and after drying $W_s = 6.78$ lb. Determine the dry density γ_d, the water content w_n, the void ratio e (assume $G = 2.65$), and the porosity n.

Answer. The dry density is

$$\gamma_d = \frac{6.78}{0.072} = 94.2 \text{ lb/ft}^3$$

The weight of water is

$$W_w = 7.25 - 6.78 = 0.47 \text{ lb}$$

The water content is

$$w_n = \frac{0.47}{6.78} \times 100 = 6.9\%$$

From Eq. (3-7),

$$e = \frac{62.4 \times 2.65}{94.2} - 1 = 0.755$$

From Eq. (3-4),

$$n = \frac{0.755}{1 + 0.755} \times 100 = 43\%$$

5-2. To what extent will the settlement of the case given in Prob. 3-4 be accelerated if sand drains of 18 in. (1.5 ft = 46 cm) diameter are driven down 8 ft (244 cm) on centers, as illustrated in Fig. 5-4? The permeability of the clay in both the vertical and the horizontal directions is the same.

Answer:

$$n = \frac{8.0}{1.5} = 5.3$$

From Fig. 4-34 and the T_h curve for radial drainage and a value of $n = 5.0$ we find that the time factor which corresponds to $U = 50$ percent consolidation is $T_{50} = 0.078$, and to $U = 90$ percent consolidation, $T_{90} = 0.28$. From Eq. (4-22) we obtain

$$t_{50} = \frac{0.078 \times 244^2}{0.0166} = 2.79 \times 10^5 \text{ min}$$

$$= 194 \text{ days} = 6.4 \text{ months}$$

and

$$t_{90} = t_{50} \frac{T_{90}}{T_{50}} = 6.4 \frac{0.280}{0.078} = 23 \text{ months}$$

Compared with the conditions of Prob. 3-4, settlement will be accelerated:

$$\frac{10.8 \times 4}{6.4/12} = 81 \text{ times} \qquad U = 50\%$$

$$\frac{46.0 \times 4}{23/12} = 96 \text{ times} \qquad U = 90\%$$

5-3. A highway embankment is to be constructed on a deep deposit of soft clay, the following properties of which were determined by means of laboratory tests:

Unconfined compressive strength: $q_u = 0.4$ ton/ft^2 = 0.4 kg$_f$/cm^2

Increase of strength in drained (consolidated) quick triaxial test: $\phi = 15°$

Modulus of volume change: $m_v' = 0.02$ cm^2/kg$_f$

$$m_v = 0.02 \times 10^{-3} \text{ cm}^2/\text{g}_f$$

Horizontal permeability: $k = 6 \times 10^{-8}$ cm/sec

Diameter of sand drains: $d_w = 18$ in. = 46 cm

Spacing of sand drains: $d_e = 10$ ft = 3.05 m

Estimate: (a) the safe height of first lift of fill and (b) the safe rate of subsequent increase of fill height.

Answer. Subject to subsequent check by a Swedish circle type of analysis (Art. 7-2) and field controls, a rough estimate can be obtained by considering the embankment load as a strip load $p = \gamma h$ and using Eq. (4-5). As in most highway embankments subjected to displacement control observations (Art. 5-2), a low factor of safety $F = 1.25$ against shear failure can be used. Then with the fill weighing $\gamma = 115$ lb/ft^3 = 1.84 g$_f$/cm^3:

Part (a):

$$h_1 = \frac{p_{max}}{\gamma F} = \frac{(5.14 \times q_u/2)}{\gamma F}$$

$$= \frac{5.14 \times 400}{115 \times 1.25} = 14 \text{ ft} = 4.3 \text{ m}$$

Part (b): If this 14-ft-high (4.3-m) lift is to be placed at a rate of 2 ft (60 cm) per week, it will be completed at the end of 7 weeks. It can be considered that the soft clay will get an additional U percent consolidation after $\frac{t}{2} = 3.5$ weeks $= 2.12 \times 10^6$ sec. Using this value for t and $d_e = 10 \times 30.5 = 305$ cm for H in Eq. (4-22) and solving for T, we obtain

$$T_h = \frac{tk}{m_v d_e \gamma_w} = \frac{(2.12 \times 10^{-6})(6 \times 10^{-8})}{(0.02 \times 10^{-3})(305^2 \times 1.0)}$$

$$= 0.0684$$

Using this value, as well as $n = d_e/d_w = 6.7$ [Eq. (5-1)], we find from Fig. 4-34 the corresponding degree of consolidation $U = 35$ percent.

The corresponding increment of effective intergranular stress (see Art. 3-4A) will be $\Delta p_e = p_e U$, where $p_e = h_1 \gamma = 14' \times 115 = 1,610$ lb/ft² $= 0.80$ kg$_f$/cm².

The increase of shearing stress during these 7 weeks will then be

$$\Delta s_1 = p_e U \tan 15° = 1,610 \times 0.35 \times 0.272°$$

$$= 154 \text{ lb/ft}^2 \ (0.077 \text{ kg}_f/\text{cm}^2)$$

The height of the second lift can then be

$$h_2 = \frac{5.14 \times 154}{115 \times 1.25} = 5.4 \text{ ft } (1.65 \text{ m})$$

The rate of placing new fill will now be reduced to 1 ft (30 cm) per week. After 5.4 weeks, the additional consolidation can be estimated as follows. The effective time of action of the full 14 ft (4.3 m) of the first lift is

$$t = \frac{7.0}{2} + 5.4 = 8.9 \text{ weeks} = 5.39 \times 10^6 \text{ sec}$$

from which value the corresponding $T_h = 0.174$ is obtained. This and Fig. 4-34 give the degree of consolidation $U = 65$ percent. Of this, 35 percent had already been taken into account in computing Δs_1. Therefore, the contribution to an additional increase of shearing strength will be:

First lift: $\Delta s_2 = 1,610 \times (0.65 - 0.35) \times 0.272 = 131 \text{ lb/ft}^2 \ (0.065 \text{ kg}_f/\text{cm}^2)$

Similarly:

Second lift: $\Delta s_2 = (5.4 \times 115)(0.30)0.272 = 51 \text{ lb/ft}^2 \ (0.025 \text{ kg}_f/\text{cm}^2)$

Total $\Delta s_2 = 182 \text{ lb/ft}^2 \ (0.090 \text{ kg}_f/\text{cm}^2)$

The height of the third lift can then be

$$h_3 = \frac{5.14 \times 182}{115 \times 1.25} = 6.5 \text{ ft } (2 \text{ m})$$

giving a total embankment height $h = 14.0 + 5.4 + 6.5 = 25.9$ ft (7.9 m) within $7.0 + 5.4 + 6.5 = 18.9$ weeks at the rates given above.

If more time is available, a somewhat greater height can be reached by following the same method of analysis but probably at a reduced rate. Where time and other considerations do not permit, a much more expensive pile-supported viaduct may have to be used instead of an embankment.

RECOMMENDED FOR FURTHER STUDY

ASCE, Ref. 14.

Johnson, Stanley J., Refs. 152 and 153.

CHAPTER 6

PILE AND CAISSON FOUNDATIONS

6-1. Types of Piles and Pile-driving Equipment. Piles are intended to transmit foundation loads to deeper soil layers [Fig. 4-1 (II) and (III)] and may be made of timber, concrete, or steel. Combinations of the three materials are also employed. Concrete piles may be either of the precast type, or may be situ-cast, i.e., cast or molded in the ground. Steel piles may be either of the so-called H-pile type, i.e., consist of wide-flanged rolled-steel sections, or of the pipe-pile type.

Depending on the nature of support provided at the selected site by the surrounding soil, the piles may be defined either as *end-bearing* or as *frictional*. The term *floating* is sometimes used instead of *frictional*. Most piles are driven into the ground, but a few of the situ-cast concrete type are bored into the ground in very much the same way as boreholes made for soil exploration. The majority of piles are vertical, but when it is necessary to offer resistance to horizontal forces, they can be driven at an angle—so-called *batter piles*. The maximum possible inclination, or *batter*, of the piles depends on the design of the pile-driving equipment available and may reach $45°$ $(1:1$ slope). *Timber piles* represent the oldest type of piling in existence. They have been employed by the human race since prehistoric days, for instance, for the so-called lake dwellings.

When fully submerged, timber piles will not decay and are likely to last for centuries. After the collapse of the campanile at Venice [see Fig. 4-24 (II)], excavation revealed that the timber piles which had been driven for the tower foundation over a thousand years before the collapse were still in such good condition that they were left in place for the foundation of the new tower, and only additional piles were driven all around the old ones to increase the total area of the foundation.

Timber piles will deteriorate rapidly if subjected to alternate drying and wetting. Creosoting and other forms of impregnation treatment of the entire mass of the pile timber by various chemical preservatives will delay the process of decay but cannot prevent it entirely. For that reason, foundations of permanent structures supported by timber piles should be carried down to an elevation where the tops of the timber piles will remain permanently below the lowest groundwater-level elevation. The probability of the groundwater table dropping progressively in urban areas because of the diversion of normal replenishment, subsurface drainage, and the use of groundwater should be considered, since expensive underpinning measures and litigation over responsibilities might ensue if the timber piles started to rot.

The portions of timber piles which protrude from the soil into free water are liable to attack by various types of *marine borers*. Most of them occur in salt water. The *molluscan* group of borers, which includes the teredos and other shipworms, grows inside timbers, whereas borers of the *crustacean* group, for instance, the limnoria, usually eat the wood from the surface. Timber piles of piers and jetties have been rapidly destroyed by such borers in some instances. Pollution of the water usually decreases the danger of the appearance of borers, but there are a great number of other factors, which vary in different localities, on which their existence depends. Expert advice should be sought before deciding whether to use timber piles in contact with free water. The borers do not penetrate through the voids of soils, even of sands, so that timber piles embedded in soil under relieving platforms with steel or reinforced-concrete sheet piling on the water side are safe from attack by borers (see Fig. 14-39).

Scour around piers (Art. 12-3) can expose the tops of timber piles to attack by marine borers. Figure 6-1 shows a bridge pier at Manasquan, New Jersey, which suddenly dropped over 3 ft (90 cm) in the 1940s, necessitating provision of a temporary roadway on top of the tilted reinforced-concrete girders until the bridge could be rebuilt across the tidal inlet. The timber piles had been driven inside a steel sheet-pile cofferdam, rectangular in plan, of the type shown in Fig. 12-3, and a concrete slab was placed by the tremie method. The cofferdam was unwatered and the pier built in the dry. Thereupon all the sheet piling was pulled. Tidal currents produced scour, exposing several feet of the timber piling, which was gradually eaten away by borers. In this case trouble could have been avoided by cutting the steel sheet piling off at the level of the concrete pile cap and leaving the lower part in place.

Impregnation of timber piles by creosote and other chemicals in vacuum chambers prolongs the useful life of timber piles (see Ref. 5), but cannot

Fig. 6-1. A bridge pier dropped several feet after scour exposed the timber piles under its concrete footing to marine-borer attack.

entirely protect them from marine-borer attack, especially in warm waters, where the borers are particularly active.   In some tropical harbors even chemically well-treated timber piles do not last more than 14 years on an average when exposed to seawater.

Bark provides some natural protection against borer attack, but it should be removed from those portions of the pile skin which are relied upon to receive some frictional support from the soil.

There usually is no difficulty in obtaining timber piles in lengths up to 60 ft (18 m).   Greater lengths have been employed, but they are difficult to obtain, especially on the Eastern and Southern coasts of the United States; West Coast timber is frequently available in greater lengths.

Great care should be exercised not to *overdrive* timber piles, i.e., not to damage them when trying to pierce a stiff layer.   This can easily happen in compact sand.   The slight permanent set S which is recorded per blow at the soil surface may then mean not that the pile penetrates the sand as one body but that it has been crushed and that its fibers are telescoped or forced past each other at the zone of failure.   If there is any suspicion that something of the kind is occurring, it is advisable to pull out one or more piles for examination.   If the piles actually have been damaged, one should either change the specification and stop the driving at a higher elevation than originally intended or resort to jetting.

Overdriving is particularly dangerous in small buildings where columns are supported by only two to three piles.   In such cases a single badly damaged timber pile may cause structurally harmful eccentric settlements of a column.

The provision of steel points is not an effective protection since it only causes the zone of crushing of timber fibers to move from the pile tip to above the steel point.

A rather unusual case, requiring subsequent localized underpinning, occurred in a paper mill where chemicals used in the preparation of pulp leaked from a faulty storage tank and damaged the tops of timber piles under adjoining footings.

Timber piles usually are not permitted to carry loads in excess of 25 to 30 tons per pile.

Precast massive reinforced-concrete piles, 12 to 18 in. (30 to 45 cm) square, can carry much heavier loads, up to 50 tons per pile, depending on the dimensions and can take fairly heavy punishment during driving. Since the piles are cast at the soil surface, close control and inspection of their manufacture are possible.

However, this type of pile has some disadvantages. The required length of the pile has to be accurately determined in advance of construction. This is not always possible. Changes in length after the pile has been driven are time-consuming and therefore expensive.

If the pile is too long, the following steps are necessary to cut it off. First, the surface concrete has to be chipped off to expose the steel reinforcement. The steel has to be burned off with a torch, and only then can the excess length be knocked off. To increase pile length is also complicated. Additional steel reinforcement has to be cut to the required length and spliced with the reinforcement of the pile proper. Often this requires chipping off the concrete of the pile to a length of 3 ft (90 cm) or so, in order to expose the steel bars and permit their splicing. Vertical forms then have to be built over the original head of the pile and removed after the extension has been cast. Driving can be resumed only after the new concrete has hardened sufficiently.

These disadvantages are not eliminated by the use of prestressing techniques when casting the piles.

Sometimes steel bars are allowed to protrude from the head of the pile in order to permit splicing with the reinforcement of the pile-capping beams. Special perforated templates are then used, both during the casting of the pile, to hold the bars in their exact positions, and during the later driving, to form an anvil over the concrete of the pile.

The casting and storage of reinforced-concrete piles require appreciable space on the site of the job itself, except on waterfront jobs where the piles can be supplied, as needed, by barges from a central casting-yard some distance away.

The greatest stresses to which precast piles are subjected are produced during their handling and lifting prior to the driving proper. For instance, a pile being lifted into position for driving by a cable from the top of the pile-driver leads will act as a beam on two supports, stressed by its own weight, if the cable is attached to its top end. Precast reinforced-concrete piles have been made in lengths exceeding 100 ft (30 m).   Prestressing has many advantages in preventing cracking.   To avoid excessive bending stresses in long piles, support at several points should be provided by means of a system of cables and pulleys at all stages of their handling.

Sometimes the piles are cast with an enlarged base in order to increase the point resistance and decrease negative friction (Art. 6-4) along their shaft. This type is of advantage for purely end-bearing piles with very soft layers above the layer in which the piles are to receive their support.   They are frequently used in Holland, where some 50 to 60 ft (15 to 18 m) of soft clay and peat are usually followed by sand.   *Precast cylindrical piles* are discussed in Art. 6-8.

Cast-in-place concrete piles present special problems, outlined in Art. 6-7.

One of the most frequently used types of *steel piles* is made of heavy wide-flanged I beams.   Such piles are usually referred to as *H-piles*.   For available sections, see handbooks of the American Institute of Steel Construction.

Compared with precast reinforced-concrete piles, they have the advantage of being easier to handle on a job.   They do not have to be of an exactly

Fig. 6-2.   Lateral deflection of a steel H-pile after hitting a boulder. (*Photo by Tschebotarioff.*)

predetermined length before driving, since an excess length can be quickly cut off by a torch or an extra length added by welding. Depending on the section used, under favorable soil conditions H-piles can be assigned loads up to 48 to 120 tons per end-bearing pile or 48 to 70 tons per friction pile.

Some engineers are apt to question the performance of end-bearing H-piles driven down to hard rock, since the rock surface may be uneven. It appears possible that an H-pile may rest on rock only at its edge and, as a result, may be subjected to appreciable bending stresses at its tip, where this condition may not be detected from the soil surface without a load test. Excavations have occasionally revealed that H-piles can be overdriven and split when the edge of a pile hit the edge of a boulder.

Figure 6-2 illustrates an H-pile deflected laterally after hitting a boulder, so that it could no longer serve as support for the timber lagging of the excavation. The situation was remedied by driving a few additional short piles in front of the boulder.

The problem of bent, or so-called *dogleg*, piles is discussed further at the end of Art. 6-2.

Figure 6-3 shows an H-pile that remained vertical but took the shape of a corkscrew after hitting some obstruction eccentrically. No special measures of remedy were required in this case.

The steel-pipe piles do not have the above disadvantages, since they can be inspected along their entire length prior to concreting. In these piles the steel shell is made of sufficient thickness to permit its driving without a

Fig. 6-3. Corkscrewlike deformation of a steel H-pile, marked *A*, due to some obstruction in the ground. (*Photo by Tschebotarioff.*)

temporary stiffening inner core; this increases the cost of such piles.   Pipe piles can be driven either closed-end or openend.   A conical steel point is welded to the tip of the *closed-end* pipes.   The resulting connection is so rugged that piles of this kind can be driven through many feet of rock riprap and underlying materials which are sometimes found over soft clay at the edge of rivers or lakes where the riprap was dumped from past rock excavations in the vicinity, creating a difficult foundation problem for later construction.   The steel point centers the reaction to the pile load when bedrock is reached.   Closed-end pipe piles displace an amount of soil equal to their volume and therefore should not be used under conditions where this may be harmful (see Art. 6-4).   H-piles or *open-end* pipe piles should then be used; the latter are driven in a few feet at a time and the soil within the pipe is cleaned out before driving is resumed.   This slows down the work and makes it more expensive than driving piles closed-end.   The removal of the soil from an open-end pipe can best be done by washing, as for borehole casings (Art. 2-3*B*).   This is not always possible in cities, since it is usually forbidden to discharge such soil-laden water into sewers, where the silt and clay particles might settle out and clog the sewers.   Compressed air may then be used to blow the soil out of the pipe.   An air-jet pipe is driven a few feet into the soil within the pipe and a few inches of water are poured over the top of the soil.   Maximum pressure is built up in the compressor tank and is suddenly released.   The resulting blast of air shoots the soil out of the pipe.

End-bearing pipe piles on rock with a wall thickness of $\frac{1}{2}$ in. (12.7 mm) and a diameter of 20 in. (51 cm) have been allowed to carry up to 150 tons per pile.   Sheet piles of the Larsen type (Fig. 11-20) welded longitudinally in pairs and provided with a welded-on point have sometimes been employed instead of pipe piles.

The problem of *corrosion* arises for all types of steel piles exposed to the action of seawater.   It is particularly serious in the splash zone.   Therefore protective concrete jackets or at least special protective paints should always cover the steel to 1 ft (30 cm) or so below low-seawater level.   *Cathodic protection* can be used at all depths below the water surface.   It consists in creating countercurrents to the electric currents which accompany the process of corrosion.   These neutralizing countercurrents can be provided either by an external source of impressed current in combination with expendable anodes of scrap iron or by using expendable anodes of metal having a higher potential than steel (see Ref. 9).

Fresh water does not create corrosion problems for steel piles and sheet piles unless it is polluted by acids.   This is often difficult to detect from the surface, to which oil substances tend to rise.   Unexpectedly for local harbor engineers and for himself, the writer found this in 1956 while inspecting in a diving suit a 15-year-old steel sheet-pile bulkhead in the Cuyahoga River at Cleveland, Ohio, on which Wiegmann inclinometer measurements were to be performed (Art. 14-3*B*).   Near the surface the steel was well protected by a layer of oil and grease, but from a depth of about 7 ft (2.1 m) all the way down to the 24-ft-deep (7.3-m) dredge level $\frac{1}{4}$-in.-thick (6-mm) rust scales could be scraped off the sheeting.

A National Bureau of Standards study showed that steel piles driven into undisturbed soil are not adversely affected by corrosion, even in soil environments which are severely corrosive to iron and steel buried under disturbed conditions in excavated trenches (Ref. 224).

Studies by Rosenqvist (Ref. 271) showed that, other conditions remaining equal, corrosion of steel is likely to begin in zones of high stress.

When considering the *selection of a suitable type of pile*, it should be remembered that no single type can be best suited to meet all of the great variety of conditions likely to be encountered in foundation work. It will be shown by the subsequent articles that each type of pile has its merits and its disadvantages. Frequently more than one type of pile may meet the technical requirements of a given job. The availability of material at the given time and place and its cost will prove the deciding factors.

The types of piles which provide the greatest safety against improper execution and which permit constant good inspection and control on the job usually cost more than less foolproof types. As a rule, they also require a larger amount of steel. This circumstance is of no particular importance in peacetime in a country like the United States which produces large quantities of steel; but it may prove prohibitive for such pile types in countries which find it difficult to import all the steel they need, even for more essential items. Local engineers are then compelled to sacrifice some of the safeguards against improper execution in favor of economic expediency, especially when the local soil conditions permit doing so without much risk. For instance, the city of Cairo in the Nile delta has many reinforced-concrete buildings 10 to 14 and more stories high; practically all the pile foundations are of the situ-cast type, Simplex, Franki, Vibro, and other similar systems (Art. 6-7). On the whole, they have a satisfactory record of performance, although few if any use permanent outer protective steel casings, as are required for situ-cast piles by the building codes of New York and of many other cities in the United States. Thus a great number of factors may influence the choice of pile types, including the general economic structure and the past engineering experiences and tradition of a given country.

Similar considerations apply to the selection of *pile-driving equipment*.

There are three main types of pile-driving hammers: the drop hammer, the single-acting steam hammer, and the double-acting steam hammer. The *drop hammer* consists of a solid piece of metal which is lifted by means of a cable operated by a winch and which is then released from the desired height by some automatic device. It is comparatively slow in operation and is seldom employed in modern heavy construction work. In the *single-acting hammer* the energy of the steam is used only to lift the ram to the desired height. The driving energy is therefore provided only by the weight of the dropping ram.   In the *double-acting hammer* the steam is first used to lift the ram, which moves inside a solid casing, and then the direction of the steam pressure applied to the ram is reversed, so that it accelerates the ram on its downward path and thereby increases its energy at impact.   The effectiveness of different types of hammers is usually compared in terms of foot-pounds of energy per blow.   A wide variety of types and sizes is available, delivering up to 80,000 ft-lb (11,000 m-kg$_f$) energy per blow.   Most double-acting types of hammer may be easily adapted for special jobs, such as pulling sheet piling, where the direction of the hammer action has to be reversed, or for driving under water.   Timber piles for temporary supporting platforms on construction jobs or in military engineering can be quickly driven by light-weight gasoline-operated hammers.   Such hammers do not require heavy driving rigs.

To avoid damage to the head of the pile, special anvils, cushions, and caps are employed during pile driving.   This is particularly important for timber and precast reinforced-concrete piles.

Selecting the weight of a pile-driving hammer to match a given type of pile and soil conditions can be facilitated by using wave equations (see Art. 6-3).

Vibratory pile drivers are coming into use (see Art. 15-6); they do not damage pile heads.

6-2. Bearing Capacity of Piles.   Figure 6-4 illustrates the forces which

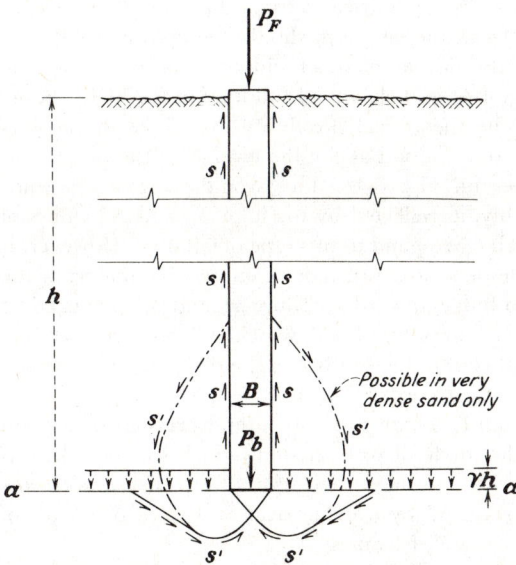

Fig. 6-4.   Forces acting on a pile.

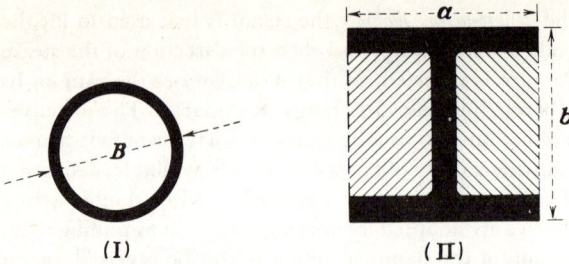

Fig. 6-5. Surfaces A_s along which the shearing stresses s of Fig. 6-4 act: (I) pipe pile; (II) H-pile.

act on a pile. P_F is the external *load at failure*. It is resisted by the end-bearing resistance P_b plus the sum of all shearing stresses $\sum s$ acting along the outer surface of the shaft

$$P_F = P_b + \sum s \tag{6-1}$$

The end-bearing resistance at failure P_b can be roughly estimated from a modification of Eq. (4-11) which is valid for strip footings. This modification was proposed by Terzaghi and Peck (Ref. 345) for square footings, B wide, and reads

$$P_b = A_b(1.2cN_c + \gamma h N_q + 0.4\gamma B N_\gamma) \tag{6-2}$$

where A_b is the cross-sectional area of tip of pile and the remaining symbols have the same significance as in Eq. (4-11).

Equation (6-2) can be used for cylindrical piles of diameter B as well, in which case the coefficient 0.4 in the last term should be replaced by 0.3.

Equation (6-2) assumes the development of sliding surfaces of the type considered by Prandtl (Fig. 4-4) and shown by full lines in Fig. 6-4. Some investigators have studied the theoretical possibility that these sliding surfaces might extend upward into the soil above the level aa of the pile tip, as shown by dash-dotted lines on Fig. 6-4. This would increase the end-bearing value P_b considerably, as reflected by the high N_c' and N_q' values of Fig. 4-7, the curves for which correspond to this type of failure. However, it can develop only in very dense sands. In more compressible materials the plane aa will simply tend to bulge upward at failure around the pile, against the weight γh of the overlying compressible soil, which will, however, serve to increase the shearing resistance s' in the soil below the plane aa, as expressed by the second term in the parentheses of Eq. (6-2).

In noncohesive soils $s = p_h \tan \delta$, where p_h is the lateral pressure of the soil against the pile and δ is the angle of wall friction, which can be taken as $\delta = 30°$. Then $\tan \delta = 0.577$, and the second term of Eq. (6-1), representing the frictional support received by a cylindrical or square pile shaft of length h from the noncohesive soil, becomes

$$\sum s = \sum A_s \, dh p_h \tan \delta = 0.577 A_s \sum p_h \, dh \tag{6-3}$$

With reference to Fig. 6-5, the value of A_s, that is, of the surface area per unit of shaft length which will have to shear past the soil at failure, should be taken as $A_s = \pi B$ for cylindrical and pipe piles and as $A_s = 2(a + b)$ for square or H-piles. Pullout tests show that usually most of the hatched area of soil in Fig. 6-5(II) adheres to the steel.

The term $\sum p_h \, dh$ in Eq. (6-3) corresponds to the area of a lateral-earth-pressure diagram against a pile, as shown on Fig. 6-6, which gives the analysis of a load test reported in Ref. 389.

This diagram is *not* intended to represent the actual distribution of lateral pressures along the length of a pile but only to give their maximum possible values at failure, providing thereby a common frame of reference for the estimation of K values from actual load tests; see Eq. (6-3a) and Table 6-1.

In the above test the failure load P_F, that is, the load at which the settlement of the 12BP53 steel H-pile rapidly increased, was found to be 105 tons

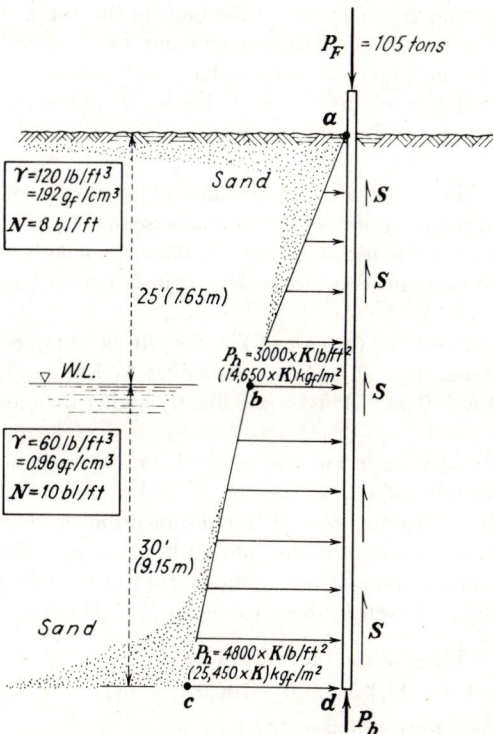

Fig. 6-6. Estimation of lateral-earth-pressure coefficient K from results of load test on a friction H-pile in sand.

(96.2 metric tons).   With $A_s = 4$ ft^2 (0.37 m^2), the frictional forces acting along the pile according to Eq. (6-3) and Fig. 6-6 will be

$$\sum s = 0.577 \times 4.0[(0.5 \times 25 \times 3{,}000K) + (30 \times 3{,}000K)$$
$$+ (0.5 \times 30 \times 1{,}800K)] = 360{,}000K \text{ lb} = 163K \text{ metric tons} \qquad (6\text{-}3a)$$

Here $K = K_y = p_h/\gamma h$, according to Eq. (10-3), is the coefficient of lateral earth pressure expressed by the ratio of lateral to vertical earth pressures along the length of the pile shaft.   Its minimum conceivable value would correspond to an active state of deformation, but it is more likely to be that of a neutral or "at rest" condition (see Art. 10-1) or be even higher in the case of dense sand and bulky displacement piles capable of inducing lateral compaction pressures.

Some early purely theoretical studies assigned lateral pressures of passive intensity to the support of piles.   This assumption has not been confirmed by the analysis of pile-load-test results, such as the one given by Fig. 6-6.

In addition, a number of so-called *static formulas* have been published over the years which attempt the evaluation of the frictional support provided to a pile by the surrounding granular soil on the basis of the angle of internal friction ϕ assigned to it.   These formulas will not be discussed further in this book since so far no practical methods have been developed for the numerical estimation of the relevant interrelationship between the angle of internal friction ϕ of the soil and the compactive effect of various types of piles.

The method described in this article provides a much more direct and verifiable approach to the estimation of the total frictional support of a pile, although the actual distribution of the frictional forces s along the length of a pile may be and probably is quite different from the one indicated in Fig. 6-6 (see Vesic, Ref. 392).

The maximum possible value of K for the case of Fig. 6-6 will be obtained by assuming the point resistance $P_b = 0$, so that, according to Eq. (6-1), $105 \times 2{,}000 = 360{,}000K$ and $K = 0.58$.   This is only slightly higher than an "at rest" value.

The minimum value of K conceivable for this case will be obtained by computing the maximum possible point resistance P_b from Eq. (6-2) and inserting its value in Eq. (6-1).   Taking $\phi = 30°$ for the medium to loose sand below the tip of the pile, we obtain from the chart of Fig. 4-7 $N_c = 50$, $N_q = 22$, and $N\gamma = 20$.   The cross-sectional area of the pile at its tip is taken to be $A_b = 1.0$ ft^2 (0.0932 m^2).   Inserting these values in Eq. (6-2) gives

$$P_b = 1.0\,[(1.2 \times 0 \times 50) + (25 \times 120 + 30 \times 60)22$$
$$+ (0.4 \times 60 \times 1.0 \times 20)] = 1.0(0 + 106{,}000 + 480)$$
$$= 106{,}480 \text{ lb} = 53.3 \text{ tons} = 48.3 \text{ metric tons}$$

From Eq. (6-1) we obtain

$$\sum s = P_F - P_b = 105.0 - 53.2 = 51.8 \text{ tons} = 47.9 \text{ metric tons}$$

and

$$K = \frac{51.8 \times 2,000}{360,000} = 0.29$$

Thus the actual value of K_y for the case of Fig. 6-6 will be somewhere between the limits of 0.29 and 0.58.   The selection procedure of a reasonable value for practical design purposes is given in Art. 6-5.

In cohesive soils with a shearing strength $s = c = q_u/2$ Eqs. (6-1) and (6-2) remain valid, but Eq. (6-3) will read

$$\sum s = \sum A_s \, dh \, cf \qquad (6-4)$$

where f is a coefficient, equal to or smaller than unity, which gives the ratio of adhesion of a clay to a steel or concrete pile to its cohesion in the natural state.   It will be seen from Fig. 6-7 that for stiffer clays its value drops to about $f = 0.35$.   The writer's own experiences confirm in a general way these trends established by Tomlinson (Ref. 348).

The end-bearing resistance P_b of a pile in clay contributes little to its overall bearing capacity.   Thus, from Eq. (6-2) and Fig. 4-7 (for $\phi = 0$) we obtain for a 1-ft² (0.0932-m²) precast-concrete pile resting on a stiff clay with an unconfined compressive strength $q_u = 1.5$ tons/ft² (1.5 kg$_f$/cm²), $c = 1,500$ lb/ft² $= 0.75$ kg$_f$/cm² at a depth of 55 ft (16.7 m) (as in Fig. 6-6):

$$P_b = 1.0[(1.2 \times 1,500 \times 6.2) + (25 \times 120 + 30 \times 60)1.0$$
$$+ (0.4 \times 60 \times 1.0 \times 0)] = 1.0(11,200 + 4,800 + 0)$$
$$= 16,000 \text{ lb} = 8.0 \text{ tons} = 7.25 \text{ metric tons}$$

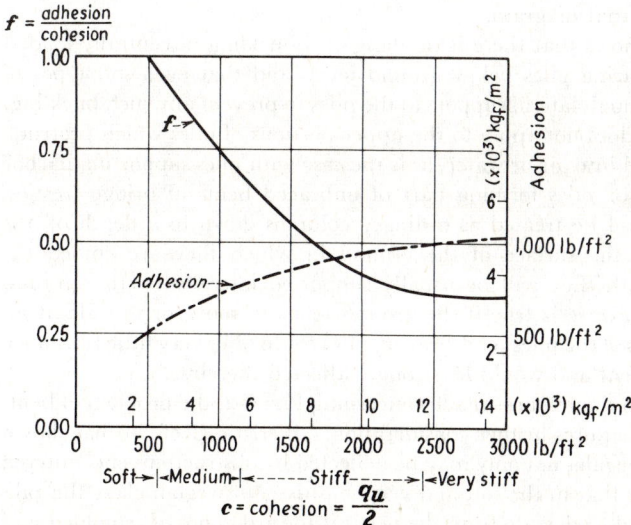

Fig. 6-7. The adhesion of clays to metal or concrete increases at a much slower rate than their shearing strength. (*After Tomlinson, Ref. 348.*)

At the same time the frictional component [Eq. (6-4) and Fig. 6-7], if c has the same value along the length of the shaft, will be

$$\sum s = 55 \times 4.0 \times 1{,}500 \times 0.53 = 175{,}000 \text{ lb}$$
$$= 87.5 \text{ tons} = 79.2 \text{ metric tons}$$

All these values refer to *failure loads* (see Art. 6-5 for *design loads*).

Sometimes it is important to determine the purely end-bearing properties of a pile. This can be done by performing first a load test of the ordinary kind, which would give the end-bearing plus the frictional resistance, followed by a pullout test, which would provide a measure of the frictional resistance alone. The difference between the values obtained by the first and the second test would indicate the end-bearing resistance of a single pile. For a time there were some doubts whether the frictional pullout resistance of a pile in sand was the same as the frictional resistance of a normally loaded pile. Small-scale model tests performed in several laboratories of different countries with model piles constructed along the lines of Fig. 2-17(I) all indicated a much smaller frictional resistance when the outer cylinder T was pulled up than when it was pushed down.

However, this seems to be an effect which is limited to the upper few inches or feet of sand, close to the surface. At any rate, the writer obtained exactly the same frictional resistance F for upward and for downward movement of the outer cylinder T of a Delft type cone [see Fig. 2-17(II)], which cylinder reached all the way to the sand surface, at four different total depths varying from 20 to 50 ft (6 to 15 m). These tests were performed during part 2 of the study illustrated by Fig. 2-18 and marked by circles and broken lines in that diagram.

Experience shows that there is no danger of buckling of centrally loaded vertical end-bearing piles below ground level, and that even soft types of clay provide enough lateral support to the piles to prevent any such buckling. Of course, this does not apply to the upper portions of piles which protrude from the ground into air or water, as is the case with piles supporting harbor piers or jetties or piles forming part of unbraced bents of bridge trestles. Such piles should be treated as ordinary columns down to a depth of 5 ft (1.5 m) below the surface of the ground in which they are embedded. Below that depth they will be usually supported laterally by the ground. However, the reverse is true if the ground tends to move or to slide at an angle to the axis of the piles; end-bearing piles could offer very little resistance to such movement and would be strongly affected thereby.

In addition to the remarks made concerning Fig. 6-2, the problem of bent, or *dogleg*, piles requires further consideration. Bjerrum (Ref. 30) has shown that long slender piles not only may be deflected by obstructions encountered at their tip, but that in the soft and very sensitive Norwegian clays the pile tip will also tend to deviate from the vertical toward zones of remolded and hence weakened clay, such as may be created by the earlier driving of another pile or by displacements of the clay at the bottom of vertical cuts.   According to Ref. 30, the Oslo building authorities reject H-piles which show a radius of curvature smaller than 1,200 ft (366 m),† as determined by a $1\frac{1}{4}$-in.-O.D. (32-mm) inclinometer lowered in a 2-in. (5-cm) tube attached to the H-pile. According to Eq. (4-16), this apparently means that no more than approximately 12,500 lb/in.² (880 kg$_f$/cm²) bending stress due to unforeseen pile deformations may be added to the 14,200 lb/in.² (1,000 kg$_f$/cm²) permissible design stress for piles less than 46 ft (14 m) long; to the 11,400 lb/in.² (800 kg$_f$/cm²) for piles 40 to 100 ft (12 to 30 m) long; and to the 9,200 lb/in.² (650 kg$_f$/cm²) for piles over 100 ft (30 m) long.

A different approach developed in the stiffer soils of the New York area. Parsons and Wilson (Ref. 242) showed by inclinometer measurements within bent dogleg cylindrical piles, followed by load tests, that there is no need to reject them, and have presented a rational method of analysis to justify their contention.   The granular soil under the bent portion of the pile was assumed to provide some vertical support.   The method was developed further by Sidney M. Johnson (Ref. 150).

6-3. Pile-driving Formulas and Records.   For over a century attempts have been made to determine the bearing capacity of a pile from its driving record.   One group of engineers equated the energy of the falling hammer to the work expended in driving the pile, i.e.,

$$WH = RS + Z \tag{6-5}$$

where W = weight of the falling hammer (or ram)
   H = height of drop of W
   R = ultimate resistance of the soil to penetration by pile
   S = penetration of pile into soil per blow (*set*)
   Z = sum of all energy losses due to any cause whatever

The practical difficulty centers on the determination of the value of Z, since there are a great number of sources of energy losses during pile driving.   To mention some: temporary compression of the ground; temporary compression in the pile; temporary compression in the driving head, including its packing; bouncing of the hammer on the pile; and elastic deformations of the hammer itself.

Another group of scientists, for instance Eytelwein (1820), based their formulas on the newtonian theory of impact, although, as shown later by A. E. Cummings (Ref. 74), Newton correctly qualified his laws of impact by reservations which precluded their use for problems similar to those of pile driving (see 1st ed., Art. 15-4).

The fundamental difference between the two approaches has not always

---

† Hanna (Ref. 119) implied that the figure of 12,000 ft in Ref. 30 is a misprint for 1,200 ft. In a personal communication to the writer Bjerrum has confirmed that 1,200 ft is correct.

been realized.   Thus the Committee on the Bearing Value of Pile Foundations of the ASCE was unable to reach agreement on the subject and published (Ref. 13a) two versions of its report.   Report A recognizes the many
limitations of pile-driving formulas but implies encouragement of the hope
that rational use of such formulas is nevertheless possible in practice if
proper judgment is exercised.   Report B carries to its logical conclusion the
recognition of these limitations by stating:

> All dynamic pile-driving formulas are subject to definite limitations and any
> dynamic pile-driving formula is nothing more than a yardstick to help the en-
> gineer secure reasonably safe and uniform results over the entire job.   The use
> of a complicated formula is not recommended since such formulas have no
> greater claim to accuracy than the more simple ones.

The writer endorses these views of Report (B).

A simple formula based on field experience and still frequently used in the
United States is the so-called *Engineering News* formula, developed by
Wellington (1888):

$$R = \frac{12WH}{S + c} \tag{6-6}$$

where c is a coefficient and the other terms have the same significance as in
Eq. (6-5).   The factor 12 is introduced because H is taken in feet and S in
inches.   With a factor of safety $F_s = 6.0$, the safe load R_s on the pile, for drop
hammers and for single-acting steam hammers, is

$$R_s = \frac{R}{6} = \frac{2WH}{S + c} \tag{6-7}$$

and for double-acting steam hammers,

$$R_s = \frac{2(W + Ap)H}{S + c} \tag{6-8}$$

where A = area of piston of ram
p = steam pressure on piston

The coefficient c is given the following values:

$$c = \begin{cases} 1.0 & \text{for drop hammers} \\ 0.1 & \text{for steam hammers} \\ 0.1P/W & \text{for steam hammers if inertia and weight of pile are con-} \\ & \text{sidered} \end{cases}$$

It should be noted that this formula is fairly satisfactory in granular soils
but does not take into account possible bouncing of the pile in saturated
cohesive soils, i.e., the considerable amount of energy which may be dissipated on the temporary compression of some of these soils.   This point can be
quite important.   The writer's interest in soil mechanics was first aroused
in 1928 when he worked as a reinforced-concrete designer for a European
construction company in Egypt and had to design new continuous foundation

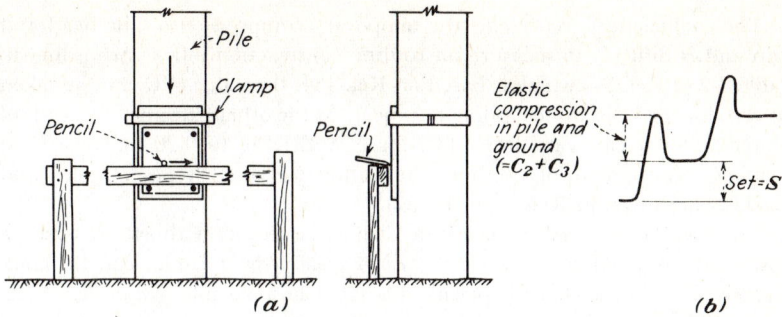

Fig. 6-8. Experimental method of determining the elastic compression in pile and ground during driving.

mats for three government buildings in the Nile delta over floating-pile foundations which had been condemned.   The static-load tests showed that the piles could carry less than one-third of the load they were supposed to carry, both according to the specifications and to a dynamic pile formula employed to check the driving.   An investigation showed that the saturated clay at that site behaved somewhat like rubber, so that the piles had little final penetration per blow but bounced considerably.   This possibility had not been taken into account by the formula and therefore had not been reported by the men on the job.   The faith in pile-driving formulas of the director of the construction company was severely shaken by the incident, and the lesson cost his firm a considerable amount of money.

A comparatively simple and yet rational formula which permits evaluation in the field of the energy losses by means of actual measurements is the Hiley formula (Ref. 131), much used in Great Britain, which reads

$$R = \frac{kWH}{S + C/2} \tag{6-9}$$

The terms R, W, H, and S have the same significance as in Eq. (6-5); H is taken in inches; k is a coefficient, always smaller than unity, which denotes the efficiency of the hammer blow, i.e., the fraction of its original energy (WH) actually transmitted to the pile; $C = C_1 + C_2 + C_3$ represents energy losses due to temporary compression of the driving head and packing (C_1), the pile (C_2), and the ground (C_3).

The values of S, C_2, and C_3 can be measured on any job by means of the arrangement shown in Fig. 6-8.   A pencil is moved by hand along a guiding board at constant speed from left to right, as shown in diagram (a).   Since at the same time the pile moves downward under the hammer blow and then moves back (upward) as it recovers partially, a record, as shown in diagram (b), is obtained on a sheet of paper clamped to the pile.   See Prob. 6-6 in this connection.

The coefficient C_1 represents the temporary compression of pile head and cap and is difficult to measure on routine construction jobs. According to table 7-2 of Ref. 57, which is based on Ref. 131, the value of C_1 can be taken as zero for the head of steel piling or pipe. At the other extreme, for heads of timber piles it can vary from 0.05 for easy driving to 0.20 for very hard driving. A number of intermediate values for other types of piles and packing are given in Refs. 131 and 57.

Since the Hiley formula permits a fairly close check on all energy losses, a lower factor of safety than for the *Engineering News* formula can be used, namely, $F = 2.0$, so that the permissible safe load on a pile will be $R_s = R/2$, where R is the value obtained from Eq. (6-9).

In some types of soils piles may "freeze" after a pause in the driving; i.e., they offer more resistance to the driving when it is resumed than they did before the halt [see Fig. 6-16(II)]. Therefore in some soils any pile-driving formula based on uninterrupted driving may give much too conservative values compared with the results of pile load tests (see Art. 6-5).

Summing up, considerable caution and judgment are necessary when estimating the actual bearing capacity of a pile by means of driving formulas. Nevertheless, driving records are very useful, since it is possible to make expensive static-load tests only, at best, on a very small fraction of the total number of piles driven, but it is a simple matter to keep a driving record of *every* pile driven on a job, and thereby to relate their performance

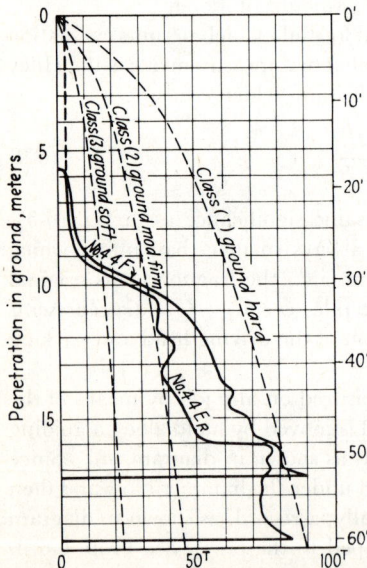

Fig. 6-9. A graphical method of recording the driving resistance of piles which facilitates the comparative evaluation of the supporting properties of the soil strata penetrated. (*British Steel Piling Co., Ltd.*)

to the results of the few static-load tests made on that site. A good way to keep such records is illustrated by Fig. 6-9. A supply of graphs is printed on tracing paper, including three curves which designate the limits of the driving resistance which is to be expected at different depths with the type of pile and hammer used on the job in class 1 ground—hard, class 2 ground—medium firm, and class 3 ground—soft. The particular three limit curves in the diagram were established on the strength of experience with the Hiley formula and different equipment in different soils. A single-acting hammer was used in Fig. 6-9, with $W = 2.0$ tons and a stroke $H = 48$ in. (12.2 cm) for pile $44E_R$ and $H = 36$ in. (9.2 cm) for pile 44F. Both were 50-ft (15.3-m) 14 by 14 in. timber piles. The final set was $S = 0.29$ in. (7.4 mm) for the first of the above two piles and $S = 0.23$ in. (5.8 mm) for the second. With these data and other equipment coefficients of the Hiley formula the actual driving record of each pile on a job can be quickly plotted on separate graph sheets, and copies can be made if needed. The driving performance of each pile on a job can be compared with the others by a glance at the file record. Any soft spots missed by the necessarily not too closely spaced borings during the soil investigation made in advance of construction are immediately revealed by a graphical record of the type shown in Fig. 6-9, which serves as a yardstick for the comparison of the performance of the piles over the entire job. The depth of penetration of individual piles can then be quickly adjusted when necessary to the actual soil condition encountered beneath each pile. However, this remark refers only to the few feet of soil around the tip of that particular pile which provides its support. All the restrictive comments of Art. 6-6 concerning the validity in respect to the entire pile foundation of load-test results on single piles apply to an equal extent to the results of pile-driving records. In other words, borings should ascertain the nature and the properties of soil layers well beneath the elevation to which the tips of the piles will reach. This is essential since otherwise detrimental settlements of the entire structure may result, as illustrated by Fig. 6-21. The piles of the bridge shown there were all driven to a satisfactory resistance, according to dynamic formulas and to the actual pile-driving records, into a fairly stiff layer of clay. Deep borings were performed only later and disclosed the presence of much softer underlying layers of clay and peat, in which the seat of the considerable surface settlements was located; these settlements reached a maximum of 6 ft 4 in. (1.95 m).

It is not always possible to drive piles, especially if they are made of timber, through a compact layer of sand without serious damage to the piles. At the same time it is often necessary to have the piles reach a deeper elevation, for instance, when there is a danger of scour or of later erosion by water currents. Pile *jetting* then must be resorted to; i.e., a water jet churns up the sand along the tip of the pile, which sinks into the sand as a result. When the desired elevation is almost reached, the jet is withdrawn, and the pile is driven to *refusal*, i.e., the minimum penetration per blow desired.

Preboring is sometimes done with an auger diameter only slightly smaller than the cross-sectional area of a pile, to avoid hard driving through a layer of stiff clay.

Increasing use of the *wave equation* has permitted a better understanding of the nature of stresses created in piles of different types by hammers of different weight during driving, as well as a rational analysis of the problem. The theoretical basis was provided over a century ago in France by St. Venant and Boussinesq, was first applied to pile driving in England (Ref. 109), and was generally advocated as a promising substitute for the questionable premises of newtonian impact-type pile-driving formulas by A. E. Cummings (Ref. 74).

In its original form the theory considered the effect of an axially centered longitudinal impact by a weight striking one end of an elastic rod of a length L with no friction along its sides which would restrain compressive waves traveling up and down the rod at a velocity

$$a = \sqrt{\frac{Eg}{w}} \qquad (6\text{-}10)$$

where g = acceleration of gravity
E = Young modulus of rod material
w = unit weight of rod material

The time for a compressive wave to travel from one end of the rod to the other is then $t = L/a$.

Even in this simplified form the wave-equation approach served to explain why in hard driving tensile cracks would appear at the top of reinforced concrete piles but in soft driving, e.g., that occurring after penetrating a stiff layer into soft clay, tips of inadequately reinforced concrete-pipe piles have been known to break off because tensile stresses are created near the tip of the pile, which lacks a firm support in an axial direction to reflect the compression waves. This condition can be crudely approximated by several billiard balls lined up against each other in the center of a billiard table to form a straight rodlike line, free at both ends. When hit axially by another billiard ball, the balls at the other free end of the continuous row will separate slightly from each other, indicating that the compressive shock wave created tension at the free end. On the other hand (to simulate hard driving of a pile), if an otherwise identical rodlike line of billiard balls is placed at right angles to an edge of the billiard table and directly against it and is then hit axially at the other, free, end by another ball, the striking ball will bounce back slightly, followed by a couple of the first balls in the line.

Nevertheless, contrary to the original assumptions of the St. Venant–Boussinesq theory, a pile does have frictional support along the length of its shaft and presents other complicating factors.   To meet these complications and permit numerical evaluation of relevant parameters, E. A. L. Smith (Ref. 304) suggested representing an actual pile, with its pile cap and hammer shown on the left-hand side of Fig. 6-10, by a series of individual weights, springs, and soil-resistance forces, as sketched on the right-hand side of Fig. 6-10.   With the help of an electronic computer and the wave equation this model permits rational evaluation of stresses at any moment during the driving of any type of pile and cap by any type of hammer, provided the real values of the soil frictional and point resistance forces are known.

These dynamic soil-resistance forces depend, among other things, on the damping characteristics of the soil.   Therefore they can be estimated only from comparative analyses of elaborate pile-driving records with subsequent load-test data on the same piles.   A step in this direction was made when Forehand and Reese (Ref. 99), under the writer's guidance, analyzed driving and loading records of 24 piles supplied through the courtesy of W. P. Kinneman and obtained numerical data on the values of the relevant damping and other dynamic soil properties.

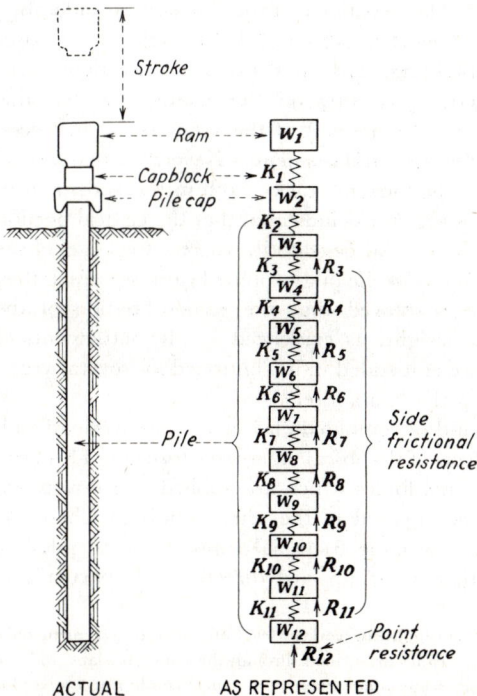

Fig. 6-10. Method of representing pile for wave-equation calculations. *(From E. A. L. Smith, Ref. 304.)*

As more such evaluations become generally available, the precision of results obtained by the wave equation will increase. It has already been used to determine the most efficient type of hammer for a given type of pile under given soil conditions. Generally speaking, the heaviest type of hammer which will not damage the pile should be used.

According to Chellis (Ref. 57), comparisons have shown that for short piles the results of Hiley type pile-driving formulas [Eq. (6-9)] agree fairly well with the results of wave-equation analysis but the former tend to underestimate the capacities of long heavy piles and mandrels.

6-4. Remolding of Clays and the Resulting Drag on Piles. The interaction between piles and the surrounding soil is one of the first points to be considered when designing a pile foundation, especially when clay layers are to be penetrated. The clay in the immediate vicinity of the piles is strongly distorted The general displacement of soil layers may not be as considerable as in an excessively deep excavation (Fig. 9-5); nevertheless, it is usually sufficient to cause detrimental settlements of sensitive clays. This was the case of the building to which Fig. 15-1 of the first edition referred. Steel-pipe piles had been driven closed-end to hardpan through over 100 ft (30 m) of varved clay. The displaced clay heaved around the building; trenches were closed thereby. The sensitivity of such clays is considerable, with average values of $S \geq 5.0$ (see Art. 3-2G and Table 4-2). A subbasement was provided in that building, and its floors and partitions were placed directly on the ground, apparently on the assumption that this should be safe, since the weight of some 6 ft of the original soil had been removed in the excavation for the subbasement. Nevertheless, signs of distress soon appeared there in the form of cracks, both in the floors and in the partitions. The location of the cracks indicated that the central portion of the floors was settling with the ground beneath it, whereas the edges of the floors were prevented from doing so by the pile-capping beams on which they rested. Accurate measurements showed that the reconsolidation of the remolded clay under its own weight, as evidenced by the settlements of special bench marks which were embedded in it, continued for several years. Mudjacking† was used to keep the floors level.

Incompletely consolidated and/or remolded clay layers can overload end-bearing piles, owing to the effects of the so-called *negative friction*. This term is employed to designate frictional forces which are applied in a downward direction to the pile surface, as opposed to the usual condition where the surrounding soil provides at least some frictional support to the piles by means of frictional forces acting in an upward direction. A particularly

---

† Mudjacking is a procedure used in highway work to level off concrete pavement slabs which settle unevenly at their joints. Holes are drilled through the concrete slabs and are connected by hoses to a *mudjack;* this is the name given to a vehicle combining a mixer for a water-soil-cement slurry and a pump which forces the "mud" slurry under the pavement and lifts ("jacks") it up to the desired elevation.

dangerous condition may arise when piles are driven through a newly placed fill, for instance, slag or gravel, and through underlying soft clay to a deeper-lying hard layer.   As the clay consolidates, the entire weight of the fill may then be transmitted through negative friction to the piles and, in some instances, may crush them.

Thus a remolded clay layer is liable to begin settling under its own weight. The surcharge by a new fill will have the same effect irrespective of remolding.   In either case, as shown in Fig. 6-11, the usual direction of the shearing stresses along the pile shaft in the clay and in the fill above it is reversed if the downward movement of the pile is prevented, for instance by its penetration into a sand layer.

Equation (6-1) remains valid, but the drag forces $\sum (-s)$ along the upper portion of the pile shaft, h_1 long, should now be added to the fraction P_{DF} of the failure load due to structural design loads

$$P_F = P_{DF} + \sum (-s) \tag{6-11}$$

This load P_F must now be resisted only by the lower portion of the pile, h_2 long, which is embedded in the sand.

The drag forces can be considerable.   Thus, in the bridge abutment shown in Figs. 2-14, 2-15, 10-34, and 10-35 the drag forces $\sum (-s)$ were estimated to equal up to 50 percent of the total load P_F when setting up the load test (see Art. 6-5).

Particularly severe effects of negative friction were observed where the lower portion of the fill consisted of slag which cemented itself into large slabs hanging on the two steel piles supporting each of the columns of a light factory shed.   Excavation revealed that both H-piles and steel-pipe piles had buckled at the clay surface aa (see Fig. 6-11).

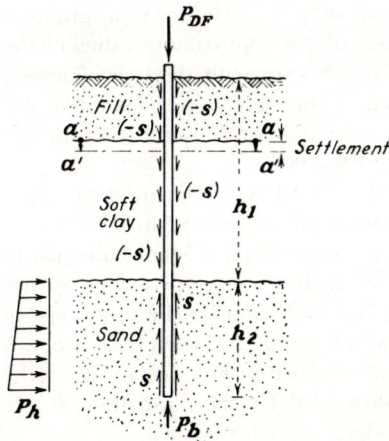

Fig. 6-11.   Any settlement of a clay layer after piles are driven creates negative friction and drag along the upper portion h_1 of a pile shaft.

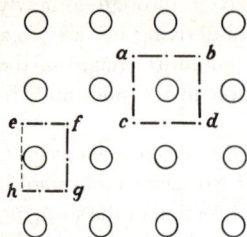

Fig. 6-12. Estimation of drag on piles in a group

The only sure way to prevent such overloading entirely is to drive the piles through a protective pipe reaching down to the clay layer, in a manner similar to the one used for load tests (see Fig. 6-13). But this is much too expensive for use with all production piles.

If no such protective measures are taken, the maximum load due to negative friction which may hang on an interior pile of a group (Fig. 6-12) is the weight of the soil column *abcd*. The maximum load which may hang on an outer pile of a group is equal to the weight of a soil column *efgh* plus the negative shearing stresses along the vertical plane *eh*. These negative stresses can be very roughly estimated in the same way as described earlier for positive shearing stresses with reference to Fig. 6-6.

The most severe remolding of a clay by pile driving occurs close to the pile-shaft surface. However, this is also the zone where remolding effects are of the shortest duration, because of the rapid dissipation of excess pore pressures created there by the pile driving. This is especially true if the pile shaft can serve as a drainage channel, e.g., for a concrete pile without any outer steel shell.

Excavation of a Simplex cast-in-place concrete pile, which the writer observed in Egypt after it had been load-tested to failure, showed that the slippage had occurred along a 22-in.-diameter cylindrical surface around an approximately 18-in.-diameter concrete shaft. A 2-in.-thick ring of stiffer overconsolidated clay adhered to the shaft.

6-5. Pile Load Tests and Their Use in Design. A pile load test is the only reliable way to determine the bearing capacity of a *single* pile. The static formulas described in Art. 6-2 are a useful tool since they permit a designer roughly to estimate the required length of piles. However, in granular soils their use depends on the knowledge of the approximate values of the coefficient of lateral pressure K, which may vary with the type of deposit encountered and type of the pile used. Therefore a pile load test still remains a necessity in a new location to permit greater assurance in the use of static formulas even for preliminary estimates.

Thus in the case of the bridge across the West River in Connecticut (Figs. 2-14, 2-15, 10-34, and 10-35) the required pile lengths at first had to be estimated on the basis of the analysis of a load test on a MonoTube pile (a thin longitudinally fluted steel shell filled with concrete) performed earlier for another bridge about a mile away but underlain by the same type of deposit. An analysis of that load test, which had been carried to failure, was made by the procedure illustrated with reference to Fig. 6-6 and gave the value of $K = 0.55$. This value was then used for the estimation of pile lengths required for the West River bridge.

Since preliminary control load tests must be carried without failure to twice the design load P_D, the pile lengths should, in general, be determined by the trial-and-error procedure of Fig. 6-6 for a failure load P'_F

$$P'_F = 2.30P_D \tag{6-12}$$

For the West River bridge the piles were tested to twice the design load, according to Figs. 6-13 and 6-14B. The design load was approximately 60 tons (54 metric tons), of which about half was due to dead and live loads of the bridge and the other half to estimated drag loads resulting from negative friction.

The validity of the assumed $K = 0.55$ value was confirmed by the load tests for the river piers, for which steel-pipe piles driven closed-end were used. They displaced approximately the same amount of soil as the MonoTube piles, possibly a little more, and hence had a similar compactive effect. However, for the abutments, for which H-piles with a lesser soil displacement were used,† the smaller $K = 0.38$ value was found.

The load-test requirement of the local authorities at that time was not

---

† Mainly because of the high fills there and hence large drag loads on the piles unless remolding was minimized.

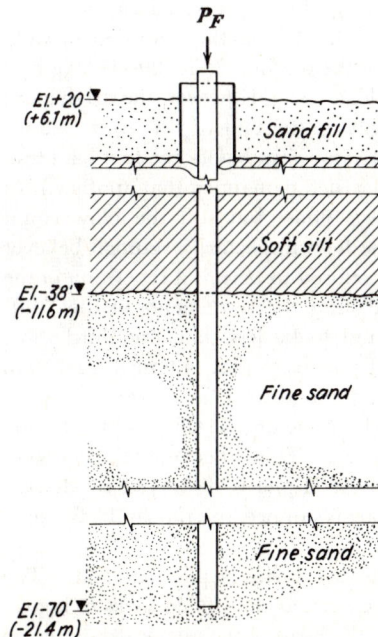

Fig. 6-13. Protective pipe around load-tested pile serves to eliminate temporary frictional support by layers which may later develop drag.

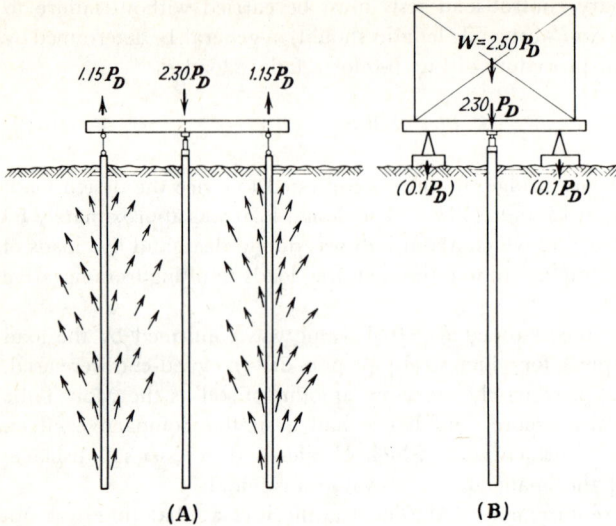

Fig. 6-14.   Two methods of performing pile load tests.   (*Ref. 374.*)

more than 0.5 in. (1.25 cm) settlement under the design load and not more than 1.5 in. (3.76 cm) under twice the design load.   A tested H-pile passed the first requirement but failed the second.   It was then decided to weld another 15-ft (4.6-m) length to the top of the original 95-ft (29-m) length of the H-pile, drive it all in, and repeat the load test.   However, the driving did not indicate any increase in blow counts at the end of the 15-ft (4.6-m) penetration compared with the recorded values just before the first load test. The field inspector of the authorities concerned demanded that another 15-ft (4.6-m) length be welded on.   This was done, but still the blow count remained approximately the same.   The field inspector, a staunch believer in dynamic pile-driving formulas, again refused to permit a repetition of the expensive load test.   He was overruled, and the settlements of the 30-ft-longer (9.2-m) friction H-pile were found to be less than one-third those recorded on the first try.   Ultimately, H-piles only 15 ft (4.6 m) longer than the 90 to 100 ft (28 to 31 m) originally estimated were used.

The incident provides another example of the unreliability of pile-driving formulas (Art. 6-3) under similar conditions.   This is because the friction of a fine saturated sand along the skin of an H-pile is destroyed by driving vibrations but is reestablished when driving is stopped and the sand "freezes" around the shaft of the pile.

There are *three main types of load application* during a pile load test.   The first, performed by placing dead weights, such as sand-filled sacks of known weight, on top of a platform attached to the head of the pile tested is now no

longer in use.   The two alternative methods now practiced are shown in
Fig. 6-14.   Both involve using calibrated hydraulic jacks pressing against a
beam attached to at least two anchor piles (Fig. 6-14A) or against a counterweight W (Fig. 6-14B).   For end-bearing piles both methods are equally
satisfactory.   However, for friction piles, especially in noncohesive soils,
method (B) is preferable because the reverse friction along the anchor piles
of method (A) spreads around them and tends to reduce the effective weight
of the sand in the vicinity of the test pile and hence its shearing strength.
This, in turn, reduces its capacity to support the loads from the shaft of the
test pile.†

† The opposite effect will be created in pullout tests when the jack is placed above the
crossbeam and its head is attached by straps to the test pile.   The two anchor piles are then
in compression and will increase the effective vertical pressures in the sand around the test
pile.

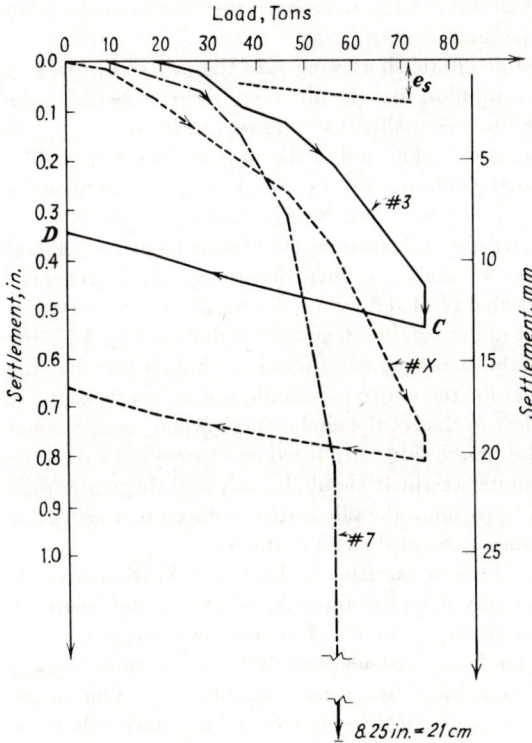

Fig. 6-15.   Pile 7 tested by method (A) of Fig. 6-14 failed, but piles 3
and X, tested by method (B), passed the test.   (*Courtesy of Philip P.
Brown, Ref. 41.*)

Figure 6-15 illustrates the point. A series of load tests was performed in
the 1950s by the U.S. Navy on H-piles driven into compact sand deposits of
the coastal plains in central New Jersey. The water table was at a depth of
8 ft (2.4 m); 10BP42 piles were used and were to sustain a test load of 75
tons (68 metric tons). The driving was done by a McKiernan-Terry 9-B-3
double-acting hammer. The *Engineering News* formula [Eq. (6-7)] gave a
safe load $R_s = 13.6$ tons (12.4 metric tons) for the 35.5-ft-long (10.8-m) pile 7;
$R_s = 13.6$ tons (12.4 metric tons) for the 35.5-ft-long (10.8-m) pile 3, and
$R_s = 10.5$ tons (9.6 metric tons) for the 34-ft-long (10.4-m) pile X.

Pile 7 was tested by method (A) of Fig. 6-14 and failed at a load of 56 tons
(51 metric tons), settling 8.25 in. (20.9 cm) under that load. On each side
of that test pile, 7 ft 2 in. (2.2 m) away, were two 52-ft-long (16-m) anchor
piles, which lifted about 3 in. (7.5 cm) out of the ground during the test.

By contrast, pile 3, located only 27 ft (8.3 m) away from pile 7, was tested
by the counterweight method (B) of Fig. 6-14 and passed the test, settling
only 0.54 in. (13.7 cm) under the test load of 75 tons (68 metric tons). This
was also true of pile X, which was located at a greater distance from pile 7 but
on the same site and in the same deposit.

The maximum conceivable elastic shortening e_s of the pile shown in Fig.
6-15 is computed on the assumption that the pile is end-bearing, with all the
test load reaching the pile tip. Actually, it should be much smaller.

An analysis by the procedure of Fig. 6-6 of the test results given by Fig.
6-15 shows that for the anchor-pile test (A) on pile 7, $K = 0.74$ and for the
counterweight type (B) tests on piles 3 and X, $K = 1.12$.

Contractors usually prefer the anchor-pile test arrangement (A) of Fig.
6-14 since it is less expensive and less time-consuming. It is generally
accepted by authorities in charge of tests since the results are conservative
and hence safe. However, under conditions similar to those of Fig. 6-15, the
advantages presented by the arrangement shown by Fig. 6-14B and the
resulting possible economies for the entire job should not be overlooked.

To avoid the reverse effect to that of the anchor pulls when using method
(B), which could be on the unsafe side since it would represent a surcharge
around the test pile, the counterweight W should be only slightly greater than
the test load. The surcharge around the pile is then reduced to a negligible
value at the most critical stage, i.e., at the end of the test.

The safety against shear failure or excessive settlement of the soil under the
spread-footing supports (usually a grid of timbers) of the counterweight W
(Fig. 6-14B) should be investigated (Chap. 4) for all stages of the test. This
is particularly important for heavy test loads of 400 tons or more when a
tilting of the counterweight can have disastrous consequences.† One of the
possible precautions is not to place all the counterweight at once before the

† During a 1970 attempt to perform a 2,000-ton load test, the largest ever, in the harbor of
Rio de Janeiro, one of the pile legs supporting the counterweight platform gave way as the
test was about to begin, causing its collapse. Eight men were killed.

TABLE 6-1. Coefficients of Lateral Pressure K Estimated from Pile Load Tests in Noncohesive Soils

Pile type	Test type	K value	Soil type
H-pile	Counterweight	0.38	Dense varved fine sand and rock-flour silt
Monotube	Counterweight	0.55	Dense varved fine sand and rock-flour silt
Pipe pile	Counterweight	0.55	Dense varved fine sand and rock-flour silt
H-pile	Anchor piles	0.29	Loose sand
H-pile	Anchor piles	0.75	Dense sand
H-pile	Counterweight	1.12	Dense sand
H-pile	Direct pull	>0.64†	Very dense sand with seams of hard silty clay
H-pile	Anchor piles (loading)	0.65‡	Medium to dense sand
H-pile	Anchor piles (pull-out)	>0.68	Same pile

† This is a *safe* K value corresponding to a maximum possible pull applied to the pile which could not make it move. Data on test courtesy of W. P. Donald, partner, Carr & Donald & Associates Ltd., Toronto, Ontario.

‡ This value was obtained from a test during the June 1972 ASCE Specialty Conference at Purdue University (Ref. 8a). The failure load of the 10-in. 57-lb HP pile was 94.0 tons. It was determined from a load-settlement diagram sent later to the writer by Prof. G. G. Goble. Using at the site the procedure illustrated by Fig. 6-6 and an estimated value of $K = 0.7$, the writer obtained a frictional limit resistance of $\sum s = 91$ tons. Adding 10 tons for the point load, the writer forecast a failure load $P_F = 101$ tons. This and another forecast of 100 tons came closest to reality. All other forecasts were higher, including a computerized on-the-spot analysis of the driving record by the CRP method (Ref. 109a).

The pull-out test raised the pile 2.0 inches (5.0 cm) at a load of 95 tons when the jack travel was exceeded.

start of the test but to do so in steps after part of the previous test weight has already been transferred in increments to the test pile.

Table 6-1 summarizes the K values obtained from a limited number of load tests analyzed by the writer according to Fig. 6-6 under the assumption that the point resistance P_R has reached its maximum value. It will be seen that there is a considerable scattering of results but with a general trend of higher K values for originally denser granular deposits for piles of larger cross section and hence displacement and for counterweight (Fig. 6-14B) type of loading.

Therefore, unless the results of a friction pile-load test in the same deposit are available, it is advisable to take reasonably low K values from Table 6-1 when determining the length of test piles. Relevant specifications should have provisions permitting the decrease of pile lengths to be ordered for the entire job once the results of the load test have been analyzed.

The test load should be applied in increments, preferably not larger than one-fourth the design load P_D. Each load increment has to be maintained until the rate of continued pile settlement reaches minimum values specified in most building codes. Sometimes this means maintaining the load for 24 hr, requiring constant observation and adjustment of the jack, since its load is liable to drop off even with slight pile settlement.

In different building codes there are a great number of definitions of allowable pile loads. The 1968 Building Code of New York City (Ref. 228, p. 120) art. C-26-1107.1(d)(4)c4 specifies that the allowable pile load shall be the lesser of two values computed as follows:

(a) Fifty (50) per cent of the applied load causing a net settlement of the pile of not more than 0.01 in. (0.254 mm) per ton (0.91 metric ton) of applied load. Net settlement in this paragraph means gross settlement due to the total test load minus the rebound after removing 100 per cent of the test load.

(b) Fifty (50) per cent of the applied load causing a net settlement of the pile of 0.75 in. (19 mm). Net settlement in this paragraph means the gross settlement as defined in 4(a) above, less the amount of elastic shortening in the pile section due to total test load.

According to this definition, pile 3 in Fig. 6-15 passed both the above criteria (a and b) for an allowable design load of $\frac{7.5}{2} = 37.5$ tons (34.2 metric tons), but pile X indicated a somewhat smaller design load of about $\frac{6.5}{2} = 32.5$ tons (29.6 metric tons).

Somewhat unclear in the above code provisions is the exact meaning of "elastic shortening" of the test pile. The maximum possible value of e_s is shown in Fig. 6-15 for the condition when the full load reaches the pile tip. This is, however, hardly ever the case. Tests on essentially end-bearing instrumented H-piles reaching to glacial hardpan through Chicago clay showed that most of the test load was transferred by adhesion to the upper clay layers without reaching the pile tip (Ref. 13, figs. 51 to 54).

The exact amount of elastic shortening e_s of a test pile is relatively unimportant for short (35 ft = 10.7 m) friction piles of the type shown in Fig. 6-15. Further, for a long (over 100 ft = 31 m) 12BP53 H-pile driven to hard point resistance by a Vulcan 06 hammer at 19,050 ft-lb (264,000 cm-kg$_f$) energy, as shown in Fig. 6-16, the e_s curve, which is drawn under the assumption of only end-point resistance, has little meaning. A much greater axial load than the design load of 28 tons = 25.5 metric tons (no drag included) could have been used, but it was not changed because of the objectives of that project (see the discussion of Figs. 10-26 to 10-32).

When interpreting the results of load tests on single piles, it should always be remembered that they provide data concerning the bearing power of only the one pile tested. Such tests therefore bring out the properties of the pile type in relation to the surrounding soil, but only in respect to the number of piles which were tested simultaneously. A careful study of the entire soil profile at the site should be made before conclusions can be drawn concerning the probable behavior of larger pile groups than the ones tested or of the entire building.   The reasons for this are similar to those which limit the usefulness of load tests on small spread footings.   This point is illustrated by Fig. 6-17.   During a load test on a single pile only a small volume of soil immediately around the test pile is stressed by the applied load.   Stresses of equal intensity will reach to a much greater depth under the building itself.

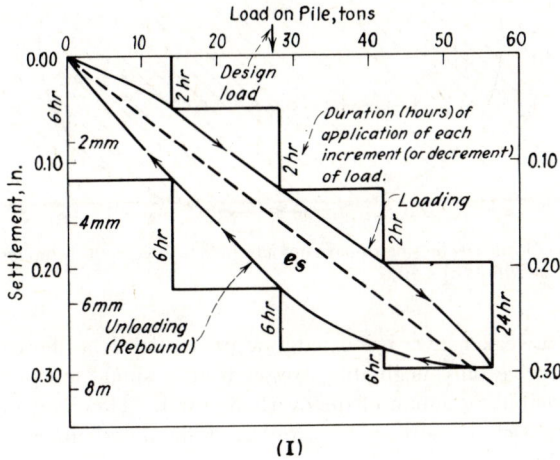

(I)

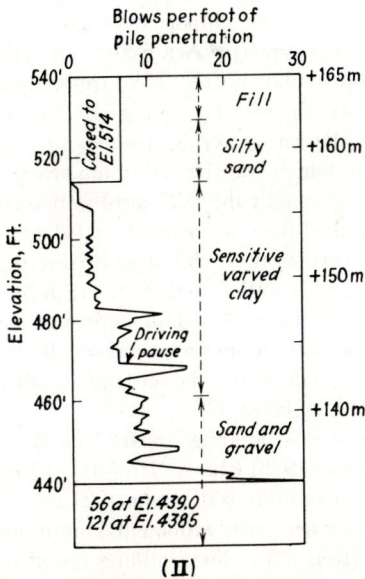

(II)

Fig. 6-16.   Test of H-pile at Allamuchy site (see Figs. 10-26 and 10-32).

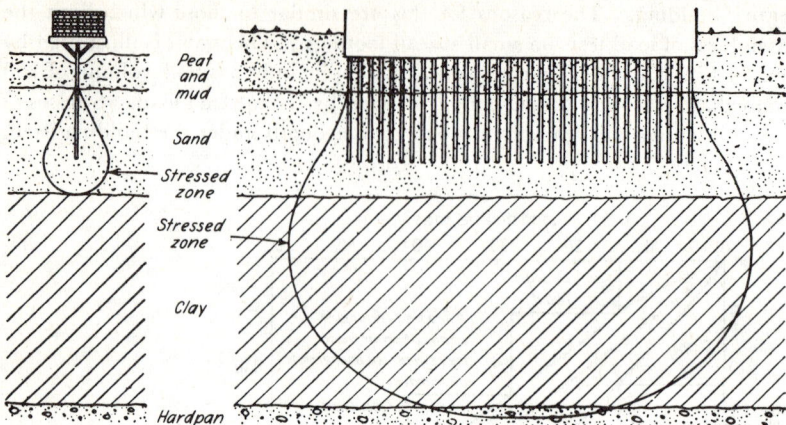

Fig. 6-17. Why the results of load tests on single piles cannot be used to forecast the behavior of the entire structure. *(From Ref. 107.)*

Should it happen that a weaker layer is located at a greater depth, as shown in Fig. 6-17, it will receive only negligible stresses from a single test pile because of the load-distributing action of the overlying sand.   However, in the case of the structure itself, the stresses transmitted to the underlying clay layer will be considerable.

6-6. Group Action of Piles.   The following field observations further illustrate the point made by Fig. 6-17.   Figure 6-18 shows the facade of the Mixed Law Courts in Cairo, Egypt.   The structure was supported by 28-ft-long (8.5-m) situ-cast concrete piles of the Simplex type (see Art. 6-7).   The piles were embedded in a stiff upper crust of brown clay, not sensitive to remolding. Load tests on single piles (of which the curve, pile II, in Fig. 15-3 of 1st ed. is representative) gave only small settlements, varying from $\frac{1}{16}$ to $\frac{1}{4}$ in. (1.6 to 6.4 mm) under 40- to 60-ton loads, which was the maximum any pile of the building had to carry.   This is less than 0.01 in. (0.25 mm) settlement per ton load, a value frequently used as one of the criteria for the satisfactory behavior of a test pile (see Art. 6-5).   Nevertheless, the building itself settled some 50 times more than the test pile; i.e., it settled over 1 ft, much of it differentially (see diagrams of building T, Ref. 352).   This happened because a softer layer C of darker clay underlay the upper oxidized stiff brown clay B in which the piles were embedded.   The seat of the settlements of the building was located in that deeper-lying clay layer (C).

Something very similar to the record of this building on the Nile River happened in the Mississippi delta to the new (1938) Charity Hospital at New Orleans, which by 1953 had sustained a maximum settlement of 21 in. (53 cm) at the center and 9 in. (23 cm) at the corner, with settlements continuing at the rate of $\frac{1}{4}$ in. (6.3 mm) per year (Ref. 32).   The building rested on short (23 ft = 7 m) timber piles, 2 ft 9 in. (84 cm) on centers, designed for 15.3 tons (14 metric tons) load.

For the Mixed Law Courts Building in Cairo (Fig. 6-18) short piles were used because of the characteristics of the Simplex cast-in-the-ground type of piles, similar to Fig. 6-22. Such piles could not be safely carried through soft clay layers below groundwater level without damage to the unprotected shaft. They were the most economical type available locally and, as a rule, did not cause trouble to isolated buildings not exceeding five to six stories height.

Settlement of floating-pile foundations of this kind, however, can cause appreciable damage to adjoining buildings in much the same manner as for mat foundations (see the discussion of Fig. 4-23). Figure 6-19 shows two buildings in Cairo, Egypt. The severely damaged old four-story reinforced-concrete frame and brick building had been safely standing for a number of years until a new eight-story building was built next to it. The foundations of both buildings consisted of short 25-ft (7.6-m) piles embedded in an upper stiff crust of clay below which softer clay was found. The settlement crater around the new building extended beneath the old one and caused a 6-in. (15-cm) differential settlement and cracking of its walls.

Recognition of the inevitability of settlements of floating-pile foundations led to the use in Cairo of longer Vibro-type cast-in-the-ground piles (Art.

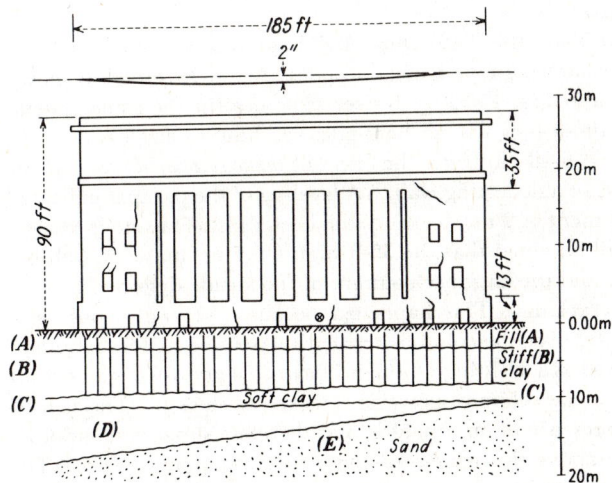

Fig. 6-18. Differential settlement and distribution of cracks over facade of a massive building on floating piles. The location of the cracks is affected by the reinforced-concrete elements embedded in the masonry. (*From Ref. 352.*)

Fig. 6-19. Damage to the old four-story building on the left and in the center of the picture was caused by the settlement crater around the adjoining new eight-story building on the right. Both were on floating piles. (*From Ref. 121.*)

6-7). This type could safely be driven down to and into the sand layers usually found at a depth of not more than 60 ft (18 m). Buildings up to 25 stories high were subsequently erected there on such foundations.

Similar developments occurred elsewhere. In New Orleans some new heavy structures have been founded on 200-ft-long (61-m) steel piles reaching to a geologically old stiff clay layer, preconsolidated to 5,000 lb/in.^{2} = 350 kg$_f$/cm^2 (Ref. 32).

In Albany, New York, the State Office Building erected in 1928 on short cast-in-the-ground standard-type Raymond piles (Art. 6-7) settled as shown on Fig. 6-20 (see also Fig. 4-33A). Newer structures in the same general area rest on over 100-ft-long (31-m) long piles reaching to hardpan.

The sketch in Fig. 6-18 illustrates the effect of *masonry reinforcement* on the formation of cracks in a deflecting wall. A leveling of the parapet indicated a differential settlement of 2 in. (5 cm) of the center of the facade in respect to its ends. It will be noted that the 35-ft-high (10.7-m) masonry wall between the parapet and the entrance columns of the facade deflected by that amount without cracking. This happened because the continuous reinforced-concrete lintel over the columns resisted the tension at the bottom of the wall, which acted as a 35-ft-high (10.7-m) beam. The 13-ft-high (4.0-m) masonry wall below the columns, however, cracked as shown. This can be attributed to the presence of an asphaltic and therefore slippery dampproof layer immediately above the reinforced-concrete pile-capping beam. The latter was intact, and the cracks, e.g., the one marked with a circle in Fig. 6-18, began in the masonry at the dampproof layer, where they were widest, and decreased in width higher up. The elevation of that layer therefore should have been staggered to key the masonry wall to the beam below.

Other similar observations indicate that the cracking of masonry buildings supported by foundations which are likely to settle can be decreased to a minimum by providing within the walls continuous reinforced-concrete tie beams all around the building, of a height corresponding to one or two brick courses, immediately above and below window openings.

The amount of settlement which can be sustained without damage by a statically determined structure is illustrated in Fig. 6-21.   This bridge could

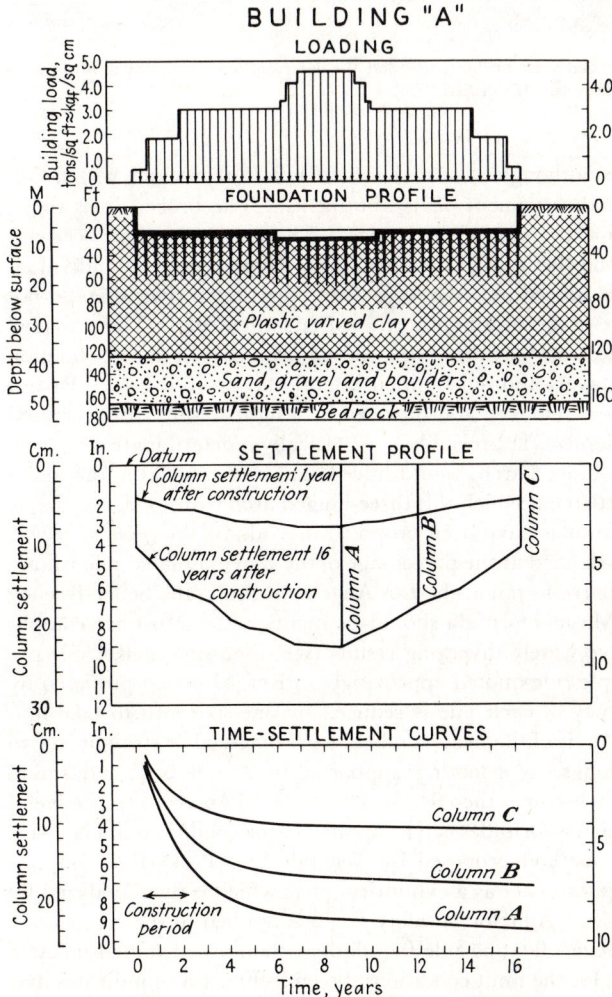

Fig. 6-20. Diagrammatic presentation of data summarizing the settlement records of a properly observed building. (*From Ref. 380.*)

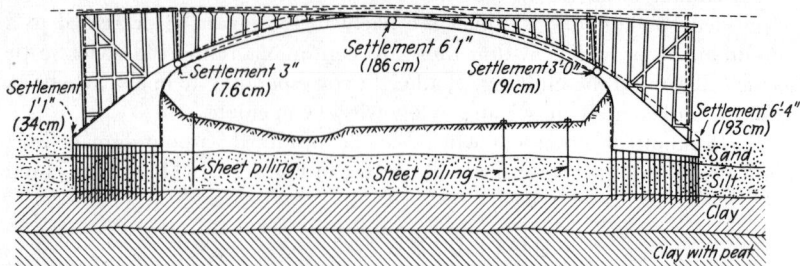

Fig. 6-21. A three-hinged arch bridge withstood the deformations caused by a 5-ft (1.5 m) settlement of its foundations. (*From Ref. 277.*)

be kept in service, although it settled some $6\frac{1}{2}$ ft (2.0 m) and had a 5-ft (1.50-m) differential settlement of its abutments. The broken lines show, to scale, the original position of the bridge. The foundation had been apparently designed on the basis of the satisfactory driving record of individual piles, an unreliable procedure. Driving sheet piles on the river side did not slow down the rate of the continuously measured settlements. This provided an additional indication that they were caused primarily by a consolidation of the underlying layers and not by their lateral and upward flow. Part of the approach fill was removed and replaced by a light trestle; this decreased the rate of the settlements appreciably. A statically indeterminate structure, for instance, a two-hinged arch, would have failed inevitably at a fraction of the differential settlement which this three-hinged arch withstood.

A number of formulas have been proposed to evaluate the *efficiency of piles in a group*, which is defined as the percentage of the sum of isolated pile values. The Converse-Labarre formula, the Los Angeles formula, the Seiler-Keeney formula and the Masters formula should be mentioned. Most are complicated and may give widely diverging results (see discussion in Ref. 57, pp. 671–676). A simple rule quoted approvingly in Ref. 57 is that proposed by Feld. The efficiency of each pile is reduced by one-sixteenth to take into account the effect on it of the nearest pile in each diagonal or straight row to which the pile belongs. For footings supported by 2, 3, 4, 5, 6, and 9 piles the group efficiency becomes then 94, 87, 82, 80, and 72 percent respectively.

None of the efficiency formulas can be applied to the conditions of Fig. 6-17.

Another simple method proposed by Terzaghi and Peck (Ref. 344) assumes a group of piles to act as a cylindrical pier, which is then analyzed by Eqs. (6-1) and (6-2). A factor of safety $F = 3$ is applied to the result.

In general, however, floating-pile foundations should be avoided unless a settlement analysis for the limit conditions shown in Fig. 4-33A indicates that the resulting settlements can be tolerated by the type of superstructure proposed.

6-7. Cast-in-place Concrete Piles.   The oldest type of cast-in-the-ground, or *situ-cast*, piles was obtained by filling a borehole of large diameter or a well with concrete.   Such *bore piles* are still used in Europe, where the casing is sunk into the ground by usual boring procedures, i.e., by augers or by washing, and is then filled with concrete.   Sometimes a special cap is fitted onto the casing.   Air or water pressure is applied to compress the concrete in the casing and at the same time lift the casing out of the ground.   Very high pressures are sometimes needed when the upper part of the casing is gripped by compact clays of a swelling type.   A danger exists then that the cement grout may be pressed out of the concrete into underlying sand layers, if present.   There are other similar practical difficulties which have to be overcome in order to have a guaranteed good execution of the job.   This type of pile is seldom used in the United States.

Another way of forming a situ-cast pile is to *drive* the casing and then to pull it up as it is filled with concrete.   In some types of piles, for instance, in the old *Simplex* type, the driving was done by means of conventional hammers, hitting on the top of the casing, which acted as a hollow pile, since it was provided with a metal or precast concrete shoe.   The shoe was left in the ground as the casing was withdrawn.   A somewhat different method, the *Franki pile* method, of driving a casing by a hammer which is later utilized as a concrete tamper is illustrated by Fig. 6-22.   This method saves the cost of the shoe.   The arching of the dry concrete plug and its friction along the inner walls of the casing were found sufficient to drive the entire casing into the ground if only light blows were delivered by the hammer-tamper, which, to that end, was lifted only slightly before each blow.   When the desired elevation was reached, the 2.5- to 5.0-ton hammer-tamper was lifted as far as

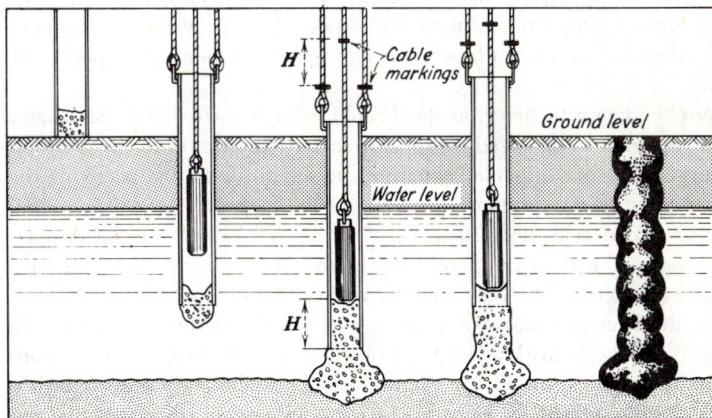

Fig. 6-22.   Steps in the formation of a cast-in-the-ground (situ-cast) concrete pile of the Franki type.   (*From a catalog of the Franki Pile Co.*)

possible and dropped, so that the concrete plug was at least partially knocked out through the bottom of the casing. From then on molding piles of the Franki, Simplex, and other similar types proceeds essentially along the lines illustrated by the third, fourth, and fifth steps in Fig. 6-22. The following essential precautions must be observed.

The distance H cannot be greater than 2 or, at the utmost, 3 times the inner diameter of the casing, since otherwise there will be serious danger that the blow of the tamper will not be sufficient to push the concrete down out of the casing, which is lifted slightly by means of cables simultaneously with each blow. This distance H is checked at the soil surface by the pile-driver operator, who must watch the relative positions of the markings on the cables attached to the casing and the tamper constantly. At the same time, it is dangerous to have too little concrete in the casing or to tamp it below the bottom of the casing, since soil might then get mixed with the concrete or even separate the concrete shaft of the pile into disconnected sections with only soil layers between them. This means that the proper execution of piles of this type depends to a very large extent on the unrelenting vigilance of the pile-driver operator. There is no way to check later, except by pile load tests, which, because of their cost, can be made only on a very small number of piles. This type of concrete piling is therefore very far from foolproof.

In addition, such piles cannot be driven through very soft sandy clays or silts or through sand lenses under a high head of water, since the lateral water pressure would then squeeze the concrete into the casing and some of the soil after it as well. In other words, this procedure simply would not function under such conditions. Reluctance to admit this shortcoming has sometimes led to serious trouble (see discussion of Figs. 6-18 and 6-19).

In recent practice this shortcoming appears to have been realized and the use of this type of pile avoided unless it was possible to provide steel lining of water-bearing sand or soft silt layers through which the pile casing had to be withdrawn.

A recent tendency to describe the Franki piles as *pressure-injected caissons* (Ref. 234) appears to be based on the special attention paid to the creation of an enlarged base of compacted concrete and soil around it by specifying the energy per blow of the tamper—usually 140,000 ft-lb (19.400 m-kg$_f$)—and the amount of concrete—from 5 to 25 ft^3 (0.14 to 0.71 m^3)—to be tamped into the base. The shaft diameter varies from 16 to 26 in. (41 to 66 cm).

Such pile-caissons can be very effective and economical when used in comparatively short lengths and when the base is formed at the surface of deep sand or gravel deposits with a low head of water, i.e., where a "quick" condition cannot occur at the start of the tamping and where the soil strength is increased by compaction. They can also be of advantage when the enlarged base can be formed on rock (Ref. 234).

In situations similar to those encountered in Egypt and illustrated by

Figs. 6-18 and 6-19 another kind of pile of the same type can be successfully employed, namely, the *Vibro* pile.   The casing is provided with a shoe and is driven to the desired elevation by a hammer hitting on its top, whereupon it is filled over its whole depth with concrete of a fairly fluid consistency.   A special type of hammer, the action of which can be reversed, is used with these piles.   The casing is pulled up as the upward-acting hammer hits an attachment of the pile casing.   The vibrations induced thereby in the casing, as well as the considerable static head of the fluid concrete, prevent its adherence to the walls of the casing and ensure a continuous shaft of the finished pile, even when the pile pierces layers of soft clay or water-bearing sand under a considerable head.   The Vibro pile is therefore essentially an end-bearing pile.   It does not have the many corrugations along the length of its shaft which are present in Simplex or in Franki piles (see Fig. 6-22), and which increase the frictional resistance along the skin of these latter types. However, this is not always a disadvantage (where drag is possible) and frequently is of little importance one way or another.   Vibro piles have been driven in lengths up to 65 ft (20 m).

All three types of situ-cast piles so far discussed, the Simplex, Franki, and Vibro, as well as other similar piles, have one further disadvantage.   Piles, especially end-bearing ones, are usually driven within a few feet of each other in clusters, so that the whole group would support a column load.   A pile driver can drive several piles a day.   The piles are driven successively next to each other.   Therefore the concrete of a pile does not have time to harden or, sometimes, even to set before the adjoining pile is driven next to it. Moving pile drivers about is a time-consuming and expensive proposition. Therefore it is not practicable to move the pile driver to operate at another location until the concrete hardens in the first pile of a cluster and then to bring the pile driver back to mold the second pile.   It may therefore happen in localities where boulders are present that the first piles of a cluster would miss a boulder.   One of the following pile casings would hit the boulder on its edge and, as it was driven in farther, would force it sideways against the still green concrete of the first piles; this would crush and destroy their shafts. For this reason many building codes of different cities in the United States forbid the use of such cast-in-the-ground concrete piles unless the concrete is protected by a steel casing permanently left in the ground.

It should be noted that this objection applies only to *concrete piles* but cannot possibly be valid in the case of *sand piles* (Art. 5-3), so that the Franki type of pile represents a very efficient way to compact a deep layer of loose sand, especially when the sand is silty.   But in incompressible plastic clay soils no compaction of the soil is possible, and driving adjoining piles may cause the remolded clay to bulge laterally and pinch off the still fresh plastic unprotected concrete of the earlier pile.   This is known to have happened in some cases with serious consequences.

Among the better-known types of American situ-cast concrete piles with

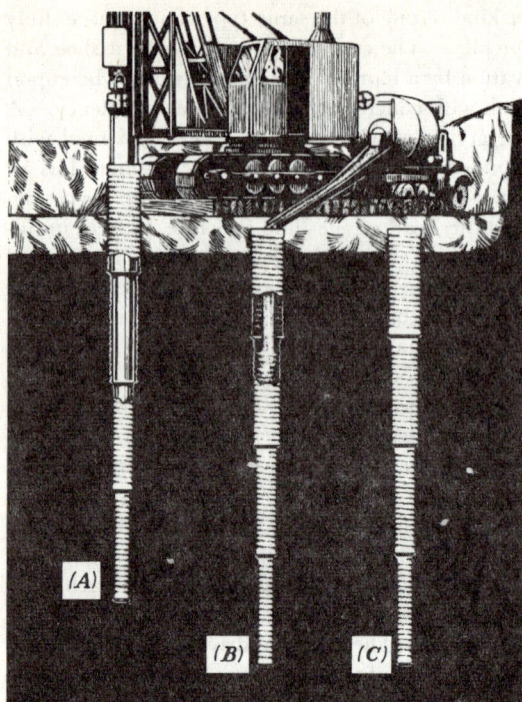

Fig. 6-23. Steps in the construction of a step-tapered Raymond pile.
(*Raymond International, Inc.*)

permanent protective casing are *Raymond tapered piles*. The shell is made of
corrugated thin sheet metal in sections of 4- to 16-ft (1.2- to 4.9-m) lengths,
which has to be stiffened by means of an inner *mandrel* or *pile core* during
driving. The mandrel is collapsible; i.e., being made of separate parts
along its entire length, it can be easily separated from the shell and withdrawn
after completed driving. During driving the parts of the core are wedged
apart by a special mechanism and are thus temporarily pressed against the
inner wall of the shell.

Raymond standard-type piles have a uniform taper and are made in
lengths of 15 to 37 ft (4.6 to 11.3 m). For greater lengths, up to 100 ft (31 m).
a heavier type, the so-called *step-tapered Raymond pile*, is used (see Fig. 6-23).
Step *A* shows the driving and step *B* the concreting after withdrawal of
mandrel and inspection of the shell; *C* shows the completed pile.

In most cased piles of this type the concrete can and should be poured in
the dry from the surface, as shown in step *B* of Fig. 6-23. It should have a
high slump to avoid the formation of voids between batches dumped into
the pile.

Some types of casing are not intended to be watertight. It should then be remembered that segregation will occur if concrete is dumped through any appreciable depth of water. The original constituents will become separated; the gravel will sink to the bottom first, and the sand will settle over it, followed by some cement. A certain proportion of the cement will remain in suspension in the water. The general picture will be similar to that obtained in a measuring cylinder during a laboratory sedimentation test for grain-size determination. It is therefore essential to prevent movement of concrete through water entirely or to reduce the distance to an insignificant minimum.

Where small quantities are involved, for instance, for concreting bore piles or small caissons, the concrete can be placed underwater by means of special buckets of the type illustrated in Fig. 6-24. Two cables are provided; the first, A, is attached to the bottom C of the bucket and is used to lower the entire concrete-filled bucket through the water. When the bucket touches the bottom of the excavation, cable A is released and the walls of the bucket are pulled up by cable B, allowing the concrete to slide into place over the sloped sides of the bottom C, which is then also pulled up by cable A, as shown by the broken line A' in Fig. 6-24(II).

Several types of caisson-piles are *cast in holes* bored in the soil *by large power-driven screw-type augers*. Some have retractable mechanical appliances for underreaming the hole to form an enlarged base in cohesive soils. This has been found advantageous in loess deposits (see Art. 5-4) of southern regions in the Soviet Union (Ref. 270). Figure 6-25 shows an excavated pile of this type at an industrial exhibit in Kiev. It is noteworthy because the bored shaft of the pile penetrates 80 cm (2 ft 8 in.) into the soil below the bottom of the enlarged base to ensure that no softer seams are located there.

Attempts have been made to provide multiple underreamed pile-shaft enlargements at more than one level in loess deposits of the lower Mississippi valley (Ref. 59).

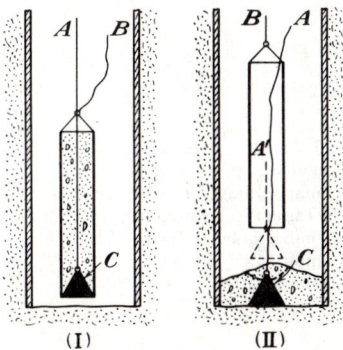

Fig. 6-24. Special buckets are used for placing small quantities of concrete underwater.

Fig. 6-25. Excavated underreamed bored pile in loess soil at 1968 Industrial Exhibit, Kiev, U.S.S.R. (*Photo by Tschebotarioff.*)

Fig. 6-26. Excavated precast reinforced-concrete pile shaft driven into enlarged base formed in loess soil by camouflet explosion at bottom of bored hole, at 1968 Industrial Exhibit, Kiev, U.S.S.R. (*Photo by Tschebotarioff.*)

Figure 6-26 illustrates an excavated *camouflet* base (Ref. 160, p. 20) of a pile in loess soil.   First, a borehole was drilled down to the desired elevation.   A small wired charge of dynamite was dropped into the hole, which was then partly filled with fluid concrete.   When the charge is exploded, some of the gas of the explosion goes up through the concrete; the remainder cools and creates a partial vacuum in the enlarged bulb formed within the compressed loess soil.   The vacuum plus gravity causes the concrete to flow into the bulb. Thereupon a precast reinforced concrete shaft of a somewhat larger cross section than the hole is immediately driven through it into the upper half of the bulb.

This method is suitable only in compressible macroporous loess soils.   The name "camouflet," which denotes an underground explosion not visible from the surface, appears to have originated in the 1850s when British army engineers unsuccessfully tried it in very compact plastic clays.

Even in loess not all excavated camouflet-type bulbs are as symmetrical about the vertical axis as the one shown on Fig. 6-26.   It seems that the same thing may happen as in swamp shooting (Art. 9-2), namely, the explosion may displace the soil in one lateral direction more than in others.

6-8. Large Driven Cylindrical Caisson–Pipe Piles.   A combination of a large steel-pipe pile with an inner steel H-pile reinforcement has been developed in the United States for heavy concentrated column loads (Fig. 6-27) and is

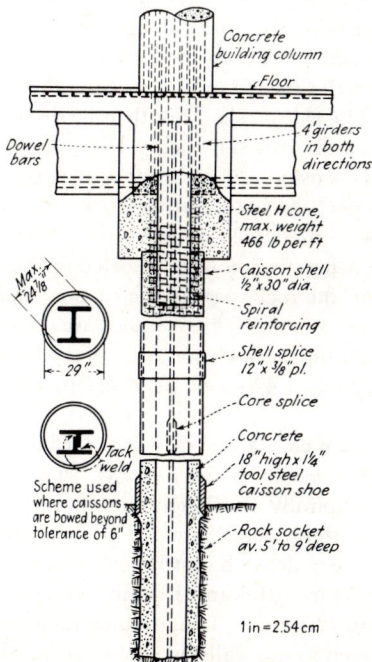

Fig. 6-27. Drilled-in caisson for heavy column loads; connection to ground floor of building. (*From Spencer, Ref. 319.*)

Fig. 6-28. Assembly and prestressing of Raymond cylinder-pile sections. (*Raymond International, Inc.*)

known under the name of *drilled-in caissons*. A 30-in.-diameter (76-cm) and
½-in.-thick (12.7-mm) caisson shell is driven down to rock through sometimes
as much as 100 ft (30 m) of clays and sands. A heavy star drill is then repeatedly dropped onto the rock surface in the caisson until a socket 5 to 9 ft
(15 to 28 m) deep is formed within it. The caisson shell can then be driven
in a little further to form a watertight seal with the rock. It is usually
possible to bail all the water out from the caisson and to lower an engineer
in a bosun's chair into the caisson to inspect the nature of the rock. After
the H-pile core is lowered into the caisson, the whole is concreted. When
bailing the water is not possible, tremie concreting must be resorted to (Fig.
6-35). Because of the drilled-in socket in the rock, part of the caisson load
is distributed through the sides of the socket to a much greater rock area than
would be true if the caisson merely rested on the rock surface. Very high
loads, varying on different jobs from 220 to 1,420 tons per caisson, have
therefore been used in actual construction.

Cylindrical caisson-pipe piles of large diameters are widely used for heavy
loads, especially in waterfront work. Noteworthy is the *Raymond cylindrical
pile*, illustrated by Figs. 6-28 and 6-29. Spirally and longitudinally lightly
reinforced sections, of a maximum 16-ft (4.9-m) length, are cast in a yard by
the spinning process, which produces a very dense high-strength concrete.
The two standard diameters are 36 and 54 in. (91.4 and 137 cm) with wall
thicknesses varying from 4 to 5 in. (10.0 to 12.1 cm). Longitudinal holes for
later prestressing by steel wires are left open in the walls by rubber cylinders
on ⅞-in. (22.2-mm) rods.

After casting, the sections are stored in the yard for curing, as shown on the left-hand side of Fig. 6-28.   Once cured, they are assembled end to end in a horizontal position with cable holes in alignment to the total desired pile length and are then prestressed to form a single unit (see the right-hand side of Fig. 6-28).   A plastic joint compound is first applied to seal the joints between the sections.   It has a high strength when set.   After tensioning by the Freyssinet method, the ends of the cables are locked temporarily by metal cones, and cement grout is pumped into the cable holes under pressure. After hardening of the grout the cones are removed.   The pile has then formed a single unit of considerable compressive and bending strength. Excess lengths can be cut off at any elevation.

Under favorable soil conditions Raymond cylindrical piles have been used for design loads exceeding 200 tons (182 metric tons) and in lengths up to 208 ft (63.5 m).   Heavy hammers must be used.   The hammer in Fig. 6-29 delivered 81,250 ft-lb (11,250 m-kg$_f$) of energy per blow on the 54-in.-diameter (137-cm) and over 100-ft.-long (31-m) piles.

The piles are transported to the construction site.   Figure 6-29 shows them arriving on a barge, marked A, moored to a Raymond owned *DeLong*

Fig. 6-29.   Driving Raymond cylinder piles from a DeLong type platform.   (*Raymond International, Inc.*)

platform, which carries the pile-driving rig.   These platforms, originally designed during World War II to permit rapid provision of pier facilities for ships at new locations, come in various sizes.   Essentially they consist of a hollow shallow steel box, usually rectangular in plan, which, when floating, can be towed by tugs from one location to another.   Through each of the four corners of the rectangular box cylindrical watertight vertical openings are provided for steel-pipe cylinders, three of which, marked *B*, are visible in Fig. 6-29.   Each cylinder has a loosely fitting jacket *C* around it, rigidly connected to the platform, with an elaborate arrangement of jacks and hydraulic vertical and horizontal (radial) grips between the jacket and the cylinder.   Once the platform has been positioned at the desired location, the radial grips on the cylinders *B* are released so that they can drop vertically down to the bottom.   The lower grips are then tightened on the cylinder, and one row of jacks forces the cylinder down, using the platform as a counterweight through the jacket *C*.   When their maximum stroke is reached, these jacks are repositioned by reversing the grips and using another battery of jacks.   The procedure is repeated until the cylinders can no longer be forced deeper into the ground, having thus acquired satisfactory bearing. If continued, this process can be used to lift the platform out of the water and above the wave crests at high tide.   The procedure is similar to the actions of a man climbing up a pole.

When the platform is to be moved, the process is reversed; the cylinders *B* are pulled up by jacks acting in the opposite direction but still using the platform as counterweight.   The three cylinders *B* seen in Fig. 6-29 protrude considerably above the platform, which is 150 by 70 ft and 13 ft high (46 by 21 m and 4 m high), since they were designed for greater depths of water than occurred at that location.   All piles in a bent can be driven without moving the platform since the pile-driving rig can be rolled laterally along its edge.

DeLong platforms permit stable and rapid driving irrespective of strong currents and moderately high waves.   The resulting advantages justify their high cost.   It is, however, essential to avoid any driving delays.

Caissons of larger dimensions will be discussed in Art. 6-10.

6-9. Underpinning.   It is sometimes necessary to carry an existing foundation to a greater depth, for instance, when a deeper basement or a subway is dug nearby.   The process is known as *underpinning*.   Either piers or piles may be used for this purpose.

In both cases a series of pits is dug under the old foundation.   A new pit is not dug until the underpinning of an already excavated adjoining pit is completed.   Usually the existing footing and the wall above it are sufficiently strong to span at first the width of the underpinning pit while it is dug and later the distance from pier to pier.   If not, the wall can be strengthened, as shown by broken lines in Fig. 6-30, section II, by casting reinforced-concrete beams *ABEF* and *CDGH* on both sides of the wall and tying them together through openings in the wall.

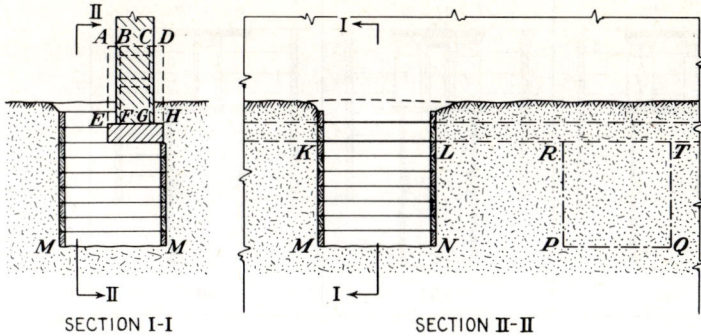

Fig. 6-30. Sketch illustrating discussion of underpinning procedures (see Fig. 6-31) and box sheeting of pits in sand.

The procedure illustrated by Fig. 6-30 is used in digging pits through moist clean sand, close to the soil surface. Such sand usually will not stand up vertically for more than a few inches. Horizontal wooden planks are then placed and nailed to form a box, which is frequently sufficiently strong to resist the lateral pressures of the sand around the shaft without any additional bracing. Spaces may be left between successive planks to permit packing with soil of the spaces between the planks and the natural ground (see Ref. 253). After packing is completed, a few tufts of hay stuck into the openings will usually be sufficient to prevent the driest of sands from running out.

When rock is at a considerable depth, underpinning piles must be used instead of piers. In order to prevent later unequal settlements of the underpinned building, especially if the new piles reach only to sand or gravel, it is often essential to *pretest* each pile to the full load it will have to carry. First a shallow pit is dug under the old footing, as shown in Fig. 6-30. Then a steel-pipe pile is pressed open-end in short sections of length L down into the soil by means of jacks supported by the old footing. Each length of pipe L is mucked out by means of specially designed tools, for instance, by the orange-peel bucket, which is similar in operation to the clamshell bucket but has four moving sections instead of two. When the underpinning pile reaches the desired elevation, it is filled with concrete, which is allowed to harden. The pile is capped with a steel plate, and another steel plate is placed and grouted against the old footing. Two hydraulic jacks are then inserted between the two plates, as shown in Fig. 6-31(I). The jacks apply to the pile the part of the building load which the pile will have to carry later. The load is maintained for a short while until all settlement of the pile ceases (see Prob. 6-4). A steel strut is then wedged in between the pile and the old footing. As shown in Fig. 6-31(II), this should be done *before* the jacks are removed, since otherwise the pile will rebound, as shown by line CD for pile 3 in Fig. 6-15, and settle again when reloaded. After removal of the

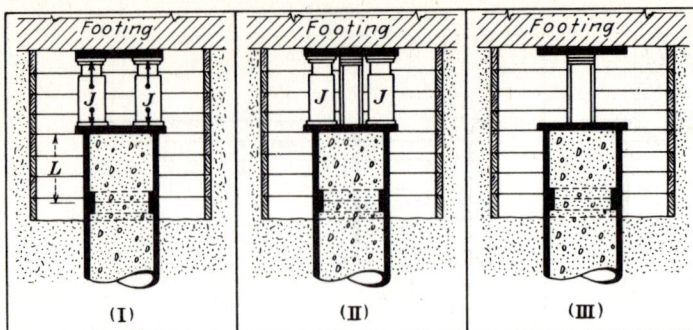

Fig. 6-31. The *pretest* method (patented) of wedging underpinning piles. (*After Prentis and White, Ref. 253.*)

jacks [Fig. 6-31(III)] and completion of the pretesting of the other piles the excavation pit can be concreted.   In this manner it is possible to transfer the entire load of a heavy structure of a new foundation without any measurable settlement.   For further details see Prentis and White (Ref. 253).   Also see the discussion of Fig. 15-25 in Art. 15-7.

6-10. Caissons.   Steel sheet piling can be used to form small caissons when the sheeting can reach down to rock and thereby cut off flow of water or soft clay toward the later excavation without the need for any or much pumping. A caisson of this kind is essentially a small cofferdam (Art. 12-3), but only light bracing and shallow-web steel sheet piling usually is needed.

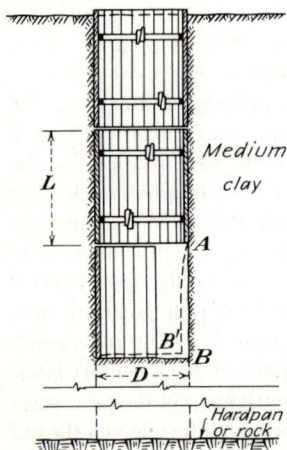

Fig. 6-32. Chicago type caisson through clay of medium stiffness to hardpan.

Figure 6-32 illustrates another type of light caisson or well which is used in clay soils.   The *Chicago caisson* is used in clays of at least medium stiffness, so that the wall of the cylindrical excavation shaft will stand up vertically to a distance L, which is usually made equal to 5 or 6 ft (1.5 to 1.8 m).   The caisson is wide enough to permit a man to work in it.   The walls of the shaft section are then lined with vertical planks, a few inches shorter than L, and are supported laterally by two pairs of steel half rings wedged apart and thus pressed against the timber lining.   In this manner the caisson can be carried down step by step to hardpan or rock.   Some *loss of ground* is bound to occur, i.e., more clay is taken out than originally occupied the volume of the excavated shaft.   This is caused during excavation by some squeezing of the clay toward the as yet unbraced shaft, as shown by the broken line AB' in Fig. 6-32. and may lead to some surface settlements (compare with Fig. 13-12 and discussion thereof).

In softer types of clay the loss of ground may become too large for the safety of adjoining structures, and in very soft clays the unbraced shaft section may close entirely. A different construction procedure is then employed. If the soft layer is shallow, cylindrical steel sections can be driven into it ahead of excavation to prevent heave of the bottom and resulting loss of ground. Or if the horizontal dimensions of the shaft and the depth of the soft clay layer are large, steel sheet piling can be used.

Small caissons sunk through plastic clay are preferable to groups of slender piles whenever the latter can be *deflected from the vertical*, whether during driving due to displacement of their tip, or by unbalanced excavation, or by the driving of adjoining piles which may displace their butts laterally much in the same manner as shown by broken lines for pile b in Fig. 11-17. A case occurred in Chicago when the tops of long slender pipe piles reaching to hardpan were found to have been displaced 2 to 3 ft laterally for this reason. Chicago caissons (Fig. 6-32) had to be substituted. Litigation followed over who should pay the extra costs.

When a stiffer, non-water-bearing stratum is reached, the base of the caisson can be *belled out*, i.e., increased conically by hand excavation, or *underreamed* to give a larger diameter of horizontal contact area with the soil much as shown on Fig. 6-25 for a mechanically formed enlargement of a bored pile base.

The piers of a bridge in deep water often have to be carried down through a greater depth of soil than land piers. The land-side bridge spans are comparatively short, and the pier loads are therefore small. The danger of scour in rivers is also smaller there, since the velocity of the flowing water is smaller at shallow depths than in the main river channel. For that reason the *land-side piers* can usually be built within sheet-pile cofferdams of the type illustrated by Fig. 12-3, where piles are sometimes driven within the coffer-dam excavation when it is necessary to extend the depth of the foundation still further.

For *deep-water piers* large caissons are customarily used. There are two main types, the *compressed-air caissons* (Fig. 6-33) and the *open caissons* (Fig. 6-34). Special problems are presented by the flotation of a caisson until it comes to rest on the soil and by the later excavation of soil below the caisson to sink it to the desired elevation. A great variety of procedures have been developed to that end, only a few of which will be outlined.

The oldest procedure consisted in building up the caisson right over its final location on a platform suspended on steel rods either from a temporary pile trestle or from anchored barges. As the caisson was built up, the plat-form was lowered by means of the suspension rods. Compressed-air locks were built into the shafts left for this purpose in the caisson, and compressed

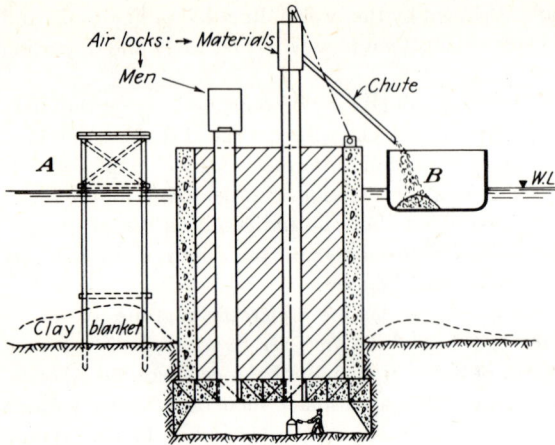

Fig. 6-33. Operation of a compressed-air caisson.

air could be used to decrease the load on the suspension rods after the caisson platform was lowered below water level. Timber and masonry were used in past construction of caissons, but in modern work they have been replaced by steel and reinforced-concrete cellular construction. It is now customary to build the cutting edge of the caisson on shore, float it out to its location, anchor it there, and build it up, as shown in Fig. 6-34, until it reaches soil firm enough to support its dead weight.

Several methods have been in use to keep the caisson afloat up to that point. The *false-bottom method of flotation* consists in providing a temporary timber bottom for each of the caisson cells, which can then be kept partially pumped out to float the caisson until it comes to rest on firm soil. The false bottom is then removed to permit further excavation within each cell. This is not always easy, since the timbers swell and jam under high uplift pressures to such an extent that sometimes they have to be hammered out piece by piece by means of long H piles. The false-bottom method is therefore suitable for shallow depths only.

Compressed air was used to float and then sink a *Moran caisson* through 120 ft (37 m) of water for one of the piers of the San Francisco–Oakland Bay Bridge (Refs. 254 and 255). Each cell of the caisson was cylindrical, steel-lined, and provided with a steel half dome. Compressed air could be applied within each cell to press the water level in it down to the desired elevation. Only part of the cells had to be put under air pressure in order to provide flotation; the remaining cells could be extended upward, provided with half domes, and, in turn, put under air pressure. The half domes could then be cut off by torches from the cells which had provided flotation up to that time, and their upward extension could be undertaken. The process of staggered extension of the cells was continued until the caisson reached firm ground.   Then all the half domes were removed, and underwater excavation was started in each cell.   That caisson was sunk to a total depth of 240 ft (73 m).

In some bridge caissons the walls of the individual cells, i.e., the space marked *GHFKEA* in Fig. 6-34, are made hollow for purposes of flotation. Temporary platforms on timber piles or on barges are still often employed to provide auxiliary surfaces for construction equipment for all modern types of caissons, as shown in Fig. 6-33, and sometimes for their anchorage, but only seldom for purposes of flotation.

In very rapidly flowing water the type of flotation and anchorage shown in Fig. 6-34 is not always possible.   The so-called *sand-island* method has been employed in some such cases, e.g., for the caissons of the Mississippi River bridge at New Orleans and for the caissons of a later bridge of the same type at Baton Rouge.   A 110-ft-diameter steel cylinder was lowered to the river bottom from a temporary platform supported by timber piles onto board mattresses and was then filled with sand, forming a huge cell or a small island, on the surface of which the cutting edge of the reinforced-concrete open caisson could be cast in the dry, and the caisson then gradually built up and sunk by dredging the cells down through the sand of the island and the underlying soil.   Later the island could be removed.

Excavation under compressed air, as shown in Fig. 6-33, is now seldom employed.   The reasons for this will become apparent from Table 6-2. Under air pressure corresponding to 115 ft (35 m) of water head a workman

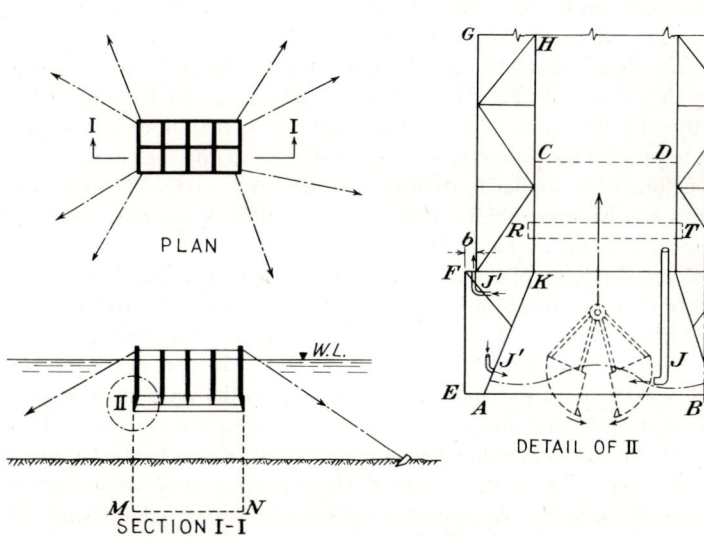

Fig. 6-34. Methods of flotation and excavation of open caissons for bridge piers.

TABLE 6-2. Customary Rules Regulating Work under Compressed Air

Maximum gage pressure		Corresponding head of water,		Time per shift, hr	Total time, hr	Rest interval, hr	Time of decompression, min
lb/in.²	kg$_f$/cm²	ft	m				
18	1.26	41	12.5	4	8	0.5	9
26	1.82	60	18.4	3	6	1	18
33	2.32	76	23.2	2	4	2	33
43	3.02	99	30.3	1	2	4	43
50	3.50	115	35.1	0.5	1	6	50

working for only 1 hr would have to be paid for a full day. No human work at all is physically possible under any appreciably higher pressures. However, it should be noted that the heads of water indicated in Table 6-2 as corresponding to certain values of gage pressure in the caisson working chamber apply only to work in pervious sandy soils. In such cases clay blankets may even be necessary around the caisson, as shown in Fig. 6-33, to prevent blowouts or excessive losses of air bubbling up through the voids of sand or gravel. But when working in impervious clay soils, gage pressures smaller than the actual head of water may be sufficient. For instance, when caisson 1 (see Fig. 2-10) reached a depth of 100 ft (30.5 m) below free-water level, a gage pressure of only 18 lb (1.26 kg$_f$/cm²) was necessary to permit manual excavation in the working chamber. In clay soils very little water will actually seep through into the working chamber of a caisson once it has penetrated sufficiently deep into the clay, and that water can be easily pumped away. Even the slightest motion of the water will dissipate part of the hydraulic head along the paths of its flow, which will be somewhat similar to those shown in Fig. 12-3. The air pressure in the working chamber can then be comparatively low, but it should be maintained at a value sufficient to prevent the plastic squeezing of the clay up into the chamber; the problem is somewhat similar to that in open cuts (Art. 11-4). Compressed-air caissons can be very useful under unusually difficult subsoil conditions, such as are illustrated by Fig. 2-10.

Underwater dredging of the individual cells of open caissons by means of clamshell buckets, as shown in Fig. 6-34, is most frequently resorted to. Jet pipes J which can be moved to any desired position are most frequently used to loosen the soil around the cutting edge, as shown in that diagram. Jet pipes and nozzles, J' in Fig. 6-34, may be built into the walls of the caisson for the same purpose and also to decrease friction along the outer skin of the caisson. This friction sometimes becomes so great that the caisson "freezes" and stops moving. This is particularly likely to happen with compressed-air caissons (see Prob. 6-5). An offset just above the cutting-edge frame will help to decrease somewhat the friction along the skin of the caisson above it.

Experience indicates that the width b of the offset (Fig. 6-34) should not exceed a few inches; otherwise it does not appear to be effective.

The gap between the walls of the caisson and the natural soil can be kept filled with a heavy thixotropic *drilling mud* to minimize wall friction.   To this end a deep trench 2 or 3 ft (60 or 90 cm) wide is dug in the natural soil around the outer periphery of the cutting edge of the caisson.   The trench is filled with drilling mud before the offset above the cutting edge frame sinks past it.   It is kept filled with mud until the caisson reaches its desired depth.

The method of placing concrete underwater by special buckets (Fig. 6-24) is too slow where large quantities of concrete are involved; the so-called *tremie method* is then resorted to (see Fig. 6-35, which illustrates the setup used for the floors of the drydock in Fig. 14-54).   Steel hoppers A are mounted on barges C and kept filled with concrete by means of belt conveyors or pumps from mixing plants usually mounted on other barges nearby.   The bottom of the hopper A is connected to a retractable funnel B, which can reach to the bottom of the excavation and can be opened or closed at its lower end by remote control.   Funnel B is kept continuously filled with plastic concrete, which slides down under the action of gravity.   The bottom end of funnel B is *kept below the surface of the concrete* so that the plastic mix is pressed outward and upward from within the already deposited mass, as shown by the arrows in Fig. 6-35.   No segregation is then possible if seepage through the freshly deposited concrete due to tidal variation and scour is prevented (see discussion of Fig. 12-4).   Grooves RT (Fig. 6-34) are left in the walls of each cell during its construction to permit better keying in of the tremie seals.   Usually the concrete seal does not fill the entire depth of the cell but extends only up to some line CD, the space above being left filled with water to decrease the pressures on the soil at the base of the caisson.   The entire caisson is then capped by a heavy concrete plate above the water level.

The depth to which caissons should reach depends on several considerations.   First of all, it should be sufficient to prevent *scour* from undermining the caisson or decreasing the overburden surcharge weight around it to a

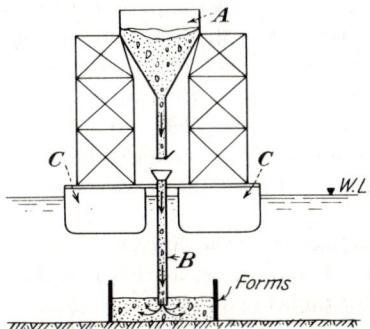

Fig. 6-35. The tremie method of placing large quantities of concrete underwater.

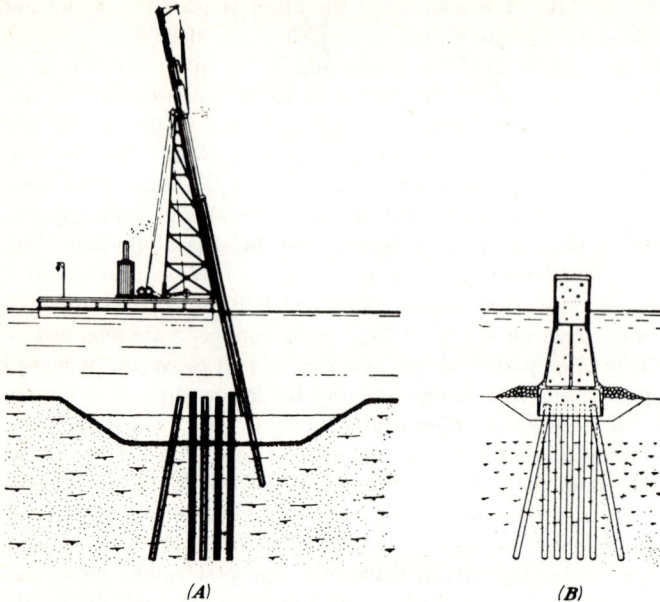

Fig. 6-36. Steps in the construction of a special type of pier in Denmark.
(*From A. Engelund, Ref. 95.*)

dangerous extent.   The bridge piers and their caissons represent an obstruction to the flow of water, so that the streamlines are crowded closer together
near the piers, in a manner similar to that illustrated by Fig. 12-2 for the
outer corners of cofferdams.   A greater velocity of flow right next to the skin
of the pier will be the result, especially during floods, when some scour of the
river bottom may occur because of the increased velocity in the main channel, even when it is not obstructed in any way.   Streamlining the caissons
and the piers may help to a certain extent, as may various types of protection
of the river bottom around the pier, such as heavy stone riprap or mattresses
woven of brush, weighted down by rocks and sunk to the river bottom (Fig.
7-25) prior to the caisson construction.   In spite of such precautions, scour
in excess of 20 to 30 ft (6 to 9 m) has been known to occur around some
bridge piers in the main channel (see discussion of Fig. 12-4).

The second consideration is that the caissons should rest on the stiffest layer
available, so that this layer can be utilized to distribute the pressures to any
weaker underlying layers.

There is a great variety of possible combinations of the different construction procedures outlined in this chapter.   For instance, as shown in Fig.
6-36, hollow precast reinforced-concrete (or timber) piles driven underwater
by means of a follower from a barge may be capped by a reinforced-concrete

caisson which was constructed on land, floated out to the site, sunk, and concreted under the use of compressed air. A trench was dredged out prior to the driving of the piles, partly to remove the upper soft mud and partly to provide room for the sand cushion needed as a support for the later rock riprap which was to serve as scour protection.

Similar procedures, but with tremie concrete used to avoid compressed air, are frequently employed in shallow water. Underwater double-acting pile drivers are usually employed instead of followers. This requires a driving rig the leads of which can be lowered over the edge of the barge down to dredge level.

In recent years the customary practice of using big individual caissons for river bridge piers has been largely replaced in the Soviet Union by the *vibratory sinking of groups of separate thin-walled reinforced-concrete caissons up to 20 ft (6 m) in diameter* connected and tied together at the water level by a heavy reinforced concrete slab on which the pier is then built up. The type of vibratory driver used for the purpose is shown in Fig. 15-20.

There are many other special types of bridge foundations, of which two should be mentioned. The *trestle* type consists of a large number of precast reinforced-concrete or steel piles (timber for a temporary structure) which extend above the water level and are braced to each other in so-called *bents* upon which rest the short beam-type (and therefore light) spans of the bridge. Such pile trestles are of particular advantage over long stretches of nonnavigable shallow water, the flow of which it is not desired to cut off by the fill of an embankment, and on poor underlying foundation material. The bridge load is then distributed over a very large area, so that deep foundations of large spans and their heavy unit loads can be avoided.

Another, but rather unusual, type of permanent structure is the *pontoon* bridge, sometimes employed to advantage over long stretches of relatively deep but calm water underlain to a great depth by poor foundation material. A notable example of such a bridge is that built near Seattle (see Andrew, Ref. 7). The cellular reinforced-concrete pontoons were cast in drydocks and then towed out and anchored at the site; they were connected to each other by specially designed elastic couplings.

6-11. Laterally Loaded Piles. There are two main types of lateral loading of piles. In the *first type* the lateral load is transmitted to the piles from the superstructure above the ground level. The design of such piles is outlined in Arts. 14-4*B* and 14-4*C*. In the *second type* the lateral load is transmitted to the pile below the ground level by lateral pressures due to the weight of adjoining new embankments or other surcharge fills. Related problems are outlined in Art. 10-9, which deals primarily with the tilting toward their backfill of bridge abutments supported by piles driven through plastic clay.

The *dowel action of piles* in resisting slides in soft clays is analyzed in Art. 7-5.

REVIEW PROBLEMS

6-1. Compare the reduction in the average unit pressure on a horizontal plane immediately beneath the tips of 30-ft-long (9.1-m) and 1.5-ft-diameter (d) (46-cm) frictional piles embedded in clay, which will be caused by the shearing resistance $s = c$ along the outer perimeter of a single pile and of a nine-pile footing, as shown in Fig. 6-37, with that of a footing of 36 piles 4 times larger. The spacing of the piles is $L = 4$ ft (1.22 m) on centers.

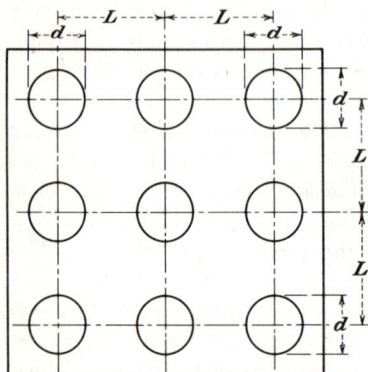

Fig. 6-37. Sketch illustrating Prob. 6-1 on the spacing of piles.

Answer. For a single pile the shearing resistance along the skin surface is $\pi \times 1.5 \times 30 \times c = 143c$; the corresponding base area of the pile is $\pi \times 0.75^2 = 1.76$ ft²; the pressure reduction per square foot of base area is then $143c/1.76 = 80.5c$. For the nine-pile footing shown in Fig. 6-37 the corresponding values will be $4(4 + 4 + 1.5)30c = 1,140c$ for the entire group of nine piles, or $126c$ per pile; the average base area per pile will be $9.5^2/9 = 10.0$ ft², and the pressure reduction will be $12.6c$ per square foot of base area. In the case of the 36-pile footing we obtain $4[(5 \times 4.0) + 1.5]30c = 2,580c$ for the entire group of 36 piles, or $72c$ per pile; the corresponding base area is $21.5^2/36 = 12.8$ ft² per pile, and the unit reduction is $72c/12.8 = 5.6c$ per square foot of base area.

It will be noted therefore that the influence of shear along the outside surface of pile groups on the reduction of pressures below the pile points decreases rapidly with the number of piles in a group, especially if the piles are closely spaced. This explains why groups of piles will settle more than a single pile under the same unit load per pile. The increase of the total base area of the pile group at the pile points has the same effect on settlements as an increase in the size of any footing, but, in addition, the unit pressures at the elevation of the pile points become larger with an increase in the number of piles.

6-2. Examine the nine sketches of different soil conditions given in Fig. 6-38 and state whether the use of piles was justified by the circumstances.

Answer. The use of piles was certainly beneficial in cases 1, 2, and 3. In case 4 there would have been no need for piles unless there was danger of later surface scour or erosion of the compact sand, for instance, close to an ocean beach. The piles would then have to be jetted. The use of sheet piles in case 6, as compared with case 5, was slightly beneficial because of the increased area of the possible surface of failure. In case 7 the question cannot be answered without more information on the degree of sensitivity of the clay to remolding. In a sensitive clay, the use of piles would be harmful; in a clay of medium sensitivity indifferent, except for the waste of money; and in a nonsensitive clay somewhat beneficial. The use of piles in the manner shown in Fig. 6-38 for cases 8 and 9 was definitely harmful if the clay was plastic. The piles should not have been driven that far and allowed to pierce the sand layer. In case 8 they should have been stopped in the upper portion of the sand layer,

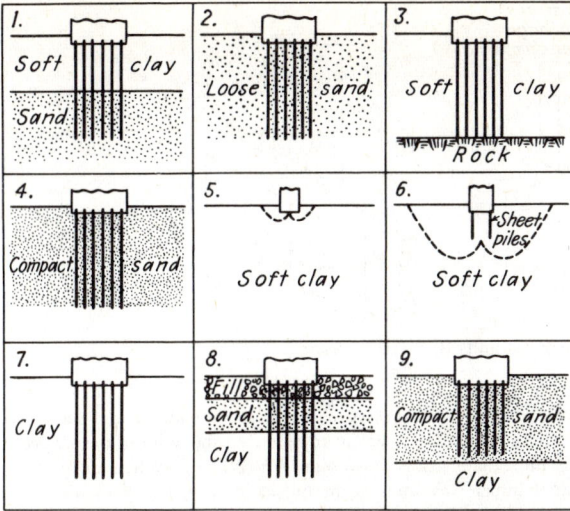

Fig. 6-38. Diagrams for Prob. 6-2. (*After Kimball, Ref. 164.*)

so that it would assist in distributing the pressures on the underlying clay. This also holds true in case 9, except that there may be no need for piles there at all, unless there is danger of scour.

6-3. A certain museum exhibited a model which had been presented to it and which purported to show the proper manner of performing a pile load test. The settlement of the pile was to be measured to 1/1,000 in. (0.025 mm) by a dial gage. The point of the gage rested against a metal strap attached to the pile, and the gage itself was supported by a stand which stood on the soil at a distance from the skin of the pipe which, in the original, would equal 4 in. (10 cm). Should you approve this arrangement on a job for which you were responsible?

Answer. No. The soil close to the test pile would also move down, forming a crater around it. Therefore the support of the gage would move down too, and the gage would register only a small fraction of the actual settlement of the pile. The gage should be attached to a horizontal beam on two supports, each of which should be several feet from the skin of the pile (see Fig. 6-14).

6-4. A small caisson of the type shown in Fig. 6-32 was carried down for underpinning purposes to a layer of very stiff but fully saturated clay. Pretesting of the caisson (see Fig. 6-31) was proposed. What would be your comments?

Answer. There would be not much point in doing this, unless the load on the pretesting jacks were maintained for days, until measurements showed that all downward movement of the caisson had stopped. Pretesting is most efficient in granular soils, where the compression occurs very rapidly.

6-5. A compressed-air caisson for a river pier of a bridge was to have been sunk through clay down to a certain elevation in a sand layer which was fixed by the specifications. Within 5 ft (1.5 m) of that goal the caisson, which had already penetrated the sand, "froze," presumably because of the lateral pressures exerted against its skin by the overlying compact clay, which was of a swelling type. Piling all available weight on top of the caisson and jetting along its sides did not help. The contractor appealed for permission to stop the caisson at the elevation reached, but this was denied by the resident supervising engineer. The

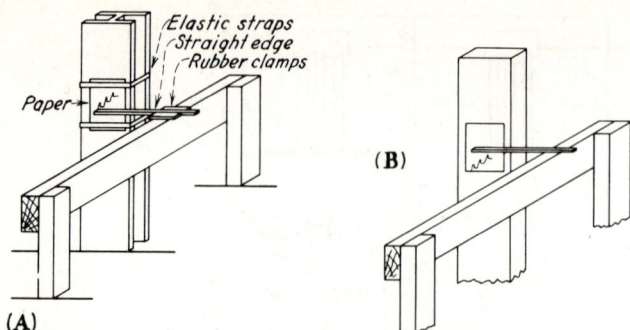

Fig. 6-39. Prob 6-6: (A) incorrect and (B) correct diagram.

contractor then ordered all men from the working chamber of the caisson and suddenly released the air pressure. This action was equivalent to removing the uplift of the air pressure from the caisson, which immediately sank down some 7 ft (2.1 m). When air pressure was reapplied, the working chamber was found to be full of sand, which was excavated, whereupon the caisson was concreted. What are your comments concerning this procedure?

Answer. The sudden removal of the air pressure created a momentary quick condition in the sand under the caisson (Árts. 8-3 and 8-4). The increased effective weight of the caisson made it move downward to, and even past, the required elevation, but simultaneously the mass of quick sand rushed upward into the 12-ft-high (3.66-m) working chamber of the caisson. The loosening effect of such a movement must have extended into the sand layer to a considerable depth below the final elevation of the bottom of the concrete-filled working chamber. Thus the letter of the specification had been complied with, but a very unsatisfactory final condition of support was created for the completed caisson. It would have been much more sensible to get permission to approve the original request of the contractor, even if it meant having to change the specifications.

6-6. Some publications have reprinted from a 1936 journal a diagram identical to Fig. 6-39A alongside one like Fig. 6-8 to illustrate further the points made concerning graphical registration of the set and rebound of a pile during driving. Is the diagram in Fig. 6-39A correct?

Answer. No, it is not. A record of this kind can be obtained only during extraction of a pile and only if the pencil is moved from right to left along the straightedge. Driving a pile with the pencil first applied, as in Fig. 6-8, will produce a diagram like Fig. 6-39B.

RECOMMENDED FOR FURTHER STUDY

Chellis, Ref. 57.
Highway Research Board, Ref. 130.
Johnson and Kavanagh, Ref. 151.
Lehigh University, Ref. 191.

CHAPTER 7

UNBRACED CUTS. SLOPE STABILITY

7-1. Stability of Unsupported Vertical Cuts. The classical approach to the analysis of the problem is illustrated by Fig. 7-1(I). The assumption is made that failure can occur only along plane surfaces, e.g., the surface 1-3 forming the angle θ with the horizontal. The component of the forces of gravity tending to produce sliding will be $W \sin \theta$. It will be resisted by the cohesive and frictional forces along surface 1-3.

A complete analysis of the equilibrium of forces along that surface (1st ed., Art. 8-1) shows that a vertical cut must have a limit height, called the *critical height* h_{cr}, which is directly proportional to the cohesion c of the soil. The cohesive resistance to sliding is proportional to the first power of the height h, whereas the forces which induce sliding, after deduction of the frictional resistance, are proportional to the second power of the height h of the cut and therefore increase more rapidly than the resistance as the height h increases. The following expression for h_{cr} results:

$$h_{cr} = \frac{4c}{\gamma} \tan\left(45° + \frac{\phi}{2}\right) = \frac{2q_u}{\gamma} \qquad (7\text{-}1)$$

Thus, so long as no additional consolidation and corresponding increase of density has occurred, the critical height may be expressed in terms of the unconfined compressive strength, whether it includes a frictional component of resistance to shear or not.

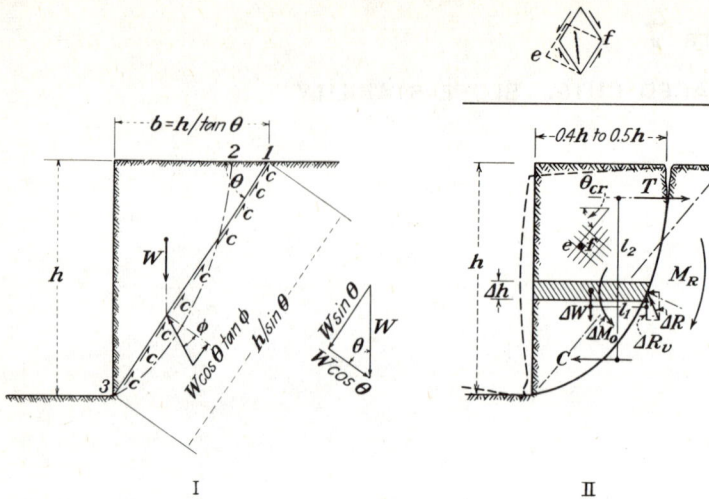

Fig. 7-1. Stability analysis of a vertical cut (I) and the causes of tension cracks at the ground surface (II).

Equation (7-1) can be presented in a somewhat different form

$$\frac{c}{\gamma h_{cr}} = 0.25 \qquad (7\text{-}2)$$

where the term $c/\gamma h_{cr}$ is called the *stability factor* and it is assumed that $c = q_u/2$ when $\phi = 0$.

The above analysis was based on the assumption of plane surfaces of failure. Observations of failures in the field, however, show that slides occur along curved surfaces of a type corresponding to curve 2-3 in Fig. 7-1. An analysis of such curved surfaces by Fellenius (Ref. 97) gave a value for h_{cr} which is only 3.5 percent smaller than the one given by Eq. (7-1) for plane surfaces of failure. Nevertheless, field experience shows that both values are too high because tensile stresses near the ground surface weaken the soil there.

The preceding conventional analysis of the equilibrium of the entire sliding wedge of soil was made without consideration of the fact that the forces taken as acting on the wedge are not concurrent. This point is illustrated by Fig. 7-1(II). Let us consider the equilibrium of a slice, Δh high, shown in that diagram. The weight ΔW of the slice will form a couple $\Delta W l_1$ with the vertical component ΔR_v of ΔR, which acts along the surface of failure as a resultant of the shearing and of the normal resistances along that surface. (Any vertical pressures transmitted to that slice from the soil above it are not shown in the diagram since they can be assumed as being balanced by reaction pressures from the soil beneath the slice.) This couple produces an overturning moment ΔM_o.   The same thing will happen with all other slices of the sliding wedge of soil.   Equilibrium will therefore require the presence of a restoring moment.

$$M_R = Tl_2 = Cl_2 = \sum \Delta M_o \tag{7-3}$$

The causes of tensile stresses near the ground surface and of the tensile cracks which have been observed there in the field prior to the failure of unsupported banks have thus been demonstrated in a qualitative manner.   However, very little is known so far about the tensile strength and the tensile strains of soils, so that no precise quantitative analysis of the problem is yet possible. Terzaghi (Ref. 338) estimates the maximum depth to which tensile cracks may reach down from the surface to be one-half of the unsupported height of the cut.   The formation of tensile cracks near the surface destroys any shearing strength of the soil there and thereby increases the shearing stresses along the lower portion of the surface of sliding.   Thus the critical height h_{cr} of a bank unweakened by tensile cracks, as given by Eq. (7-1), will be reduced by such cracks to a value h'_{cr}, which can be determined in accordance with the above conservative assumption of Terzaghi from

$$h'_{cr} = \frac{2.58s}{\gamma} = \frac{1.29q_u}{\gamma} \tag{7-4}$$

(as shown in the 1st ed., Art. 8-2).

A progressive failure of a vertical cut was illustrated by a series of model experiments with gelatine performed by Harroun in Housel's laboratory at the University of Michigan (Ref. 125).   The results are summarized in Fig. 7-2.   Molten gelatine was poured in a cold room between two lubricated

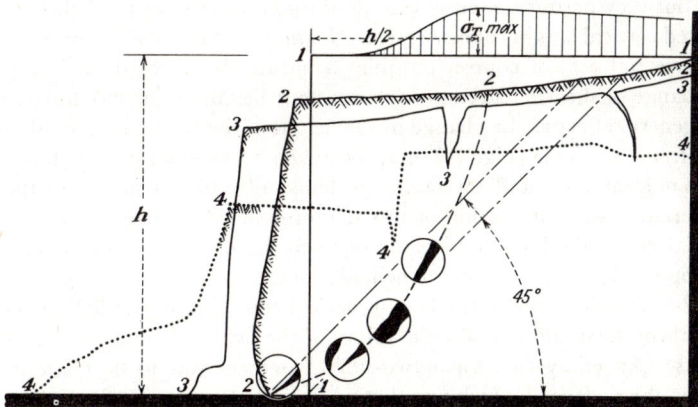

Fig. 7-2. Successive stages in the failure of a vertical bank of cohesive material. Model laboratory tests with gelatine. (*After Harroun, Ref. 125, and Terzaghi, Ref. 338.*)

vertical glass plates parallel to the plane of the drawing.   After the gelatine cooled and solidified, the temporary vertical support 1-1 was removed; as a result the gelatine bank sagged to position 2.   It will be noted from Fig. 7-2 that in position 2 no tension cracks had as yet developed.   Tension at the upper surface of the bank, however, is indicated by the relatively greater outward movement of the lower portion of the bank.   The start of the development of a curved surface of shearing failure was revealed there by four photoelastic pictures, shown ringed by circles in Fig. 7-2.

During the third stage of the experiment (marked 3 in the diagram) the temperature of the room was raised somewhat.   This decreased the shearing strength of the gelatine and induced further deformations of the bank. Pronounced tension cracks appeared on its upper surface, and some crushing of the material occurred at the toe.

It was only during the fourth stage of the experiment (marked 4), when the temperature of the room was raised further, that sliding occurred along the curved surface of failure, which was somewhat displaced compared with its original position.   The gelatine sloughed out at the toe as a result of this sliding.

At approximately the same time, Terzaghi (Ref. 338) reported the results of measurements performed at his Vienna laboratory on gelatine of a somewhat stiffer consistency than the one used by Harroun.   The tensile strains were actually measured at the upper surface of the unsupported gelatine bank prior to the appearance of tensile cracks.   Their general trend is plotted in Fig. 7-2.   The greatest value of the tensile strain, and therefore of the tensile stress, was reached at a distance from the edge of the cut equal to approximately one-half of its height.

No precise quantitative evaluations can be made from experiments of this type, but they permit the visualization of the mechanics of the failure of unsupported vertical cuts in cohesive soils.   No similar changes in the strength of a cohesive soil are, of course, possible in nature, but according to Eq. (7-4), a change of shearing strength at a constant height of cut should have the same general effect as the change in the height of the cut in a material of constant strength.   Thus Fig. 7-2 may be taken to represent, at reduced scales, the deformations and the failure of banks of different height in the same material.   An examination of this diagram shows that the nature of the material below the horizontal plane through the toe of the bank should have an appreciable influence on the behavior of the bank.

Figure 7-3 illustrates one of the few numerical comparisons carried out so far of the theoretical and actual field values of the critical height of unsupported cuts   An excavation for a two-story basement was to be made in varved clay, the surface of which was sloping so that at one edge of the cut it was 9.5 ft (2.9 m) lower than at the opposite side.   The excavation was made without any bracing to the full depth required, with a height of vertical cut of 22.0 ft (6.7 m) on one side and 31.5 ft (9.6 m) on the other.   Then the

(I)

(II)

Fig. 7-3. Failure of a cut 31.5 ft (9.6 m) deep in varved clay. Since the cross-stiffening timbers of the bracing, as shown in (I), were not in place at the time of failure, the cut was unsupported. (I) Photograph just before failure; (II) photograph just after failure.

installation of the timber bracing was begun.   Figure 7-3(I) shows the stage
it had reached just before the failure of the higher side of the cut.   It may
be seen that the cross bracing was not yet in place, except in part at the
surface.   Thus no cross stiffening at all was available to the main braces at
the lower level, where, as a result, the cut was entirely unsupported.   Figure
7-3(II) shows the same location after the failure of the 31.5-ft-high (9.6-m)
side of the cut.   The opposite 22.0-ft-high (6.7-m) side did not fail.

None of the modern methods of clay testing had been developed at the
time.   However, a very careful laboratory study was made on undisturbed
samples extracted from an adjoining site.   The average unconfined compressive strength of selected samples was found to be $q_u = 1.05$ tons/ft^2
(1.05 kg$_f$/cm^2) and the unit weight of the clay $\gamma = 120$ lb/ft$^3 = 0.06$ ton/ft$^3 =$
1.92 g$_f$/cm^3.   Inserting these values in Eqs. (7-1) and (7-4), we obtain
$h_{cr} = 35$ ft (10.7 m) and $h'_{cr} = 22.6$ ft (6.9 m).   This latter value is in quite
good agreement with the situation illustrated by Fig. 7-3.   The failure
occurred in upper New York State in March.   It is therefore possible that it
was temporarily retarded by the increased tensile strength of the partially
frozen upper crust of the ground, which disappeared when the thaw set in,
as it did at the time of the failure.

It would thus appear that the weakening of the ground surface by tensile
cracks should be taken into account when designing unbraced cuts of
excavations.   Equation (7-4) appears to take care of this in a reasonably
conservative manner.   However, further comparative field studies of this
type in respect to both stable and unstable past cuts are needed to provide
further checks.

For rigidly braced cuts (Chap. 11), as compared with unbraced cuts,
there is naturally much less tendency for tensile cracks to develop since the
upper braces counteract the overturning moment M_R of Eq. (7-3).

**7-2. Analysis of the Stability of Slopes by the Swedish Cylindrical-surface
Method.**   The large number of embankment slides on soft clays in Sweden
prompted the appointment by the State Railroad Administration of a
special Geotechnical Commission (1913) for their study.   The work of the
commission and of other Swedish engineers led to the development of a
method of slope-stability analysis which has become generally known as the
Swedish cylindrical-surface (or circular-arc) method, first proposed by
Petterson (Ref. 250).   Figure 7-4 illustrates the kind of field observations
which formed the basis for this method.

The full lines in Fig. 7-4 give the cross section of a 25-ft (7.6-m) water-
depth quay wall of Gothenburg harbor.   Since the deposit of soft clay was
over 150 ft (45.8 m) deep, some 50 ft (15.3 m) of it was dredged out, as
shown in the sketch, and replaced by sand fill into which the piles supporting
the cellular-type reinforced-concrete relieving platform (Art. 14-5) of the
quay wall were driven.

On March 5, 1916 several hundred feet of the quay wall slid out seaward, coming to rest in a position indicated by lighter lines in Fig. 7-4. This position, the exposed part *GG'* of the slip surface, as well as the heave of the harbor bottom (shown by broken lines), indicated that a rotational type of failure had taken place. Since modern methods of undisturbed sampling from deep borings and of testing the shear strength of soft clays had not yet been developed, trial computations were performed later by Fellenius (Ref. 97), involving various assumptions concerning possible limit combinations of the cohesion *c* and of the angle of friction ϕ which would correspond to a factor of safety of unity along different possible cylindrical surfaces of failure. Only one end, point *G* of the break at ground surface, was common to all such possible surfaces of failure. The other end would have to pass somewhere between points *A* and *E*, point *B* being one of the most probable ones. With these limiting conditions in mind, a large number of trial computations were performed with various possible positions of the center *O*. The positions indicated in Fig. 7-4 were found to give the most unfavorable values for any of the centers *O* tried. It may be seen that the assumption of a purely frictional resistance ($c = 0$) to sliding gave the *shallowest* arc *GE*. This is logical, since the assumption of $\phi > 0$ means that the shearing strength of a soil increases with depth, thus making deep-seated failures unlikely.

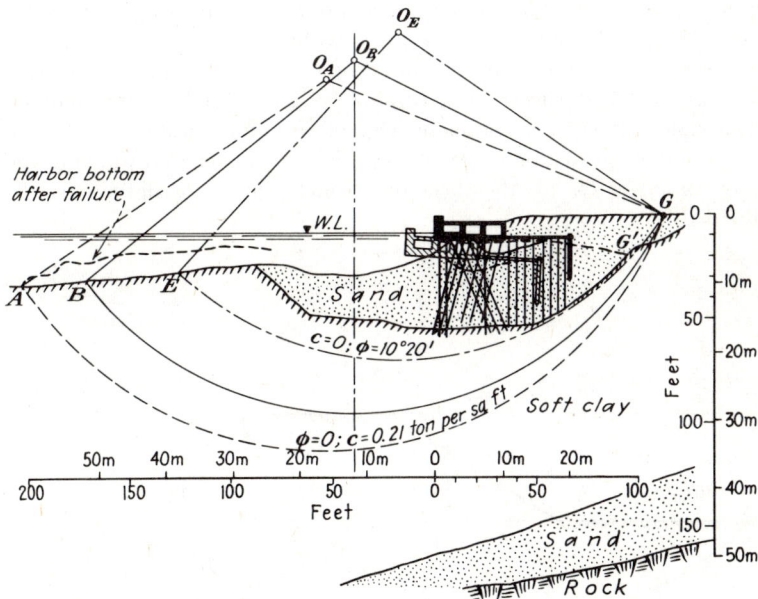

Fig. 7-4.   Harbor of Gothenburg (Sweden) quay-wall failure, March 5, 1916.   (*After Petterson, Ref. 250, and Fellenius, Ref. 97.*)

For similar reasons the assumption of $\phi = 0$ gave the deepest arc GA.   The intermediate arc GB corresponded to intermediate values of c and ϕ ($\phi = 4°$). A somewhat flatter arc GB than the one shown in Fig. 7-4 had been originally drawn by Petterson (Ref. 250) under the assumption of $c = 0$ and gave a value of $\phi = 9°40'$ for a factor of safety of unity.   This means that a purely frictional failure along GB is somewhat less likely than along GE, since a higher shearing strength of the soil along GE corresponding to $\phi = 10°20'$ would be required to produce equilibrium just on the verge of failure.

This discussion shows that the rotational character of some slides along curved surfaces in deep layers of soft clay is established beyond any doubt. It also shows, however, that slight variations in the assumed location of the sliding surface have much less effect on the actual overall stability than changes in the assumed shearing strength of the clay.

In the cylindrical-surface method, as shown in Fig. 7-7, the soil mass above the failure surface was subdivided into *slices*—nine slices in the case illustrated by that diagram.   The equilibrium of each slice, e.g., that of the third slice of Fig. 7-7 represented by the trapezoid $mnm'n'$, is considered independently of the others.   This requires simplifying assumptions, such as that the forces on the faces mm' and nn' of the slice are equal and opposite to each other and that the nonconcurrent nature of the weight W_3 of the slice and of the shearing resistance along the surface $m'n'$ may be overlooked. Graphical procedures of analysis were then developed, in part by means of the so-called ϕ-*circle* method.   Once a center of rotation has been selected, a small circle can be drawn around the center with the radius $r' = R \sin \phi$. The resultants for all slices, formed by the weight W and by the frictional resistance along the corresponding segment of the failure surface, will then be tangent to the so-called ϕ circle of radius r'.   This helps in drawing the polygon of forces for all the slices into which the entire sliding mass is subdivided.

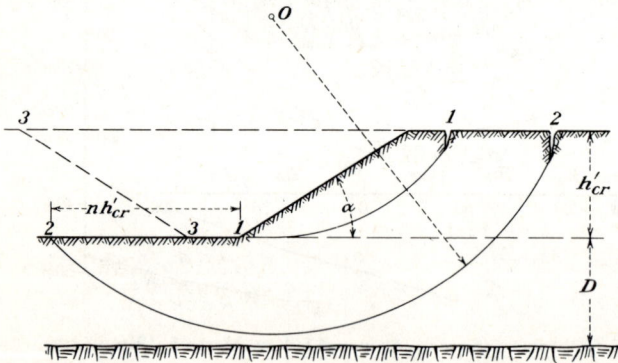

Fig. 7-5.   Key to the symbols used in Fig. 7-6.

Taylor (Ref. 330) utilized this method to compute tables and charts which give the relationship between the angle α of the slope and its critical height h_{cr}, on the one hand, and the properties of the soil, as expressed by its unit weight γ, its cohesion c, and its angle of internal friction ϕ, on the other. The numerical values of the *stability factor* $c/F_s \gamma h$, where F_s is the factor of safety [compare with Eq. (7-2), where it equals unity], were given in terms of the angle α of the slope and of the *depth factor* $h + D/h$.   Each point on the charts was obtained after 10 to 20 trial computations, which proved necessary to determine the most unfavorable location of the center of rotation O.   No consideration was given to the weakening of the bank by tension cracks. Similar charts had been developed by Fellenius (Ref. 97).

The above data were used as a basis for the computation of the charts given in Fig. 7-6.   The significance of the symbols used is illustrated by Fig. 7-5.   The values of h'_{cr} corresponding to $F_s = 1.00$ are given directly in feet for different angles of slope α as a function of the cohesion c of the soil and for depths D of the same soil below the toe of the slope equal to 0, 20, 50, and 100 ft, followed by strata with higher shearing strength, such as sand or rock. The values of h'_{cr} were in all cases taken to equal two-thirds of the height h_{cr} unweakened by tension cracks at the surface.   As explained earlier, no precise data are available on this point, but the above assumption is believed to be conservative and safe.   The charts of Fig. 7-6 have been computed for an effective unit weight of the soil $\gamma = 100$ lb/ft^3 (1.6g$_f$/cm^3).   If the actual unit weight of the soil has a different value γ', the values of h'_{cr} obtained from the charts of Fig. 7-6 should be multiplied by $100/\gamma'$.   This is rigorously correct only when $D = 0$.   However, the error involved when $D > 0$ is slight and is on the safe side.   The charts also give the values of n by which the corresponding values of h'_{cr} should be multiplied if one wishes to estimate the length nh'_{cr} of the possible *mud wave* which may occur in the case of a slide, as shown in Fig. 7-5.   None of the charts of Fig. 7-6 are valid when the toe of the opposite slope, if any, of the cut falls within the distance nh'_{cr}, thereby restricting the development of the sliding surface 2-2 assumed for the computation of the charts.   In such an eventuality reference is made to Taylor's original article (Ref. 330), which considers in its charts the case when points 1 and 3 of the toes of the opposite slopes coincide.

It will be noted that only Fig. 7-6(I), for $D = 0$, gives curves involving a value of $\phi > 0$, namely, $\phi = 10°$.   For other values see Ref. 330.   This is true because the most unfavorable failure surface for any soil with $\phi > 0$, that is, for a soil whose shearing strength increases with depth, tends to pass through the toe of the slope but not beneath it.   This will also be the case if $\phi = 0$, but $\alpha > 53°$.

The critical height of cohesionless soils ($c = 0$) is infinitely great so long as the angle of slope α is equal to or smaller than the natural angle of repose of the soil.

Uniform soil conditions of the type illustrated by Fig. 7-5 are seldom

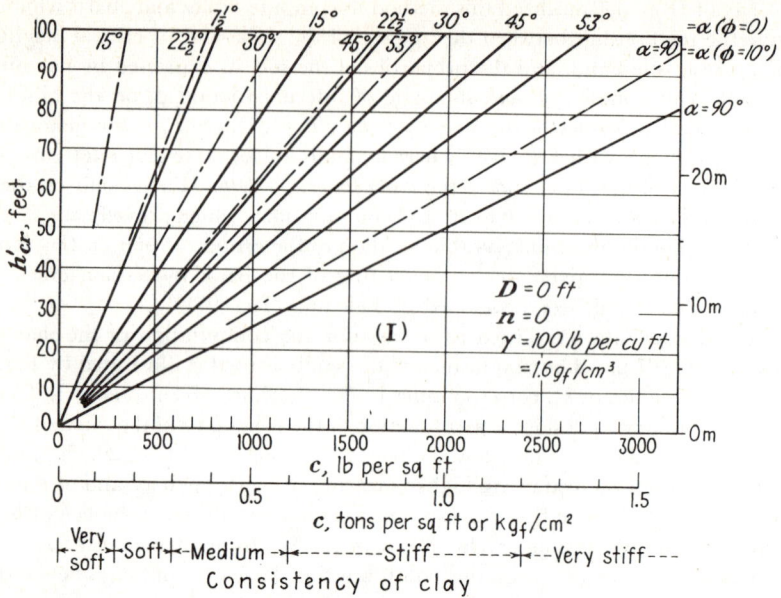

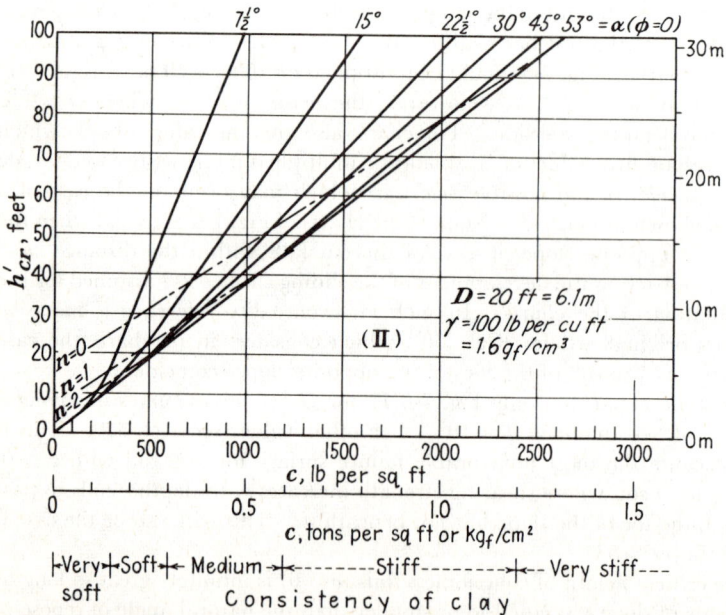

Fig. 7-6a. Four diagrams illustrating the relationship between the critical height h_{cr}' of different slopes and the cohesion c of a clay weighing 100 lb/ft³ (1.6 g_f/cm³). (*Developed from Taylor, Ref. 330.*)

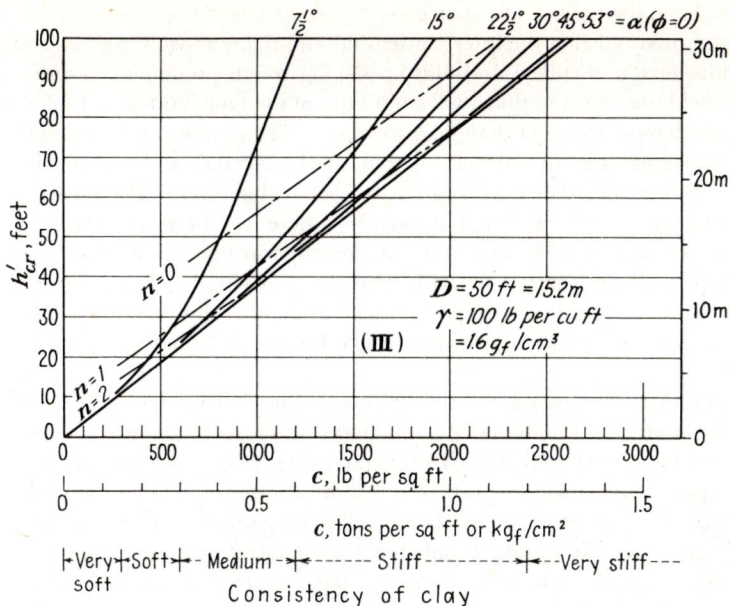

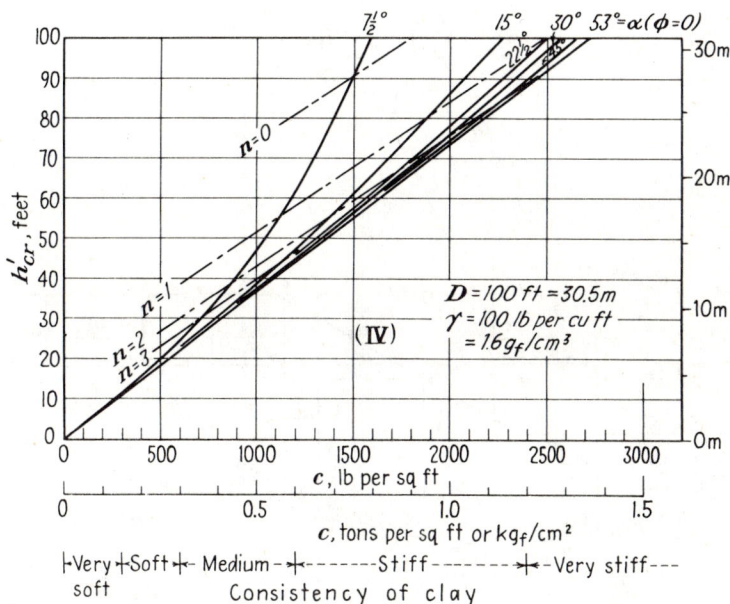

Fig. 7-6*b*.   (*Continued*).

encountered in the field.   The data given by the charts of Fig. 7-6, however, are helpful in visualizing the interrelationship and the relative importance of the various factors involved and also in making rough preliminary estimations for field use.   Nonuniform soil conditions of the type illustrated by Fig. 7-7 are much more frequent than uniform ones.   The effective unit weight of the soil above the free-water level ± 0.00 has to be taken in accordance with Eq. (3-8) and in accordance with Eq. (3-10) below that level.   The shearing strength of the soil layers A and B may be different.   Thus the surface of failure shown in Fig. 7-7 is drawn on the assumption that the deeper-lying layer B has a lower shearing strength than the overlying layer A.   Several trial computations and their comparison with each other, however, would be necessary to determine the most unfavorable surface and the location of its center O.

The customary computation procedure is as follows.   After selection of the surface of failure, the soil above it is subdivided in cross section, as shown in Fig. 7-7, into a number of slices.   The effective total weight W of each slice is then computed, as shown for parts of slice 7 by Prob. 7-4.   The product of each weight W and the distance r from its line of action to the vertical line through the center of rotation O contributes to the overturning moment M_o, the forces to the right of that line by increasing that moment, and the forces to the left of the line by decreasing it.   Thus, with reference to Fig. 7-7,

$$M_o = \sum_5^9 Wr - \sum_1^4 Wr \qquad (7\text{-}5)$$

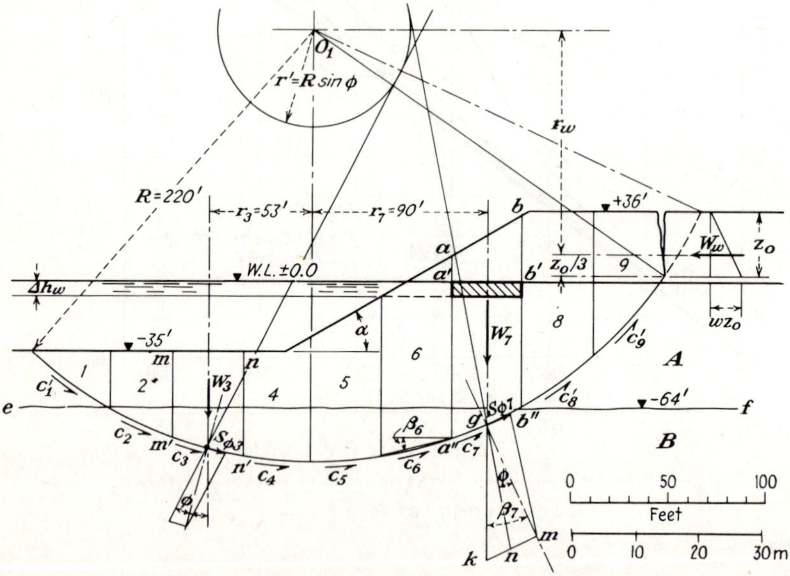

Fig. 7-7.   Example of slope-stability computations for nonuniform soil conditions.

The resisting moment M_r is governed by the sum of the cohesive and frictional forces acting along the surface of failure. Thus, if we take slice 7 as an example, the component of the resisting moment provided by its cohesive resistance will be $cl_7 R$, where l_7 is the length $a''b''$. Similarly, the component of its frictional resistance will be $W_7 \cos \beta_7 \tan \phi$, where β_7 is the angle formed by the line $a''b''$ with the horizontal and $W_7 \cos \beta_7$ is the component of the weight of slice 7 normal to the line $a''b''$. Accordingly,

$$M_r = R \sum_1^9 cl + R \sum_1^9 W \cos \beta \tan \phi \qquad (7\text{-}6)$$

The values of c and ϕ corresponding to the properties of the soil layer at the bottom of each slice should be used in the above summation.

The factor of safety F against sliding is then determined from

$$F = \frac{M_r}{M_o} \qquad (7\text{-}7)$$

As an additional precaution, the possible effect of the accumulation of rainwater in tension cracks at the ground surface may be taken into account by adding to the overturning moment M_o the value $W_w r_w$.

The value of the depth z_o to which tension cracks may reach is usually taken as one-half of the critical height of an unsupported vertical cut, as given by Eq. (7-1), that is, $z_o = q_u/\gamma$. Saturation with water above the free-water level increases the effective unit weight of the soil somewhat. An examination of Fig. 7-7 shows that this will increase the weight of slices 6, 7, 8, and 9 and therefore also the overturning moment.

A similar but even more pronounced effect is caused by a sudden drawdown, i.e., by a drop of the water level, caused by, for instance, rapid tidal variations in estuaries. Suppose the free-water level in the channel dropped by the amount Δh_w, as shown in Fig. 7-7. Some time will elapse before the water in the soil will drain out and adjust itself to that new level. Meanwhile the weight of, say, slice 7 will be increased, since the effective weight of the prism $a'b'$ long and Δh_w thick depended on the buoyed unit weight of the soil prior to the drawdown and will depend on the unbuoyed saturated weight of the soil after the drawdown. Thus the effective unit weight of that prism is almost doubled (Prob. 7-4).

The construction of flow nets for drawdown conditions is even more difficult and uncertain, since the saturation line usually is not known and has to be estimated. Thus the alternative procedure illustrated by Fig. 7-7 for the estimation of sudden drawdown effects appears preferable in view of its simplicity.

The main uncertainty involved in the performance of stability evaluations of the type described in this article lies in the proper estimation of the shearing strength of the soil, as expressed by the values c and ϕ.   Therefore computations of this type should not be attempted for design use without the participation of experienced soil engineers. No opportunity should be

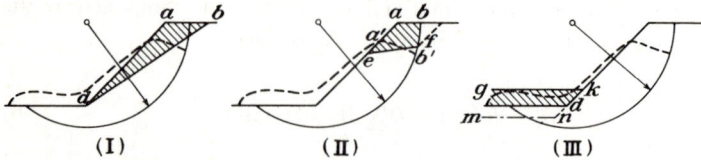

Fig. 7-8. Three types of measures to stabilize a slope which had failed along a cylindrical surface.

missed to perform postmortem analyses of actual slides in conjunction with modern methods of determining the shearing strength of soils.   This is the only way to perfect existing techniques.

Any measure which decreases the overturning moment M_o in Eq. (7-5) will increase the stability of a slope.   This may be done, for instance, by cutting it back, as shown in Fig. 7-8(I), from da to db to decrease the angle of the slope.   The overturning moment will then be decreased by the moment of the area shown hatched in the diagram.   A similar result may be achieved after a slide, as shown in Fig. 7-8(II), by not building the surface $a'b'$ of the mass of soil which has slipped out up to its original position ab but cutting it down to ef prior to restoring the original slope.

A third method is shown by Fig. 7-8(III).   It consists in leaving some of the soil which has slid out at the toe of the slope.   A similar procedure employed to permit the construction of railway or highway embankments on very soft clay is illustrated by Fig. 7-9 and consists in the use of so-called *loading berms* to decrease the overturning moments both of possible shallow slides 1-1 and of deep slides 2-2.

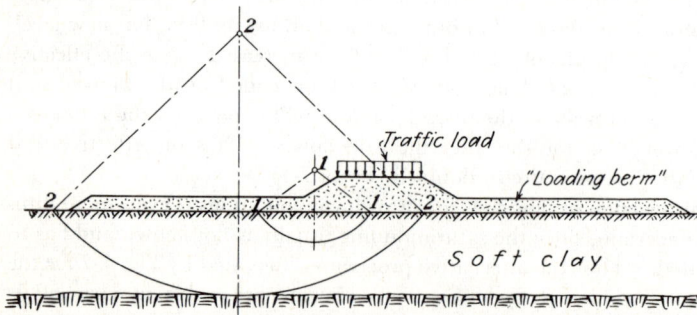

Fig. 7-9. The use of loading berms to permit the construction of embankments on beds of soft clay.

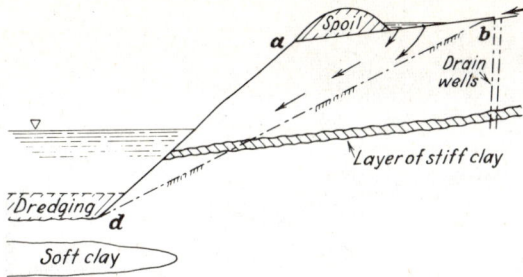

Fig. 7-10.   Causes and remedies of slide during 1936 deepening of the Chesapeake- Delaware canal.

With reference to Fig. 7-8(III), it should be noted that a reverse procedure, i.e., deepening the cut by excavation, for instance, to the level *mn*, will increase the overturning moment and thereby increase the danger of sliding. Some slides of canal banks have been caused by dredging to deepen the channel.

The creation of conditions of the type illustrated by Fig. 7-10 should be avoided under all circumstances.   First of all, the overturning moment is increased by the weight of the excavated material placed at the top of the cut.   In addition, the free runoff of surface water is prevented.   The seeping water weakens the soil in the zone of possible failure and increases its unit weight.   The resisting moment is thereby decreased, and the overturning moment is increased.

Figure 7-10 refers in sketch form to an actual slide during a 1936 deepening of the Chesapeake-Delaware canal.   The dredged soil was placed close to the top of the existing canal bank, damming up rainwater runoff from the sloping ground surface.   Seepage from the newly formed pond saturated and weakened most of the sandy clay soil of the slope overlying a comparatively impervious layer of stiff clay.   Seepage forces (Art. 8-3) decreased the stability further.   The presence of a deeper lens of soft clay aggravated the situation, and several hundred feet of the canal bank slid into it.

The slope had to be flattened appreciably to the line *db*, and surface water flowing toward it was intercepted by a row of large-diameter drain wells, as sketched in Fig. 7-10.

The presence of thin horizontal lenses of sand in a bank of clay at times may have a very detrimental effect on its stability if such lenses are connected to an adjoining large mass of sand.   During rainy seasons the free-water level in the sand mass may rise considerably and thereby produce considerable uplift pressures in the sand seams and lenses.   Thus the tendency to slide out may be increased (see Fig. 8-8).

In such cases a particularly effective measure of remedy is to drill *horizontal drains* into the face of the bank.   They can range in size from tunnels

Fig. 7-11. Effects of deep underwater slide. (*Original photo from Ref. 96.*)

large enough for a man to walk through to perforated corrugated sheet-metal pipes pushed in by bulldozers or jacks and washed out by jets.   Periodic washing out of the pipes is then usually required, whereas for the larger drains installed in tunnels or in trenches clogging can be prevented by pervious-concrete linings and/or *graded filters* (see the discussion of Fig. 7-28).

Figure 7-11 illustrates the need for careful soil investigations whenever land fill is placed along the banks of a waterway.   Such fill had been slowly built out into the water of a bay over a number of years and was being enlarged up to the line shown in the photograph when suddenly over 1 million cubic yards of soil slid out into the water, creating such a tidal wave that it tore motor boats from their moorings along the opposite shore.   The water was some 70 ft (21 m) deep where the fill had extended 7 ft (2.1 m) above water level before the slide.   Some 300 ft (90 m) of railroad embankment, which had been in place for over 90 years, also went out with the new fill.   Subsequent borings and shear tests of undisturbed clay samples from the area gave a factor of safety which was less than unity for stability analyses by the cylindrical-surface method.

A method for the approximate estimation of the shear strength of incompletely consolidated clays has been proposed by Maslov (Ref. 210); see also Ref. 211.

The customarily used *design factors of safety* are quite low, compared with those for other structural materials having much more clearly definable strength properties. In most highway-embankment work a minimum factor of safety of only $F = 1.25$ is required when no structures can be endangered by a potential slide and $F = 1.50$ when such structures are present.

7-3. Block Slides. This type of slide may occur along a horizontal plane of weakness in shear. Sloughing of the slope will then result. An example is provided by Figs. 7-12 and 7-13, illustrating the consequences of an outward sloughing of the end slope of a 55-ft-high (16.8-m) embankment next to a bridge across a river. Horizontal sliding occurred along the base of the embankment where some submerged uncompacted sand fill had been dumped through the water to replace the excavated very soft mud. The lateral pressures developed by the fill of the embankment as it slid outward overturned the two partially completed adjoining bridge piers, one of which is seen in the photograph.

A borehole put down immediately after the slide at the location marked P in Fig. 7-12(I) revealed that not all the soft mud a had been removed by the contractor and that a layer several feet thick remained over the shale. A piezometer (Art. 2-5) was installed at the bottom of the hole and within a short time revealed a buildup of pore pressures in the mud which almost equaled the full effective weight of the newly placed embankment. Thus there is no doubt that the sliding must have started in the remaining mud layer. However, repairs of the overturned bridge pier showed that its

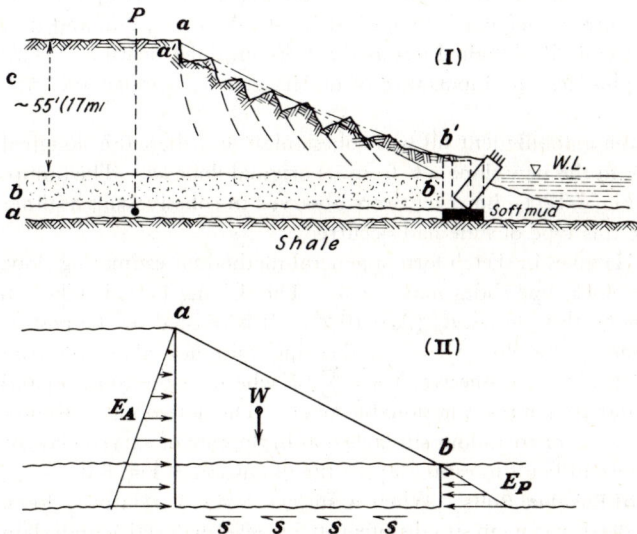

Fig. 7-12. (I) Block-type slide, causing sloughing of embankment and slope, which overturned a bridge pier under construction (see Fig. 7-13). (II) General procedure for estimating block-type stability.

Fig. 7-13. A bridge pier under construction pushed over by the pressure developed when the end slope of the adjoining 55-ft-high (16.8-m) embankment sloughed out. See Fig. 7-12(I). (*Photograph by Tschebotarioff.*)

foundation slab, built within a steel sheet-pile cofferdam, had not been displaced laterally, thus suggesting that the actual sliding occurred at a somewhat higher level within the loose underwater sand fill. Presumably the initial deformations of the overstressed mud triggered a collapse of the loose sand structure, liquefying it momentarily (see Arts. 7-7, 8-3, and 8-4) so that the overlying fill sloughed out as if it were on roller bearings. This probability emphasizes the importance of underwater-fill compaction (Art. 5-3).

In this case the embankment fill was cohesionless and therefore sloughed fairly uniformly to the new slope $a'b'$ from its original slope ab. The humps sketched in on Fig. 7-12(I), however, were observed in cohesive soils at other locations where this type of slide had occurred.

Figure 7-12(II) gives in sketch form a general method for estimating slope stability where block-type slides may occur. The driving force is taken to equal the active earth pressure E_A (Art. 10-2). It is resisted by the passive resistance E_P and by the sum $\sum s$ of the shearing resistances along the weak layer. If the weak layer is cohesive, $\sum s = \sum cA$, where c is the cohesion and A is the horizontal area of the questionable layer. The horizontal resistance of saturated fine sand or rock-flour silt layers, as in the case of varved clays or silts, is much more difficult to estimate; see the discussion of Fig. 8-8.

7-4. Slides of Residual Soils. When a surface layer of relatively loose and permeable detritus, i.e., in situ disintegrated *residual* material, is underlain by a layer of compact impervious shale, water is liable to percolate through the detritus and along the surface of the shale, thereby softening it up and

making it slippery.   If a cut, say for a highway, is made under such conditions as are illustrated by Fig. 7-14, then the entire surface detritus layer is
liable to start *sliding into the cut along the shale surface.*

The two photographs of Fig. 7-15 illustrate a case of this type.   Photograph I shows the face of the cut and its intersection with the plane of slippage.   Photograph II shows an uncovered portion of the surface of slippage
with scratches left by pebbles of the overlying and moving detritus on the
softened surface of the shale.   Proper surface drainage is the most effective
remedy.   It can be facilitated by providing impervious (clay) surfacing at
points where water is likely to accumulate, for instance *a* and *b* in Fig. 7-14,
and channels to carry the water away.

In humid climates dangerous slides of this type may occur periodically
even without a cut, once the detritus cover of steep slopes gets sufficiently
sodden.   Alternating sloping layers of waterbearing porous sandstone and
shale may aggravate the situation further.   Draining the water away is the
only effective remedy in such cases.   Drainage tunnels may be used in
extreme cases.   Conventional laboratory strength tests are of little use in
such cases.   Accumulated local experience in related geological areas is the
best guide.

Figure 7-16 illustrates an incipient slide along a slippery surface that
started developing because of improper compaction of the backfill in a new
sewer trench at the toe of a future slope.   The ground surface was to be
leveled for a future warehouse, as shown in the sketch.   The part to be filled
was not yet completed when surface cracks in the compacted cohesive fill
indicated lateral movements of the slope.   Borings with continuous SPT
sampling (Art. 2-4A) were then made both through the backfilled trench and
the adjoining natural soil overlying the shale.   Both the SPT blow counts N
and the laboratory liquidity indices I_L [Eq. (3-17)] indicated that the backfill
in the trench was much less dense than the adjoining natural soil (Ref. 167).

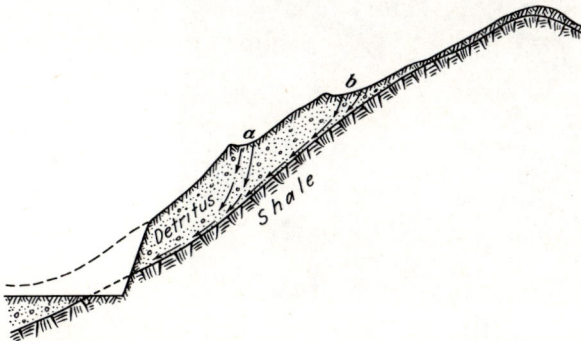

Fig. 7-14.   Profile showing drainage conditions which facilitate
detritus slides into cuts of the type illustrated by Fig. 7-15.

Presumably its lateral compression permitted small movements of the slope fill which might continue later and produce cracking of the warehouse walls if they were founded on the compacted-fill surface near the top of the slope.

In climates of alternating rainy and dry seasons slow *downhill creep* of otherwise stable surface layers may occur, especially if they consist of highly colloidal CH type ($w_L \geq 50$ percent) clays. Shrinkage cracks will develop

(I)

(II)

Fig. 7-15. Movement of a detrital bank along a wet slippery plane on top of hard shales (see Fig. 7-14). (*Courtesy of H. F. Peckworth.*)

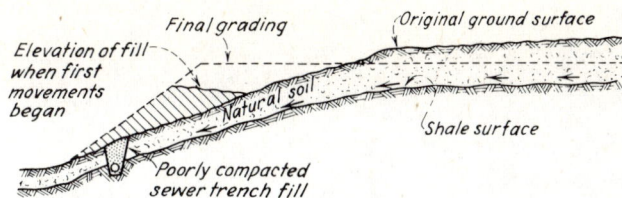

Fig. 7-16. An improperly compacted sewer-trench backfill which affected stability of the new slope above it. (*Ref. 167.*)

on their surface during the dry season but will be quickly filled up at the start of the rainy season by soil washed down the slope. As the wet clay gradually swells, it is unable to regain its original volume and therefore exerts a lateral force on the surface soil elements adjoining it on the downhill side. The process is repeated seasonally, producing downhill creep.

Sliding along a single slippery surface, however, is only one of the simpler types of movements possible in residual soils. A state of the art paper by Deere and Patton and six related papers (Ref. 85) show the complexities involved because of varying weathering and permeability profiles in different basic rock types and related factors. Measures to forestall possible disastrous slides in weathered material were found to be so uncertain that in some new housing developments near San Juan, Puerto Rico, the creation of fairly level surfaces by razing low hilltops to fill adjoining ravines was resorted to.

7-5. Dowel Action of Piles in Soft Soils. Several field cases came to the attention of the writer where lateral displacements of pile-supported footings near the top of an unstable slope took place before they gradually stopped. In one such case trestles supported by light timber piles under a conveyor belt along a short causeway from a river finger pier had to be repeatedly adjusted to meet a 12-in. (30-cm) lateral and 6-in. (15-cm) vertical (downward) movement of the pile tops. Subsequent undisturbed sampling of the underlying soft clay, testing, and stability analyses along cylindrical failure surfaces gave a factor of safety $F = 0.92$, indicating that a complete sliding failure of the slope would have been inevitable if no piles had been present. The use of Eq. (7-10) with $L = 7d$, however, increased the factor of safety to $F = 1.08$. That equation was developed as follows.

J. Brinch Hansen made an early attempt (Ref. 123) to evaluate numerically the stabilizing effect of piles. On the strength of purely theoretical considerations he suggested that the resistance against a dowel of rectangular section moving transversely through a cohesive plastic mass would be $p = 11.4hc$ per unit of dowel length. Then he analyzed a short rigid dowel intersecting a slip surface. He assumed soil reactions alternated in a way similar to that shown in Fig. 7-18(I), but took them to be of the same intensity p throughout the dowel length a (Fig. 7-17) on each side of the slip surface. He then

Fig. 7-17.   Deformations of model piles after direct shear test.   (*Ref. 78.*)

computed the transverse force T which such a dowel could transmit across it [Eq. (7-8)] and suggested that a pile could transmit no less than a dowel would:

$$T = 0.414pa \qquad\qquad (7-8)$$

How the value of a was to be determined for a pile was not specified.

The writer initiated some relevant model tests at Princeton University. First, Mackenzie's model tests on rectangular anchor rods (Ref. 205) showed that Hansen's $p = 11.4ch$ value [Eq. (14-24)] should be reduced to $p = 8.5ch$ [Eq. (14-27)], where $h = d =$ height of anchor or diameter of pile (see also Figs. 14-28 and 14-29 and discussion thereof).

Then Dastidar (Ref. 78) performed a series of direct shear and unconfined compression tests on 4-in.-diameter (10.2-cm) plastic clay cylinders in which 6-in.-long (15.3-cm) and $\frac{1}{8}$-in.-diameter (3.2-mm) $(d = h)$ model hardwood piles (hospital applicators) were embedded.   Groups of 4 to 16 piles at spacings of $4d$, $6d$, and $8d$ were tested, as well as cylinders with no piles at all.

A black, highly compressible clay, completely remolded and homogenized under the addition of water, common in Harris County, Texas, was used in the tests.   This clay has liquid and plastic limits of 92 and 30 percent, respectively, which give it a plasticity index of 62 percent.   Its parent material is limestone, and its basic clay mineral is montmorillonite.   This clay contains 66 percent clay size material, 22 percent silt, and 12 percent sand.

Figure 7-17 shows a cross section through a nine-pile group at the end of a direct shear test with zero surcharge when a 0.5-in. (12.7-cm) lateral displacement had occurred along the slip plane.   It will be seen from the photo that the pile deformation was essentially of the type sketched as $A'A'$ in Fig. 7-18(I), where the dash-dotted line AA represents the original position of the pile.   This deformation had to be accompanied by the kind of deformations indicated on that sketch.

Since it is not yet practicable to determine the exact distribution of the soil reactions along the model pile length (see Art. 1-9), the following procedure for estimating the dowel effect of the piles was adopted.   The shearing resistance developed during a test with piles was compared with the resistance in tests where no piles were used.   It was found that in all cases the resistance increment was proportional to the number of piles installed, irrespective of their spacing, which was never smaller than $4d$.   The resistance increment increased with the shearing deformations.   The simplifying assumption was then made that the increment of shearing resistance per pile T could be represented by pressure triangle with a constant maximum value $p_m = 8.5cd$

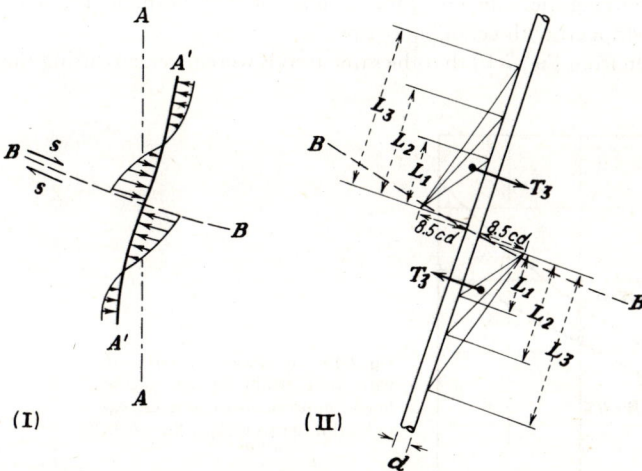

Fig. 7-18.   (I) Probable distribution of clay reactions corresponding to Fig. 7-17.   (II) Simplified estimation from model-test results of force T transmitted by pile across slip surface.

at the slip surface and $p = 0$ at a distance L from it, as sketched in Fig. 7-18(II) and expressed by

$$T = \tfrac{1}{2} p_m L \qquad (7\text{-}9)$$

Since the value of T obtained from the tests increased with increasing shearing deformations, the value of L, according to Eq. (7-9), would also increase correspondingly.   Actually both p and L would probably increase simultaneously until p reached its value of p_m.

By expressing L in terms of the pile diameter d it was found that for a 0.5-in. (12.7-mm) displacement in the direct shear test (Fig. 7-17) $L = 14d$ and $L = 10d$ for a 0.2-in. (5.1-mm) displacement.   Intermediate values fell in an approximately straight line, which, when extrapolated, gave $L = 7d$ for zero displacement.   The water content of the clay samples tested varied from 44 to 49 percent with an average of 47 percent.   At this water content the remolded soil had an approximate shearing strength $c = 1.25$ lb/in.^{2} (88 g$_f$/cm^2) in direct shear and $c = 2.55$ lb/in.^{2} (179 g$_f$/cm^2) in unconfined compression tests.

The absence of a surcharge in the direct shear tests probably accounted for the comparatively low c value they gave.   However, probably for the same reason, the direct shear tests gave a comparatively higher L value for zero displacement, so that its actual T value was in line with those of the unconfined compressive-strength test, as shown by the comparison which follows.

In the unconfined compressive-strength tests the pile butts and tips ended in the clay $\tfrac{3}{4}$ in. (19 mm) from the top and bottom metal plates.   To prevent the clay from bulging there the end $\tfrac{3}{4}$ in. (19 mm) of the 6-in.-high (15.3-cm) cylinder was wrapped with cellophane tape.

It will be seen from Fig. 7-19 that the same trends were revealed during the

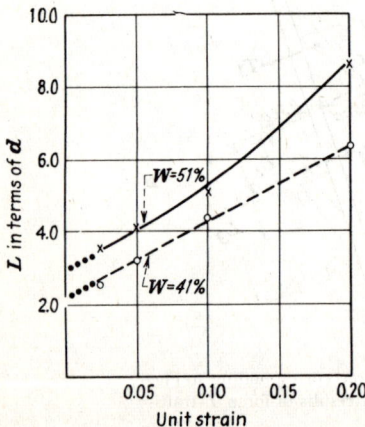

Fig. 7-19. Increase of force T with unit strain in an unconfined compression-strength test, expressed in terms of L in Eq. (7-9).

unconfined compressive-strength tests as in the direct shear tests, but with lower values of L. The extrapolation to zero strain of the curves on Fig. 7-19 gives $L = 2.2d$ for $w = 41$ percent and $L = 2.9d$ for $w = 51$ percent. The corresponding shearing strengths were $c = 4.3$ lb/in.^{2} (302 g$_f$/cm^2) and $c = 1.70$ lb/in.^{2} (120 g$_f$/cm^2).

By inserting these values and those for the direct shear test in Eq. (7-9) we obtain

$$w = 41\%: \quad T = \tfrac{1}{2} \times 8.5 \times 4.3 \times 0.125 \times 2.2 \times 0.125$$
$$= 0.628 \text{ lb} \ (285 \text{ kg}_f)$$

$$w = 47\%: \quad T = \tfrac{1}{2} \times 8.5 \times 1.25 \times 0.125 \times 7.0 \times 0.125$$
$$= 0.580 \text{ lb} \ (263 \text{ kg}_f)$$

$$w = 51\%: \quad T = \tfrac{1}{2} \times 8.5 \times 1.70 \times 0.125 \times 2.9 \times 0.125$$
$$= 0.328 \text{ lb} \ (149 \text{ kg}_f)$$

If we insert the same c value for $w = 41$ percent in Hansen's purely theoretical equation (7-8) for rigid dowels, as well as the coefficient 11.4 from his eq. 14-26 instead of 8.5 and the value $a = 2$ in. from Fig. 7-17, we obtain:

$$w = 41\%: \quad T = 0.414 \times 11.4 \times 4.3 \times 0.125 \times 2.0$$
$$= 0.507 \text{ lb} \ (230 \text{ kg}_f)$$

This is 81 percent of the 0.682 lb (285 kg$_f$) obtained from the experiments with flexible model piles. A similar comparison for $w = 51$ percent gives 61 percent.

The agreement is sufficiently close to suggest the use for rough preliminary estimates in practice of the following equation, which is obtained by inserting $L = 3d$ and $p = 8.5cd$ in Eq. (7-9):

$$T = \tfrac{1}{2} \times 8.5cd \times 3d = 12.7cd^2 \tag{7-10}$$

The exact value of T will naturally depend on the flexibility of the pile too. More field inclinometer determinations of the horizontal subgrade reaction (Arts. 1-9 and 14-4C) of laterally loaded piles will be needed before practically useful methods of analysis related to the influence of pile flexibility can be developed. Meanwhile Eq. (7-10) provides what the writer considers to be a crude but safe method of estimating the stabilizing force T which a pile of diameter d can develop at its intersection with a surface of shear slippage. Equation (7-10) is conservative since it refers to zero movement and the force T will increase appreciably if some deformations can be permitted.

With reference to Fig. 11-17 and its discussion in Art. 11-4, the resisting moment M_r in Eq. (7-7) can then be increased by

$$\Delta M_r = nTR \tag{7-11}$$

where $n =$ number of piles intersecting cylindrical failure surface

$T =$ value in Eq. (7-10)

$R =$ radius of cylindrical surface

The dowel action of piles is known to have prevented an unstable slope of largely granular hydraulic fill from sliding out (see discussion of Fig. 14-45).

In general, the dowel resistance of piles should not be counted on in original designs, and the use of Eq. (7-10) is recommended only in connection with the analysis of the need or otherwise for remedial measures once movements have begun to develop.

Short rigid dowels consisting of steel beams concreted in drilled holes have been successfully used in stabilizing a slope in decomposed schist rock (see De Beer and Wallays, Ref. 82).

7-6. Stability of Cuts in Stiff-fissured and Overconsolidated Clays. None of the methods described in the preceding articles for the numerical estimation of the stability of vertical cuts or of slopes in homogeneous plastic clay can be applied to overconsolidated so-called *stiff-fissured clays*. Terzaghi (Ref. 336) gave a sound explanation of the causes of sudden failures of clay banks which should have had an ample factor of safety if their behavior had been governed by the strength of the unfissured portions of the clay mass. An excavation produces tensile stresses in the upper zone of the slope or cut (Art. 7-1). The resulting expansion opens up the fissures of the clay in that zone, especially near the soil surface. Water can then gradually seep into the fissures, thereby softening the adjoining clay. After a while, the resistance to shear of the clay mass will be governed, down to a considerable depth, by the strength of these softened thin layers. Four of the five cases quoted by Terzaghi in the above reference indicated that failure had occurred at effective shear strengths of approximately 0.30 ton/ft², whereas the compressive strength of samples of the unweakened clay between the fissures was 10 to 20 times greater. One case corresponded to a failure strength of 1.0 ton/ft² (1.0kg$_f$/cm²).

Stiff-fissured, sometimes referred to as *slickensided*, clays of the above type have caused many troublesome slides in England. Attempts have been made, by means of field studies of such slides, to evaluate the softening of the clay in the fissures as a function of the time elapsed since the cut was made. The results of such studies, reported by Skempton (Ref. 299), indicate that this is a promising line of approach to the problem. Of course, separate field studies have to be performed for different geological formations in different regions. They are not likely to have universal validity.

Slickensided clays of the stiff-fissured type in the so-called cucaracha formation caused repeated trouble during the construction of the Panama Canal. The strength at failure was found to vary between 15 and 28 percent of the undisturbed shear strength (Ref. 29). Nevertheless, it was several times higher than the failure strength of most of the clays reported by Terzaghi (Ref. 336) or that of the English clays reported by Skempton in Refs. 299 and 301.

Figure 21 of Ref. 301 shows that a zone of softened clay extended about 1 in. (2.5 cm) on either side of slip planes recorded in the field at the site of three major slides in the London area, the water content increasing in that zone from an approximate value of $w = 28$ percent within the clay mass to a maximum of $w = 35$ percent at the slip plane, i.e., by some 20 percent. This supports Terzaghi's 1936 explanation (in Ref. 336) of the special nature of stiff-fissured clay slides, yet this simple fact seems to have been forgotten even by some university faculty members. Thus the writer, in his capacity of General Reporter to a session of the Third Pan-American Conference on Soil Mechanics and Foundation Engineering, had to comment unfavorably (Ref. 373) on a paper published there which recommended a general increase of factors of safety in design practice, using the slides on the Panama Canal and in England as illustrations without saying anything about the special nature of slides in the stiff-fissured clays there.

Overconsolidated clays, even when not of the stiff-fissured type, can create stability problems for conventionally designed slopes of open cuts. An example are the clays in the *Seattle area*. Numerous slides of highway cuts in that region prompted an extensive investigation, reported by Sherif in Refs. 289 to 292. The Seattle varved clays are of glacial origin and were consolidated during successive glaciations by great masses of ice up to 3,000 ft (910 m) thick. This produced precompression pressures of 375 lb/in.² (27 kg$_f$/cm²) as determined by consolidation tests. As a result, although photographs of thin vertical clay slices exhibit a pattern of varves generally similar to the one shown on Fig. 2-6 for the clays of the Albany, New York, area, the average water contents are much lower for the Seattle clays and residual lateral pressures are left in the clay in the aftermath of the melting of the ice surcharge. Evidence of this is the coefficient of lateral earth pressure at rest, K_0 (see Art. 10-1), which was determined experimentally in a special laboratory device and found to be greater than unity.

A highway cut removes the lateral restraint on the soil of a slope, which then starts slowly expanding and hence losing some of its original shearing strength in the process. Sherif reports (Ref. 291) results of laboratory tests which show that this lateral stress relief causes the Seattle overconsolidated clays to lose about 23 percent of their initial strength and that the design strength to be used in calculating the stability of unretained slopes should be about 27 percent of the initial short-term strength of these soils and not more than 50 percent of the laboratory strength determined by conventional quickly performed tests. This means that a factor of safety of at least $F = 2.0$ and preferably $F = 3.7$ should be used there in conjunction with the customary quick unconfined compression or triaxial tests.

7-7. Flow Slides. The two main types are *mudflows* and *slides of liquefied sand*. Mudflows can be divided into a number of subcategories and have related types of slides in clay (see Skempton and Hutchinson, Ref. 303). Usually they consist of random remnants of clay debris in a soft clayey matrix weakened by water. Similar are slides in the *quick clays* of Norway and eastern Canada.   An initial rotational slip remolds the extremely sensitive clay, which then flows out like a liquid with lumps of the dried-out stiffer crust floating on it.   The related problems are of considerable but mainly regional importance.

Of more general importance to engineers are cases of flow slides in saturated loose sands or other noncohesive granular materials.

Ehrenberg (Ref. 93) described a flow slide of loose sand in a soft-coal mine in Germany.   The soft coal was covered by a 155-ft-thick (47-m) layer of sand, which was removed to permit open-pit mining, and which was dumped in parts of the excavation where the coal had already been taken out.   One of these sand dumps reached a height of 62 ft (19 m) above the open level of the adjoining coal surface and was partially saturated with water seeping down a slope into the pit.   Without any warning over a million cubic yards of that sand flowed out into the pit, spreading out within a few minutes over the uncovered coal to a distance of 2,300 ft (700 m).   Fortunately the slide occurred in the evening when only four men operating emergency equipment were in the pit.   Two were close enough to the far edge and succeeded in climbing out in time; the other two perished.

Similar flow slides have been known to occur in high dumps of noncohesive chemical waste products of the fine rock-flour silt grain size.   In one case a dried-out surface crust gave a misleading appearance of stability until some

Fig. 7-20.   Sudden localized flow slide of saturated clean sand.   (*From Ref. 349.*)

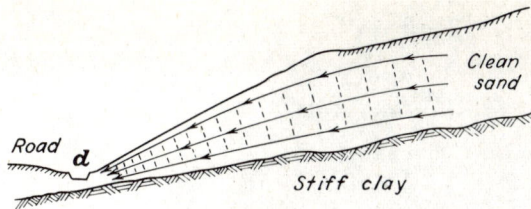

Fig. 7-21. Soil profile and the probable resulting flow net during heavy rain at location of slide shown in Fig. 7-20.

shock or vibrations suddenly liquefied the saturated interior, which flowed out, engulfing a neighboring village with heavy loss of life.

Large underwater slides of the flow type reported from Holland involved the complete liquefaction of a mass of loose sand which then spread out on very flat slopes.

The preventive measure against such flow slides is the proper compaction (Art. 5-3) of the sand (see Art. 8-4 for a discussion of relevant criteria).

Figure 7-20 shows a localized flow slide of clean coarse to fine sand along an inadequate drainpipe which caused the saturation of the sand around and above it. The slide occurred in an approach-road embankment to the New Jersey Turnpike after very heavy rains and happened quite suddenly, just as a car with two passengers was passing. The driver saw the moving mass of fluid sand and tried to avoid it by swerving to the left but was engulfed by it. The car doors could not be opened, and both occupants had to get out through the windows.

Subsequent borings revealed the soil profile shown in Fig. 7-21. A sloping layer of stiff clay passed just under the ditch d of the approach road, so that the flow net (Art. 8-2) of the seeping rainwater must have had the approximate shape shown in Fig. 7-21. The converging flow lines must have created a quick condition (Art. 8-3) at the ditch d, triggering the liquefaction of the entire saturated sand mass around and above the drainpipe which was supposed to channel away water from a ditch paralleling the turnpike. The writer visited the site that day after the slide, when the road had already been cleared of the sand flow and the embankment had been restored. Yet the coarse to fine sand at the bottom of the ditch d was still in a semiquick condition: when the writer stepped on it, his foot sank in well above the ankle. In this connection see the discussion of Figs. 7-12 and 7-13, as well as of 1st ed., Fig. 8-11.

7-8. Cuts in Loess Soil. Experience with such cuts has shown that a vertical or almost vertical cut of the kind illustrated in Fig. 7-22 proves to be most stable and lasting because of the predominantly silty composition of loess soils (Art. 3-7E) and because of their resulting low cohesion, which renders them very susceptible to rapid erosion by rainwater trickling down inclined slopes.

Fig. 7-22. A vertical cut in loess soil along a highway near Vicksburg, Mississippi. (*Photo by Tschebotarioff.*)

With vertical cuts most of the rainwater will not reach the edge of the cut and flow over it but will seep into the loess surface behind the slope.   This is particularly pronounced for loess soils in their primary deposit, since the vertical permeability in such cases is much greater than the horizontal permeability.   Draining water away from the cut is usually advisable, however.

Turnbull (Ref. 387) reported good results with similar techniques during the construction of canals in Nebraska.   Back slopes of 1 on ¼ were used up to a height of 40 ft (12 m) in sandy loess and up to a height of 55 ft (17 m) in silty loess.   This applies to the slope above the water level.   Special treat-

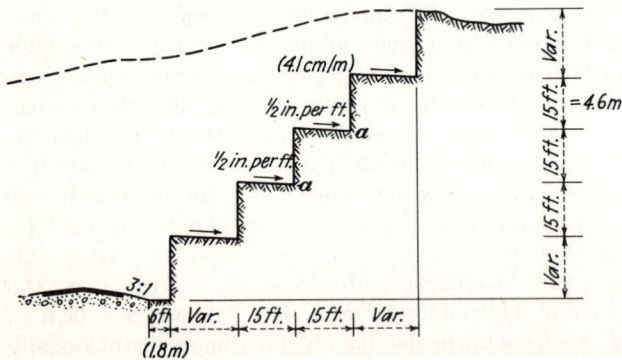

Fig. 7-23.   Deep stepped cut with vertical faces in loess soil on a highway in Iowa. (Ref. 141.)

ment such as sand berms, flatter slopes, and blanketing with treated material was needed below water level.

Figure 7-23 illustrates a method used for an 80-ft-deep (24.5-m) cut in the construction of a highway in Iowa (Ref. 141).   It had approximately 15-ft-high (4.6-m) steps with vertical faces.   A slight (1 on 24) slope was provided to drain water away from the edge of each cut.   To avoid erosion of the toe of the next higher step, the region a was paved, and the drainage of the accumulating water was facilitated in a longitudinal direction, i.e., at right angles to the plane of the drawing, by provision of a gentle slope in that direction.

7-9. Protection of Slopes.   Growing grass is one of the simplest and least expensive means for protecting slopes against *erosion by wind and rainwater action*.   Once a good turf has been formed, the grass will absorb most of the impact of rain drops, and its roots will hold the surrounding soil in place and prevent it from being washed down the slope.

It is very important to permit the grass to form a continuous cover before erosion has time to develop.   Otherwise seeding will be entirely ineffective. Erosion is apt to develop particularly rapidly on slopes formed by soils with little cohesion, i.e., true silts, very fine sands, rock flour, or loess.   Covering the slope with sod, when available, is an effective but expensive countermeasure.   Soil of this type on a gentle slope can be held down with cheesecloth long enough for the grass to take root.   Otherwise the soil would be blown or washed away together with the grass seeds.

On steep slopes the velocity of the water flowing down the slope can be greatly decreased by the method illustrated in Fig. 7-24.   It is similar to the

Fig. 7-24.   Protection of a highway slope by a method similar to contour plowing or terracing of the U.S. Soil Conservation Service.   (*Photo by Tschebotarioff.*)

so-called *contour plowing* or *terracing* used for soil-conservation purposes in agricultural work. Water then tends to flow slowly along the gently inclined grooves between the plowed ridges, which run almost parallel to the toe of the slope. The erosive power of the water is thereby reduced to a minimum.

In addition to eroding the surface of embankment slopes, heavy rains may frequently cause several foot-deep pockets, from which soil has flowed down the slope. This means that the surface soil was less pervious than the embankment soil behind it so that the resulting buildup of water pressure caused it to "pop out." To prevent repetition the pocket should be repaired by filling with pervious gravel or broken stone and not with the same soil that flowed out.

Special precautions are required for the protection of slopes close to the waterline of canals, lakes, or dams against *erosion by wave action*. This is usually accomplished with rock riprap, where the size of the blocks of rock has to be increased with the height of the waves to be expected. A sufficient weight of such blocks prevents their displacement by the impact of waves. In addition, it is necessary to prevent gradual washing out of the soil between the blocks by water running down the slope as each wave recedes. Something in the nature of an inverted filter is helpful for this purpose. A layer of sand is placed immediately on top of the natural soil of the slope and is followed by layers of gravel, broken stone, and finally rock riprap.

Protection of underwater slopes against *erosion by scour* is usually accomplished by wood mattresses fabricated on land, launched, and then sunk at the desired location by dumping rock riprap on the mattress. Figure 7-25

Fig. 7-25. Fabrication, launching, and temporary flotation of mangrove mattresses for scour protection of flood drainage-channel underwater slope. (*Raymond International, Inc.*)

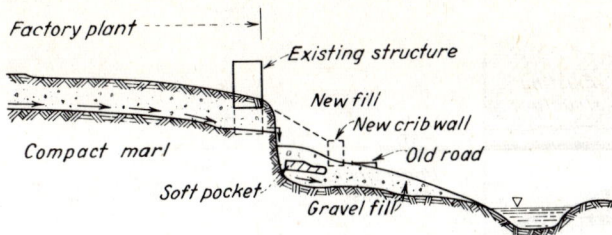

Fig. 7-26. Erosion of the detritus bank threatened an existing building. The new crib wall and protective backfill behind it slid out due to an unsuspected soft pocket of old factory waste.

illustrates the process on a Raymond-Emkay project. The type of mangrove wood locally available would not float, and the reusable wood boxes shown on the left of the photo were filled with foam rubber to provide temporary flotation.

Figures 7-26 to 7-28 illustrate the *treatment of bank-erosion problems* in an existing and expanding factory plant. Water seeping along an underlying inclined layer of very compact marl (unconfined compressive strength $q_u = 12$ tons/ft$^2 = 12$ kg$_f$/cm^2) was eroding a steep bank of detritus above it and threatening thereby the stability of an important existing old structure founded on shallow spread footings.

First, an attempt was made to build a new crib wall next to an existing old road and place backfill behind it, as shown in Fig. 7-26, to protect the face of the bank from further erosion. However, just as the backfill was being completed, it slid out together with its retaining wall to some distance down the slope. Borings were then made which revealed the previously unsuspected presence of a 14-ft-thick (4.3-m) soft pocket of decaying cellulose waste which had been dumped over and along the edge of the bank by the past owners of the plant and then covered up by them with gravel fill to make a road.

Underpinning of the existing building had to be resorted to, as shown in Fig. 7-27. Individual underpinning buttresses were carried down and into the very stiff marl. Precast reinforced-concrete planks, backed and fronted by a gravel filter, retained the detritus behind the structure.

Figure 7-28 illustrates the measures which were taken for the foundation of a high new chimney in the same plant to which Figs. 7-26 and 7-27 refer. The bank in the area was generally unstable, as evidenced by the performance of a new parking lot which required placing of new fill at the edge of the bank: it slid out before the fill was completed. Piles could not penetrate into the compact marl or provide substantial restraint to the bank if it started to slide. A reinforced-concrete box caisson, open at the bottom, was therefore built up on the ground surface and sunk into the marl by excavating its interior. Its bottom slab was then concreted.

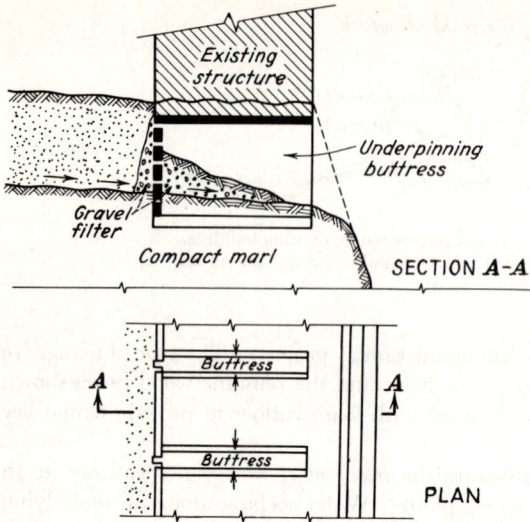

Fig. 7-27. Underpinning by buttresses was the solution to the problem illustrated by Fig. 7-26.

To improve the stability of the bank itself, an open trench was dug along the river side of the chimney caisson to intercept water flowing downhill along the marl surface; existing structures prevented this from being done on the uphill side of the caisson. A perforated steel pipe, surrounded by a graded filter, was placed in the trench and backfilled with clean sand covered by a clay blanket. The water accumulating in the perforated pipe was carried away to the creek by smaller pipes placed every 30 ft (9.1 m) or so at right angles to it.

The three-layered *graded filter* was used around the perforated pipe to prevent it from eventually getting clogged.

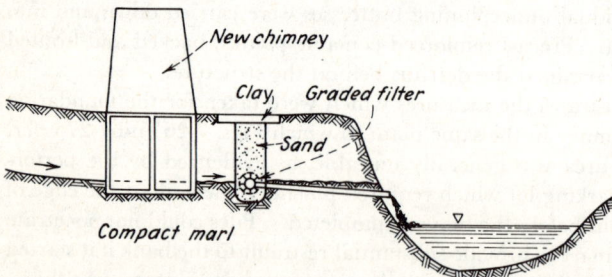

Fig. 7-28. Caisson foundation for high new chimney and stabilization of adjoining detritus bank by deep drain in the factory area illustrated by Figs. 7-26 and 7-27.

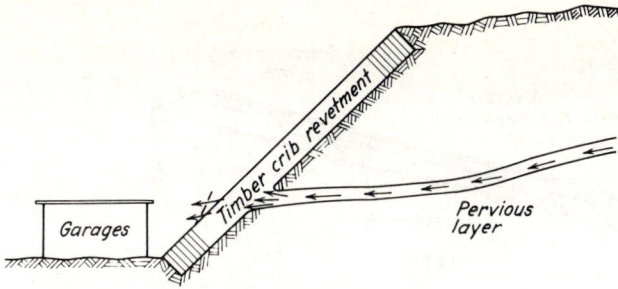

Fig. 7-29. Failure of timber-crib protective revetment because of insufficiently pervious fill in the crib.

The following general principles apply to the design of any type of drain. If a coarse-gravel drain is laid in a trench dug through clay soil, seepage and other pressures will gradually squeeze the clay into the gravel until all its voids are filled with clay, i.e., clogged, and the drain ceases to function. Studies by Bertram and others (Ref. 26) indicate that a satisfactory performance of the filter can be expected if the following conditions are observed. The grain-size curves of soils for the proposed filter layers are determined and are plotted as shown in Fig. 3-1. The grain sizes of each soil corresponding to 15 percent of the total (D_{15}) and to 85 percent of the total (D_{85}) are read off from the grain-size curves. There will be no danger of the finer soil being squeezed into the voids of the coarser soil if the D_{85} of the finer soil is not smaller than one-fourth to one-fifth of the D_{15} of the adjoining coarser soil; this is the requirement needed to prevent clogging.

Cribs (Art. 10-7) can be quite effective in preventing slope erosion, but it is essential to fill them with clean sand or gravel no less *pervious* than the most pervious seam in the soil of the slope to be protected. Otherwise trouble of the kind illustrated by Fig. 7-29 may result. A high slope was being eroded by rainwater, and the soil washed down from it caused clean-up trouble to the owners of garages at its toe. A creosoted-timber crib revetment was then used to face the slope. It was filled with random mixed soil from the slope. Apparently it was less pervious than some pervious layer at about one-third the slope height because during a period of heavy rains the entire crib revetment was pushed out by water pressure at that level. The upper two-thirds of the crib lost their support and came crashing down the slope onto the garages, causing much damage.

A special problem of *slope treatment in permafrost regions* confronting highway construction in the far north is illustrated by Fig. 7-30(I). In early winter the active layer starts freezing from the surface. The frozen zone of the active layer reaches the permanently frozen soil first under an embankment. Elsewhere the cover of vegetation and snow, which acts as an insulation, delays freezing somewhat, but all vegetation is removed from under an embankment during its construction and the roadway has to be kept cleared of snow to permit traffic. When an embankment is located on the side of a hill, ground-

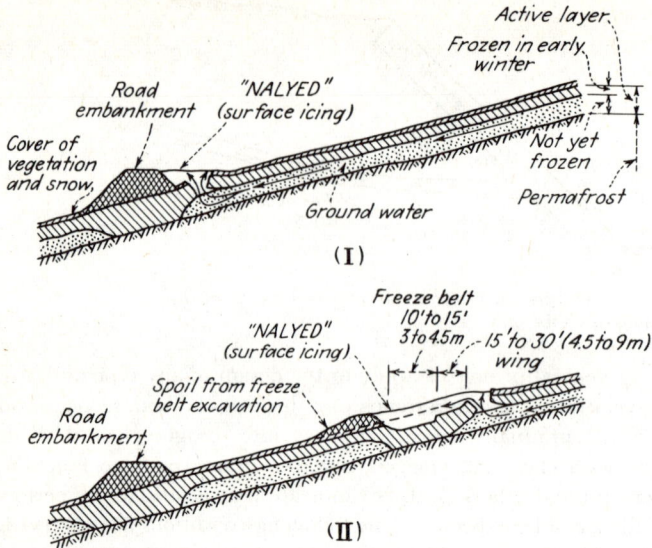

Fig. 7-30. Formation of large quantities of surface ice (*nalyed*) on slopes in permafrost regions is (I) detrimental when occurring next to unprotected embankment but (II) not dangerous when controlled by excavation of a suitably located freeze belt. (*After Tchekotillo, Ref. 333.*)

water may continue flowing through the still unfrozen lower part of the active soil layer until it encounters the completely frozen active layer under the embankment, which then acts as a dam.   If a sufficient head is built up, the water may break out to the surface through the upper frozen part of the active layer and freeze there, forming large masses of *surface ice* (other names are *nalyed* or *icing*) along the embankment.   In some extreme cases it may even overflow and cover the roadway.   In the spring, this ice will provide large quantities of meltwater, which softens the soil and thereby endangers the stability of the embankment and the roadbed.

A preventive measure worked out by Soviet engineers in Siberia is illustrated by Fig. 7-30(II).   It aims at intercepting the groundwater and forcing the inevitable development of surface ice at locations where it cannot harm the highway.   To that end, the vegetation and turf cover is removed, and a shallow excavation is made along a so-called *freeze belt*, some distance uphill from the highway and parallel to it.   The belt is cleared of snow during the first month or so of the winter.   As a result of these measures the active layer freezes through under the belt before it freezes under the road embankment, and the surface ice is formed in the belt, where it will do no harm.   Drainage ditches are provided to carry away part of the surface water and the melt water from the belt in the spring.   Several consecutive belts of this type have to be provided in some locations (Ref. 333).

Drainage ditches must be protected from freezing by special *warmth-retention* measures. Similar measures are required under small bridges, since otherwise the ice under the bridge will be covered with less snow than on open stretches and the river channel will be liable to freeze under the bridge right down to the bottom before it does so elsewhere. Surface ice may then form in front of the bridge and may destroy it. Freeze belts, cut into the ice during early winter at shallow spots upstream of the bridge,

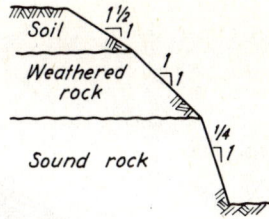

Fig. 7-31. Some suggested slopes for deep highway cuts. (*After Ref. 251.*)

may be used in some cases (see Tchekotillo, Ref. 333 and Tsytovich, Ref. 386).

7-10. Rockslides and Rockfalls. The slopes shown in Fig. 7-31 for deep highway cuts have been suggested as safe. These slopes are required to avoid large slides. Individual blocks of rock, however, may become separated from the face of the slope at any inclination thereof and roll down along it, bounce off it, or come down in a free fall, as sketched in Fig. 7-32. In all these cases the falling rocks present a real danger to traffic at the bottom of the slope. Possible protective measures include a ditch at the toe of the slope. It is suggested in Ref. 267 that it be made $D = 4$ ft (1.2 m) deep when used with a protective rock fence at the edge of the highway. Check fences can be provided on long slopes. A suggestion† that remains untried is to

† By James S. Peet in 1969 term paper at the University of Delaware.

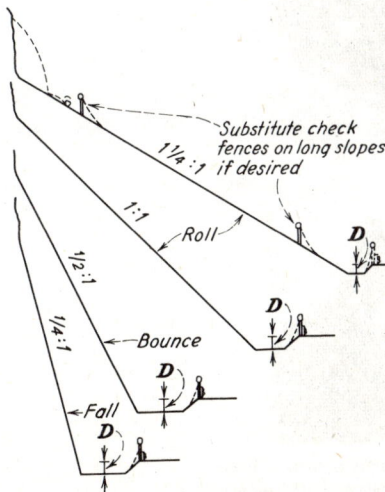

Fig. 7-32. Rock fences to protect highways from bouncing rocks and fences on slopes to check rolling rocks. (*From Ref. 267.*)

Fig. 7-33.   Rock and snow fence at the top edge of a railway cut in the Swiss Alps.   (*Photo by Tschebotarioff.*)

Fig. 7-34.   Steel rods anchor upper slabs of laminated rock to lower ones along a railway cut in the Swiss Alps.   (*Photo by Tschebotarioff.*)

Fig. 7-35.   Protective reinforced-concrete roof over a roadway in the Swiss Alps at the toe of a steep slope with frequent rockfalls.   (*Photo by Tschebotarioff.*)

Fig. 7-36.   Protective antirockfall and antisnowslide tunnellike structure at a hairpin turn of a highway in the Soviet Caucasus.   (*Photo by Tschebotarioff.*)

fill the ditch with some shock-absorbing material such as slag or expanded lightweight aggregate.

Figure 7-33 shows a protective fence at the top of a steep railroad cut to stop rocks rolling down a natural slope above. The fence consists of old rails concreted as posts into holes drilled into the rock, two rails per hole, with horizontal wooden logs between them.

Very large loose blocks of rock can be anchored back individually in a manner similar to that described with reference to Figs. 11-22 and 11-23. Wiremesh screens, hung from the top of steep cuts, are sometimes used as a temporary protective measure.

Laminated rocks, especially if thin decomposed claylike seams are present between the laminations, can present special problems when they are sloping toward a cut. In the photo of Fig. 7-34 slides had been occurring along the bedding planes inclined under almost 45° toward the railroad cut. It proved necessary to fit the slope of the cut to the inclination of the bedding planes and to use steel rods to dowel the upper layers to the lower ones.

In some cases there is no room for protective ditches along the toe of a slope with frequent rockfalls. Then, as shown by Fig. 7-35, a protective reinforced-concrete roof must be provided over the road and designed to resist the impact of heavy rocks. Figure 7-36 shows a similar tunnellike structure for protection of a highway curve.

REVIEW PROBLEMS

7-1. An unsupported vertical cut 23 ft (7.04 m) deep is to be made in a stiff clay layer, the relevant properties of which have been determined in the laboratory from tests on undisturbed samples as follows: $q_u = 1.40$ tons/ft² (1.4 kg$_f$/cm²), $\gamma = 125$lb/ft³ (2.0g$_f$/cm³). What will be the factor of safety F against rupture of the bank?

Answer. According to Eq. (7-4):

$$h'_{cr} = \frac{1.29 \times 1.40 \times 2,000}{125} = 28.9 \text{ ft } (8.8 \text{ m})$$

$$F = \frac{28.9}{23.0} = 1.26$$

7-2. On what approximate slope would one have to make a 23-ft-deep (7.0 m) cut to obtain a factor of safety $F = 1.26$ if the clay is softer than that in Prob. 7-1 ($q_u = 0.70$ ton/ft², $\gamma = 110$ lb/ft³), reaches to a depth $D = 30$ ft (9.1 m) below the bottom of the cut, and is followed by much stiffer material at a greater depth?

Answer. According to Eq. (3-19) $c = q_u/2 = 700$ lb/ft². To obtain a factor of safety $F = 1.26$ one should calculate a value of c to be used in the computations as follows: $c = 700/1.26 = 560$ lb/ft², corrected further to $560\frac{100}{110} = 510$ lb/ft², since the unit weight of the soil is greater than that used in the charts. From Fig. 7-6(III), where $D = 50$ ft (15.3 m), we find $\alpha = 10°$ (1 : 5.7), and from Fig. 7-6(II), where $D = 20$ ft (6.1 m), we find $\alpha = 16°$ (1 : 3.5). Extrapolating, we obtain a slope of 1 : 4, which should be satisfactory for purposes of preliminary estimation. Note that the corresponding value of n is 1.5; i.e., a steeper slope would be permissible if the width of the base of the cut is smaller than $1.5 \times 23 = 34.5$ ft (10.5 m).

7-3. What slope would be permissible if the clay of the cut is underlain by stiffer material, i.e., if $D = 0$, all other conditions remaining the same as in Prob. 7-2?

Answer. From Fig. 7-6(I) we find $\alpha = 45°$ (1 : 1).

7-4. By what value would the overturning moment of slice 7 in Fig. 7-7 be increased as a result of sudden drawdown $h_w = 7.5$ ft (2.3 m)? The void ratio of the soil is $e = 0.84$, and its buoyed weight, according to Eq. (3-10) and a value of $G = 2.65$, is 56 lb/ft³ (0.895 g_f/cm³).

Answer. According to Eq. (3-8), the unit weight immediately after the drawdown within its zone, which is shown hatched for slice 7 in Fig. 7-7, would be

$$56.0 \times \frac{2.65 + 0.84}{2.65 - 1.00} = 118.4 \text{ lb/ft}^3 \ (1.9 \text{ g}_f/\text{cm}^3)$$

The unit increase would be $118.4 - 56.0 = 62.4$ lb/ft³. Thus it is equal to the removal of the effect of buoyancy per unit of total volume (voids + solids) of the soil. The distance $a'b'$ being equal to 36 ft, the total increase of weight in slice 7 (1 ft = 30.5 cm deep) will be $62.4 \times 7.5 \times 36.0 \times 1.0 = 16,850$ lb $= 16.58$ kips. The corresponding increase in the overturning moment will be $16.85 \times 90.0 = 1,515$ ft-kips (22,450 kg_f/cm).

RECOMMENDED FOR FURTHER STUDY

Skempton and Hutchinson, Ref. 303.

CHAPTER 8

SEEPAGE AND CAPILLARITY. EARTH DAMS

8-1. Permeability of Soils. *Permeability* is the property of a soil which allows water to flow through it. Computations of gravitational permeability are based on the *law of Darcy* (1856), according to which the velocity of percolation is directly proportional to the *hydraulic gradient* (see Fig. 8-1).

$$v_p = k_p i \tag{8-1}$$

where v_p = actual velocity of percolating water

k_p = coefficient of percolation, i.e., actual average velocity of flow through the voids of the soil when $i = 1.0$

i = hydraulic gradient = h/L

h = difference between the groundwater levels on either side of a soil layer, i.e., the drop of head over distance L

L = thickness of the soil layer measured in the direction of flow

The law of Darcy is valid for laminar flow; no turbulence of flow is possible in most natural soils, except in coarse sands or gravels of uniform size.

In practical problems it is more convenient to deal with the total cross-sectional area A of a soil mass than with the average area of the voids. Accordingly, the *coefficient of permeability* k of a soil is defined as the imaginary average velocity of flow v which will occur under the action of a hydraulic gradient of unity ($i = 1.0$) through the total cross-sectional area (voids + solids) of the soil.

$$v = ki \tag{8-2}$$

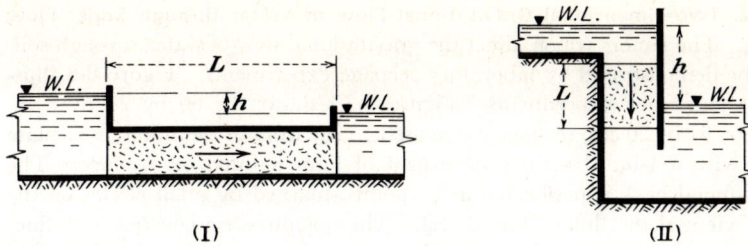

Fig. 8-1. Significance of the term *hydraulic gradient* $(i = h/L)$ for (I) horizontal and (II) vertical direction of gravitational flow of water through soils.

The assumption is made that the average area of the voids is directly proportional to the volume of the voids V_v. With reference to Eq. (3-12), the following relationship will exist between the coefficient of permeability k and the coefficient of percolation k_p:

$$k = \frac{V_v}{V} k_p = \frac{n}{100} k_p = \frac{e}{1 + e} k_p \tag{8-3}$$

The discharge Q during the time t through a total cross-sectional area of soil A can then be computed from

$$Q = kiAt \tag{8-4}$$

The coefficient of permeability k is expressed in the metric system in centimeters per minute or centimeters per second. The latter units have the advantage of providing a simple relationship with English measures:

$$1 \text{ ft/year} = 0.96 \times 10^{-6} \text{ cm/sec} \approx 1.0 \times 10^{-6} \text{ cm/sec} \tag{8-5}$$

Figure 8-2 gives the wide range of the variation of coefficients of permeability k for different types of natural soils.

Test methods for determining the coefficient of permeability are given in the first edition, Art. 5-2; see also ASTM Designation D-2434-68, Ref. 18, Permeability of Granular Soils, Constant Head.

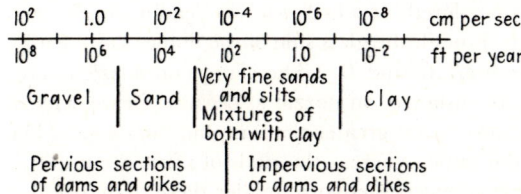

Fig. 8-2. Permeability coefficient k of different types of soils. (*After Ref. 48.*)

8-2. Two-dimensional Gravitational Flow of Water through Soils; Flow Nets. The factors which affect the gravitational flow of water through soils can be demonstrated by laboratory seepage experiments. Figure 8-3 illustrates some such experiments. Figure 8-3A shows the 60 by 24 by 8 in. (153 by 61 by 20 cm) seepage flume used. The front of the flume is of plate glass with a 4-in. (10-cm) square grid of lines painted on its face. The sheet-metal back is perforated at 27 points, marked by small circles on the front view of the flume (Fig. 8-3A). The openings are covered with fine-mesh wire screens. Each opening is connected to a glass standpipe.

An overflow T is provided at one end of the flume to take care of excessive inflow from the faucet R when the outlet faucet U is closed or when the total discharge through an earth dam in the flume is smaller than the inflow.

When the flume is filled with water only, no soil at all being added, the water in all 27 standpipes will rise to the same elevation, irrespective of the fact that these standpipes are connected to the flume at four different elevations, I, II, III, and IV. One then says that the *head* at all these elevations is the same. Thus a head represents a potential, not a pressure.

Things will be different if we fill the tank with sand. For instance, form an earth dam as shown in Fig. 8-3C and D and open both faucets R and U to provide constant water levels at the upstream and the downstream faces of the dam, the difference between these two levels being equal to h. It will then be noticed that the water in the standpipes will rise to elevations having intermediate values between those of the upstream and the downstream free-water levels. These elevations are read and written down on a special mimeographed sheet similar to Fig. 8-3A, each opposite the point marking the corresponding standpipe. Lines of equal head (*equipotential lines*) can then be drawn in between the 27 points at which the head was measured, in a manner similar to the procedure employed when drawing contour lines in land surveying. They are shown by broken lines in Fig. 8-3B, C, and D.

Colored liquid (fluorescein is used as dye) is then allowed to seep into the upstream face of the dam at selected points. A special small tank (not shown in the drawings) is used for the purpose. Several rubber tubes with glass nozzles lead from that tank. Their nozzles are pressed into the sand at the points a, b, c, d, e, f, and g on the upstream side next to the glass plate. Clamps fitted to the rubber tubes are loosened so as to release a slight trickle of the fluorescein. A green-colored so-called *flow line* leading from each nozzle can then be observed through the glass side of the flume, as shown by full lines and arrows in Fig. 8-3B, C, and D. The clamps on nozzle a have to be loosened more than, for instance, on nozzle g, because the velocity of the inflowing water around nozzle a is greater than around nozzle g. (The head lost in both cases is the same, whereas the path of percolation at g is greater, and the hydraulic gradient is therefore smaller there than at a.)

The system of interrelated equipotential lines and flow lines is termed a *flow net*. It will be noted that the equipotential lines intersect the flow lines

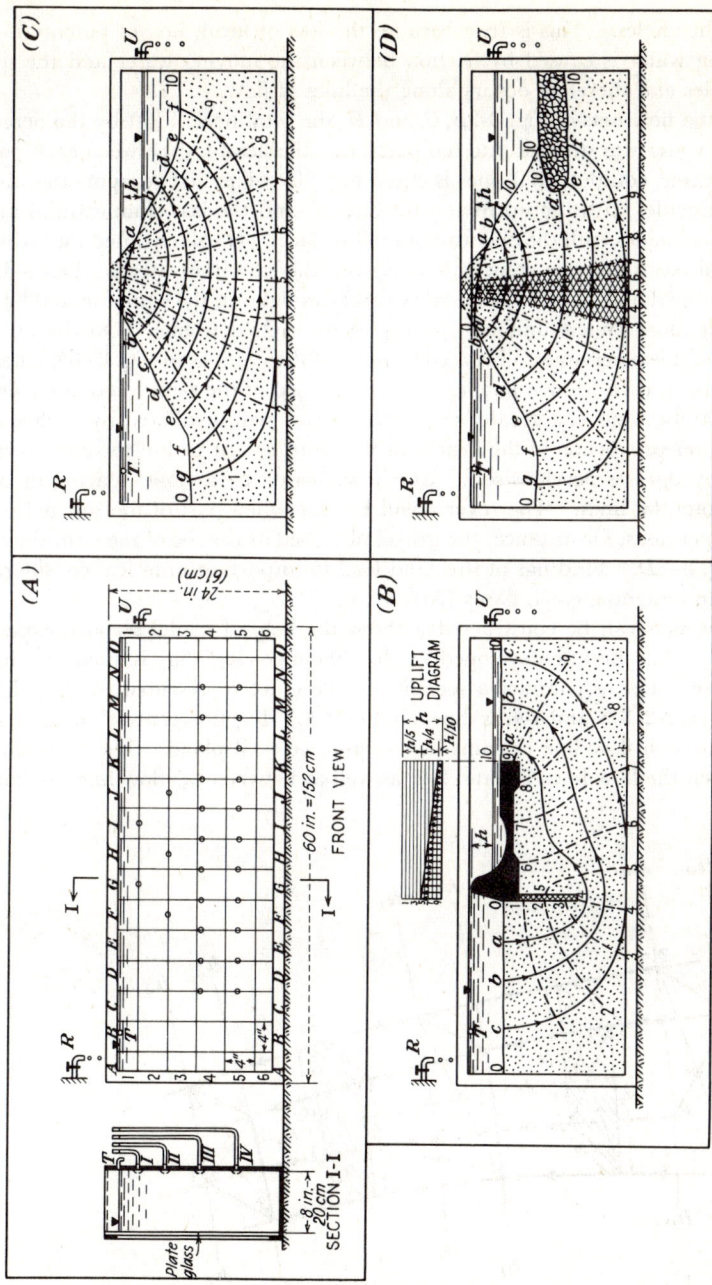

Fig. 8-3. Gravitational flow of water through soils. The general dimensions of the flume employed for the laboratory seepage demonstrations are shown in *A*.

at right angles. This is true because the loss of head, i.e., of potential, of seeping water is caused by friction between the moving water and the soil particles and therefore occurs along the lines of flow.

In the flow nets of Fig. 8-3B, C, and D, the total head h lost by the percolating water was divided into ten parts, i.e., the head lost between each pair of adjacent equipotential lines is equal to $h/10$. The first equipotential line 0-0 coincides with the upstream soil surface, and the last equipotential line 10-10 coincides with the downstream soil surface. It will be noted that when the soil has a uniform composition, e.g., in the case illustrated by Fig. 8-3C, where the dam was built of the same sand throughout, the equipotential lines have a more or less uniform spacing along each flow line. On the other hand, if a less pervious soil is used in parts of the dam, as in Fig. 8-3D, where the central core (shown hatched) was composed of the sand fraction passing the 100-mesh sieve, a greater resistance to flow will be offered by such soil. A greater proportion of the head will therefore be lost within the zone occupied by the less pervious soil. This is indicated by a closer spacing of the equipotential lines. The reverse will be true when part of the soil mass is more pervious, for instance, the gravel filter bed at the toe of the dam shown in Fig. 8–3D. Findings of this kind lead to important practical considerations in designing earth dams (Art. 8-10).

Flow nets can be constructed without the help of model seepage experiments. A technique developed by Forchheimer (Ref. 98) is used for that purpose. Let us consider a section of a flow net represented by four flow lines 1-1, 2-2, 3-3, and 4-4, as shown in Fig. 8-4. The flow is two-dimensional, so that each flow line remains in the same vertical plane. The distance b between the flow lines 1-1 and 2-2, as well as between the flow lines 3-3 and

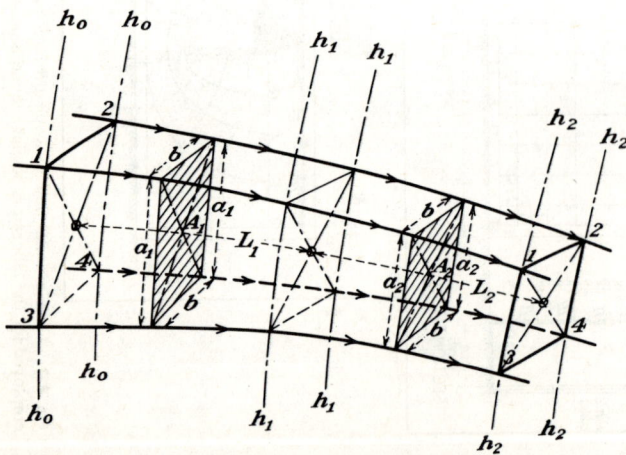

Fig. 8-4. The principles of flow-net construction.

4-4, will then remain constant.   The discharge Q through the soil enclosed by these four flow lines will also remain constant at all cross sections.   This follows from the definition of a flow line as the path followed by a particle of water.   Since only nonturbulent laminar flow is considered, none of these paths can intersect another one.   The water within the four flow lines shown in Fig. 8-4 behaves essentially as if it were flowing through a pipe limited by these lines.   Where the flow lines come closer together, so that the soil cross section bounded by them decreases, the discharge remains the same but the velocity of flow is increased.   Thus the discharge Q_1 through the cross section A_1 must be equal to the discharge Q_2 through the cross section A_2.   According to Eq. (8-4),

$$Q_1 = ki_1 A_1 t = Q_2 = ki_2 A_2 t \qquad (8\text{-}6)$$

In a homogeneous soil the coefficient of permeability k will have a constant value throughout.   The hydraulic gradients i and the cross sections A will equal

$$i_1 = \frac{h_0 - h_1}{L_1} \quad \text{and} \quad i_2 = \frac{h_1 - h_2}{L_2} \qquad (8\text{-}7)$$

$$A_1 = a_1 b \qquad A_2 = a_2 b \qquad (8\text{-}8)$$

If we decide to draw our equipotential lines in such a way that the drop of head Δh between each pair of adjacent equipotential lines is the same, then

$$\Delta h = (h_0 - h_1) = (h_1 - h_2) = \text{constant} \qquad (8\text{-}9)$$

By substituting the values of Eqs. (8-7) to (8-9) in Eq. (8-6) we obtain

$$k \frac{\Delta h}{L_1} a_1 bt = k \frac{\Delta h}{L_2} a_2 bt$$

or

$$\frac{a_1}{L_1} = \frac{a_2}{L_2} \qquad (8\text{-}10)$$

The physical significance of Eq. (8-10) is that the ratio of the sides of every rectangle of a flow net formed by intersecting flow lines and equipotential lines must have a constant value if the flow net has been drawn correctly. Thus, if one rectangle of a flow net has been drawn as an approximate square with $a_1 = L_1$, then all other rectangles of the flow net must also be approximate squares.   This circumstance can be utilized to draw flow nets by a trial-and-error procedure (see Ref. 332, pp. 161–166).   In the case of earth dams the line of saturation has to be determined first; this can be done by means of an approximate method developed by Casagrande (Ref. 50).

When water flows through soils of different permeability, Eq. (8-6) is simplified to read

$$\frac{k_1 a_1}{L_1} = \frac{k_2 a_2}{L_2} \qquad (8\text{-}11)$$

Let us assume that the more permeable soil has the permeability coefficient k_1 and that we have begun drawing our flow net in that zone as a system of squares; that is, we have made $a_1 = L_1$. It will then follow from Eq. (8-11) that

$$\frac{a_2}{L_2} = \frac{k_1}{k_2} \tag{8-12}$$

In other words, in the zone of the less permeable soil $(k_2 < k_1)$ the flow net will consist of a system of rectangles with the side a_2 being larger than the side L_2 in proportion to the ratio k_1/k_2 of the coefficients of permeability of the two adjoining soil zones. The results of the experiment shown in Fig. 8-3D illustrate this point in a general way.

Tridimensional flow involves the use of a variable value b in Eq. (8-6). This complicates the problem to such an extent that graphical solutions become impracticable. An exception is the case of radial flow, which can be treated as a modified two-dimensional flow problem by a method given by Taylor (Ref. 332).

8-3. Quicksand Conditions. The loss of head along a flow line occurs because of friction between the water and the soil through which it flows. The soil skeleton resists this friction. So-called *seepage forces*, representing differences of head or potential, are exerted against the soil in the direction in which the water flows. The seepage force J acting against an area A along length L where the loss of head Δh occurs will be

$$J = \Delta h \, A \gamma_f \tag{8-13}$$

where γ_f is the unit weight of the fluid $(=1.0$ for fresh water if the metric system is used).

The seepage force j exerted by water per unit of volume of the soil $(A = 1.0)$ is

$$j = \frac{\Delta h}{L} \times 1.0 \times 1.0 = i \tag{8-14}$$

where $i = \Delta h/L$ is the hydraulic gradient. In English measures,

$$j = i \times 62.4 \tag{8-15}$$

If a flow line intersects a slope of sand, the seepage force may affect the natural angle of repose α_R (Fig. 3-20) of the soil. On the downstream face of a dam the seepage forces j will decrease α_R near the free-water level, since the horizontal components of j along the flow lines aa will tend to increase the tangential sliding forces (see Fig. 8-3C and D). This circumstance may be partly responsible for the erroneous idea expressed in many old textbooks that the angle of repose of a submerged clean sand is smaller than that of a dry clean sand. Similar conditions are liable to arise after a heavy rainfall on any embankment leading down to a free body of water. The water is seldom clear enough to permit noticing from the bank that, under such conditions, the angle of repose of the sand deeper down is greater than at the water level.

Water flowing into a slope, for instance, on the upstream face of a dam, exerts a stabilizing influence, since the seepage forces increase the tangential resisting forces to sliding. This circumstance is utilized to facilitate cuts in rock-flour types of fine-grained soils with little cohesion by means of suitably located well points with or without electroosmosis (Fig. 9-14).

In some cases, for instance, on the inner faces of some types of cofferdams [Fig. 12-1(I)], water will flow vertically upward at right angles to the excavation surface if the cofferdam is pumped out. The seepage forces j will then be also directed upward and will be resisted by the unit weight γ' of the buoyed sand. According to Eqs. (8-15) and (3-10), at limit equilibrium

$$j = i_{cr} \times 62.4 = \frac{G-1}{1+e} \times 62.4 \qquad (8\text{-}16)$$

so that the critical hydraulic gradient which corresponds to this limit equilibrium is

$$i_{cr} = \frac{G-1}{1+e} \qquad (8\text{-}17)$$

The absolute specific gravity G of quartz sands is 2.65 and, according to Fig. 3-6, the void ratio e of some naturally deposited sands may vary between the values of 0.57 and 0.95. With these values we obtain from Eq. (8-17) for the loosest possible state of submerged sand $i_{cr} = 0.85$ and for the densest state $i_{cr} = 1.05$. An approximate average value of the critical hydraulic gradient can be taken to equal unity. The corresponding void ratio is then $e = 0.65$ and, according to Eq. (3-4), the porosity $n = 39.3$ percent.

The significance of the critical hydraulic gradient can be demonstrated in the laboratory with the help of a device illustrated in Figs. 8-5 and 8-6, which give its vertical cross section. It is a metal box, 1 by 1 by 1 ft (30 by 30 by 30 cm), with a glass window on one side. Water can flow into the bottom of the box when the stopcock C is opened. A porous filter plate A is located an inch or so above the bottom of the box. The space above that filter plate can be filled with sand almost up to the overflow level. The standpipe B is connected to the free space below the filter plate.

As soon as the stopcock C is opened, water will start to flow vertically upward through the filter plate and the sand. It will be noticed then that the water level in the standpipe B will rise above the free-water level in the box by a height h, which will increase with the velocity of the flow as the stopcock C is opened wider. This height h therefore represents the loss of head of the flowing water due to friction against the solid skeleton of the filter plate and of the sand above it. The flow lines, of which ten, a to j, are shown in Fig. 8-5, are all directed vertically upward. The equipotential lines, by their

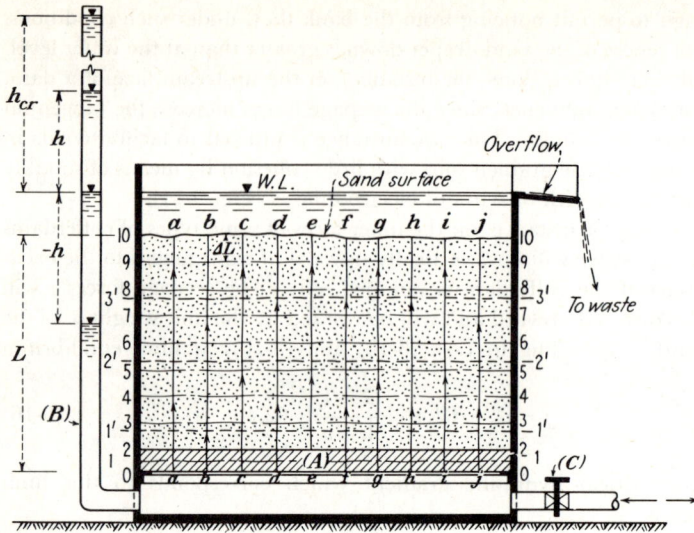

Fig. 8-5. Laboratory demonstration of quicksand action.

very nature, have to intersect the flow lines at right angles and, in this case, are therefore horizontal.   If we draw the equipotential lines in such a way that the distance between them represents the same value of lost head $\Delta h =$ constant, the number of equipotential lines will increase with the hydraulic gradient $i = h/L$ as the stopcock C is opened wider.   Their spacing ΔL will decrease correspondingly.   Thus, as shown in Fig. 8-5, if the equipotential lines 0'-0' to 3'-3' correspond to the loss of head h, a greater loss of head with increasing velocity of flow will produce a closer spaced system of equipotential lines, for instance 0-0 to 10-10 as shown.

Finally, a critical condition will be reached when the entire sand mass begins to *boil;* it becomes *quick* as it is loosened up and held in suspension by the upward-flowing water.   This is the condition expressed by Eq. (8-17) and $i_{cr} = \Delta h/\Delta L_{cr}$.   In this quick condition the sand loses its supporting power; any object placed on the sand surface will sink into it if its unit weight is greater than the unit weight of the fluid sand-water mixture.   It should be noted, however, that placing a solid object on the sand surface modifies the entire pattern of the flow net (see Fig. 8-6 and compare to Fig. 8-5).   Visible boiling of the sand will begin around the edges of the solid object W.   This is caused by the greater local velocity of flow, as indicated by the more closely spaced flow lines deflected by the object from their original path.

Similarly, it has been observed on underdesigned cofferdams in the field that a quick condition usually begins to develop at their inside corners, where the concentration of flow lines is greatest.

In the laboratory the direction of the flow can be reversed (Fig. 8-5) by connecting the stopcock C to the waste and opening it. It will then be observed that the water level in the standpipe B will drop below the freewater level in the box. The value of this *negative head* $-h$ will increase with the escape velocity of the water through the stopcock C. The direction of the seepage forces is now reversed, and their effect is added to the effect of gravity. Thus they will have a tendency to compact the soil slightly and to increase its shearing strength.

The preceding discussion shows that any sand can become a *quicksand* and remain continuously in that condition so long as a flow of water and a critical hydraulic gradient have been developed and are maintained by pumping during inadequately planned construction operations, or by special drainage conditions, such as under improperly designed dams built on a bed of sand. Thus a quicksand is *not* a type of material but a condition which can be prevented by appropriate measures.

A special type of a localized quick condition is provided by so-called *piping*, where a stream formed by a liquefied sand-water mixture moves through surrounding stable sand as if it were flowing through a pipe. Figure 14-40 illustrates a laboratory demonstration of that effect in the seepage flume shown in Fig. 8-3A. A temporary vertical partition was placed across the flume. It had, at a quarter of its height above the bottom, a small (diameter $= 2$ in. $= 5$ cm) semicircular hole next to the plate-glass side of the flume. The hole was plugged with a removable stopper, and the flume was filled with fine beach sand on one side of the partition. Artificially colored, black sand was placed in horizontal layers at 2-in. (5-cm) elevation intervals.

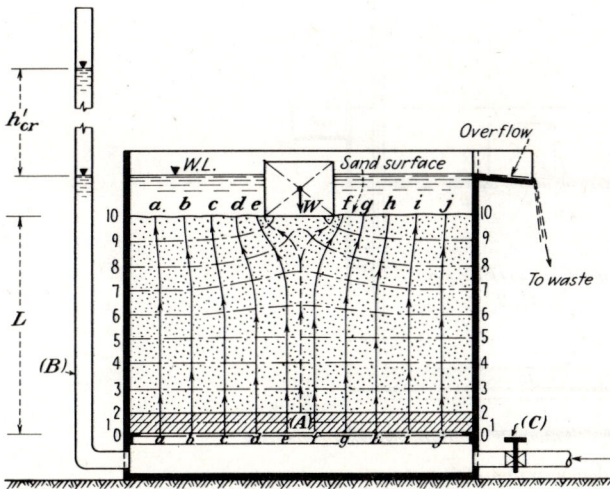

Fig. 8-6. Laboratory demonstration of localized quicksand action.

The photographs in Fig. 14-40 show the setup after completed filling. When the stopper was removed and sand began to trickle out laterally through the hole, a column of sand immediately above the hole appeared to be liquefied and was set into downward motion as if it were moving along a pipe. A crater was formed at the surface. Its slope corresponded to the natural angle of repose. The sand rolled down along that slope toward the "pipe," which had almost vertical walls. The lateral pressure exerted by the heavy fluid sand-water mixture must therefore have been sufficient to keep the surrounding sand in place by counterbalancing its active lateral pressure. The latter, of course, must have been relatively small because of arching phenomena around the fluid "pipe," similar to those likely to occur around shafts.

A special condition may arise in uncompacted, loosely deposited, fully saturated sands, the *loose grain structure* of which may collapse as a result of a *sudden shock*, so that the whole mass may be momentarily liquefied, *become momentarily quick*, with unpleasant consequences. Some uncompacted, very fine, uniformly loose sands may be particularly susceptible to such momentary liquefaction. Shearing stresses imposed by construction operations may favor momentary liquefaction in all loose, fully saturated sands.

The liquefaction of a loose sand as a result of a sudden shock can be demonstrated in the laboratory. The metal box shown in Fig. 8-7 is filled with sand. The stopcock c is connected to a waterline and is opened wide. Water is thus allowed to surge through the filter stone a upward through the sand and out over the overflow d; this completely loosens up the sand. The stopcock c is then closed; it is disconnected from the water-line and is opened

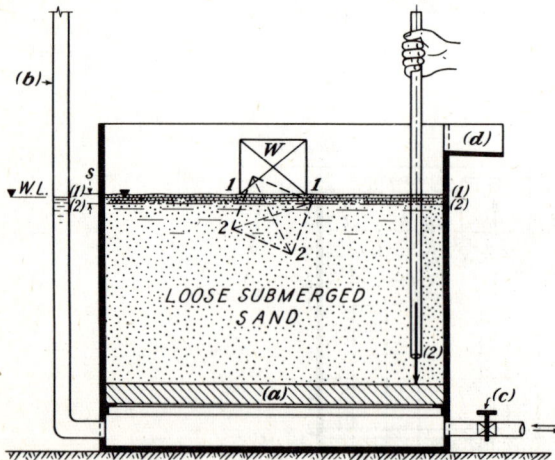

Fig. 8-7. Laboratory demonstration of the contraction and temporary loss of supporting capacity of a loose submerged sand as a result of a sudden strong shock.

to permit downward drainage of the water at a rate sufficiently slow to avoid compacting the loose structure of the sand. When the water level drops approximately $\frac{1}{4}$ in. (6.3 mm) below surface 1-1 of the sand (as seen from the glass standpipe *b*), the stopcock *c* is closed, and a weight *W* is carefully placed on the sand surface. A metal rod is then rammed through the sand, so as to hit the bottom of the box and jar it. Two things will then be observed. The entire surface of the sand will fall by the amount *s* to the level 2-2 and will sink slightly below the water level. Thus the shock will have caused the compaction of the entire mass of the saturated loose sand. The weight *W* will, however, be found to have sunk down to the position 2-2 by an amount several times greater than the settlement *s* of the sand surface. This indicates that immediately after the shock the whole mass of the sand was liquefied for a few moments. In this condition it had no shearing strength whatsoever and could not offer any resistance to the shearing stresses which are always caused in the soil by a load resting on its surface (Fig. 4-3).

8-4. Critical Sand Density at Liquefaction. Since dense sands expand and loose sands contract during shear (Art. 3-5*A*), there must be an intermediate density at which shearing deformation can take place without any change of volume. The void ratio which corresponds to this intermediate density has been termed *critical void ratio* by Casagrande (Ref. 48).

Direct shear tests are not well suited for the determination of the critical void ratio of sands; triaxial tests on completely saturated sands must be used. The change of volume of a sand specimen during the test is measured by recording the variations of the water level in the graduated glass burette attached to stopcock 2, which is kept open, as shown in Fig. 3-25. At least three to four separate triaxial tests, with as many different initial sand densities, must be performed in order to determine the critical void ratio for a given intensity of the minor principal stress σ_3. As shown in the first edition, Fig. 7-25, the volume change at the failure load of each test is plotted against the initial void ratio at which the sand specimen was put into the apparatus for testing (it is necessary to have at least one test with very dense sand and another with very loose sand). A line is then drawn, as shown in the diagram, through the points thus obtained. Its intersection with the line representing the ordinates of zero volume change gives the value of the critical void ratio e_{cr}.

It may then be seen that an increase in the value of the confining pressure σ_3 brings about a decrease in the recorded value of e_{cr}. This means that if the sand used for the tests illustrated by that diagram had an initial void ratio of, say 0.80, then under a confining lateral pressure of $\sigma_3 = 1$ kip/ft² (= 0.5 ton/ft²) it would tend to expand during shear, whereas under a higher confining lateral pressure of $\sigma_3 = 6$ kips/ft² it would tend to contract.

All the above considerations are of considerable practical importance in connection with *liquefaction* phenomena of saturated loose sands, which sometimes lead to the so-called *flow slides* of embankments or earth dams (Art 7-7).

The critical-void-ratio concept leads to the conclusion that any contraction of sand during shear may cause its liquefaction and that therefore a sand of medium density which would be safe at shallow depths might nevertheless liquefy at greater depths. The static laboratory tests of Castro (Ref. 53) appear to support this conclusion.

By contrast, extensive studies of full-scale sand-liquefaction phenomena in earthquake regions and laboratory cyclic loading tests (Ref. 285) have led Seed to state (Ref. 286) that under earthquake loading conditions "the liquefaction potential of a soil is reduced by an increase in confining pressure." In general, fine sands were found to liquefy more easily than coarse sands and uniformly graded materials more easily than well-graded materials. For earthquakes of moderate intensity (acceleration $a = 0.1g$) Seed concluded (fig. 18, Ref. 286) that liquefaction of fully submerged sands was unlikely to occur under any conditions when the SPT field test gave values of at least $N = 7$ blows/ft at a depth of 5 ft (1.5 m) and increased from there linearly to at least $N = 16$ blows/ft at a depth of 70 ft (21 m).

With reference to Fig. 2-16, which relates the N values of an SPT test to relative densities at different depths, a compaction of submerged sands to a relative density of at least 70 percent should be the aim for safe designs.

This should be satisfactory for static conditions too (see the discussion of Figs. 7-12 and 7-13 and Art. 5-3), since it does not seem logical to assume that there would be more danger of liquefaction of a deep sand layer under static conditions than there would be during a moderate earthquake.

The more stringent requirement always to compact submerged sand to densities below their critical void ratio, even at considerable depths, appears to be in need of confirmation by full-scale observational data.

8-5. Underground Erosion. It has already been mentioned (Art. 7-2) that the presence of thin horizontal layers of sand in a bank of clay may have a detrimental effect on its stability. If such a sand layer happens to be connected to free water at a higher elevation, as shown in Fig. 8-8, a horizontal force equal to $\frac{1}{2}\gamma_w h^2$ will be exerted on the block of clay. At the same time the frictional resistance to sliding along its base will be reduced by the uplift component of the pressures in the water seeping along the sand layer. Sliding of the entire block may result, or sand may be eroded by the seeping water at

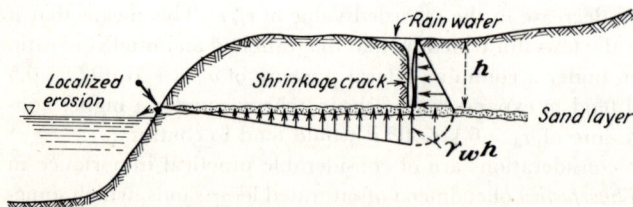

Fig. 8-8. Stability of a bank can be undermined by seeping water and the resulting underground erosion.

Fig. 8-9. Two buildings damaged by underground erosion.   (*From Ref. 269.*)

the edge of the bank and may undermine it locally.   The resulting soil settlements above the sand layer may severely damage houses built on the surface of the ground, as shown by Fig. 8-9.

Figure 8-10 shows that such localized "loss of ground" may take place even in a large mass of sand when water seeps toward a point A, a broken pipe in this case, into which sand is being gradually washed and carried away. Above a slope corresponding to the natural angle of repose of the saturated sand, shown by a heavy inclined line on Fig. 8-10, a cavern gradually develops in the moist sand and extends up the slope until the surface cover finally caves in.   The process is similar to the formation of sinkholes in limestone areas (see Fig. 4-47; compare also with Fig. 14-40).

8-6. Nongravitational Flow of Water; Frost Heaving.   The most commonly known form of nongravitational flow of water through soils is caused by capillary attraction.   This phenomenon is due to the affinity of water to most soils and the ability of water to resist surface tension.

Another but less well-known form of nongravitational water movement is the flow which is caused by differences of temperature within a soil layer, known by the general name of *thermoosmosis*.   It has been demonstrated by Bouyoucos (Ref. 36) that the affinity of water to soil increases with decreasing temperature.   This accounts for the observed migration of water from a warmer section of a soil layer to a colder one.   Such migration of water in a fluid phase is sometimes accompanied by condensation of water vapor in the air-filled voids of colder sections of not fully saturated soil layers.

Thermoosmosis is one of the explanations offered for the heaving of the center of light structures erected on swelling clays (see Fig. 4-43).

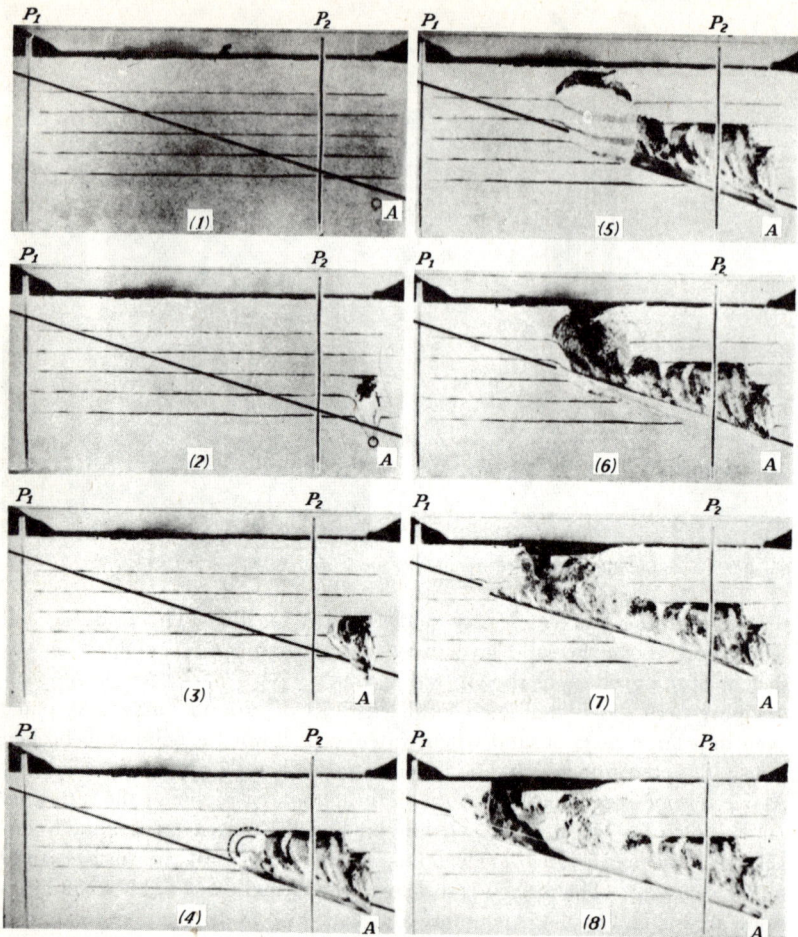

Fig. 8-10. Eight stages in laboratory demonstration of underground erosion due to gradual washing away of sand at point A. (*From Ref. 269.*)

A closely related phenomenon is *electroosmosis*. It was shown as early as 1808 by Reuss (Ref. 264) that the application of an electric potential will produce water movement in a capillary tube. Since then the theory of such movement has been developed by a number of investigators. The water migrates from the anode ($+$) to the cathode ($-$). Winterkorn (Ref. 407), has shown the direct interrelationship which exists between electroosmotic and thermoosmotic phenomena. Water moving through soil under the influence of a thermic potential creates thereby an electric potential.

Findings in the field of thermic effects on engineering behavior of soils are given in the proceedings of an international conference on the topic (Ref. 130).   That conference was dedicated to Winterkorn.

Electroosmosis has found direct practical application in facilitating excavation work through otherwise unstable rock-flour types of soils (Fig. 9-14). Thermoosmosis is closely related to frost-heaving phenomena.

Observations have shown that the surface of frozen soil layers is liable to heave under certain conditions.   Heaves of 10 in. and more have been recorded.   The main factors which influence the heaving have been found to be:

1. Presence of a free-water table below the depth of frost penetration at a distance H (see Fig. 8-11) when that distance is smaller than the height of capillary rise H_{max} [Table 3-2]

2. The value of the height of capillary rise H_{max}

3. The permeability of the soil

4. The duration of the frost.

Excavations in frozen soil which heaved have disclosed the presence of lenses or layers of solid ice, as shown in Fig. 8-11, indicating that the

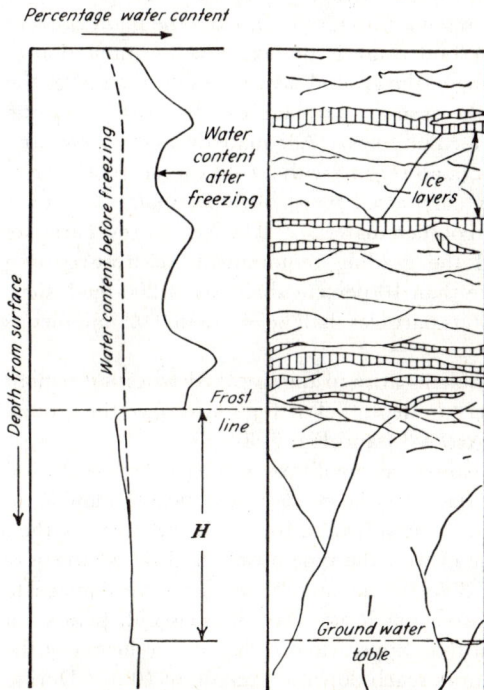

Fig. 8-11.   Increase in the water content of a frozen soil layer located close to the groundwater table.   (*After Refs. 28 and 238.*)

heaving is caused not just by an expansion of water during freezing but by a steady growth of the ice crystals as a result of the continuous capillary migration of water from the free-water table into the frozen zone. The ice lenses grow in size with time when the frost continues. See Fig. 4-42 in this connection.

Clean sands are not subject to frost heaving because of their negligible height of capillary rise. Clays are liable to heave only when the frost lasts for a long time. Although clays have a considerable height of capillary rise, their permeability is so low that only little additional water can be supplied through them by capillarity to the frost zone. The most dangerous frost-heaving soils are the silts, which have intermediate values of the height of capillary rise and of permeability, thus allowing the rapid growth of ice layers. Sands with such a high silt content that all the spaces between the sand grains are filled with silt are likely to heave as if they were silts.

The danger of frost heaving exists not only when there is a continuous water table within a silt layer underlying a structure such as a road. Particularly dangerous are cases when the silt forms pockets penetrating into a clay layer on a slope. Percolating rainwater can then accumulate in these pockets and later cause irregular frost heaving.

The irregularity in the heaving of a frozen soil surface is the main cause of damage to structures. The second cause is the excessive accumulation of water and the resulting softening of the ground near the soil surface after the thawing of the ice lenses in the spring. Damage can be avoided by the measures outlined in Art. 4-1 for buildings. Adequate drainage is essential for highways, and, in addition, in all regions with a cold winter, base courses have to be built of thoroughly compacted *frost-resistant material*. There are some variations in the definition of such material. The New Jersey Turnpike Authority (Ref. 226) defined the grading requirements of frost-resisting material as follows: "not more than 10 percent shall pass a 200 mesh sieve and not more than 5 percent of its particles shall be less than 0.02 millimeters in size."

Special civil engineering problems arise in the so-called *permafrost* regions of the far north, where at a certain depth below the soil surface the ground remains eternally frozen (see Art. 4-8*A* and Fig. 7-30).

Water movements may be caused seasonally by growing vegetation and produce volume changes in surface clay layers detrimental to shallow foundations of buildings and roads. The spread of roots and the depth of their penetration vary with the type of tree, the type of soil, and the intensity of summer rainfall. Ward (Ref. 395), in his analysis of extensive damage to buildings with shallow foundations on heavy clays in England, points out that the average root spread of trees approximately equals the height of the tree, and that the roots sometimes reach down to a depth of 10 ft. During dry spells trees and shrubs will absorb moisture from the soil around their roots. If the soil is heavy clay, uneven shrinkage may result in the zone of root penetration, accompanied by differential settlements of any shallow foundations founded within that zone.   Damage is likely to be considerable when only part of the foundation rests on the zone of root penetration.

Reference 19 provides data on moisture changes in soils beneath covered areas.   All such changes are due to nongravitational flow of water.

8-7. Types of Dams and the Principles Which Govern Their Choice.   Dams may be made of timber, steel, concrete, or rock and earth fill.   To fulfill its purpose a dam must be designed to prevent at a minimum cost excessive or dangerous seepage both through the dam itself and through the soil or rock beneath and around the dam.   The pressures transmitted by the dam to the underlying soil should not create a danger of shear failures in that soil or excessive settlements and deformations thereof which might damage the dam itself and thereby endanger its stability.

It follows that concrete dams are best fitted for erection on sites where they can be founded on stiff and impervious material, i.e., preferably on sound rock.   Earth dams are not limited by this restriction; because of their large dimensions, the pressures which they transmit to the underlying soil are distributed over considerable areas.   For the same reason seepage losses and the danger of a quick condition are decreased, since the length of the paths of percolation under the dam is increased considerably.   The earth dam itself can deform without much difficulty to adjust itself to deformations of the underlying soil which would destroy the much more brittle concrete.

Timber dams are seldom used and then only for small and temporary structures.   Steel is employed in dams mainly as an accessory material of construction.

The nature of the material available at the site is an important consideration in the choice of the type of dam to be built.   Thus rock-fill dams are of advantage in distant mountain valleys where there is little or no soil suitable for the construction of the dam.   The rock fill ensures the structural stability of the dam, and it is rendered watertight by a membrane covering its upstream face.   A blanket of rolled-clay fill is best suited for this purpose. However, in some cases where no suitable soil at all was available within easy reach, thin reinforced-concrete, steel, or timber blankets have been used.

The factors affecting the choice between an earth dam of rolled fill and one of hydraulic fill are outlined in the next articles.

8-8. Hydraulic-fill Dams.   The 95-ft-high (29-m) Sardis Dam, built by the U.S. Engineers across a tributary of the Mississippi River, will be used for the discussion of hydraulic-fill dam-construction procedures.   The methods used for the placing the hydraulic fill are illustrated by Figs. 8-12 to 8-14.

A dredge, of a type similar to those employed for underwater excavations, cuts its way from the river to the borrow area.   The mixture of soil and water cut up by the suction head of the dredge is pumped, sometimes over a distance of several miles, to the site of the dam.   The pipeline is laid along both edges of the dam, as shown in Fig. 8-13.   Each length of 10 ft (3 m) or so of the pipe is provided with a slot on its lower face which can be opened or closed manually by means of a sliding metal plate. Usually the soil-water mixture is discharged through not more than three or four slots opened at one time (see Fig. 8-14). The discharge can thus be located at any point

Fig. 8-12. Cross section showing construction procedure for a hydraulic-fill dam at the stage illustrated by Fig. 8-13.

of the pipeline around the dam. The pipeline is so placed that the water it discharges will flow toward the centerline of the dam. The sand is deposited first, close to the pipe, and forms the pervious outer *shell* or *shoulder*, whereas silt and clay flow toward the inner core *pool*, where they settle out and form an impervious *core* for the dam. The fine colloidal clay remains in suspension for a considerable time and in modern construction work is usually pumped away by a small pump floating on a raft on the core pool (Fig. 8-13). The permeability of the silty clay core is so low that the discharge through the dam will be insignificant, even without the finer colloidal-sized particles, whereas the rate of consolidation, and therefore the rate of increase in the shearing strength, of the core will be greatly improved by the removal of colloids. A clamshell (Fig. 8-13) is used to stir up the sediment of the core pool in order to prevent the deposition of streaks of sand which might form undesirable and even dangerous pervious channels through the core.

When the sand reaches the level of the pipe, a new temporary supporting

Fig. 8-13. The Sardis Dam under construction by the U.S. Engineer Department. General layout of the hydraulic-fill pipelines. (*Photograph by Tschebotarioff.*)

Fig. 8-14. View of a discharge point along a hydraulic-fill pipeline employed by the U.S. Engineer Department for repairs of the Fort Peck Dam slide. (*Photograph by Tschebotarioff.*)

timber trestle is provided.   The pipeline is disconnected and is raised to the new trestle.   In this manner the pipeline is successively raised, as shown in Fig. 8-12, from the position 1-1 to 5-5, and further on until the dam is completed.   A bulldozer is used to provide the first small embankment at 1-1.

Hydraulic-fill dams can be constructed in any weather, and in this respect they have a considerable advantage over rolled-fill earth dams.   However, the very nature of the hydraulic-fill process, as described above, limits its application in earth-dam construction to sites where the soil in the local borrow areas consists of mixtures of sand, silt, and clay.   Where such soils are available, the hydraulic-fill method provides a comparatively inexpensive method for the transportation and the deposition of very large masses of soil. The Fort Peck Dam was built by hydraulic-fill methods which involved some 100 million cubic yards of soil.   A considerable disadvantage of the hydraulic-fill method is that the sand is deposited in a comparatively loose condition and may be therefore susceptible to flow slides (see Arts. 7-7, 8-3, and 8-4).   Some compaction may be obtained by letting a tractor with caterpillar tread roll back and forth over the newly deposited sand.

8-9. Rolled-fill Dams.   Figure 8-15 gives the cross sections of two rolled-fill earth dams built by the U.S. Bureau of Reclamation.   The Deer Creek Dam (Fig. 8-15*A*) is of a somewhat later construction, when careful selection of soils and field control were already employed as a matter of routine.   Relatively impervious soil was placed in zone 1.   Granular material was placed in the outer zone 2.   The impervious core was extended down to rock by means of a *cutoff trench*.   A concrete *cutoff wall* reaching into rock was placed along the bottom of the cutoff trench and extended upward along the walls

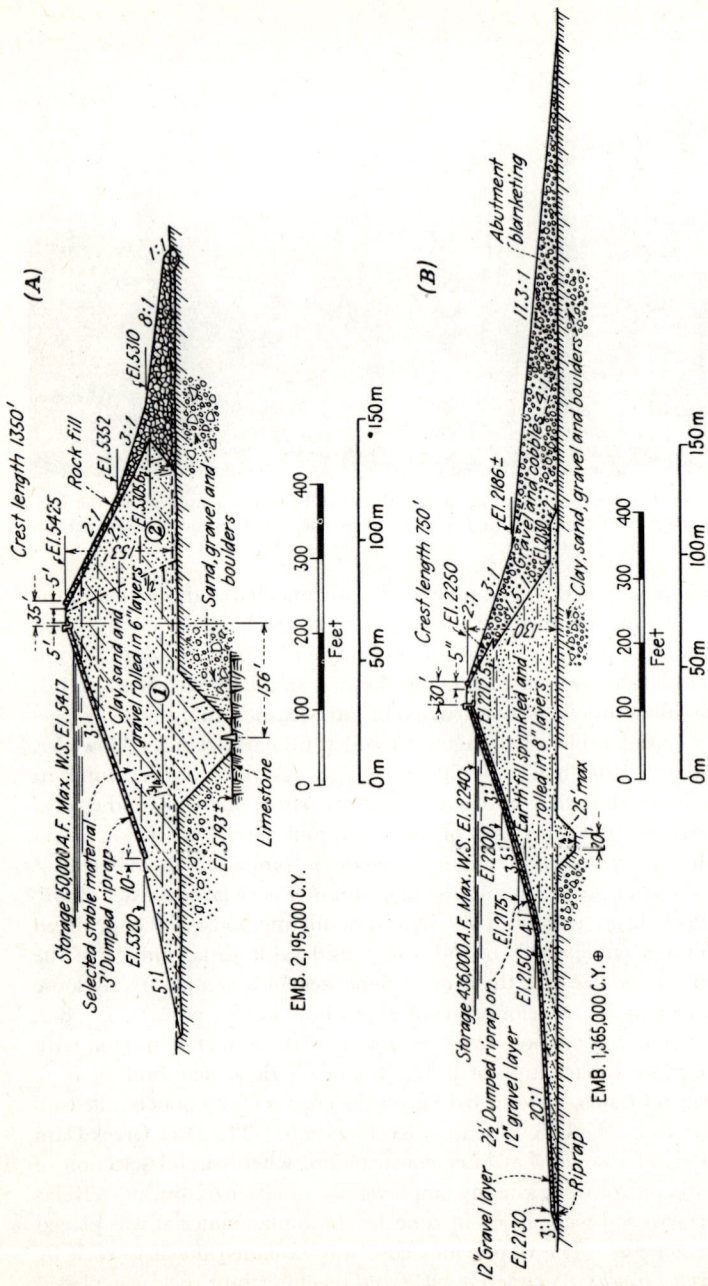

Fig. 8-15. (*A*) Cross section through the rolled-fill Deer Creek Dam, built in 1937 by the U.S. Bureau of Reclamation. The cutoff trench reached to rock. (*Courtesy of the U.S. Bureau of Reclamation.*) (*B*) Cross section through the rolled-fill Cle Elum Dam, built in 1931 by the U.S. Bureau of Reclamation on a deep bed of sedimentary deposits. (*Courtesy of the U.S. Bureau of Reclamation.*)

of the canyon.   The purpose of such cutoff walls is to decrease the danger of seepage along the plane of contact between natural soil or rock and the rolled fill, since such a contact plane always represents a zone of weakness.   The purpose of the cutoff trench, as implied by its name, is to prevent seepage under the dam.   Well-points may have to be employed for the excavation of the cutoff trench in water-bearing sandy soils, where the trench may have to be built in sections and the river temporarily diverted through specially built tunnels or other types of outlet structures.

Steel sheet piling is sometimes used to provide a cutoff under a dam when digging a deep trench is not practicable.   This was done under the Fort Peck Dam but did not prove fully effective.   On sites where boulders prevent the driving of sheet piling, the use of compressed-air caissons (Art. 6-10) has been tried successfully.   This was the case at the Quabbin Dam (Ref. 88). Small reinforced-concrete caissons were successively sunk side by side to rock at depths up to 100 ft (30 m).   The individual caissons were then connected, also under compressed air, to form a continuous core wall under the dam.

In some cases the rock is at such considerable depth under a dam that it is not possible to reach it by any type of cutoff wall or trench.   It then becomes necessary to design the dam so that its stability will not be affected by uplift pressures created by water seeping through the soil under the dam.   Figure 8-15B illustrates the design of a rolled-fill dam under such conditions.

Cutoff walls also have to be provided at the junction between a dam and rocky valley walls.   They are concreted in trenches cut into the sloping rock of a valley wall where the fill of a dam abuts against it, to prevent seepage and the formation of "pipes" along the contact surfaces of the rock and the fill.   Figure 8-16 shows such a cutoff wall in the Swiss high Alps.   In the foreground is the compacted rolled fill of the clay core of the dam which had to be placed here under unusually difficult conditions.   The short and rainy summer construction season at the high altitude did not permit any natural drying out of the only clay material available within an economic hauling distance.   Because of this, before rolling, that clay first had to be dried out to its optimum moisture content (Art. 5-5) in a rotary kiln at the site.

Compaction of the fill must be performed in accordance with the general principles discussed in Art. 5-5.   Soil of any composition can be dug up by shovels in borrow pits and transported to any designated section of the dam by heavy rubber-tired equipment, which can materially assist the special rollers in compacting the fill.   The cost per unit of volume of rolled fill is appreciably higher than that of hydraulic fill.

The fill should be rolled on the "dry side," i.e., at water contents at least 2 percent below the optimum, for reasons explained in Art. 8-10.   Exceptions may be made for low dams on a very compressible foundation since the probable deformations may produce cracks in a dry and hence brittle fill with a danger of "piping" developing along these cracks.

In bringing the fill to the water content desired for its compaction it is

Fig. 8-16.   Concrete cutoff wall at the Marmorera Dam.   (*Photograph by Tschebotarioff.*)

always easier to add water than to remove it by drying.   The water may be added either at the site of the dam or by sprinklers in the borrow-pit area when the soil there is very dry.   A combination of both methods may be employed.   Work has to be interrupted during protracted periods of rain.

Care should be taken not to have less pervious material placed on the downstream face of the dam if one wishes to avoid disastrous blowout of the downstream layers by water pressure built up against them inside of the dam. Impervious material (clay) is usually placed in the center of the dam; sometimes an upstream blanket is employed.   The latter method has a disadvantage in that small animals may bore holes into it.   Also, sloughing of the blanket in cylindrical surface slides thereof may occur in case of a sudden drawdown, i.e., a rapid drop in the upstream water elevation.   Somewhat flatter upstream slopes may be required to prevent such slides.   Continuous field control of the density and water content of the fill is essential in all cases; the methods of such control are outlined in Art. 5-5.

When any smooth-walled pipes or conduits are embedded in the fill of a dam, they should be provided with *antiseep collars*, the purpose and function of which are similar to that of cutoff walls just described.   Figure 8-17 gives a sketch of the layout of antiseep collars recommended by the Soil Conservation

Service of the U.S. Department of Agriculture (Ref. 73).   This service builds mainly single-purpose small dams of the *flood-retarding* type to decrease soil erosion, up to 30 to 50 ft (9 to 15 m) high.   The resulting siltation of larger reservoirs in the lower reaches of a drainage basin is also decreased thereby.

Failure to provide seep collars along conduits can have serious consequences (see Figs. 8-20 and 8-21).

The Soil Conservation Service (Ref. 305) requires the equal spacing of the collars within the saturation zone but at distances not more than 25 ft (7.6 m). Their number n is determined from

$$\frac{L + 2nV}{L} = 1.15 \qquad (8\text{-}18)$$

where $L =$ length, in feet, of that part of the barrel of a drop inlet or culvert lying within the zone of saturation, measured from the downstream side of the riser to the toe drain or point where the phreatic line intercepts the conduit

$V =$ vertical projection and minimum horizontal projection of the antiseep collar, in feet

For small dams with a height of 50 ft (15 m) or less the side slopes on a good foundation, i.e., in about 80 percent of the cases in the Soil Conservation Service practice, are controlled by the minimum requirement for maintenance of the vegetative cover by mowing.   A slope of 2.5 horizontal to 1 vertical is about the minimum slope for safe mechanical mowing.   On a very weak foundation stability analyses may show the need for flatter slopes (12 or 15 to 1) in the lower half of the dam (Ref. 73).

A *levee* is an embankment built along the shores of a river to contain its floodwaters and prevent them from inundating adjoining lands; it is essentially a small dam.   Some levees must be built on very soft and unstable ground.   Figure 8-18 shows the preparation of a base for a small levee in a mangrove swamp.   A dragline, operated by a caterpillar-track crane from a sectionally movable timber platform, was first used to remove surface

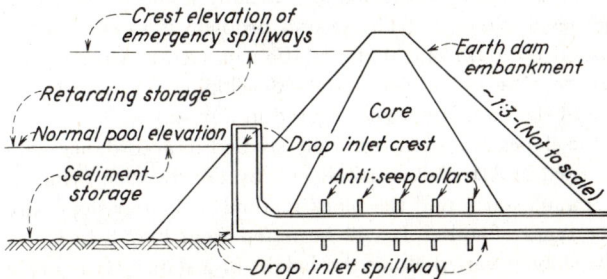

Fig. 8-17.   Sketch section showing typical elements of a U.S. Soil Conservation Service flood-retarding dam.   Not to scale.   (*Ref. 73.*)

Fig. 8-18.   A corduroy base for a levee along the edge of a future flood-control channel in a mangrove swamp.   (*Photograph by Tschebotarioff.*)

vegetation.   Then a *corduroy* road base, i.e., logs laid together transversely, and rocks on top of it were placed.   The levee embankment can then be built up over the rocks in compacted layers.   This somewhat improves the overall stability; a slip circle cannot pass through the corduroy layer without shearing the logs.

8-10. Stability of Earth Dams; Cases of Failure.   The failure of any type of dam after its completion is more disastrous in its consequences than the failure of any other type of structure.   The stability of a dam should therefore be the subject of particularly careful studies.   The study of both geological and engineering features is necessary to ensure a stable dam.   Close cooperation and understanding between geologists and soil engineers are therefore even more important for the design of all types of dams than they are for other foundation studies.

Soil engineers are mainly concerned with earth dams and must study two principal factors on which their stability depends.   First of all, the strength of the soil in the dam itself and in the foundation beneath it should be sufficient to resist the shearing stresses which are induced under any sloping earth surface.   In other words, the slopes selected for the dam should be related to the shearing properties of the soil.   The second problem is to control the seepage forces through the dam and its foundation in such a manner that there is no possibility of a quick condition's developing anywhere and the general stability of the dam is not endangered in any way.

The stability of the slopes of a dam is usually studied in accordance with the procedures discussed in Arts. 7-2 and 7-3, i.e., by the Swedish cylindrical-failure-surface (circular-arc) and the block methods.   Flatter slopes are required on weaker types of soils.   It will be noted from Fig. 8-15*A* and *B* that, as a rule, the slope is varied along the height of a dam.   It is made steeper near the top and is flattened out toward the base.

Some compaction of sand fills, especially in earthquake regions, is essential to prevent flow slides (Art 7-7).   On the other hand, there is some question whether excessive compaction of any type of fill is necessary when the underlying soil is comparatively weak.   It appears possible that such overcompaction of cohesive soils may even be detrimental, since it will provide a comparatively rigid superstructure which may be overstressed while adapting itself to the deformations of the underlying weaker material.

Rolled-fill material should be compacted on the dry side (Arts. 5-5 and 8-9), since otherwise excessive pore pressures may be developed in the fill.   Control observations are therefore essential and may indicate the need for changes of the original design.   The development of excessive pore pressures u decreases the frictional component of the shearing strength of a granular rolled fill, in accordance with Eq. (3-54).

In cohesive soils high pore pressures indicate that no further consolidation and no further corresponding increase of density and of shearing strength of the fill are taking place.

The *field measurement of pore pressures* in different sections of a dam provides essential information which cannot be obtained by any other means.   Purely theoretical analyses cannot take fully into account the great complexity and accidental variations in the composition of the soil in different parts of a large dam.   A number of devices have been developed for the purpose of measuring pore pressures.   Prior to the construction of the dam a hole is drilled down to the elevation in the natural soil where it is later desired to measure the pore pressure.   A plastic pipe is inserted into the hole.   Metal pipes are not advisable, since their interaction with some soils may develop gases which increase the pressure in the water of the pipe to values well in excess of the actual pressure in the voids of the soil around the lower end of the pipe. This end is perforated, and the space between the pipe and the walls of the hole is backfilled with granular material for a distance of 12 in. (30 cm) from a clay slurry plug above the bottom.   Higher up that space is also filled with a clay slurry.   It is essential that the slurry be of a highly impervious type, since otherwise the device will register the highest pore pressure in any one of the soil layers intersected by the pipe, instead of the pressure at its lower end.

The top end of the plastic pipe, above the natural soil surface, is covered by a cemented plastic piezometer tip.   The lower end of the tip is protected by a porous disk, and a double line of plastic tubing is connected to the upper end of the tip.   Both branches of the tubing are then carried through specially dug and backfilled (tamped) trenches to a terminal well on the downstream face of the dam.   Some 14 pipes of this type ean be placed in a trench 2 ft (61 cm) wide.   The purpose of the double line of tubing is to permit the periodical control flushing of any air or gas bubbles from the tubing and the piezometer tip.

A similar but somewhat simplified installation is used within the rolled fill. No vertical pipe is needed.

A large number of such devices have been installed on new dams for control purposes. For instance, pore pressures were measured at 40 points by as many separate piezometer tips on the Boysen Dam. All tips were connected by tubing to one terminal well, where a system of brass pipes and valves permitted their connection to two bourdon-tube-type altitude pressure gages which were used for the measurement of the pore pressures (see Ref. 394).

According to Ref. 393, systematic performance measurements of dams constructed by the U.S. Bureau of Reclamation have permitted continuous design improvements.

The *stability of a hydraulic-fill dam* presents special problems during the period of its construction (Art. 8-8). The outer shell, or "shoulder," which is composed of granular material, has to resist lateral outward fluid pressures of the slowly consolidating inner clay core. Measures to accelerate consolidation of the clay core are sometimes employed (Art. 8-8).

The *control of seepage forces* in earth dams is effected by placing the less pervious soil at the center or on the upstream face of the dam. The seepage forces will then be dissipated within that less pervious material (see Fig. 8-3*D*) at a safe distance from the downstream face. This is intended to prevent the development of a quick condition there (Art. 8-3) and to ensure stability by having a sufficient thickness of soil between the zone where the seepage forces are absorbed and the downstream face. It will be noted that this procedure was employed in the two dams illustrated in Fig. 8-15*A* and 8-15*B*, where the outward grading of the soil types was done in several steps, with cobbles and rock fill following the gravel. The slopes were flattened out considerably near the base of the dam shown in Fig. 8-15*B*, thereby appreciably lengthening the path of the water percolating under the dam and decreasing the hydraulic gradient (Art. 8-1). It will be noted that the cutoff trench of that dam did not reach down to rock.

The flat slopes of a hydraulic-fill dam are therefore well suited to conditions where the underlying soil is pervious to a considerable depth. Additional precautionary measures may be possible and necessary, for instance when a thin layer of loam covered a deep bed of sand, thus forming a natural impervious blanket over it. This blanket was not disturbed under most of the dam and upstream thereof, except for the stripping of the upper 6 in. of soil, which were perforated by a considerable amount of grass roots. The dam (see 1st ed., Fig. 17-5) was built directly on top of this blanket, except for the portion under the downstream toe where the topsoil was removed all the way down to the sand and drainpipes were installed. This ensured the relief of possible excessive uplift pressures near the toe of the dam in a manner similar to, but somewhat more effective than, that of the short drain at the toe of the model dam shown in Fig. 8-3*D*. No special grading of the filter material appears to have been undertaken in this case, since any clogging of the filter with time would be compensated for by the favorable effect of the increased thickness of the impervious upstream blanket due to the deposition of silt from the usually muddy waters of the particular river behind that dam.

Very little or no pervious material (sand or gravel) is available at some dam sites. Toe drains are then sometimes used, but they require careful grading of the filter material if they are not to become rapidly clogged (see Art 7-9, discussion of Fig. 7-28).

Graded horizontal filters may be employed to prevent a quick condition by loading with their weight the underlying surface of the soil within which *all* of the seepage forces are to be dissipated; these are the so-called *weighted* or *reversed* filters.   The D_{15} of the coarser layers of such filters should be 4 to 5 times greater than the D_{85} of the underlying finer layers.

If later pore-pressure measurements appear to indicate that horizontal drains are not fully effective, dangerous uplift pressures may be reduced, even at any time after construction, by drilling a row of relief wells along the toe of a dam.   For instance, uplift pressures corresponding to some 40 ft (12 m) of water head were measured after completion of the 240-ft-high (73-m) Fort Peck Dam in the sand and gravel layers underlying the toe of that dam.   The steel sheet piling used as a cutoff wall apparently was not fully effective.   Drilling a row of relief wells, however, decreased the uplift pressures at the toe of the dam to insignificant values.   Similar measures were used at other dams with reported success.

Borrow areas for the fill of a dam can sometimes be utilized for the relief of uplift pressure.   It is therefore often advisable to locate such borrow areas on the downstream side of the dam.   They should not be located on the upstream side if this would perforate a natural impervious blanket.

Much can be learned from past failures that will be of value for future designs.   This is true in all soil-engineering work and especially in the field of dam construction.

The first requirement for the satisfactory performance of any dam is that it should be built on a site with geological features permitting the storage of water in the reservoir behind the dam.   This is not necessarily the case of all sites in regions of cavernous limestone.   Intensive grouting as a possible remedial measure in such locations was successfully employed by the Tennessee Valley Authority.

Trouble of this kind, however, is not limited to limestone regions; leakage can develop through *open tension cracks* in massive sandstone bedrock.   A case of this kind in Arizona is described in the first edition, Art. 17-2.

The writer was asked to help in a somewhat similar small-scale case in Vermont when a swimming pool cut into a hillside would not hold any water at all because of the coarse-grained nature and resulting high permeability of the glacial till at that spot which was used to dam up a creek flowing down the hill.   Several bags of commercially available granulated (VollClay) Wyoming sodium *bentonite* (Art. 3-1*B*), mixed with the coarse sand and gravel of the till, solved the problem.   The mixing was done simply by throwing handfuls of the granulated bentonite onto the soil as it was being pushed forward by the blade of a bulldozer to form an impervious layer on the inner slope of the dam and on the pool bottom behind it.   The bentonite mixture, once saturated, gets so soft that one cannot step on it without sinking in; it should therefore be covered, before flooding, by a rolled layer of at least 2 ft (60 cm) of natural noncohesive soil to form a "walking mat" once the pool is in use.

Geological and soil-engineering studies should be extended wll beyond the site of the dam proper and should cover not only the floor but also any natural embankment walls of the reservoir.   Disregard of this circumstance may lead to trouble, as illustrated by Fig. 8-19, which in addition provide further evidence of the freak soil formations which may occur in regions of former glaciation.   The glacial ice had moved *up* a valley, forming a moraine embankment across it.   As the embankment grew, the level of Cedar Lake above the glacier was raised with it from 1-1 in ancient times to the level 2-2. This latter level was maintained prior to the construction of a concrete dam across the postglacial valley marked by the broken line *BB* in Fig. 8-19. This valley was cut through the natural embankment by the postglacial Cedar Creek, which provided an overflow for the waters of Cedar Lake.

The construction of the concrete dam raised the water in the lake to the level 3-3 and saturated well above the line *BB* the glacial outwash gravels which formed the core of the natural embankment adjoining the dam.   The water in the gravel could not escape, since the outer face of the moraine embankment was covered by a layer of varying thickness of glacial till and boulder clay.   This is a tentative explanation of the failure, as given by Mackin in Ref. 207.   As the water pressure grew against the outer impervious layer, it finally gave way at one of the weaker zones.   Within approximately an hour over a million cubic yards of detritus was washed out from the embankment, forming an amphitheater-shaped crater (marked *AA* in Fig. 8-19)

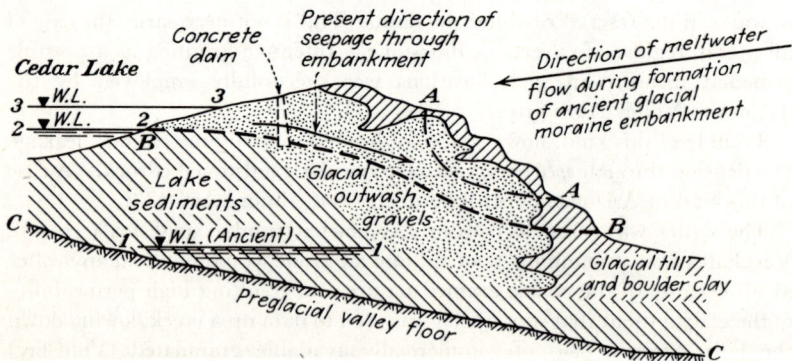

Fig. 8-19. Geological profile 6,000 ft (1,835 m) away from the concrete Cedar Creek Dam through natural embankment in the failure zone *AA*. (*From Mackin, Ref. 202.*)

in its face.   Its walls were found to be formed of bedded gravels, whereas the narrow throat with steep walls was cut through till.   The floodwaters which rushed down the valley through that amphitheater destroyed railroad tracks, a sawmill, and a small village.   The discharge through the amphitheater decreased very quickly and continued at a slow rate for several months until the water level in Cedar Lake dropped appreciably.

Thin horizontal water-bearing seams represent another important geological feature, since, if they are overlooked, the uplift pressures at the toe of dams in such seams may reduce frictional shearing resistance along these seams and produce failure.   Geologists can detect such features better than engineers.   According to Ref. 132, neglect of uplift was the cause of the 1911 failure of the concrete dam at Austin, Pennsylvania, with a loss of over 100 lives.   Relief wells can prevent such disasters.   The dam was built on sandstone and shale, and uplift had not been anticipated.

Geological studies without engineering strength testing of rocks and soils, however, may be inadequate.   The disastrous consequences of weak foundation material under a concrete dam are illustrated by the failure of the 205-ft-high (63-m) St. Francis Dam in California; the cause thereof lay in defective foundations.   At the east end the dam rested on mica schist and at the west end on reddish conglomerate, which became soft when wet.   This latter property was apparently ascertained only after the failure.   Both end portions of the dam failed suddenly.   Huge chunks of concrete, measuring 50 to 100 ft (15 to 30 m) side length, were carried half a mile from the original site by the suddenly released torrent, which caused much damage downstream of the dam.   There were 236 known dead and 200 missing (see 1st ed., Art. 17-2).

Failures of earth dams due to weak underlying soil strata also occur. Usually the failure takes place during construction and is evidenced by a slumping of one of the slopes in a manner indicating a rotational type of slide. As a rule, an underlying saturated clay layer is found to be responsible for the failure.   This was true of the Chingford Dam in England (Ref. 298) and the Marshall Creek Dam in the United States (Ref. 261).   Reconstruction of that dam at flatter slopes proved to be an effective remedy.

A failure of a hydraulic-fill dam due to what appeared to be the combined action of sliding along a weak stratum in the natural soil and a flow slide in the loose hydraulic fill was illustrated by Fig. 8-11 of the first edition.

The most frequent cause of earth-dam failures is provided by inadequate spillways.   Careful hydrological studies of maximum precipitation and runoff toward all tributary streams are therefore of greatest importance.   An earth dam cannot resist erosion by water flowing rapidly over its crest; therefore if an earth dam is *topped*, it is certain to be destroyed.   Spillways must therefore be designed to take care with an ample margin of safety of the greatest possible flood that may ever occur.   They are built of concrete and are usually placed in a cut through natural ground at one of the ends of the

Fig. 8-20. Upstream view of 50-ft-wide (15-m) break in a concrete-lined 35-ft-high (10.7-m) earth dike of a water reservoir (see also Fig. 8-21). (*Photograph by Tschebotarioff.*)

dam. A disastrous failure of a dam was caused by an inadequate spillway and the topping of the earth fill at South Fork Dam in Pennsylvania (see Ref. 62). The released mass of water swept down the valley causing what is often referred to as the Johnstown Flood, since Johnstown was the locality which suffered most. In all, 2,280 lives were lost and 1,675 bodies were recovered. The material damage was enormous.

Fig. 8-21. Downstream view of the break in the earth dike shown in Fig. 8-20. Note absence of antiseep collars and cutoff wall along the rock abutment face. (*Photo by Tschebotarioff.*)

The silting up of a reservoir may increase lateral pressures against a dam, as compared with usual design assumptions which consider only water pressure. The increase in pressure may become dangerous in an underdesigned concrete dam, and at least one failure was attributed to this cause (see Ref. 132). The increase in lateral pressure may be estimated to equal five-tenths of the buoyed weight of the silt.

The *lack of antiseep collars* along a conduit or of cutoff walls along the rock abutment of an earth dam (Art. 8-9) may cause the failure of the entire structure.

Figure 8-20 shows the view from upstream and Fig. 8-21 the view from downstream of a 50-ft-wide (15-m) break in an earth dike which occurred when the reservoir behind it was being test-filled, the water level having reached a height of about 20 ft (6 m), or about two-thirds the design level. It will be seen from Fig. 8-21 that no seep collars had been provided (Fig. 8-17) along the smooth concrete pipe passing through the dike from the intake tower. Nor was a cutoff wall (Fig. 8-16) built into the rock abutment. These two omissions appear to have been the main causes of the failure.

REVIEW PROBLEMS

8-1. A proposed weir on sandy soil, similar to the one illustrated in Fig. 8-3B but somewhat shorter, was analyzed with respect to safety against the development of a quick condition at its downstream end. A flow net was drawn to a suitably large scale, and a section of its downstream part is given in Fig. 8-22(I). The relevant dimensions were measured to

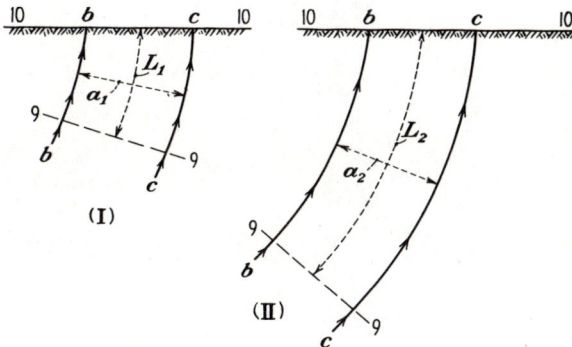

Fig. 8-22. Illustration of Prob. 8-1.

scale on the flow net and were found to be $L_1 = 1.56$ ft (47.6 cm) and $a_1 = 1.60$ ft (49 cm). The total difference of head between the upstream and downstream water levels was $h = 25$ ft (7.6 m); the head lost between the equipotential lines 9-9 and 10-10 was $\Delta h = \frac{25}{10} = 2.5$ ft (76 cm). It was then decided to place a clay blanket on the sand surface behind the weir to some distance upstream of it. The resistance to flow offered by that clay blanket absorbed a large portion of the total head h. A new flow net was drawn to take into account this new condition, and Fig. 8-22(II) shows the resulting changes in the section of the downstream part which is being examined. It was found that the distance between the flow lines bb and cc had not changed, remaining $a_2 = a_1 = 1.60$ ft (49 cm), but the distance L_2 increased to 3.65 ft (1.11 m).

Assuming that the sand has a porosity $n = 35$ percent (void ratio $e = 0.54$), compute the factors of safety against the development of a quick condition in the two cases illustrated by Fig. 8-22.

Answer. The critical hydraulic gradient will be [Eq. (8-17)]

$$S_{cr} = \frac{2.65 - 1}{1 + 0.54} = 1.07$$

The actual hydraulic gradient in the case illustrated by Fig. 8-22(I) will be $S_1 = \Delta h/L_1 = 2.50/1.56 = 1.6$, and the corresponding factor of safety $F_1 = S_{cr}/S_1 = 1.07/1.60 = 0.67$. Thus failure will occur.

In the case illustrated by Fig. 8-22(II) $S_2 = \Delta h/L_2 = 2.50/3.65 = 0.685$, and the factor of safety $F_2 = S_{cr}/S_2 = 1.07/0.685 = 1.57$.

8-2. What will be the discharge per square foot of downstream sand surface area between the flow lines bb and cc in the case illustrated by Fig. 8-22(II) if the permeability coefficient of the sand is $k = 2 \times 10^{-2}$ cm/sec $= 2 \times 10^4$ ft/year?

Answer. According to Eq. (8-4),

$$Q = 2 \times 10^4 \times 0.685 \times 1.0 \times 1.0 = 13,700 \text{ ft}^3/\text{year} = 3,950 \text{ m}^3/\text{year.}$$

RECOMMENDED FOR FURTHER STUDY

U.S. Bureau of Reclamation: *Earth Manual*, Commissioner's Office, Denver, Colorado.†
U.S. Soil Conservation Service: *Engineering Memoranda, Earth Dams*, Washington, D.C.†

† Periodically revised to reflect current practice.

CHAPTER 9

EXCAVATIONS AND GROUNDWATER LOWERING

9-1. Removal of Soft Soils by Excavation and by Surcharge Displacement. Peat and other soft soils with a high organic content are liable to continue settling for a long time when loaded by the weight of the fill, even if no outright shear failure occurs through the embankment and the underlying soil. Such settlements may be due only in part to consolidation; gradual lateral plastic yielding may also be a contributing factor, as well as the decay of organic matter. Drainage of adjoining areas for agricultural purposes may increase such settlements. Peat soils in Louisiana, when dried, are reported to shrink to 40 percent of their original volume. In the fenland districts of England drainage of the peat soils caused continuous surface settlements measured over periods of 60 years and more; the settlements exceeded 40 percent of the original thickness of the soft layer.

The replacement of soft mud and peat by granular material is therefore often advisable in order to provide a proper foundation for an embankment. When the depth of the soft layer of peat or mud does not exceed 10 ft, complete excavation of the soft material can be performed without difficulty. Usually this is done by means of clamshell buckets or draglines operated by cranes from the end of the fill embankment. In some cases, when the proposed embankment approaches the edge of a waterway, it is possible to remove entirely even a greater depth of soft soil by underwater excavation of a wide trench from a floating dredge. The trench is then backfilled hydraulically (Art. 8-8) with granular material.

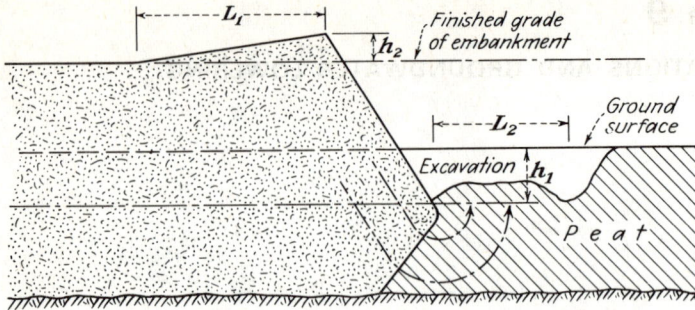

Fig. 9-1. Longitudinal section of embankment under construction showing how excavation of upper 10 ft (3 m) of swamp can be combined with a backfilling procedure to displace the underlying peat by temporary surcharge.

For depths greater than 10 ft (3 m), a procedure illustrated by Fig. 9-1 is usually employed. It consists in the excavation of the upper part of the swamp to a depth $h_1 = 10$ ft (3 m) and to a distance L_2 corresponding to the reach of the crane operated from the top of the fill, which is dumped without compaction to a height h_2 above the finished grade of the embankment. This is done to increase the height of the end slope of the embankment and to facilitate its outward sliding and the displacement of the soft peat, as indicated by dash-dotted lines in Fig. 9-1. Only clean uncompacted granular material should be used for the fill. Excavation of the peat ahead of the fill should be combined with saturation of the fill by jetting in order to destroy any apparent cohesion which might give it some temporary strength. The fill of the embankment is frequently advanced first along the centerline of the embankment, so that it takes on, in plan, the shape of a wedge. The excavating is then done on both sides of the wedge, and most of the peat is displaced laterally.

The temporary fill is then removed down to the water line and is reused for further surcharge and mud displacement by end-dumping operations off

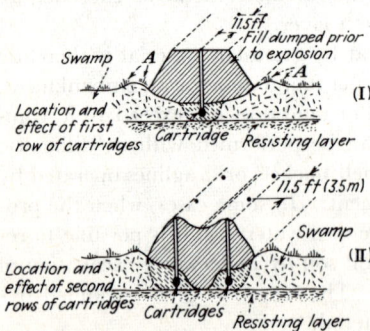

Fig. 9-2. Underfill method of swamp-mud and peat displacement under an embankment by blasting. (*After Leo Casagrande and T. A. Wheeler in Ref. 34.*)

the advancing embankment head, as illustrated by Fig. 9-1.   The permanent body of the embankment is built up in layers and is compacted above the water level by rolling.

9-2. Displacement of Soft Soils by Blasting. The usual procedure is illustrated by Fig. 9-2.   The sand fill is dumped on the surface of the swamp, sinks somewhat into it, and displaces some of the underlying mud or peat laterally. It is essential to remove the vegetation cover not only under the fill itself but also to some distance around it.   Otherwise this cover, which has some tensile strength, would restrain the displacement of the mud in the zones *A* of Fig. 9-2.   One to three rows of cartridges are then placed under the fill by jetting from its surface, and the central rows are detonated 1 sec later than the outer rows.   The mud is shot out laterally by the force of the explosion, and the sand fill sinks into the space thus formed between it and the deeper, more resisting layers.   The detonation of a single central row of cartridges usually does not produce sufficient displacement of the mud under the toe of the embankment (Fig. 9-3), and supplementary shots then become necessary if a condition of this kind is revealed by check borings.

Operations of this type were frequently performed in the lake districts of Michigan and Minnesota during the early 1920s.   They were also used in harbor work in Scandinavian countries and for German highways in the 1930s.   Observations of the later performance of highways and of harbor retaining-wall backfills provided with a foundation by such "swamp-shooting" methods, however, often disclosed uneven surface settlements which were traced to individual pockets of undisplaced mud.   The risk of the formation of such pockets is always considerable, since the force of the explosion does not appear to be distributed uniformly but is frequently channeled in an unpredictable manner.   The displacement of soft muds and clays by blasting, therefore, does not represent a fully reliable foundation embankment-construction procedure.

Sometimes blasting is used as an accessory to the displacement procedure

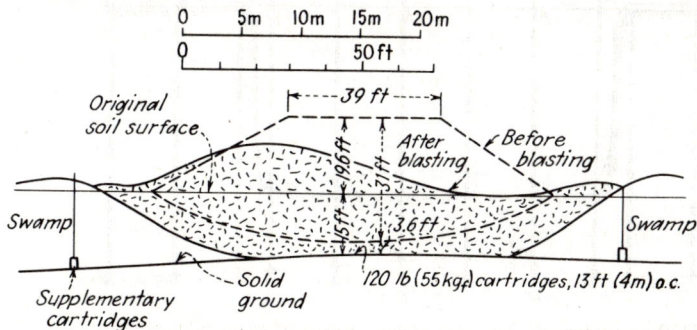

Fig. 9-3.   Example of the results of blasting peat by the underfill method.   (*After Leo Casagrande and Siedek in Ref. 34.*)

illustrated by Fig. 9-1. Cartridges are detonated below the bottom of the excavated trench in order to liquefy the mud there.

In marine work blasting is inadmissible in all areas where it might adversely affect the local fishing industry.

9-3. Deformations of Open Cuts in Soft Clays. Figure 9-4 illustrates the nature of the heaving movement which was measured by Cuevas (Ref. 72) in Mexico City. The upward movement of soil layers at the center of the pit reached 4 ft (1.22 m). Peck (Ref. 245) measured lateral and upward movements of the underlying clay when the weight of the excavation in the Chicago subway cut shown in Fig. 11-4 reached the approximate value of the unconfined compressive strength $q_u = 0.67$ ton/ft^2 (0.67 kg$_f$/cm^2) of the underlying clay of medium sensitivity—S varied from 3 to 4—(most of the movement occurred while the depth of excavation was increased from 10 to 13 ft, prior to placing the first brace). Model tests with gelatine, reported by Tschebotarioff and Schuyler (Ref. 380), demonstrated, as shown in Fig. 9-5, that a deep unbraced excavation induced not only displacements of the bottom and the side walls of the pit but also considerable deformations of the entire underlying and surrounding mass. The displacements were much larger than the ones induced by pile driving and could therefore cause appreciable remolding and weakening of a sensitive clay. These conclusions found further support in full-scale observations. Settlements of the structure erected on the site illustrated by Fig. 7-3 were found in the area of the slide to be at least twice as large as in the part where no slide had taken place owing to more adequate precautions during the subsequent excavation. Thus unchecked excessive deformations of the clay during construction may have later detrimental consequences for the completed structure.

It should be noted that bracing the walls of the cut to resist the lateral

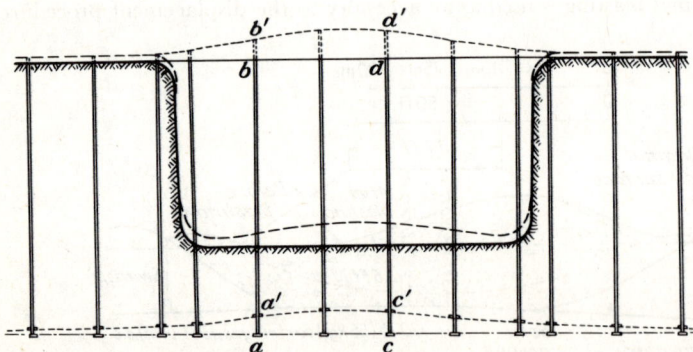

Fig. 9-4. The heave of the soft clay in and around an excavation pit in Mexico City. The heave of an underlying layer *ac* was measured by means of underground bench marks. (*After Cuevas, Ref. 72.*)

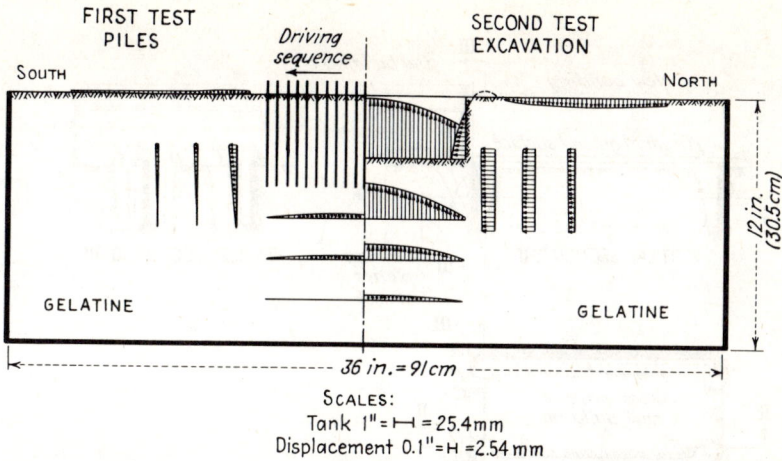

Fig. 9-5. Comparison of displacements by model tests. (*From Tschebotarioff and Schuyler, Ref. 380.*)

pressures of the clay against them is not always sufficient to ensure a safe execution of the excavation. The possibility of heaving of the bottom of the pit should be taken into account, as shown by the analysis in Art. 11-4.

9-4. Open Excavations in Rocks and Stiff Clays. As a rule, excavations of this type do not present any special problems for foundations of buildings. Vertical cuts can usually be made to the required depth without any lateral bracing or support. There are, however, exceptions. One such case is illustrated by Fig. 9-6. Blasting of an open cut for the basement of a new building was begun in the usual manner at one of its corners, but an adjoining old building, which had no basement, soon developed signs of distress. The origin of the trouble was traced to the inclined planes of the folded bedrock, along which slipping movement began to develop when they were deprived of lateral support by the excavation.

The following procedure solved the problem. Trenches were blasted with small charges and were dug out for the cross walls, leaving intact the rock blocks between these trenches. The individual rock seams under the outer footing of the adjoining old building were able to span the gaps *AC*, *DG*, etc., which were formed by the trenches. The cross walls of the new building and their footings were then concreted in their trenches. After the concrete of the cross walls hardened, the excavation of the rock was completed between the original cross trenches. The individual rock seams under the old building spanned the gaps *BE*, etc., between the cross walls, which were able to take up the entire thrust from the rock seams.

See Art. 15-7 for the estimation of the effect of blasting on adjoining buildings.

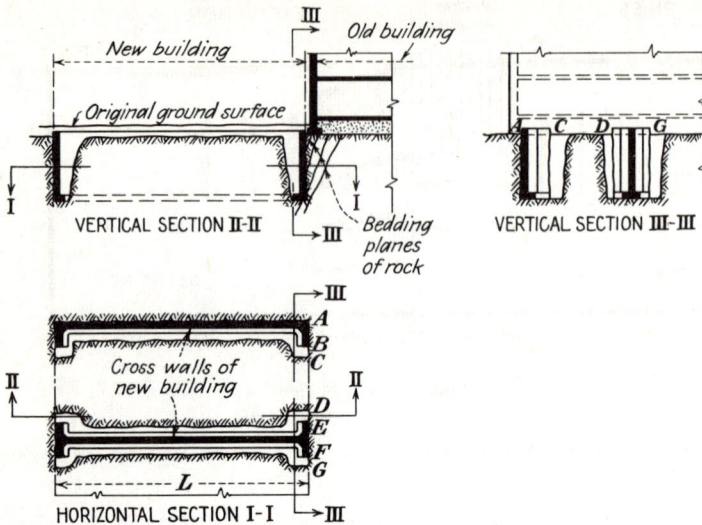

Fig. 9-6. Normal type of excavation for the basement of a new building damaged an adjoining old wall, owing to sliding of underlying rock along inclined bedding planes. Alternating excavation and construction of cross walls in new basement, the first step of which is shown in this sketch, solved the problem. (*From unpublished data of Spencer, White and Prentis, Inc.*)

In many stiff cohesive soils steep slopes of open cuts are possible. Plastic cover sheets are then often used to protect them from erosion by rainwater while the excavation remains open during foundation construction.

9-5. Future of Excavations by Nuclear Explosions. Extensive research is being conducted in this field, including full-scale experiments (Refs. 235 and 80). The future possibilities for excavating exceptionally large masses of soil and rock for important civil engineering works, such as large canals, by creating a series of adjoining detonation craters appear to be very promising once really "clean" nuclear explosives without dangerous radiation effects are assured. A more detailed discussion of this topic is beyond the scope of this book.

9-6. Groundwater Lowering. The unwatering of excavations is a problem mainly in sand soils. The bottom of excavations in sand is not susceptible to heave due to excessive shearing stresses, as is the case with excavations in clays. Such heaving involved shear failures of the clay at considerable depths below the bottom of the cut. This type of failure is possible in clays because they frequently have a constant shearing strength which is independent of the weight of the overburden, but it is unlikely in most types of granular soils, such as sands. The shearing strength of sands depends on frictional and not on cohesive properties and therefore increases with depth below the soil surface.

Sands, when fully saturated, may however cause a different type of trouble in excavations, namely, they are liable to become quick (Art. 8-3) unless special precautions are taken for the unwatering.

The simplest type of unwatering—by *pumping from sump pits*—is the most likely to cause localized quick conditions (see the discussion of Fig. 12-3). In most excavations in sand it therefore becomes necessary to divert the direction of water flow away from any exposed free sand surface by pumping from wells.   Three main types of devices are used for this purpose:

1. *Well points*
2. *Deep wells*
3. *Eductors*, also known as *ejectors*

Each type has its own merits and limitations which govern its selection for specific soil and excavation conditions.   They will now be outlined.

The principle of operation of a well point is illustrated by Fig. 9-7.   A steel

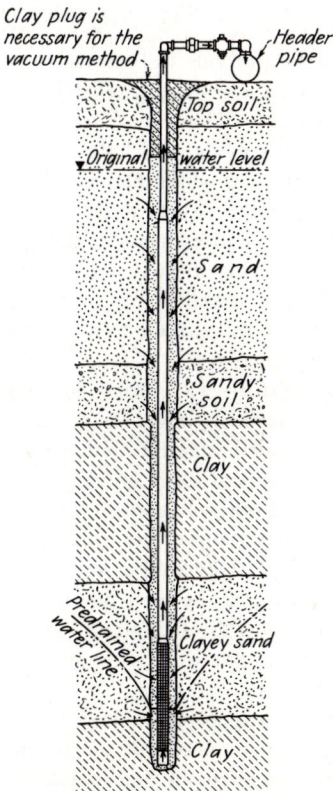

Fig. 9-7. Vertical cross section through a well point in operation. (*Moretrench Corp.*)

Fig. 9-8. Closeup view of well-point connections to their header pipe. (*Photo by Tschebotarioff.*)

pipe of approximately $1\frac{1}{2}$ in. diameter, with perforated side walls at its lower end, covered with a wire-mesh filter screen, i.e., the so-called *well point*, is jetted into the ground by pumping water through it. The water rises to the surface past the outer walls of the pipe and forms a cylindrical hole around the well point, which can be gradually filled with sand while the velocity of the jetting water is decreased. Water from all pervious layers above the tip of the well point can then reach it, irrespective of the presence or of the absence of any horizontal impervious seams which might otherwise cut off the flow from some of the intermediate pervious layers. Well points are jetted in rows, where each well point is connected at the soil surface to a header pipe which, in turn, connects with a pump (see Fig. 9-8).

In very fine sands with some silt and clay admixtures a very close spacing of ordinary well points may become necessary in order to lower the groundwater table around them adequately. The so-called vacuum method can then be employed to increase the normal gravitational head under whose action water will flow through these layers toward the well point. An airtight clay plug is provided at the soil surface over the top of the cylindrical sand filter around the well point (see Fig. 9-7). Unwatering creates a partial vacuum in the cylindrical sand filter around the well point; the gravitational head under whose action water will flow toward the well point is then increased by the difference between the atmospheric pressure and the partial vacuum pressure in the voids of the sand filter.

Unwatering by well points is a comparatively inexpensive method which permits handling large volumes of water. Its main disadvantage is the limited depth to which it can be used. This is inherent in the suction by vacuum on which the well-point procedure depends. A perfect vacuum cannot be achieved by commercial machinery in practice, and experience shows that the partial vacuum in a single row of well points succeeds in lowering the water table by some 15 ft (4.6 m) only. When that depth is reached by the excavation, a second row of well points with its own header pipe has to be placed there, as shown in Fig. 9-9. Up to four such successive rows, or stages, have been used in some cases, the fourth row only 11 to 12 ft (3.3 to 3.6 m) below the third, but this method presents many other disadvantages in cases similar to those illustrated by Figs. 11-15 and 11-16. Ordinary well points cannot be used outside the cofferdam sheeting. Hence, if any splits in the interlocks occur where boulders are encountered, the full unrelieved water pressure from outside the sheeting will "blow" sand or rock-flour soils into the excavation as it approaches the top of the split, sometimes even before the split can be detected and attempts made to patch it.

The use of *deep wells* is much more advantageous in such cases since they can be operated from the original soil surface, without any excavation, to lower the groundwater 40 to 50 ft (12 to 15 m) in one stage and over 100 ft (31 m) in multiple stages. This is possible because submerged centrifugal pumps are placed at the bottom of the well which then force the water up the pipe. No vacuum-type suction is involved. Sometimes the motor which drives the pump is located at the soil surface, as shown in Fig. 9-10. This photograph shows one of four deep wells located at the corners of a

Fig. 9-9. Regular well points must be used in rows at successively lower elevations when the required depth of groundwater lowering exceeds 15 ft (4.6 m). (*Photo by Tschebotarioff.*)

Fig. 9-10. An individual deep well with centrifugal pump at the bottom and motor at the surface. (*Photo by Tschebotarioff.*)

rectangular cofferdam for the New Jersey anchorage abutment of the Walt Whitman suspension bridge across the Delaware to South Philadelphia. These four deep wells were used to relieve uplift water pressures in a deep sand layer to prevent a blowout as the excavation within the cofferdam approached the surface of that layer.

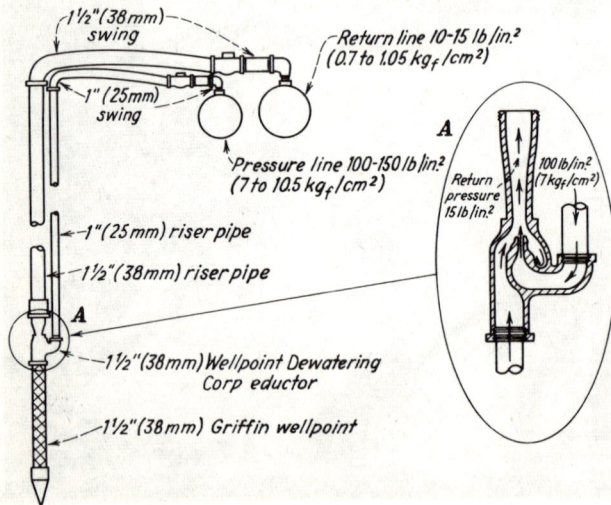

Fig. 9-11. Operation of a Griffin eductor well point. (*Ref. 397.*)

Deep wells were developed in Europe in the 1920s and can be successfully used outside the sheeting of cofferdams to prevent blows of noncohesive water-bearing soils through split interlocks where the regular well points developed in the United States cannot be employed.

To meet situations of this kind, an *eductor (or ejector)* well-point type has come into use. Its operation is illustrated by Fig. 9-11. A vacuum is created at the well-point tip by means of a high-speed flow of water through a jet nozzle. Thus the water from the soil has to be sucked up only a very short distance and is then forced up the return pipe.

Various other types of eductor-ejector nozzles are used to achieve the same purpose. Figure 9-12 gives a relevant example of groundwater lowering *outside* the cofferdam sheeting. In general, this method permits unwatering to 80-ft (25-m) depths but requires two pipes connected to each well point and high-pressure pumps which consume 5 to 10 times more power on a given project than other dewatering systems (Ref. 108). It is therefore more expensive.

Electroosmosis (Art. 8-6), when used in connection with well points (Fig. 9-14), may create an additional head which will force the movement of water even through relatively impervious silt and rock-flour types of soils. Leo Casagrande reported a number of cases where excavations in such soils became possible through the use of electroosmosis. Rows of well electrodes acted in combination with adjoining rows of rod electrodes. One of the

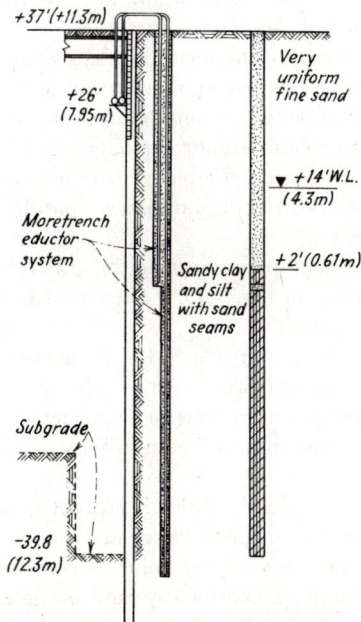

Fig. 9-12. Moretrench ejector system installed outside of cofferdam sheeting for a B.A.R.T. tunnel in San Francisco Bay area. (*Ref. 221.*)

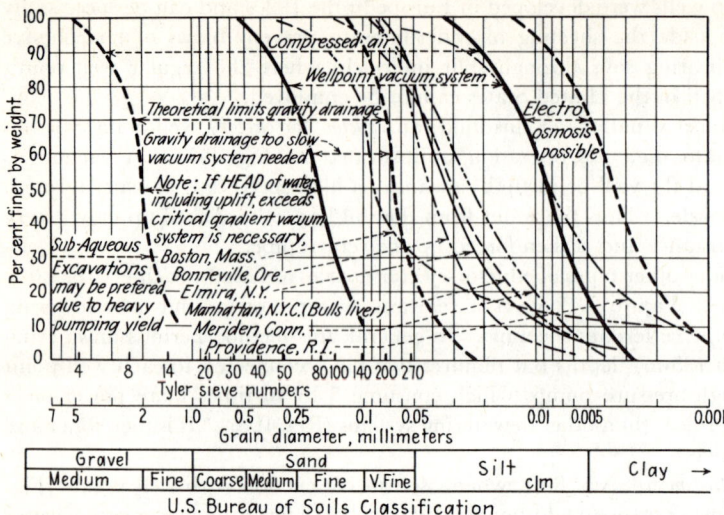

Fig. 9-13. Delineating limits of soil-dewatering methods. Successful well-point drainage installations in fine-grained soils. (*Moretrench Corp.*)

examples given is that of a U-boat pen at Trondhjem, Norway, where all ordinary measures failed for a 46-ft-deep (14-m) excavation next to the ocean. The unsuccessful measures included sloping of the sides of the excavation and their protection by 60-ft-long (18-m) sheet piles embedded 50 ft (15 m) in the ground. Before the cut could be completed, deep-seated slides occurred, distorting the piling, and moving it a considerable distance toward the excavation. However, after an electroosmotic drainage installation was put into operation, the construction was completed without any further difficulty (Ref. 51). However, the power consumption is considerable, making the method quite expensive.

The grain-size curves of soils in which well-point drainage of different types can be successfully employed are shown in Fig. 9-13. They are based on the experiences of the Moretrench Corporation.

The range of ejector-system use is not indicated in Fig. 9-13. The lower limit will be approximately the same as for regular well points. The upper, more pervious limit is governed by the horsepower requirements, which depend on the total depth of unwatering in addition to the permeability of the soil (from Ref. 108).

9-7. Effects of Groundwater Lowering. A quick condition is prevented by the use of well points or deep wells, since the seepage forces are directed down or horizontally toward the metal filter mesh of the point, which can resist them, and which does not permit the movement of any sand particles through the filter. By driving the well points below the elevation of the bottom of a sheeted excavation the seepage forces are diverted from their upward direction toward the excavation.   The bottom of the pit is thereby ensured against the development of a quick condition.

The stability of slopes can also be greatly improved by using properly placed well points (Fig. 9-14), since it is then possible to reverse the natural direction of the flow of water toward the face of the cut.   The reversed seepage forces then contribute to the stability of the cut, instead of undermining it.

However, the lowering of the groundwater table reduces the buoyancy and thereby increases the effective weight of the soil within the depth of the lowered groundwater table (see Prob. 9-1).   As a result, that layer and the soil layers beneath it receive an additional load and undergo additional consolidation.   Surface settlements will follow if these layers are soft.

An example is provided by the very careful measurements performed during the construction of the Rotterdam tunnel.   Well points relieved the uplift pressures in a sand layer which underlay soft clay and peat.   As shown in Fig. 9-15, the groundwater level in observation wells, which reached to the sand, dropped at times to 42 ft (12.8 m).   The settlements of the ground surface were greatest close to the line of well points and observation wells, 20 in. (51 cm) at a distance of 30 ft (9.1 m) but decreased with distance; for instance, they equaled 3 in. (7.6 cm) some 360 ft (110 m) away.   The rate of settlement closely followed the variations in the water head of the sand layer.

In all similar work, careful studies should be made of the effect which differential settlements of the ground surface may have on existing structures in the vicinity.   Such settlements will naturally increase with the depth to which groundwater is lowered and with the duration of the pumping.   The usual procedures of settlement analysis (Art. 4-6) are applied to the solution of the problem, where the loads which produce settlement are determined in a manner similar to that outlined in Prob. 9-1.   The T_v values from Fig. 4-34 should be used for the computation of the rate of settlement of layers, the effective weight of which has been increased by lowering the groundwater.

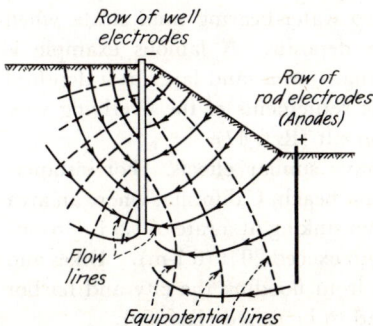

Fig. 9-14.   Electroosmosis causes flow of water through fine silt and rock-flour types of soil toward well-point electrodes.   Proper location of well points permits open cuts on slopes which otherwise would not be stable.   (*After Leo Casagrande, Ref. 52.*)

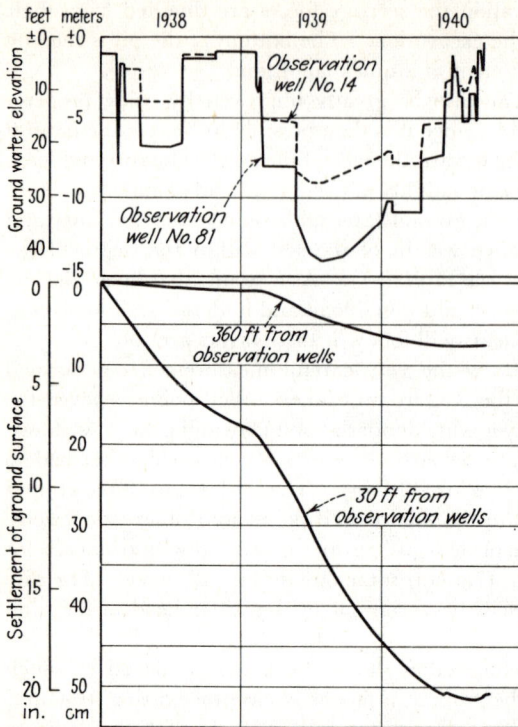

Fig. 9-15. Effect of the lowering of the groundwater table on surface settlements during the construction of the Rotterdam tunnel. (*After van Bruggen, Ref. 42.*)

Recharging, i.e., pumping water back into the water-bearing stratum but nearer to the structures liable to be damaged by subsidence of this type, sometimes had to be used (Ref. 241).

Considerable settlements of an entire large area can be caused by *continued pumping for water-supply purposes* from deep water-bearing sand strata when they are overlain by soft compressible deposits. A famous example is Mexico City, where water-supply pumping from a sand layer at a depth of about 100 ft (31 m) caused considerable settlements of the overlying very soft saturated deposits of volcanic ash and silt (Ref. 47).

Pumping oil from deep strata can have similar effects. For instance, serious problems have been created at Long Beach, California, where an area several miles wide along the coast has been sinking at a rate of 1.5 ft (46 cm) per year. The settlements are estimated to exceed 20 ft (6.1 m). Dikes and locks had to be built to keep high tides from flooding the city and harbor area; bridges over navigable channels had to be raised (Ref. 56).

9-8. Waterproofing.   The basement of a small house will be used as an example of advisable waterproofing procedures (Fig. 9-16).   If the footings, walls, and floor of a basement are made of solid monolithic concrete, this may keep the water from actually flowing into the basement, provided no cracks have developed anywhere.   Nevertheless, the basement may be damp, since the permeability of concretes falls within approximately the same range as that of clays.   The inner surfaces of the walls and floors of a basement may therefore appear dry, whereas actually a steady slow flow of water may be occurring from the outside through the concrete toward a surface of evaporation within the concrete.

A continuous membrane of waterproofing material should therefore be applied to the outside of the walls and below the floor, as shown in Fig. 9-16. Cold asphalts should not be used, since they are susceptible to deterioration due to soil bacteria action.   Asphalts placed hot are satisfactory but require very careful inspection, since they are apt to form bubbles which leave small openings in the membrane unless it is composed of alternating layers of asphalt and fabric.   Bubbles are particularly liable to appear at the joints of cinder or cement blocks when they are used for the construction of the walls; quite a lot of water may then seep into the basement through a tiny hole. The practice of dumping the outside fill against the wall without compaction, and of leaving it to settle down over a period of years because of frost action, usually aggravates this condition.   The fill gets sodden after the first heavy rain and then, after a dry spell, shrinks away from the wall, as shown by the broken line *BC* in Fig. 9-16.   The crack between soil and wall may be very small; nevertheless, when filled with water, it may develop a head of several feet against a small gap in the membrane, forcing a lot of water into a hollow block.   Proper compaction of the backfill is therefore advisable; it should form a slope *AF* immediately after the waterproofing of the walls.

A number of chemical compounds are now available which effectively seal the pores of the concrete and which can be substituted for hot asphalt when forming the outer waterproofing membrane.   A so-called *vapor barrier* should be formed by the use of such compounds on the inner face *DE* of a basement

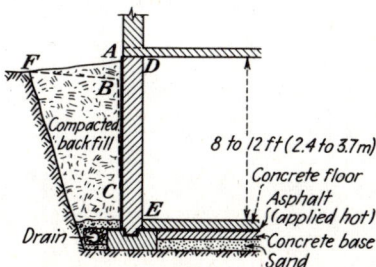

8 to 12 ft (2.4 to 3.7 m)

Concrete floor
Asphalt
(applied hot)
Concrete base
Sand

F   A   D
B
Compacted
backfill
C   E
Drain

Fig. 9-16.   Basement waterproofing of a small house.

wall when it is built of hollow cement or cinder blocks. Otherwise condensation is likely to occur on humid hot summer days inside the hollow wall, followed by evaporation of the condensed water back into the basement during drier weather, so that the basement is constantly humid.

Drains should be placed along the outside of the footings whenever it is possible to provide an outlet for them somewhere along an adjoining slope. A sand blanket under the floor should then also be connected to such outlet to prevent the development of uplift against the floor. The filter drains should be graded, as discussed in Art. 7-9 with reference to Fig. 7-28.

In heavy construction and deep excavations a protective outer *sand wall* is placed between the waterproofing and the soil. It is poured right against the sheeting. The purpose of the sand wall is to provide protection to the subway waterproofing and to permit placing it against a smooth surface. The so-called *three-ply-membrane type of waterproofing* is customarily used, i.e., a coat of hot asphalt alternating three times with a coat of impregnated linen fabric. The walls of the structure are then concreted against the waterproofing membrane.

REVIEW PROBLEM

9-1. With reference to Fig. 4-30, by what amount will the effective vertical pressures on the underlying layers be changed by a 4.5-m (14.7-ft) fluctuation of the groundwater level? Assume that the soil within the range of water-level variation remains fully saturated at all times, that its specific gravity is $G = 2.7$, and that its void ratio is $e = 1.00$.

Answer. With reference to Eqs. (3-7) and (3-10), we find that, when saturated by capillarity, the soil weighs

$$\frac{2.7 + 1.0}{1 + 1.0} \times 62.4 = 115.5 \text{ lb/ft}^3 = 2.08 \text{ g}_f/\text{cm}^3$$

When buoyed, it weighs

$$\frac{2.7 - 1}{1 + 1.0} \times 62.4 = 53.1 \text{ lb/ft}^3 = 0.956 \text{ g}_f/\text{cm}^3$$

The difference per foot depth is $115.5 - 53.1 = 62.4$ lb/ft^3. Thus full buoyancy is effective, and a rise of the water level shown in Fig. 4-30 will decrease the effective pressures on the underlying layers by $62.4 \times 14.7 = 908$ lb/ft$^2 = 0.45$ ton/ft$^2 = 0.45$ kg$_f$/cm^2.

CHAPTER 10

GRAVITY RETAINING WALLS

10-1. Lateral Earth Pressures; General Concepts. Let us assume that a massive gravity retaining wall shown in Fig. 10-1(III) rests on a hard but slippery layer 3-3′ of shale. The backfill behind the wall will exert a lateral pressure E_A, the so-called *active lateral earth pressure*, which will tend to push the wall to the left to a position shown by the dash-dotted lines. The stress condition of a small element of the backfill close to the wall, if we neglect the friction between the wall and the soil, will be very similar to the condition illustrated in Fig. 10-1(I). The vertical unit pressure σ_1, which usually can be taken as being equal to the weight of the overburden γh, is greater than the lateral unit pressure σ_3. Thus the so-called *active state* of deformation or of rupture in a soil mass is taken to represent a condition where lateral expansion of the soil is possible and is induced by the weight of the soil or by a surcharge resting on its surface.

The ratio of lateral to vertical pressure in the active state is termed the *coefficient of active lateral earth pressure* K_A. The limit value at failure will be

$$K_A = \frac{\sigma_3}{\sigma_1} = \tan^2\left(45° - \frac{\phi}{2}\right) - \frac{2c}{\sigma_1}\tan\left(45° - \frac{\phi}{2}\right) \tag{10-1}$$

(The derivation of this equation was given in Arts. 7-8 and 10-1, 1st ed.)

Unless horizontal arching or wall friction (Art. 10-3) relieves the vertical pressure σ_1, it will be equal to

$$\sigma_1 = \gamma h \tag{10-2}$$

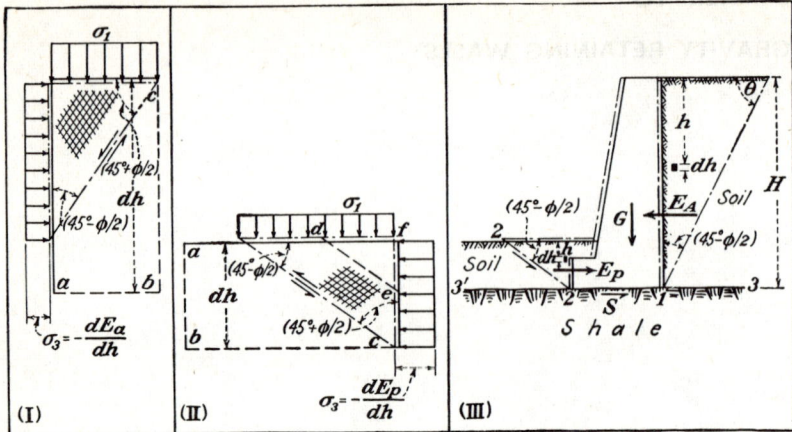

Fig. 10-1. Diagrams illustrating the terms *active* and *passive earth pressure*. (I) Active state: $\sigma_1 > \sigma_3$. (II) Passive state: $\sigma_3 > \sigma_1$. (III) Active and passive earth pressure for a massive gravity wall slipping along plane 3-3′, if wall friction is neglected.

so that

$$K_A = K_\gamma = \frac{\sigma_3}{\sigma_1} = \frac{p_h}{\gamma h} \tag{10-3}$$

where K_γ is the ratio of the actual lateral pressure p_h to the unrelieved unit weight of the overburden at that elevation. Then

$$K_A = \tan^2\left(45° - \frac{\phi}{2}\right) - \frac{2c}{\gamma h} \tan\left(45° - \frac{\phi}{2}\right) \tag{10-4}$$

For a granular cohesionless soil ($c = 0$),

$$K_A = \tan^2\left(45° - \frac{\phi}{2}\right) \tag{10-5}$$

The coefficient K_A for granular cohesionless soils is sometimes expressed by means of another equation:

$$K_A = \frac{1 - \sin\phi}{1 + \sin\phi} \tag{10-6}$$

Equation (10-6) was originally derived by Rankine (Ref. 260), and is commonly used in England; Eq. (10-5) is more frequently used on the continent of Europe. Either of these equations can be derived from the other by direct trigonometric transformation. Equation (10-5) will be used in this book.

For a frictionless cohesive soil ($\phi = 0$) Eq. (10-4) will read

$$K_A = 1 - \frac{2c}{\gamma h} \qquad (10\text{-}7)$$

or, under consideration of Eq. (3-19),

$$K_A = 1 - \frac{q_u}{\gamma h} \qquad (10\text{-}8)$$

As the wall shown in Fig. 10-1(III) slips outward along the plane 3-3′ under the influence of the active earth pressure E_A, its movement will be resisted by the soil in front of its toe, i.e., by the so-called *passive lateral earth pressure* E_p. The stress condition of a small element of the soil close to and in front of the wall, again neglecting the friction between the wall and the soil, is shown in larger scale in Fig. (10-1)II. Essentially it represents the condition of the prism shown in Fig. 10-1(I) if it were laid on its side by rotating it clockwise through 90°. The procedure of the analysis is exactly the same in both cases, except that σ_3 is now greater than σ_1 and can be interchanged with it.

Thus the so-called *passive state* of deformation or of rupture in a soil mass is taken to represent a condition where vertical expansion of the soil occurs as a result of lateral contraction produced by lateral pressures transmitted to the soil by a structure or by a part thereof. The weight of the soil itself and any surcharge resting on its surface will contribute to the *passive pressure*, i.e., to the *resistance* offered by the soil to this type of deformation. The unit vertical pressure will have to be much smaller than the lateral external pressure if this type of failure is to occur.

The ratio of lateral to vertical pressure in the passive state is termed the *coefficient of passive lateral earth pressure* K_p. Assuming that Eq. (10-2) is valid, the limit value at failure will be

$$K_p = \frac{\sigma_3}{\sigma_1} = \tan^2\left(45° + \frac{\phi}{2}\right) + \frac{2c}{\gamma h} \tan\left(45° + \frac{\phi}{2}\right) \qquad (10\text{-}9)$$

For a cohesionless granular soil ($c = 0$) this expression is simplified to

$$K_p = \tan^2\left(45° + \frac{\phi}{2}\right) \qquad (10\text{-}10)$$

Therefore, $$K_p = \frac{1}{K_A} \qquad (10\text{-}11)$$

For a frictionless cohesive soil ($\phi = 0$) Eq. (10-9) will read

$$K_p = 1 + \frac{2c}{\gamma h} = 1 + \frac{q_u}{\gamma h} \qquad (10\text{-}12)$$

The values of K_A and of K_p given by the preceding equations represent the limit values which are reached at the point of failure, where the assumption is made that both the full frictional resistance and the full cohesive resistance reach their maximum values simultaneously after the same amount of deformation and maintain both these maximum values even after further deformation. This assumption is somewhat questionable from a quantitative point of view, but it is acceptable for a preliminary qualitative description of the influence exerted by these factors. K_A will always be smaller than unity [see Eq. (10-1)], whereas K_p will always be greater than unity [see Eq. (10-9)]. Their limit values, as given by these two equations, represent the minimum value of K_A which is reached as a result of full lateral expansion of the soil prior to failure and the maximum value of K_p which is reached as a result of full lateral compression of the soil prior to failure. It therefore follows that for a soil in its natural condition in situ, i.e., for a soil which neither expanded nor contracted laterally after its formation, the lateral pressure within its undisturbed and undeformed mass must have some intermediate value between the values of the active and the passive pressures of the same soil. This value of the lateral earth pressure existing in the undeformed mass of natural soil is called the *lateral earth pressure at rest*. Other terms used to designate the same condition are the *neutral lateral earth pressure* or the *lateral earth pressure at consolidated equilibrium*. The ratio of lateral to vertical earth pressure in this natural state is termed the *coefficient of earth pressure at rest* K_0.

As shown in Art. 10-8 of the first edition, according to the theory of elasticity the coefficient of earth pressure at rest K_0 depends solely on the value of the Poisson ratio ν:

$$K_0 = \frac{\sigma_3}{\sigma_1} = \frac{\nu}{1 - \nu} \tag{10-13}$$

The Poisson ratio ν has its maximum value of $\nu = 0.5$ for a completely incompressible material. The corresponding value of K_0 is then 1.00, as actually measured for unconsolidated clays in a semifluid condition. For smaller values of $\nu = 0.4$, 0.3, or 0.2, Eq. (10-13) gives smaller values of $K_0 = 0.67$, 0.43, and 0.25 respectively.

Attempts have been made to establish a theoretical relationship between the strength properties of a soil and its coefficient of earth pressure at rest by Jaky (see 1st ed., Art. 10-11 and Ref. 144), Kezdi (Ref. 161), and Sowada (Refs. 308 and 309).

Compaction of granular soils against an unyielding wall can produce high *compaction pressures*, corresponding to values of $K_y = 1.00$ and higher (see 1st ed., Fig. 7-20).

Still higher K_y values may result from *swelling pressures* of cohesive clay fills, the use of which should therefore be avoided behind retaining structures.

10-2. The "Classical" Theories of Coulomb and Rankine; Validity for Gravity Walls. Several experimental earth-pressure studies were made during the early part of the eighteenth century. None of them led to the development of a rigorous basis for the design of earth-retaining structures. Coulomb (Ref. 67) was the first to succeed in developing one as a result of a purely theoretical study. He considered the limit equilibrium of the entire wedge of soil behind a retaining wall in very much the same manner as in Fig. 10-1 for an infinitely small element of soil. Accordingly, the limit value of the earth pressure at failure of the soil was expressed by him in terms of the total pressure E and not of unit pressures.

By differential calculus Coulomb determined the plane cb (Fig. 10-2C) along which the resistance-to-sliding/sliding-force ratio would be a minimum, compared with other possible sliding planes through point c. To this sliding plane cb there is a corresponding maximum value of the lateral pressure E against the retaining structure. (Relevant derivations are given in 1st ed., Arts. 7-12 and 10-1.)

Coulomb did his work at a time when trigonometric functions were not yet in use; accordingly, he expressed all his values as ratios. Brown (Ref. 40) transformed Coulomb's original (1776) equation to correspond to present terminology and obtained

$$E_A = \frac{\gamma H^2}{2} \tan^2\left(45° - \frac{\phi}{2}\right) - 2cH \tan\left(45° - \frac{\phi}{2}\right) \tag{10-14}$$

Coulomb's analysis was limited to plane surfaces of failure, in order to simplify the mathematics involved. Nevertheless, he admitted the possibility of curved surfaces of failure, as shown by his original diagrams.

In his original analysis Coulomb ignored the effects of wall friction; i.e., the angle δ in Fig. 10-2A was taken as $\delta = 0$, the direction of E becoming

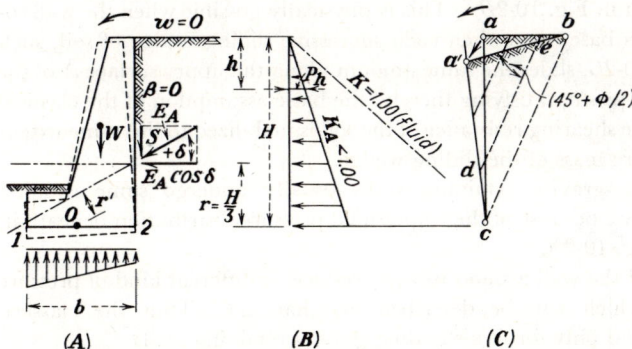

Fig. 10-2. Displacements of a gravity wall are essentially a rotation around its base. This satisfies basic assumptions of the Coulomb theory, and pressure distribution is hydrostatic.

horizontal. Rankine (Ref. 260) studied the state of stress within a loose granular mass with zero cohesion. His analysis was based on the assumption that the slightest deformation of the soil is sufficient to bring into play its full frictional resistance and immediately to produce an "active state" if the soil tends to expand parallel to its surface, and a "passive state" if it tends to compress parallel to its surface.

Another basic assumption of the Rankine theory was that the pressure on a vertical plane must be parallel to the soil surface. Model tests have shown this to be incorrect in the vicinity of a retaining wall, since friction between the soil and the wall has a very strong influence on the direction and magnitude of the resulting pressure on the wall.

Rankine's analysis was extended by Résal (Ref. 263) to include a soil with both friction and cohesion. The same objections apply to this extension.

It should be noted that the derivation of Rankine's equation is based on the use of conjugate pressures and the stress ellipse. The procedure therefore involves techniques which are somewhat less generally familiar in the United States than the ones used by Coulomb and in the preceding articles of this book. At the same time, the equations obtained in both cases for the unit and for the total lateral pressures are identical if the soil surface is horizontal and if the friction between the wall and the soil is taken to be zero (Art. 10-1). The Coulomb approach of "wedge of least resistance" permits a clearer analysis of the effect on lateral earth pressures of wall friction of various intensities (Art. 10-3) than the Rankine-Résal "state of stress" approach. This factor is very important in its influence on passive pressures. A further description of the Rankine methods of analysis and the derivation of his formula will therefore be omitted as unnecessary ballast for the general civil engineering practitioner.

The *distribution of lateral earth pressures* which corresponds to Eq. (10-14) is hydrostatic, and the lateral-earth-pressure diagram has the shape of a triangle, as shown in Fig. 10-2B. This is physically possible when the wall rotates around its base, since then each successive sliding wedge of soil, such as *ade* in Fig. 10-2C, slides the same amount along the upper surface *de* of the underlying soil prism, satisfying thereby the basic assumption of the classical theories that the shearing resistance of the soil is mobilized to the same extent within the entire mass of the sliding wedge.

Free-standing gravity retaining walls usually undergo some rotation around their base because of the trapezoidal pressure distribution beneath it, as shown in Fig. 10-2A.

A rotation of the wall around its top produces a different kind of pressure distribution, which will be described in Chap. 11. Thus the classical theories are valid only for free-standing gravity retaining walls.

The *inclination of the back of the wall* and the *slope of the backfill* behind it also affect the magnitude of the lateral pressures, as expressed by the relevant K

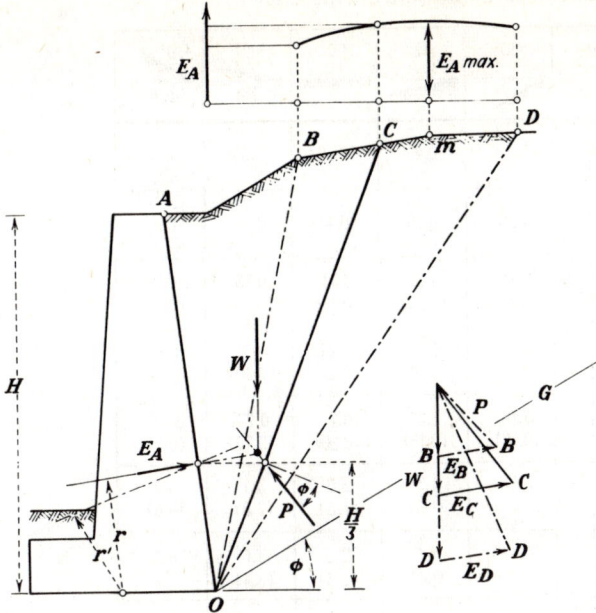

Fig. 10-3. Graphical method for determining the maximum active earth pressure for an irregular soil surface.

values. This is illustrated by Table 10-1, which is valid for a cohesionless soil, a zero angle δ of wall friction, and plane surfaces of failure. The values in parentheses correspond to curved surfaces of failures, which should always be considered for reasons explained in the Art. 10-3.

For an irregular soil surface behind a retaining structure, a graphical procedure illustrated by Fig. 10-3 can be employed. A point C is arbitrarily selected on the soil surface, and the line OC is drawn. The center of gravity of the soil cross-sectional area OAC and its weight W are determined. The point of application of the other two forces E_A and P acting on the wedge OAC can be assumed to be located at a distance $H/3$ above the base line. Their direction is known, and their magnitude can be determined by means of a conventional polygon of forces shown in Fig. 10-3. This procedure is repeated for other possible sliding surfaces, for example, OB and OD. The E_A values obtained for each sliding surface from a polygon of forces are plotted above the ground line and are connected by a curve as shown in Fig. 10-3. The maximum value of E_A and the sliding surface Om which produces it can then be picked off the plot.

The distribution of lateral pressures σ_3 along the depth of a retaining wall

TABLE 10-1.   Lateral-earth-pressure Coefficients†

ω =		-30°	-12°	±0°	+12°	+30°
					1:4.7	1:1.7
$\beta = +20°$	K_A Values	0.34	0.43	0.50	0.59	1.17
+10°		0.30	0.36	0.41	0.48	0.92
±0°		0.26 (0.26)	0.30 (0.30)	0.33 (0.33)	0.38 (0.38)	0.75 (0.85)
-10°		0.22 (0.22)	0.25 (0.24)	0.27 (0.26)	0.31 (0.30)	0.61 (0.63)
-20°		0.18 (0.18)	0.20 (0.18)	0.21 (0.20)	0.24 (0.22)	0.50 (0.45)
$\beta = +20°$	K_P Values	0.50	1.5 (1.0)	2.3 (1.8)	3.1 (2.8)	4.9 (4.6)
+10°		0.62	1.8 (1.4)	2.5 (2.3)	3.6 (3.4)	6.2 (5.9)
±0°		0.75 (0.40)	2.1 (1.8)	3.3 (3.1)	4.4 (4.2)	8.8 (7.4)
-10°		0.92 (0.52)	2.6 (2.4)	3.8 (3.6)	5.9 (5.7)	16.7 (9.3)
-20°		1.17 (0.67)	3.4 (3.0)	5.3 (4.8)	9.6 (7.2)	45.7 (11.6)
$c = 0$;			$\phi = 30°$;		$\delta = 0°$	

† K values in parentheses refer to curved surfaces of failure.

when the soil has both friction and cohesion is illustrated by Fig. 10-4. If $\sigma_1 = \gamma h$, Eq. (10-1) gives us

$$\sigma_3 = \gamma h \tan^2\left(45° - \frac{\phi}{2}\right) - 2c \tan\left(45° - \frac{\phi}{2}\right) \qquad (10\text{-}15)$$

The surface of the ground is horizontal, and friction between the wall ab and the soil behind it is assumed to be zero.   If the soil had no shearing strength whatsoever ($c = 0$, $\phi = 0$), then at all depths the lateral pressures would be equal to the weight of the overburden γh, as in a fluid.   The distribution of lateral pressures against the wall would correspond to the line $K_A = 1.00$ in Fig. 10-4A.   If the soil has both friction and cohesion, the distribution of active lateral earth pressures follows the K_A line in Fig. 10-4B, and there is tension between the wall and the soil down to a depth z_0. The value of this depth can be computed from the ratio $H/(H - z_0) = \gamma H \tan^2(45° - \phi/2)/\sigma_3$ to read

$$z_0 = \frac{2c}{\gamma} \tan\left(45° + \frac{\phi}{2}\right) \qquad (10\text{-}16)$$

An examination of Eq. (10-14) and Fig. 10-4 shows that the equations giving the total lateral earth pressure E_A acting against a wall, when based on the Coulomb and on the Rankine-Résal analyses, involve the assumption that the soil will adhere to the material of the wall, i.e., masonry, concrete, steel, or timber, so strongly that the bond developed between the soil and the wall will be able to withstand appreciable tension. This assumption is not in qualitative agreement with actual experience, although practically no exact numerical data are yet available on the actual tensile strength of such a bond.

The Rankine-Résal analyses of lateral pressures of clay soils are all based on the assumption that the ultimate shearing strength of the soil has been reached and maintained along the entire depth of the wall. They can therefore be referred to as the *strength theories*.

On the other hand, there are many indications that plastic clays in general, and especially those of low sensitivity to remolding, can deform while maintaining or rapidly regaining a definite *neutral* or *consolidated equilibrium ratio* (K_0 or K_{ce}) of lateral to vertical pressures (see 1st ed., Arts. 10-7 to 10-9, 10-11, 10-20, 16-5, and 16-6; also Refs. 398 and 412). The application of this *neutral-earth-pressure theory* to practical designs is discussed further in Art. 10-5.

10-3. Effect of Wall Friction and Its Direction on the Active Pressures and Passive Resistance of Soils. The equations derived in the preceding articles

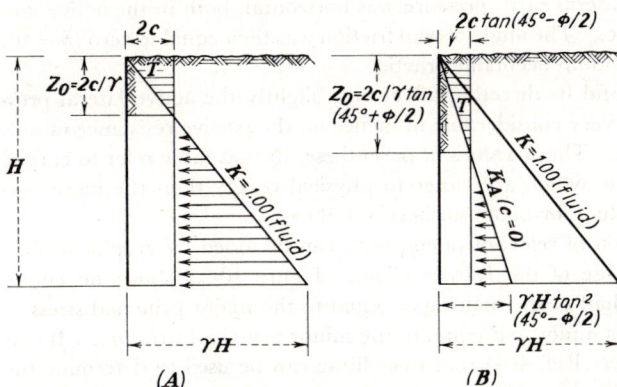

Fig. 10-4. Distribution of lateral pressures according to Coulomb and Rankine-Résal theories: (*A*) for soil with cohesion only; (*B*) for soil with both friction and cohesion.

TABLE 10-2.   Lateral-earth-pressure Coefficients for $\omega = 0$†

δ	Values of K_A ϕ				Values of K_p ϕ			
	25°	30°	35°	40°	25°	30°	35°	40°
$-40°$				0.77 (0.88)				92.3 (17.5)
$-30°$		0.87 (0.98)	0.50	0.36		10.0 (6.4)	15.3 (9.7)	25.1 (14.6)
$-20°$	0.61	0.47 (0.48)	0.36	0.28	4.6 (4.1)	6.1 (5.4)	8.3 (7.5)	11.9 (10.4)
$-10°$	0.47	0.38	0.30	0.24	3.3 (3.3)	4.2 (4.2)	5.3 (5.3)	7.0 (7.0)
$\pm 0°$	0.41 (0.41)	0.33 (0.33)	0.27 (0.27)	0.22 (0.22)	2.5 (2.5)	3.0 (3.0)	3.7 (3.7)	4.6 (4.6)
$+10°$	0.37	0.31	0.25	0.21	1.9	2.3	2.7	3.3
$+20°$	0.36	0.30 (0.30)	0.25	0.20	1.4	1.7	2.0	2.4
$+30°$		0.30 (0.31)	0.25	0.20		0.87 (0.53)	1.3	1.7
$+40°$				0.20 (0.22)				0.77 (0.52)

† See also Table 10-1. K values in parentheses refer to curved surfaces of failure.

were based on the simplifying assumption that no shearing stresses were being transmitted to the soil along the vertical face of the wall, so that the direction of the resultant lateral earth pressure was horizontal, both in the active and in the passive case.   The angle of wall friction was then equal to zero ($\delta = 0$). This condition seldom occurs in practice.

Wall friction and its direction affect only slightly the active lateral pressures but have a very considerable influence on the passive resistance of soils (see Table 10-2).   The K values in parentheses in that table refer to curved surfaces of failure, which are closer to physical reality than the more customarily used values for plane surfaces of failure.

The explanation of relevant phenomena can be aided by graphical illustrations making use of the *Winkler ellipse*.   Figure 10-5A shows an ellipse drawn with one-half of the major axis equal to the major principal stress σ_1 and one-half of its minor axis equal to the minor principal stress σ_3.   It was shown by Winkler (Ref. 404) that this ellipse can be used to determine the magnitude and direction of any stress as the radial distance to the center of the ellipse when that stress is acting on any plane passing through the same point of application as the principal stresses σ_1 and σ_3.

The inclination of failure planes in respect to the principal planes, as sketched in Fig. 10-1, is expressed by

$$\theta_{cr} = 45° + \frac{\phi}{2} \tag{10-17}$$

This angle can be indicated on the stress ellipse, as shown in Fig. 10-5A.

A procedure for *orienting the stress ellipse at the face of a wall* with a known angle of wall friction δ was given by Krey (Ref. 175, pp. 34–36). This orientation consists in determining the angle θ between the plane FO of the face of the wall and the major principal plane (see Fig. 10-5A). This procedure was used to determine the orientation of the stress ellipse in Figs. 10-6 to 10-8. The actual drawing of the stress ellipse, however, was omitted on these diagrams, and only the principal axes thereof are shown, as in Fig. 10-5B.

For the *active case* the *effect of wall friction* on the stress conditions near a rigid wall rotating around its base is illustrated by Fig. 10-6. If no wall friction existed, the stress ellipses along the wall would have the same orientation as shown in Fig. 10-6(III) along the failure plane BC for the angle of wall friction $\delta = 0$; that is, the major principal stress σ_1 would be vertical and equal to the effective weight of the overburden whereas the minor principal stress σ_3 would be horizontal.

However, wall friction will be present since the rotation of the wall around its base B (as is the case for rigid gravity walls) will cause the soil surface near the wall to drop from A to A''. The earth pressure $+E_A$ on the wall will then be directed as shown in Fig. 10-6(I) and the wall reactions against the soil as shown in Fig. 10-6(II) (compare with Fig. 10-2). The orientation of

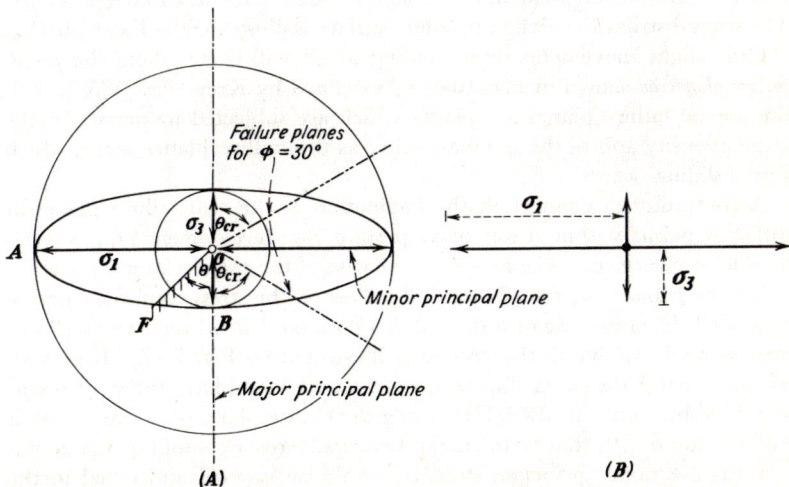

Fig. 10-5. The Winkler stress ellipse.

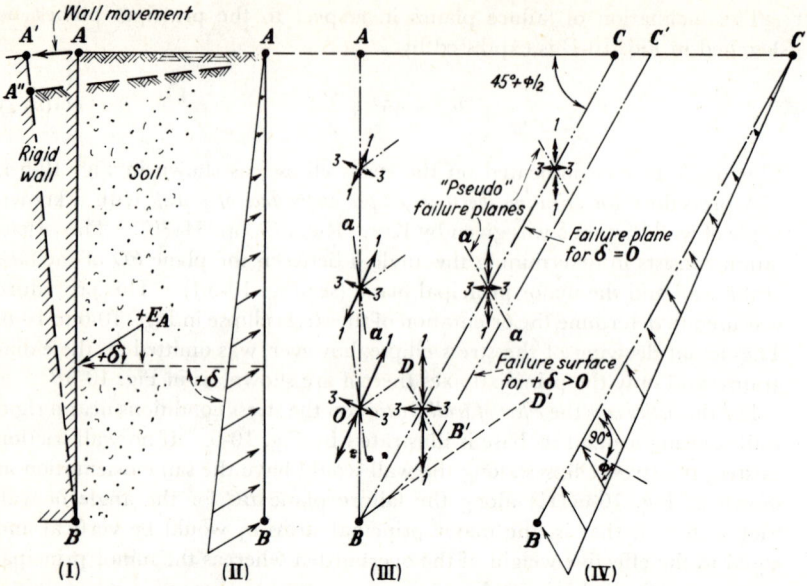

Fig. 10-6. Effect of wall friction on shape of failure surface for active case when wall rotates around base away from fill.

the stress ellipse at the face of the wall can then be determined by the procedure just outlined with reference to Fig. 10-5A.   Close to the face of the wall the failure planes will then have the inclination BD'—parallel to OD in Fig. 10-6(III)—which explains the slightly curved actual surface of failure. The stress distribution along the failure surface is illustrated by Fig. 10-6(IV).

Only slight movements or no sliding at all will occur along the *pseudo failure planes aa* shown in Fig. 10-6.   As defined by Krey (Ref. 175, p. 41), the pseudo failure planes are planes which are subjected to stresses of the same intensity and of the same obliquity as the failure planes along which actual sliding occurs.

A continuity of changes in the inclination of the real failure planes at different points within a soil mass permits the development of a continuous failure surface.   The reverse is the case of the pseudo failure planes.

For the *passive case*, the *effect of wall friction* on the stress conditions near a rigid wall AB pressed against the soil to a position $A'B'$ without any wall displacements in the vertical direction is illustrated by Fig. 10-7.   If no wall friction existed, the stress ellipses along the wall would have the same orientation as shown in Fig. 10-7(III), along the failure plane BC for an angle of wall friction $\delta = 0$; that is, the major principal stress σ_1 would be horizontal whereas the minor principal stress σ_3 would be vertical and equal to the effective weight of the overburden.

However, wall friction will be present since the displacement of the wall will cause the soil surface near the wall to rise from A to A''. The earth pressure $+E_p$ on the wall will then be directed as shown in Fig. 10-7(I), and the wall pressures on the soil will be directed as shown in Fig. 10-7(II). The orientation of the stress ellipses at the face of the wall can again be determined by the procedure outlined above with reference to Fig. 10-5. Close to the face of the wall the failure planes will have the inclination BD', parallel to OD in Fig. 10-7(III).

This explains the curvature of the actual surface of failure. Although such a curved surface BC' will have a greater area than a plane surface BC, the resistance to sliding along the curved surface BC' will be smaller.   Figure 10-7(III) serves to explain the cause for this by showing that close to the toe of the wall the friction along its face increases the vertical pressures to such an extent that the major principal stress would be almost perpendicular to a plane surface of failure BC (see also Ref. 126).   Hence, the assumption of plane surfaces of failure leads to much too high values of passive resistance for values of $\phi > 10°$, as shown by Tables 10-1 and 10-2 for *negative values of δ*, where the K_p values corresponding to curved surfaces of failure are enclosed in parentheses.   However, the passive resistance even for curved surfaces of failure will be a multiple of the theoretical values obtained for the assumption of zero wall friction.

The reverse is true for *positive values of the angle of wall friction* δ, i.e., in the not too frequent case when the wall is pulled out of the ground, as illustrated by Fig. 10-8.   If the wall moves from the position AB to $A'B'$ [Fig. 10-8(I)], the earth pressure $+E_p$ on the wall will be directed as shown in Fig. 10-8(I) and the wall pressures on the soil will be directed as shown in Fig. 10-8(II).

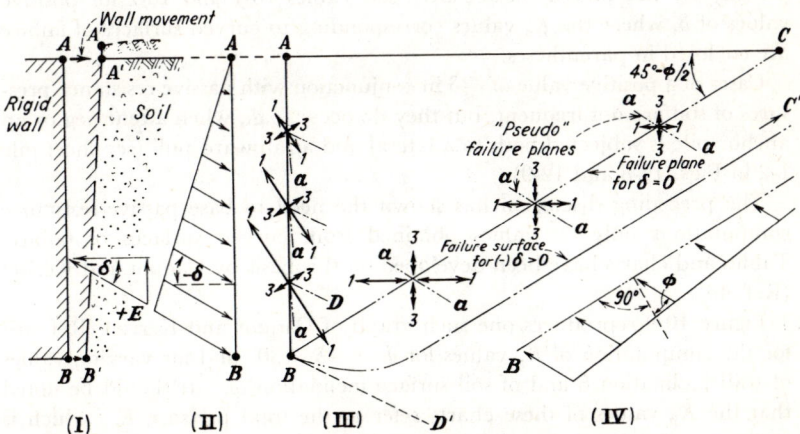

Fig. 10-7.   Effect of wall friction on shape of failure surface for passive case when wall is pushed horizontally against soil.

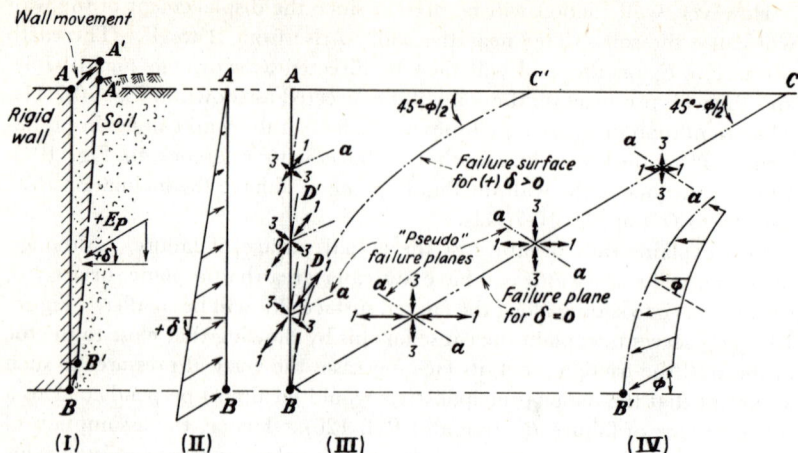

Fig. 10-8. Effect of wall friction on shape of failure surface for passive case when wall is pulled toward and out of the soil.

The orientation of the stress ellipse at the face of the wall will then be as shown in Fig. 10-8(III).   Close to the face of the wall the failure planes will have the inclination BD, parallel to OD'.   The resulting failure surface will have the shape shown by the curve BC'.

Since the area of the curved failure surface BC' is now smaller than that of the plane surface BC, and since the weight of the overburden above these failure surfaces is reduced by wall friction, the resistance to sliding along both surfaces will be smaller than for the case of assumed zero wall friction, especially for the curved surface BC'; see Tables 10-1 and 10-2 for positive values of δ, where the K_p values corresponding to curved surfaces of failure are enclosed in parentheses.

Cases of a positive value of $+\delta$ in conjunction with passive resistance pressures of soil are not frequent, but they do occur, e.g., when a tent peg or an anchor pile is subjected both to a lateral and an upward pull (see sheet pile 1-2 in Figs. 12-8 and 12-9).

The preceding discussion has shown the need to base passive-resistance computations only on values obtained from curved surfaces of failure. Tables and charts have been developed on this basis by Caquot and Kérisel (Ref. 46).

Figure 10-9 reproduces one such graph of Caquot and Kérisel (Ref. 46) for the computation of K_p values for $\phi = -\delta = 30°$ and for varying values of wall inclination β and of soil surface inclination ω.   It should be noted that the K_p values of these charts refer to the total pressure E_p, which is inclined under the angle $-\delta$ in respect to the normal to the back of the wall. Therefore, if one wishes to obtain the earth-resistance component normal to the wall, the E_p values should be multiplied by cos δ.   To obtain the horizontal component of earth resistance, the E_p values based on Fig. 10-9 should be multiplied by cos $(\delta - \beta)$.

If the chart of Fig. 10-9 is to be used in conjunction with anchor blocks or other structural elements where the wall friction is mobilized only as a result of the upward displacement of the soil, the K_p values should be reduced by multiplication with 0.75 for Fig. 10-9.   This is because in such cases the maximum values of wall friction δ and of internal friction ϕ are not reached simultaneously, as shown by Edmund Johnson's 1953 medium scale model tests with dense sand (see Refs. 402, 149, 158, and 363).   These tests fully confirmed the results of the Caquot-Kérisel theoretical analysis in the case where a progressively increasing downward thrust was exerted on the

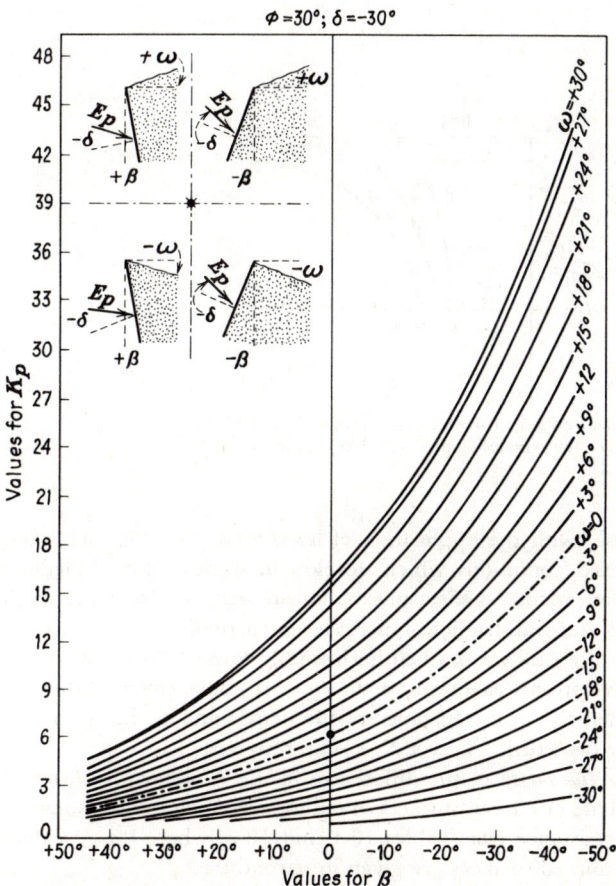

Fig. 10-9.   Graph for the computation of K_p values for varying values of β and ω and for $\phi = -\delta = 30°$.   (*After Caquot and Kérisel, Ref. 46.*)

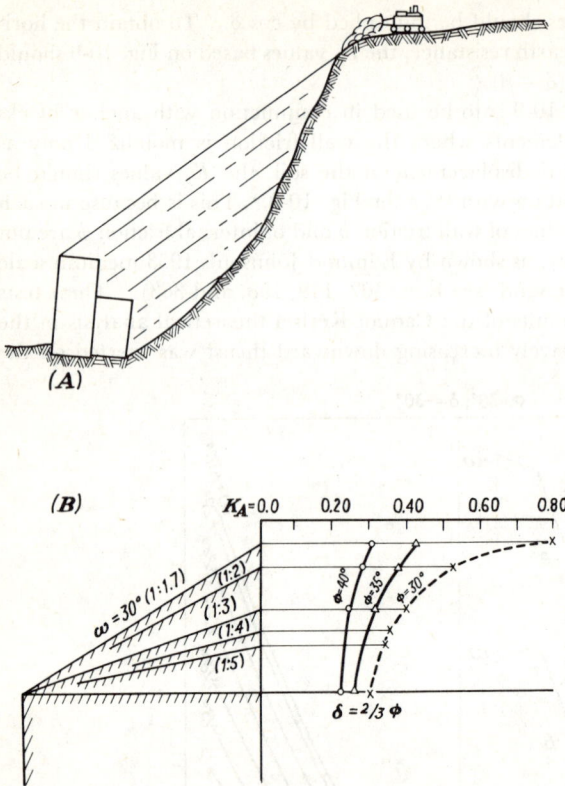

Fig. 10-10. (*A*) Damage to a 24-ft-high (7.3-m) crib wall backfilled by sand bulldozed over the edge of slope. (*B*) Explanation of the causes of trouble in (*A*).

wall simultaneously with the application of horizontal pressure. This test procedure simulated conditions which develop in front of the embedded lower portion of an anchored sheet-pile bulkhead (Art. 14-3*B*) when both internal friction ϕ and wall friction δ increase concurrently.

However, when the wall was pushed horizontally toward the fill, wall friction could fully develop only as a result of an upward displacement of the soil, which started when the peak resistance of the dense sand (point *a* on Fig. 3-27) was already exceeded. Lower K_p values resulted.

In the case of *active pressures*, the differences in the K values which result from the use of plane or curved surfaces of failure are much less pronounced than for passive resistance (see Tables 10-1 and 10-2, where the K values corresponding to curved surfaces are given in parentheses).

In the most frequent active case of wall friction corresponding to $+\delta$ values, which is the one of most gravity walls, the effect of wall friction on the K_A values is so small that it can well be neglected in that respect. Instead, its overall effect can be expressed by the change of direction of the total lateral earth pressure E_A, namely, by using the r' values instead of the r values, as shown in Figs. 10-2 and 10-3, when computing the overturning moment which will be somewhat reduced thereby.

The *change of direction of* E_A, however, can have a very considerable and detrimental effect if it is the result of an infrequent case of a complete reversal in the direction of wall friction (see Art. 10-7 and Figs. 10-20 to 10-24, which describe the failure of a twin-cell crib wall).

Figure 10-10A illustrates another failure, this time of a 24-ft-high (7.3-m) twin-cell crib wall where a further contributing cause was the *manner of back-filling*, which greatly increased the active lateral pressures E_A.   Sand backfill was bulldozed over the edge of higher ground so that it assumed a natural slope of about $1:1.7$.   It was uncompacted and hence could not have had a ϕ value much in excess of $30°$.   The lateral pressures of sloping backfill increase considerably when the slope angle ω approaches the value of the angle of internal friction ϕ, which, for loose sand, corresponds approximately to its angle of repose.   It can be seen from Fig. 10-10B that for a slope of $1:1.7$ ($\omega = 30°$) and $\phi = 30°$, $K_A = 0.80$.   In other words, it is then 2.6 times greater than the $K_A = 0.30$ for the same slope had the fill been compacted in layers, thus raising its ϕ value to at least $40°$.

10-4. Surcharge Effects.   It is convenient to express a uniformly distributed surcharge p_s in terms of a layer of soil having the same density γ as the underlying soil and a weight equal to p_s.   The height of this soil layer will then be $h_s = p_s/\gamma$, and the lateral pressures exerted by it from the surface of the soil downward will equal, as shown in Fig. 10-11(I),

$$p_{hs} = h_s \gamma K = p_s K \qquad (10\text{-}18)$$

The coefficient K in Eq. (10-18) should have the same value as that assigned to it for the determination of the lateral pressures exerted by the underlying soil.   The rectangular lateral-pressure diagram of the surcharge

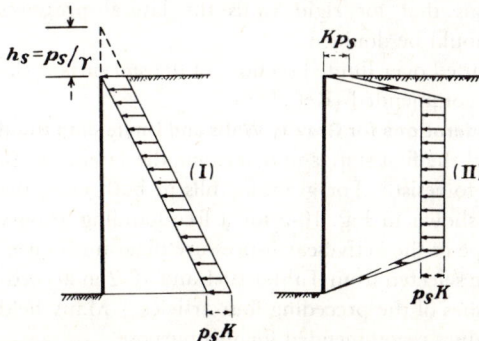

Fig. 10-11.   Lateral-pressure distribution produced by surcharges p_s uniformly distributed over the soil surface.

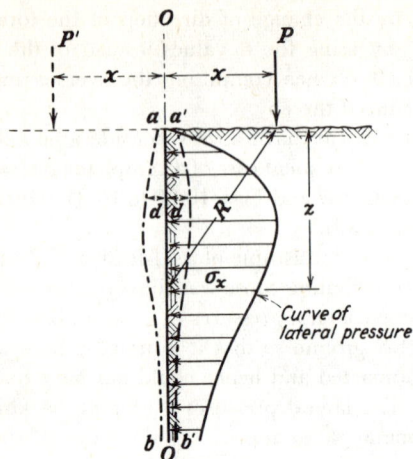

Fig. 10-12   Lateral-pressure distribution produced by a concentrated load P. Mirror-image effect doubles the lateral pressure σ_x for a rigid unyielding wall.

should be added to the corresponding lateral-earth-pressure diagrams of the triangular or of the trapezoidal (Chap. 11) types, as the case may be, in the manner illustrated by Fig. 10-11(I) and (II).

For concentrated loads and noncohesive backfills, Spangler's (Ref. 312) and other experiments have shown that Boussinesq's equation can be brought into good agreement with the measured data (1st ed., Art. 10-21). Cohesive soils should behave in a similar manner. For a Poisson ratio $\nu = 0.5$, the lateral pressure σ_x will be a maximum:

$$\sigma_x = \frac{p}{2\pi} \, 3x^2 z R^{-5} \qquad (10\text{-}19)$$

The above value was obtained from an analysis of a semi-infinite elastic solid. This meant that the soil was supposed to extend beyond the face OO of the wall, which would deform to the position ab shown in Fig. 10-12.

If the wall is rigid, no such deformation can occur. The effect is equivalent to applying a mirror-image load P', as shown, to neutralize the lateral displacements d. This means that for rigid walls the lateral pressures obtained from Eq. (10-19) should be doubled.

For surcharge loads distributed over limited sections of the soil surface the use of Newmark's charts is recommended (Ref. 227).

10-5. General Design Considerations for Gravity Walls and Unyielding Rigid Walls.
For both types of wall the first step is to determine the lateral earth pressure which the wall has to resist. For granular fills in both cases the distribution is triangular, as shown in Fig. 10-2 for a free-standing gravity wall. For such walls the slope of the active-earth-pressure diagram is given by the K_A value which can be selected from Tables 10-1 and 10-2 in accordance with the general guidelines of the preceding four articles. Many field measurements support the values recommended for this purpose.

For an unyielding rigid wall, however, no soil deformations are possible of the type needed to reduce the lateral earth pressures to their active values. Therefore, the slope of the design lateral earth-pressure-diagram will be governed by the *neutral, or at-rest, condition* to which an earth-pressure-coefficient value varying from $K_0 = 0.4$ to $K_0 = 0.5$ corresponds. These limits are based on experimental laboratory cell tests and on field measurements (see the references to the first edition at the end of Art. 10-2).

An example of the results of such field measurements is given by Fig. 10-13. It gives the results of measurements against a 79-ft-high (24-m) wall which was backfilled with loose clean sand in the manner indicated in the diagram. The wall formed part of a massive reinforced-concrete structure for an underground factory. It could therefore be considered as absolutely rigid and unyielding.

The lateral pressures were measured by means of large (diameter = 12.0 in. = 30.5 cm) Maihak (vibrating-wire) type cells.

The area of the cell in contact with the soil was increased by placing specially designed metal plates between the soil and two of the cells. The outer surface of each plate was flush with the surface of the masonry. In this manner, pressures against 54 percent of the height of the wall were measured over a width of 2 ft (61 cm). This method gives a much smoother sequence of measured pressures than can be obtained by the use of small individual cells.

The factory was built in an open excavation and then backfilled with clean sand. Laboratory direct shear tests gave for that sand a value of the angle of internal friction $\phi = 42°$. The angle of repose in a dry state was found to be $\alpha_R = 34°$.

The backfilling proceeded from the surface of the ground at the edge of the excavation toward the building, as shown in Fig. 10-13, and took about 4 months to complete. All compaction of the sand was avoided; its unit

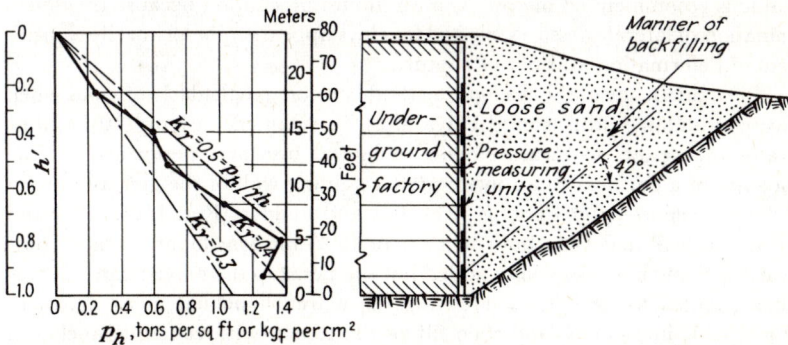

Fig. 10-13. Lateral earth pressures acting against a 79-ft-high (24-m) massive concrete wall of underground German factory, as measured in 1942. (*After H. Muhs, Ref. 222.*)

weight after placing was estimated at $\gamma = 100$ lb/ft³ (1.6 g$_f$/cm³). Because of its slightly moist condition and the resulting apparent cohesion, the angle of repose during backfilling in the field was higher than in the laboratory and equaled 42°.

Taking the lowest of these values, $\phi = 34°$, we obtain, by setting the angle of wall friction equal to zero, from Eq. (10-4) the highest possible value of $K_A = 0.28$. It will, however, be noted from Fig. 10-13 that the actually observed average coefficient of earth pressure was $K = 0.42$. This value was reached a year after construction, having increased slightly, by approximately 5 percent, during that period. The increase of pressure was presumably due to the slight increase of density of the sand by traffic vibrations and percolating rainwater. Thus the pressures actually observed in this structure came very close to the at-rest values obtained for loose sand in the laboratory and by model tests, as was to be expected for an unyielding rigid wall. The pressure distribution was essentially hydrostatic; i.e., it increased linearly with depth.

A new method for the in situ measurement of lateral pressure in normally consolidated clays reported by Bjerrum and Andersen (Ref. 31) is based on the principle of *hydraulic fracturing*. A piezometer is inserted into a clay deposit, and a vertical crack is initiated in the clay at the level of the piezometer tip by controlled hydraulic pressure. The fluid pressure is then reduced until the crack closes, as evidenced by a decrease of flow of water into the piezometer. The fluid pressure at that moment is considered to equal the natural lateral pressure at rest within the clay deposit. In this manner values of $K_0 = 0.40$ to 0.50 were determined in the "quick" Norwegian clays and $K_0 = 0.50$ to 0.60 for clays of normal sensitivity.

Clay backfills are to be avoided. If for some reason this cannot be done, the use of the Rankine-Résal strength theories illustrated by Fig. 10-4 does not appear advisable, as indicated in the end of Art. 10-2. The use of a triangular earth-pressure diagram, as shown in Fig. 10-2B, with a $K_0 = 0.5$ value is recommended instead as a minimum precaution because the determination of lateral pressures exerted by clays appears to be primarily a problem of deformation and not of rupture.

The inadequacy of the strength method becomes particularly obvious when overconsolidated stiff-fissured clays must be retained. Figure 10-14 illustrates the results of measurements of lateral pressures performed on the bracing of a cut next to an inadequate retaining wall of the gravity type in London, reported by Cooling (Ref. 65) and Golder (Ref. 110). The old retaining wall had been built in 1901 to 1902 and was found to move outward. Some buttresses were added but did not stop the movement. It was then decided to strengthen it by digging a trench behind it, as shown in Fig. 10-14, in sections, and then filling the trench with concrete, anchored by steel tie rods to the old wall. As the trench was dug, measurements were performed on the timber struts. Preliminary calibrations of the selected struts in the laboratory indicated that compressive strains of the wood could

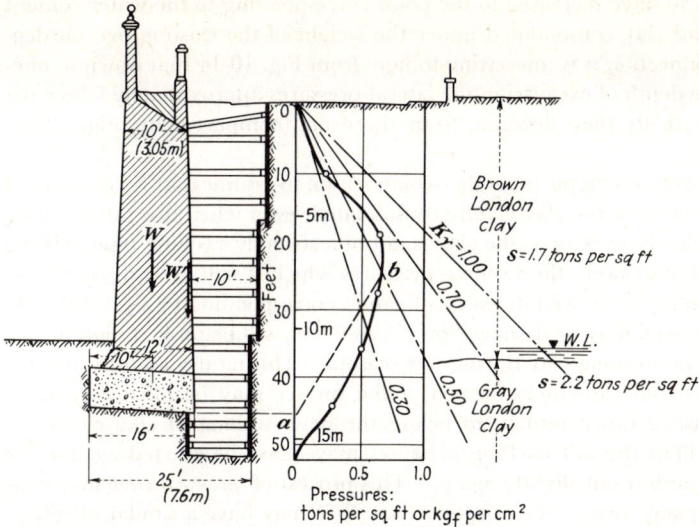

Fig. 10-14. Observations of earth pressure for distribution on timbering of a 52-ft-deep (16-m) cut in stiff-fissured London clay. (*After Cooling, Ref. 65, and Golder, Ref. 110; the lines of the hydrostatic pressure ratio K have been superimposed on the original drawing.*)

give fairly accurate values of the loads applied, provided they were measured over a 5-ft gage length to 0.01 mm, using special metal points screwed into the interior of the wood through a shallow recess subsequently filled with wax. This and other techniques eliminated the otherwise considerable effect of the surface strains of the wood, which are caused by moisture changes (Ref. 110).

The clay behind the wall was of the stiff-fissured or slickensided type, over-consolidated during its past geological history. As stated by Golder (Ref. 110), "the behavior of the London clay in stability problems is usually con-trolled by the strength, not of the mass of clay, but of the clay surfaces exposed in the fissures." This is typical of other clays of this kind (Art. 7-6). According to Eq. (7-4), a vertical bank in the weakest layer encountered ($s = 1.7$ tons/ft$^2 = 1.7$ kg$_f$/cm^2, $\gamma = 120$ lb/ft$^3 = 1.92$ g$_f$/cm^3) in the cut shown in Fig. 10-14 should have been able to stand unsupported up to a height of $(2.58 \times 1.7)/0.06 = 73$ ft (22.3 m). Nevertheless, definite lateral pressures exerted by that clay were measured at a depth of only 52 ft (15.9 m). The intensity of the lateral pressures varied in different sections of the trench with the time of the year. It was smallest during the dry summer months. Figure 10-14 shows the maximum values which were recorded in a section built during December, January, and February, when it was reasonable to assume that the fissures of the overconsolidated clay had been soaked with water and, as a result, were filled with softer clay, the water content of which was likely to have increased to the point corresponding to the water content of semifluid clay consolidated under the weight of the existing overburden. In this connection it is interesting to note from Fig. 10-14 that down to one-half of the depth of excavation the lateral pressures approximately follow the line $K_y = 0.50$; they decrease from there on (compare with Fig. 14-11, curve B).

For general design purposes there is no reason to assume that K_A will exceed the value of 0.5 if the clay is fully consolidated, even when it is saturated by receding floods, so long as the clay is not of a strongly swelling type.   If the clay is liable to swell, the swelling pressures which it will exert against a retaining wall may be well in excess of values corresponding to $K_A = 1.0$.   As a result the wall may be damaged or will *creep*, i.e., will be pushed slightly outward by the swelling clay during wet seasons.   During dry seasons the clay will shrink, but the cracks formed at the surface may be filled by surface debris washed down into them before the new swelling of clay closes the cracks.   Thus the full swelling pressures may again be exerted against the wall and push it out slightly again.   This process of outward *creep* may continue for many years.   Frost action (Art. 8-6) may have a similar effect.

The entire problem of pressures exerted by clay backfills represents a suitable subject for systematic regional research.   Until more experimental data become available, walls backfilled with mixtures of sand and clay should be designed, according to Fig. 10-2, for a value of $K_A = 0.5$, which should take care of unfavorable conditions of saturation of the backfill.   Weep holes should be provided in the walls or continuous graded gravel drains installed behind the walls to allow for drainage and to prevent full water pressures from building up against the wall.   They should be protected from freezing. Gutters should be provided to carry the water away before it seeps into the soil near the wall.   The use of clay backfills likely to swell should be avoided.

With reference to Fig. 10-2, *the dimensions of a gravity retaining wall are determined as follows:* the width b at the base must be such that the *stabilizing moment* of the weight W of the wall around edge 1 is *greater than the overturning moment* of the earth pressure E around the same edge; the resultant R must fall within the middle third of the base, so that edge 2 will still be pressed against the ground; the *pressure p_1 beneath edge 1 should not exceed the permissible pressure on the ground* (Art. 4-7); the shearing resistance along plane 1-2 of the base should be greater than the earth pressure E, since *sliding* would otherwise result.   Passive earth pressure against the toe is usually neglected (see Prob. 10-1).   The right dimension is arrived at by trial.   For the first attempt one may take $b = 0.4h$.

For clay soils the *shearing resistance along* plane 1-2 of the *base* can be taken to equal one-half of the unconfined compressive strength q_u of the clay.   If this value is low, piling (including batter piles) may have to be resorted to (see Art. 10-8).

Reinforced-concrete retaining walls are frequently used instead of massive gravity walls. The lateral pressure distribution and the overall dimensions of the wall are determined in the same way as indicated above for gravity walls. The weight of the soil above the heel of the wall is to be included in the overall stability computations. The weight of the soil above the toe may be included if no danger exists of its later removal. Once the lateral pressures and the soil reactions are determined, the detailed design of the component parts of the wall is undertaken in the same manner as for concrete subject to bending.

Sliding of a wall is a not infrequent occurrence when the underlying soil is clay. The presence of a thin seam of soft plastic clay below the wall footing can often be undetected by borings and cause considerable trouble later. A case of this kind is illustrated by Fig. 10-15. A reinforced-concrete wall was built on stiff clay to retain a road which crossed at right angles a depression in a slope. The wall was highest, 32 ft (9.8 m), at the deepest point of the depression. As the backfilling was completed and the surfacing of the upper road begun, signs multiplied that the wall was moving laterally. Transit and level surveys were then made daily, a plot of which showed that no tilting was involved but only a lateral horizontal displacement of several inches. A time-displacement plot showed that the movement was not slowing down but was even accelerating somewhat, reaching a maximum value of 15 in. (38 cm). A complete failure of the wall appeared imminent, but the following emergency measures saved it. Within a few hours trucks brought in temporary fill which was spread by bulldozers in front of the wall and above its toe (zone 1 in Fig. 10-15). At the same time the backfill in zone 2 was removed by a clamshell bucket operated by a crane standing beyond the limits of the primary sliding wedge, limits which were indicated by cracks in the ground surface parallel to the wall. The backfill from zone 2 was dumped over the wall to zone 1 by the swinging boom of that crane. These temporary measures stopped all wall movements and permitted the initiation of permanent measures of remedy.

In other cases, where slippage along a plane of disturbed clay immediately

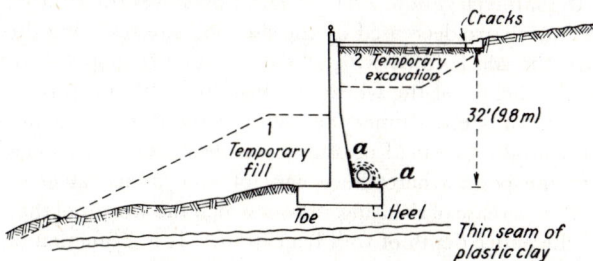

Fig. 10-15. Measures required to stop the sliding of a 32-ft-high (9.8-m) reinforced-concrete wall and other generally advisable precautions.

beneath the footing is feared, a key under the heel of the wall can be helpful if it forms an integral part of the reinforced-concrete footing.

Details in the installation of drainage pipes behind the wall can be very important.   The surfaces *aa* (Fig. 10-15) at the back of the wall and the top of the footing should be waterproofed, especially at the expansion joints in the concrete of the footing.   This had not been done in a case where the drainpipe got clogged and built up a head of water because of seepage toward it from neighboring septic tanks.   This water then percolated down through the expansion joint, softening the clay just under the footing.   Lateral creep of the abutment resulted.

10-6. Pressures in Silos and Bins.   Observations made of grain silos and bins show that the increase of pressure on the bottom of the silo and against its side walls is not proportional to the height of grain over the point where the pressures are measured.   Numerous experiments have been performed, both on models and on full-sized bins.   Figure 10-16 gives the results of a typical example of carefully performed full-scale measurements on an actual structure, reported by Jamieson (Ref. 145).   One of the silo cells, 67 ft (20 m) deep and having a horizontal 12 by 13.5 ft (3.7 by 4.1 m) cross section, was selected for the tests.   The vertical pressures p_v and the horizontal pressures p_h were measured by means of hydraulically operated pressure cells located at the bottom of the silo cell and in the lower part of the side wall, as shown in Fig. 10-16.   The adjoining diagram shows the increase of the measured pressures as a function of the corresponding depth h of the grain above the points of measurement.   The unit weight of the wheat used during the tests was 49.4 lb/ft³ (0.79 g$_f$/cm³).   Its angle of repose was $\alpha_R = 28°$.

It will be noted from Fig. 10-16 that both the vertical and the horizontal pressures increased at a decreasing rate as the value of h increased.   This happened because of the increasing influence of the frictional shearing stresses s between the wheat and the walls of the silo cell.   These shearing stresses are active along the entire depth of wheat and are a function of the corresponding horizontal pressures, the latter, in turn, being a function of the corresponding vertical pressures at the same elevation.   The vertical pressures transmitted to the bottom of the silo cell are decreased by the shearing stresses along the entire height to which the silo is filled with wheat.   It will be noted from Fig. 10-16 that when the height of the wheat reached 40 ft (12.2 m) above the silo bottom, or approximately 3 times the width of the cell, no further increase of either horizontal or vertical pressures was measured.   This elevation corresponds to the point where the weight of each added layer of wheat is balanced by the increase of shearing stresses which the weight of that layer produces along the entire depth of wall beneath it.   It is a function of the width of the cell (compare with Art. 13-4).

The ratio of the actually measured horizontal and vertical pressures increases somewhat with h from $K_\gamma = p_h/p_v = 0.54$ to $K_\gamma = 0.64$.   The decrease

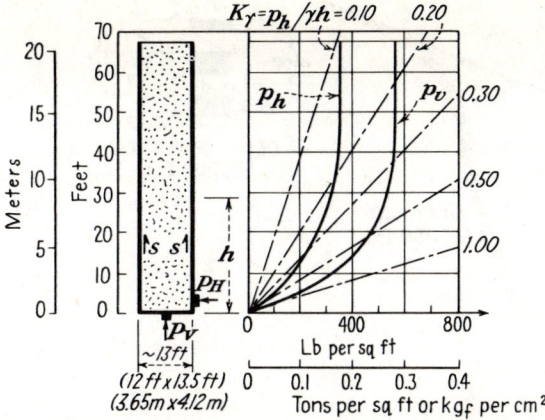

Fig. 10-16. Results of pressure measurements in a wooden silo filled with Manitoba wheat in Canada. (*After Jamieson, Ref. 145.*)

with depth of the coefficient K_γ is only apparent, since K_γ is customarily computed for purposes of convenience as the ratio $p_h/\gamma h$, that is, under the assumption of a constant vertical fluid pressure equal to the full weight of the overburden $p_v = \gamma h$; this assumption is not correct.   The vertical pressure changes and not the actual value of K.   Nevertheless, the method of relating the measured lateral pressures to the weight of the overburden will be maintained, since it provides the most convenient way for the comparison of the results of field measurements on different types of structures and at different localities.   These data help illustrate the action of soil fill within the cells of crib walls.

It should be clearly understood, however, that the pressure distribution sketched in Fig. 10-16 refers to *static conditions only*.   A number of cases have been recorded when, during discharging, cracks appeared in the walls of a silo above the silo bottom at a height equal to approximately twice the silo diameter.   No trouble has been observed during silo filling.

Mackey and Mason (Ref. 206) have reported the results of model experiments showing that in what they termed the *pipe zone* of a silo temporary arches were formed at the time of discharge which increased the lateral pressures on the silo walls to values corresponding to $K = 1.95$ and $K = 1.68$ for loose and dense sand fills, respectively.

10-7. Crib Walls.   Gravity retaining walls in the form of a *crib* are sometimes employed.   They are modeled after timber-crib cofferdams (Art. 12-2) but are usually built of interlocking prefabricated reinforced-concrete units of two types, A and B (Fig. 10-17).   The spaces between these units are filled with soil.   The width b of the crib is determined in the same way as indicated above for an ordinary gravity wall.   The dimensions of the prefabricated

DETAIL OF VERTICAL
SECTION I-I

VERTICAL
SECTION I-I

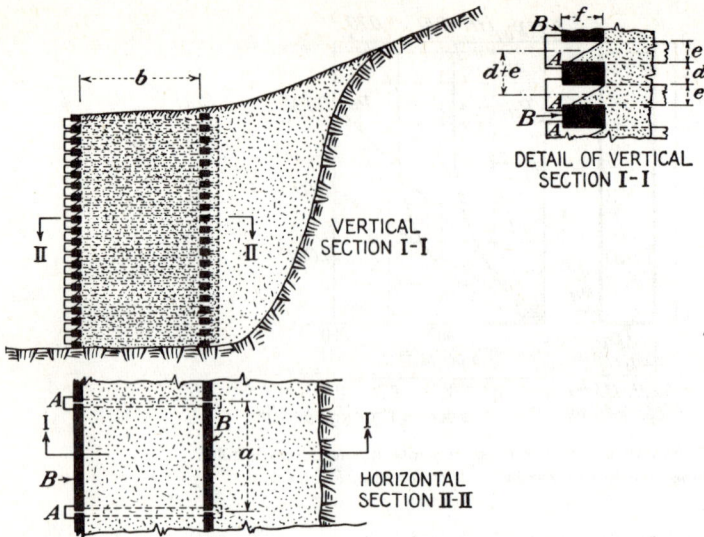

Fig. 10-17.   Design of crib retaining wall.   Precast reinforced-concrete units.

units should be chosen so that $f \geq 2e$; otherwise dry granular fill will not be retained within the crib.   The prefabricated units of type B (*stretchers*) are designed to resist in bending, as beams of span a on two supports, a maximum total lateral pressure equal to $(d + e)a \times 0.5\gamma b$, where γ is the unit weight of the soil.   The B units should also resist one-half of the total vertical pressure indicated below for the A units.   This lateral pressure will correspond to that in a silo and will be developed if the crib is filled with soil prior to backfilling. The active pressures after backfilling should not create any greater bending moments.   Symmetrical tensile and compressive reinforcement should be used for both types of units.   The A units (*headers*) should be reinforced to take up in tension the total lateral force exerted against a B unit; the head of the A units should be designed to take up that force in shear.   In addition, the A units should be designed to resist in bending, as beams of span b on two supports, a total vertical force assumed transmitted to it by friction from both sides and equal to $(d + e)b \times 0.5\gamma a \times 0.58$, where the first part of the equation represents the total lateral pressure ($K_n = 0.5$) and the coefficient of wall friction is taken to equal $\tan \delta = 0.58$ ($\delta = 30°$).

Crib walls of this type permit some economy of concrete and can be quickly erected if a stockpile of prefabricated units is available.   They permit excellent drainage of the backfill, which should always be granular.

The precast concrete stretcher units A at the outer face of the wall can be either of the *open* type, as in Figs. 10-17 and 10-18, or the *closed* type, as in Figs. 10-20 and 10-22.   The closed type permits the safe use of sand backfill

Fig. 10-18. Longitudinal deformations of crib wing wall due to settlements and soil movements shown in Fig. 10-19.   (*Photo by Tschebotarioff.*)

throughout the cell, whereas in the open type crushed rock is usually placed against the outer face of the wall to ensure that the sand is not washed out after the fill gets saturated by heavy rains.

Reinforced-concrete crib walls easily adjust themselves to longitudinal deformations caused by differential settlements, as illustrated by Fig. 10-18.

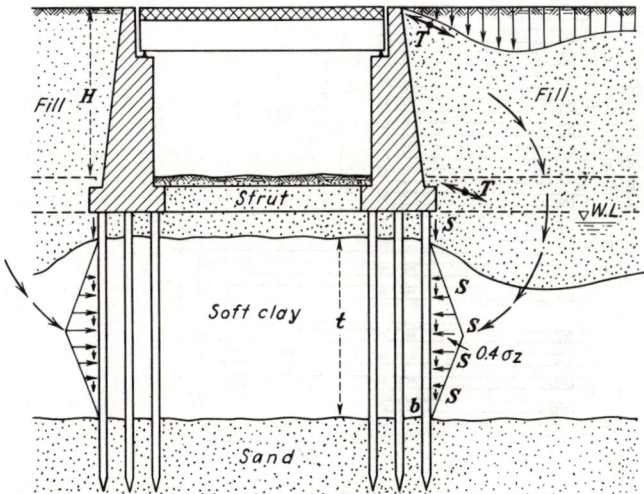

Fig. 10-19. Cross section through underpass adjoining the crib wing wall shown in Fig. 10-18.

Fig. 10-20. General view of damaged 34-ft-high (10.4-m) concave crib wall.

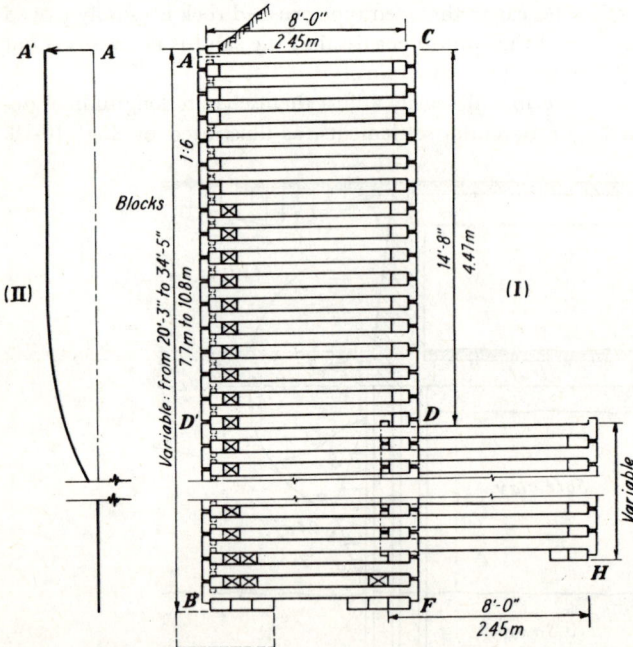

Fig. 10-21. (I) Cross section of concave twin-cell 34-ft-high (10.4-m) crib wall as originally designed. (II) Deformations of upper single-cell section of crib wall shown in Fig. 10-20.

The differential settlement between the 25-ft-high (7.6-m) fill and the pile-supported abutment (Fig. 10-19) exceeded 2 ft (60 cm). Nevertheless the reinforced-concrete crib wing wall adapted itself to the resulting deformations without damage. The lateral pressures against the piles under the abutment indicated in Fig. 10-19 will be discussed in Art. 10-9.

The width of a single-cell crib wall is limited by the length of the precast headers, which are customarily supplied in 6- and 8-ft (1.83- and 2.44-m) standard lengths. An 8-ft (2.44-m) header limits the safe height of a single-cell crib wall to a maximum of about 16 ft (4.9 m). For greater wall heights interlocking twin-cell crib walls must be resorted to. A height of such twin walls in excess of 24 ft (7.3 m), however, can create special problems, as illustrated by Figs. 10-20 to 10-24, since they can be *very sensitive to transverse differential settlements* (Ref. 371).

Fig. 10-20 gives a general view of a concave 24-ft to 34-ft-high (7.3-m to 10.4-m) crib wall. Its cross section is shown in Fig. 10-21. Immediately after backfilling was completed the upper one-cell-wide portion of the wall began showing visible signs of distress (Fig. 10-22) where the wall height

Fig. 10-22. Outward bulge of upper part of concave 34-ft-high (10.4-m) crib wall (see Fig. 10-21). (*Photo by Tschebotarioff.*)

exceeded 20 ft (6.1 m). Part of the upper backfill had to be removed and dumped in front of the wall (Fig. 10-20). That stopped the movement.

A stability analysis was then performed in the conventional manner, as shown in Fig. 10-23(I), indicating that the factor of safety was quite satisfactory, namely

$$F = \frac{23.5 \times 0.649}{5.4} = 2.82$$

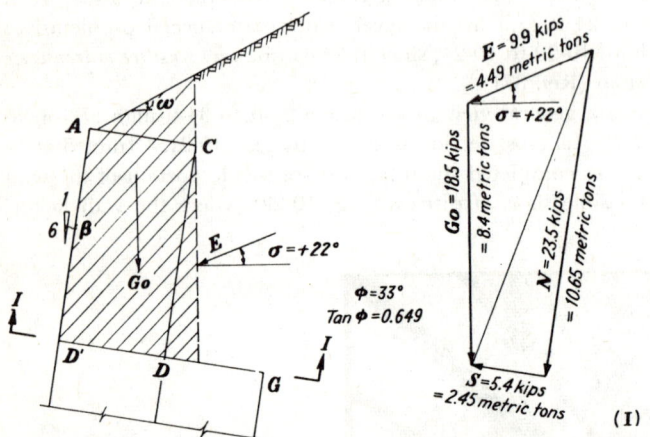

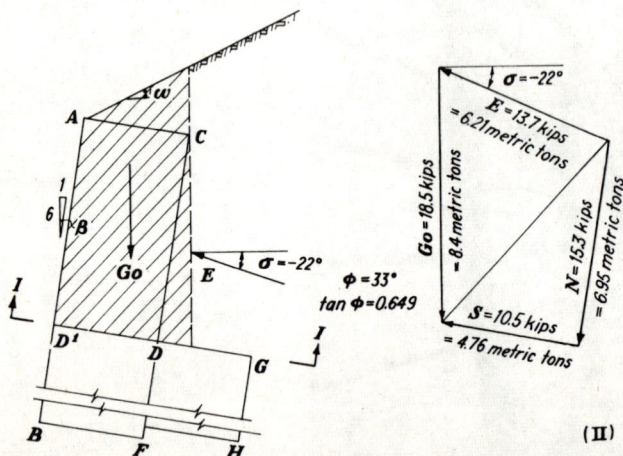

Fig. 10.23. (I) Conventional analysis of upper single-cell section of concave crib wall. (II) Stability analysis of upper single-cell section of crib wall if *CDF* settled more than *AD'B* and *GH*.

The trouble was then analyzed and explained as follows (Ref. 371). An examination of the upper surface AC of the crib wall (Fig. 10-21) indicated that the fill within the cells must have settled after it had been placed. Further, construction records showed that the placing of the fill within the upper part $ACDD'$ of the wall (Fig. 10-21) was done in freezing weather when adequate compaction was not possible. However, the fill behind the wall was compacted by construction equipment passing over it.

The lowest value of the angle of internal friction determined in the laboratory for the loosest state of the fill was $\phi = 28°$. The actual slope of the fill surface immediately behind the wall was not as steep as assumed in the original design but was appreciably flatter ($\omega = !2°$). By repeating the analysis of Fig. 10-23(I) with $\phi = 28°$, $\delta = +18°$, $\beta = -9°$, and $\omega = +12°$, a satisfactory factor of safety against sliding equal to $F = 2.1$ was obtained. Thus the low original shearing strength of the fill within the cells could not explain the actual sliding. The following deductions, however, fitted all the observed facts.

Settlement of the fill within the cells was bound to produce so-called "arching" or "bin effects" within the cells. This, as well as the 1 : 6 batter of the crib, loaded its inner longitudinal wall CDF to a greater extent than the outer walls $AD'B$ and GH.

The greater loading of the central longitudinal wall produced its greater settlement, as a consequence of which the conventionally assumed direction of the angle of wall friction $+\delta$ was changed to $-\delta$. The stability analysis was therefore repeated for this changed condition [Fig. 10-23(II)], all other assumptions of Fig. 10-23(I) remaining unchanged. This analysis indicated that the reversal of the direction of wall friction decreased the safety against sliding to

$$F = \frac{15.3 \times 0.649}{10.5} = 0.95$$

Actually this factor must have been even smaller when sliding began since the angle of internal friction must have been smaller than $\phi = 33°$ before seasonal temperature and saturation variations, in combination with shearing deformations, compacted the originally loose frozen sand fill to its present satisfactory density.

The tendency toward greater settlement of the central longitudinal wall of the crib skeleton was accentuated by the details of its foundation. In accordance with the customary assumption that a crib wall acts like a massive gravity wall, a substantial continuous reinforced-concrete footing was provided at its toe (B). It is shown by broken lines in Fig. 10-21. However, only three precast stretcher units were laid down below the longitudinal center wall (F). They were not structurally connected to each other transversely, except by the headers. A numerical estimation of the downward force P, transmitted by the longitudinal wall of the crib skeleton in the case of some soil bin action within its cells, indicated that the headers above and below the stretchers and the block could not have transmitted the resulting loads to the soil through the stretchers without cracking.

To check this point, three cells were fully excavated and the anticipated cracks were actually found in the headers.   The measured deflection of the headers indicated that the central longitudinal crib wall must have settled at least 2 in. more than the outer face of the crib.

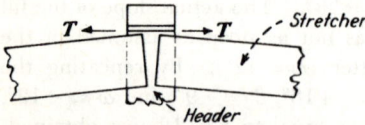

Fig. 10-24.   Outward lateral movement of concave crib wall induces transverse tensile stresses in headers.

It should be noted that a convex crib wall of approximately the same height in the vicinity did not show any signs of distress, presumably because the entire wall, in plan, formed a compressed arch.   The severe cracking of the reinforced-concrete headers and stretchers of the concave concrete wall (Fig. 10-22) had to be attributed, therefore, to tensile stresses T induced in the headers as a result of the outward sliding of the upper one-cell-wide portion of the wall and the accompanying tendency of the stretchers to slide laterally at their support on the headers (Fig. 10-24).

For the reconstruction of this wall it proved necessary first to demolish entirely the part thereof which was higher than 24 ft (7.3 m) down to within 6 ft (1.8 m) from its bottom.   The remaining part of the cells was then excavated individually and filled with lean concrete to form a solid block.   The wall was rebuilt thereon to a height of 24 ft (7.3 m) with a longer and flatter slope behind its top.

The subsoil in this case consisted of a compact sand and gravel glacial deposit.

When a high twin-cell wall is underlain by poorer material, the provision of a solid reinforced-concrete footing across its width may be insufficient, and piles may have to be used.

10-8. Gravity Walls and Abutments on Piles; Conventional Approach and Its Limitations.   A pile foundation should be selected for a retaining wall or abutment whenever there might otherwise be a danger of shear failure of the soil under the toe of the wall and/or whenever excessive settlements could occur because of the compression or consolidation of the underlying soil.

Customarily, pile layouts are made for the conventional assumptions, illustrated by Fig. 10-25A, that the only external forces acting on the piles are the same ones which would act on an abutment without piles above line 1-1 of the bottom of its footing.   The methods of analysis employed until recently permitted the determination only of axial stresses in the piles, leaving out of consideration possible flexural stresses.

When evaluating this approach, differentiation is essential between two possible limit soil conditions, between which a precise demarcation line cannot always be clearly drawn.

In the first extreme case, the piles are driven through loose predominantly sand and gravel soils with little or some silt and clay content. Such soil deposits may undergo excessive local deformations under the high toe pressures of a retaining wall on spread footings, but they will not undergo any further settlement under their own weight even when piles are driven through or into them. Compressive or shearing deformations of such deposits under the added weight of new backfill are slight. Under such conditions flexural stresses in the piles are negligible and can be ignored even if a lateral thrust of 1 ton is assigned to each vertical or battered pile, as this is conventionally done. The type of pile selected and its resistance to bending are then of secondary importance. Displacement piles, timber or concrete, even if the latter have little reinforcement or only thin outer steel shells, may even be of advantage by compressing and densifying the easily drainable soil. (Methods of evaluating bending stresses in piles subjected to lateral loads transmitted by the superstructure are outlined in Arts. 14-4B and 14-4C.)

The conventional approach to pile design, which assumes axial loads only, is satisfactory for such conditions and will be examined further in this article. However, this conventional approach can lead to considerable trouble when applied to the opposite extreme case when the piles are driven through a sensitive plastic clay (Fig. 10-28). Special measures become necessary then to meet the loading conditions of Fig. 10-25B. They will be discussed in Art. 10-9.

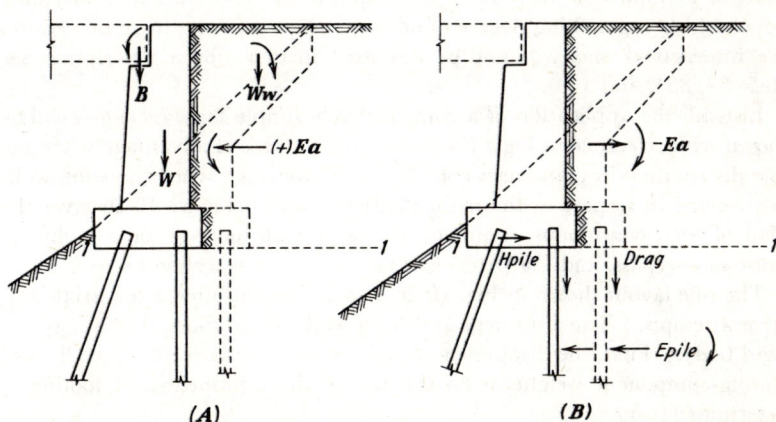

Fig. 10-25. Sketch of design loads: (A) Conventional; (B) additional when piles are driven through plastic clay. (*From Ref. 375.*)

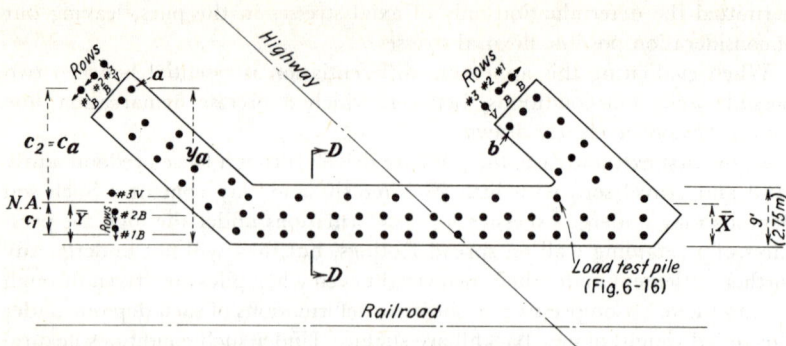

Fig. 10-26. Analytical procedure for conventional computations of axial pile loads under an abutment. See Fig. 10-27 for section DD.

A number of graphical and analytical procedures have been developed for determining axial stresses in piles once the resultant R of the active earth pressure E_A and weight W of the wall are known. E_A and W are obtained as outlined in Arts. 10-2 and 10-5.   Most of these procedures assume that the piles are hinged at both ends, so that no bending moments can be transmitted there.

Historically, one of the earliest such procedures is that of Culmann (1866), still frequently employed because it uses simple graphical statics.   A much more complicated procedure is that of the *center-of-rotation* method, attributed to Westergaard, which considers the axial elongations of piles but unjustifiably ignores the deformations of the surrounding soil.   Finally, several *elastic* procedures of increasing complexity have been proposed, some of the latest requiring computers for the solution of several simultaneous equations. Since it is impossible to provide the requisite soil constants with anything approaching a matching degree of accuracy, in most cases these procedures are impractical and will not be discussed further (for a description see Refs. 37, 334, and 100).

Instead, the application of a comparatively simple *analytical method* will be shown with reference to Figs. 10-26 and 10-27.   It is of advantage when the pile distribution in plan has a complicated shape, e.g., when the wing walls are skewed in respect to the main abutment wall.   Figure 10-26 gives the plan of such continuous abutment and wing-wall footings for a highway-railroad overpass, and Fig. 10-27 gives a vertical cross section thereof.

The pile layout shown in Fig. 10-26 was arrived at after a few trial-and-error attempts.   The abutment and wing walls are considered to act as one rigid body.   First, the distance $\bar{X}$ of the center of gravity of all wall- and footing-component weights from the toe of the abutment-wall footing is determined from

$$\bar{X} = \frac{\sum (Wx)}{\sum W}$$

(10-20)

where W = weights of individual wall components

x = distance of each W from toe of abutment-wall footing

The distance $\bar{Y}$ of the neutral axis of the pile configuration from the toe of the abutment-wall footing is established in a similar manner from

$$\bar{Y} = \frac{\sum (y)}{n} \tag{10-21}$$

where y = distance of each individual pile from toe of abutment-wall footing

n = total number of piles

The moment of inertia I_p of all piles in respect to the neutral axis defined by Eq. (10-21) is then

$$I_p = \sum (c^2) \tag{10-22}$$

where c is the distance of each individual pile from the neutral axis.

Then, with the eccentricity $e = \bar{Y} - \bar{X}$, the vertical load V on any pile is

$$V = \frac{\sum W}{n} + \frac{(\sum W)ec}{I_p} \tag{10-23}$$

The number n_b of the batter piles, as well as their batter, is then determined by trial and error from

$$H = \frac{E_A}{n_b} \quad \text{and} \quad N = \sqrt{H^2 + V^2}$$

where H = horizontal component to be taken up axially by each batter pile

N = axial load on any pile

N should not exceed the maximum permissible pile load N_m. Normally, the batter should not be steeper than 1 horizontal in 3 vertical since otherwise driving costs may be increased and hence the bid prices too.

For further details see Prob. 10-3, which gives the numerical values of pile loads resulting from this conventional analysis of the abutment illustrated by Figs. 10-26 and 10-27. This abutment and some of the piles beneath it were instrumented for research purposes. The results obtained are given in Art. 10-9.

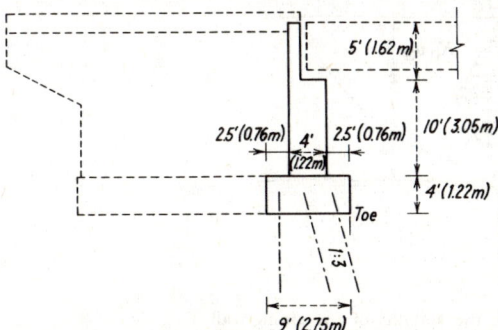

Fig. 10-27. Section *DD* of Fig. 10-26.

10-9. Nonaxial Stresses in Piles Driven through Plastic Clay under Walls and Abutments.

As a first step in a situation similar to that illustrated by Fig. 10-28, one should investigate the safety against a rotational failure of the entire structure, for instance along a cylindrical surface AB (see Art. 7-2). The piles may increase somewhat the overall resistance to rotation by acting as dowels across the slip surface (Art. 7-5) but may at the same time weaken the clay soil by remolding it. The sensitivity of the clay should be taken into account in this connection. In extreme cases the piles may even be sheared off; see, for example, Ref. 367, fig. 5-47, when a quay wall failed completely. It was successfully rebuilt on spread footings after sand drains were driven through the soft clay, permitting its consolidation under a temporary surcharge, with a resulting increase of the shearing strength of the clay.

Even if the factor of safety against rotational failure has a value of 1.5 (usually considered satisfactory for embankments near structures), the deformations of the underlying clay may nevertheless cause additional loads on the piles which restrain the deformations of the clay. These loads are shown on Fig. 10-25B and will now be discussed in connection with the observed phenomenon of abutment movements toward their backfill. These *additional loads* are the vertical drag on the piles, the horizontal thrust H from the front row of batter piles at the toe of abutment footing, a couple formed by a lateral thrust E_{pile} against the piles under the abutment heel, and a decrease of lateral pressure $-E_a$ against the abutment proper.

The drag develops when the piles are driven through a sensitive plastic clay which cannot be compressed but only displaced and remolded by pile

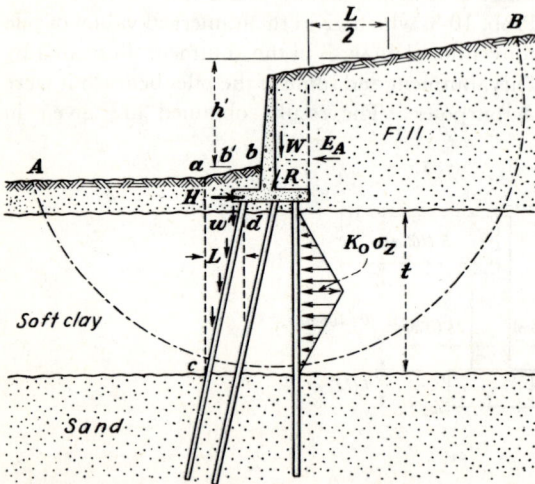

Fig. 10-28. Forces which influence the stability of a retaining-wall pile foundation.

driving.   Such remolded clays are liable to consolidate further under their own weight, and especially so under the added weight of backfills.   The direction of shearing stresses between the soil and the piles is then reversed. Instead of providing some support to the piles, as such soils do during and shortly after pile driving, because of its slow consolidation, the remolded clay gradually develops so-called *negative friction* along the faces of the piles, which transfers to them vertical pressures equal to the weight not only of some of the surrounding clay but also of the fill above the clay.   The latter load component usually is particularly large because of the greater unit weight of the unbuoyed denser fill (see Art. 6-4).

In the case of batter piles, most of the temporary clay support below their lower inner faces will then be lost.   The outer front batter piles (Fig. 10-28) will then carry the weight of the soil prism *abdc* and will act as a beam loaded by the vertical pressures ω' and spanning the horizontal projection L of the pile length *cd*.   This loading will develop a *horizontal thrust H* of the batter piles at point *d* of Fig. 10-28.   This thrust is also indicated in Fig. 10-25B.

The *decrease of lateral pressures* $-E_a$ against the abutment wall is a result of plastic deformations within the underlying consolidating clay layer.   This was demonstrated during model tests conducted by the writer in the 1940s (see Art. 14-3B).   As a result of these plastic deformations in the clay an overlying thin sand layer, saturated by capillarity and thus having some tensile strength, actually pulled away from the wall as consolidation of the clay progressed (see Fig. 14-11).   Similar effects were observed by the writer on full-scale structures (see Figs. 10-18 and 10-19).   The curvature in the fill layers indicates that horizontal tensile stresses T are induced in the fill close to the wall.   At the same time, the vertical piles under the heel of the abutment will be stressed by *lateral pressures of the consolidating clay* E_{pile} which will induce bending stresses in the piles.

In the absence of any relevant measurements, the writer attempted in 1962 a very rough estimation of these lateral pressures E_{pile} (see Ref. 367, pp. 490–494).   The lateral pressure E_{pile} was presented in the form of a triangle which reached a maximum value p_H at the center of the clay layer:

$$p_H = 2bK_{ce}\gamma H' = 0.8b\gamma H' \tag{10-24}$$

where b = width of pile

$K_{ce} = 0.4$ = coefficient of consolidated equilibrium (Art. 10-2)

$\gamma H'$ = weight of difference H' in height of fill at toe and at heel of abutment

In view of the results of field measurements on an abutment at Allamuchy, New Jersey (Ref. 170, 230, and 376), which will be summarized on the following pages, the writer maintained the triangular pressure distribution, as shown in Figs. 10-19 and 10-28, but recommended (Ref. 376) a decrease of p_H to

$$p_H = K_{ce}\sigma_z b \tag{10-25}$$

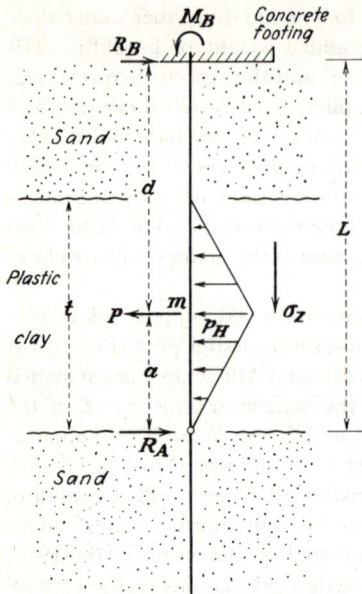

Fig. 10-29.　Procedure for estimating bending stresses in piles under the heel of an abutment.

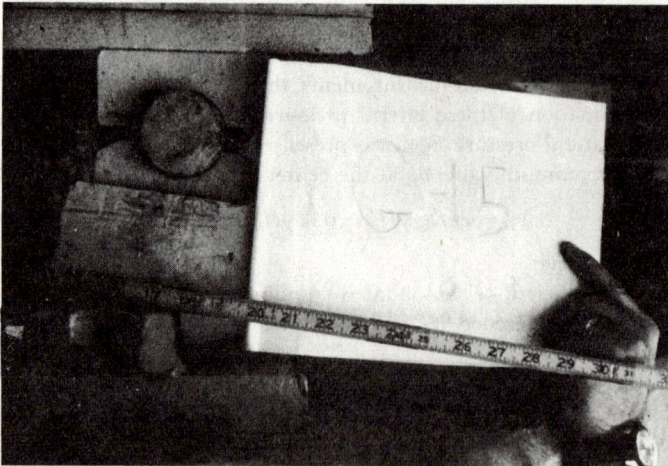

Fig. 10-30.　Tilting of a bridge rocker on Allamuchy research project because of abutment movement toward its backfill.　Scale in inches.　*(From Ref. 170; photo by Tschebotarioff.)*

where σ_z is the increment of vertical stress at the center of the clay layer under the heel of the abutment due to the weight of the backfill.   The bending moments in the pile can then be estimated in accordance with Fig. 10-29 from equations in structural handbooks:

$$M_B = -\frac{Pa(L^2 - a^2)}{2L^2} \tag{10-26}$$

$$M_m = +\left(P\frac{a}{2}\right)\left(2 - \frac{3a}{L} + \frac{a^3}{L^3}\right) \tag{10-27}$$

where
$$P = 0.9\frac{P_H t}{2} \tag{10-28}$$

(see Prob. 10-4).

The resulting bending stresses in piles account for the observed tilting of pile-supported abutments toward their backfill.   It was known for some time (see the first edition, 1948, of Ref. 344) that an abutment on a spread footing would tend to tilt toward its backfill since its base, located at the edge of the area loaded by the backfill, is bound to become inclined toward the central and deeper part of the settlement crater.   The heel of the abutment footing will then settle more than its toe, thus inducing a rotational movement of the abutment and a horizontal displacement at rocker level (Fig. 10-30).

Several unpublicized cases occurred in the 1950s where this kind of movement proved troublesome even on pile-supported bridge abutments. This could only mean that the vertical piles under the heel of the abutment had buckled because of lateral pressures exerted against them by the clay layer loaded by the weight of the embankment, or because of drag along their length, or because of a combination of both factors.

Figure 10-31 illustrates a particularly severe case in a northern state where the abutment moved laterally 10.0 in. (25.4 cm) toward the embankment fill, requiring rebuilding of the bridge rocker sill.

It should be noted here that the 10.0-in. (25.4-cm) horizontal rocker displacement reflected the movement in opposite directions of both abutments, including the one with fixed support.   Thus, if the lateral displacement of each abutment is a, the displacement of the rocker will be $2a$.

Serious trouble of this kind at several bridge abutments of a new Canadian highway was reported in 1968 (Ref. 322).   The piles there were end-bearing on rock.

A research project, sponsored by the New Jersey State Department of Transportation, was initiated in 1966 to check the performance of a conventionally designed abutment.   A site of a proposed new skewed highway-railroad overpass was selected near Allamuchy, where the thickness of the plastic clay layer was smaller and its strength greater than in informally known cases where trouble had developed elsewhere (compare Figs. 10-31

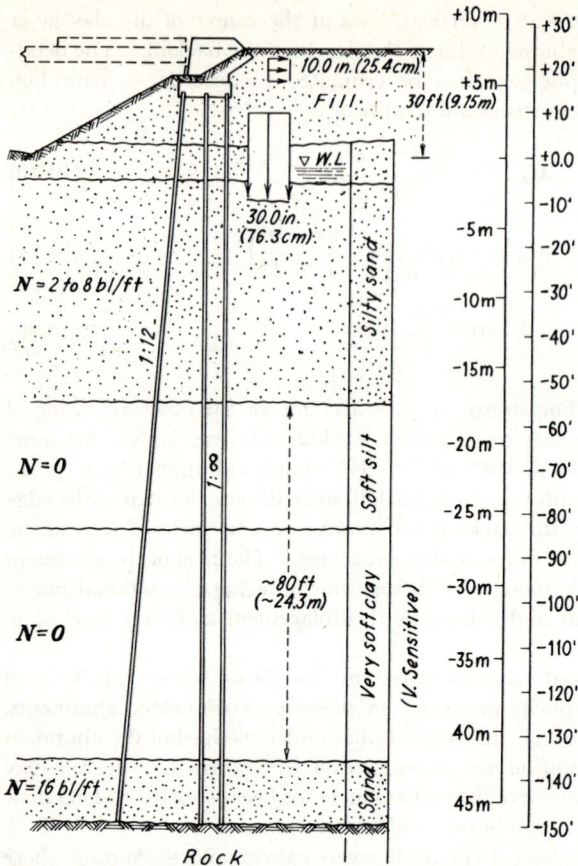

Fig. 10-31. Observed movements of a railroad overpass abutment in a northern state. *(From Ref. 375.)*

and 10-32). Thus some measurable deformations characteristic of the problem could be expected to occur without reaching damaging proportions. This expectation was realized when the construction was completed in 1970.

The following were the most significant findings:

1. The measured lateral earth pressures against the abutment proper decreased from values corresponding to conventional design coefficients of $K = 0.32$ (38 lb/ft^3 = 0.61 g$_f$/cm^3 fluid pressure) to $K = 0.13$ (16 lb/ft^3 = 0.26 g$_f$/cm^3 fluid pressure). Most of the pressure drop occurred after the entire fill was in place.

2. During the same period the measured settlements of the surface of the original ground under the backfill behind the abutment were approximately 5 in. (12.7 cm).

3. The settlements of the abutment wall were negligible, but it moved slightly toward the backfill and tilted toward it because the tips of the wing walls settled 2.0 in. (5.1 cm). During the same period the adjoining original ground surface settled 2.5 in. (6.3 cm).

4. The settlement of the wing-wall tips began after the height of the backfill reached 22 ft (6.7 m), when its weight equaled approximately 3.0 times the original shearing strength $c = 900$ lb/ft^2 (4,400 kg$_f$/m^2) of the underlying clay (see Fig. 10-33).

5. The lateral movement of the rocker support began at the same time, reaching a maximum of about 1.5 in. (3.8 cm) (see Fig. 10-30).

6. Strain measurements at the four flange corners of a few instrumented H-piles right under the concrete footing of the main abutment indicated appreciable bending stresses, especially near the junction with the wing wall, where the piles were oriented at right angles to the face of the wing wall.

7. Slope-indicator measurements on these H-piles also clearly indicated lateral bending thereof in the clay layer.

8. A 6-month winter construction pause permitted some consolidation and corresponding increase of the shearing strength in the varved clay, with the result that the completion of the fill in the spring did not produce any significant further movements.

9. A slight tendency of the entire abutment to rotate in plan around a vertical axis was observed, presumably because of the unsymmetrical pile layout associated with the skewed wing walls.

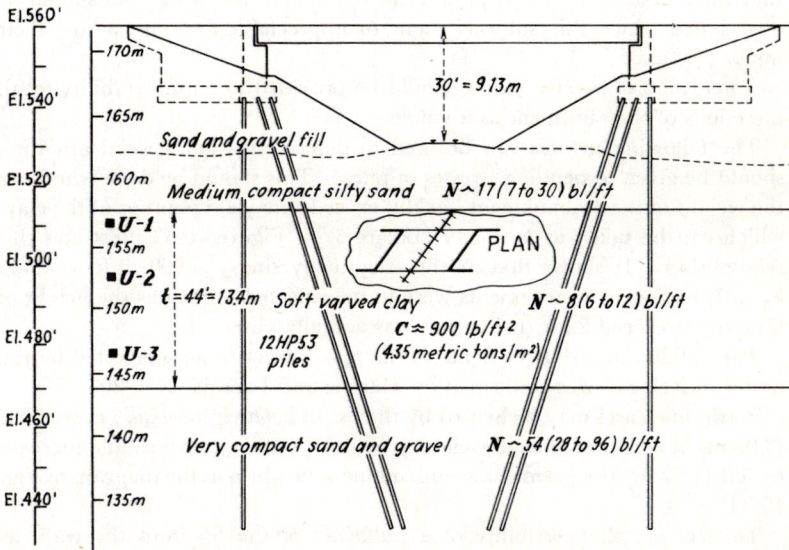

Fig. 10-32.   Soil profile at Allamuchy research project.   (*From Ref. 170.*)

Let us now compare these findings with the results of the conventional analysis according to which this abutment was originally designed (see Figs. 10-26 and 10-27, their discussion in Art. 10-8, and Prob. 10-3).

The heaviest load was found, conventionally, to be axial and equal to 50.0 kips (22.7 metric tons) per pile. The 12HP53 piles have a cross-sectional area of 15.6 in.² (101 cm²), giving a design unit compressive stress of only 3.2 kips/cm² (225 kg$_f$/cm²). The measured extreme fiber corner compressive stress of a batter pile near the junction of abutment and wing walls was found to be 25 kips/in.² (1.760 kg$_f$/cm²), or 8 times greater.

The lightest load according to the conventional analysis was that of pile a under the tip of the wing wall. It was supposed to carry a load of only 25 kips (11.3 metric tons). The permissible design load was 28 tons = 56 kips (25.4 metric tons). Under that load a test pile (Fig. 6-16) settled 0.12 in. (3 mm). Yet the tip of the wing wall over pile a settled 2.0 in. (5.1 cm), almost as much as the 2.5 in. (6.4 cm) of the adjoining original ground surface during the same period of time, indicating that this pile a and the adjoining ones must have buckled.

It is therefore obvious that consideration of bending stresses in piles is a must under similar conditions.

This mean that, *first*, only piles with adequate flexural resistance and a minimum capacity for remolding should be used in such cases. H-piles or pipe piles driven open end and washed out continuously during driving meet this requirement.

Second, the present practice of orienting all H-piles under wing walls so that their main (xx) axis is parallel to the face of the wing wall should be abandoned, since this subjects them to appreciable bending across their minor (yy) axis.

Third, piles of reverse batter should be provided to ensure stability in all directions of the abutment as a whole.

The following *criterion* can be used to determine when special attention should be given to bending stresses in piles. This should be done whenever the weight of the embankment backfill exceeds the yield point p_y of the clay, which can be taken as $p_y = 3.0c$ [Eq. (4-3)]. Figure 10-33 illustrates this relationship. It shows that at the Allamuchy site ($c = 900$ lb/ft² = 4,400 kg$_f$/m²) no unusual movements were to be expected so long as the height of fill did not exceed 22 ft (6.7 m), as was actually observed.

The validity as a danger signal of the $p_y = 3.0c$ criterion suggested by the writer in Ref. 375 was confirmed by Marche and Lacroix (Ref. 209).

Borderline cases may be helped by the use of *lightweight backfill;* every 10 ft (3.05 m) of height of backfill weighing 60 lb/ft³ (0.96 g$_f$/cm³) should increase by 5 ft (1.52 m) the permissible embankment height h in the diagram of Fig. 10-33.

To decrease the possibility of a pullaway of the fill from the wall, as manifested by a decrease of its lateral pressures, a tension-breaking 1-ft-

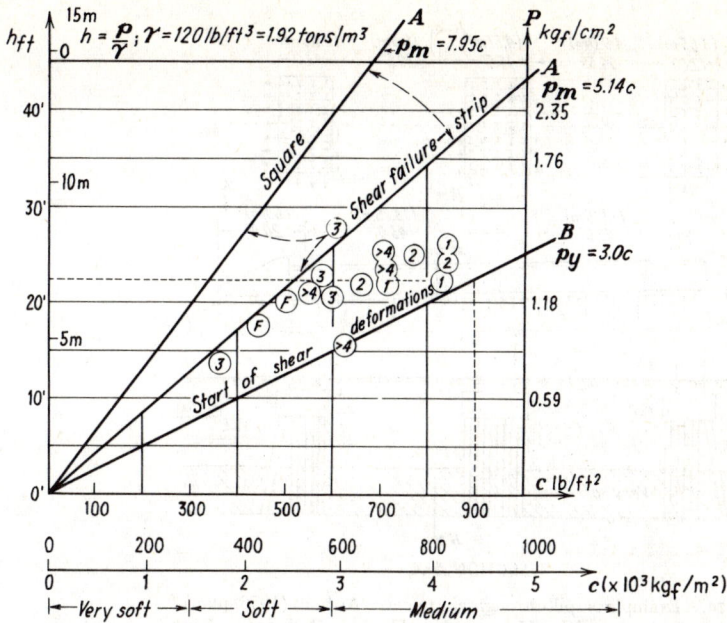

Fig. 10-33.   Limit stresses in underlying clay layer and its strength versus embankment height.   (*From Ref. 375.*)   The circled figures refer to backward tilting (in inches) of 16 bridges analyzed by Marche and Lacroix; F = failure.   (*Ref. 209.*)

thick (30-cm) layer of pea gravel could be placed behind the wall sloping away from its top (Ref. 375, fig. 6).

Preloading the abutment area under a separate preconstruction contract can be used to increase the shearing strength of the clay appreciably (Art. 5-2).

The *spill-through type of abutment* appears to provide the most rational solution for particularly difficult cases involving very weak clay layers.   An abutment of this type (Figs. 10-34 and 10-35) has two main advantages: (1) The total lateral pressure transmitted to the spill-through abutment below the continuous lateral-stiffening upper cross-strut, i.e., below elevation $+20.0$ ft ($+6.1$ m) in Fig. 10-35, and to the piles is cut down to almost half of the total lateral pressure against a continuous type of abutment.   (2) The provision of several more rows of piles as compared with a continuous abutment leads to a relatively greater number of piles being free of bending stresses.

Figure 10-34 shows the writer's as-built design, which was dominated by considerations of drag only (see Art. 6-4).   Its cross section is shown in fig. 5-51, Ref. 367.   The piles used were 14HP73 piles 95 ft (29 m) long.   The average axial design load was 62 tons per pile, of which 37 tons were due to dead and live loads of the bridge and abutment and 25 tons were due to negative-friction loads of the soil.   The depth of penetration into the layer of very fine sand and rock-flour-type silt was determined by load testing the

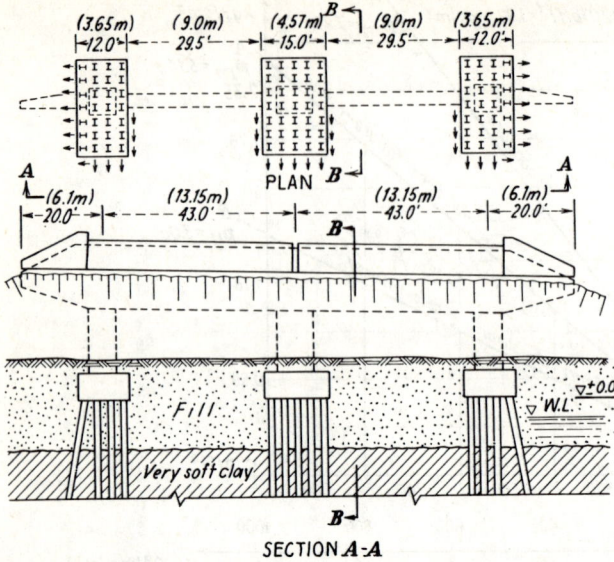

Fig. 10-34. Example of spill-through abutment. As-built (1956) plan of West River Bridge from West Haven to New Haven. Designed by King and Gavaris, New York City, for the Connecticut State Highway Department.

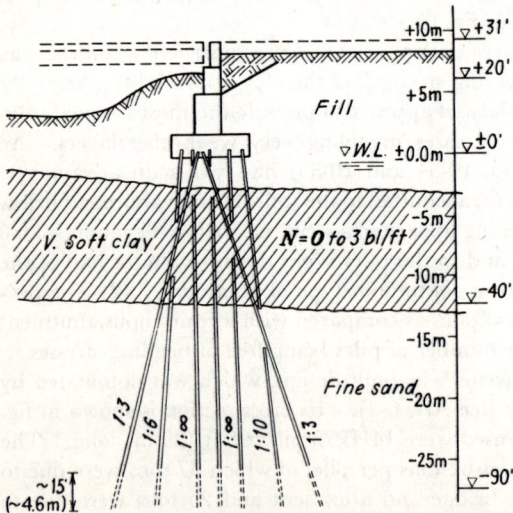

Fig. 10-35. Section *BB* of Fig. 10-34, showing possible minor improvements in the pile layout.

H-piles to twice the design load. To eliminate temporary support from the fill and clay, 30-in.-diameter (76-cm) steel pipe sleeves were driven down to the top of the fine sand and were washed out. The H-piles were driven inside these protecting sleeves and were then load-tested (see Fig. 6-13). No abutment movements whatsoever have been observed since its construction in 1956.

In the light of observations made since then, a somewhat more rational and economic pile layout can be obtained, as tentatively shown on the cross section in Fig. 10-35 (for corresponding plan thereof see Ref. 375, fig. 9). An increase of 15 ft (4.7 m) in pile penetration would permit a reduction in the number of piles, the reverse batter of some of them, and the relocation of batter piles to give them maximum screening by the footing above them from bending by the weight of the fill.

The consequences of ignoring lateral pressures on abutment piles of a bridge are illustrated by Fig. 10-36. The spill-through type of abutment was used, but the number and type of situ-cast reinforced-concrete piles

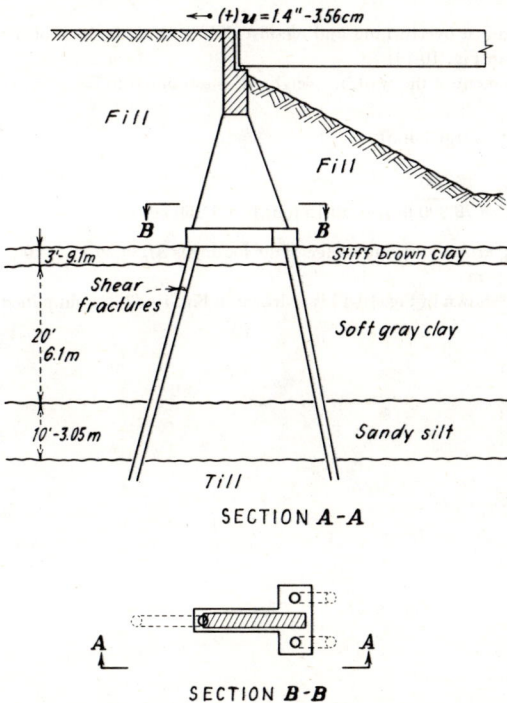

Fig. 10-36. Excavation revealed that situ-cast single reinforced-concrete piles under heels of spill-through bridge-abutment pillars, which had tilted toward its backfill, had been fractured in shear. (*After Ref. 209.*)

employed suggest that only axial loads were fully taken into account.   The resulting movements prompted an excavation which revealed that four piles had been fractured in shear, as shown on the sketch.

Another example of severe damage to piles due to lateral pressures transmitted to them by soft cohesive layers from a fill is given by Leussink and Wenz (Ref. 193).   The well-instrumented piles formed part of a preliminary test section at a proposed iron-ore storage yard.   The measurement results caused the abandonment of the original plan to support the portal-crane rail tracks on piles.   Gradual preloading of the soft cohesive deposit, in conjunction with sand drains (Art. 5-2), was resorted to instead.

A method for estimating lateral pressures against piles transmitted to them by plastic cohesive layers has been given above with reference to Figs. 10-25B, 10-28, and 10-29 and Eqs. (10-25) to (10-28).

Another method has been proposed by De Beer and Wallays at the Madrid Conference (Ref. 83).

REVIEW PROBLEMS

10-1. Determine the safety against overturning and against sliding along its base of the gravity retaining wall illustrated in Fig. 10-14.

Answer.   Prior to the reinforcement of the wall, its weight W is estimated to be

$$\frac{12 + 10}{2} \times 42 \times 140 = 64{,}800 \text{ lb/ft}$$

$$16 \times 5 \times 150 = \overline{13{,}500}$$

$$W = \overline{78{,}300} \text{ lb/ft} = 39.15 \text{ tons/ft} = 1{,}160 \text{ kg}_f/\text{cm}$$

The moment resisting overturning around the outer edge of the footing is $M_r = 39.15 \times 10 = 391.5$ ft-tons/ft $= 3.54 \times 10^5$ m-kg$_f$/m.

The maximum lateral pressure shown in Fig. 10-14 is redrawn in Fig. 10-37 in a simplified

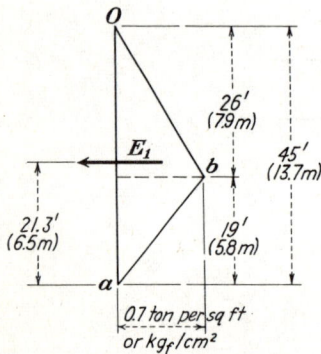

Fig. 10-37.

form to correspond to the conditions which may be assumed to have existed before the reinforcement of the wall.   The total lateral earth pressure E is then

$$E = 0.7 \times \tfrac{1}{2}(26 + 19) = 15.8 \text{ tons/ft} = 472 \text{ kg}_f/\text{cm}$$

The overturning moment is

$$M_o = 15.8 \times 21.3 = 336.0 \text{ ft-tons/ft} = 3.05 \times 10^5 \text{ m-kg}_f/\text{m}$$

and the factor of safety against overturning is

$$\frac{M_r}{M_o} = \frac{391.5}{336.0} = 1.16$$

The shearing stress along the 15-ft-wide (4.57-m) base is

$$\tau = \frac{16.0 \times 1.0}{15.8} = 0.99 \text{ ton/ft}^2 = 0.99 \text{ kg}_f/\text{cm}^2$$

The factor of safety against sliding due to shear failure of the underlying gray London clay with a shear strength $s = 2.2$ tons/ft² is $s/\tau = 2.20/0.99 = 2.22$. Thus it is almost twice as large as the factor of safety against overturning even if the passive resistance at the toe is neglected. Nevertheless, the wall failed by slow outward sliding and had to be reinforced. This shows again that in stiff-fissured clays the strength at the contact surfaces of the fissures governs the behavior of the clay mass, and not the strength s of the intermediate intact lumps of clay.

10-2. To what values of the angle of internal friction ϕ and of the cohesion c may the coefficient of earth pressure $K_y = 0.554$ correspond on the basis of conventional strength theories so long as no pressure redistribution has taken place?

Answer. Any combination of the values ϕ and c given by the line in Fig. 10-38 will satisfy

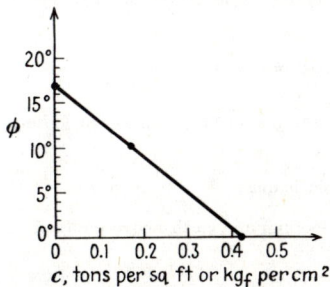

Fig. 10-38.

the value of $K_y = 0.554$, according to Eq. (10-4). Thus, if we set $c = 0$ in that equation, we obtain

$$\tan^2\left(45° - \frac{\phi}{2}\right) = 0.554$$

$$\tan\left(45° - \frac{\phi}{2}\right) = 0.747$$

$$45° - \frac{\phi}{2} = 36.7°$$

$$\phi = 16.6°$$

If we set $\phi = 0°$ in Eq. (10-4), we obtain

$$1.00 - \frac{2c}{1.90} = 0.554$$

$$c = 0.446 \frac{1.90}{2} = 0.424 \text{ ton/ft}^2 = 0.424 \text{ kg}_f/\text{cm}^2$$

By setting $\phi = 10°$ in Eq. (10-4), we obtain

$$\tan^2 40° - \frac{2c}{1.90} \tan 40° = 0.554$$

$$0.708 - \frac{2c}{1.90} 0.842 = 0.554$$

$$c = 0.174 \text{ ton/ft}^2 = 0.174 \text{ kg}_f/\text{cm}^2$$

Other points of the line shown in Fig. 10.38 can be obtained in a similar manner.

10-3. Determine the pile loads under abutment illustrated by Figs. 10-26 and 10-27. Maximum permissible load per pile is $N_m = 28$ tons $= 56$ kips $= 25.4$ metric tons. Batter not to exceed 1 : 3.

Answer. The abutment and wing walls and footings are considered to act as a monolithic unit. First, the following values are determined for use in Eqs. (10-20) to (10-23):

$$E_A = 532 \text{ kips (241 metric tons)}.$$

This is the total horizontal pressure of backfill, assumed to develop fluid pressure of 35 lb/ft^3 = 0.56 g$_f$/cm^3 ($K = 0.30$), including effect of surcharge assumed to equal weight of 2 ft (61 cm) of fill.

$$E_A \times \frac{h}{3} = 3,590 \text{ ft-kips (496 metric ton-meters)}$$

This is the moment of the total earth pressure in respect to the toe of the abutment footing. Wall friction has been neglected.

$$\sum W = 2,774 \text{ kips (1,257 metric tons)}$$

This is the total weight of abutment and wing walls, footing, and earth above the footings plus dead and live load from bridge superstructure.

$$\sum (Wx) = 22,770 \text{ ft-kips (3,090 metric ton-meters)}$$

This is the sum of the moments of the individual weights W in respect to the toe of abutment footing.

$$n = 66 \text{ piles}$$

This is the total number of piles.

$$\sum (y) = 521 \text{ pile-ft (159 pile-m)}$$

This is the sum of all distances y of individual piles from toe of abutment footing.

With these values we obtain:

$$X = \frac{22,770 - 3,590}{2,774} = 6.9 \text{ ft (2.10 m)}$$

This is the distance of resultant in the plane of abutment footing from its toe.

$$\bar{Y} = \tfrac{521}{66} = 7.9 \text{ ft (2.41 m)}$$

This is the distance of neutral axis of entire pile group from toe of abutment footing.

$$\varepsilon = \bar{Y} - \bar{X} = 1.0 \text{ ft (30.5 cm)}$$

This is the eccentricity of resultant R in respect to neutral axis of entire pile group.

The distances c of the individual piles to the neutral axis of their group are then taken off from the plan (Fig. 10-26), and the sum of their squares gives the moment of inertia of the group:

$$I_p = 2.972 \text{ pile-ft}^2 = 279 \text{ pile-m}^2$$

The distance from the neutral axis to the front row of batter piles is $c_1 = 7.9 - 1.5 = 6.4$ ft. This row will receive the largest vertical load of

$$V = \frac{2,774}{66} + \frac{2,774 \times 1.0 \times 6.4}{2,972} = 42.0 + 5.9$$

$$= 47.9 \text{ kips (21.8 metric tons) per pile}$$

Similarly, the second row of batter piles will receive $V = 45.1$ kips (20.5 metric tons) per pile, and the third row of vertical piles at the heel of the abutment will get $V = N = 42.4$ kips (19.3 metric tons) per pile.

The smallest vertical load will be that of the pile furthest away from the neutral axis of the pile group. That will be pile a at the tip of one of the wing walls (Fig. 10-26), for which $c_a = c_2 = 18.3$ ft (5.58 m) and

$$V_a = N_a = \frac{2,774}{66} - \frac{2,774 \times 1.0 \times 18.3}{2,972} = 42.0 - 17.0$$

$$= 25 \text{ kips} = 12.5 \text{ tons} = 11.35 \text{ metric tons}$$

A horizontal load of 0.5 kips (454 kg_f) is then assigned to each pile, i.e., a total of 33 kips (15 metric tons) for all 66 piles. The remaining $532 - 33 = 499$ kips (227 metric tons) of the total lateral earth pressure are then assigned to the 34 batter piles, giving $\frac{499}{34} = 14.7$ kips (6.7 metric tons) per pile. For the front row a batter of 1 in $47.9/14.7 = 3.25$ will be needed. A 1:3 batter will be used for all batter piles.

The resulting axial load in the piles of the front row will be $N = \sqrt{14.7^2 + 47.9^2} = 50.0$ kips = 25 tons (22.7 metric tons) per pile. This should be the largest axial load of any pile under the abutment according to conventional procedures. Since it is smaller than the permissible design load of $N_m = 56$ kips = 28 tons (25.4 metric tons), the pile layout is satisfactory.

For the limitations of this and of other conventional methods, see Art. 10-9.

10-4. Strain-meter measurements on a vertical H-pile under the heel of abutment wall (Fig. 10-27) indicated a moment of fixation $M_B = -57.5$ kip-ft (7.96 metric ton-meters). Estimate the probable corresponding magnitude of lateral earth pressure against pile at center of clay layer.

Answer. From Figs. 10-29 and 10-32 we find $t = 44$ ft (13.45 m); $a = 22$ ft (6.72 m); $d = 48$ ft (14.7 m); $L = 70$ ft (21.4 m). Inserting these values in Eq. (10-26) and solving for P, we find $P = 5.82$ kips and from Eq. (10-28) $p_H = 0.300$ kip/ft$^2 = 1,465$ kg_f/m^2.

A separate stress-distribution analysis (fig. 29, Ref. 170) using the Newmark chart (Art. 4-3) shows that 26 ft (8.55 m) of fill above original ground level, weighing 3.12 kips/ft^2 (15,250 kg_f/m^2), will produce a vertical stress $\sigma_z = 1.25$ kips/ft$^2 = 6,120$ kg_f/m^2 at the center of the clay layer opposite the pile where the above moment M_B was recorded. The width of that 12HP53 pile was $b = 1$ ft (30.5 cm). From Eq. (10-25) we then obtain $K_{ce} = K_0 = 0.300/1.25 = 0.24$.

10-5. Using the same procedure as in Prob. 10-4, estimate the probable bending stresses in pile *a* under the tip of the wing wall (see Fig. 10-26).

Answer. From the contour lines of equal stress in fig. 29 of Ref. 170, at the center of clay layer we find that at the location of pile *a*: $\sigma_z = 1.80$ kips/ft² (8,880 kg$_f$/m²). Using the $K_{ce} = 0.24$ value obtained in the preceding problem, we get $p_H/b' = 1.8 \times 0.24 = 0.432$ kip/ft² (2,110 kg$_f$/m²). The $b = 12$-in.-wide (30.5-cm) piles under the skewed wing walls project a width $b' = 1.35b$ on a plane parallel to the main abutment wall. The lateral pressure $p_H = 0.432 \times 1.35 = 0.582$ kip/ft (0.865 metric ton/m) on that width will be distributed to the major and minor principal axes of the pile in proportion to their moments of inertia $I_x = 394$ in.⁴ (16,450 cm⁴) and $I_y = 127$ in.⁴ (5,290 cm⁴). The xx axis will get $394/(394 + 127) = 0.755$ and the yy axis $127/(394 + 127) = 0.245$ of the load or bending moment.

The total concentrated load on the pile is obtained from Eq. (10-28). With $t = 44$ ft (13.5 m), we get $P = 11.55$ kips $= 5.13$ metric tons, and from Eq. (10-32)

$$M_m = +138 \text{ ft-kips} = 1,670 \text{ in.-kips} = 19.25 \text{ metric ton-meters}$$

The bending stress in respect to the xx and yy axes will be

$$f_z = \frac{0.755 \times 1,670 \times 6}{394} = 19.0 \text{ kips/in.}^2 = 1,333 \text{ kg}_f/\text{cm}^2$$

$$f_y = \frac{0.245 \times 1,690 \times 6}{127} = 19.3 \text{ kips/in.}^2 = 1,357 \text{ kg}_f/\text{cm}^2$$

Corner bending stress $\qquad = \overline{38.3}$ kips/in.² $= \overline{2{,}690}$ kg$_f$/cm²
Axial compressive stress (from
   design in Art. 10-9) $= 25.0/15.6 = \underline{1.6}$ kips/in.² $= \underline{115}$ kg$_f$/cm²
Total corner compressive stress $= \overline{39.9}$ kips/in.² $= \overline{2{,}805}$ kg$_f$/cm²

This value does not include any allowance for possible drag but is quite sufficient to have initiated by itself the observed buckling of pile *a* (see Art. 10-9), especially if we consider that the piles under the tips of the wing walls, such as pile *a*, are more exposed to possible lateral pressure and drag concentrations than the instrumented piles from which the $K = 0.24$ value of Prob. 10-4 was obtained.

RECOMMENDED FOR FURTHER STUDY

Morgenstern, N. R., and Z. Eisenstein: Methods of Estimating Lateral Loads and Deformations, in Ref. 15, pp. 51–102 (to be reprinted in *ASCE Proceedings*).

CHAPTER 11

BRACED AND ANCHORED CUTS

11-1. Nonhydrostatic Distribution of Lateral Earth Pressures against Sheeting of Horizontally Braced Cuts. The construction of subways in New York City at the turn of the century was carried out in deep braced cuts in sandy, noncohesive soils. Experience soon indicated that Coulomb's triangular distribution of lateral earth pressures (Fig. 10-2B) did not correspond to reality under such conditions. The upper braces gave evidence of being overstressed even when they were designed for lateral-pressure values twice as large as the ones to be expected from a triangular pressure distribution.

In the 1930s Taylor (Ref. 331) extended Terzaghi's large-scale model tests (Ref. 335), which had shown that Coulomb's pressure distribution was essentially correct for the case of a wall rotating around its bottom or being displaced horizontally. Using small two-dimensional models (backfill of steel cylindrical rods), Taylor found that the cases of rotation around the toe of a wall and of its parallel displacement gave results essentially similar to the earlier data obtained by Terzaghi. However, the case of rotation of a wall around its top indicated not only a parabolic distribution of lateral pressures but also an appreciable increase of the total pressure as compared with the Coulomb theory.

Later measurements showed that the lateral movements of sheeting during the excavation of a braced cut closely corresponded to the conditions of rotation of a wall around its top. Thus the results of model tests and full-scale field experiments and observations were in full agreement.

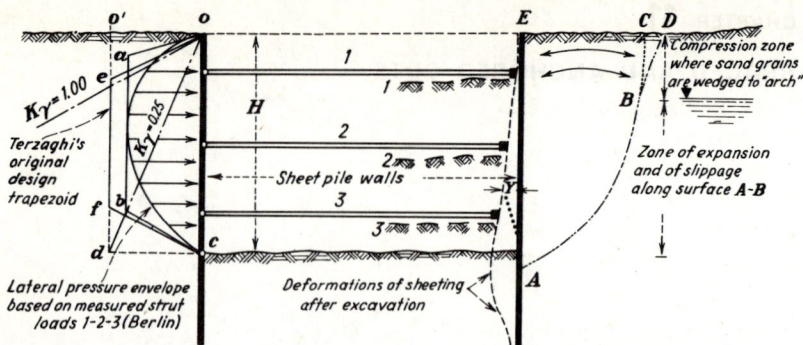

Fig. 11-1. Deformations of sheeting and soil and the resulting pressure distribution in braced cuts in sand.

Figures 11-1 and 11-2 illustrate the mechanical processes involved.   The construction procedure is as follows.   After both sheet-pile walls are driven, the soil between them is excavated to level 1 and the first brace 1 is installed and wedged against the wales.   This precludes any further deflection of sheeting at that level except as a result of axial compressive strains in strut 1 due to further increases of the lateral load.   As the excavation is continued to level 2, the sheeting will deflect at and below that level, as shown by dotted lines on the right-hand side of Fig. 11-1.   The installation of strut 2 will prevent further movements there, but the process will be repeated below it as the excavation proceeds to lower levels.   As a result, the final shape of the deflection curve y will be as shown by broken lines on an exaggerated scale at the right-hand side of Fig. 11-1.   Essentially, these deflections represent a rotation of the sheet-pile wall around its top strut, i.e., the reverse of a gravity-wall rotation around its base, for which the Coulomb design procedure was developed and has been found valid (Art. 10-2).   For a braced cut the shearing resistance of the soil can no longer be mobilized to the same extent within the entire mass of the sliding wedge.

This is illustrated by Fig. 11-2.   The photo, taken through a glass sidewall of a testing tank, shows the movement of sand particles behind a wall rotating around point O.   It was used by J. Brinch Hansen in connection with an analysis based on sliding along a curved surface of failure ABC.   A close look at Fig. 11-2, however, will show that, in addition to the major rotational movement along the nearly circular surface ABC, there is also a downward movement of sand grains between BC and BD.   Since the distance ED is larger than OB, this means that the sand grains at and above the level OB are wedging themselves in between each other.   In the process of doing so they are bound to produce what the writer has termed a condition of *true arching* (see Ref. 357).   Part of the weight of the sand above the level OB is then carried by an arch of hard sand grains as the sand below that level expands due to the outward movement of the sheet piling. Compared with the Coulomb triangular pressure distribution, this should lead to an increase of lateral pressures in the zone of the upper strut and to a decrease of pressures in the zone of the lower struts.

The term *arching* has been frequently and somewhat loosely used in the past to explain any observed departure from the triangular Coulomb earth-pressure distribution. Sometimes arching has been equated with bin action in silos (see Art. 10-6). This is not entirely correct. The mechanical processes involved are similar but not identical. In both cases there is a reduction of vertical pressures in the lower layers because of the transfer of

Fig. 11-2. Movements of sand behind model wall rotating around point *O*. (*After J. Brinch Hansen, Ref. 122.*)

part of the weight of the upper layers to the vertical bin walls due to fill friction along these walls.   However, in a bin this happens in connection with lateral pressures, which cannot exceed active or neutral values, so that the relevant coefficient of lateral pressure $K \leq 0.5$ or ≤ 0.6 at the most.   In the case of true arching this coefficient should be greater than unity, that is, $K \geq 1.00$, since it would then reflect the progressive wedging and jamming of individual sand grains, i.e., a process which is the reverse of sliding.

Thus, for every arch there is also a transfer of pressures by shear, but not every case of transfer of pressures by shear produces a state of true arching.

In this connection the writer has analyzed (Ref. 357, fig. 13) a case reported in 1945 by Pennoyer involving the washing out of the lower part of a sand-gravel fill from inside three diaphragm-type (see Fig. 12-6B) cofferdam cells, each cell having in plan a horizontal section 35 by 27 ft (11.7 by 8.2 m). The interlocks of the sheet piling were ruptured in several places where boulders were encountered.   Water coming through the cofferdam had washed out the original soil through the gaps in the piling up to the top of the breaks, some 12 ft (3.7 m) above the rock, leaving several cells completely empty to about that elevation.   Above it, the sand and gravel formed a perfectly stable dome.   The writer's analysis in Ref. 357 showed that this could have happened only if the minimum ratio of horizontal to vertical pressure at the walls was $K \geq 1.13$ and that in all probability it was appreciably higher.   Thus, this seems to be a case of true arching.

A stable condition of true arching can develop only if the walls forming an abutment for the arch are unyielding and if the individual soil grains are hard and nondeformable; thus it cannot develop in plastic clays.

Another condition is that the natural sand deposit should not be too loose; otherwise, especially if the sand is submerged and thus lacks the apparent cohesion of a moist sand, the downward movement and wedging of the sand grains will at first result only in densifying the sand before a stable arch can develop and exert an increased lateral thrust (see the discussion of Fig. 11-8 in Art. 11-3C).

Another condition for the stability of true arching is that the movements must be small enough to prevent a condition of flow from developing (see Ref. 357 and Fig. 11-3, where strut loads decreased after a slide into excavation of silt near its bottom).

A factor which is usually ignored is the *effect of steel-sheeting continuity*, which can in part account for an increase of loads in the top strut, compared with values obtained from a triangular pressure distribution.   For plastic clays it can even account for the full difference, as will be outlined in the next article.

11-2. Early Field Measurements and Observations in Horizontal Braced Cuts.   The results of strut-load measurements performed during open-cut subway construction in deep sand deposits at Berlin were reported by Spilker in 1937 (Ref. 321).   Groundwater lowering was used.   The strut loads varied considerably at the three stations where measurements were made.

Analyzing these results in 1941, Terzaghi (Ref. 338) suggested ignoring the vertical continuity of the sheeting and soldier beams and computing the lateral pressure distribution from the measured strut loads by assuming hinges in the vertical sheeting opposite each strut. The envelope of pressures obtained in this manner from strut loads at all three stations had a parabolic shape (as indicated on the left-hand side of Fig. 11-1), and Terzaghi proposed the use of a pressure trapezoid *oefc* for design purposes.

There was at first some reluctance to accept these findings, it being suggested that erratic hand wedging of struts might account for the observed variations in the strut loads. This could not be disproved by the Berlin measurements, which were made only after all struts were in place. However, this contention was refuted soon after by a series of measurements which were performed—also in sand—in a test section for a proposed subway at Munich (Ref. 171). They were repeated after each row of struts was installed and indicated that pressures in the upper and middle struts increased as the excavation progressed.[†]

At about the same time, similar measurements were performed in New York on the Sixth Avenue Subway and were reported by Prentis and White (Ref. 253), as shown in Fig. 11-3, for a 120-ft-long (37-m) cut in sand. Here again higher lateral pressures, which exceeded values corresponding to $K_y = 1.00$, were measured against the upper half of the bracing of the excavation, thus indicating that a redistribution of pressures was the most important of the factors producing the observed shape of the pressure-distribution curve.

The trapezoidal pressure line *oabc* shown in Fig. 11-3 represents the diagram suggested by Tschebotarioff (see 1st ed., Art. 10-18) for the design of the bracing of excavations in sand, as a modification of Terzaghi's original proposals on the matter.

One of the first known series of extensive measurements of lateral pressures against the timbering of open cuts through plastic clay was performed during the construction of the Chicago subways and reported by Peck (Ref. 245). Figure 11-4 gives a typical result of these measurements (for contract S-1A). Of particular interest is the observation according to which an appreciable inward displacement of the MZ38 sheet piling (Art. 11-6) took place Jan. 3, 1941, when the depth of excavation had reached only 12 ft (3.67 m). The ground next to the sheet piling had been excavated down to a depth of 8 ft (2.45 m) and had not yet been backfilled; thus the lateral displacement of the sheet piling was induced by deep-seated movements of the clay toward the excavation, as evidenced by cracks in the old freight tunnel far beneath it. The point is of importance in connection with all excavation problems (Art. 11-4).

[†] In the 1950s the writer had the opportunity of measuring the stress induced in a WF steel strut of about 20 in.² (129 cm²) cross section by steel wedges driven in by a heavy sledgehammer. It proved impossible to induce in this manner a compressive stress in excess of about 1 kip/in.² (70 kg$_f$/cm²), or 20 kips (9,100 kg$_f$) of total compressive force.

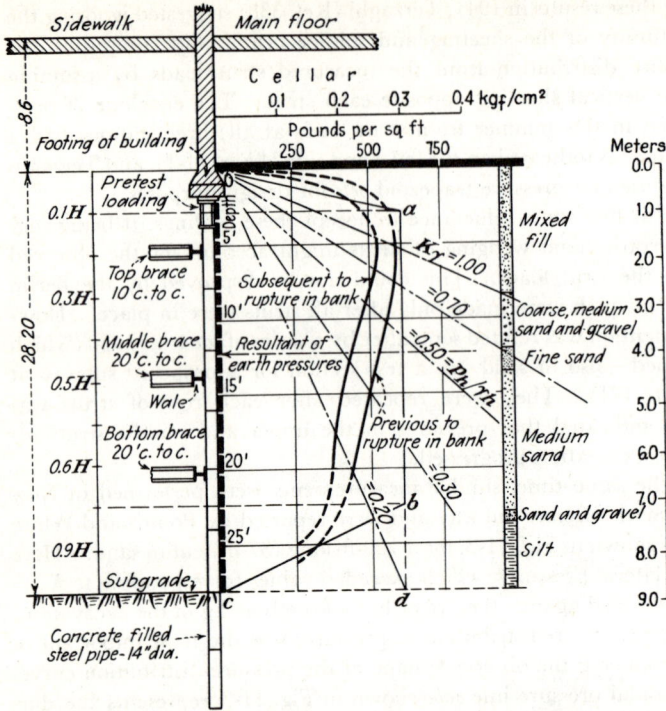

Fig. 11-3. Hydraulically measured lateral earth pressures against braces of subway excavation at Sixth Avenue and 16th Street, New York City. (*After Prentis and White, Ref. 253; the lines of the hydrostatic pressure ratio K have been super-imposed on the original drawing.*)

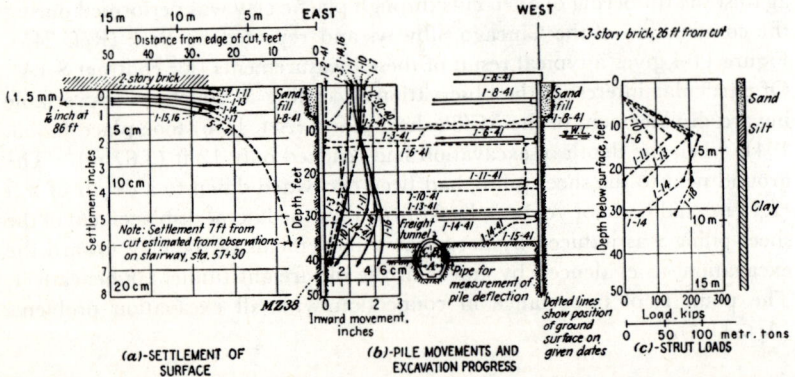

Fig. 11-4. Example of the results obtained by lateral-earth-pressure measurements on the bracing of open cuts through Chicago clay during subway construction (contract S-1A). (*After Peck, Ref. 245.*)

The clay at Chicago is of glacial origin and was found to range from a soft consistency with an unconfined compressive strength of $q_u = 0.3$ ton/ft², a natural water content of $w_n = 50$ percent, a liquid limit $w_L = 55$ percent, and a plasticity index $I_p = 35$ percent, to a stiff consistency with $q_u = 0.7$ ton/ft², $w_n = 22$ percent, $w_L = 32$ percent, and $I_p = 12$ percent (Ref. 245). A layer of sand overlay the clay in most places.

Peck attempted to relate the measured lateral pressures to the shearing strength of the clay at failure, as determined from unconfined compressive-strength tests. Terzaghi (Ref. 340) made the assumptions on which that analysis was based. A correction factor (which changed q_u to q_a) was introduced to take care of the presence of sand layers above the clay. A trapezoidal pressure diagram, similar to the one proposed earlier by Terzaghi and shown in Fig. 11-1 for sands, was suggested for design purposes on the basis of the field measurements, good agreement with which was claimed (Ref. 245).

The highest possible value of lateral pressures, according to that diagram, was stated to be

$$p_h = \gamma H K_a \tag{11-1}$$

where H is the total depth of the cut and

$$K_a = 1 - \frac{2q_a}{\gamma H} \tag{11-2}$$

It is also noted that the value of K_a, as expressed by the Terzaghi-Peck equation (11-2), is based on the total pressure E_A; that is, it can be obtained from Eq. (10-14) by setting the angle of internal friction $\phi = 0$ and dividing the remaining values by the total fluid pressure $\gamma H^2/2$. A different expression, and a smaller value of K, as compared with those based on unit pressures, is obtained thereby [see Eq. (10-8)]. The difference is caused by the fact that Eq. (10-14) for the total pressure E_A assumes that tension between the piling and the clay is fully active in the upper soil layers. On the other hand, Eq. (10-8), which is based on unit pressures, will give positive values of K only below the depth of the tensile zone (Fig. 10-4). The use of the total Rankine-Résal pressures for the computation of the K values, as introduced by Terzaghi and Peck and expressed by Eq. (11-2), represents a departure from many previous concepts of the matter, for instance, from those of Cain (see 1st ed., Art. 10-4). Cain's views, however, appear to be more rational, since the bond between soil and wall usually cannot resist tension, and it seems logical to ignore it, as he suggested.

All these unexplained contradictions made Tschebotarioff surmise (Ref. 353) that the agreement, reported by Peck (Ref. 245), between the lateral pressures as measured in the Chicago subway cuts and as computed from

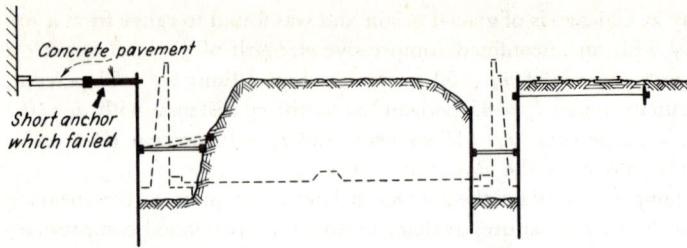

Fig. 11-5. Profile of construction job to which Fig. 11-6 refers.

Eq. (11-2) might have definite limitations.   An analysis of the data given by Peck in his paper (Ref. 245) was thereupon performed by Brown (Ref. 40) and confirmed this point of view.   Figure 10-26 in the first edition summarizes Brown's analysis.   When the depth of excavation equaled $H = 15.3$ ft (4.66 m), the Terzaghi-Peck equation (11-2) gave a value of $K_a = 0$. Nevertheless, a definite pressure, approximately equal to $K_y = 0.10$, was recorded on the single upper strut which had been placed by that time.   The same discrepancy was found when the depth of excavation reached $H = 27.1$ ft (8.26 m).   The Terzaghi-Peck equation (11-2) still gave a value of $K_a = 0$, whereas all three struts recorded definite pressures.   The pressures against the upper strut, however, had increased and corresponded to a value of $K_y = 0.30$.   This one strut was located within the depth of the sand layer. The other two struts were located within the depth of the underlying plastic clay layer, and the pressures against them corresponded to a value of $K_y = 0.20$.

It was only when the excavation reached depths of $H = 40.6$ ft (12.4 m) and $H = 44.0$ ft (13.5 m), the latter value being the greatest on that particular job, that approximate agreement was obtained between values based on Eq. (11-2) and the actually measured pressures.   Down to approximately one-half of the depth H the lateral pressures approximately followed the line $K_y = 0.45$; farther on they decreased.

In 1969 (Ref. 249, p. 276) Peck acknowledged the validity of this critique and modified his design recommendations as outlined in Art. 11-3.

In 1939 and 1940 an important series of measurements was performed in Holland in up to 46-ft-deep (14.1-m) *braced cuts on the approaches to the Maas River Tunnel at Rotterdam* in soft clay† and peat.   The design was based on *neutral earth pressures* (Art. 10-1), the intergranular lateral pressures being taken as one-half the corresponding vertical pressures (the latter not being considered as decreased by the removal of part of the original overburden) to which was added the full water pressure.   A graphical comparison of the design pressure curves with the observed and the Terzaghi-Peck values is given in the first edition by Figs. 10-28 and 10-29.   The design and observed values were in reasonable agreement.   The same trend was evident as in

† Approximate equivalent value $q_u = 0.5$ ton/ft^2 = 0.5 kg$_f$/cm^2.

the Chicago measurement; i.e., Eq. (11-2) gave unsafe values of lateral pressures for depths of excavation smaller than 34 ft (10.4 m).

A very important *field study at Shellhaven, England*, was reported by Skempton and Ward in 1952 (Ref. 302). The steel sheeting of a 32-ft-deep (9.8-m) cut in sensitive soft clay ($c = 300$ to 400 lb/ft$^2 = 1,470$ to $1,960$ kg$_f$/m^2) was braced at three levels. The loads measured in the struts and in the wales were found to be of the same order of magnitude as resulted from the use of the original Terzaghi-Peck diagram, Fig. 11-7(I).

However, it was shown that *consideration of the continuity of the sheet piling and of its deflections* also gave good agreement with the measured results on the basis of an essentially triangular pressure-loading diagram obtained from

$$p_h = \gamma z - \gamma_w h - 2c \sqrt{\frac{1 + c_w}{c}} + \gamma_w h \qquad (11\text{-}3)$$

where p_h = component of active earth pressure normal to sheet piling
  γ = full density of soil
  γ_w = density of water
  h = head of groundwater above point considered
  c = shear strength of clay
  c_w = wall adhesion
  z = depth below ground surface of point considered

The slope of the resulting triangular pressure diagram (see fig. 10, Ref. 302) appears to closely approach the one for $K = 0.5$.

However, unless continuity is considered, a triangular design pressure diagram can be definitely dangerous, even for comparatively small depths of excavation, as illustrated by Figs. 11-5 and 11-6.

Fig. 11-6. Collapse of sheet-pile wall due to failure of short anchors which were rigidly tied into a concrete roadway but designed for a triangular pressure distribution. (*Photo by Tschebotarioff.*)

An underpass had to be built in a populated area for a new throughway. The groundwater was below the excavation level. The soil above that level consisted of fill and of granular material. First, steel sheeting was driven to permit the excavation for one of the gravity retaining walls, as shown on the right-hand side of Fig. 11-5. The upper brace was replaced by a long anchor tied to a deadman. Although trains occasionally passed over it, the resulting vibrations caused none of the trouble which was feared and the wall was satisfactorily completed. The lower brace was easily removed in the process of construction. This encouraged the contractor to omit one row of steel sheeting for the opposite wall and brace the lower strut against a timber wale placed against the face of the bank, the space between it and the natural soil being merely filled with gravel. As a result, when the overall failure started at the short upper anchor, the wale of the lower strut slipped up the embankment slope, as shown by dotted lines in Fig. 11-5. But this was only a contributing factor to the overloading of the short stiffly un-yielding anchors, the deadmen of which were embedded in the concrete pavement but were designed for a triangular pressure distribution against the sheeting. A check by a trapezoidal pressure distribution (Fig. 11-1) showed that the anchors were stressed up to their yield point. The failure shown in Fig. 11-6 resulted.

11-3. The Design of Horizontal Bracing in Cuts. *(A). Design Loading for Cuts in Sand.* The dimensions of the original (1941, Ref. 338) Terzaghi design trapezoid shown in Fig. 11-1 were as follows: the distance $O'e = 0.2H$; $ef = 0.8H$; $fd = 0.2H$; $cd = 0.7\gamma HK_A$.

In 1948 (see the first edition of Ref. 344) Terzaghi recommended increasing the dimension cd to

$$cd = 0.8 \cos \delta \, \gamma HK_A$$

where δ is the angle of wall friction.

Analyzing the results of measurements on the Sixth Avenue subway in New York City, the writer (1st ed., Fig. 10-22) suggested decreasing the distance $O'e$ to $0.1H$ and setting the distance $cd = 0.20\gamma H$, as shown by the trapezoid *oabc* in Figs. 11-1 and 11-3.

In 1967 (Ref. 344) and in 1969 (Ref. 249) Peck recommended using $cd = 0.65\gamma HK_A$ and a rectangular lateral-pressure diagram $OO'dc$ (see Fig. 11-1) instead of a trapezoid. Since the coefficient of active pressure K_A is depen-dent on the angle of internal friction ϕ, this recommendation is equivalent to suggesting the multiplication of the unbuoyed unit vertical pressure γH of the soil behind the wall at the level of the excavation by a variable coeffi-cient $K = 0.65K_A$, which also becomes dependent on the value of ϕ. With reference to Table 10-2, we find that this coefficient K will vary as shown in Table 11-1.

The angle of internal friction of sands increases with the density of the deposit (Art. 3-4A). It therefore follows from Table 11-1 that Peck's 1969 rectangular design diagram for sands should give smaller lateral pressures for

TABLE 11-1.

ϕ	K_A	$K = 0.65K_A$
40°	0.22	0.143
35°	0.27	0.176
30°	0.33	0.218
25°	0.41	0.267

dense sands. This certainly cannot be true for the upper strut, where the arching phenomena and the resulting increase of lateral pressures are likely to be greatest for originally dense sands (see Art. 11-1 and the discussion which follows under C).

The variations in the dimensions of the design trapezoids outlined above are comparatively minor and reflect attempts to make them fit the results of different sets of field measurements. These results, which are outlined in Art. 11-2, as well as later ones, including the Cologne subway measurements reported in 1968 by Briske and Pirlet (Ref. 39), disclosed the same general trends.

Field determinations of the angle of internal friction ϕ for sand deposits are expensive and time-consuming and cannot be done with any degree of representative reliability. For that reason they are seldom performed. It therefore seems at least impractical to base essentially empirical designs for braced cuts on the theoretical values of the coefficient of active lateral earth pressures K_A, the relevance of which to the mechanical processes involved is questionable. Its continued use seems to be dictated mainly by habit and tradition.

At the present stage of our knowledge it therefore seems sufficient to define a design trapezoid, or rectangle, by setting the value of its lateral pressure $cd = K_\gamma \gamma H = 0.25 \gamma H$, as shown in Fig. 11-1. Here γ is the unbuoyed unit weight of the saturated soil.

The use of the hydrostatic pressure ratio K_γ facilitates the rapid comparison of design and observed values, as shown by the lines for varying values of K_γ drawn in Figs. 11-3, 10-13, 10-14, and others.

For further points of importance in the design of bracing in sands see sections C and D of this article.

(B). Design Loading for Cuts in Clay. The development of the original Terzaghi-Peck loading diagram shown by Fig. 11-7(I) has been discussed in Art. 11-2 with reference to the first Chicago measurements. Subsequent measurements elsewhere, especially in Oslo, Norway, and in Mexico City, induced Peck (Ref. 249) to recommend in 1969 the design diagram shown by Fig. 11-7(II). The lateral pressure is now given by $\gamma H - m4c_u$, where the newly introduced coefficient m can vary between 1.0 and 0.4 and is intended to reflect the decrease of the shearing strength s_u of the clay beside and beneath the cut due to deep-seated shearing deformations.

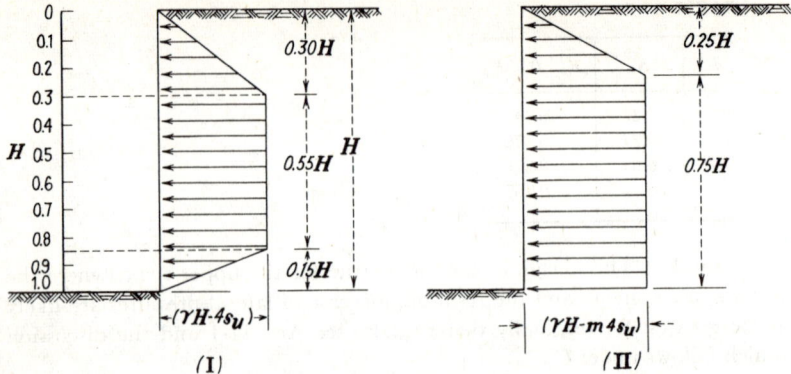

Fig. 11-7. The Terzaghi-Peck lateral-earth-pressure diagram for the design of braced open cuts in plastic clay, based on the ultimate strength of the clay.   [(I), *Ref. 245;* (II), *Ref. 344.*]

The value of $m = 1.0$ was found to fit most cuts observed so far and $m = 0.4$ the Oslo and Mexico City cuts.   The clays of both these cities have rather unusual properties.   In Oslo the undisturbed shearing strength of the clay is quite low, varying from 200 to 500 lb/ft² (980 to 2,450 kg$_f$/m²), with a sensitivity of about 4 and a natural water content close to the liquid limit $w_L = 40$ percent (Refs. 138 and 94).   In Mexico City the average undisturbed shearing strength of the upper nonoxidized clay layers is about 730 lb/ft² (3,570 kg$_f$/m²), but its natural water content of $w_n = 280$ percent is close to its liquid limit $w_L = 289$ percent (Ref. 133, p. 114).   It is therefore not surprising that deep-seated movements of the clay beneath the bottom of a cut, of the type leading to failures analyzed in Art. 11-4, can appreciably remold and weaken such materials even if no overall shear failure occurs.

The neutral earth-pressure-ratio method, consisting in the use of a triangular pressure diagram for $K_0 = K_{ce} = 0.5$, with or without consideration of a sheet pile or soldier-beam continuity, cannot be used in such cases since the "consolidated equilibrium" of the clay is destroyed by remolding, with a resulting increase in the K value.

As a preliminary danger signal the criterion suggested by Peck (Ref. 249) can be used, namely, the value of the *stability number* $N = H/s_u$.   When this value exceeds $N = 6$, caution is indicated, especially if the clay is sensitive and the value of s_u refers to the strength of the clay for some distance beneath the bottom of the cut.   For cuts less than 20 ft (6.1 m) deep with $N = 3$ or 4, no special investigations are required.

Peck correctly points out (Ref. 249) that these criteria are only broad generalizations.   The practical conclusion is that on all important new jobs, especially in localities where no similar previous experience is available, the first construction sections should be designed as carefully instrumented trial test sections on the basis of unfavorable assumptions.   Specifications should be flexible, to permit changes of the original design for subsequent job sections on the strength of the measurement results.

The *neutral-earth-pressure method of design* is based on a different theoretical concept than the Terzaghi-Peck trapezoids, which were developed from the cohesive failure strength of soils (see 1st ed., Art. 16-5). The state of *consolidated equilibrium* of a plastic clay is considered to represent a condition of incipient failure within a deposit of plastic clay, which can therefore be related to the coefficient K_n of neutral lateral earth pressure, also termed the coefficient K_0 of lateral pressure at rest.

The lateral-earth-pressure diagrams of Fig. 11-7a reflect this concept. Swatek, Asrow, and Seitz successfully used this diagram for the design of the bracing of a large 70-ft-deep (21.3-m) excavation in Chicago clay (Ref. 327). This was a record depth for Chicago. The strut loads were determined under consideration of strut overloads, step by step at each strut level for each excavation increment. The design strut-load envelope determined in this manner was found to agree very closely with the envelope of strut loads actually measured in four panels. On the other hand, the Terzaghi-Peck trapezoidal strut-load envelope gave at least 65 percent higher strut loads.

This had been anticipated (see discussion of Fig. 10-26 in 1st ed., Art. 10-20).

It should be mentioned in this connection that cell tests on a large sample of undisturbed Chicago clay, performed in the late 1950s in the writer's laboratory at Princeton University, showed that an induced slight lateral expansion resulted in a sudden drop of the lateral pressure of the clay and, hence, of the $K_n = K_0 \approx K_{ce}$ value. However, because of creep, the K_0 value was gradually built up back to almost its original value.

Further clarification of the performance of plastic clays can be expected from the development of methods for the in situ measurement of lateral

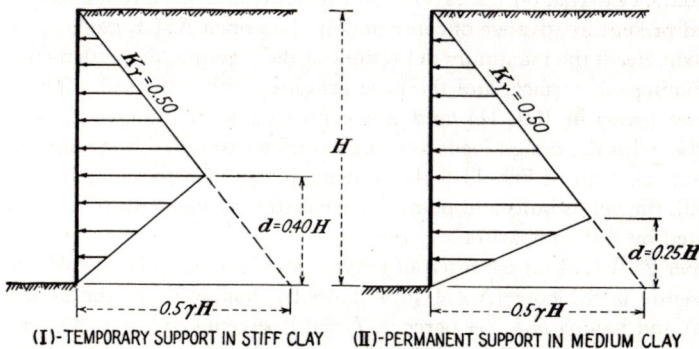

(I)-TEMPORARY SUPPORT IN STIFF CLAY   (II)-PERMANENT SUPPORT IN MEDIUM CLAY

Fig. 11-7a. Neutral-earth-pressure-ratio method. Lateral-earth-pressure diagram proposed for the design of braced open cuts in plastic clay. Note: for soft clays, $d = 0$ in all cases. (*After Ref. 356.*)

pressures, and hence of the K_0 values that exist in natural deposits. Note-worthy in this respect is Bjerrum's "hydraulic fracturing" method (Ref. 31) and the French *sonde autoforeuse des Ponts et Chaussées* (see Art. 2-5).

In cold climates the formation and growth of ice lenses during *prolonged periods of frost* in the soil next to the sheeting have been known to increase lateral pressures on struts appreciably. Thawing by hot air and similar measures sometimes have to be resorted to.

(C). Design Loadings for Cuts in Layered Soils. The design for the worst possible assumptions was followed during the construction of a *subway in Tokyo*, reported in 1963 by K. Ishihara and Y. Yuasa (Ref. 143). The 66-ft-deep (20.2-m) cut with six rows of struts was made through alternating layers of clay and sand: 13 ft (4 m) of silty clay near the surface, then 20 ft (6.1 m) of gravelly sand, then 13 ft of silty clay, then 20 ft (6.1 m) of gravelly sand. The unconfined compressive strengths of the silty clays varied from $q_u = 0.5$ ton/ft^2 to $q_u = 0.8$ ton/ft$^2 = 0.8$ kg$_f$/cm^2. The sand layers appear to have been of medium density, the standard penetration test values varying from $N = 10$ to $N = 20$ blows/ft.

The bracing was designed for the Terzaghi-Peck trapezoid in clay, Fig. 11-7(I), which gave lateral-pressure intensities approximately 2.5 times larger than the trapezoid for sand (Fig. 11-1). The average unbuoyed unit weight of about 107 lb/ft^3 (1.71 g$_f$/cm^3) of all soil layers was used in determining the trapezoid dimensions. The measured apparent-pressure diagram based on the strut loads fell within the pressure trapezoid for sand, except at a depth of about 40 ft (12.2 m) opposite the central clay layer, where an increase of pressures by about 50 percent in excess of the sand trapezoid values was recorded.

An important set of comparative measurements for a 60-ft-deep (18.3-m) *subway cut in Boston* was organized by Lambe and is described in Refs. 111 and 183. Four engineeers (Golder, Gould, Tschebotarioff, and Wilson) were given the data available on the layered soil deposits and were requested to predict and present in advance of construction at an open ASCE meeting in 1967 the strut loads, the maximum deflections of the sheeting, the settlements of the adjoining soil surface, and the pore pressures within the soil. Their forecasts are given in Ref. 111 and are compared by Lambe (Ref. 183, pp. 149–218) with the design loads and the values measured. None agreed fully. With the help of Fig. 11-8 the writer will now briefly compare his forecast with the field results and point out the further refinements of reasoning indicated by this comparison.

The upper 25 ft (7.6 m) consisted of gravel, sand, silt, and clay fill which was apparently fairly loose ($N = 1$ to 4 blows/ft), nonplastic in the upper 10 ft (3 m) and having $w_L = 34$ percent, $I_p = 15$ percent, and $w_n = 30$ percent in the lower 15 ft (4.6 m). The free-water level was at a depth of approximately 7 ft (2.1 m).

Then followed 20 ft (6.1 m) of silt, the upper 12 ft (3.6 m) of which had

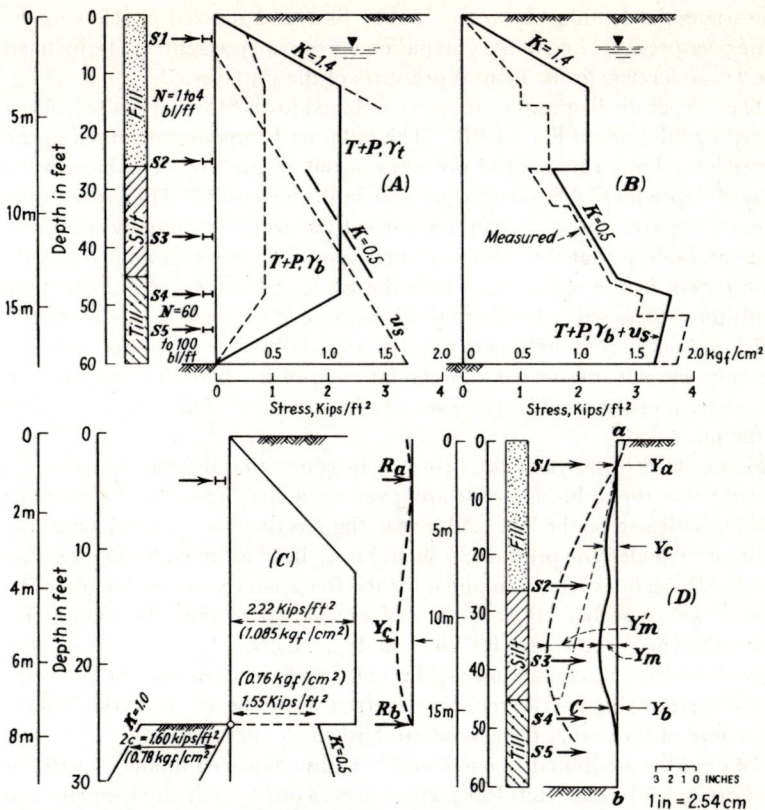

Fig. 11-8. Comparison of predicted (by the writer) and measured apparent lateral pressures and deflections in a cut for a Boston subway. (*Ref. 111.*)

$w_L = 30$ percent, $I_p = 8$ percent, $w = 26$ percent, and $s = q_u/2 = 800$ to 1,000 lb/ft² (3,900 to 4,900 kg$_f$/m²). The lower 8 ft (2.4 m) were organic with $w_L = 123$ percent, $I_p = 62$ percent, $w_n = 80$ percent, and $s = q_u/2 = 860$ lb/ft² (4,300 kg$_f$/m²).

From a depth of 45 ft (14.1 m) down was compact till ($N = 60$ to 100 blows/ft) with $w_L = 23$ percent, $I_p = 11$ percent, and $w_n = 12$ percent.

The steel sheeting was of the PZ38V55 cross section (see Art. 11-6). All struts were steel and, except for the top-level one, were prestressed to one-half the design load.

Figure 11-8A gives the loading conditions considered by the writer. The trapezoid shown by full lines and marked $T + P$ represents the Terzaghi-Peck trapezoid for sands and an unbuoyed wet-soil weight γ_T; the trapezoid shown by broken lines was similarly obtained for a buoyed soil unit weight γ_b.

The triangular loading shown by broken lines and marked u_s refers to the static pore pressure, i.e., to the gravitational free-water weight.   The inclined line $K = 0.5$ refers to the neutral pressures of the silt layer.

These separate diagrams were then combined to give the composite loading shown by full lines in Fig. 11-8B.   The unbuoyed trapezoid was used in the upper fill, followed by neutral pressures in the silt and by a combination of buoyed trapezoid and free-water pressure in the lower till.   The broken lines show the apparent-pressure diagram based on the strut loads actually measured.

It can be seen that the agreement between prediction and reality is fairly good except in the upper fill, where the measured values were about two-thirds those expected.   Probably this is because of the loose nature of the fill, which did not permit arching to develop, especially since the upper strut was the only one not prestressed.   A combination of the buoyed trapezoid and free-water pressure would have given closer agreement with values measured in the fill.

Figure 11-8C illustrates the first step in computing deflections to be expected.   On the right-hand side are given the active pressures; the soil resistance is indicated on the left.   A hinge in the sheeting was assumed where the resistance equaled the pressure; it should have been assumed lower (see Fig. 11-1).   Deflections were computed for the free span above the hinge.   The process was repeated for each step of excavation to give the cumulative deflection curve shown by full lines in Fig. 11-8D.   It was assumed that there would be practically no yielding of the sheeting in the compact till; this is where the biggest discrepancy occurred, as can be seen from the broken-line curve of the actual deflections established by inclinometers.

This can be attributed to considerable and unexpected inflow of water at the bottom of the cut (Ref. 183), which loosened the originally compact and supposedly impervious till and decreased its lateral resistance (see Art. 12-3).

All this demonstrates again the importance of acquiring measured information on the actual performance of local deposits and of providing test sections for all important jobs in localities where such information is unavailable or inadequate.

The settlements of the adjoining soil surface, which to a large extent depend on the amount of lateral yield of the sheeting, were also larger than expected.   Consolidation of the silt, when water lowering was attempted, also influenced the settlements (see Art. 9-7).

(D). Details of Bracing.   Struts should be designed to take into account possible variations in individual strut loads by up to 50 percent as compared to their average.   Figure 11-9 illustrates some of the methods employed for bracing open cuts.   Each *brace* or *strut b* should be installed as soon as the excavation reaches its elevation.   This is less important in shallow cuts (10 to 12 ft = 3 to 4 m) through compact cohesive soil [Fig. 11-9(IV)], but it is essential in shallow cuts through softer soils and for all soils with deep cuts if accidents of the type illustrated by Fig. 7-3 are to be avoided.

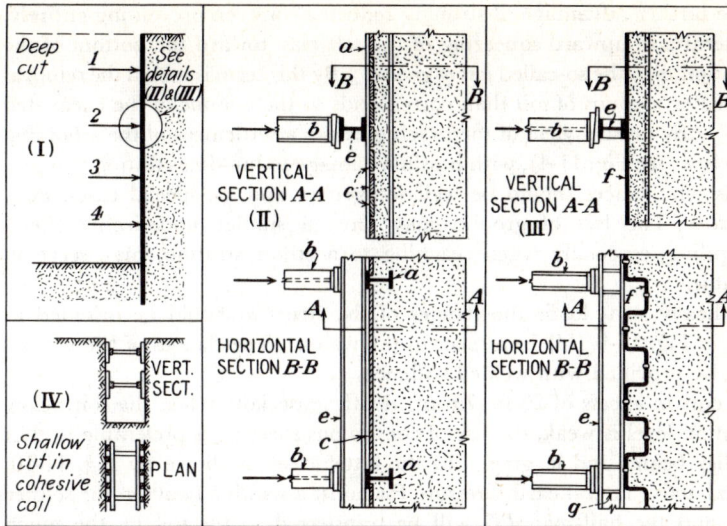

Fig. 11-9. Some types of bracing in open cuts.

There are two main types of wall lining in deep cuts, illustrated in Fig. 11-9(II) and (III).   In the first type wide-flange steel *H-piles a* are driven from the surface into the ground, 5 to 6 ft (1.5 to 1.8 m) on centers, before the excavation is begun.   *Horizontal timber sheeting*, or *lagging*, *c* is then inserted, board by board, behind the flanges of the H-piles as excavation progresses. Sometimes gaps of $\frac{1}{2}$ to 1.0 in. (12 to 25 mm) height are left between adjacent boards to facilitate drainage.   The gaps are stuffed with hay if the soil is sandy, to prevent the soil from trickling out through the gaps after drying. When the elevation of a row of struts *b* is reached, a horizontal *wale e* is placed against the H-piles, and the struts or braces *b* are tightly wedged against it.   The horizontal spacing of the braces usually is a multiple of the spacing of the H-piles.   It may vary from row to row and frequently is made smaller in the upper rows than in the lower ones.   Both the wales and the braces can be made of heavy timbers, up to 12 to 14 in. (30 to 37 cm) square, or of steel H beams.

In the second type of cut lining [Fig. 11-9(III)] a continuous row *f* of steel sheet piles is driven into the ground instead of H-piles.   No horizontal timber lagging is then needed, but a much greater quantity of steel is used in this type of lining, which, as a result, is comparatively more expensive than that shown in Fig. 11-9(II).   The use of continuous steel sheet piling becomes necessary with soft clay soil, especially if it alternates with thin water-bearing layers which are difficult to unwater.   In the latter case sheet piling will keep the water out of the excavation, but the bracing may have to be designed to resist full water pressure.   Continuous sheet piling has the further advantage of strongly reducing, or even preventing entirely, the lateral and upward squeezing of the soft clay toward the bottom of the excavation, i.e., the so-called *loss of ground*.   By this term is meant the removal of a greater amount of soil than corresponds to the volume of the excavated space.   Any inward yield of the bracing causes a settlement of the adjoining soil surface (see Fig. 11-4), with possible damage to buildings resting thereon. That is why braces should be well wedged in and, in special cases, even *prestressed*.   The loss of ground may have a similar undesirable effect. Sheet piling, especially when reaching to a stiffer stratum, may serve to prevent it.

For heavy strut loads the flanges of the struts *b* should be oriented as shown in Fig. 11-9(III) in respect to the wales.   The flanges of the wales *e* should be provided with welded stiffeners *g*.

For cuts in excess of 25 ft (7.6 m) depth, especially when the soil below excavation level is weak, the use of continuous sheeting is preferable to that of soldier beams and lagging.   In the latter case, as shown by Fig. 11-10, the total active lateral earth pressure *P* against a width *b* between the soldier beams and the half-span $L/2$ will be transferred to the soil by the much smaller width *b'* of the soldier beam.   The resulting intensity of pressure may exceed the passive resistance of the soil (see Art. 11-5 and Fig. 11-15).

Lateral yielding of the bracing should be minimized to decrease settlement of the adjoining soil surface which may damage buildings resting thereon.

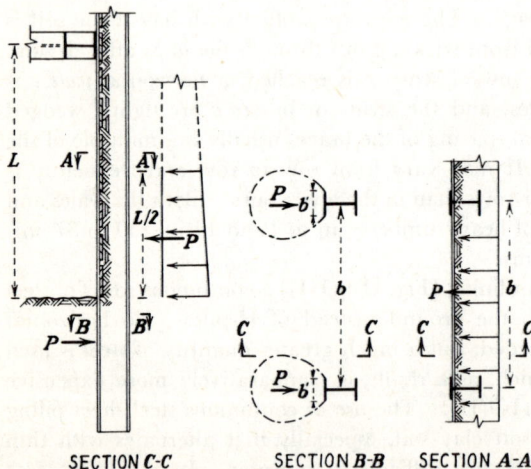

Fig. 11-10. Check of balance of forces at excavation level for soldier beams with lagging.

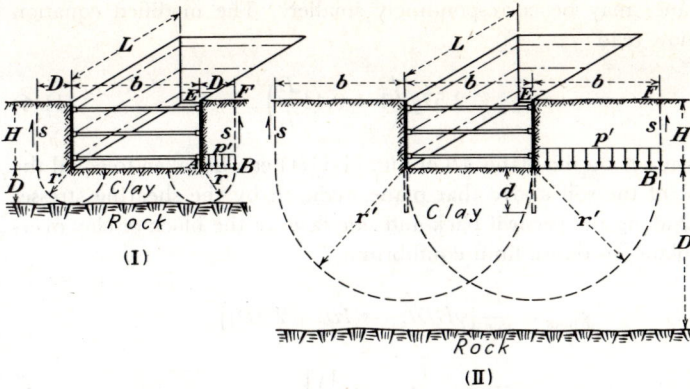

Fig. 11-11. Cuts in plastic clay. The sketch illustrates conditions governing safety against heaving of the bottom of the cut.

Observations in London reported orally by W. H. Ward† showed that lateral tensions in the surface soil layers behind a yielding retaining structure could damage buildings even more severely than vertical settlements. This point and possible countermeasures appear to merit more attention than they have so far received elsewhere.

11-4. Heaving of Clay Bottoms in Horizontally Braced Cuts. The heaving of the bottom of unbraced excavations has been discussed in Art. 9-3. Bracing the walls of the cut to resist the lateral pressures of the clay against them is not always sufficient to ensure a safe execution of the excavation. The possibility of heaving of the bottom of the pit should be taken into account, as shown by the following analysis, illustrated by Fig. 11-11. It represents a development of earlier work by Housel (Ref. 136) and by Terzaghi (Ref. 341). Two cases have to be considered.

In the first case [Fig. 11-11(I)] the depth D of the soft clay between the bottom of the pit and the upper surface of an underlying nonplastic layer (such as rock or sand) is smaller than the width b of the cut. With reference to Art. 4-2, failure of the clay is likely to occur along a cylindrical surface of an approximate radius $r = D$, as shown in Fig. 11-11(I). The failure will be caused by the weight of the overlying soil, namely, by the pressure p' which the soil will exert on the plane AB. Equation (4-8) can then be applied to the stability analysis of the clay beneath the plane AB, with the following modifications: $h = 0$; D now stands for the symbol b of Eq. (4-8); the coefficient $5.52c$ should preferably be reduced to the original Prandtl value to read $5-14c = 2.57q_u$, since the radius r in Fig. 11-11 may actually be somewhat greater than D, and the reduction of p' by shearing stresses along

---

† During panel discussion, Session V, ASCE Special Conference on Performance of Earth and Earth Supported Structures (Ref. 16a).

vertical planes may be correspondingly smaller. The modified equation (4-8) will now read

$$p'_{max} = 2.57q_u\left(1 + 0.44\frac{D}{L}\right) \tag{11-4}$$

The pressure p' on the plane AB of Fig. 11-11(I) can be taken to equal the unit weight of the soil above that plane, reduced by the shearing stresses $s = c = q_u/2$ along the vertical back and side faces of the block of clay overlying that plane, so that a limit equilibrium,

$$p'_{max} = \frac{1}{DL}\left[\gamma HDL - s(HL + 2HD)\right]$$

$$= H\left[\gamma - q_u\left(\frac{1}{2D} + \frac{1}{L}\right)\right] \tag{11-5}$$

Combining Eqs. (11-4) and (11-5), we obtain the limit depth of a braced cut which is compatible with equilibrium against heaving of the bottom:

$$H_{max} = \frac{2.57q_u(1 + 0.44D/L)}{\gamma - q_u(1/2D + 1/L)} \tag{11-6}$$

If the length L of the cut is greater than the depth D $(L \geq D)$, local squeezing may occur in soft clays at the center of L; it is then advisable to ignore partially the restraining end effects and to transform Eq. (11-6) for that purpose as follows:

$$H_{max} = \frac{2.57q_u\left(1 + 0.44\dfrac{2D - L}{L}\right)}{\gamma - q_u\left(\dfrac{1}{2D} + \dfrac{2D - L}{DL}\right)} \tag{11-7}$$

valid for $D < L < 2D$ and $b > D$.

It will be noted that for $L = D$ Eq. (11-7) is identical with Eq. (11-6), whereas for $L = 2D$ it takes on the following simplified form, which is equivalent to the omission of the restraining end effects:

$$H_{max} = \frac{2.57q_u}{\gamma - q_u/2D} \tag{11-8}$$

valid for $L \geq 2D$ and $b > D$.

In the second case [Fig. 11-11(II)], when the depth D of the clay is greater than the width b of the cut, a similar derivation gives equations which in all respects are identical with Eqs. (11-7) and (11-8), except that b should be substituted for D.

In order to obtain the permissible safe depth of braced excavations, the values of q_u should be divided by the factors of safety suggested in Table 4-2,

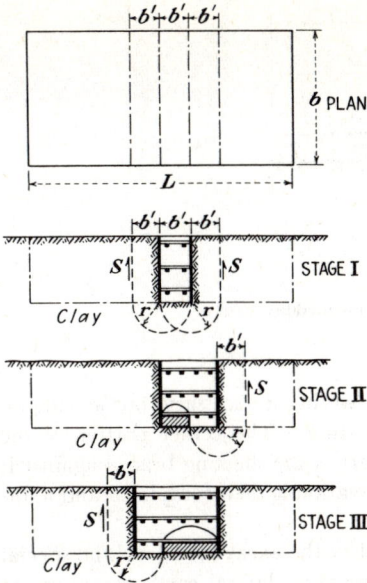

Fig. 11-12. Excavating and concreting the bottom slab in small sections increase the safety against heaving of the bottom of a cut in clay.

and the q_u/F_s values substituted for q_u in Eqs. (11-7) and (11-8) [see part (c) of Prob. 11-2].

Steel sheet piling extended to a distance d below the point A [see Fig. 11-11(II)] is beneficial, especially if stiffer clay is encountered below the depth d. Stability evaluations are then somewhat more elaborate than the ones just given but follow the same general lines.

An examination of Eqs. (11-6) to (11-8) shows that the value of $H_{\max}$ will increase with a decreasing value of L. This circumstance can be utilized in the case of long cuts with a large value of L. The excavation is then carried out in successive stages, as shown in Fig. 11-12. As soon as the excavation of each narrow section of cut is completed, the corresponding section of the foundation mat is concreted and weighted down still further, if necessary, by temporarily placing over the mat some of the clay that is removed from the next adjoining section of the cut or by concreting parts of the cross walls.

Another auxiliary method, successfully used in Norway, consists in placing between the longitudinal walls of the cut rigid *transverse diaphragms* below the bottom of the excavation. This is done from the surface before the excavation is started. Adhesion of the clay to the diaphragm walls helps resist the tendency of the soft clay to heave.

11-5. Inclined Bracing of Wide Cuts against Center Slab. When the cuts are too wide for convenient strutting of one wall against the wall across the cut the procedure illustrated by Fig. 11-13 is often resorted to. First, the sheeting is driven around the entire proposed cut. Then the soil at the

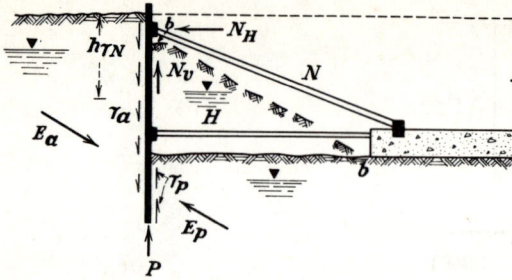

Fig. 11-13. Forces acting on the sheeting and the inclined braces of a cut in stable ground.

center is excavated, using groundwater lowering if necessary, but leaving on a slope bb a wedge of soil against the sheeting. The center portion of the foundation is concreted and the upper part of the sheeting braced against it by means of inclined struts N. The excavation is then completed and additional struts H installed.

When the ground is firm, especially below the excavation level, no special difficulties should be expected. The horizontal lateral earth pressures are given by the trapezoidal loading diagrams indicated in Art. 11-3, and the horizontal component N_H of the inclined-strut load N is determined from the trapezoid selected. The corresponding vertical component N_V will be balanced by the frictional component τ_a of the active pressures along a certain depth $h_{\tau N}$; the remaining frictional forces τ_a will be balanced by the point resistance P of the sheeting and by the frictional component τ_p of the passive soil resistance beneath the excavation level.

When the adequacy of the soil strength beneath that level is questionable, stability analyses (Art. 7-2) are indicated. Factors of safety of at least 1.7 are needed to prevent the possibility of plastic deformations. An assured speed of operation by experienced teams may sometimes permit a reduction of this value. In other borderline cases, the *method of excavating by sections can be used to increase the factor of safety* by bringing the shearing strength of the soil behind the wall and below the cut into play on planes perpendicular to the wall. An example is given by Fig. 11-14, which refers to the undercutting of a high bank of clay. The completed portions of the foundation mat served a double purpose in this case. First, they loaded by their weight the surface of the clay and thereby prevented excessive heaving. Second, they served as abutment to the steel braces which shored the sheeted vertical soldier H beams. Thus they resisted the lateral earth pressure which the bank exerted against these supports of the cut. The safety against horizontal sliding of the mat should be determined. The total lateral earth pressure E_A, multiplied by a factor of safety F, should not exceed the product of the horizontal area of the mat which is in contact with the clay and the shearing strength $s = c = q_u/2$ of the clay.   Since the surface clay layer immediately under the foundation mat is likely to have been somewhat remolded and weakened by construction operations, it is advisable to provide keys, A in Fig. 11-14, which anchor the mat in undisturbed zones of the clay. Such keys were not necessary in this particular case, since the mat received sufficient passive earth support at the other end of the excavation.

When the soil below excavation level is so poor that piling is required to support the foundation mat of the new structure, *conventionally designed inclined braces may be overloaded by any one of several factors* or a combination thereof. This is illustrated by the sketch in Fig. 11-15, which refers to an actual case in a geological region of past glaciation.   The depth of the cut h was approximately 50 ft (15 m).   Rock was at a depth of some 110 ft (34 m) and was overlain by 10 to 20 ft (3 to 6 m) of sand, gravel, and boulder till.   From there up to close to its surface the soil consisted mainly of alternating (varved) layers of fine sand, silt, and clay.   The foundation mat was to be supported on H-piles.   The sheeting consisted of continuous flat-arch web sheet piles *sp* driven behind heavy soldier H beams *sb*, which were spaced 4 ft (1.2 m) on centers.   These soldier beams were driven into the till; the sheet-pile wall was driven to some 20 ft (6 m) below excavation level but was not riveted or

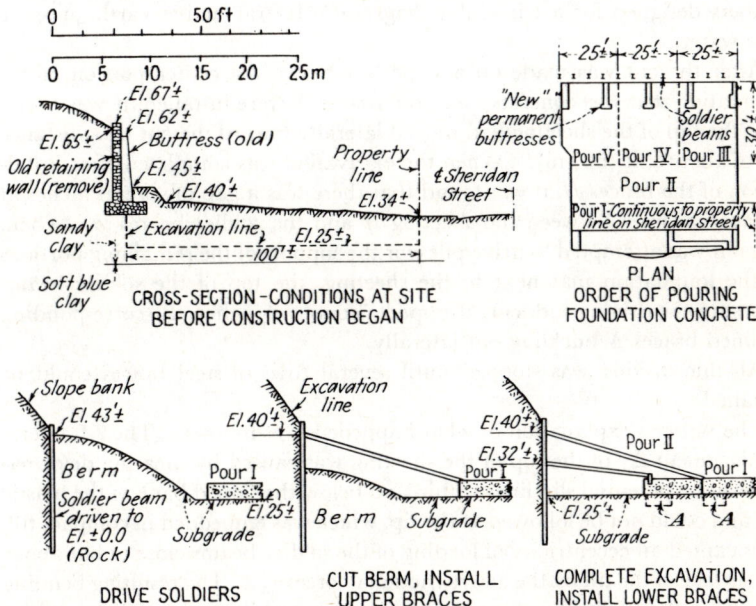

Fig. 11-14.   The sequence of excavation, concreting, and bracing necessary to ensure stability of bank and safety against heaving of bottom of cut for a new building at Albany, New York.   *(After Charles B. Spencer, Ref. 320.)*

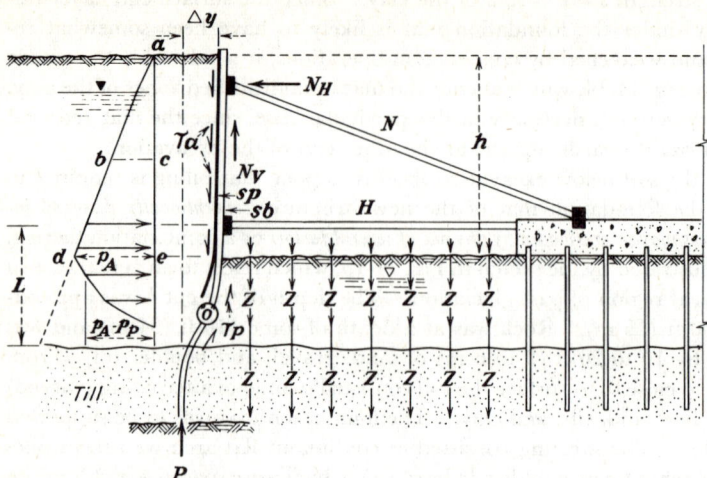

Fig. 11-15.   Overloading of an inclined brace in unstable ground.

welded to the soldier beams.   The groundwater lowering was done by rows
of stepped well points within the sheet-pile wall.†   The braces N were heavy
timbers designed for a triangular diagram of lateral active earth pressure
plus water.

After the cut was made on a slope but before the center portion of the
foundation mat was concreted and the braces N were installed, it was found
that the top of the sheeting had moved laterally toward the cut by a distance
Δy of about 2 ft (60 cm).   When the excavation was completed after installation of the braces H, it was found that there was a gap of several inches at
excavation level between the sheeting sp and the soldier beams sb.   Then,
when it was attempted to drive piles for the support of the remaining portions
of the foundation mat next to the sheeting, the top of the soldier beams
closest to the driving suddenly dropped a couple of inches, the corresponding
inclined braces N buckling out laterally.

All pile driving was stopped until several rows of steel braces could be
installed.

The writer's explanation of what happened is as follows.   The 2-ft lateral
displacement Δy of the top of the sheeting was caused by shearing deformations along potential slip lines within and below the sloped bank of the plastic
soil and could not be followed at the tip, which was embedded in compact till.
This caused an eccentricity of loading of the soldier beams close to but above
the surface of the till by the active frictional forces τ_a.   The resulting bending
stresses in the soldier beams were increased by additional bending stresses
due to the $p_A - p_P$ lateral pressures shown in Fig. 11-15.   The conditions

† More suitable methods are available; see Art. 9-6.

here, as evidenced by the separation at excavation level between sheeting and soldier beams, were very similar to those illustrated by Fig. 11-10 and discussed in Art. 11-3.   The vibrations during the pile driving close to the sheeting must have greatly reduced the lateral passive resistance p_P of the already overloaded soil in front of the soldier beams, as well as its frictional resistance τ_p.   This momentarily increased still further the bending stresses in the soldier beams so that a plastic hinge O must have developed, with resulting buckling there of the soldier beams, which stopped when driving was halted.

The inclined braces also started buckling because they could not support the vertical load of the entire frictional component of the active earth pressure at the time the frictional resistance τ_p was rendered temporarily inactive by pile-driving vibrations.

Some time later the writer had the opportunity to organize load measurements on inclined struts of a similar but even deeper cut in the same general area.   The results are shown in Fig. 11-16.

The full lines A refer to one side of the cut where measurements could be made on the three upper rows of struts only.   This is because the measurements were initiated after the entire 56-ft-deep (17.1-m) cut was accidentally flooded during a "blow" through breaks in the sheeting as the excavation advanced some 50 ft ahead (in plan) of the locations summarized by Fig. 11-16. By that time the piles had been driven and the floor slab concreted over them at these locations, enclosing the struts (4) within it.   The loads acting on the three upper rows of wide-flange steel struts were determined by means of Whittemore strain-gage readings (Art. 1-9) at the four flange corners, by comparison with readings taken after the struts were removed and carried no load at all.   The pressure curves A shown in Fig. 11-16 represent for each strut elevation an average of strut readings taken at five adjoining strut stations, the two extreme stations being 37 ft (11.3 m) apart.

The dash-dotted lines B and the broken lines C in Fig. 11-16 refer to the opposite side of the wide cut where the zero-load readings on the steel struts were taken before their installation.   The lines B give the average of four adjoining strut stations, the outer ones being 26 ft (8 m) apart, and refer to the construction stage when the excavation was 52 ft (15.9 m) deep and four rows of struts were installed.   The lines C refer to the same stations and the completed 66-ft-deep (20.2-m) excavation with all six rows of struts in place and the groundwater level outside the sheeting lowered by two deep wells, as shown in Fig. 11-16.   The maximum deviations in each horizontal row of struts from the average shown were ± 60 percent in row 1 and ± 27 percent in row 5.

The lateral-earth-pressure curves were obtained from the horizontal component $N_H = N \cos \alpha$ of the measured axial strut loads N by the procedure outlined in Art. 11-2; i.e., the continuity of the sheeting was ignored, and hinges were assumed in the sheeting at the level of each strut.

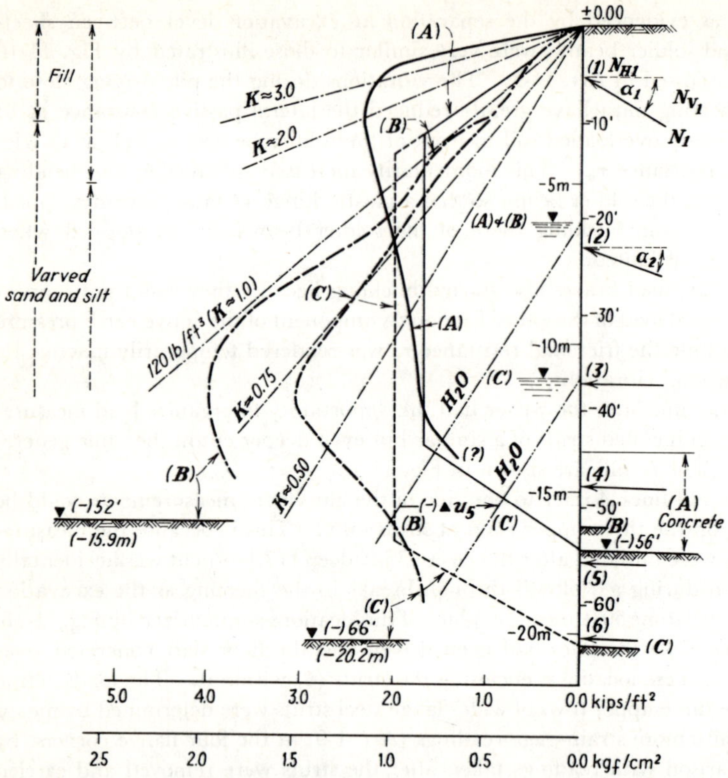

Fig. 11-16. Results of field load measurements on inclined and horizontal braces in a deep cut through deposits of glacial origin.

The very high pressures of curve A against the upper strut 1 can be attributed to the arching of the granular fill at that location, which was accentuated by the loosening of the underlying layers due to loss of ground through breaks in the sheeting during a blow and accidental flooding in the adjoining section.

The reason for the high ($K \approx 0.75$) triangular pressure distribution of curve C above the lowered groundwater table is not immediately apparent. This again demonstrates the need for great caution when designing the bracing of new types of cuts and for control measurements during construction.

The driving of piles from el. -66 ft to support the floor slab had only a very slight effect here, and that only on the lower horizontal strut loads, presumably because of the operation of two deep wells outside the sheeting at the time and the resulting downward flow of water on both sides of the sheeting, which had a stabilizing influence on the sand and rock-flour silt layers into which all the sheeting penetrated.

In similar uncertain cases it nevertheless appears prudent to design the inclined braces for the entire frictional component $E_A \sin \delta$ of the full active lateral earth pressure E_A as given by whatever lateral-earth-pressure diagram is selected.   When several inclined braces are provided, as in Fig. 11-16, this frictional component $E_A \sin \delta$ can be distributed between the individual braces in proportion to their inclination, as expressed by their $\sin \alpha$ values. Thus, the maximum frictional load N_{F1} on strut 1 would be

$$N_{F1} = \frac{E_A \sin \delta \sin \alpha_1}{\sin \alpha_1 + \sin \alpha_2} \tag{11-9}$$

If the horizontal load component N_H of a strut is based solely on the lateral-earth-pressure diagram selected, its corresponding vertical component N_V is

$$N_V = N_H \tan \alpha \tag{11-10}$$

and the axial load N is

$$N = \frac{N_H}{\cos \alpha} = \frac{N_V}{\sin \alpha} \tag{11-11}$$

The vertical load component N_V of Eq. (11-10) will normally counterbalance some of the frictional forces τ_a along a certain length $h\tau_N$, as schematically indicated in Fig. 11-13.   However, if the conditions of Fig. 11-15 prevail for which Eq. (11-9) is set up, and if the value N_F for a strut is larger than its value N_V from Eq. (11-10), the strut load N should be determined from

$$N = \frac{N_F}{\sin \alpha} \tag{11-12}$$

Of course, the lateral earth pressures against the strut will be increased accordingly by some passive resistance required for equilibrium, a point which should be remembered when analyzing and evaluating the results of field measurements.

In the structural design of struts it should be remembered that individual strut loads may be 50 to 60 percent greater than the average values given by Eq. (11-11) or (11-12).

Driving piles with followers from the ground surface is sometimes attempted to avoid problems of the type illustrated by Fig. 11-15 when piles are driven from the bottom of the completed excavation.   However, other problems may then arise in plastic clays, as illustrated by Fig. 11-17.   Shearing deformations in the clay before the first inclined braces e can be installed may induce plastic creep along a slip surface below the tip of the land cofferdam sheeting and tilt the piles *abc* out of plumb, as shown by broken lines for piles b, impairing thereby their usefulness as a permanent support of the floor mat.

To prevent or minimize such creep a factor of safety of at least $F = 1.7$ is desirable along possible sliding surfaces. The dowel action of piles and their resistance T for zero movement (see Art. 7-5) can be included in this safety-factor value, as well as the resistance ΔV to pullout of piles type a and to settlement of piles type c.

Speed of excavation and of concreting the center portion of the floor mat is also essential to permit rapid installation of the inclined braces e. The excavation to level 1 and installation of the wales d and diagonal corner braces f before proceeding with the excavation to level 2 in the central portion of the cofferdam can also be of some help in reducing undesirable deformations.

An interesting and novel method for a 90-ft-deep (27.5-m) excavation 400 by 500 ft (122 by 153 m) in plan was used in *Johannesburg* and is illustrated in sketch form by Fig. 11-18 (Refs. 148, 128, 262, and 399). The cut had to be made in residual soils with an approximate shearing strength of 2,600 lb/ft² (12,750 kg$_f$/m²). The water table varied at the south and north ends of the cut, as shown in Fig. 11-18. It was lowered further by filter wells. Then 3.5-ft-diameter (1.07-m) situ-cast concrete piles a were installed 7.5 ft (2.23 m) on centers around the periphery of the cut, and Gunite arches b were formed between them as the excavation progressed. When the

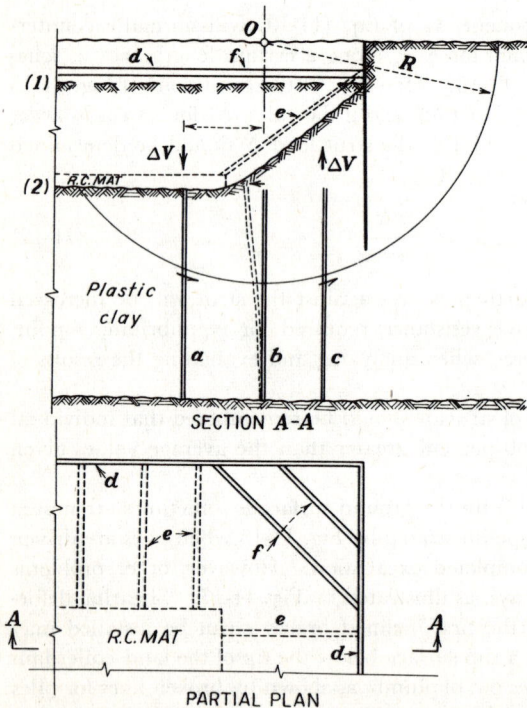

Fig. 11-17. Stability during later excavation of piles driven with followers.

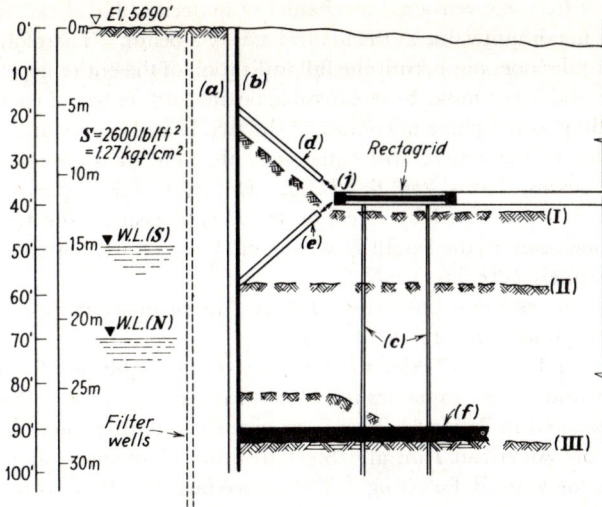

Fig. 11-18. Sketch of part section of 90-ft-deep (27.5-m) excavation for the Carlton Center in Johannesburg. (*Courtesy of J. E. Jennings, Paul Weidlinger, and Ove Arup & Partners.*)

excavation reached level I, temporary light piles *c* were installed to support a *rectagrid*, or reinforced-concrete horizontal girder, forming a closed inner ring with a few pile-supported cross braces to allow for nonuniform circumferential loading. The rectagrid was prestressed, and precast inclined struts *d* were installed and also prestressed by jacks *j*. These jacks were further used to control possible later wall movements due to temperature effects on the rectagrid system. A similar procedure was used for the installation of the precast struts *e* after the excavation reached level II.

11-6. Characteristics of Different Types of Sheet Piles. As their name implies, piles of this type are driven very closely next to each other so that they form a continuous wall or *sheet*. The purpose of such a wall of sheet piling may be either to cut off the flow of water through the soil or to keep the water and the soil out of an excavation which requires vertical cuts too deep to stand without support. Sheet piles may be made of steel, reinforced concrete, or wood. *Steel sheet piles will be discussed first.*

When steel sheet piles must resist lateral pressures of water or soil by serving as vertical beams supported by wales and struts (see Fig. 12-3), their resistance to bending, as governed by their section modulus, is of paramount importance. Sheet piles with deep webs, for instance, the PZ or the PDA types shown in Fig. 11-19, are then employed. The PDA (deep arch piling) of the U sheet-pile type is the older type and corresponds to the one known under the name of *Larssen* sheet piles in Europe (Fig. 11-20). It will be noted that the interlocks of this type of sheet pile coincide with the neutral axis of the wall. It will also be recalled from conventional mechanics of materials that shearing stresses reach their maximum value at the neutral axis of a beam. Therefore the U type of sheet piles does not permit the full utilization of the entire depth of the wall section and acts similar to rectangular beams laid on top of each other. Unless sliding at the plane of contact of the two beams is prevented, the section modulus of the system will equal only the sum of the section moduli of the two beams, that is, $2bh^2/6 = bh^2/3$. However, if sliding along the plane of contact is prevented by rivets or by other measures, the two beams will act as one beam of the height $2h$ which will have a 2 times greater section modulus, namely $b(2h)^2/6 = 2bh^2/3$.

Table 11-1 gives the essential properties of some American sections, and Fig. 11-19 gives the dimensions of four of them.

The values given in Table 11-2 refer to sheet piles of the Bethlehem Steel Co., but U.S. Steel and other companies roll almost identical sections. The section designations used in Table 11-2 conform to the standard nomenclature prepared by the American Iron and Steel Institute. All sheet piling sections begin with the letter P, for piling. The succeeding letter Z, or other letters define the shape, such as:

$$DA = \text{deep arch}$$
$$MA = \text{medium arch}$$
$$SA = \text{shallow arch}$$
$$S = \text{straight}$$
$$SX = \text{straight, extra-strength interlock}$$

The two-digit numbers represent the weight of the section in pounds per square foot of wall.

Figure 11-20 shows some types of European sections with different interlocks. Type E is of interest because of the special steel interlock provided as an entirely separate unit. By driving the piles with the bulb forward, filling

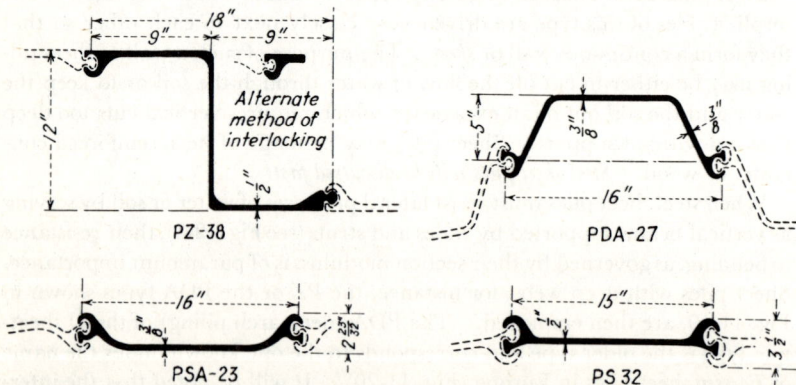

Fig. 11-19. Some types and dimensions of American steel sheet piles. (*Bethlehem Steel Co.*)

TABLE 11-2.   Essential Properties of Some Bethlehem Steel Sheet Piles

Section no. (standardized nomenclature)	Area		Width		Weight		Section modulus		Interlock† strength	
	in.²	cm²	in.	cm	lb/ft²	kg_f/m^2	in.³/linear ft	cm³/m	lb/in.	kg_f/cm
PZ38	16.77	108.2	18	45.7	38.0	186	46.8	2,510	8,000	1,425
PZ32	16.47	100.2	21	53.3	32.0	156	38.3	2,290	8,000	1,425
PZ27	11.91	77.0	18	45.7	27.0	132	30.2	1,620	8,000	1,425
PDA27	10.59	68.4	16	40.6	27.0	132	10.7	585	8,000	1,425
PMA22	10.59	68.4	19⅝	49.8	22.0	107	5.4	290	8,000	1,425
PSA23	8.99	58.0	16	40.6	23.0	112	2.4	128	12,000	2,140
PSA28	10.98	70.8	16	40.6	28.0	136	2.5	134	12,000	2,140
PS28	10.29	66.4	15	38.1	28.0	136	2.4	128	16,000	2,850
PS32	11.76	75.9	15	38.1	32.0	156	2.4	128	16,000	2,850
PSX35	13.09	84.5	15¼	38.8	35.0	171	2.6	145	28,000	4,810

† See catalogs for additional information.

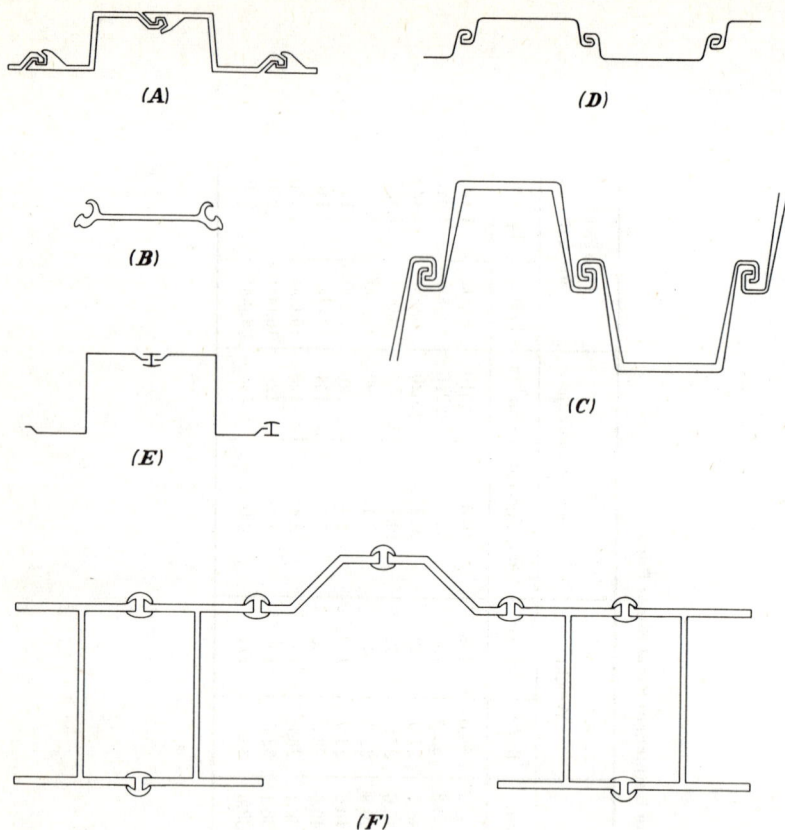

Fig. 11-20. Some types of European sheet piles: (*A*) Hoesch and Frodingham; (*B*) Arbed-Belval; (*C*) and (*D*) Larssen; (*E*) Krupp; (*F*) Peine.

the groove with sand is avoided and the danger of splitting the interlocks reduced. These separate interlock units also fit the Peine caisson sheet piles (Type *F*) so that the two types can be combined. Driving a continuous wall of Peine caisson sheet piles without splitting interlocks presents practical difficulties in any soil where large stones or other obstructions may be encountered. The combination of Krupp and Peine sheet piles, however, has much better driving properties. The heavy Peine piles can take considerable vertical loads in addition to lateral loads. The intermediate lighter Krupp piles are used as fillers only and are not considered in the computation of the section moduli of the combined section.

Similar results can be achieved by using American wide-flanged steel girder profiles as soldier beams in combination with shallow-arch sheet piles,

PSA23, welded or riveted to a flange of the wide-flanged section to ensure the esential proper structural interaction of the unit.   This fabrication work raises the cost appreciably.

Figure 11-21 shows the much greater range of resistance values covered by the Peine piling compared with standard American sheet piles.   The heaviest of the latter, the PZ38 section, has a section modulus of 46.8 in.^{3}/ft (2,510 cm^3/m) of wall.   By riveting or welding on cover plates, this value can be increased up to a maximum of some 92 in.^{3}/ft (4,840 cm^3/m).   The heaviest Peine sheet piles have 256 in.^{3}/ft (13,770 cm^3/m) and have a favorable weight-section modulus ratio.   The availability of such piles may have a decisive influence on the selection of the type of retaining structures.

In addition to a greater weight range of European sheet piles, European and American practice differ in another important respect, the treatment of the U types of piles.   The American catalogs consider that no shear will be transmitted through the interlocks of such sheet piles located in the neutral axis of the wall.   This gives them a very low efficiency as compared with the Z types of sheet piles.   On the other hand, the catalogs of most European firms give the section-moduli values for their U-type sheet piles as if the wall acted as one unit capable of transmitting full shear through the interlocks in its neutral axis.   In Germany, the studies of this questionable point by

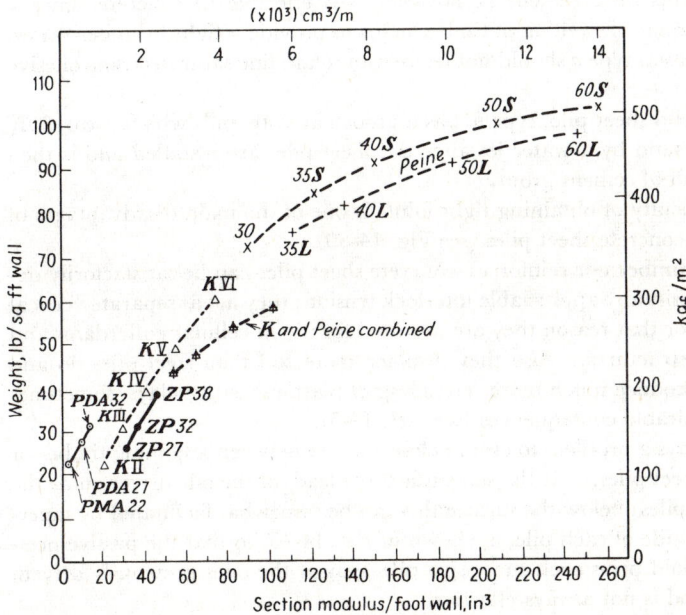

Fig. 11-21. Comparison of American Z and U types of pilings; of Krupp (K), of Peine, and of combined Krupp-Peine sheet piles.

Lohmeyer (Ref. 198) led to the driving of double U piles, i.e., in pairs, their joints having been first pressed together.   This advisable practice is not always followed elsewhere.   It is an open question what happens when U sheet piles are driven singly.   In sand, the interlocks may get so jammed by hard grains that sliding along them is hindered appreciably.   But this is very doubtful in plastic clays, or oystershell beds (Ref. 369), and caution is then indicated as to what values of section moduli should be used.

Customarily, American steel sheet piles are rolled of A328 steel with a yield point of 38.5 kips/in.^{2} (2,710 kg$_f$/cm^2), which satisfies other ASTM requirements for this type of steel.   Some companies provide sheeting of ASTM steel A572 grades with yield points of 45, 50, or 55 kips/in.^{2} (3,180, 3,520, or 3,870 kg$_f$/cm^2).   These *high-yield steels* have special advantages for some anchored bulkhead designs (see Art. 14-3).   Corrosion problems are treated in Art. 6-1.

Timber sheet piles are seldom used at present.   The thickness of tongue-and-groove sheet piles varies from 4 to 12 in. (10 to 30 cm); the width is approximately 10 in. (25 cm), and the length seldom exceeds 40 ft (12 m).   The comments in Art. 6-1 concerning driving, jetting, and durability of timber piles apply to timber sheet piles as well.

Reinforced-concrete sheet piles are of two types.   Type *a* is provided with a tongue and groove, similar to the ones used on timber sheet piles (see Fig. 14-39).   This arrangement is, however, less effective in concrete, since a certain amount of swelling of timber helps to provide a tight fit under water. For that reason type *a* should not be used to retain fine saturated noncohesive soils.

The second sheet pile, type *b*, has a groove at both ends which is carefully cleaned of sand by a water jet after the sheet piles are installed and is then pumped full of cement grout.

The difficulty of obtaining tight joints is one of the main disadvantages of reinforced-concrete sheet piles (see Fig. 14-39).

Neither timber nor reinforced-concrete sheet piles can be satisfactorily designed to resist any appreciable interlock tension; they act as separate vertical beams.   For that reason they are unsuited for use in cellular cofferdams and in similar structures.   Also they displace more soil than steel piles do and therefore produce much more remolding of plastic sensitive clays, sometimes with undesirable consequences (see Art. 14-5).

It is always a problem to ensure close contact between adjoining timber or concrete sheet piles.   At the soil surface the leads of the pile driver guide the individual piles; below the surface this can be somewhat facilitated by tapering off one side of each pile, as shown in Fig. 14-43, so that the passive pressure E_p would press each successive pile against the ones previously driven. This method is not always effective.

Some other problems related to sheet-pile *driving* are outlined in Art. 14-6.

Only high-quality concrete with 4,000 to 5,000 lb/in.^{2} (280 to 350 kg$_f$/cm^2),

28-day strength should be used for the sheeting.   The longitudinal reinforcement of the sheet piles is designed to take care of bending stresses caused by handling the piles during transportation and installation, as well as by lateral pressures in the completed structure.   Prestressing as such has advantages, especially in seawater, since the cracking of the bent concrete in the tension zone is thereby largely eliminated and the danger of corrosion of the reinforcement is correspondingly decreased.   However, the reversal of bending stress above and below the dredge line in most bulkheads reduces the economic effectiveness of normal types of prestressing.

11-7. Anchorage of Deep-cut Linings; Slurry Walls.   Anchorages are frequently resorted to instead of braces in deep and wide cuts.   They become indispensable for holding back the lining of a deep vertical cut into the side of a hill.   Figure 11-22 illustrates the construction sequence used since 1957 in Brazil for cuts into rock (Ref. 66).   As a first step, trenches are excavated for alternate anchors of the first upper row.   From the work platforms thus created holes are drilled, in the second step, into the rock; anchor rods are inserted into these holes, and their end lengths L are pressure-grouted into sound rock with cement.   Then precast reinforced-concrete plates with laterally protruding dowels are slipped over each individual anchor onto a cement bed.   After hardening of the cement each anchor is posttensioned to the desired test load.   Then the anchors are locked against their plates at the design work load, and the remaining length of the hole is filled with plastic grout.

In the third step, the preceding operations are repeated for the remaining alternate anchors of the first row.   In the fourth step the reinforced-concrete lining is poured around the first row of anchor plates to form a continuous wale beam, and the operations of step 1 are repeated for alternate anchors of the second row.   In step 5 all the preceding operations are completed for the second row of anchors.   The excavation is then continued in the same manner for one row of anchors at a time until the desired depth is reached.   Multistoried buildings have been built in this way in Rio de Janeiro right against vertical cuts in rock.   Figure 11-23 shows a three-anchor-row retaining wall of this type which permitted a vertical cut at the face of an existing building without any underpinning thereof being needed.   The anchors should be sufficiently long to permit their cement grouting in sound rock only.   Careful advance geological exploration is therefore essential for adequate designs.

Similar anchorage procedures have been used in soils too.   The following points, illustrated by Fig. 11-24, should be considered in this connection.   Cement grouting of anchors for a distance L required to develop the desired bond to the soil is quite inadequate if the distance L is measured from the critical failure plane OC, even if the individual pretesting of all anchors gave satisfactory results.   This is because, as shown in Fig. 10-3, the critical failure plane OC is only one of many possible failure planes, so that the entire

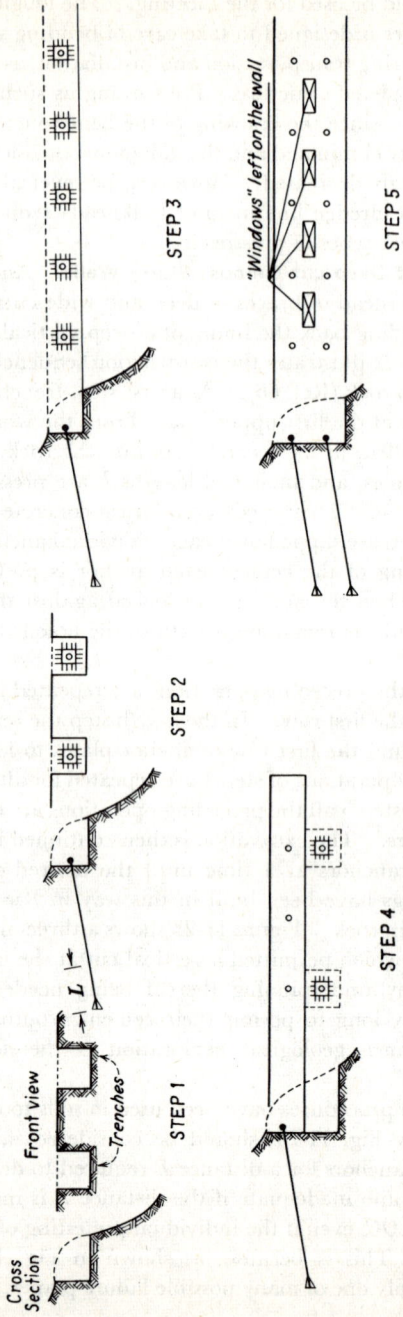

Fig. 11-22. Steps of execution for anchored walls (Tecnosolo system). *(From Ref. 66.)*

Fig. 11-23. Anchored wall supporting a slope above which a construction is located. (*From Ref. 66.*)

soil mass above the surface of natural repose OG of noncohesive soils, as determined by the angle of internal friction ϕ, is inherently unstable. Therefore, the upper anchor rows of Fig. 11-24A would offer much less resistance to a general slide than the lower rows, and the top row (1) would offer no resistance at all.

It is therefore necessary to extend all the cement-grouted portion L of the

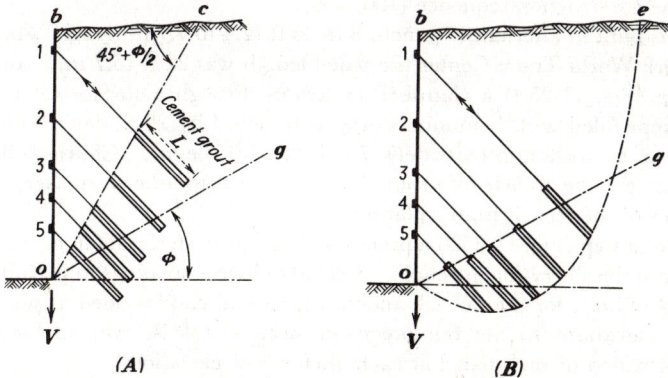

Fig. 11-24. (*A*) Inadequate length of anchors in noncohesive soil. (*B*) A high factor of safety against sliding along surface *oe* is needed in cohesive soils.

anchors into a stable soil zone, as shown in Fig. 11-24*B*. The length *L* itself can be determined from prestressing load tests.

In cohesive or semicohesive soils a check should be made of the safety against sliding (Art. 7-2) along a curved surface *oe* passing below the anchor tips and the bottom of the wall lining. Precise numerical recommendations cannot be made until more measurements have been performed, published, and analyzed. At the present stage of our knowledge it appears prudent to aim at a factor of safety not less than $F = 2.0$ if undesirable deformations are to be avoided.

Special attention should be paid to the bearing of the lining wall *ob* at level *o* or beneath it. The axial pulls of the anchor rods will introduce vertical compressive forces into the wall *ob* which will produce a cumulative downward force *V* at the level *o*. If no adequate support is provided there, a settlement of the entire wall *ob* will result and will introduce dangerous stresses into the anchor rods. As already stated, the space between the rods and the drill-hole walls above the cement grout should be filled with *plastic* anticorrosion grout to prevent slight wall movements from overstressing the anchors. However, this measure is insufficient to eliminate such overstressing by larger wall movements, which should be prevented by adequate design.

When geological conditions permit, the most satisfactory solution is to have the lining wall bear on rock and to cement-grout all anchors within rock only, as shown in Fig. 11-26 for the 70-ft-deep (21.4-m) basement excavation of the World Trade Center in New York City, above which rise two twin towers, each 110 stories high.

The 3-ft-thick (91-cm) cast-in-the-ground reinforced-concrete lining around the perimeter of the approximately 500-ft-wide (152-m) and 1,000-ft-long (305-m) excavation was built by the *slurry wall* technique, developed in Italy and France and now widely used throughout the world. Figure 11-25 illustrates the construction sequence (Ref. 156).

The wall is built in alternating panels, 8 to 25 ft (2.4 to 7.7 m) long. For the New York World Trade Center the panel length was 22 ft (6.7 m). In the first step (Fig. 11-25*A*) a clamshell excavates through a surface ditch, constantly kept filled with bentonite slurry, a trench 3 by 22 ft (90 cm by 6.7 m) down to rock approximately 70 ft (21 m) below. Churn-drill chopping rigs cut the trench into sound rock. The bentonite slurry keeps the side walls of the trench from collapsing.

In the second step (Fig. 11-25*B*) a prefabricated cage of steel reinforcement is lowered into the slurry-filled trench. Steel plates with openings to permit later drilling of holes for the tieback anchor rods are already welded at predetermined elevations to the reinforcement steel. At least two anchors should be provided in each panel at each anchor-row elevation.

In the third step (Fig. 11-25*C*) the panel is concreted by the tremie method (Art. 6-10). Then the intermediate panels are excavated, reinforced, and

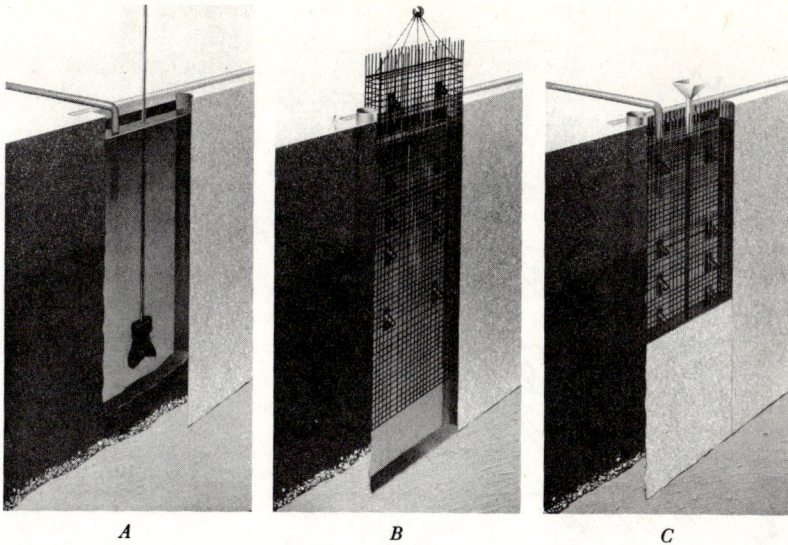

Fig. 11-25. Sequence of slurry-wall construction at the World Trade Center in New York City. (*Ref. 156.*)

tremie-concreted in the same manner until a continuous cast-in-the-ground perimeter wall has been constructed around the area to be excavated.

The excavation proceeds down to the first anchor level. Then inclined boreholes, cased through soil layers when necessary, are drilled into sound rock, and the anchor rods or cables are dropped into the holes and cement-pressure-grouted within the rock (Fig. 11-26). Each anchor tieback is pretested by jacks and is left posttensioned at the design working load. This procedure is repeated at each anchor tieback level until the excavation is completed. Concrete buttresses are provided in rock below the lowest basement floor.

For the New York World Trade Center the anchor tiebacks will not be relied on for permanent lateral support of the perimeter wall. This support is to be provided by the basement floor concrete slabs. After they are completed, the anchors are to be cut.

A conventional watertight sheet-pile wall of this depth could not have been built at this site. It would have been impossible to drive steel sheeting into the rock through the boulders in the hardpan layer just above it, at least without rupturing many interlocks. The slurry-wall method permitted chopping through the boulders. Higher up, old timber cribs and rocks in the fill also presented obstacles to sheet-pile driving but created only minor difficulties for the slurry wall. When much slurry was lost into the voids of a rock-filled crib, a wider trench was first cut into the rocks and filled with low-grade concrete, through which the slurry trench was then cut.

STREET

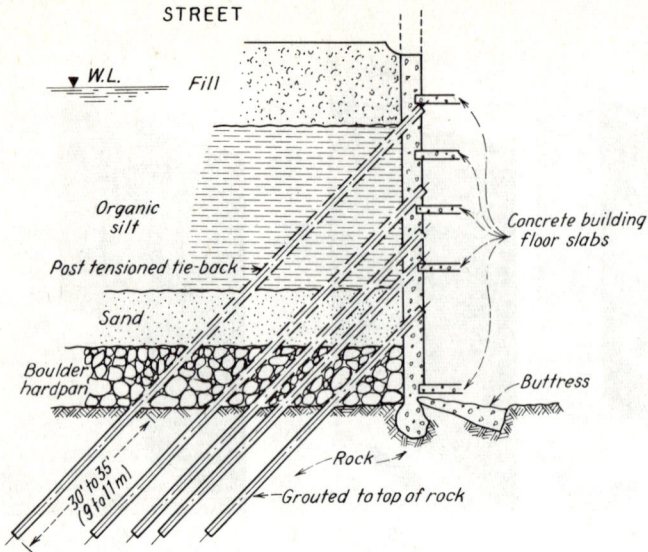

Fig. 11-26. Typical section through completed basement perimeter wall of the World Trade Center in New York City. (*Ref. 156.*)

Thus the slurry-trench method has proved itself invaluable in practice, but it still lacks a firm theoretical basis. During a 1963 debate at a Conference on Grouts and Drilling Muds in London (Ref. 116) there was no unanimity as to why slurry-filled trench cuts are stable. The specific gravity of the bentonitic slurry is seldom higher than 1.06 and cannot alone account for the stability of long cuts when the water level is high. Suggestions were then made that "reverse" electroosmotic phenomena (Art. 9-6) may contribute to the stability. At the time of the 1969 International Conference in Mexico City (Ref. 214) this point still was not clarified. There is no doubt that the bentonite in the slurry helps to form a cake or crustlike coating along the soil walls of the trench, which prevents the vertical soil face from disintegrating grain by grain. But the interplay of forces which produces overall stability is less clear.

Figure 11-27 illustrates the relevant points, with reference to the New York World Trade Center conditions (Ref. 373). The line ab represents the outward lateral pressure exerted on the soil walls of the trench by the slurry when its surface is at ground level, el. $+13$ ft. The slurry weighs $62.4 \times 1.06 = 66.2$ lb/ft^3 (1.06 g$_f$/cm^3). The line aCe represents the active earth and water counterpressure when the water level outside the trench is not lowered below its natural ± 0.0 elevation. It can be seen that the outward pressure of the slurry then exceeds the inward pressures only in the upper 30 ft (9.1 m) of the 73-ft-deep (22.3-m) cut. This is important since it eliminates the tensile stresses and the fissures from which most slips and slides originate and develop (Art. 7-2).   Shearing stresses along a horizontal plane fg through the sliding wedge at this depth of 30 ft (9.1 m) will produce some redistribution of lateral pressures and increase the stability of the lower 40 ft (12.2 m) of the wedge.   Also, in practice, construction procedures, usually limiting the excavation panel length to a maximum of 20 ft (6 m) or so, introduce helpful restraints along vertical boundaries.

Further, a temporary groundwater lowering by only 10 ft (3 m) outside the slurry-filled trench would shift the line of inward pressure aCe to $aC'e'$ and would thereby create an excess of slurry pressures in the upper 65 ft (20 m) of the 73-ft-deep (22.3-m) cut.   It did not prove necessary to resort to this emergency measure on this job.

Problems also arise with the structural design of the reinforced-concrete wall.   The successive installation and prestressing of several tiers of anchor tiebacks as the excavation progresses downward may produce alternating active and passive earth-pressure conditions along the height of the wall. The reinforcement of the wall was designed to meet the most unfavorable combination of possible conditions.   Extensive field-control measurements were performed during the construction.   They included strain meters on

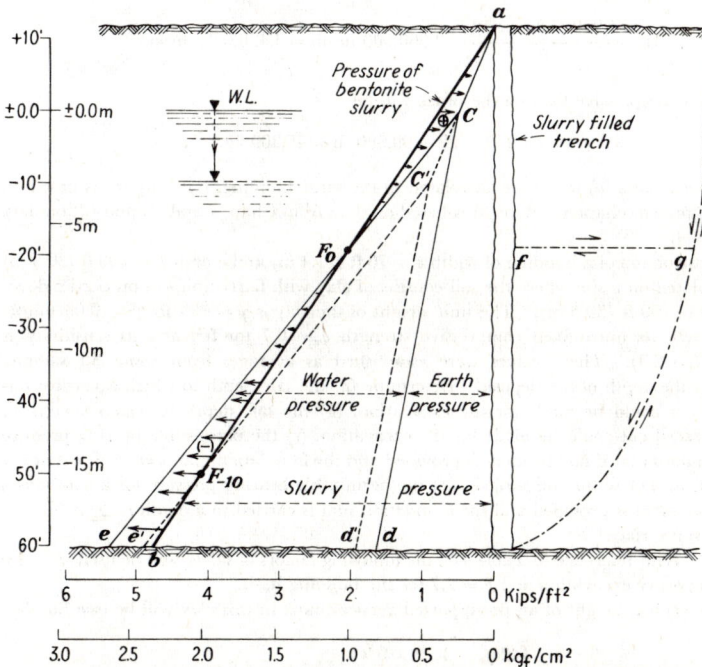

Fig. 11-27.   Factors affecting stability of excavated slurry trench.   (*Ref. 373.*)

the steel reinforcing rods of the perimeter wall, checks of anchor pull values, and Wilson inclinometer (Arts. 1-9 and 10-9) readings in vertical guide pipes embedded in the wall itself and in the soil nearby.

REVIEW PROBLEMS

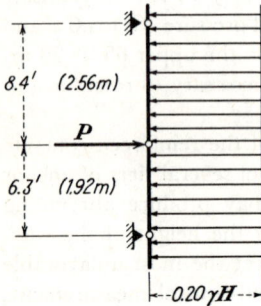

$8.4'$ (2.56m)

P

$6.3'$ (1.92m)

$-0.20\gamma H-$

Fig. 11-28.

11-1. Determine the bending moments for the wale and the strut load of the middle braces of the cut in sand illustrated by Fig. 11-3 in accordance with the design diagrams of that drawing and Fig. 11-1.

Answer. The relevant portion of the lateral-pressure diagram is drawn in Fig. 11-28. The unit lateral earth pressure is

$$0.20\gamma H = 0.20 \times 120 \times 28.2 = 676 \text{ lb /ft}^2 = 3,300 \text{ kg}_f/\text{m}^2$$

The pressure against the wale is

$$676(8.4 + 6.3)\tfrac{1}{2} = 4,940 \text{ lb/ft} = 7,380 \text{ kg}_f/\text{m}$$

Assuming that the wale does not extend for more than two spans of 20 ft (6.1 m) between the individual middle braces, the maximum bending moment that it will have to resist is

$$M = \frac{4,940 \times 20^2 \times 12}{8} = 2,960,000 \text{ in.-lb} = 3,420,000 \text{ cm-kg}_f$$

The axial compressive load on the brace will be

$$P = 4,940 \times 20 = 99,880 \text{ lb} = 45,300 \text{ kg}_f$$

11-2. *Note:* parts (*a*) to (*d*) are all related to the same building, but only (*b*) is based on data of the present chapter. Part (*a*) is based on data from Chap. 7 and (*c*) and (*d*) on data from Chap. 4.

The construction of a building of width $b = 70$ ft (21.4 m) and length $L = 100$ ft (30.5 m) is contemplated on a site where the soil consists of clay with fairly uniform properties down to a depth of 100 ft (30.5 m). The unit weight of the clay is $\gamma = 120$ lb/ft³ = 0.06 ton/ft³ (1.92 g$_f$/cm³), its unconfined compressive strength $q_v = 0.7$ ton/ft², and its sensitivity is medium ($S = 2.3$). These values were established as averages from some 30 samples throughout the depth of the deposit. Determine (*a*) the safe depth to which a vertical unsupported cut could be made for the excavation, (*b*) the safe depth to which a vertical, laterally braced cut could be made for the excavation, (*c*) the permissible bearing pressure for a continuous mat if no basement is provided and the foundation mat is carried to a depth of 5 ft (1.52 m) below the soil surface, (*d*) the permissible bearing pressure for a continuous mat if a basement is provided and the foundation mat is carried to a depth of 20 ft (6.1 m) below the soil surface.

Answer. With reference to Table 4-2, the following factors of safety will be used: $F = 2.0$ for the temporary excavation and $F = 2.7$ for the building itself.

(*a*) The critical height of an unsupported vertical bank in this clay will be (see Eq. 7-4)

$$h'_{cr} = \frac{1.29 q_u}{\gamma} = \frac{1.29 \times 0.7}{0.06} = 15.1 \text{ ft} = 4.6 \text{ m}$$

The safe height will be

$$h_0 = \frac{h'_{cr}}{F} = \frac{15.1}{2.0} = 7.5 \text{ ft} = 2.29 \text{ m}$$

(b) With reference to Eq. (11-7), for H_{max} and $F = 2.0$, noting that $b < D$, so that the values of b should be used instead of D in Eq. (11-7), the safe depth of simultaneous excavation of the entire area will be

$$H_0 = \frac{2.57 \dfrac{0.7}{2.0} \left(1 + 0.44 \dfrac{2 \times 70 - 100}{100}\right)}{0.06 - \dfrac{0.7}{2.0} \left(\dfrac{1}{140} + \dfrac{2 \times 70 - 100}{70 \times 100}\right)} = 22.5 \text{ ft} = 6.86 \text{ m}$$

The limit depth H_{max} is obtained by using in the above equation $q_u = 0.7$ instead of $0.7/2.0$

$$H_{max} = 36 \text{ ft} = 10.98 \text{ m}$$

(c) The 5 ft (1.53 m) of excavated soil will be almost entirely replaced by the foundation mat. No load reduction will therefore be possible. With reference to Eq. (4-8),

$$p_{max} = 2.76 \times 0.7(1 + 0.38\tfrac{5}{70} + 0.44\tfrac{70}{100}) = 2.60 \text{ tons/ft}^2$$

$$p_0 = \frac{p_{max}}{F} = \frac{2.60}{2.70} = 0.97 \text{ ton/ft}^2$$

(d) The additional 15 ft (4.58 m) of excavated soil will be replaced in part by columns, walls, and floors. Therefore only some 85 percent of the weight of the soil removed can be taken to represent an effective reduction of load as compared with case (c). Without that reduction,

$$p_{max} = 2.76 \times 0.7(1 + 0.38\tfrac{20}{70} + 0.44\tfrac{70}{100}) = 2.74 \text{ tons/ft}^2$$

and with that reduction the safe load is

$$p_0 = \frac{p_{max}}{F} + 0.06 \times 15 \times 0.85 = 1.01 + 0.76 = 1.77 \text{ tons/ft}^2$$

The provision of a 15-ft (4.6-m) basement has thus increased the permissible load by 80 percent. A greater increase might be achieved by the provision of two basements, but the deeper excavation would be possible only if carried out in narrow sections (see Fig. 11-12).

RECOMMENDED FOR FURTHER STUDY

Mexico 1969, Ref. 214.
Peck, Ref. 249, pt. 2, Deep Excavations, pp. 259–290.
Proc. ASCE Conf. Performance of Earth and Earth Supported Struct. Purdue Univ., 1972, especially Ref. 76 (performance of slurry walls) and Refs. 159, 38, 185, 327, 12, 187 (performance of braced or of tied-back walls).
Proc. 5th Eur. Conf. Soil Mech. Found. Eng. Madrid, 1972.

CHAPTER 12

COFFERDAMS

12-1. Purpose and Types of Cofferdams. The name *cofferdam* is given to a variety of temporary structures employed to keep water and earth out of excavations made for the construction of permanent structures. Sheeted and braced open cuts of a rectangular or circular plan are sometimes referred to as *land cofferdams* when the groundwater level is located below the soil surface. They have already been discussed in Art. 11-3. The present chapter deals with temporary cofferdams having free water on one or more sides. Some cofferdam types in this category are illustrated by Fig. 12-1.

Cellular cofferdams have features similar to the double-walled cofferdam shown in Fig. 12-1(IV); they are discussed in Arts. 12-4 and 12-5. Cellular cofferdams are sometimes used as *permanent structures* in river and harbor engineering work as wharves and dolphins. Their design has then some special features which are given in Art. 14-8.

When cofferdams are used to permit the construction of a dam across a river, the procedure illustrated by Fig. 12-2 is employed unless it is possible temporarily to divert the whole river into a new channel, which is practicable only with some small rivers. For large rivers construction in stages becomes necessary. A cofferdam is built next to one of the river banks, as shown in Fig. 12-2(I). The enclosed space is unwatered, so that excavation can proceed to the desired level. A section of the concrete dam is then built in the dry within the enclosure, whereupon the cofferdam is removed and transferred to the other bank [Fig. 12-2(II)], where the whole operation is re-

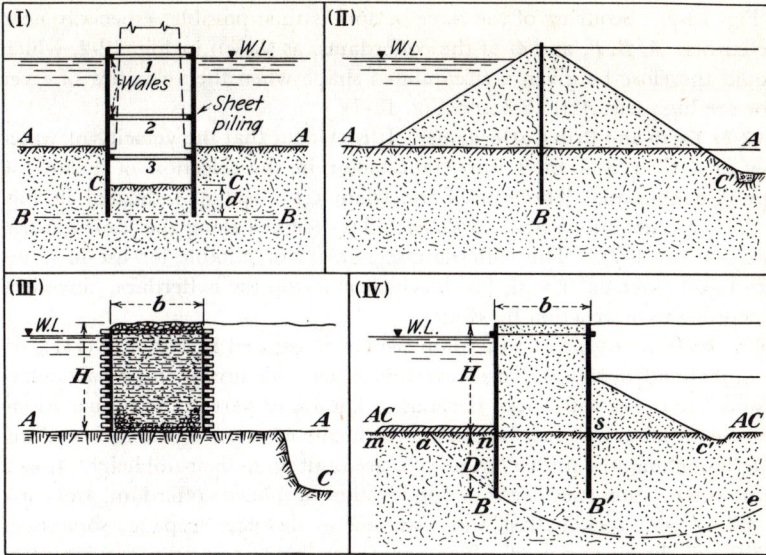

Fig. 12-1.   Some types of cofferdams.

peated.   Sometimes more than two construction stages are necessary in order to keep a sufficiently large section of the river channel open before the dam is completed [Fig. 12-2(III)].

The cofferdams temporarily block off part of the river channel, so that the velocity of the flow of water is increased in the open part, especially next to the cofferdam, where the flow lines squeeze themselves together, as sketched

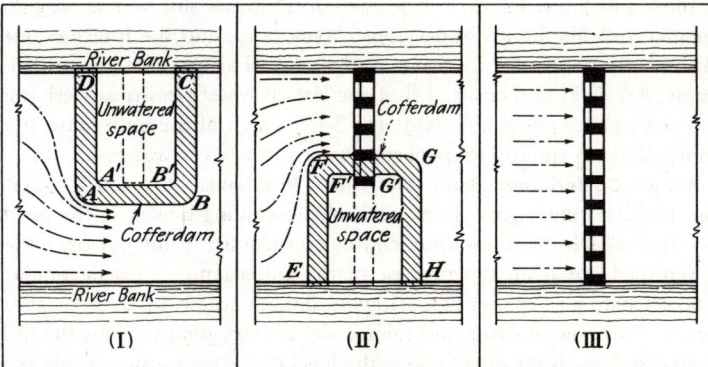

Fig. 12-2.   Using cofferdams for the construction in stages of a permanent dam across a large river.

in Fig. 12-2. Scouring of the river bottom is then possible, especially near the corners *A, B, F,* and *G* of the cofferdams, as shown in Fig. 12-2, which should therefore be given a streamlined shape when the velocities of river flow are high (see Art. 12-3 and Fig. 12-7).

12-2. Earth and Crib Cofferdams. It is evident that the velocity of water flow in a river is a most important factor in the selection of a suitable type of cofferdam. The type of cofferdam cross section indicated in Fig. 12-2(II) is essentially a *small earth dam* and is designed along the same general lines (see Art. 8-7). This cofferdam section is not suitable for use in rivers with rapid currents or with floods which may top the cofferdam, since it is susceptible to destruction by scour.

The *timber-crib* type of cofferdam section illustrated in Fig. 12-1(III), on the other hand, may be well used in rivers with rapid current and is particularly suited to rivers with rocky bottoms. The lower part of the timber frame is made on land and may be tailored to fit the contours of the rock surface. After launching, the timber-frame cells are built up to their full height, towed out to the position they are to occupy in the completed cofferdam, and sunk by filling with rock ballast and with soil to decrease seepage; sometimes additional sheeting is used. The completed block acts as a gravity dam, and its resistance to overturning and sliding is analyzed in the same manner as for gravity retaining walls (Art. 10-5). For large cofferdams the cribs are composed of more than one cell. The timbering of each cell is designed to resist the lateral pressures of its fill. These pressures are estimated in the same way as the pressures in bins (Ref. 401 and Art. 10-6). For the Bonneville Dam (Ref. 401) the individual crib pockets or cells had a maximum size of 12 by 12 ft (3.76 by 3.76 m). The maximum height *H* of the Bonneville cofferdam was 65 ft (19.8 m), its maximum width *b* was 60 ft (18.3 m) = 0.9*H*. This appears to be the highest cofferdam of this type.

The row of 12 by 12 ft (3.76 by 3.76 m) pockets on the side of the excavation was filled with broken rock. The row on the water side was lined with timber planks and filled with impervious clayey sand, and the intermediate rows were filled with bank-run gravel and sand. This provided a graded-filter action (Art. 7-9) and ensured that the lateral water pressures were not dissipated throughout the whole 60-ft (18.3-m) width of the cofferdam but were absorbed along the row of pockets closest to the river water.

12-3. Braced Cofferdams; Scour and Uplift Problems. A braced coffer-dam [Fig. 12-1(I)] consists of a single wall of sheet piling driven in the form of a box within which the foundation can be constructed in the dry once the water is pumped out from the interior of the cofferdam. This particular illustration refers to a river pier of a bridge in shallow water, up to 30 or 35 ft (9 to 11 m). The row of struts and their wales are designed to resist the full lateral water and earth pressures above the level of the excavation inside the cofferdam. The sheet piling is usually steel of the deep web type (Art. 11-6), of a section chosen to resist bending as a beam spanning vertically the distance between the wales of adjacent rows of struts. After the pier is completed, the sheet piling is removed either by pulling it from the ground or by cutting it at the level *AA* of the bottom. Pulling the full length of the piling for the purpose of reusing it is seldom possible if the concrete adheres to it over part of its length. Divers and special torches are used for underwater cutting.

The depth *d* to which the sheet piling is driven into the ground below the level *CC* of the excavation inside of the cofferdam should be sufficient to ensure stability of the bottom of that excavation. If the soil is sand to a considerable depth, the greatest danger will be that of a quick condition (Art. 8-3) as a result of the unwatering of the cofferdam. This is illustrated by Fig. 12-3, which gives a vertical section through a sheet-pile cofferdam driven through shallow water for the purpose of construction of a bridge pier within that cofferdam. The base of the pier was to rest on sand at el. −40 ft (−12.3 m). If the unwatering of the excavation were attempted by pumping from a sump pit, the flow of water toward the sump pit would follow the pattern and form the flow net shown in Fig. 12-3. According to Prob. 12-1, a quick condition would then result in and around the sump pit. In other words, the sand at the bottom of the excavation would start to "boil" and would be partially liquefied and pushed upward into the excavation. In addition, since in a quick condition sand has no supporting power either for lateral or vertical loads, the sheet piles of the cofferdams would lose the support they previously had at their lower ends in the sand. Excessive load would then be thrown onto the lower struts of the cofferdam bracing, so that a progressive collapse of the bracing and an inward displacement of the sheet piling might become imminent. This danger is decreased by a greater length *d* of the sheet piles, since this will increase the length of the paths of percolating water. The exact length of *d* can be determined by trial, where a

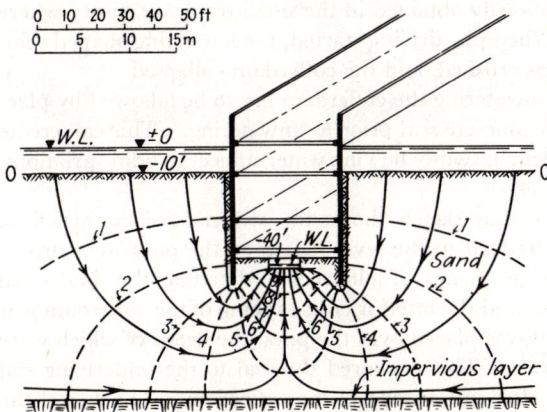

Fig. 12-3. Unwatering excavations in sand by pumping from sump pits may create a dangerous quick condition.

flow net (Art. 8-2) is constructed for each trial value of the depth d selected. Seepage into the cofferdam may be strongly reduced if a slightly less pervious layer is located at the elevation BB of the pile points.

Placing a horizontal clay blanket on the river bottom around the braced cofferdam, similar to the blanket mn in Fig. 12-1(IV), may strongly reduce seepage while active, but it is not reliable if scour occurs.

If the entire soil to a considerable depth is composed of plastic clay, the stability of the bottom of the excavation against shear failure and upward heaving should be investigated (see Art. 11-4). In some cases it may prove advisable to place the pier on piles if a stiffer layer is available deeper down.

Piles must be used under bridge piers supporting heavy loads of large spans even when all the underlying soil is sand. They serve to increase the safe load per unit of horizontal area of pier foundation since the shearing strength of noncohesive soils increases with depth. In such cases the piles are preferably driven *before* the sheeting of the cofferdam. If for some reason this proves inexpedient, then at least the piles should be driven within the cofferdam, with the help of followers, but *before* unwatering. Otherwise the vibrations caused by the driving may completely liquefy the sand, which is already buoyed by the upward flow of water toward a sump pit, and cause considerable trouble.

The following case illustrates this point. A single-wall steel sheet-pile cofferdam, similar to the one shown on Fig. 10-1(I), was installed in a river with a sand bottom. The future bridge pier was circular in plan, and so was the cofferdam. This permitted the provision of ring-shaped reinforced-concrete wales, which normally could be expected to be entirely in compression. All interior cross bracing could therefore be eliminated. The steel sheet piles were long enough to prevent a quick condition under static loading only. The cofferdam was successfully unwatered using a sump pit; well points could not be easily obtained in the small tropical country where the site was located. When pile driving started, the lower ring-shaped reinforced-concrete wale was crushed, and the cofferdam collapsed.

Driving piles before unwatering the cofferdam has to be followed by placing a tremie (Art. 6-10) concrete seal prior to unwatering. This can create a different kind of problem in swiftly flowing water subject to tidal variations, as illustrated by Fig. 12-4.

The left-hand side of that sketch shows the sequence of construction. First, the bottom was dredged to the level AA; then the piles were driven from the water surface by means of followers. After that the single-wall steel sheeting was driven, and the interior cross bracing of the cofferdam was installed. A tremie seal was placed over the piles, the heads of which were embedded in the concrete. This anchored the seal to the underlying soil against uplift pressures after unwatering of the cofferdam. The rest of the pier could then be completed in the dry.

However, some unexpected difficulties developed after the steel sheeting was in place, as sketched on the right-hand side of Fig. 12-4.   The velocity of the tidal river current at times exceeded 10 ft/sec (3 m/sec), and some 30-ft-deep (9.1-m) pockets were *scoured* out at some locations around the cofferdam, which had a rectangular shape in plan.   Driving the steel sheeting deeper than level B was not possible because of the outer batter piles, which were in the way.   So the scour pockets were filled with fascines and rock.   This controlled the further development of scour.   Thereupon the tremie seal was placed under customary controls.

When the unwatering was completed, visual inspection of the exposed seal showed that the concrete was of exceptionally poor quality, considerable segregation having occurred.   Underwater inspection by divers of the outer lower rim of the cofferdam showed that in some places cement laitance had accumulated between the rocks near the steel sheeting.

These facts suggested the following explanation of the trouble by Kennedy.   The fascines and rock fill of the scour pockets must have been quite pervious.   Therefore, the over 10-ft (3-m) tidal variation outside the cofferdam could produce a flow of water of alternating direction and sufficient velocity to induce localized quick conditions and *piping* (Art. 8-3) under the sheet-pile tips, as sketched on the right-hand side of Fig. 12-4.   John F.

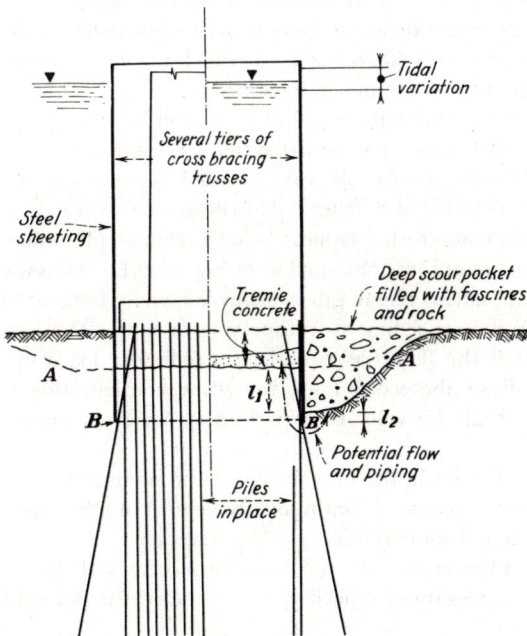

Fig. 12-4.   Trouble resulting from scour on the outer face of a cofferdam.

Kennedy (Ref. 157) showed that the *weighted creep ratio* C_c, taken as the length of the path of percolation $(l_1 + l_2)$ along the sheeting, divided by the differential head (taken as one-half of tidal variation), was much smaller than the minimum safe value of 7.0 for fine sand suggested by Terzaghi and Peck (Ref. 344, p. 617). It proved necessary to reflood the cofferdam and then remove portions of the tremie seal, replacing it by means of a procedure which included the use of Prepakt concrete.

The depth of scour can be decreased by *streamlining* the pier and the cofferdam around it, but only by some 10 percent to a maximum of 30 percent as compared to values for a rectangular-nose form of piers aligned with flow (Ref. 188).

The *alignment* factor can be quite important, as shown by Fig. 12-5B. Thus, the depth of scour may be increased by some 50 percent for a 45° angle of attack against a blunt-nosed pier twice as long as it is wide (Ref. 188). This circumstance should therefore be borne in mind, together with other factors, when deciding the location and alignment of a bridge in rapidly flowing rivers with erodable bottoms.

Figure 12-5A can be used for a rough estimate of the maximum depth of likely scour. It was developed from extensive model tests at the University of Iowa, in cooperation with the Iowa State Highway Commission and the Bureau of Public Roads (Ref. 188), and gives conservative results. The velocity of flow does not affect the diagram since all tests were made at the same approach velocity of 1.25 ft/sec (0.38 m/sec), at which the movement of sand particles along the bottom was found to have begun.

Velocity may have an effect although the question of its effect on scour is still an open one. Thus, later tests have indicated that for approach velocities of 9 ft/sec (2.8 m/sec) the depth of scour was increased by some 45 to 60 percent compared with a velocity of 4 ft/sec. However, at 9 ft/sec these later tests and the resulting complicated equations gave scour depth values ranging from 100 to 50 percent of those obtained from Fig. 10-5A. Thus the use of that diagram is quite safe. The depth of scour is heavily influenced by whether the oncoming flow is sediment-transporting or not. The best available evidence is that if the flow has equilibrium sediment loads upstream and downstream from the scour hole, the scour configuration is affected only slightly if at all by velocity variations (John F. Kennedy, Ref. 157).

When measuring depth of scour in the field it should also be remembered that it can fluctuate with time because of continuous movement of submerged sand dunes along the bottom of some rivers.

The question of *uplift pressures* against the tremie-concrete seal should always be given careful consideration, especially when the seal is not held down by piles.

The presence around the cofferdam of an impervious layer of mud above sand into which the sheeting is driven is not a guarantee that full uplift

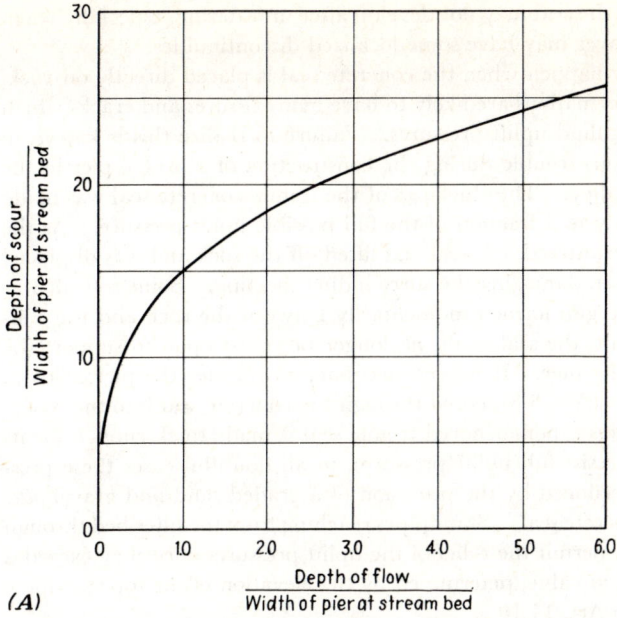

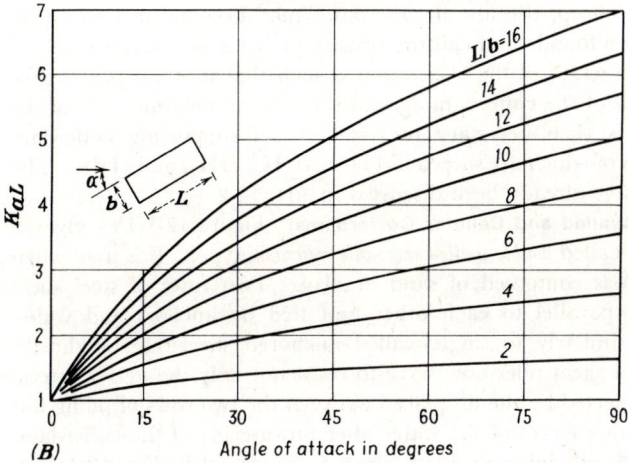

Fig. 12-5. (*A*) Basic design curve for depth of scour at zero angle α of attack. (*B*) Multiplying factors for piers not aligned with flow. (*From Laursen and Toch, Ref. 188.*)

pressures against the seal may not develop after unwatering, especially when the impervious layer may have some localized discontinuities.

The same may happen when the concrete seal is placed directly on rock, since most rock formations are likely to have many fissures and cracks which will transmit full fluid uplift pressures. Failure to realize this is known to have caused serious trouble during the construction of a bridge pier in the Hudson River valley. The thickness of the tremie-concrete seal was made to correspond only to a fraction of the full possible uplift pressure. As the cofferdam was unwatered, the seal was lifted off the rock and was displaced laterally somewhat, damaging the surrounding sheeting. Some soft silt was squeezed into the gap formed momentarily between the rock and the concrete. As a result, the seal could no longer be relied upon to support the design loads of the pier. It proved necessary to transfer the pier loads to drilled-in caissons (Art. 6-8), cored through the concrete seal into the rock.

Therefore, unless a nonanchored tremie seal is made thick enough for its weight alone to resist full uplift pressures, in all doubtful cases these pressures should be reduced by the provision of a graded sand and gravel *filter bed* under the concrete seal. Standpipes reaching from the filter bed through the seal can then permit the relief of the uplift pressures once they exceed a specified maximum value, determined by the elevation of the top standpipe opening (see also Art. 14-10).

If the water is deep, the use of cofferdams may become uneconomical. The piers are then founded on caissons of various types (see Art. 6-10).

Frequently the width of the excavation is such that it is not practicable to brace one wall of the cofferdam against the wall on the other side of the excavation. It is then necessary to resort to self-supporting cofferdam walls, some types of which are shown in Fig. 12-1(II), (III), and (IV). The first two types have already been discussed in Art. 12-2.

12-4. Double-walled and Cellular Cofferdams. Figure 12-1(IV) gives a section of the so-called *double-walled sheet-pile cofferdam* type. It is used when the river bottom is composed of sand or clay. Two rows of steel sheet piles are driven parallel to each other and tied by anchors and wales. Each row acts similarly to single-walled anchored sheet-pile bulkheads. But the anchored sheet piles now have to resist not only the active lateral earth pressures exerted by the fill placed between the two rows of piling but also the overturning forces of the water after unwatering of the cofferdam. Inner berms with adjoining drainage ditch C, as shown in Fig. 12-1(IV), are helpful in reducing the danger of a quick condition and are used whenever there is space for their construction. Otherwise the width b of the double-walled cofferdam has to be made almost equal to its height H, and the depth of penetration D of the sheet piling may have to equal $0.65H$ (Ref. 342). If the soil is clay, the stability analysis should include a study of the safety against shearing rupture of the clay along various possible curved surfaces of sliding, such as ae.

Figure 12-6 shows, in plan, two of the most frequently used types of *cellular cofferdams*, the cellular type (*A*) and the diaphragm type (*B*).   In both types the radial lateral outward pressures of the fill in the cells induce tensile stresses in the arched sections of the sheet piling.   Accordingly, straight-web sections with high interlock strength (see Art. 11-6) are employed in cellular cofferdams, whereas in double-wall cofferdams [Fig. 12-1(IV)] the sheet piles have to resist bending, so that arch-web sections with high values of their section moduli have to be employed.

In the *circular type* (Fig. 12-6*A*) the tensile stresses of each closed ring balance each other out, so that each cell is self-contained.   This type can therefore be used for permanent structures too, such as dolphins or mooring towers (see Art. 14-4*C*), which require isolated cells.   Further, serious damage to one cell, including its complete collapse, will not affect neighboring cells (see Fig. 12-13).

In the *diaphragm type* (Fig. 12-6*B*) the cross walls serve the same purpose as the anchor rods in a double-walled cofferdam [Fig. 12-1(IV)].   Since these cross walls are built of straight-web sections, they have very little flexural resistance to differences in lateral pressures from the fill, as well as the water, in the adjoining cells.   Therefore, they are not only very sensitive to damage of an adjoining cell but are apt to deflect and be distorted even by uneven filling or by water-level differences in adjoining cells during construction.

The design calculations for both types of cellular cofferdams are made in respect to an equivalent rectangular width *E* (see Fig. 12-6), which can be taken as roughly equal to 0.85 times the cell diameter *D*.   Exact values for different sized cofferdams are given in most sheet-pile catalogs of steel-producing companies.   In this respect the stability computations for the double-walled cofferdam and for both types of cellular cofferdams follow the same general lines.

Similarly, *scour problems* of all these cofferdam types can be treated in the

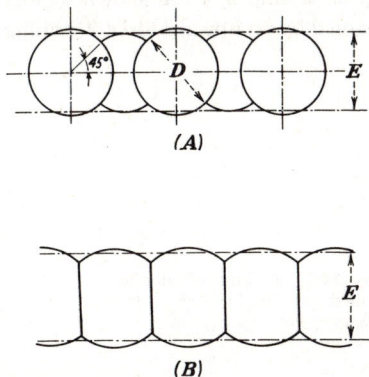

(A)

(B)

Fig. 12-6. Main types of cellular cofferdams: (*A*) circular and (*B*) diaphragm.

same manner.   Figure 12-7 sketches a simple way of safeguarding a cofferdam against being undermined by the eddies of rapidly flowing water.   A
curved sheet-pile wall is built out into the river from the outer upstream
corner of the cofferdam and braced against timber piles driven on its inboard (concave) side.   Model tests conducted in the hydraulic laboratory
of the University of Iowa by the U.S. Engineer Corps showed that this
streamlining transfers the deep erosion scour pockets from the cofferdam
corner a, where they are dangerous, to a', where they are harmless.   Later
full-scale construction by Spencer, White and Prentis on the Mississippi river
confirmed this (Ref. 401, pp. 43–47).

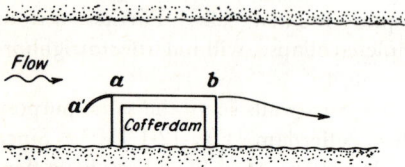

Fig. 12-7.   Streamlining   a   cofferdam.   (*From
White and Prentis, Ref. 401.*)

Until the 1940s it had been customary to analyze a cellular cofferdam
resting on rock as a gravity retaining wall, specifically with respect to its
resistance against sliding along its base and against overturning.   This
approach was sometimes extended even to cellular cofferdams the sheet piles
of which penetrated into sand.   One of the first to publish data demonstrating the inadequacy of this customary approach was Rimstad (Ref. 266).
The tests he performed on a model of a double-walled cofferdam with a dry
sand base and fill disclosed a failure mechanism which it is important to
understand and which is shown in sketch form by Figs. 12-8 and 12-9.

The application of a horizontal force H to simulate the one-sided water
pressure on an unwatered cofferdam produced a tilting of the originally
vertical walls 1-2 and 3-4 to the positions 1'-2' and 3'-4', as shown in Fig.
12-8.   This tilting was obviously accompanied by an upward force T pulling

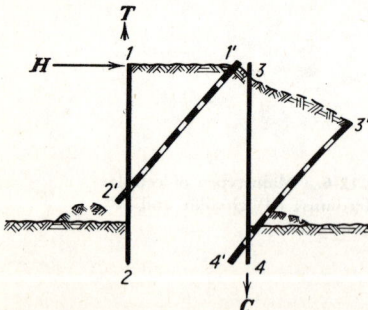

Fig. 12-8.   Failure of double-
walled cofferdam model.   (*After
Rimstad, Ref. 266.*)

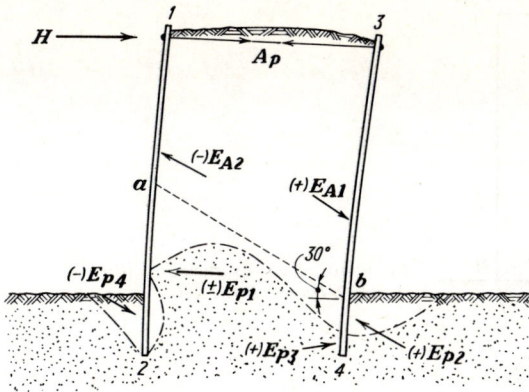

Fig. 12-9. Slip surfaces in sand at start of test shown in Fig. 12-8. (*After Rimstad, Ref. 266.*)

the waterside sheet 1-2 out of the ground and forming a couple with the downward force C on sheet 3-4. A photographic technique similar to the one outlined in Art. 11-1 with reference to Fig. 11-2 was used to determine the zones of the sand base and fill which did not move in the early stages of the test when the deformations were quite small. The limits of these areas are shown by dash-dotted lines in Fig. 12-9. These lines represent the limits of the slip or rupture surfaces. Their shape is related to the direction and nature of the lateral earth pressures on the sheeting, which the writer has approximately indicated by arrows and symbols on Fig. 12-9. They are discussed as follows, with reference to Art. 10-3.

Sheet 3-4 is subjected to the same kind of active and passive earth pressures as a fixed-end anchored bulkhead (Art. 14-3A and Fig. 14-8). But sheet 1-2 is acted upon by a passive lateral earth pressure $-E_{p4}$, the intensity of which is much smaller than that of $+E_{p2}$ because of a change in direction of the angles of wall friction; sheet 1-2 is pulled out of the soil whereas sheet 3-4 is pushed into it. For the same reason the intensity of the active earth pressure $-E_{A2}$ is greater than that of $+E_{A1}$. However, both are in equilibrium with the same anchor pull A_p because $-E_{A2}$ acts along a shorter length of sheeting than $+E_{A1}$ does. The direction of $\pm E_{p1}$ is shown as horizontal since it seems doubtful that wall friction could affect it.

A detailed numerical analysis along these lines for practical designs does not appear feasible at present. But the Rimstad model tests served the very useful purpose of emphasizing the role of fill stability as a most important factor in the overall stability of a double-walled or cellular cofferdam.

Several simplified approaches to this problem developed. Figure 12-10 illustrates the solution proposed by J. Brinch Hansen (Refs. 266 and 122) in respect to a cofferdam on rock. He assumes that the lowest slip surface within the sand fill is a logarithmic spiral passing through points A and B,

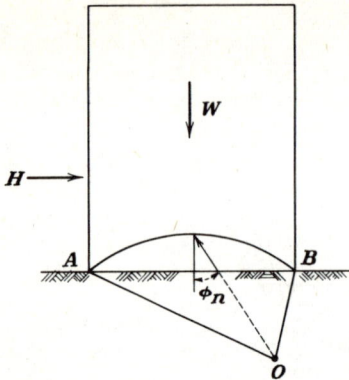

Fig. 12-10. Failure surfaces. (*After J. Brinch Hansen, Ref. 122.*)

along which rotational tilting of the cofferdam can occur.   If the angle of internal friction of the fill is ϕ and the desired factor of safety is F, the logarithmic spiral is drawn for an angle ϕ_n obtained from

$$\tan \phi_n = \frac{\tan \phi}{F} \qquad (12\text{-}1)$$

All internal stresses along the spiral form an angle ϕ_n with the normal and pass through the pole O.   The only remaining forces acting on the unstable mass of soil above the spiral are its weight W and the lateral force H.   If the moment of W around the pole O is greater than the moment of the overturning force H around the same pole, the structure is stable.   Several positions of the pole O have to be investigated.   Of course, this procedure is applicable only to entirely noncohesive fill.

The Brinch Hansen approach has been extended and refined in Denmark by Krebs Ovesen on the basis of extensive model tests analyzed in Ref. 239. In France, a somewhat similar approach involving slip surfaces in the shape of inclined circular arcs has been used by Schneebeli (Ref. 281).

Terzaghi (Ref. 342) recommended investigation of the safety against tilting due to sliding along the centerline of the cofferdam, as shown in Fig. 12-11A.

The shearing force Q along the centerline is computed from the overturning moment M and the cofferdam width b to equal

$$Q = \frac{3M}{2b} \qquad (12\text{-}2)$$

The vertical pressures on the rock at the base of the cofferdam can be represented by the trapezoid $abcd$ assuming that it acts approximately as a rigid body.   Then the value of the shear Q is equal to the area of each of the shaded triangles in Fig. 10-11A.

For a unit of cofferdam length the shearing resistance R along the vertical centerline is assumed to equal the total lateral active earth pressure against it [Eq. (10-14)], multiplied by the coefficient of internal friction $\tan \phi$ of the soil, increased by the frictional resistance f in the sheet-pile interlocks

$$R = \frac{\gamma H^2}{2} \tan^2\left(45 - \frac{\phi}{2}\right)(\tan \phi + f) \tag{12-3}$$

The relevant factor of safety is then

$$F = \frac{R}{Q} \tag{12-4}$$

In the same place (Ref. 342, p. 1095) Terzaghi suggests that the interlock-friction value be taken as $f = 0.3$. The use of Eq. (12-3) is linked to the assumption that the greatest active lateral earth pressure and hence the greatest interlock tension occurs at the rock line.

Actually, the greatest tension must occur at a height of approximately $h/4$ above the rock line, judging by the visible deformations of fully filled cells. There usually is some slack in the interlocks immediately after driving, causing an increase of cell diameter after it is filled. This diameter should be proportional to the intensity of interlock tension. Observations show that, after filling, the cell tends to assume a barrel shape with the largest diameter approximately $h/4$ above the rock line, along which shearing stresses and in which the toehold of the sheeting exert a restraining influence.

The use of Eq. (12-3), however, is quite safe since there is reason to believe

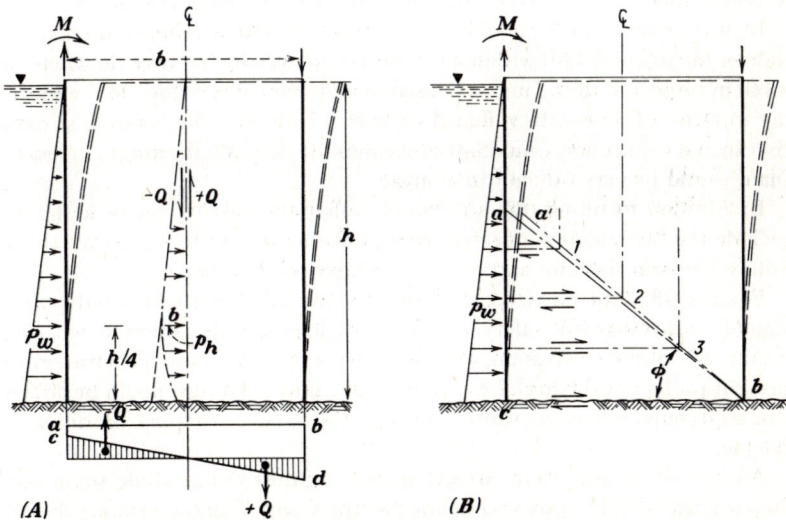

Fig. 12-11.   Failure surfaces.   [(A) *after Terzaghi, Ref. 342; (B) after E. M. Cummings, Ref. 75.*]

that the lateral pressures within the cell are greater than the active values assumed in Eq. (12-3) and may correspond to neutral values.

The Terzaghi analysis of slippage along a vertical plane, as in Fig. 12-11A, corresponds to only one of the possible modes of failure within the fill. A second possibility is slippage along horizontal surfaces, safety against which can be investigated by the procedure proposed by E. M. Cummings (Ref. 75) and illustrated by Fig. 12-11B.

Cummings assumes that only the fill below the line ab remains stable, the line ab being inclined under the angle of internal friction ϕ with the horizontal. Cummings arrived at this assumption indirectly, on the basis of his own simple but ingenious small-scale model tests (Ref. 75). It is, however, in approximate agreement with the result of the Rimstad tests; see Fig. 12-8, where the line ab is shown broken.

The triangular section of stable soil abc is divided into slices, and the resistance developed by each slice is taken to equal the weight of the entire soil above its base multiplied by the friction coefficient (tan ϕ). For clays, this resistance equals the cohesion multiplied by the total horizontal area of the slice.

When the entire mass of soil within the cell is composed of noncohesive free-draining sand and gravel, as should be the case if the entire mass is composed of fill, either one of the two methods most frequently used in the United States, the Terzaghi or the Cummings method, should ensure a cofferdam stable against tilting. However, if the soil in the lower part of a cell consists of nonexcavated natural soil left in place and containing clay layers, a check by the Cummings method should always be made, since the Terzaghi method deals with only one of the possible modes of failure.

In this connection it should also be realized that a reinforced-concrete slab on the top of the fill within a cell cannot materially improve the safety of a cell in respect to tilting unless the slab reinforcement is welded to the sheeting to form a frame with stiffened corners. However, the bending stresses that such a connection would introduce into the flat-web sheeting, curved in plan, would be very difficult to analyze.

In addition to tilting, the analysis of cofferdam stability on rock should include the investigation of safety against sliding on the base; against shear failure between sheeting and fill; and of interlock tension.

For a cofferdam on deep sand or clay the following additional points should be investigated: safety against a bearing-capacity failure at toe, i.e., on the side of the excavation, and the adequacy of sheet-pile penetration to prevent pullout at the heel, i.e., on the water side. To this should be added (for sands only) a flow-net study to prevent the danger of a quick condition at the toe.

An overall stability study involving safety against sliding along some surface ae [Fig. 12-1(IV)] passing below the tips B and B' of the sheeting should always be performed.

The first cellular cofferdam was constructed in 1910 for raising the battleship *Maine* from the bottom of Havana Harbor in 35 ft (10.7 m) of water. The underlying soil and the fill in the cells were clay, so that the cofferdam began to tilt dangerously when the water level was lowered by 15 ft (4.6 m). It had to be braced against the hull of the ship before unwatering could e successfully completed (Ref. 342).

Figure 12-12 illustrates the circular type of cell used for the cellular cofferdam which enclosed, during its construction, the Kentucky Dam of the Tennessee Valley Authority.   With a total height of 98 ft (30 m) this is the highest cofferdam built so far.   The use of an inner berm permitted a small diameter of the cells equal to $0.59H$.   Freely supported cofferdams usually have a width of the cells equal to $0.85H$ or $1.00H$.   [Design calculations for the Kentucky cofferdam (Fig. 12-12) are given on pp. 111–115 of Ref. 288; other stability calculations can be found in Refs. 191 and 15.]

The interlock friction is a function of the interlock tension; according to Terzaghi's analysis (Ref. 342), it may increase the total shearing resistance along vertical planes by some 50 percent, so that the presence of transversal sheet-pile wall sections should constitute an important advantage of the cellular type of cofferdam compared with the plain double-wall type. Lubrication of the locks should be avoided, even though it facilitates pulling

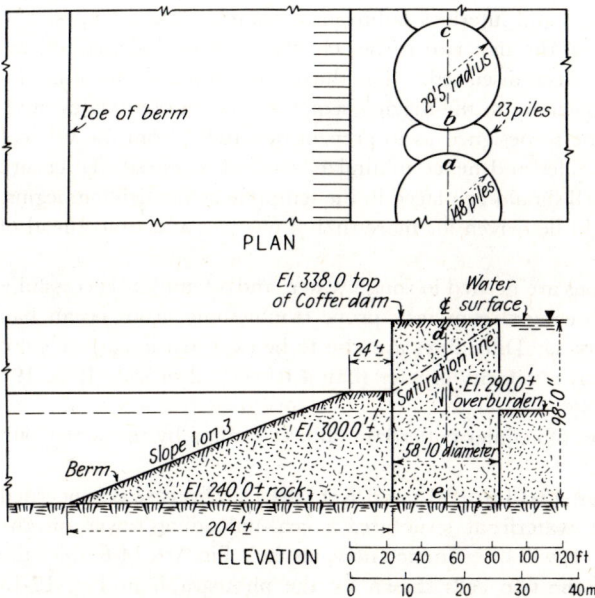

Fig. 12-12.   Cellular cofferdam used for the construction of the Kentucky Dam, Tennessee Valley Authority.   (*After Colburn, Ref. 61.*)

the sheet piles for reuse. Since the use of berms may decrease somewhat the interlock tension along the plane *de* and hence the interlock friction and resistance to sliding along that plane, differences of opinion exist (Ref. 342) concerning the advantages of using such berms in connection with cellular cofferdams.

When the sheet piles of the cofferdam are driven into sand, the upward seepage pressures of the percolating water may decrease the passive resistance of the sand along the inner face *sB'* [Fig. 12-1(IV)] of the inner row of sheet piling unless berms with drainage ditches *C'* to lengthen and flatten the paths of percolation, or similar measures, are used for cellular cofferdams as well as for double-wall cofferdams, to which Fig. 12-1(IV) refers.

12-5. Failures of Cellular Cofferdams. White and Prentis (Ref. 401) report some cofferdam failures on the Mississippi River which were caused by the absence of measures to counteract the detrimental effects of seepage forces. Inner corners are particularly dangerous in this respect, since flow lines converging on the corner from two directions at right angles to each other squeeze themselves closely together there, with a resulting increase in the velocity of flow.

Reference 15 lists 11 different causes or failure modes of cellular-cofferdam failures reported in answers to a questionnaire circulated by the authors. The three most frequent causes, with several failures each, were (1) scour and partial loss of cell fill; (2) partial shearing of silt and clay fill; (3) failure at connection sheet piles and interlock failure near connection sheet piles.

The elimination of the first two causes chiefly involves design problems which have already been discussed. The third cause is related to construction procedures, especially to the driving sequence and the templates used. Templates should be so designed as to prevent deviations from the vertical of individual sheet piles and hence minimize interlock stresses. To ensure this *all* sheets in a cell should be placed in the template before driving begins, and no sheets should be driven for more than a few feet at a time ahead of the remainder.

Special precautions are needed in rough water, and a template successfully used in a slowly flowing stream may prove troublesome in an ocean bay exposed to high waves. Difficulties are also to be expected in surface calm water which flows at a velocity greater than 4 ft/sec (1.2 m/sec) (Refs. 191 and 15).

Two specific cases of cellular cofferdam failures studied by the writer will now be described.

Case 1. (See Figs. 12-13 to 12-15 and Ref. 364.) This case is concerned with a permanent waterfront structure, a coal-unloading tower on the Mississippi River. It will be examined now, instead of in Art. 14-8, since the collapse of one of the two cells shown by the photograph in Fig. 12-13 originated in a defective tee connection. This cause is possible in all types of cellular cofferdams, temporary as well as permanent.

Fig. 12-13.   Case 1: coal-unloading tower cell after failure.   (*From Tschebotarioff, Ref. 364.*)

A series of individual cells was built along the riverbank for mooring coal barges.   Two large cells, 13 and 14, were joined to form an unloading platform.   The cell dimensions are shown on Fig. 12-14.

The failure occurred due to bursting of cell 13 at the tee connection marked X on the plan.   Hydraulic filling of both main cells had already been completed, and filling of the connecting cells was underway, reaching the elevations shown on section AA at the time the tee failure occurred.

Because of considerable water-level fluctuations in the river, the cells had an unusually large free height of 77 ft (23.5 m) above river bottom.   Consequently, the hydraulic filling of the cells could produce appreciably higher axial tensions T_F in the flange and in the stem T_s of the tee connection than would have resulted from dry filling.   This is because rapid hydraulic filling is not likely to permit the excess water to escape immediately, even when weep holes are provided.   Therefore, the cell bulges under the action of the combined fluid weight of water and soil.   Some contraction of cell diameter will then take place after the fill fully consolidates and will be resisted by greater than neutral radial pressures of the drained fill.

Nevertheless, the maximum possible interlock stresses which would result from hydraulic filling would exceed by only some 25 percent the 8,000 lb/in. (1,425 kg_f/cm) stress indicated as permissible for the type of section used (see Table 11-2).

A series of tests on three kinds of tees were then initiated at Lehigh University by Burns & Roe, Consulting Engineers.   The results are shown in

CONDITIONS AT TIME OF FAILURE

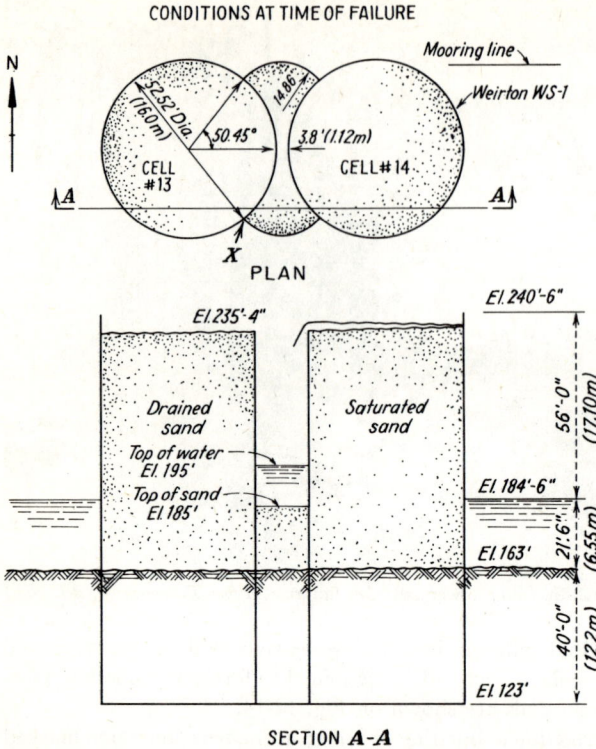

Fig. 12-14. Case 1: conditions of filling at time of failure shown by Fig. 12-13. (*From Tschebotarioff, Ref. 364.*)

Fig. 12-15. The tee type *A* was the conventional shop-welded kind and type *C* the shop-riveted kind. Type *B* had been field-welded by the contractor on the job site. An angle iron was first welded on one side of the flange and the stem to hold them in place while they were welded together at their direction connection. These *B*-type samples used for the tests were cut from one of the cell 13 tees which had not failed.

The tees were subjected to gradually increasing stem pulls T_s after application of a flange pull $T_F = 11,000$ lb/in. (1,960 kg$_f$/cm) through arcs composed of 3.5 sheet pile sections on each side of the tee. Some typical results are given on Fig. 12-15. They prove that the maximum stem pull T_s which a tee could resist was a function of its ability to undergo plastic deformations, as expressed by the value *y*. The angle welded on one side of the type *B* tee prevented these deformations. A riveted connection type *C* permits them by allowing some slippage between the angles and the flange of the sheet.

The cellular cofferdam was successfully rebuilt as originally designed, but after replacing all previously field-welded tees by riveted tees. The cells were sand-filled by dry procedures, i.e., by using clamshell buckets.

Welding tees even in shops under carefully supervised conditions requires x-ray checks of the absence of slag inclusions in the metal. Such inclusions are apt to be rolled into the shape of flat lenses within the web of sheet piles, greatly weakening them in respect to any transverse forces transferred by a tee stem welded to their surface. Field welding of tees should not be permitted.

Since a tee cannot become effective before plastic deformations in the metal of the flange have taken place, some designers use a so-called Y connection, where the forces in the three legs are in static equilibrium without any overstressing of the flange to deform it plastically. Such Y connections have been used on the Kentucky dam cofferdam, as shown in Fig. 12-12.

Case 2. (See Figs. 12-16 to 12-19.) A circular cofferdam was being built to permit construction in the dry of an intake to the water-supply tunnel of a neighboring city (Ref. 169). Four cells had been completed, and a crane had been moved out on cell 4, from which to set up the sheets for the fifth and last cell, 3. Sometime during the night cell 4 collapsed. Its fill, most of the sheeting, and the crane disappeared under the surface of the water.

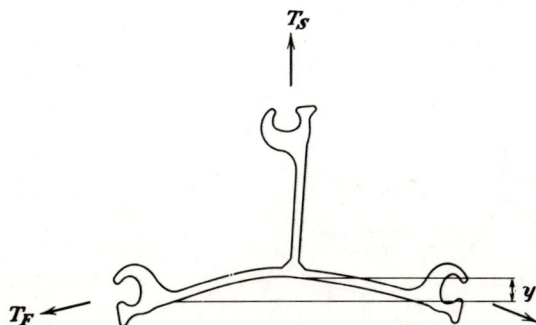

Test	y In.	y Cm	T_S Kips/in.	T_S kgf/cm	
A	1.3	3.2	6.7	1,190	(Fillet shop weld)
B	0.6	1.5	1.6	285	(Angle-stiffened field weld)
C	1.7	4.3	8.5	1,510	(Shop-riveted)

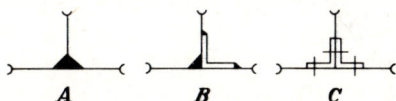

Fig. 12-15. Case 1: results of comparative tests on three types of tees. (*From Tschebotarioff, Ref. 364.*)

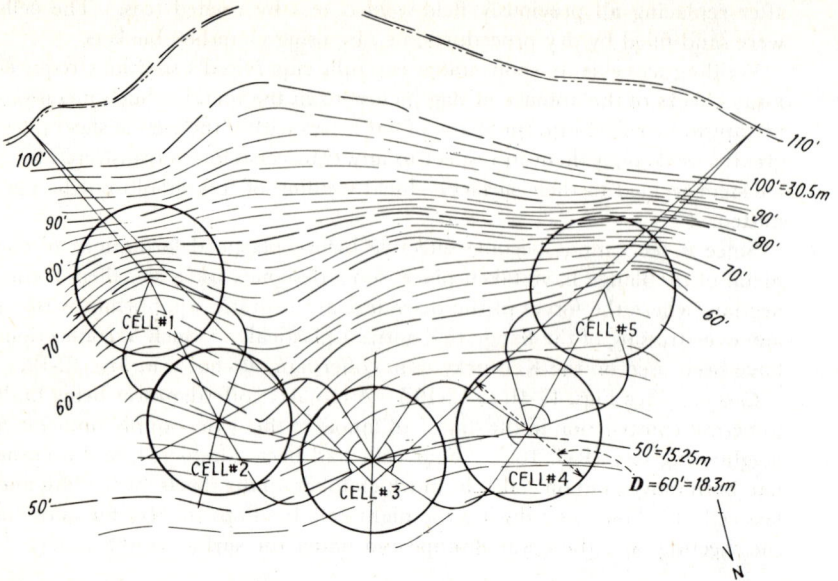

Fig. 12-16. Case 2: general layout of the five cells of the cofferdam, illustrated by Figs. 12-17 to 12-19. (*Ref 169.*)

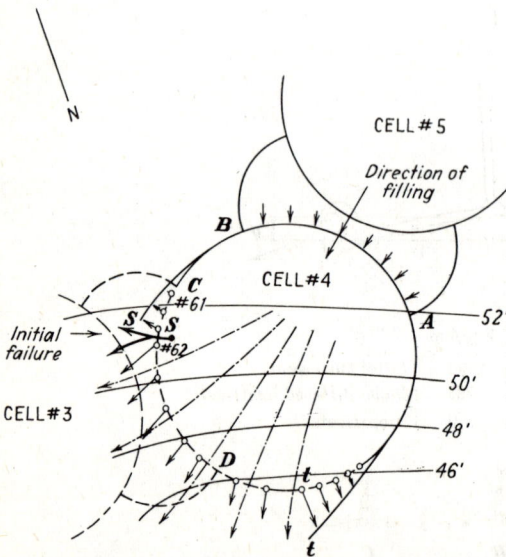

Fig. 12-17. Case 2: sketch of probable displacement of fill within cell #4 after its failure (see Fig. 12-16). (*Ref. 169.*)

Underwater examination of the wreckage by divers showed that the cell had burst at the interlock between sheets 61 and 62, the location of which in plan is shown on Fig. 12-17. When these sheets were recovered, it was found that the lower few inches of the interlock had opened; higher up the thumb of the interlock of sheet 61 was ripped off, retaining its connection to the interlock of sheet 62. The pattern of the fracture indicated to metallurgists that this is where the fracture started, proceeding upward.

A recovered spud H-pile, which had supported the timber template for driving the sheeting, came up with several feet of soft silt still left within its flanges, indicating that the silt had not been removed by the contractor before starting to fill the cell.

These facts suggested the following explanation by the writer in Ref. 169. The cells were filled by bulldozing alternate truckloads of bank-run gravel and rock-tunnel spoil over the edge of cell 5. Thus the fill was dropped through the water on the uphill side of the sloping rock surface and would be bound to displace the silt in a mud wave outward, as tentatively indicated by arrows in Fig. 12-18.

This completely remolded silt would have very little shearing strength, and its lateral pressures would be of the kind produced by a fluid with a lateral-earth-pressure-coefficient value $K = 1.00$. The diagram on the left-hand side of Fig. 12-18 indicates the resulting radial pressures within the cell. Their values are computed in Prob. 12-4, which also gives the resulting interlock pulls T if the sheets formed a closed ring at the relevant elevations. It will be noted that these interlock pulls T would be of the order of 13,000

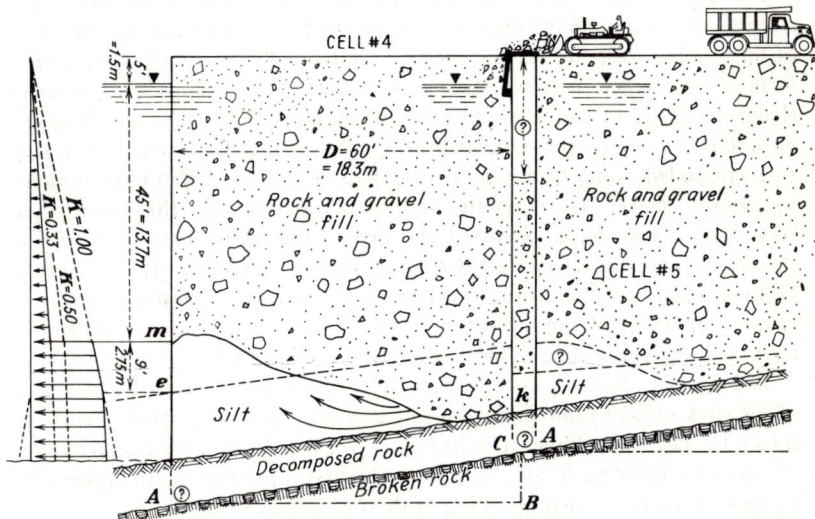

Fig. 12-18. Case 2: relationship between lateral earth pressures and probable height of mud wave created by unsymmetrical filling of cell (see Fig. 12-17). (*Ref. 169.*)

Fig. 12-19. Case 2: metallurgists examining sheeting from collapsed cell; see Fig. 12-17. (*Photo by Tschebotarioff, Ref. 169.*)

lb/in. (2,300 kg$_f$/cm), which is 60 percent greater than the maximum recommended design values of 8,000 lb/in. (1,425 kg$_f$/cm) but still well below the minimum interlock strength of 16,000 lb/in. (2,850 kg$_f$/cm).

The failure that occurred therefore has to be accounted for by additional stresses, which must have been created by the fact that at the downhill end of the sloping rock surface the sheets were longest and therefore could not form closed rings. Between the tees C and D (Fig. 12-17) each successive sheet of the arc in cell 4 would penetrate some 2 in. (5 cm) less than the elevation reached by the outboard sheet. At the interlocks where each ring segment ended, some additional stresses had to be transmitted to the adjoining shorter sheet. Hard points, such as boulders within the decomposed rock layers, may have increased the penetration differences of adjoining sheets and hence the localized stress increments. The cumulative effect of all these stress increments must have reached a maximum in the area where, in plan, the circle of the cell sheeting intersected at right angles the contour lines of the rock surface. This is where the failure started (Fig. 12-17).

This negative factor was caused by the absence of any prepared benching of the rock surface prior to driving the sheeting, i.e., excavation of rock, as shown by dash-dotted lines ABC in Fig. 12-18, to provide a horizontal surface for all sheet tips of each cell. It is reported that contractors with higher bids for this job had included benching in their proposals.

12-6. Responsibility for Cofferdam Performance. Until recently it has been customary to make the contractor solely responsible for cofferdam performance, even though his design was usually subject to review by the engineers of the owner of the structure under construction. This procedure seems to have its origin in a desire to permit competitive use of different construction methods supposedly best known to the contractors who propose them.

This century has seen a steady growth in the size of different types of structures, with a corresponding increase in the size and complexity of their substructures. Greater depths of excavation and greater water depths to operate in frequently became necessary in a variety of conditions, not always fully covered by the previous experience of individual contracting firms.

The growth of relevant engineering knowledge due to new developments in the fields of applied soil and fluid mechanics is also continuing, but all too often its rational application to practical field problems of cofferdam design requires careful and time-consuming studies and on-the-spot investigations which cannot be performed by contractors in the short time usually made available for the preparation of their bids. Low bids, based on risky guesses and assumptions, are often the result of this situation and are sometimes followed by failures, with subsequent litigation, costly both in money and in lost time for everyone concerned, whatever the ultimate disposition of such cases by the courts may be.

It is therefore essential that the designers of complex substructures carefully consider the methods by which they can be built, including the possible designs of cofferdams when such will be needed. All preliminary soil- and hydraulic-engineering investigations necessary for cofferdam design should be made by the designers of the substructure. The cofferdam and the sub-structure designs should be correlated at the time the latter is made. Much later grief can thereby be avoided. In some complex cases this may mean that the engineers will have to assume full responsibility on behalf of the owner of the structure for the cofferdam design. The writer is familiar with a case where this actually had to be done.

REVIEW PROBLEMS

12-1. With reference to the flow net drawn in Fig. 12-3, what is the danger of a quick condition developing in the sump pit?

Answer. The total head lost is $h = 40$ ft (12-2 m). Ten equipotential lines have been drawn in Fig. 12-3, so that the head lost between each pair of adjacent lines is $\Delta h = 4.0$ ft (1.2 m). When drawn to a larger scale, the distance between the last two equipotential lines i.e., between the one marked 9 in Fig. 12-3 and the bottom of the sump pit, can be measured: $L = 1.9$ ft (58 cm). According to Eq. (8-14), the hydraulic gradient below the bottom of the sump pit will be

$$ S = \frac{\Delta h}{L} = \frac{4.0}{1.9} = 2.1 $$

Failure due to the development of a quick condition will be inevitable, since the highest possible value of the critical hydraulic gradient for very dense sand (see Art. 8-4) is $S_{cr} = 1.05$. Thus the factor of safety is much smaller than unity: $F = S_{cr}/S = 1.05/2.1 = 0.50$.

12-2. Prior to unwatering the cofferdam shown in Fig. 12-3, the surface of the excavation was covered by a graded filter, and a 5-ft-thick (1.53-m) seal of concrete was placed over it. Several overflow standpipes reaching into the filter layer were left embedded in the concrete. Estimate the factor of safety against uplift of the concrete seal.

Answer. It has been shown in Prob. 12-1 that within the upper 1.9 ft (58 cm) of soil a head of 4.0 ft (1.2 m) of water was dissipated. The flow net which corresponds to the conditions of the present problem will differ somewhat from the one drawn in Fig. 12-3, but not much. If we make the unfavorable assumption that only the weight of the seal will resist a head of 4.0 ft (1.2 m) of water, the factor of safety against uplift will still be adequate: $F = (5 \times 140)/(4 \times 62.5) = 2.81$.

12-3. Estimate the possible depth of scour around a bridge pier 20 ft (6.1 m) wide at a river bottom composed of a deep sand layer. The pier is aligned with the direction of the flow, the approach velocity of which can reach 5 ft/sec (1.5 m/sec) at flood stage. The water depth will then be 25 ft (7.6 m).

Answer. The velocity is sufficient to produce scour. To use the design diagram Fig. 12-5A, we obtain the relevant abscissa $\frac{25}{20} = 1.25$ and from the curve find the corresponding ordinate to be 0.85. The maximum likely depth of a scour pocket will then be $0.85 \times 20 = 17$ ft (5.2 m).

12-4. Compute the horizontal pressures at levels m and e of Fig. 12-18 and the resulting interlock pulls T.

Answer. The vertical pressure at level m is approximately $P_v = 5 \times 125 + 45 \times 65 = 3,550$ lb/ft^2 (17,350 kg$_f$/m^2). Below the mud-wave surface $K = 1.00$, and the horizontal pressure $p_h = p_v$. With a cell diameter $D = 60$ ft (18.3 m), the interlock pull will then be $T = 3,750 \times \frac{60}{2} = 11,250$ lb/in. (2,000 kg$_f$/cm). At level e the horizontal pressures will be increased by $9 \times 65 = 595$ lb/ft^2 (2,910 kg$_f$/m^2) and the interlock pull then becomes $T = 13,000$ lb/in. (2,300 kg$_f$/cm). If all silt had been removed, the above values would have been only one-third as large.

RECOMMENDED FOR FURTHER STUDY

Lacroix, Yves, Melvin I. Esrig, and Ulrich Luscher, Design, Construction and Performance of Cellular Cofferdams, Ref. 15, pp. 271–328.
Lehigh University, Ref. 191, pp. 319–439.

CHAPTER 13

TUNNELS AND CONDUITS

13-1. Rock Tunnels. Field exploration, including borings, should always be performed at key locations of a proposed tunnel alignment to check geologic opinions on the character of strata to be encountered. Failure to do so may lead to tragic consequences, as during the construction in 1908 of the Loetschberg tunnel (Ref. 416, fig. 22, p. 89) illustrated by Fig. 13-1. The 9-mile-long (14-m) tunnel pierces the alpine mountain chain and at a distance of about 1.6 miles (2.6 km) from its north-northwest portal was to pass below the Gastern Valley. A commission of geologists estimated that the tunnel would be overlaid by more than 300 ft (90 m) of rock in that area. They were mistaken. The tunnel encountered a much deeper ancient valley filled with water-bearing sand and gravel, and an underground mud slide suddenly filled it for a distance of about a mile. Twenty-five men lost their lives. Part of the tunnel had to be relocated.

If the rock is entirely sound, no special supports may be required to carry the weight of the tunnel roof during construction. On the other hand, elaborate precautions and a special sequence of construction operations may be necessary if preliminary information indicates that the rock is shattered or that other hazards are to be expected. Figure 13-2 illustrates the construction procedure employed for the short (540 ft = 165 m) but very wide (79 ft = 24.2 m at the springline) tunnel through the shattered interbedded sandstones and shales of Yerba Buena Island, connecting the two parts of the

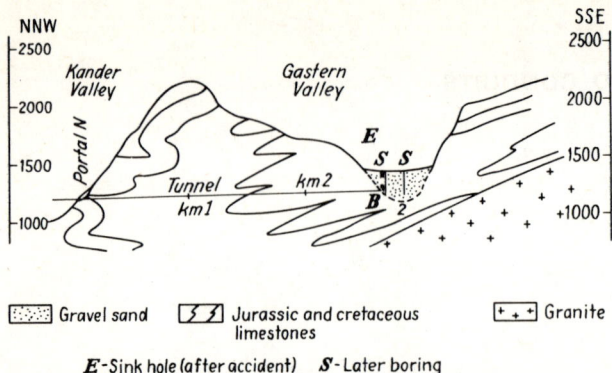

Fig. 13-1. Profile of the north section of the Loetschberg tunnel where failure occurred under the Gastern Valley. (*From Ref. 416.*)

San Francisco–Oakland Bay Bridge. Similar procedures are employed when tunneling through other weakened types of rocks.

First of all, as shown in Fig. 13-2*A*, a small pilot tunnel ("monkey drift") is advanced at the crown. This has the advantage of permitting the consulting geologists, who should always be present on important jobs of this

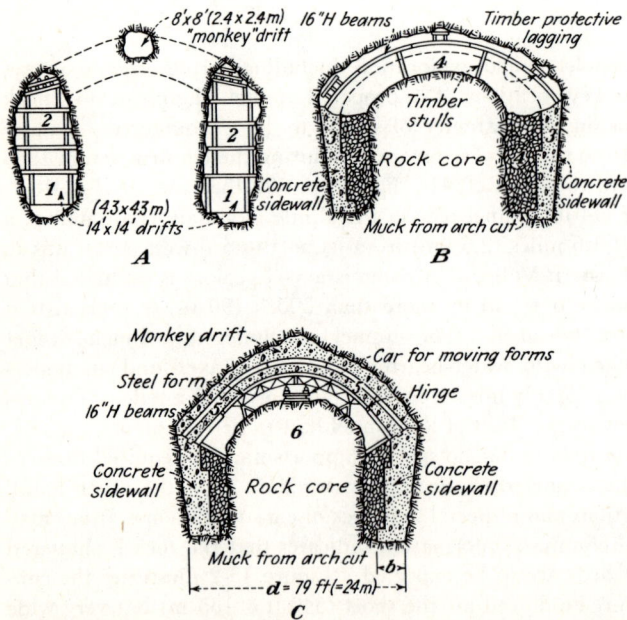

Fig. 13-2. Sequence of construction operations, Yerba Buena Tunnel. (*After Proctor, Ref. 254.*)

type, to verify, as the work progresses, the preliminary evaluations of the state of the rock which they had made from core-drill borings and surface examination of the geology of the site. Necessary changes of construction procedure can then be made in time. Sidewall drifts are advanced shortly after.

During the next stage, illustrated by Fig. 13-2B, the concrete sidewalls are built, and the roof is excavated in shallow sections which are temporarily braced against the central rock core left intact for that purpose.

Finally, as shown in Fig. 13-2C, the concrete of the roof arch is placed either by gravity from the center monkey drift or by forced pumping. Additional grouting of spaces between the lining and the rock and of the rock seams is sometimes resorted to.

As a last step, the rock core is removed. Many modifications in the details of the above procedure are possible, of course, depending on local conditions.

Methods of estimating rock pressures against the tunnel lining have been considerably advanced in recent years by the development of *rock mechanics*, discussion of which is beyond the scope of this book.

13-2. Tunnels in Soil. When tunneling through stiff clay, procedures similar to those in rock, as illustrated by Fig. 13-2, have frequently been employed. They are usually referred to as the *liner-plate method*, since light liner plates, strengthened by steel arch ribs, are installed to support the clay before concreting the permanent lining. The factors on which the success of this method depends are the shearing strength of the clay and the width of the tunnel as well as the overburden pressure on its crown. The unit pressure over the width b of the continuous footing for the temporary lining (see Fig. 13-2, where this value refers to the permanent lining) increases with the value of the diameter d of the tunnel and with the overburden pressure. If this unit pressure of the footing becomes excessive, compared with the shearing strength of the clay, excessive settlements of the footing will follow and may even lead to a shear failure and upward squeezing of the underlying clay when the central clay core of the tunnel is removed. Considerable loss of ground would then result, i.e., more clay would be removed than corresponds to the volume of the tunnel. This would be accompanied by uneven settlements of the ground surface and by damage to structures erected thereon.

The use of compressed air during construction may partially relieve the clay pressures transmitted to the temporary footing and permit the installation of a permanent lining, which in such cases is given a base over the full width of the tunnel, so that it forms a monolith with the side walls and roof.

Chicago experience has shown (Ref. 340) that the liner-plate method could be successfully employed there for tunneling under compressed air of small sewer tunnels, but that for wider subway tunnels the much more expensive shield method must be resorted to in sections where there is softer clay.   Terzaghi (Ref. 340) has given a method for the numerical estimation of the limit conditions under which the liner-plate method may still be safely used.   The sketch in Fig. 13-3 illustrates this method, with some minor modifications.

If no compressed air is used, the vertical pressure V (per linear foot of tunnel) transmitted to the footing of liner plate ribs equals

$$V = W - S \tag{13-1}$$

where $W =$ weight of soil above one-half tunnel width

$\quad\quad S =$ shearing resistance along vertical plane above liner-plate wall

The resistance S can be based on one-half the average unconfined compressive strength of clay layers [Eq. (3-19)] above the arched portion of the tunnel.   It appears safe to do so, but only during construction, since vertical pressures in tunnels may build up to the full overburden weight value within a few years, as shown by Housel's measurements discussed below with reference to Fig. 13-5.

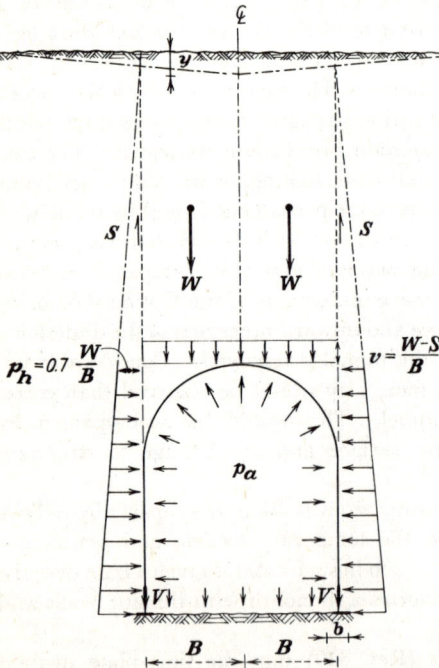

Fig. 13-3.   Forces acting on the ribbed-plate lining of a tunnel.   (*After Terzaghi, Ref. 340.*)

Using Eq. (4-5) for ultimate bearing capacity and a factor of safety F, we obtain the safe minimum width b of a continuous-strip footing:

$$b = \frac{VF}{5.14c_u} = \frac{p_v BF}{5.14c_u} \tag{13-2}$$

where c_u is one-half of the average unconfined strength q_u of the clay at the level of the tunnel invert and below it. Since this is a temporary construction, the value of F can be taken between $F = 1.6$ and $F = 2.5$ depending on the sensitivity of the clay (see Table 4-2). It is not practical to make the width b greater than 2.0 to 2.5 ft (60 to 75 cm) because of eccentricity of loading which would otherwise result. If Eq. (13-2) gives impractically large values, the use of compressed air should be considered since it not only decreases the vertical pressure on the footing but also acts like a surcharge in Eq. (4-6) in respect to the clay surface at invert level. If the air pressure is p_a, Eq. (13-2) becomes

$$b = \frac{(p_v - p_a)BF}{5.14c_u + p_a} \tag{13-3}$$

If Eq. (13-3) still gives impractically high values for b, the use of *shield tunnels* should be considered. Such tunnels are usually given a circular cross section. The relevant construction techniques are discussed in Art. 13-3 on subaqueous tunnels with reference to Fig. 13-6. Shield tunnels are much more expensive than liner-plate tunnels; nevertheless they had to be used in Chicago for several miles of subway tunnels (25 ft = 7.6 m diameter) south of the Chicago River (Ref. 339), where the unconfined compressive strength below the level of the tunnel invert was found to vary from $q_u = 0.4$ to $q_u = 0.8$ ton/ft^2 (0.8 kg$_f$/cm^2). North of the river the upper and lower strength limits of the clay were about twice as large, so that horseshoe-shaped plate liners (Fig. 13-3) for tunnels 20 ft (6.1 m) wide were successfully employed.

Using shield tunnels under city streets presents great difficulties. Depending on how large or how small the shield opening is made, either some loss of ground into the tunnel or some pushing of soil away from the tunnel head will occur. Both types of soil displacement are liable to remold the clay and induce its later reconsolidation, with resulting settlement of the street surface.

For sewer liner-plate work circular tunnel sections are customarily used (see Art. 13-5) in preference to the horseshoe section of Fig. 13-3, which is related to some of the subway work in Chicago.

The final concrete lining of the tunnel should be poured as soon as possible. As illustrated by Fig. 13-5, the full weight of the overburden will come to rest on the tunnel crown some time after construction if the soil is plastic clay. For that reason the permanent lining should be designed to carry that full weight. The lateral pressures to be expected have not yet been fully determined, especially the passive resistance which a plastic clay can be relied upon to maintain permanently in the case of flexible ring-shaped tunnel linings and deformations of the type illustrated by Fig. 13-11(II). Therefore the range of variation from $K = \frac{1}{2}$ to $K = \frac{2}{3}$, used for the design of the Chicago subway tubes, without surcharge, appears reasonable until more data become available on this subject [see reports by Nicolet and Gunlock on the design and the construction of the tubes and stations (Ref. 229)]. Heavy wall sections are the consequence of such assumptions; further experimental studies may permit their reduction in future structures.

Purely theoretical considerations are of little importance for problems of this type when compared with the results of actual measurements and observations. Only a very limited number of such records is available. One of the more noteworthy and complete sets of such observations was obtained and reported by Housel (Ref. 136) from Detroit during construction of sewer tunnels at a depth of some 60 ft (18 m) below the soil surface. The overlying and surrounding soft plastic clay was fully saturated with water and had a natural water content varying from $w_n = 26$ percent to $w_n = 37$ percent. The liquid and plastic limits of the clay were not stated, but it would appear from other analyses of the Detroit clay that it is of the same general type as the Chicago clay. Housel stated (Ref. 136) that the shearing strength of the clay, except for a stiffer surface crust, varied between 150 and 200 lb/ft² (733 and 976 kg$_f$/m²). These values were obtained by direct slow undrained-ring double-shearing tests (Art. 3-5B). Such tests give the yield value, which for clays of this type is 5 times smaller than the ultimate shearing strength (see 1st ed., Fig. 7-32). It would therefore appear that the unconfined compressive strength of the Detroit clay was approximately equal to $q_u = 0.75$ ton/ft².

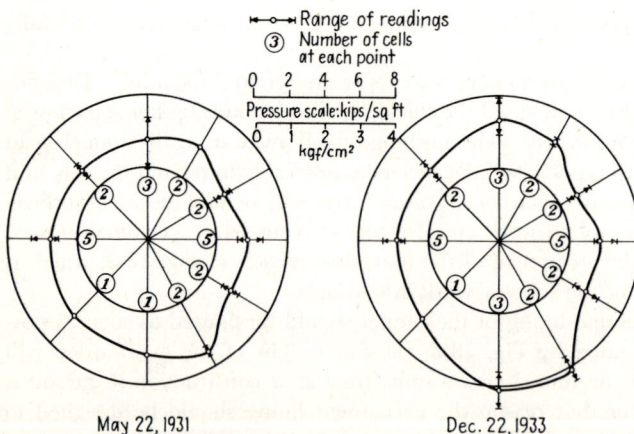

Fig. 13-4. Some sample readings of Goldbeck pressure cells on Detroit sewer tunnels. (*After Housel, Ref. 136.*)

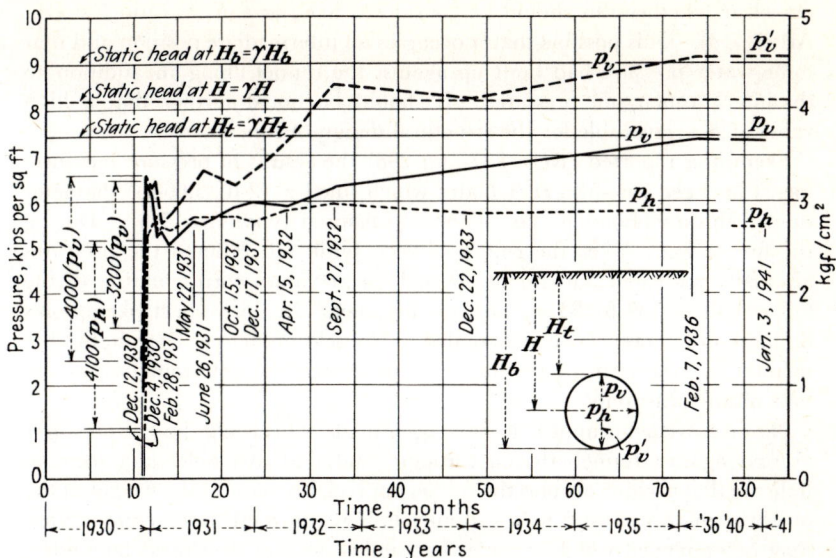

Fig. 13-5. Measured variations with time of the pressures exerted against sewer tunnels at Detroit. (*After Housel, Ref. 136.*)

The sewer tunnel cross section had the shape of rings of $9\frac{1}{3}$ ft (2.9 m) I.D. and $17\frac{1}{3}$ in. (44.5 cm) wall thickness. Goldbeck pressure cells were installed on the outer face of the concrete tunnel lining. The large number of individual cells employed compensated somewhat for the unreliability of this type of cell when used over long periods of time and for the inevitable scattering of readings, based on the measurement of pressures over small areas of contact with the soil (Art. 1-9). Figure 13-4 illustrates the general layout of the cells and some typical readings.

A summary of the results obtained over a period of 10 years of observation is given in Fig. 13-5. The tunnel was built with the use of compressed air to minimize the loss of ground and the resulting surface settlements of buildings. After completion of the tunnel and release of the compressed air on Dec. 12, 1930, as shown in Fig. 13-5, all cells recorded an increase of soil pressure which corresponded fairly closely to the drop in air pressure of 3,880 lb/ft² (1.9 kg_f/cm²). Then for a period of 3 months the pressures decreased somewhat. The horizontal pressures remained practically unchanged thereafter, but during the following 5 years the vertical pressures increased steadily until they stabilized themselves at values corresponding to the weight of the overburden at the respective elevations, referred to as *static head* by Housel. There were no significant changes in the next 5 years. The ratio of lateral to vertical pressure in this *reconsolidated-equilibrium* condition, according to Fig. 13-4, was equal to $K_n = 5.4/8.2 = 0.66$. It is not clear whether this should be considered a K_s or a K_{s+w} ratio (1st ed., Art. 10-13). It is possible that it occupies an intermediate position and that some water pressure had built up against the tunnel lining in addition to the intergranular soil pressures. It should be noted further that a high value of K is favorable for the structural design of tunnels.

Skempton reported (Refs. 297 and 298) the results of pressure measurements between cast-iron ring plates which lined a 12-ft (3.66-m) diameter tunnel through London clay of the stiff-fissured type (Art. 7-6). During the first 2 weeks after the ring had been built and grouted the pressures gradually increased and finally leveled off at values corresponding to the full weight of 109 ft (33 m) of overlying clay. In this respect Skempton's findings on London clay corresponded to Housel's findings at Detroit, but the method of measurement he employed permitted the determination of the maximum thrust only.

No measurements appear to have been made concerning the soil pressures exerted against tunnels driven through sand, but available data seem to indicate that arching around the tunnel appreciably reduces the weight of the overburden transmitted to the tunnel lining. A method of computation may be employed which is somewhat similar to that developed for underground conduits in trenches, described in Art. 13-4.

Equation (13-5) may be used for the estimation of the total load which the tunnel lining may have to carry, where the coefficient C_d may be determined from Fig. 13-9 by the substitution of the ratio $H/2r$ for the ratio H/b of that diagram, r being the tunnel radius, and of $2r$ for b.

Great care must be taken to prevent any escape of sand into the tunnel during its construction. Moist sand will usually arch over small openings and will not cause trouble in this respect; but entirely dry sand, which is sometimes encountered, is liable to trickle into the tunnel through the smallest gaps in the temporary lining. Sand movements of this kind destroy most if not all of the arching around the tunnel, with a resulting strong increase of both vertical and horizontal pressures on the supports of the lining. Such cases have been recorded and cause considerable difficulties. An efficient countermeasure was provided by chemical grouting and solidification (see Art. 5-7) from the tunnel face of the sand ahead of it, prior to tunneling through troublesome sections where the sand was completely dry (Ref. 411).

13-3. Subaqueous Tunnels. The principle of the *shield method* of tunneling is illustrated by Fig. 13-6 as applied to the construction of a subaqueous tunnel. A specially constructed metal shield S is pressed forward into the ground by a battery of some 20 or 30 hydraulic jacks J placed around the circumference of the shield in such a way that the completed cylindrical body of the tunnel lining may be used by the jacks as a support. The stroke of the jacks is made to correspond to the width b of each ring of the steel lining, and the number of jacks corresponds to the number of the steel-segment units of the ring. Thus, after completing a forward thrust, it is possible to relieve the pressure on the jacks, one by one, and to replace them by the steel segments of the lining, which can then serve as a support for the next thrust.

No loss of ground can occur in a radial direction, since the shield overlaps the completed lining at all stages. Neither will any loss of ground occur at the face of a shield in the case of a subaqueous tunnel, where it is even advantageous to push some of the soil ahead of the shield. This can be done, as shown in Fig. 13-6, by having only a very small opening in the shield through which the soil is squeezed into the interior of the tunnel. The amount of expensive removal of soil through the tunnel is then decreased to a minimum. A ridge Δt high is formed by the soil which is pushed up over the tunnel; it can be subsequently dredged away. This type of procedure can be successfully used only in plastic clay or mud of low shearing strength; examples are the Holland Tunnel and the Lincoln Tunnel tubes under the Hudson River at New York (Ref. 165). Compressed air is employed in all cases during construction to minimize the amount of water seeping into the tunnel at its face.

To prevent any infiltration the air pressure should correspond to the head of water H_{wb} at the bottom of the tube (see Fig. 13-6). However, this is dangerous since it means that there will be an excess air pressure in respect to the head of water H_{wt} at the top of the tube, thereby creating the danger of a blowout. This actually did happen during the construction of a tunnel under the East River in New York City when three men were blown out of the tube by suddenly outrushing air. Only one came out alive, shooting out of the water in an air bubble.

When subaqueous tunneling is through sand or other pervious strata with high frictional resistance, it is no longer possible to push some of the soil out of the way of the tunnel and it becomes necessary to remove it all through openings in the shield, a procedure which requires considerable skill and

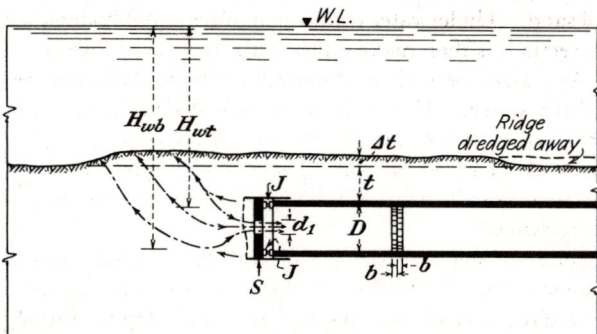

Fig. 13-6. Longitudinal section of subaqueous tunnel, showing principle of shield method of construction through mud or soft clay.

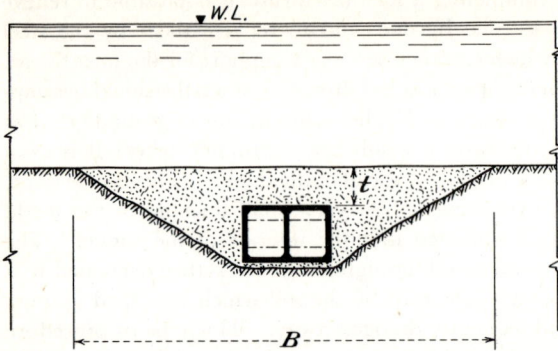

Fig. 13-7. Cross section of subaqueous tunnel, showing principle of the trench method of construction.

experience.   Care has to be taken to prevent blowouts at the tunnel face due to escape of compressed air to the surface through the shield and the overlying pervious strata.   To that end, temporary clay blankets sometimes have to be placed over the sandy bottom, as was done during the construction of the Queens Tunnel under the East River at New York (Ref. 296).

The shield method of subaqueous tunneling is advantageous in harbors where the waterfront is crowded with structures which might be damaged by the extensive dredging necessary in connection with the *trench method* of subaqueous tunneling, the principle of which is illustrated by Fig. 13-7.   A trench is dredged to the required depth.   The slopes depend not only on the properties of the soil material but may be strongly affected by the prevailing velocites of the current in the overlying body of water.   The tunnel shell is built on land or in a shipyard of reinforced concrete and steel in sections, the ends of which are closed by temporary bulkheads to permit flotation.   The sections are towed one by one to their locations, filled with water, and sunk to a prepared bed of sand.   Underwater connection of the suitably designed ends of the separate sections is then made either with the help of divers and tremie concreting (Art. 6-10) or with compressed-air diving bells lowered from the surface of the water.   The underlying bed of sand is pressure-grouted to eliminate cavities between it and the tunnel body and to ensure uniform distribution of the load on the soil.   Divers remove the end partitions of the tunnel sections from its interior, from which water is then pumped out.   The trench is backfilled.

The minimum depth t of soil over the top of both types of subaqueous tunnels is selected to ensure a safe distribution of the load of an accidentally sunken ship which would not crush the tunnel shell.   This depth t usually varies between 15 and 20 ft (4.6 and 6.1 m).

The connection of both types of subaqueous tunnels to the land approaches is usually made at the ventilating towers placed on each shore. Shield tunnels are also frequently started through an opening in the sidewalls of the caisson of a ventilation tower.

13-4. Conduits. Extensive studies of the problem of pressures against underground conduits have been carried out since 1910 at the Iowa Engineering Experiment Station by Marston and his successors. A review of these and of other related studies was published by Spangler (Ref. 313). Figure 13-8 illustrates Marston's analysis of a pipe conduit in a trench, where it is assumed that cohesion is inactive and only frictional forces come into play. By equating the vertical forces acting on an element of backfill, dh thick, within the trench, the following equation is obtained:

$$W + dW + 2K_A \frac{W}{b} \tan \delta \, dh = W + \gamma b \, dh \qquad (13\text{-}4)$$

The solution of this linear differential equation reads

$$W = \gamma b^2 C_d \qquad (13\text{-}5)$$

where

$$C_d = \frac{1 - e^{-\alpha h}}{2K_A \tan \delta} \qquad (13\text{-}6)$$

and

$$\alpha = \frac{2K_A \tan \delta}{b} \qquad (13\text{-}7)$$

where K_A = coefficient of active earth pressure, defined by Eq. (10-5) or
  (10-6)
  δ = angle of wall friction between backfill and wall of trench
  e = base of natural logarithms
  γ = unit weight of backfill

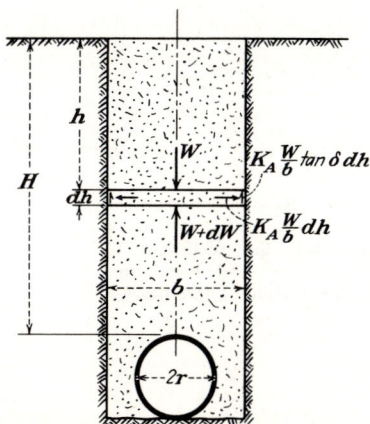

Fig. 13-8. Diagram illustrating Marston's analysis of vertical loads on pipe conduits in trenches. (*After Spangler, Ref. 313.*)

Figure 13-9 gives the variation of the coefficient C_d as a function of the depth-to-width ratio H/b of a trench. The angle of wall friction δ was set equal to the angle of internal friction ϕ of the backfill. The four curves of Fig. 13-9 were computed for the following values of $K_A \tan \delta$:

Curve a: $K_A \tan \delta = 0.192$ minimum for granular materials
Curve b: $K_A \tan \delta = 0.165$ maximum for granular materials
Curve c: $K_A \tan \delta = 0.130$ maximum for clay
Curve d: $K_A \tan \delta = 0.110$ maximum for saturated clay

In this connection it should be noted that if $\delta = \phi$,

ϕ	$K_A \tan \delta$
30°	0.192
25°	0.187
20°	0.178
15°	0.156
10°	0.124
8°	0.105

Thus the reduction of the vertical load P due to friction along the walls of the trench theoretically is not very sensitive to changes in the frictional properties of the soil. The curves given in Fig. 13-9 are claimed to have been established by actual tests which corroborated the above theory. Nevertheless it is advisable to use granular fill only, since clay fill cannot be effectively compacted and homogenized within a narrow trench.

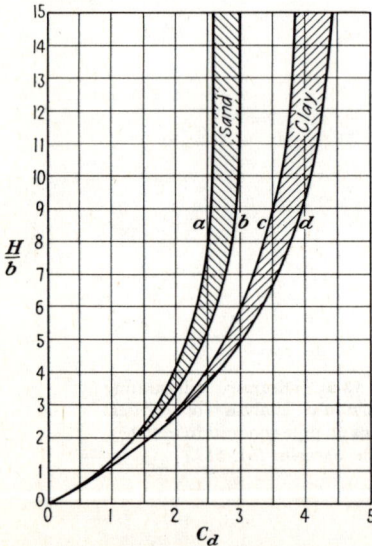

Fig. 13-9. Relationship between the depth-to-width ratio of a trench and the coefficient C_d governing the load transmitted to a pipe conduit. (*After Spangler, Ref. 313.*)

It should be noted from Fig. 13-9 that curve a ($\phi = 30°$) indicates that no further increase of the pressure on the pipe conduit is to be expected if the depth of the trench exceeds nine times its width.   This is in reasonable agreement with the results of measurements on silos, where an even greater reduction of vertical loads is to be expected and actually takes place owing to friction along all *four* walls of the silo.   For instance, it will be noted from Fig. 10-16 that no further increase of vertical pressure was recorded after the depth of grain in the silo exceeded 3 times its average width.

A completely different and even reversed situation arises if the pipe conduit is covered by embankment fill.   If the conduit is rigid, it may receive more load than the actual weight of the fill immediately above it. The stiffness of the pipe conduit itself, the type of its bedding, the compaction of the fill around it, all will influence the results.

If the embankment fill around and above a conduit is compressible, the compression of a layer of thickness $2r$ may be greater than the decrease of the vertical diameter of the conduit under the same load.   In that case the picture of load redistribution given in Fig. 13-8 for a trench may be reversed, and not only will the conduit have to carry the full weight of the overburden above it, but some of the weight of the surrounding soil may be transferred to it by what is sometimes called *negative friction*.   The term is used in a similar problem of end-bearing piles driven through soft soil which consolidates further under its own weight (Art. 6-4).   It is advisable to prevent the development of such undesirable increases of load on the conduit by suitable construction operations along the lines indicated in Fig. 13-10.   The pipe is laid in a prepared bed of compacted soil partly below the level of the natural soil.   Selected granular material A is thoroughly rolled and compacted on both sides of the pipe to an elevation reaching somewhat above the top of the pipe.   The space B immediately next to the pipe is compacted by mechanical tamping.   The space C is filled by loosely dumped soil, and the space D is subjected to normal embankment-compaction procedure.   A condition partially resembling the trench bedding is thereby created.

Spangler (Ref. 314) refers to a conduit resting within a fill on the surface of natural soil (line aa in Fig. 13-10) as a *positive projecting conduit* if none of the operations marked A, B, and C on Fig. 13-10 are performed and the fill D is compacted uniformly throughout.   When a conduit is placed in a trench dug within the natural soil, as shown by broken lines in Fig. 13-10, Spangler refers to it as a *negative projecting conduit*.   A conduit placed in a trench dug entirely within natural soil (Fig. 13-8) is referred to as a *ditch conduit*.   When a relieving partial excavation within a compacted fill (C in Fig. 13-10) is backfilled with loose material, the pipe below it is referred to as an *imperfect ditch conduit*.   This terminology appears to have been generally accepted.

In Ref. 314 Spangler has given graphs (similar to the one of C_d on Fig. 13-9, which refers to a ditch conduit) for a coefficient C_n which can be used

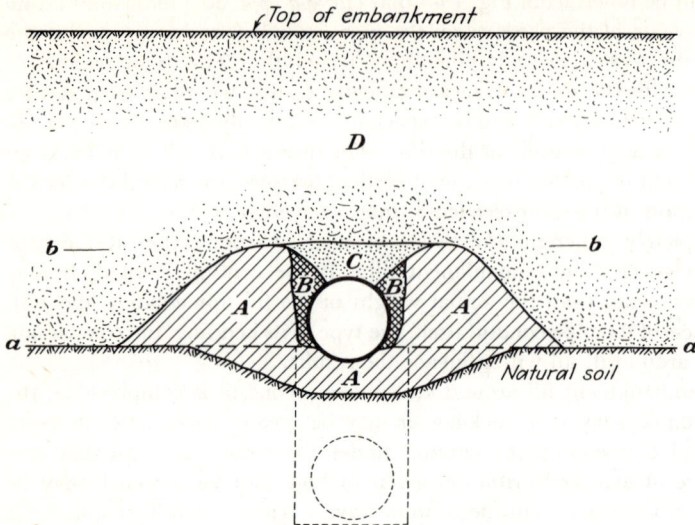

Fig. 13-10. Procedure for constructing embankments over conduits.

instead of C_d in Eq. (13-5) for different ratios of embankment height to depth of ditch below natural ground surface and their relative compressibilities.

To be effective, the imperfect-ditch method requires very careful field supervision of all operations, especially of density controls. This seems to be one of the reasons why the method has not been used very widely so far. Also, some engineers have been reluctant to incorporate in a permanent structure organic substance, such as bales of straw or hay, to provide assurance of a really compressible layer in an imperfect ditch.

Nevertheless published reports of successful uses of this procedure throughout the country are increasing. Thus, Spangler reported a case in the city of Atlanta (Ref. 316) where a 15-ft-deep (4.6-m) imperfect trench was dug into the natural ground above an existing 48-in. (1.22-m) reinforced concrete pipe and was filled with alternating layers of loose soil and leaves. This permitted placing a 60- to 78-ft-high (18- to 24-m) new embankment above the fill. The operation cost less than one-tenth the cost of building a new sewer capable of carrying the full weight of the new fill or of providing a reinforced-concrete protective slab above the old sewer.

Scheer and Willett in Ref. 279 report the successful reconstruction of an 18.5-ft-diameter (5.6-m) structural plate culvert under 83 ft (25.4 m) of cover in Montana. The original culvert failed, apparently because of the too brittle A490 high-strength steel bolts. The new culvert was rebuilt using larger A325 bolts of milder steel. In the reconstruction a 3-ft-thick (90-cm) layer of baled straw was placed above the culvert and served as the primary element of an imperfect trench.   The new culvert was instrumented with Carlson soil stress meters and electric-resistivity strain gages.   The results showed that the vertical load on the culvert was much less than the weight of the overlying column of earth, correlating well with the Marston theory, as emphasized in Spangler's discussion of Ref. 279.

In Ref. 87 Deen compares the performance of a 48-in.-diameter (1.22-m) reinforced-concrete pipe culvert built in Kentucky under a 36-ft-high (11-m) embankment.   One section was built as a positive projecting conduit and was badly damaged.   A second section was built using the imperfect-trench method, whereby one-third of the depth of the trench was filled with straw. The pipe in this section suffered no damage.

Earlier studies by Timmers (Ref. 345) had shown that filling the imperfect trench with loose friable soil is insufficient to develop the potential of the method fully.   As pointed out by Spangler in his discussion, very compressible material, such as straw or hay, is needed as backfill of at least part of the imperfect trench.

Davis and Bacher (Ref. 79) have given a progress report of an extensive research program of instrumented field measurements on actual structures by the California Division of Highways involving arch culverts, rigid concrete and flexible structural-plate steel pipes, as well as positive-projection and imperfect-ditch methods of backfill, including the use of baled straw for the trench.

The finite method of analysis (Arts. 1-11 and 14-10) has been used to supplement the California study (Ref. 79); see also Ref. 243.

Flexible pipes appear to bear up particularly well under heavy loading if the surrounding fill is granular.   Peck and Peck (Ref. 244) have reported the results of a survey of the performance of 18 flexible corrugated steel-pipe culverts under railway embankments with depths of overburden (selected granular fill) reaching up to 50 ft (15.3 m).   The satisfactory performance of these culverts indicated that a state of approximately equal all-round pressures must have been reached as a result of deformations similar to those illustrated by section AA of Fig. 13-11.   Under the weight of the fill the pipe is compressed in the vertical direction, and its originally circular cross section acquires an elliptical shape.   The vertical diameter is shortened, whereas the horizontal diameter is lengthened, because of the tendency of the pipe to bulge out laterally.   The lateral displacement of the adjoining soil induced by this deformation increases the lateral pressures against the pipe beyond the active and the neutral values.   A condition of passive resistance is thus created.   Some of the compaction measures suggested in Fig. 13-10 were used in a few cases.   The measured shortening of the vertical diameter of these culverts varied considerably but did not exceed 7.1 percent.

To compensate for such compression, a preliminary vertical elongation of a flexible steel-plate pipe by some 3 percent, using temporary timber struts

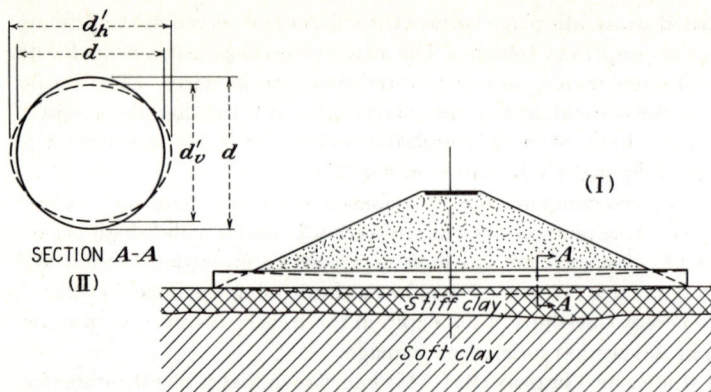

Fig. 13-11.   Transverse and longitudinal deformation of a flexible conduit.

and wedges, has been suggested in Ref. 317.   The struts remain in place until the entire embankment has been completed.   They are then removed.

When the depth of the overburden is 50 ft (15.3 m) (Ref. 244), its weight can be assumed to equal $50 \times 120 = 6,000$ lb/ft² (2.93 kg$_f$/cm²).   Assuming a uniform all-around pressure distribution of the above intensity against the 10-ft-diameter (3.05-m) culvert, we obtain a value of $6,000 \times \frac{10}{2} = 30,000$ lb (13,600 kg$_f$) compressive force per foot length of each of the two walls of the culvert.   The method of computation is identical with that employed for the determination of tensile stresses in the walls of a boiler.   The metal-wall thickness of this culvert was 0.2813 in. (7.42 mm), giving a cross-sectional area of 3.37 in.² and a unit compressive stress in the steel of $30,000/3.37 =$ 8,800 lb/in.² (616 kg$_f$/cm²).   This is, of course, only a very rough estimation for a hypothetical load distribution, and much more work, including more precise field measurements, will be needed before the design of such culverts can be placed on a fully reliable and rational basis.

When the soil beneath the embankment is composed of soft clay, settlements of the original ground surface may be induced by the consolidation of the clay under the weight of the embankment.   As a result, the conduit will be deformed longitudinally, as shown in Fig. 13-11, since the settlements will be greatest beneath the center of the embankment.   In some such cases it is advisable to provide flexible joints between the longitudinal sections of pipe, and to place the conduit with a camber equal to about one-half the estimated settlement under the centerline of the embankment.

When pipe conduits are laid just beneath the ground surface over mud or very soft clay, their support on piles may become necessary.

The customary methods of structural design were criticized in 1967 by Spangler as being too severe in respect to reinforced-concrete conduits (Ref. 317).   The same reference suggests procedures for in situ repairs of damaged concrete conduits.

A symposium assessing the state of the art of subsurface soil-structure inter-action was held at the 1972 annual meeting of the Highway Research Board. A comprehensive summary was given by Selig (Ref. 286c). Regrettably here again, as by Bjerrum in Ref. 31a, the term "arching" was used to designate all "transfers of pressures by shear." As explained in Art. 11-1, two different physical phenomena—wedging and sliding—are expressed by the two above terms so that differentiation between them is essential for the clarity of relevant future research.

The results of another comprehensive study in this field at Northwestern University were published in Ref. 175a.

13-5. Construction Controls. All types of tunneling in soft ground or of sheeted trench excavation for conduits are inevitably associated with some *loss of ground*, meaning thereby the excavation of more soil than originally occupied the excavated space. Although loss of ground cannot be pre-vented entirely, every effort should be made to minimize it in built-up areas to avoid damage to adjoining structures and subsequent litigation. Field measurements are essential to check numerically the effectiveness of the con-struction procedures used and show whether changes are needed.

Figure 13-12 illustrates a method of control suggested by Terzaghi in connection with shield construction work for Chicago subways.

The use of the shield method in land tunneling minimizes radial loss of

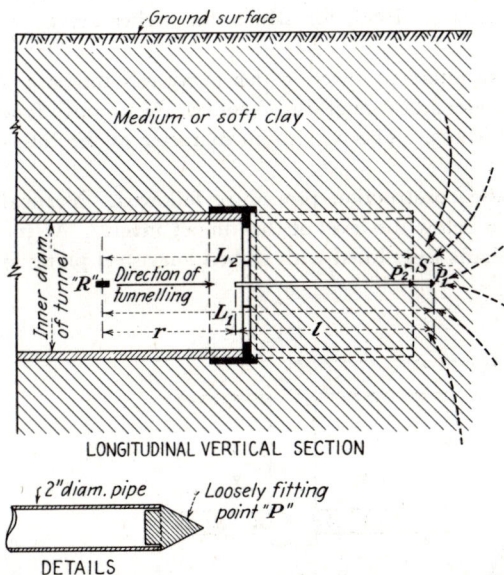

LONGITUDINAL VERTICAL SECTION

DETAILS

Fig. 13-12. Method of estimating amount of loss of ground due to squeezing of medium or soft clay into face of tunnel. (*After Terzaghi, Refs. 339 and 340.*)

ground toward the tunnel shaft; it is, however, not possible to push any soil out of the way of the advancing tunnel, as can be done sometimes in subaqueous work (see Fig. 13-6). The ground heave might cause as much, or more, damage to buildings on the surface as would a loss of ground. Therefore most of the shield face has to be left open. The amount of the resulting loss of ground can be estimated by the method illustrated in Fig. 13-12. A loosely fitting point P is attached to a 2-in. (5-cm) pipe of known length l and pressed horizontally into the clay ahead of the face of the tunnel. The distance r from the rear end of the pipe to a reference mark R on the completed tunnel lining is measured and recorded. The pipe is then withdrawn, leaving the point P in the clay. When the excavation reaches that point, the distance L_2 between the point P and the reference R is measured; $s = r + l - L_2$ will then represent the linear dimension of the excess ground excavated ("lost") at that elevation. If this amount is excessive and this fact is confirmed by surface settlements, which should always be measured, the air pressure may be increased to reduce it.

The variations in the engineering properties of glacially deposited clays in Chicago were sufficiently small to permit advance decisions on the type of tunneling work to be adopted. Elsewhere soil conditions may be much more erratic, requiring special methods of control.

Some relevant possibilities will now be outlined with reference to the construction of the East Branch Ohio River Interceptor by the Cincinnati Metropolitan Sewerage District in 1956, for which the writer served as consultant (Ref. 218).

Six miles of tunnels were to intercept sewers which previously discharged into the Ohio river. The interceptor tunnel was to convey the sanitary flow to new sewerage treatment works. The maximum diameter of the interceptor was 8 ft (2.44 m).

Figure 13-13 illustrates the construction procedure followed. Vertical shafts were first dug down to below the level of the tunnel invert. As the excavation progressed, the shafts were lined with ribbed liner steel plates of

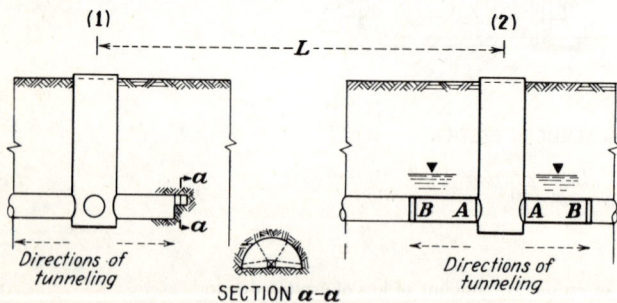

Fig. 13-13. Sewer-tunnel construction procedures.

Fig. 13-14.   Photograph looking down a tunnel shaft in Cincinnati.   (*Photo by Tschebotarioff.*)

the same type as the ones used for the tunnel lining but of a curvature corresponding to the shaft's larger diameter.   The photograph on Fig. 13-14 is taken from the soil surface looking down over the edge of a shaft.   It shows the ribs along all four edges of the curved liner plates and the bolts which hold the plates together.   Pipes for compressed air, etc., can also be seen.

When necessary, well points were used for a temporary drawdown of the water level in order to install the concrete-lined airlocks, with airtight doors *A* and *B*, as shown in respect to shaft 2.   Shafts are always provided at locations where existing sewers have to be intercepted.   Otherwise the selection of distance *L* between them is usually left to the contractor, subject to approval by the engineer, since it is based on a balance between the cost of a shaft and the cost of hauling excavated material to the shaft over an increased distance *L*/2.

In general, the contractor was permitted to pick the method of construction, but careful studies by the city helped guide him in his decisions.

As in most river deposits, soil conditions were quite erratic along the tunnel route.   Figure 13-15 shows the soil properties disclosed by one of the borings. Since these properties could change considerably in an unpredictable manner over short distances, only a very limited number of borings were performed at key locations.   The following control measures were developed instead.

First, a very careful survey was made of the entire route and several critical problem areas were designated as such.   They included several large but old structures and a potential slide area.   Photographs were taken of all visible preconstruction cracks or of other damage along the tunnel route with one or two engineers in the picture holding a small blackboard on which the date of the photograph was written.   Bench marks were established and their elevations determined on critical buildings and in the street surface

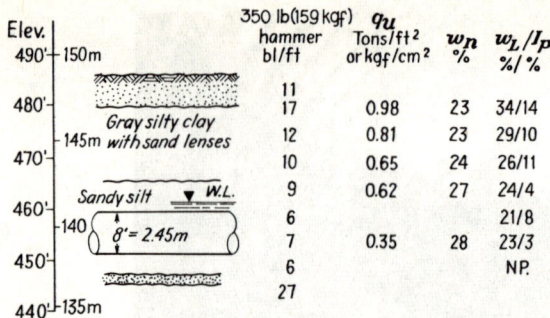

Elev.	350 lb(159 kgf) hammer bl/ft	q_u Tons/ft² or kgf/cm²	w_n %	w_L/I_p %/%
490'┬150m				
	11			
480'─	17	0.98	23	34/14
Gray silty clay	12	0.81	23	29/10
145m *with sand lenses*				
470'─	10	0.65	24	26/11
Sandy silt ▼ W.L.	9	0.62	27	24/4
460'─ 140	6			21/8
ϐ'= 2.45m	7	0.35	28	23/3
450'─	6			N.P.
	27			
440'┴135m				

Fig. 13-15.   Soil properties along a boring for Cincinnati sewer tunnels.

along a line at right angles to the tunnel centerline. Seven bench marks were used to establish a settlement profile along that line—one over the tunnel centerline and others at 4, 12.5, and 25 ft (1.2, 3.8, and 7.6 m) distance from the centerline on either side of it (see Fig. 13-16). Such settlement profiles were measured at 100-ft (30-m) intervals and at 25-ft (7.6-m) intervals in particularly critical areas.

Work was begun in areas where no trouble was to be expected, so as to gain some experience of the measured effects of using compressed air and the time lag between the mining and the grouting operations, as well as needle beams (see section *aa* in Fig. 13-13). The mining consists in excavating the soil in the heading for 1 ft (30 cm) or so and then immediately lining it with a ring of steel plates. It is inevitable that the excavation diameter be irregular and somewhat larger than the diameter of the steel lining plates. Pressure grouting, from inside the tunnel through openings left in the lining plates for that purpose, with a 1:12 (cement-sand) zero-slump grout was used to fill the voids. From the point of view of the contractor's cost of operations it is desirable to do the grouting as infrequently as possible in order to minimize the effect of time loss connected with setting up and dismantling the grouting equipment. However, a delay of the grouting increases the probability that soil will be squeezed into the voids left outside the lining. Settlement measurements made after completion of the mining and repeated after the grouting help to establish a reasonable balance between these conflicting requirements.

Tunneling contracts of the magnitude of the one at Cincinnati permit some advantageous seasonal scheduling of operations. First, no tunneling was planned during the river flood season in areas likely to be affected by rising waters. Second, the tunneling alongside an old gas holder could be scheduled for a period of low seasonal gas consumption so that the gas company could shut it down, if necessary, and rely on other gas holders in the city. It was suspected that the cylindrical brick masonry walls of a deep underground caisson under the gas holder, filled with water to act as a gas seal, might have been cracked, saturating the surrounding soil. A disastrous sudden inflow of water into the tunnel through some sand or gravel seam might have resulted if the caisson under the gas holder remained filled with water.

This precaution was shown to be fully justified. As the tunnel approached the gas holder, early evidence of soil saturation was obtained at the tunnel heading, which at first was not reflected by the street-settlement profile (Fig. 13-16*A* at station 70 + 75). The gas tank, which was located between stations 71 + 70 and 73 + 00, was then unwatered. Considerably more settlement of the street surface nevertheless resulted there, as shown by Fig. 13-16*B* at station 72 + 75. The profile is unsymmetrical, since the street surface settlements on the south side were decreased by friction along the caisson walls, the face of which was only 16 ft (4.9 m) away from the tunnel centerline at its closest point. The final maximum settlement of the street surface at this location was 0.32 ft = 3.8 in. (9.8 cm). The holder itself did not settle, its foundation reaching several feet below the level of the tunnel invert.

Air pressure used at other critical locations did not exceed 10 lb/in.^{2} (0.7 kg$_f$/cm^2). Maximum street settlements were of the order of 1 in. (2.5 cm). No structures were damaged, and no underpinning was required even

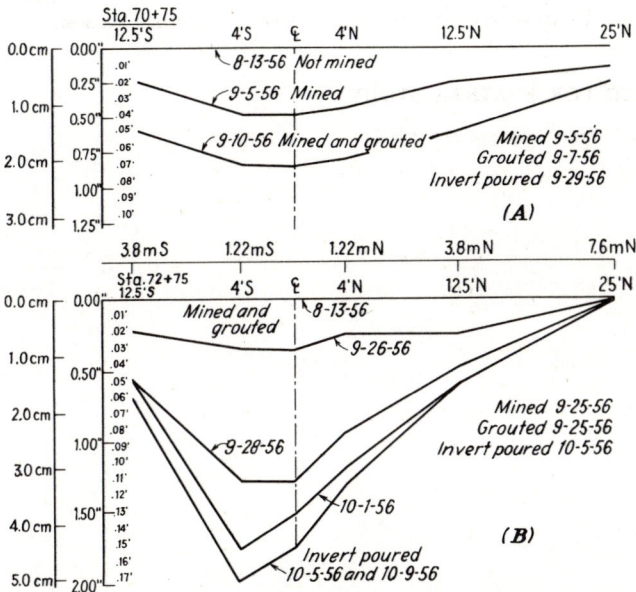

Fig. 13-16. Settlement profile of street surface during Cincinnati sewer-tunnel construction: (*A*) under normal conditions; (*B*) opposite emptied gas holder which had previously leaked seal water from its caisson foundation.

when the foundations were at elevations above that of the tunnel invert but at a sufficient distance away.

Some rock tunneling, involving blasting, had to be done in an area where detritus slides (Art. 7-4) along sloping rock surfaces had occurred in the past. Work in that area was therefore scheduled for a time of the year with greatest likelihood of dry weather. All blasting was done with light shots, using millisecond delays, to decrease the blast energy. This was checked by accelerograph measurements and the Crandell energy ratio (Art. 15-5) and was found to be within safe limits.

All these precautions were looked upon as insurance. They paid off in a generally smooth operation and the absence not only of any real damage but even of otherwise not infrequent claims of damage and related litigation.

Similar precautions and controls are advisable in all cases where sewers are placed in deep open cuts through soft soils within sheeted and braced trenches. As in all work of this kind some loss of ground will inevitably result. Additional loss of ground may be caused by pulling steel sheeting out of plastic clay, since some of it is apt to come out of the ground sticking within the recesses of U-shaped sheets and—even of Z-shaped sheets when they are pulled in pairs, as is usually the case. Sometimes it is advisable to plan on leaving the sheeting permanently in the ground. If this is not done to avoid the expense, specially careful surveys and settlement measurements should be made before, during, and after construction as insurance against the sometimes wildly exaggerated later court claims for compensation.

RECOMMENDED FOR FURTHER STUDY

Peck, Ref. 249, pt 1, Tunneling, pp. 225–258.

CHAPTER **14**

WATERFRONT STRUCTURES

14-1. General Considerations. A marine structure for tying up vessels is generally called a *dock*. When a dock parallels the shore, it is called a *wharf* or *quay*. A *pier* is a dock which extends from the shoreline into the water. Seven structural types of docks are shown in Fig. 14-1.

Figure 14-1(1) shows a reinforced-concrete caisson, i.e., a box which is representative of *massive quay walls* discussed in next Art. 14-2.

For less favorable soil conditions and depths of water not exceeding 30 to 35 ft (9.15 to 10.7 m), the *anchored bulkhead* (type 4 in Fig. 14-1) is generally the most economical in the United States. Greater depths are possible under favorable soil conditions if heavier European steel sheeting is used. The design procedures of anchored bulkheads are given in Art. 14-3.

Economically, a close second to type 4 is type 6, a *platform on timber piles with bulkhead on the land side*. However, in tropical and subtropical seas, timber piles cannot be used for type 6 or for type 7, since even properly creosoted piles there undergo severe damage from marine borers within a period of 15 years or less. In northern seas or in partially polluted harbors where marine borers are not active, even untreated timber piles can be used below water, so that type 6 becomes very advantageous, especially if the costs of type 4 are increased by the need of cathodic protection against corrosion of the steel by salt water.

Water depths of 40 to 50 ft (12 to 15 m) can be obtained by the use of the structure types 2, 3, 5, 6, and 7 shown in Fig. 14-1.

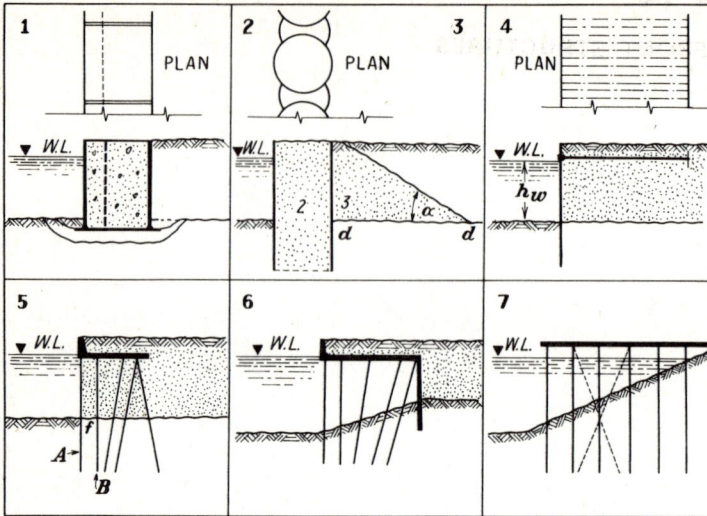

Fig. 14-1.   Some types of quay-wall structures.

Types 6 and 7 are analyzed in Art. 14-7.   Type 7 is of advantage in areas of severe earthquakes, where other more massive structures are more susceptible to damage.   Type 5, *relieving platforms*, is analyzed in Art. 14-5, and type 2, *cellular cofferdams*, in Art. 14-8.

A *sand dike* (type 3, shown next to type 2) can be used with other types of retaining structures too, e.g., 1, 4, and 6, to reduce fluid ($K = 1.00$) lateral pressures of hydraulic fills with high clay content.   When placed at the natural angle of repose α of the sand, or flatter, the dike will exert lateral pressures on the retaining structure no greater than for a backfill composed entirely of clean sand.   The action of the dike consists in transmitting by shear the fluid pressures ($K = 1.00$) of the hydraulic fill to the base dd of the dike.   Therefore, to be effective, the dike must rest on firm soil at and below elevation dd (Ref. 356).   Availability of materials and economic factors varies so much at different times and localities that it frequently becomes necessary to prepare several alternative designs before the selection of the most suitable type of retaining structure is possible.

Often more than one structure will satisfactorily meet the soil conditions at the same site from a soil-engineering point of view.   This is illustrated by the photograph in Fig. 14-2, taken during an extension of the Antwerp harbor.   The work required the construction on land of a quay alongside an existing waterway and the subsequent dredging away of the soil in front of the completed quay.   In the foreground of Fig. 14-2 can be seen the excavation and the start of concreting for a massive gravity wall.   In the adjoining section at the back of the cut can be seen a completed platform on precast reinforced-concrete piles.

In similar cases sometimes only direct competitive bidding can show which type of structure will cost the least.   A contracting firm which happens to have idle excavating and water-lowering machinery may submit the lowest bid for a gravity-wall option of a wharf section large enough to keep most of its available equipment busy.   But another contracting firm with idle pile drivers may submit the lowest bid for a platform-type option of another wharf section.

14-2. Massive Quay Walls.   Such walls are essentially gravity walls, and their design follows the same lines as that of gravity retaining walls (see Art. 10-5).   However, as in the design of all waterfront structures, the lateral forces due to possible *tidal lag* should be added to those of the earth backfill. If the tidal lag is a ft, the resulting lateral pressure will be $a \times 62.4$ lb/ft² $= a \times 305$ kg$_f$/m², which can be taken as uniformly distributed down to the dredge-line level (see Fig. 14-21).

Gravity walls are satisfactory only if the soil layers beneath their base are firm and will not cause shear failure or settlements.   This type of quay wall is not very frequently used in the United States because of high labor costs and the amount of labor involved in preparing the formwork and placing the reinforcing steel.   On the other hand, such walls are frequently used in countries with lower labor costs, especially when they have to import their steel and timber piles.

Fig. 14-2.   Use of a gravity wall and a platform on piles in adjoining sections of a new wharf in Antwerp.   (*Photo by Tschebotarioff, 1958.*)

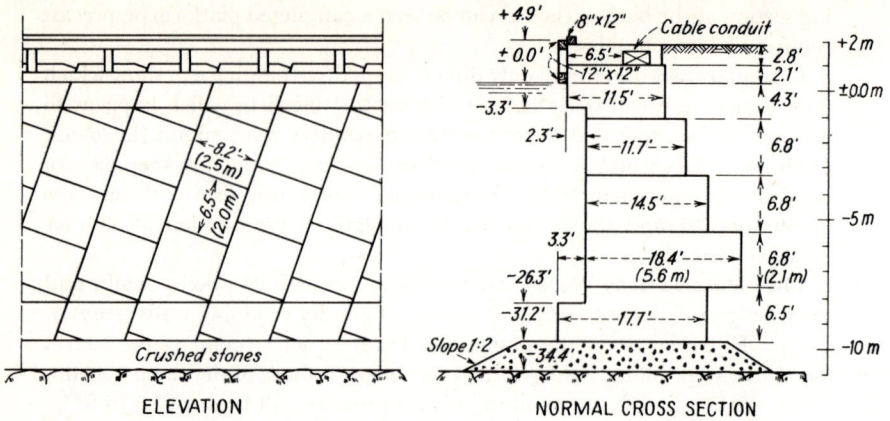

ELEVATION   NORMAL CROSS SECTION

Fig. 14-3. Quay wall at Aruba, showing method of bonding precast concrete blocks. (*Reproduced from Ref. 114 by permission of the Editor, The Dock and Harbour Authority.*)

In addition, the excavation for the type of massive wall shown in the foreground of Fig. 14-2 requires the use of independent deep wells *a* which force the water up the pipes *b* to a collector pipe *c*. As explained in Art. 9-6, this type of dewatering is more frequently used in Europe than in the United States.

Under favorable soil conditions massive gravity quay walls built of large precast concrete blocks, so-called *cyclopean masonry*, can be used to advantage. The most frequently used type consists of large concrete blocks which are precast on shore, where good quality control of the concrete is possible. The blocks are then transported by barge and lowered into place by a floating crane onto a bed of sand, gravel, or crushed stone, which has been smoothed out first by a diver.

The joints of such mortarless masonry usually are horizontal and vertical. Figure 14-3 shows a quay wall in Aruba Harbor (Netherland Antilles), where the bonding between the precast blocks was achieved by having all joints inclined. This has the advantage of developing friction, and hence resistance to displacement, along all joints, not merely along the horizontal ones, as is the case of conventional block walls. The weight of some precast blocks of the Aruba wall was 62 tons. Heavier blocks have been used elsewhere. The size is limited by the capacity of the available floating crane.

By making the blocks of the second row from the bottom particularly large and by moving them inward, as shown in Fig. 14-3, the toe pressures of the wall are decreased and a more uniform distribution of wall pressures on the crushed-stone bed is achieved.

Some attempts have been made, notably in Sweden, to install *in situ*, with the help of divers, thin prefabricated reinforced-concrete units, so as to pro-

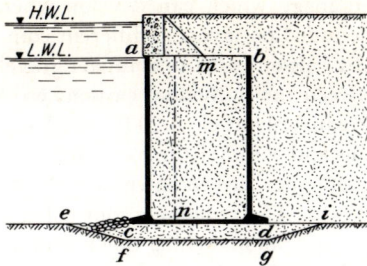

Fig. 14-4. Cellular reinforced-concrete caisson type of quay wall.

vide high-quality concrete outer facing of the massive quay wall and also to serve as forms for the underwater placing of the bulk of the wall concrete by tremie methods.

Rock-filled timber cribs (Art. 12-4) can be used below water level for shallow depths of water not exceeding 15 to 20 ft (4.6 to 6.1 m) if there is no danger of marine-borer attack.

Figures 14-1(I) and 14-4 illustrate the *caisson type of quay-wall construction*, which has considerable advantages in marine and waterfront work.   A reinforced-concrete caisson of cellular design is built at a convenient location, floated, towed to the place of the new structure, and then filled with water to make it sink over the exact spot designated for it.   Other caissons are then placed in the same manner next to it to form a continuous wall or to act as piers for intermediate cellular-type girders.

The latter method was successfully used in the case illustrated by Fig. 14-5,

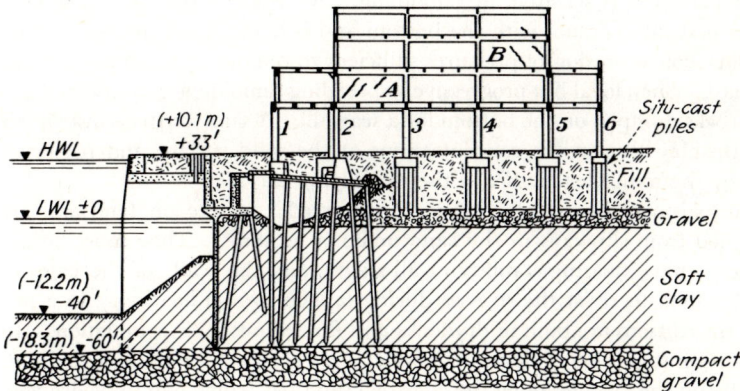

Fig. 14-5. Differential settlements and the resulting damage to the superstructure of the transatlantic pier in the harbor of Le Havre required the underpinning of rows 3, 4, 5, and 6 of columns and the transfer of their loads to the layer of compact gravel at el. −60 ft (−18.3 m).   *(After Freyssinet, Ref. 102, and Rodio, Ref. 268.)*

which, however, also demonstrates the damage which can develop when different parts of the same structure are founded on layers of different compressibility. The quay wall was formed by caissons sunk to compact gravel at el. -60 ft (-18.3 m). The gaps between the individual caissons were bridged by reinforced-concrete slabs approximately at el. $+20$ ft ($+6.1$ m). Column rows 1 and 2 of the pier building and some of the earth fill were supported by long precast reinforced-concrete piles, driven down to the same compact gravel layer at el. -60 ft (-18.3 m). The remaining four column rows 3 to 6, however, were supported by short piles reaching down into an upper layer of gravel approximately at el. ± 0.0. The inclination of the cracks at points A and B indicates that the consolidation of the soft clay below that gravel layer would have induced a greater settlement of the center of the pier building even if all its column rows were supported by the upper gravel layer [compare with Fig. 4-25(II)]. Column rows 3 to 6 therefore had to be underpinned by long piles reaching down to el. -60 ft (-18.3 m). Nevertheless, the severe cracking at A was undoubtedly aggravated by the unyielding support originally provided to column rows 1 and 2.

Frequently part of the soft natural bottom is dredged away and the trench filled with sand, as shown in Fig. 14-4, forming a mattress *efgi* to distribute the load of the caisson on the underlying soil. When the latter consists of soft mud, the mattress has in some cases been made 20 ft (6.1 m) thick. In addition, a temporary sand dike reaching above the final ground level at the wharf has sometimes been used to consolidate by its weight the soft mud beneath the future wharf and to increase thereby the shearing strength of the soil. This was successfully done at Rotterdam, Holland, and at Surabaya, Belawan, and Samarang in Indonesia.

The use of a thin *sand mattress* is frequently advisable even over a bed of stiffer clay if it is sensitive to remolding. An edge of the caisson usually comes first into contact with the bottom and is liable to create there a momentary concentration of pressures sufficient to remold and thereby weaken the clay. Such local but progressively spreading remolding may also develop with rocks dumped on the bottom for a seawall. A sand mattress distributes over the clay all pressure concentrations at the sand surface and preserves thereby the natural structure of the underlying clay.

The caissons are usually built of reinforced concrete on land and are launched from slipways in the same manner as ships. They must be designed to have floating stability at all stages, and the walls of the caissons are designed to resist the stresses during launching and floating. In a few cases the caissons are built in drydocks and floated out after completion. In the harbor at Gdynia, Poland, economies were achieved by building caissons directly on the ground along the edge of a sand bar which had to be dredged away as part of the harbor development. Expensive launching arrangements could be dispensed with, as a result, and the caissons were floated simply by pumping the sand away from around and beneath them by means of the suction heads of hydraulic dredges.

The walls of the caisson cells vary from 6 to 12 in. (15 to 30 cm) in thickness. Apart from launching and floating stresses, they should resist lateral pressures of the sand with which the cells are filled once the caisson is in place. On the water side they should, in addition, resist pressures engendered by the impact of waves and of ships. Wave pressures vary considerably at different locations (see Art. 14-9).

The need for a thicker wall of the caisson on the water side, *ac* in Fig. 14-4, is sometimes met by providing a second thin wall *mn* and then filling the space between it and the outer wall *ac* with concrete, once the caisson is in place. A considerable variety of designs of the caisson itself and its superstructure is possible.

Once the caisson is in place, is filled with sand and/or concrete, and is back filled, it acts essentially as a massive gravity retaining wall.

In sheltered locations but with uncertain soil conditions the outer cells *amnc* can be left empty to decrease the pressures on the ground under the toe of the caisson.

14-3. Anchored Bulkheads. (*A*). *Development of Design Theories.* The so-called *free-earth-support* method for anchored-bulkhead design is the oldest and most conservative of all such procedures. It is still used occasionally, although it is based on the questionable assumption that all the soil below the dredge line has reached its limit shearing strength throughout the depth of sheet-pile embedment and is therefore incapable of producing effective restraint of the sheet piling to the extent necessary to induce negative bending moments. The pressure distribution *in a granular soil* which corresponds to this assumption is shown in Fig. 14-6 for a minimum depth of embedment D' compatible with equilibrium, i.e., when the factor of safety in respect to the limit value of the passive resistance of the soil in front of the bulkhead is equal to unity ($F_s = 1.00$).

Figure 14-6(I) refers to a condition where the depth of embedment is just sufficient for limit equilibrium, assuming that the maximum possible passive resistance is fully mobilized. The anchor pull can then be determined from the condition that the sum of the horizontal forces is equal to zero:

$$A_P = E_A - E_P \tag{14-1}$$

where

$$E_A = [\tfrac{1}{2}(a+b)^2\gamma K_A] + [\gamma(a+b)K_A(H_w + D')]$$
$$+ [\tfrac{1}{2}\gamma'(H_w + D')^2 K_A] \tag{14-2}$$

and

$$E_P = \tfrac{1}{2}\gamma'D'^2 K_P \tag{14-3}$$

In the above equations γ refers to the unbuoyed and γ' to the buoyed unit weight of the granular soil; all the other symbols are as shown in Fig. 14-6(I). The first bracketed expression in Eq. (14-2) represents the area *def* of the lateral-earth pressure-diagram [Fig. 14-6(III)], the second represents the area *efgh*, and the third represents the area *emh*. Equation (14-3) represents the

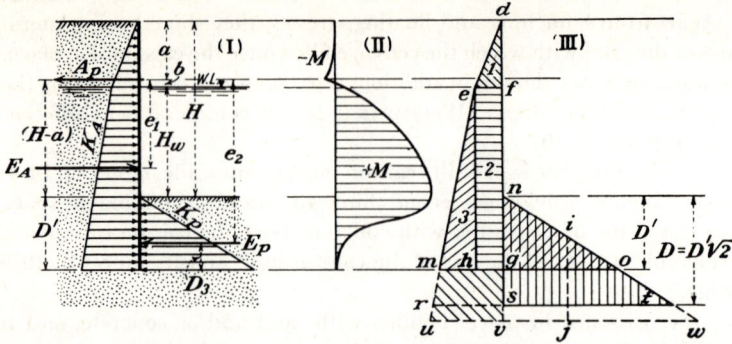

Fig. 14-6. The free-earth-support method of anchored-bulkhead design in sand: (I) equilibrium of forces for depth of embedment giving a factor of safety of unity; (II) shape of bending-moment diagram; (III) pressure diagrams for other depths of embedment.

area ngo. The depth of embedment D', which will correspond to the limit equilibrium, can be determined from the condition that the sum of the moments around the point where the anchor connects with the bulkhead must equal zero:

$$E_A e_1 = E_P e_2 \qquad (14\text{-}4)$$

where

$$E_A e_1 = -\left[\tfrac{1}{2}(a+b)^2 \gamma K_A \left(\frac{a+b}{3} - b \right) \right]$$

$$+ \left[\gamma'(a+b)K_A(H_w + D') \left(\frac{H_w + D'}{2} + b \right) \right]$$

$$+ \tfrac{1}{2}\gamma'(H_w + D')^2 K_A [\tfrac{2}{3}(H_w + D') + b] \qquad (14\text{-}5)$$

and
$$E_P e_2 = \tfrac{1}{2}\gamma' D'^2 K_P(H_w + b + \tfrac{2}{3}D') \qquad (14\text{-}6)$$

In actual design all values contained in Eqs. (14-5) and (14-6) are selected and are numerically known, with the one exception of the depth of embedment D'. Thus after insertion of the corresponding figures into these equations, Eq. (14-4) may be given the form

$$C_1 D'^3 + C_2 D'^2 - C_3 D' - C_4 = 0 \qquad (14\text{-}7)$$

where C_1, C_2, C_3, and C_4 are numerical coefficients, so that the value of D' can be determined. Substitution of trial values is one of the simplest ways to solve the cubic equation (14-7). For instance, if after consideration of all relevant points we select $K_A = 0.30$, $K_P = 3.00$, $\gamma = 115$ lb/ft$_3$ (1.84 g$_f$/cm³) $\gamma' = 69$ lb/ft³ (1.105 g$_f$/cm³), $H_w = 28$ ft (8.55 m), $a = 15$ ft (4.6 m) and

$b = 2$ ft (61 cm), and substitute these values into Eqs. (14-5) and (14-6), they can be transformed into a cubic equation of the above type, from which, by trial, a value of $D' = 18$ ft (5.5 m), corresponding to a ratio $D/H = 18/(28 + 2 + 15) = \frac{18}{45} = 0.40$, is obtained.

Once D' is known, E_A and E_P are determined from Eqs. (14-5) and (14-6) and the anchor pull A_P from Eq. (14-1). The numerical values of all forces acting upon the bulkhead are then known. The bending moments induced by these forces can be determined in accordance with the customary procedures of mechanics of materials. Figure 14-6(II) indicates the shape of the bending-moment curve which will result from such computations.

The actual depth of embedment D is made greater than D' to obtain the desired factor of safety against rupture of the soil in front of the bulkhead and against failure of the entire structure. A factor of safety of 2 $(F = 2.00)$ is sometimes chosen to that end. One of the frequently used methods of computation assumes that the effectively mobilized portion of the passive earth pressure has the shape of a trapezoid $nvji$, the area of which is equal to one-half of the maximum theoretically possible triangular resistance area nwv, as shown in Fig. 14-6(III). This assumption complicates the relevant computations to an extent which does not appear justified, since so many other approximations are involved in the basic assumptions of this design method. For that reason the Danish rules, outlined in the following part of this article, permit determining the actual depth of embedment D from

$$D = \sqrt{2}D' = 1.42D' \qquad (14\text{-}8)$$

This relationship appears to be based on the fact that, as shown in Fig. 14-6(III), the area of the triangle ngo will be one-half of the area of the triangle nst if ng is made equal to D' and ns to D, as indicated by Eq. (14-8). This leaves out of consideration the theoretical increase of the total active pressure by the area $mgsr$. Therefore Eq. (14-8) would provide an approximate factor of safety $F = 1.7$, and not 2.0, as assumed. If $F = 2.0$ is desired, D should be made equal to

$$D = 1.7D' \qquad (14\text{-}9)$$

It should be realized that an increase of the depth of embedment in sand beyond the value D', essential as this is to prevent a toe-kickout type of failure, automatically invalidates the assumption on which this method is based, namely, that the soil below the dredge line has reached its limit shearing strength throughout the depth of embedment. Some fixation of the pile tip is therefore bound to occur, as disclosed by recent measurements (Art. 14-3B). The conventional *application of the free-earth-support method to bulkhead design in clay soils* is illustrated by Fig. 14-7. In accordance with Eq. (10-7), the active pressures are obtained from the fluid pressure $(K_y = 1.00)$ by subtracting from it $2s$, taken to equal $2c$. Below the dredge line fda the areas

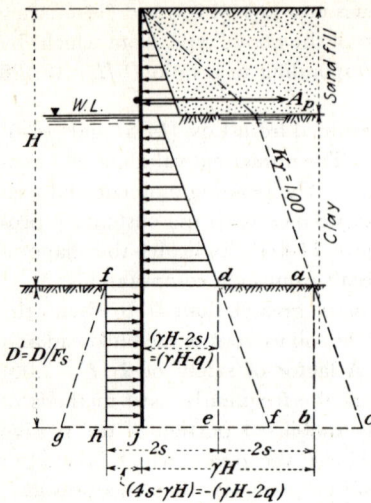

Fig. 14-7. The free-earth-support method of anchored-bulkhead design in clay when based on the ultimate strength of the soil. (*After Skempton, Ref. 298.*)

of the active-pressure triangles *abc* and *def* are equal and cancel the area of the passive-fluid-pressure triangle *fgh*.   The residual unit passive pressure *hj* is then equal to

$$p'' = p_P - p_A = 4s - \gamma H \tag{14-10}$$

Equation (10-15) forms the basis for the determination of p_P.   A prerequisite for equilibrium is the condition that

$$s = c \geq \frac{\gamma H}{4} \tag{14-11}$$

or

$$q_u \geq 0.5 \gamma H \tag{14-12}$$

Otherwise, in accordance with Eq. (14-10), no positive value of the residual unit passive pressure can be obtained in front of the bulkhead at any depth of embedment.   In other words, there exists a critical height:

$$H_{cr} = \frac{2q_u}{\gamma} \tag{14-13}$$

This is a familiar relationship [Art. 7-1 and Eq. (7-1)].

This procedure appears to be entirely rational insofar as the determination of the maximum possible passive resistance is concerned, since it is quite logical to base the theoretical maximum resistance to rupture on the ultimate strength of the soil.   As regards the active pressures, however, the same inconsistencies of this method are possible as have been established for cuts in clay soils (Art. 10-2; also see 11-3B in this connection).   Once a depth of embedment has been established which is safe against rupture, no rupture can occur above the dredge line either, and the bulkhead deformations and not the ultimate strength of the clay will govern the active pressures.

The method illustrated by Fig. 14-7 leads to the following procedure of design. Once the lateral-pressure diagram has been determined as shown in that sketch, the minimum depth of embedment D' compatible with equilibrium is established by taking moments around the point of application of the anchor pull A_P, in a manner similar to that just described for sands. The actual depth of embedment D, however, is now made equal to $D'F$. If the factor of safety is to be $F = 2.0$, then $D = 2D'$.

The *fixed-earth support method in noncohesive soils* is based on the assumption that the bulkhead deflections y are such that the elastic line of the bulkhead will take the shape indicated by the broken line in Fig. 14-8(I). This line reverses its curvature at the point of contraflexure c. This is equivalent to assuming that the soil beneath the dredge line exercises effective restraint on the bulkhead deformations. As a result, the bulkhead acts like a partially built-in beam subjected to bending moments, the diagram of which has the shape indicated by Fig. 14-8(II).

The classical method of computation involves a number of arbitrary simplifying assumptions. The passive resistance of the soil behind the bulkhead at its lowest tip is replaced by a concentrated force R_D at a distance ti above that tip equal to $0.2D'$. The elastic line of the bulkhead is assumed to be tangent to the vertical at the point t.

The residual line of passive pressures is then drawn, as shown in Fig. 14-8(I), by subtracting the active from the passive pressures. To that end,

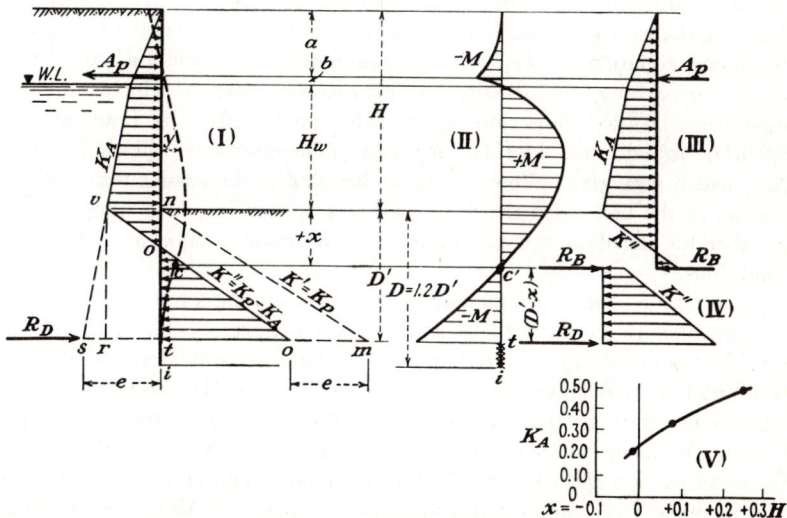

Fig. 14-8. The fixed-earth-support method of anchored-bulkhead design in sand.

the distance st is made equal to om, and a line is drawn to connect the points v and o.   An arbitrary value is selected for D', and a deflection line, otherwise termed the elastic line, of the bulkhead is determined for the known loading and made tangent to the vertical through t.   Graphical methods (Ref. 341) are preferable in this connection.   If the elastic line thus determined does not intersect the vertical at anchor-level elevation (assumption: lateral displacement there is $y = 0$), then the depth D' has been estimated incorrectly and is not compatible with the conditions of equilibrium imposed. A new value has then to be selected for D', and the entire procedure of determining the elastic line has to be repeated for the new depth until a value of D' is found at which the elastic line will intersect the vertical at anchor level. This is the so-called *elastic-line method*.   It is extremely time-consuming and, for that reason, is seldom used in practice.   It will therefore not be elaborated upon further in this book.

The use of the elastic-line method, however, permitted the development by Blum (Ref. 33, 1931) of a much simpler procedure, known as the *equivalent-beam method*.   By repeated trial computations involving different values of ϕ, where K_A was based on Eq. (10-5) and K_P was taken to equal $2/K_A$, Blum succeeded in establishing a theoretical relationship between ϕ and the distance x from the dredge line to the point of contraflexure c.   Figure 14-8(V) gives this relationship, where ϕ is expressed in terms of K_A.   It should be noted in this connection that doubling the K_P value, compared with the value obtained from Eq. (10-5), was undertaken by Blum not because he considered the beneficial effect of wall friction (Art. 10-3), but because of the results of previous tests by Franzius (Ref. 101, 1927) at Hannover.   During these tests Franzius obtained very high values of passive resistance and recommended doubling the values of passive resistance obtained by the use of the heretofore customary equation (10-11).   The direction of the wall friction (Art. 10-3) was not given any consideration by this recommendation, which therefore should not be used indiscriminately.   The test box used by Franzius was 3.3 ft (1.0 m) wide and 4.9 ft (1.5 m) high.   Therefore side wall friction may have had a very great influence on the increase of the passive resistance of the soil in the box when the front wall was pushed in.   It is questionable whether his test data can be applied to a normally long wall under field conditions.

Blum's equivalent-beam method consists in assuming a hinge at the point of contraflexure c, where the bending moment is zero.   The part of the bulkhead above the hinge can then be treated as a separate, freely supported beam with an overhanging end, as shown in Fig. 14-8(III), and its reactions (the anchor pull A_P and the shear R_B at the point of contraflexure) and bending moments can be determined in the customary manner.   After that, the lower portion of the bulkhead below the point of contraflexure c is treated as a separate, freely supported beam on two supports.   All the loads acting on that beam are known, since K'' is given, except the reaction R_D.   The span $(D' - x)$ of that beam, compatible with equilibrium, is also not yet known. This span, however, can easily be determined by equating the moments of the loads shown in Fig. 14-8(IV) around the point of application of R_D.   Once $(D' - x)$ is computed, the final depth of embedment is determined from

$$D = 1.2(D' - x + x) = 1.2D' \qquad (14\text{-}14)$$

The fixed-earth-support method has sometimes been criticized because of some of its allegedly doubtful assumptions.   Later elaborate experimental investigations (Ref. 356), however, have shown that it comes very close to reality where backfilled bulkheads are concerned (see the design recommendations made in Art. 14-3C).

A purely empirical design procedure, known as the *Danish rules*, seems to have grown from a design philosophy expressed as follows in 1898 by a leading Danish designer: " Quay walls are never calculated in practice, but are made in accordance with established rules."

When a new material, reinforced concrete, was introduced at the turn of the century, a daring experiment was made by two Danish engineers, Christiani and Nielsen, who in 1906 built a pier at Aalborg which could not have stood up, according to the then conventional applications of Coulomb's theory to the free-earth-support method of bulkhead design.

Although underdesigned, even according to the later so-called Danish rules, the Aalborg pier, when visited by the writer in 1953, appeared to be in excellent condition.

The stability of the Aalborg pier was attributed to a reduction of active lateral pressures in the mid-span zone between the anchor and the dredge-line levels.   This pressure reduction was assumed to be caused by the deflection of the sheet piling and the resulting arching of the soil in a vertical direction between these two levels.

This concept was supported by the results of medium-scale-model tests by Stroyer on flexible 3 by 3 ft (91.5 by 91.5 cm) metal sheets, rigidly supported and allowed to deflect only after backfilling was completed.

The Danish Society of Engineers adopted these concepts and promulgated rules for design and a pressure distribution based on the above concept of vertical arching.   Details of this procedure are given in the first edition, Art. 16-12.   The method will not be discussed further now since in no known case of model or of field measurements was a pressure distribution obtained similar to the one given by the Danish rules.   Further, the theoretical validity of these rules no longer seems to be defended by leading Danish engineers after the results of tests conducted in the 1940s by the writer became better and more generally known.   The very concept of arching was not even discussed in an outstanding 1953 theoretical treatise (Ref. 122) by Brinch Hansen, as pointed out by the writer in Ref. 364b.

The large-scale-model tests performed in 1943 to 1949 by Tschebotarioff

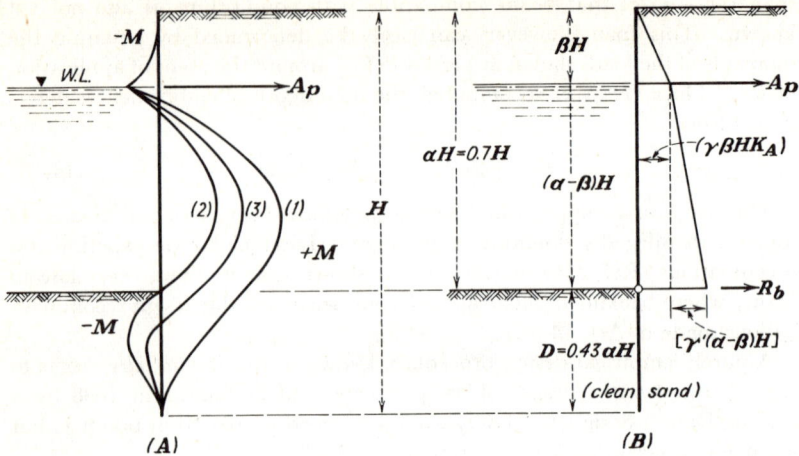

Fig. 14-9. (*A*) Influence of degree of sheet-pile fixation below the dredge line on the shape of the bending-moment curves. (*B*) The hinge-at-dredge-line method, which corresponds to curve 2 in (*A*).

at Princeton University under the sponsorship of the Bureau of Yards and Docks, U.S. Navy, showed that an appreciable reduction of bending moments did take place but because of previously unsuspected features of the passive resistance of sand below the dredge line. This resistance was much greater and was concentrated closer to the dredge line than expected, thus reducing the effective span of the sheeting and hence the bending moment. The reduction, however, was not as great as that obtained following the Danish rules; bending moments computed on the basis of these rules equaled approximately 75 percent of actually measured values.

For a depth of embedment in clean sand of medium to compact density equal to $D = 0.43\alpha H = 0.30H$ (see Fig. 14-9) good fixation of the sheeting developed below the dredge line with a corresponding bending-moment curve of type 2. At the dredge line the bending moment was zero. This led the writer to propose a simplification of Blum's equivalent-beam method, the *hinge-at-the-dredge-line method*, shown in Fig. 14-9*B*. It will be discussed further in sections *B* and *C* of this article.

Rowe published in 1952 (Ref. 272) the results of extensive medium-scale-model tests on dry sand with a greater range of bulkhead flexibilities. *Rowe established* a general relationship between *the reduction of bending moments* computed by the free-earth-support method and the flexibility number ρ of a bulkhead (Fig. 14-10):

$$\rho = \frac{H^4}{EI} \qquad (14\text{-}15)$$

where $H =$ total length of sheet piling, ft

$E =$ young modulus of sheet-pile material, lb/in.^{2}

$I =$ moment of inertia of sheet pile, in.^{4}/ft.

The diagram shown in Fig. 14-10 refers to sand soil, to a zero surcharge $p_s = 0$, and to $\alpha = 0.7$ and $\beta = 0.2$. These two coefficients, α and β, define the freeboard and embedment dimensions in respect to the total length H when the anchor level corresponds with the water level as shown in Fig. 14-9.

If the experimentally obtained moment-reduction curves are plotted in terms of the unit moment $\tau = M/H^3$ vs. the flexibility number $\rho = H^4/EI$, they become independent of the scale of the structure and are referred to as *operating curves* for the structure. The $M_1 = 100$ percent shown in Fig. 14-10 is $M_1 = M_{max}/H^3$, where M_{max} is the maximum moment computed for free-earth-support conditions, i.e., taken from curve 1 in Fig. 14-9.

On the same diagram can then be plotted the *structural curves* for a given profile and material of a sheet pile and for a given bending stress. These curves indicate the unit moment which varying lengths H of such a sheet pile can withstand.

The structural curves A in Fig. 14-10 show the unit resistance moments to bending of steel sheet piles of the US sections PZ-27, PZ-32, and PZ-38 for a permissible stress of 22,000 lb/in.$^2 = 1,545$ kg$_f$/cm^2.

The intersection of the structural curve of a given section with the reduction curve for a given sand density gives the value of log ρ, and hence of the total pile length H, which corresponds to the permissible stresses and other constants selected for that particular chart.

If a point of a structural curve corresponding to a given log ρ value of the section selected is located *above* the operating curve, this means that the bending stresses in the piling will be smaller than the stress for which the structural curve has been computed. Similarly, if a point of a structural curve is located *below* the operating curve, this will mean that the bending stresses in

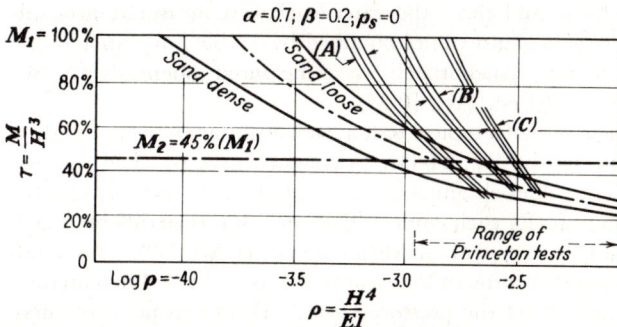

Fig. 14-10.   Rowe's method of anchored-bulkhead design. Relationship between M/M_{max} and log ρ.   (*From Ref. 369.*)

the piling will be higher than the stress of the structural curve. These considerations permit the selection of a suitable section.

It will be noted from Fig. 14-10 that Rowe's average-density curve, the structural curves of the five steel sheet-pile profiles, and the reduction value corresponding to Tschebotarioff's hinge-at-dredge-line procedure all intersect around the same point; i.e., they give almost identical values. This is because although Rowe starts with the free-earth-support moment curve 1 in Fig. 14-9, he applies to it empirical reduction coefficients which reduce its maximum M value to that of the moment curve 2.

The method of Rowe greatly facilitates understanding the fundamentals of the problem. Thus, if we plot in Fig. 14-10 the resistance curves B for the same sheet-pile sections for which we had plotted the curves A but for the additional deflection which would correspond to the first limit of elasticity of the metal at 33,000-lb/in.^{2} (2,310 kg$_f$/cm^2), then the corresponding experimental moment will decrease from 45 percent of M_1 to 36 percent of M_1, as shown in Fig. 14-10. In other words, this indicates the presence of an additional factor of safety equal to $\frac{45}{63} = 1.25$ if one designs a steel sheet-pile wall for the stresses of 22,000 lb/in.^{2} (1,545 kg$_f$/cm^2) usually considered permissible in the United States for A328 steel. The advantage of using sheeting rolled from ASTM steel A572 with high yield points of 45,000, 50,000, or 55,000 lb/in.^{2} (3,170, 3,520, or 3,870 kg$_f$/cm^2) becomes evident by following a reasoning similar to the one just given.

Thus, the group of curves C on Fig. 14-10 corresponds to a further increase of the working stress to the 45,000 lb/in.^{2} (3,170 kg$_f$/cm^2) yield point of a V45 steel. This will introduce an additional "hidden" factor of safety equal to approximately $F = 0.36/0.32 = 1.12$, compared with a working stress of 33,000 lb/in.^{2} (2,325 kg$_f$/cm^2).

(B). *Measurements and Field Observations.* The 1943 to 1948 1 : 10 *model scale tests at Princeton University* were performed under conditions of complete model similarity. Bending strains were measured in the steel sheets by numerous (105 pairs) electric-resistivity strain gages. Deflections above the dredge level, both below and above the water level, were measured mechanically and were checked against values obtained by double integration of the bending-moment curves. Anchor pulls were measured independently (see Refs. 354 and 356 and 1st ed., Art. 10-23).

The general dimensions of a typical test, as well as the analytical procedure followed, are illustrated by Fig. 14-11. A smooth curve was laid through the bending-moment values obtained at 35 elevations as an average of three pairs of SR-4 strain gages for each point. This curve was then differentiated, taking points from the curve, to obtain shear values (see Art. 1-9). A smooth shear curve was then laid through these shear points and the differentiation process was repeated to get the pressure curve. From this pressure curve the bending moments were computed back as a check by conventional strength of materials methods. Differences of more than 7 percent between

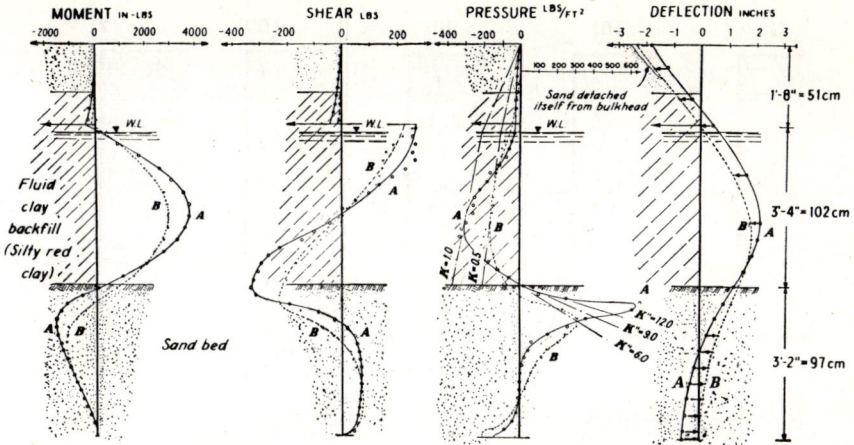

Fig. 14-11. Model bulkhead bending moments, shears, lateral pressures, and deflections at (A) the initial and (B) final stages of originally fluid clay backfill consolidation during Princeton test 21. (*After Tschebotarioff and Welch, Ref. 382.*)

points of the originally measured and recomputed curves normally did not occur, demonstrating thereby the adequate accuracy of the method.

Figure 14-12 gives a summary of the main types of pressure distribution established during the Princeton tests with *sands*. It was found that differentiation is essential between conditions created by backfilling behind a flexible anchored sheet-pile bulkhead or by dredging in front of a sunk wall. No clear differentiation between these two conditions had been made in previously published theoretical investigations of the subject of arching in soils. No evidence of vertical arching was found when the model bulkheads were backfilled with sand [Fig. 14-12(I) and (II)]. This is true because vertical arching, as a result of the flatness of the arches, is the least stable type. Similarly to horizontal arching (Art. 11-1), it does not develop noticeably behind an anchored bulkhead while backfilling is done, since no soil is present during most of the backfilling to provide an abutment for the arch at and above the anchor level. Further, the elastic elongation of the anchor and the yield of its supports progressively increase as backfilling goes on. This induces the breakdown of any arches in the uncemented sand. Definite evidence of arching was obtained at Princeton only during the stages of a test which simulated dredging in front of a sunk wall, i.e., when all the backfill was in place, the bulkhead having been driven or "sunk" through it, the anchor support of which did not yield any further [Fig. 14-12(V)]. Of all the theoretical pressure-distribution curves so far advanced which assume arching of sands, only the one proposed by Ohde [Ref. 237] closely corresponded to the one determined at Princeton under the above conditions. If the anchor support is immovable, the strong outward movement of the

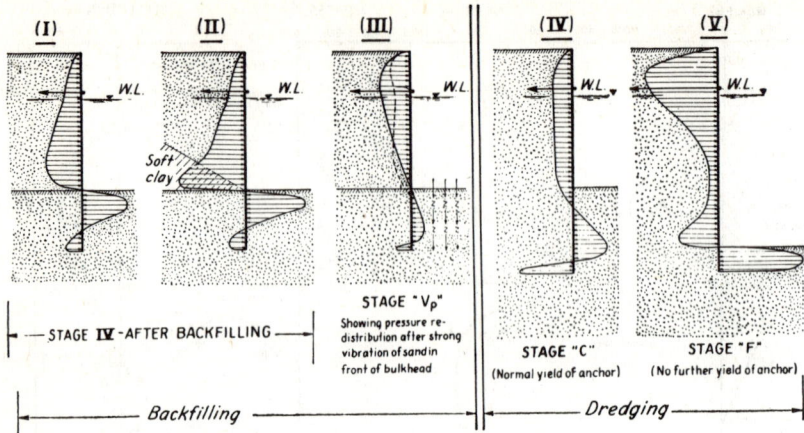

Fig. 14-12. Five main lateral-earth-pressure distribution types determined during the Princeton tests with model flexible bulkheads. *(From Tschebotarioff and Brown, Ref. 379, 1948.)*

embedded lower portion of the bulkhead will press the upper portion of the bulkhead against the soil behind it and will induce passive pressures of a high magnitude.

Severe vibration of the sand below the dredge line in front of a completely backfilled bulkhead [Fig. 14-12(III)], has an effect similar to dredging. However, even a slight simultaneous natural yield of the anchor strongly reduces the effect on the pressure redistribution of both types of arching and of the passive pressures above anchor level [Fig. 14-12(IV)].

Exceptionally severe vibration of the sand backfill behind the bulkhead by spud vibrators increased lateral pressures, so that the resulting bending moments in the bulkhead were increased by 60 percent and more, compared with values obtained after normal backfilling.

The resultant of the residual passive pressures was located much closer to the dredge line than this is usually assumed, these pressures being a function of the bulkhead displacements (see Fig. 14-13). This and the decrease of the active pressures just above the dredge line by shearing stresses, and not by vertical arching, were found to be the main causes of smaller bending moments in the model sheet piling, compared with values obtained by conventional methods. The flexibility of the bulkhead was of importance to the extent that the bulkhead displacement y at the dredge line (Fig. 14-13) increased the shearing stresses along that boundary and decreased the active pressures behind the bulkhead at that boundary.

This is the probable physical explanation of Rowe's findings (Fig. 14-10) concerning the decrease of bending moments with an increased bulkhead flexibility. The distribution of passive resistance pressures below the dredge line alone does not seem to explain this finding. During the Princeton model tests the passive pressures below the dredge line in front of the bulkhead reached Kp values which in some cases were 3 to 4 times greater than the maximum values which are theoretically possible if the effect of wall friction is neglected. This finding approximately corresponds to the result of the theoretical analysis of the problem of passive resistance (see Table 10-2 and Fig. 10-9) for the condition where the angles of internal friction ϕ and of wall friction are assumed to be equal, and the bulkhead sinks somewhat into the soil (Art. 10-3 and Fig. 10-7).

Figure 14-13 illustrates the nature of pressure distributions against the embedded portion of an anchored flexible sheet-pile bulkhead. As the backfilling proceeds, the total active pressures above the dredge line gradually increase, as well as the deflections y of the sheeting from the original position 1. The sheeting successively occupies the positions 2, 3, and 4, and as a result the corresponding actual resistance curves 2, 3, and 4 extend farther and farther down along the limiting maximum $K_p \gamma h$ line.

The elevation of the point of contraflexure, which is equivalent to a hinge where the bending moment is zero, will drop in the process as indicated by circles in Fig. 14-13.

A similar phenomenon was observed during Princeton model tests with varying depths of embedment during which all other factors, such as the flexibility of the bulkhead and the distance between the dredge line and the anchor level, remained unchanged. For smaller depths of embedment the point of contraflexure would drop, as shown by small circles in Fig. 14-13,

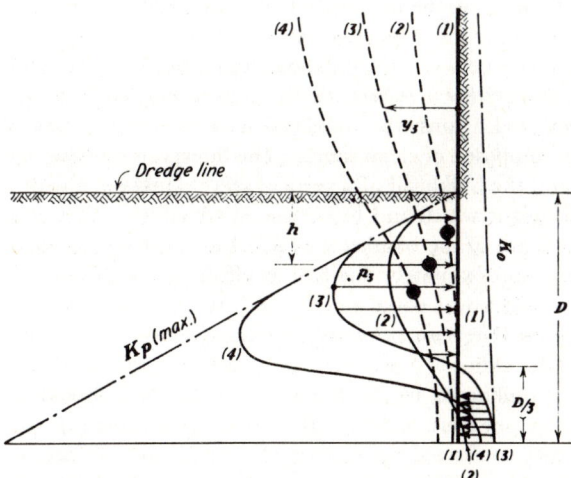

Fig. 14-13. Relationship between the deflections and the earth-resistance distribution of a flexible anchored bulkhead below the dredge line.

if the depth D in that diagram is assumed variable and curve 4 is taken to show the relative deflection for the smallest depth of embedment, compared with curves 3 and 2 representing deflections for progressively larger embedments. With a decreasing depth of embedment D the shape of the entire bending-moment curve would change from 2 in Fig. 14-9A to 3 and finally to 1.

It is noteworthy that fixation at the tip of the sheeting was found to be produced by neutral or active pressures only, not exceeding the K_0-line values (see Fig. 14-13). This explains why fixation of the tip, as evidenced by a reversal of measured bending strains there, was present even when the tip had moved slightly outward.

The lateral pressures of originally fluid clay backfills were found to decrease with time as a function of the consolidation of the clay and without any outward movement of the bulkhead being necessary to achieve the pressure reduction. As a result of the spring action of the deflected bulkhead it even moved back toward the backfill during its consolidation (see Fig. 14-11). After complete consolidation the lateral pressures of the clay corresponded to a value of $K = 0.50$ (curve B, Fig. 14-11), except in the immediate vicinity of more rigid restraining horizontal boundaries.

A further induced expansion of the consolidated-clay backfills did not reduce their lateral pressures any further in the upper half of the backfill during tests where the water level reached to the backfill surface so that no restraining layer capable of resisting some tension because of capillary saturation was present there. In other words, the active pressures of the consolidated nonsensitive plastic clay backfill were found to equal its neutral pressures, further confirming laboratory findings on the matter (1st ed., Arts. 10-9 and 10-12).

Another important finding of the Princeton tests was that a *sand dike* placed at its natural angle of repose between the bulkhead and a fluid-clay backfill [see Fig. 14-1 (III)] *was fully effective in reducing the lateral pressures of the fluid clay.* The lateral pressures exerted against the bulkhead were no greater than if the entire backfill were composed of clean sand. The interposition between the fluid-clay backfill and the bulkhead of a vertical sand blanket of a width equal to the bulkhead height was found to be just as effective as that of a sand dike. When the width of the blanket was equal to one-half the bulkhead height, it was only approximately one-half as effective and it was not effective at all when its width was equal to one-tenth the bulkhead height.

Field measurements with the Wiegmann inclinometer were performed in the 1950s with the sponsorship of the Office of Naval Research under the writer's direction on several existing bulkheads in the harbors of Baltimore, Brooklyn, Cleveland, and Galveston (see Refs. 383 to 385). Although performed only above the dredge line, they confirmed the findings of the preceding Princeton model tests and brought out additional points outlined in the following articles.

The *construction of a new Pier 11 by the Port of New York Authority in Brooklyn* (Refs. 155 and 178) provided an opportunity of performing Wiegmann in-

clinometer measurements from the start of construction and down almost to
the very tip of the sheeting.   Three special hollow box piles, of the same
moment of inertia and the same neutral axis as the PZ38 sheeting of the bulkhead and interlocking with it, were specially designed for the purpose and
were driven at intervals of over 200 ft (60 m) as an integral part of the
2,000-ft-long (600-m) bulkhead.

The anchor pulls of rods opposite the three test piles were measured
directly by means of two Carlson strain meters on each anchor rod.   It was
found that the anchor rods were subjected to appreciable bending stresses,
which were superimposed on the normal tensile stresses close to their connection to the wales (see also Art. 14-4B).

The results of slope change measurements on the three test piles are shown

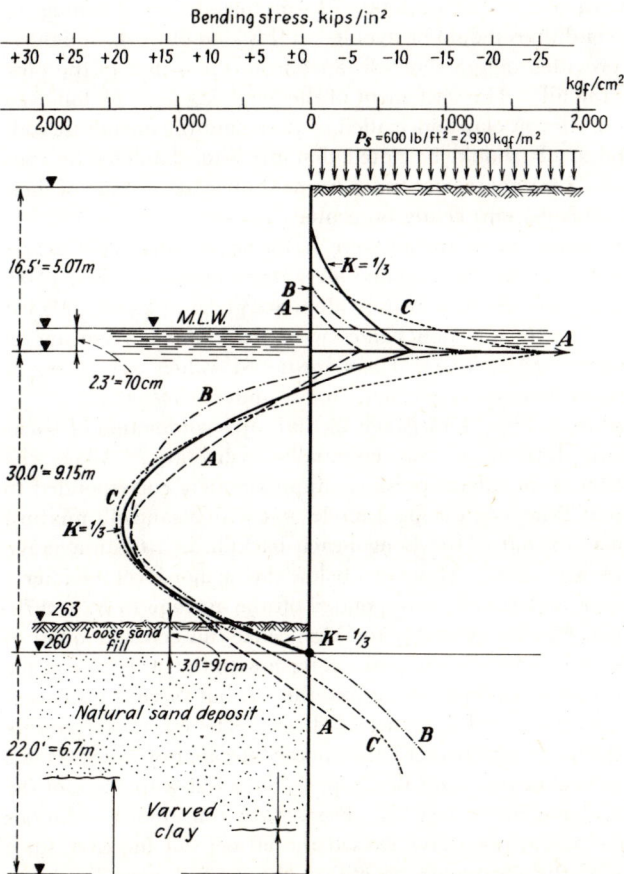

Fig. 14-14.   Bending-moment curves obtained from Wiegmann inclinometer measurements on three hollow boxpiles *A*, *B*, and *C* of Pier 11,
Brooklyn, New York.   (*Ref. 364a*).

in Fig. 14-14.   The theoretical bending-moment curve shown by a full line
on that diagram was computed in accordance with the design diagram Fig.
14-18 for a value of $K_A = \frac{1}{3}$.   It will be noted that the points of zero moment
(hinges) of the three test piles are either at the surface of the natural sand
layer (for pile B) or 2 (pile C) to 4 (pile A) ft (30 to 60 cm) beneath it (Ref.
364*a*).

Direct measurements of lateral earth pressures against a full-sized anchored
bulkhead of Pier C in Long Beach harbor, California, were reported in 1950
by Duke (Refs. 89 and 361).   The general dimensions of the bulkhead are
shown in cross section in Fig. 14-15.   The surface of the hydraulic fill settled
over a foot as the fill consolidated.   A large part of this settlement could be
attributed to the 5- to 6-ft-thick (1.5 to 1.8-m) layer of silty clay deposited
ahead of the sand fill proper from the fill water which was allowed to flow
all along the length of the 2,365-ft-long (720 m) pier before reaching an
overflow.   Such conditions should be avoided in this kind of work, and over-
flows should be provided only a short distance from the orifice of the pipe
which discharges the fill.   The settlement of the overlying sand fill followed
the consolidation of the soft clay and loaded by its weight the anchor tie rods
and the batter piles.   It should be noted that the 3-in.-diameter tie rods
were spaced 6 ft (1.82 m) apart, and the A-frame timber batter piles of their
anchorages only 3.0 ft (91 cm) center on center.

Lateral-earth-pressure measurements were performed by means of Carlson
pressure cells, marked by the letters P and a reference number in Fig. 14-15
(stage 1).   The measured earth-pressure values are given in kips (1,000 lb)
per square foot.   The anchor pull values were determined by means of
Carlson strain meters (Art. 1-9).   Their measured values are given in
Fig. 14-15 in kips per foot (see conversion factors under *Notation*).

It will be noted from Fig. 14-15 (stage 2) that after completion of backfilling the pressure distribution was essentially hydrostatic.   Above the
anchor level at stage 2 the lateral pressures approximately corresponded to
the ones obtained at Princeton during a model test with a sand-silt mixture
of a grading similar to that of the Long Beach backfill, i.e., to an average
value of $K_y = 0.44$ (Ref. 356).   However, below the anchor level the lateral
pressures were much higher and corresponded on the average to $K_y = 0.70$.
The readings of cell P8 were probably too high, since this cell was found to
have been dislodged from its original position flush with the inner face of the
bulkhead, so that it protruded somewhat into the fill; but there is no reason
to doubt the overall accuracy of the other readings.   There are two possible
explanations for the 60 percent higher values of the lateral pressures at stage 2
below the anchor level of the Long Beach pier compared with those of the
corresponding Princeton model test 59.   First, slight continuous vibrations
produced by wave action may have caused the 60 percent increase, since
strong vibrations of the completed backfill of this type during Princeton
test 59 had demonstrated its considerable susceptibility to vibrations and

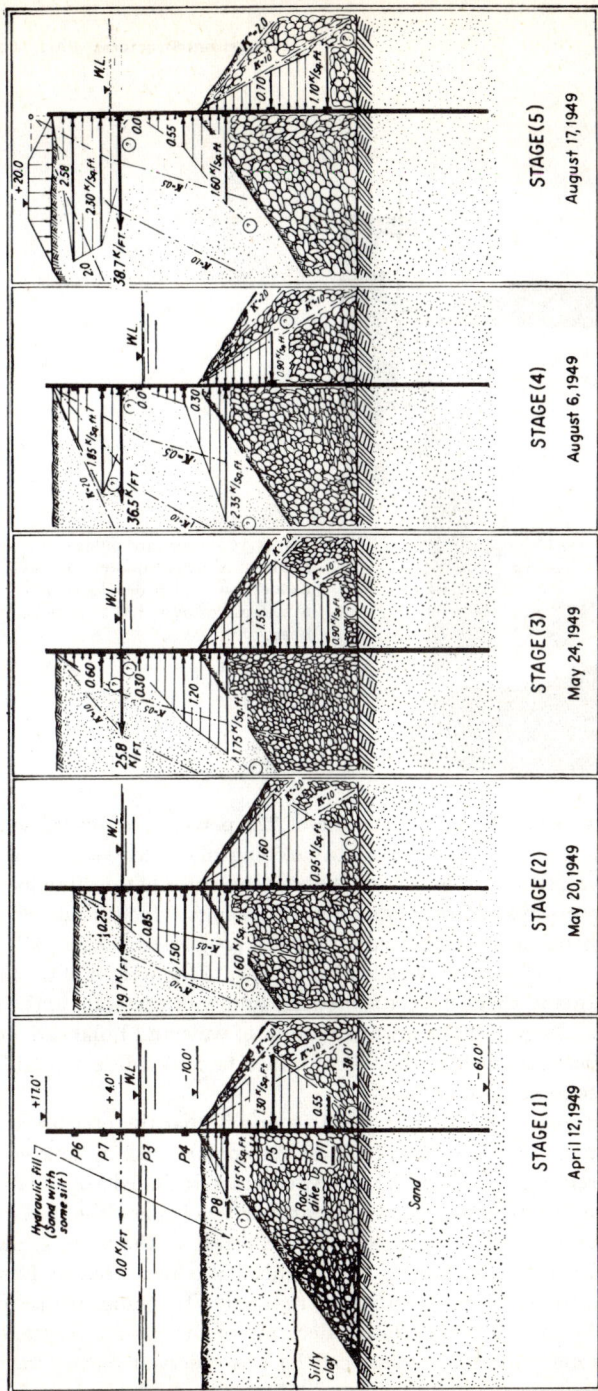

Fig. 14-15. Analysis of the Long Beach Pier C bulkhead-test data. The observed redistribution of lateral pressures after consolidation of the hydraulic fill is attributed to overloading of the anchors, which produces a tendency of the wale to move inward, with resulting accentuation of horizontal arching above the anchor level. (*From Tschebotarioff, Ref. 361 discussion of G. Martin Duke's Ref. 89.*)

Fig. 14-16. Outward bulge due to failure of inadequate anchor connection, which developed into a collapse of over 100 ft of bulkhead.

produced an almost 4 times greater increase of 227 percent, compared with static lateral pressures. Second, horizontal arching may have caused this increase. However, there can be no doubt about the causes of the subsequent redistribution of pressures and of overloading of anchors which occurred as the consolidation of the fill and of the underlying clay progressed (see stages 3, 4, and 5, Fig. 14-15). The anchors were loaded by part of the weight of the fill. This would have made them deflect somewhat and pull the wale and the bulkhead inward. Even a slight inward motion of wale and bulkhead, not exceeding a fraction of an inch, as the fill continued to consolidate, should be sufficient to induce horizontal arching.

It will be noted from Fig. 14-15, stages 3, 4, and 5, that the pressure was zero below the anchor level. The previously customary assumptions concerning vertical arching of the Danish rules by contrast, included appreciably increased pressures immediately below the anchor level, since the arching was supposed to be a product of the primary deflection of the sheet piling. However, no additional deflection of the bulkhead was measured at Long Beach Pier C after stage 2 (Fig. 14-15) was reached. It should further be noted from Fig. 14-15 that a progressive decrease of the passive resistance pressures of the outer rock dike against cell P5 was observed during stages 2 to 5. This observation excludes any possibility of vertical arching, since the outer dike would then have to act as an outer abutment to any such vertical arches and to provide an increased resistance to their load.   The observed *decrease* of the passive resistance, however, is entirely consistent with the explanation that the weight of the soil loaded and pulled in the anchor, and through it the bulkhead, and thereby decreased the passive resistance pressures at the top of the outer dike.   Finally, the conventional assumptions concerning vertical arching, as presented by the Danish rules, do not lead to any increase of the anchor pulls, as compared with the free- or fixed-earth-support methods.   The Ohde method is more reasonable and leads to an increase of some 60 percent in the anchor-pull values.   However, there was an increase of 85 percent in the anchor pull at Long Beach Pier C between stages 2 and 4, or of over 140 percent as compared with normal assumptions. The anchors were stressed almost up to the elastic limit, and some bolts and other minor connections actually failed in places.   The need to avoid over-loading of the anchors by the weight of the fill is therefore apparent.

Cases of *anchor failures* are not infrequent and will be discussed further in Arts. 14-4*B* and 14-6.   The photograph in Fig. 14-16 shows the initial appearance of an outward bulge of the concrete capping which developed into a complete failure by outward tilting of over 100 ft of bulkhead because of an inadequate anchorage connection.

Figure 14-17 shows the appearance of an inward bulge of the concrete

Fig. 14-17.   Inward bulge due to toe kickout of old bulkhead because of later inadvertent localized overdredging.

capping of an anchored bulkhead due to a *toe kickout*. This was an old bulk-head with only 18 ft (5.5 m) of water which lost part of its original embed-ment around the point of failure because of later inadvertent localized *over-dredging* by some 4 ft (1.20 m) during channel deepening for a new pier across the slip.

(*C*). *Advisable Design Procedures.* Before the studies just described were completed in the 1950s, bending stresses in steel sheet piling with sand back-fills computed by various existing and frequently used methods could vary by as much as 300 percent, depending on whether the most liberal method (the Danish rules) or the most conservative method (the free-earth-support method) was followed. The selection of the method depended largely on the temperament of the designer.

The Danish rules have now been shown to have no real theoretical basis and to lead to factors of safety smaller than those claimed or customarily required.

In spite of some early assertions to the contrary, Rowe's design procedure and the simplified equivalent-beam method proposed by the writer have been shown to be in complete agreement with each other under similar soil con-ditions for steel sheet piling (Refs. 362 and 31*a*). Rowe applied to the free-earth-support moments (to curve 1 on Fig. 14-9*A*) empirical moment-reduc-tion coefficients to obtain curve 2, which was given directly by the writer's hinge-at-the-dredge-line procedure. This latter procedure is based on a verifiable physical factor, the location of the zero-moment point, which is identical with the point of contraflexure, i.e., the hinge. Further, it requires much simpler computations compared with the roundabout way of first solving cubic equations [Eq. (14-7)] for the free-earth-support method and the subsequent use of flexibility vs. moment-reduction charts.

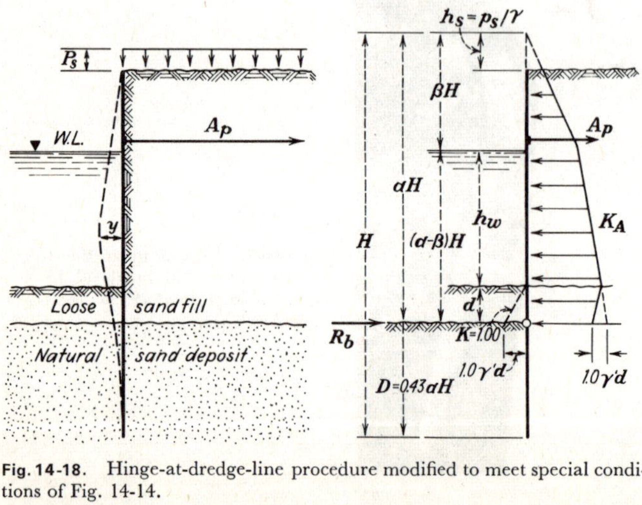

Fig. 14-18. Hinge-at-dredge-line procedure modified to meet special condi-tions of Fig. 14-14.

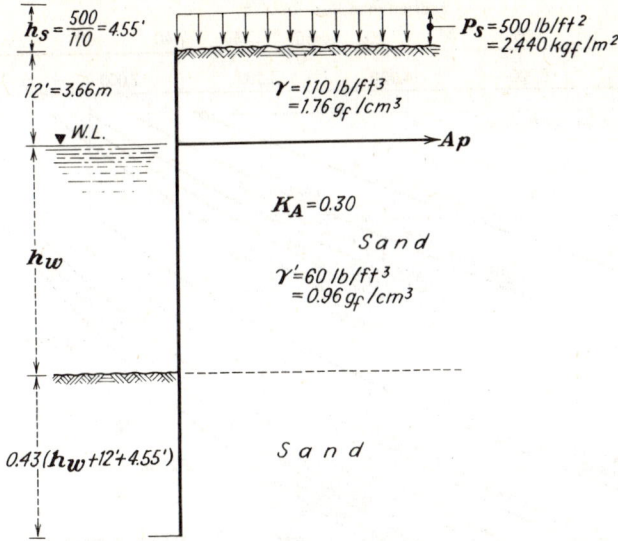

Fig. 14-19. Dimensions of an anchored bulkhead used for the comparative graph of Fig. 14-20.

Further, the simplified equivalent-beam method can easily be developed for application to complex soil conditions below the dredge line not covered by Rowe's extensive but necessarily limited and simplified range of model tests or by Blum's original determination of the hinge location solely as a function of the value of the angle of internal friction ϕ and the corresponding K_A value, assumed to remain constant below the dredge-line [Fig. 14-8(V)].

The miniaturization of inclinometers (Art. 10-9), compared with the large original Wiegmann inclinometer, makes it much easier to perform appropriate measurements on new bulkheads and to establish in the field the actual point of contraflexure, the hinge, which determines the degree of fixation of the bulkhead in the ground. Once the elevation of this hinge for certain soil conditions is known, it can be predicted for similar soil conditions, and the computation of the bending moments in the sheeting can then be reduced to the application of elementary statics to a beam on two supports with an overhanging end. Figure 14-18 shows such a diagram, corresponding to the soil conditions and measurement results of Fig. 14-14.

The advantages of using the hinge-at-the-dredge-line method for sands, compared with the unrealistically conservative free-earth-support method, are illustrated by Fig. 14-20, which indicates the maximum permissible water depths for the other dimensions of the bulkhead and the soil and load conditions given by Fig. 14-19 on the basis of the two design methods for different types of steel sheet piling.

It will be seen from Fig. 14-20 that only a 20-ft (6.1-m) water depth is

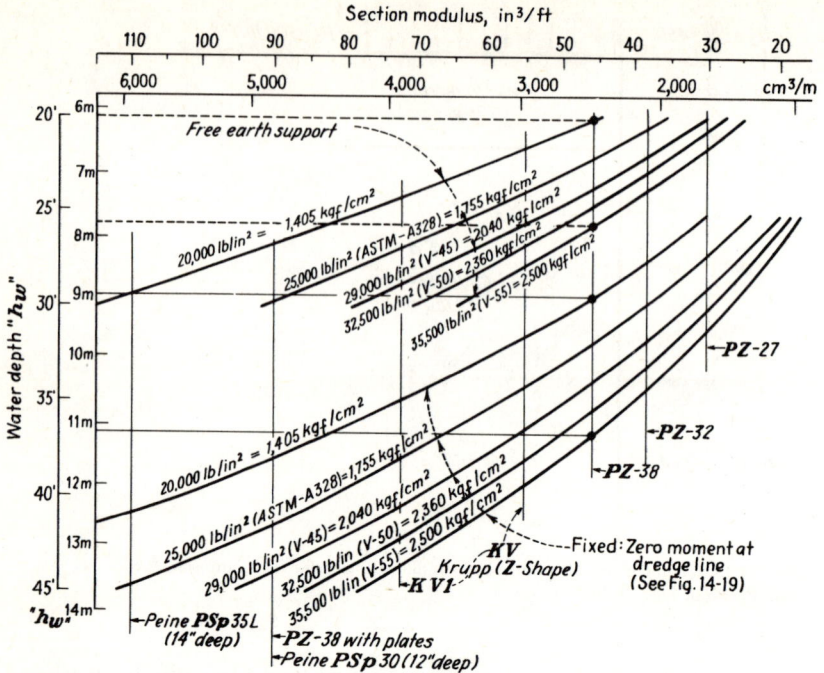

Fig. 14-20. Comparison of maximum permissible water depths for two design methods and different types of steel and sheet piles of the anchored bulkhead shown in Fig. 14-19. (*From Tschebotarioff, Ref. 369.*)

permissible according to the free-earth-support method for a bulkhead of the heaviest American sheeting (ZP38; see Art. 11-6) stressed to a maximum of 20,000 lb/in.^{2} (1,400 kg$_f$/cm^2) but that this depth can be increased to 29.5 ft (8.85 m) according to the hinge-at-the-dredge-line procedure. If this procedure is combined with sheeting of V55 high-yield steel, the water depth can be increased to 37 ft (11.3 m).

It will also be noted from Fig. 14-20 that greater water depths become possible for anchored bulkheads by using some types of European sheet piles without resorting to the use of special steels. This lag in the United States apparently results because these greater water depths, up to 50 ft (15.3 m) so far, can be obtained by using cellular cofferdams (Art. 14-8), which were developed in the United States but not generally used in Europe until after World War II. Thus there was a greater incentive for European steel companies to roll heavier profiles.

Positive bending moments in the sheeting can be reduced by dropping the anchor level, as was successfully done at the Brooklyn Pier 11 (see Fig. 14-14). However, if any repairs become necessary later, as was true for the pier illustrated by Fig. 14-16, well points have to be used first to lower the water below the anchor levl.

At low tide the free-water level drops faster than the level of the water in the backfill behind the sheet-pile bulkhead. Appreciable lateral pressures may be exerted against the sheet piling as a result of such a *tidal lag* (see Fig. 14-21). The effect is somewhat similar to that of a surcharge (Fig. 10-11); it should be considered in designs. The amount of lag varies with the magnitude of the local tidal variation and with the nature of the backfill. It should be determined experimentally in advance of construction, for instance, by observing the water-level variations in perforated pipes sunk into the soil near existing waterfront structures.

Timber sheeting has been shown by Rowe to have a greater relative flexibility than steel, so that it is safe to design it in accordance with the procedures developed for steel. Further, higher bending stresses should be permitted for timber sheeting than for separate rectangular timbers. Factors of safety as high as 5 or 6 are customarily required for the latter to take care of knots and other possible localized defects in the wood. However, in a continuous wall of good-quality timber sheeting such localized defects cannot be expected to occur at the same elevation in several adjoining sheets, and the excessive yielding of any one sheet will be transmitted by soil action to the adjoining ones and thereby relieved.

Things are different for *reinforced-concrete sheeting*. According to Rowe, its flexibility is smaller than that of steel sheeting, but no comparable field measurements on concrete sheeting appear to have been made so far. Caution is therefore indicated, especially in sensitive clays, where the greater bulk of the concrete sheet piles will produce much more displacement and hence remolding of the clay than steel sheeting. It should also be remembered that in concrete sheeting consideration of the negative bending moments below the dredge line cannot be neglected as is done for steel sheeting. These moments will be smaller than the positive moments above the dredge line which govern the selection of the sheet-pile section. But the steel reinforcement of concrete sheeting must take the reversal of bending moments

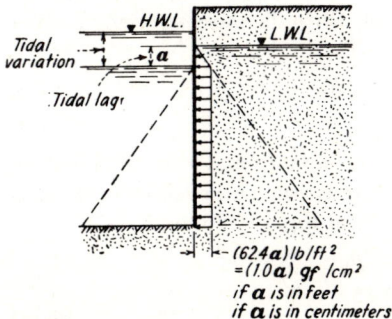

Fig. 14-21. Lateral pressures exerted against a row of sheet piling as a result of a lag in the tidal variation of the water level in the backfill.

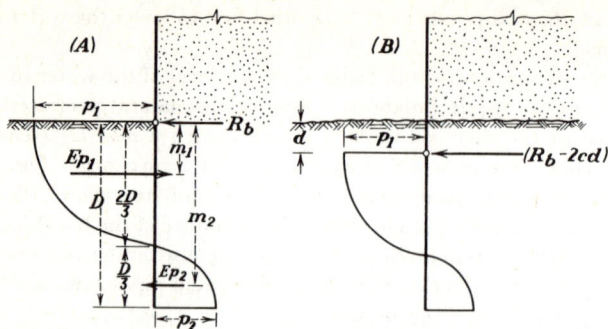

Fig. 14-22.   Computation of safety factors for sheet-pile fixation in clay. (*From Tschebotarioff, Ref. 383.*)

below the dredge line into account should fixation develop there.   Uncertainties over this point complicate economical designs, especially of pre-stressed sheeting.

The design of all types of *sheeting penetrating into medium to soft plastic clay* should follow the conservative free-earth-support method as given above with reference to Fig. 14-7.

Evidence has been obtained that steel sheeting driven into stiff over-consolidated and nonsensitive clay does get effective fixation in such material (see Ref. 383, figs 4 to 7).

A rough estimate of the magnitude of such fixation can be made by a trial-and-error procedure, the first step of which is illustrated by Fig. 14-22*A*. The fixation is governed by the lateral pressures p_1 and p_2 on the clay.   These pressures are to be resisted without shearing or consolidation deformations of the clay if the fixation is to take place as assumed.   This can be checked as follows.

A hinge is assumed at the dredge line; R_b is computed as the lower reaction of the equivalent beam (see Fig. 14-18); the active pressures of the clay below the dredge line are ignored if the vertical pressure at the dredge-line level behind the bulkhead is smaller than $2c$.   This will normally be the case for depths of water not exceeding 30 ft (9.1 m) when the shearing strength of the clay is $c = 1,500$ lb/ft² (7,340 kg$_f$/cm²).   Then

$$E_{p1} - E_{p2} = R_b \tag{14-16}$$

$$E_{p1} \times m_1 = E_{p2} \times m_2 \tag{14-17}$$

On the strength of model measurements on sands and a depth of embedment $D = 0.3H$ it is assumed that passive-resistance pressures vary parabolically and change signs at $\frac{2}{3}D$; then, from Eqs. (14-16) and (14-17),

$$p_2 = 0.57p_1 \tag{14-18}$$

$$p_1 = \frac{3.15}{R_b/D} \tag{14-19}$$

The safety factor F' against shear is

$$F' = \frac{2c}{p_1} \tag{14-20}$$

For the anchored bulkhead B analyzed in Ref. 383 and found to have satisfactory fixation, $F' = 4.17$ and $c = 1,500$ lb/ft² (7,340 kg$_f$/m²). This factor of safety against shear should be at least $F' = 3.00$ to prevent creep. Otherwise the checking procedure should be repeated for a lower elevation of the hinge as shown in Fig. 14-22B.

So far no cases of sheet-pile bending failures in anchored bulkheads have been reported.   Caution is nevertheless indicated when applying sophisticated design methods to soil conditions not fully covered by published experimental investigations, especially when dealing with sensitive clays and using concrete or U types of steel sheet piling (see Art. 11-6).

In determining the depth of sheet-pile embedment the possibility of inadvertent overdredging should always be kept in mind.   For that reason the theoretically required depth D should be increased by 4 ft (1.20 m) for 15- to 25-ft (4.6- to 7.7-m) water depths and by 3 ft (90 cm) for greater depths.

This requirement can be partially compensated for by staggering the penetration of every alternating pair of sheet piles, as sketched in elevation on Fig. 14-23.   With this economical arrangement, successfully used in Sweden, the passive resistance to fixation at the tips of the deeper sheets will be no less than when the entire wall reached continuously down to the elevation aa (see the discussion of Fig. 14-25, which follows).   It can also be seen from

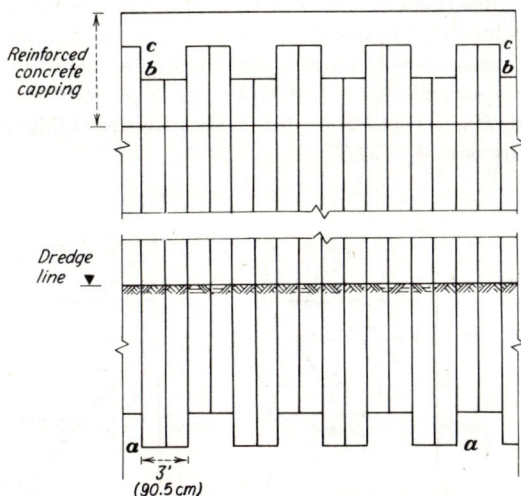

Fig. 14-23. The advantages of staggering the embedment penetrations of alternating pairs of steel sheet piles.

Figs 14-13 and 14-22 that the passive resistance p_2 at the back of the tip of the sheeting is comparatively small.   At the top of the sheets a better embedment in the reinforced concrete cap will be obtained with a decrease of stress concentrations and with less probability of a horizontal shrinkage crack than when all the sheets ended at one of the elevations *bb* or *cc*.   Yet the length of all the sheets is only *ab*.

Most of the trouble encountered in anchored bulkheads is caused by their anchorages, especially at the connections between the anchors and the bulkheads.

14-4. Bulkhead Anchorages and Dolphins.   Figure 14-24 illustrates three main types of bulkhead anchorage: (A) the anchor block, or deadman anchorage; (B) the A-frame pile anchorage; (C) the tension batter-pile anchorage directly connected to the sheeting.

(A). *Deadman Anchorages.*   The anchor blocks should be placed far enough back from the bulkhead to ensure that their passive-resistance wedges of soil *bdc* do not encroach appreciably on the active soil wedge *aeg* of the bulkhead itself, as sketched on Fig. 14-24A.   In addition, the overall stability along a potential sliding surface *fedc* should be investigated.

The problem of lateral resistance in sand in front of an anchor block at some distance below the soil surface is illustrated by Figs. 14-25 and 14-26. In the past it was customary to consider only the resistance along the height h of the block taken from a conventional pressure diagram as shown by horizontal arrows in Fig. 14-25.   Since this was coupled with low K_p values based on $\delta = 0$, the results were much too conservative, as was shown by experimental data.   Figure 14-26 is based on the results of experiments by Buchholtz (Ref. 44), further described by Streck (Ref. 117).   The tests were carried out at the Franzius Institut, Hannover.   The charts show the comparative resistances of continuous anchor blocks at different depths below the soil surface and of separate square blocks of a width $b = h$.   The charts can well be used within the limits $H/h = 1.5$ to $H/h = 5.5$.   They were established for a sand of medium density with $\phi = 32.5°$.

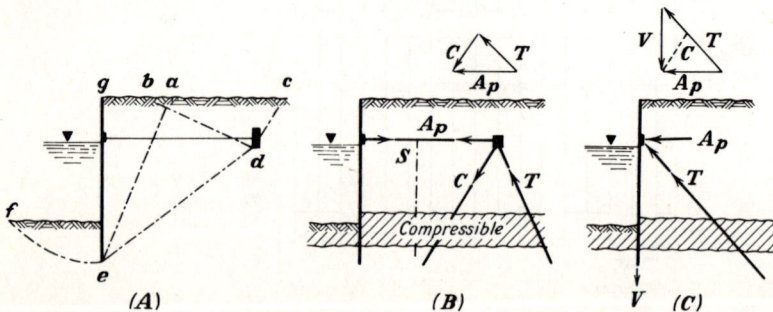

Fig. 14-24. Types of bulkhead anchorages.

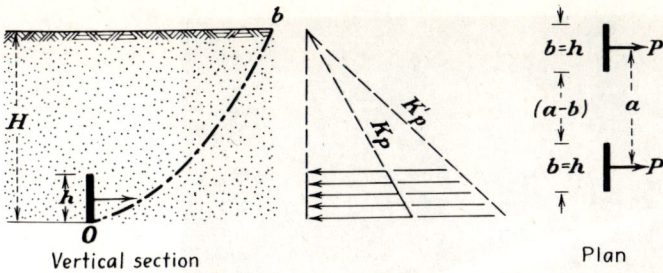

Fig. 14-25. Soil resistance to anchor blocks in sand below its surface (see Fig. 14-26). (*After Buchholtz, Ref. 44.*)

The resistance of a continuous block per unit of width is then computed from

$$E_p = \frac{\gamma H^2}{2} K_p$$

where the K_p values are taken from Fig. 14-26. It will be noted that an increase of the ratio H/h, that is, of the depth of the anchor block below the sand surface, has very little effect on the overall resistance. It is as if the entire wedge *ob* of Fig. 14-25 were offering its resistance for $\delta = 0$.

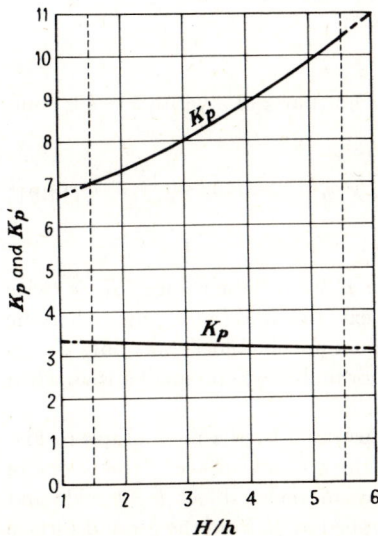

Fig. 14-26. Earth-resistance coefficients for anchor blocks in sand below its surface (see Fig.14-25). (*After Buchholtz, Ref. 44.*)

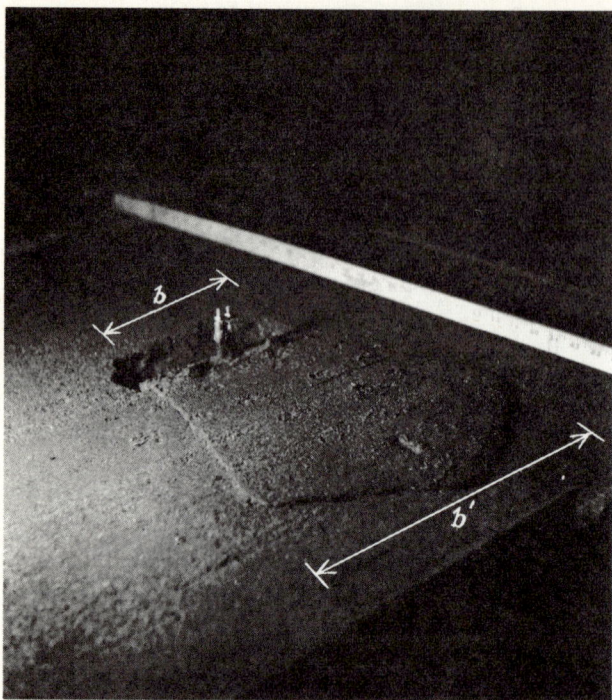

Fig. 14-27. Surface appearance of moist-sand wedge displaced at failure by individual small anchor block. (*From Merkin, Ref. 213.*)

The resistance of a separate square anchor block of a width $b = h$ is computed from

$$E_p = \frac{\gamma H^2}{2} K_p' b \tag{14-21}$$

The K_p' values are taken from Fig. 14-26.

It will be noted from Fig. 14-26 that for $H/h = 1.0$ the value of K_p' is twice as large as that of K_p. This reflects the experimental finding that when the spacing between the centerlines of individual anchor blocks was only $a = 2b$ (see Fig. 14-25), the resistance to the anchor pulls P was no smaller than when the anchor blocks were continuous.

The physical explanation for this is illustrated by the photograph in Fig. 14-27, which shows the shape in plan at the ground surface of the wedge of slightly moist sand displaced at failure by an anchor block $b = h$ wide and $H/h = 1.0$ high, with the anchor pulls applied at $\frac{2}{3}h$ from the ground surface through cables within small bentonite-slurry–filled cylindrical channels in the sand (see Ref. 213). It will be noted that at its widest point the wedge width is b', or approximately twice as large as that of the anchor block b. Thus the wedges would merge if the open spaces between individual anchor blocks were b wide.

In plastic clay soils with $\phi = 0$ and $c > 0$ a continuous anchor block H high, according to the Coulomb and the Rankine-Résal theories, will offer resistance to lateral displacement expressed by

$$E_p = \frac{\gamma H^2}{2} + 2cH \tag{14-22}$$

At depth h below the soil surface, the lateral resistance will be

$$p_h = \gamma h + 2c \tag{14-23}$$

The above expressions refer to a wall or to an anchor block reaching up to the soil surface. Equation (14-22) is obtained from Eq. (10-12) by multiplying it with $\gamma H^2/2$, that is, the value of the full fluid pressure corresponding to $K = 1.00$. The case of an anchor block located at some distance below the clay surface is illustrated by Figs. 14-28 and 14-29.

J. Brinch Hansen (Ref. 123) considered the case of an anchor block of rectangular cross section pulled through a plastic-clay soil as shown in Fig. 14-28A. It was assumed that the clay cannot change its volume and must therefore flow around the block, offering to such motion a shearing resistance $s = c$ along the slip surfaces shown by dash-dotted lines. The total resistance P per unit of anchor-block width will be

$$P = 11.4ch \tag{14-24}$$

Mackenzie (Ref. 205) performed small-scale-model tests with two plastic clays. In these tests the γh component of Eq. (14-23) was quite small compared with the $2c$ value. Possibly for that reason the deformations of the

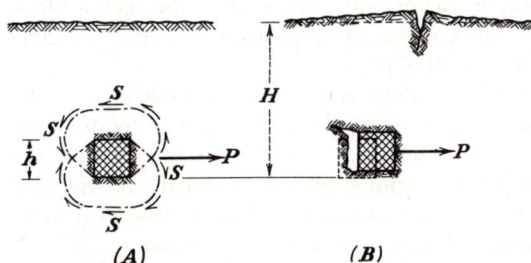

Fig. 14-28. Failure surfaces in clay around anchor blocks below soil surface: (A) theoretical considerations by Brinch Hansen (Ref. 123); (B) experimental results by Mackenzie (Ref. 205).

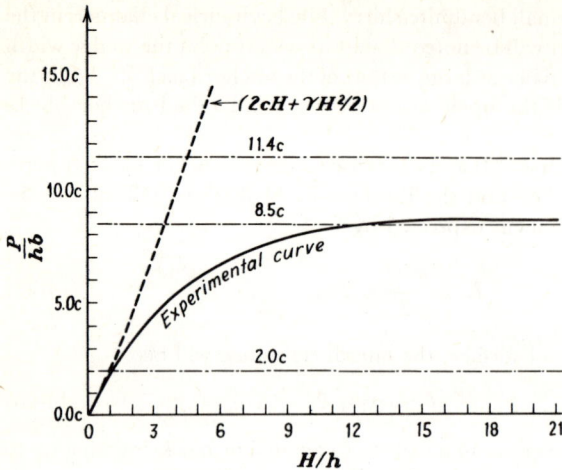

Fig. 14-29.   Resistance of plastic clay to anchor blocks.   Summary of experimental and theoretical results.   (*After Mackenzie, Ref. 205.*)

clay around the anchor block were as shown in Fig. 14-28B, and the limit resistance P was smaller than Brinch Hansen's value [Eq. (14-24)] and read

$$P = 8.5ch \qquad (14\text{-}25)$$

It will be noted from Fig. 14-29 that the full resistance $2cH$ of the wedge in front of the block was effective only for a ratio $H/h = 1.0$, i.e., when the anchor block reached to the soil surface   For larger H/h values the resistance gradually became smaller than the values given by Eq. (14-22), reaching the values of Eq. (14-25) as a limit.

The experimental curve of limit resistances shown in Fig. 14-29 can be used for design purposes under consideration of proper factors of safety. The results should be slightly on the conservative side if one neglects the γh component on both the passive and active sides of the anchor block.

The elevation of the point of anchor-pull application to the anchor block, as well as the shape of the block itself, can influence the overall resistance [see Merkin (Ref. 213) and Cox (Ref. 68)].

(B). *Piled Anchorages.*   Whenever there is a soft compressible layer at and below the dredge line which cannot be conveniently removed by dredging, piling has to be used for the anchorage.   For the A-frame type of pile anchorage shown in Fig. 14-24, two tension piles T are usually provided for every compression pile C since in most cases a pile of equal length can carry approximately twice as much load in compression as in tension.

Batter piles are essential to prevent anchorage displacements of the type illustrated by Fig. 14-30, which refers to a concrete relieving platform on piles, built in 1929 to 1930, anchored back to pile clusters over a distance of

375 ft (115 m) by means of 2-in.-diameter (5-cm) steel anchor tie rods spaced 5 ft (1.52 m) apart.   At their other end the anchors connected to the outer pier leg of the craneway.   A layer of soft clay was located at some depth below the anchors.   Hydraulic fill was placed up to the level of the anchors, granulated slag was placed around, and cold slag above the anchors.   Stock piles of iron ore were placed on the completed fill, loading its surface to 3 tons/ft^2.   The first indication of trouble was that the outer pier leg of the craneway was found to have moved inward almost 6 in. ($5\frac{5}{16}$ in. $= 13.8$ cm). When the ore stockpiles were removed, it was found that the fill surface had formed craters with a maximum settlement of about 3 ft (92 cm) at their centers.   An excavation revealed that the anchors had been deflected by the same amount and in the same manner from their original elevation (see Fig. 14-30).

Arrangements of the type shown on Fig. 14-31 can protect anchors from loading by the weight of the overlying fill if the diameter of the protective concrete pipe is made somewhat larger than the settlement of the fill to be expected at that elevation due to the consolidation of underlying compressible layers.   A similar method was successfully used in Sweden, where hollow concrete boxes were placed around the anchors (see 1st ed., Fig. 16-29). Failure of some anchors occurred where such precautions had not been taken.

In most cases the anchors adjust themselves by plastic deformations of the metal without failing to the deflections imposed on them.   It is therefore essential to avoid the use of nonductile steels, such as old rails.   In the harbor at Dunkirk, France (see Ref. 190), a 200-ft-long (61-m) section of a bulkhead-type quay wall suddenly slid out to sea.   It was found that the anchors had failed.   They were made of rolled-steel channels which showed signs of cracks, possibly caused in the first place by the impact of wartime explosions

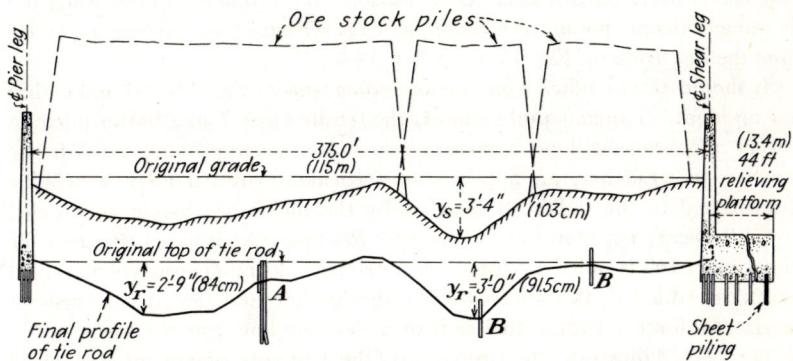

Fig. 14-30. The 3-ft (90-cm) differential settlement of the soil surface and of the 375-ft-long (115-m) anchor tie rods of a relieving platform due to consolidation of underlying clay by the surcharge weight of ore piles.   The pier leg of the overhead craneway was pulled $5\frac{7}{16}$ in. (13.8 cm) toward the shear leg which formed part of the relieving platform.   (*Courtesy of M. D. Ayers, Steel Company of Canada, Ltd.*)

from which rusting had spread and weakened the section further.   The use of steel cables for the anchorage of bulkheads has been considered instead of more rigid profiles.   Of course, the cables would have to be specially well protected against rusting.

Particular attention should be given to details of the connections between

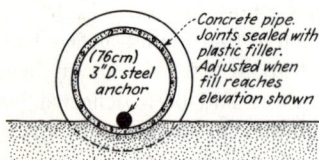

Fig. 14-31.   Possible method of protecting anchors against overloading by later settlements of fill.

anchors and bulkhead since the bolts or welds connecting them—directly or through wales—cannot undergo plastic deformations when overstressed and should therefore be designed with high factors of safety.

Anchor deflections due to the consolidation of underlying fill and natural soil are accompanied by the development of negative bending moments near the sheeting if the connection there is rigid.   To prevent its resulting overloading German steel companies supply short anchor-length connections with built-in double hinges.   This prudent practice does not seem to have been followed elsewhere.

Using battered steel piles for direct anchorage (Fig. 14-24C) eliminates anchors entirely but, by itself, does not solve the problem of preventing the loading of the anchorage as a consequence of settlements of underlying layers (see the discussion of Fig. 14-45 in Art. 14-6).

It should also be noted from the force diagrams of Fig. 14-24B and C that for an identical anchor-pull value A_p the tensile force T in a batter pile of a direct anchorage will be approximately twice as large as for an A-frame anchorage.   Further, an appreciable vertical downward force V will be transmitted to the bulkhead sheeting by the direct batter-pile anchorage.

C. Dolphins; Use of Modulus of Subgrade Reaction.   An isolated structure for mooring vessels is called a *dolphin*.   In its simplest form it consists of a vertical shaft embedded in the soil below the dredge line and designed to resist a horizontal force P transmitted to it by a mooring line from a vessel.

Fig. 14-32A illustrates the estimation of the depth of embedment D required for safe stability in sand of a single pile dolphin.   The maximum possible passive resistance of the sand at a depth D is

$$p_{max} = \gamma D(K_P - K_A) \tag{14-26}$$

Equilibrium requires that

$$P = E_1 - E_2 \tag{14-27}$$

$$Ph = E_2 e_2 - E_1 e_1 \tag{14-28}$$

The value of E_1 is governed by $p = p_{max}/F$, whereby the factor of safety should be $F \geq 2.5$.   The force E_1 can be taken to equal the area abc multiplied by $2d$, where d is the shaft diameter.   The factor 2 is introduced for reasons explained above in the discussion of Figs. 14-25 and 14-27.

On the other hand, the force E_2 can be taken to equal the area cfd multiplied by $2d$ since its localized concentration near the tip of the shaft will in itself provide a hidden factor of safety in respect to the $(K_P - K_A)$ line.

The K_P value can be selected from Table 10-2 for an angle of wall friction $\delta = 0$.   If the force P is likely to have a downward component, the K_P value may be increased to values of $-\delta > 0 \leq \frac{2}{3}\phi$.   Similarly, if P is likely to have an upward component, the K_P value should be decreased to values of $+\delta > 0 \leq \frac{2}{3}\phi$.

The simplest way to estimate D is by trial and error.   After drawing a diagram of the type shown in Fig. 14-32A, select the point c so that the force E_1 will be somewhat larger than P.   Then pick the point f so that E_2 will satisfy Eq. (14-28).   Check whether this value of E_2 satisfies Eq. (14-27). If not, repeat this procedure for a different depth D.

The bending moments and shears in the shaft can then be determined by simple statics from the force P and the earth-pressure diagram $abcdf$ on Fig. 14-32A.   The result will be on the safe side compared with the probable actual pressure distribution indicated by dotted lines.

Figure 14-32B refers to the stability of a vertical pile embedded in clay. The procedure is the same as that given above with reference to Fig. 14-32A

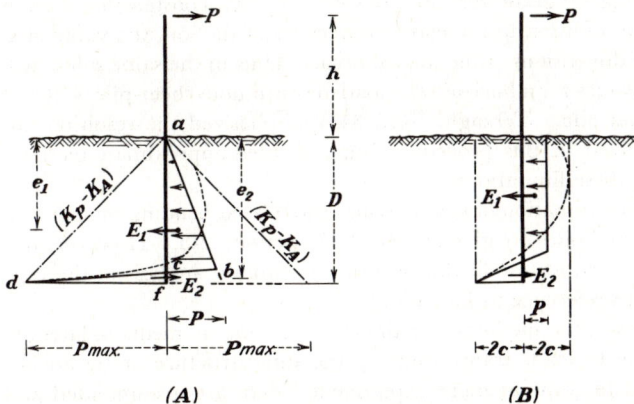

Fig. 14-32.   Determination of embedment depth D for vertical shaft subjected to a horizontal force: (A) in sand; (B) in clay.

except that special caution is indicated when selecting the c value of sensitive clays susceptible to remolding.

A more sophisticated procedure for determining shears and bending moments in a slender vertical shaft or pile is based on its flexibility and on the deformation characteristics of the adjoining soil. This procedure involves using the so-called *modulus of subgrade reaction*, the significance of which will be briefly outlined. Until recently its practical use was limited to the design of rigid concrete pavements. As shown in the first edition, Art. 19-6, this was because the basic assumption of the procedure is approximately valid for concentrated loads only. This assumption, often referred to as the *Winkler hypothesis*, is that the reaction pressures p of the soil under any point of the pavement are proportional to the deflection, or settlement, y of the soil surface.

$$p = k_s y \qquad (14\text{-}29)$$

where k_s was at first believed to represent a constant for a given type of soil. This coefficient is the modulus of subgrade reaction. The assumption expressed by Eq. (14-29) can be valid only for an imaginary soil with no shearing strength, such as would be simulated by a viscous liquid or by a bed of helical springs set side by side. In an actual soil Eq. (14-29) approximately corresponds to reality only in the case of a fairly flexible structural element acted upon by concentrated loads, for instance, a railroad tie. Another similar condition is presented by the portion of a steel sheet-pile bulkhead embedded in the ground (see Fig. 14-11), where the function of a concentrated load is performed by the shear transmitted at dredge level to the soil beneath it through the sheet piling. Equation (14-29) can be applied for the analysis of such and other similar problems, as was attempted by Palmer and Thompson (Ref. 240).

The modulus of subgrade reaction, however, is *not* a constant for a given type of soil. In addition to the elastic properties of the soil, the value of k_s depends on the dimensions of the loaded area. Thus in the same soil k_s will have different values for a horizontally loaded continuous sheet-pile wall and for an individual pile. Terzaghi (Ref. 343) emphasized the resulting uncertainties involved in this procedure but indicated approximate methods for overcoming these limitations.

Graphs for the estimation of k_s values and the related bending moments in horizontally loaded piles are given in Ref. 225, section 13-5. However, this procedure is *not* a substitute for an overall soil-stability analysis of the type given above with reference to Fig. 14-32.

Improvements in the methods of estimating bending moments in laterally loaded piles due to loads transmitted by the superstructure or by anchor pulls are bound to come as more experimental data are accumulated and correlated.

Several papers on the topic published in the Proceedings of the Fifth European Conference on Soil Mechanics and Foundation Engineering

(Madrid, 1972) give the results of model and of full-scale lateral-load tests on different types of piles and their theoretical analysis.

A very *important series of tests* is in progress *at Bucknell University.* As reported by Kim, Brungraber, and Kindig (Ref. 163) 20 well-instrumented steel H-piles, 40 ft (12.2 m) long, driven to refusal against limestone rock, two of them isolated and the rest in three groups, were subjected to systematic testing by lateral and vertical loads.

The lateral loads in the first series of the Bucknell tests reported in Ref. 163 were light and were not intended to produce failure. Two main conclusions were arrived at. The first conclusion was that "caps supported on pile groups containing unsymmetrically placed batter piles may undergo appreciable lateral deflections when subjected to vertical loads alone." This finding supports the writer's theoretical deduction illustrated by Figs. 10-25 and 10-28 concerning the existence of a lateral thrust H exerted by batter piles against their cap under a bridge abutment (see also fig. 3 of Ref. 375). The second conclusion was that "contrary to the usual experience with piles in groups under vertical loads, piles in groups are considerably more effective in resisting lateral loads than are isolated single piles."

The authors correctly attribute this result to the increased lateral stiffness of piles in groups when joined by a rigid cap. Such piles in a group were found to deflect in a double curvature, whereas isolated single piles were bent in single curvature, as sketched in Fig. 14-33.

Since in the Bucknell tests all piles rested on rock, the relevant findings concerning effectiveness of group action cannot be extended to radically different soil conditions, e.g., of the type illustrated by Figs. 14-35 and 14-36, which frequently occur in harbor work. The piles of the model dolphins penetrated here into plastic clay so that, just as in the case of vertical pile loading, the soil deformations and not the structural rigidity of the dolphins governed the displacements. Thus a 20-in. (51-cm) horizontal displacement of the top of the model piles (level A in Fig. 14-35) occurred at a load of 40 lb (18.2 kg$_f$) for single piles but at a load of only 30 lb (13.6 kg$_f$) per pile of a

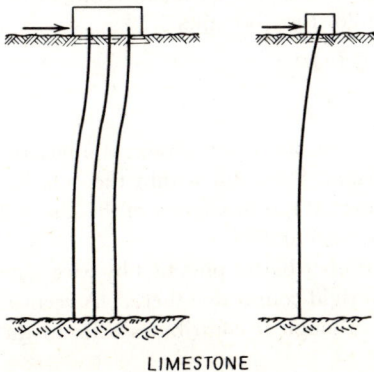

Fig. 14-33. During first series of Bucknell tests on piles reaching to rock (Ref. 163) the structural rigidity of the pile-cap system rather than soil deformations governed the effectiveness of resistance to lateral forces. The reverse had been found for soil conditions of Figs. 14-35 and 14-36 (Ref. 358).

LIMESTONE

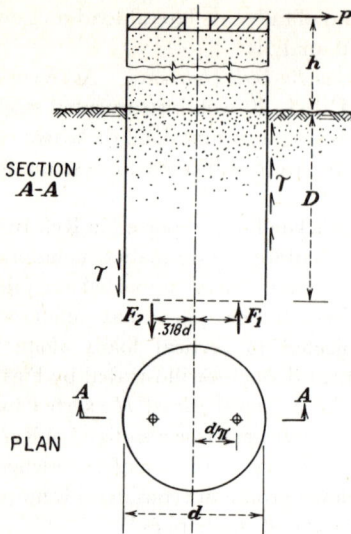

**SECTION
A-A**

PLAN

Fig. 14-34. Frictional forces contributing to stability of sheet-pile dolphin in sand.

three-pile dolphin and at a still smaller load of 22 lb (10.0 kg$_f$) per pile of a seven-pile dolphin (see Ref. 358, fig. 4).

Steel sheet piles forming an isolated cylindrical sand-filled caisson of 5 to 15 ft (1.5 to 4.6 m) diameter are sometimes used for dolphins. Their stability is then similar to that of an isolated cellular cofferdam. With reference to Fig. 12-8, frictional forces F_1 and F_2 shown in Fig. 14-34 will provide additional resistance to overturning, supplementing the effect of the horizontal forces illustrated by Fig. 14-32. These additional forces can be estimated as follows.

By assuming $\phi = 30°$ and the angle of wall friction $\delta = \frac{2}{3}\phi = 20°$, we get $F_1 = E_1 \tan \delta = 0.36E_1$. Both vertical forces will be applied, in plan, at the center of gravity of the half-ring along the outer periphery of which they will be acting, so that their resisting moment in respect to the centerline of the cylinder will be $0.318dF$. Equation (14-28) then becomes

$$Ph = E_2 e_2 - E_1 e_1 + 0.12dE_2 + 0.12dE_1 \qquad (14\text{-}30)$$
$$= E_2(0.12d + e_2) - E_1(e_1 - 0.12d)$$

A concrete stiffening slab at the top of the sheet-pile caisson is advisable with an opening to permit addition of sand if the fill within the cylinder settles. Independently of this slab an internal stability check of the sand fill should be made in accordance with Arts. 12-4 and 14-8.

Frequently dolphins consist of 3 to 19 timber batter piles tied by wire rope and bolted together at their top to form a rigid connection there. A vertical pile at the center is called a *king pile*, although it contributes little to the lateral stability of the pile cluster.

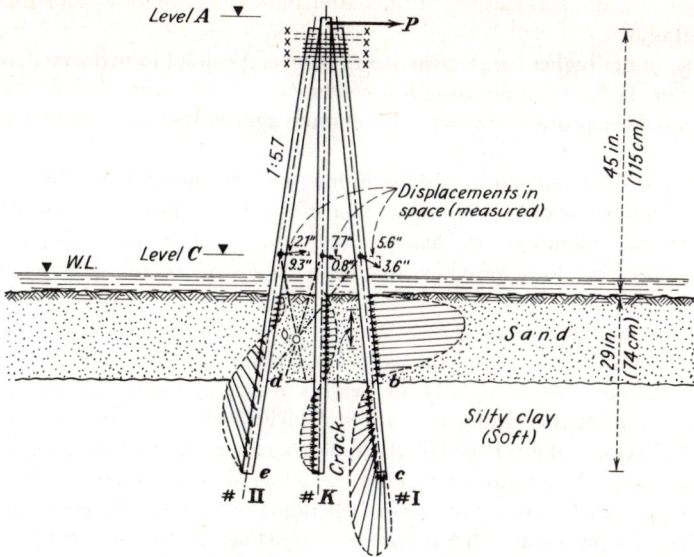

Fig. 14-35. Probable distribution of soil reactions at failure during a pullover test of three-pile model dolphin. (*From Tschebotarioff, Ref. 358.*)

Figures 14-35 and 14-36 illustrate a model test performed on a three-wood-pile dolphin (Ref. 358). For purposes of test analysis all three piles were located in the same vertical plane. Separate vertical load tests indicated that individual piles offered only 75 lb (34 kg$_f$) resistance to axial pull and reached the yield point of the soil around them at 80 to 90 lb (36.3 to 40.9 kg$_f$) in compression. Using the force diagram of Fig. 14-24B, ignoring the king pile, and setting $C = T = 75$ lb (34 kg$_f$), we obtain graphically $A_p = 26$ lb (11.8 kg$_f$). Under this load the horizontal displacement of the three-pile dolphin at level A was negligible—about $\frac{1}{2}$ in. (12.7 mm). This appears to indicate that the conventional procedure of assuming a hinge at the top of

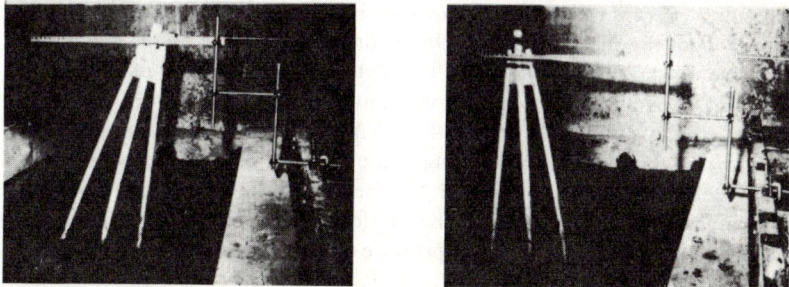

Fig. 14-36. Tilting three-pile model dolphin during pullover test illustrated by Fig. 14-35.

the A-frame and an axial loading of the batter piles gives safe results for this type of dolphin.

Actually, under higher loading carried to failure, the dolphin performed as one semirigid body, rotating around a center O. Visible deflection of the piles indicated the probable pressure distribution against them as sketched in Fig. 14-35.

The force P to be resisted by a dolphin may be transmitted either by the pull of a mooring line or by the impact of a ship. In the latter case special fender systems, mounted on heavy pile-supported reinforced-concrete platforms, may have to be provided to absorb the energy of a large moving ship (see Ref. 259, art. 5.9).

14-5. Relieving Platforms. These structures, as their name indicates, are heavy platforms which carry the weight of surcharge loads and of most of the fill above the water level. These weights are then transmitted by the piles which support the platform to the soil layers below the dredge line, thereby "relieving" the fill behind the bulkhead sheeting of these weights and so decreasing the lateral pressures of the fill against the sheeting.

There are two main types of platform, depending on whether the bulkhead sheeting is on the land side or on the water side [see Figs. 14-1(6) and 14-1(5)]. Platforms with sheeting on the land side will be discussed in Art. 14-7. The present article will deal with platforms having sheeting on the water side, i.e., with relieving platforms in the strict sense of that term.

Insofar as design procedures are concerned, the main difference between various current approaches to the problem lies in the degree of consideration given to the screening effect of the piles under the platform in respect to lateral pressures against the bulkhead sheeting on the water side. The conventional active lateral-earth-pressure diagram against a vertical plane passing through the intersection of the land-side tensile pile T and the dredge-line level is represented by CBG on Fig. 14-37.

An important question is: How much of this pressure diagram CBG is transmitted to the sheeting? If the width AD of the platform were infinite and the presence of the battered compression piles C and tension piles T were ignored, the lateral-pressure diagram against the sheeting would be represented by the triangle ABM. Since the width of the platform is finite, its screening effect is estimated as shown in Fig. 14-37. From the inner lower corner D of the platform a line DF' is drawn under the angle ϕ, which in this case was taken to equal 30°. This determines the point F of the pressure diagram above which no pressures from beyond the platform are transmitted to the sheeting. Then a line DN' is drawn under the angle $\theta = 45° + \phi/2$, which defines the sliding plane through D of the active wedge of soil. Below the point N opposite N', the lateral pressure is taken to equal the values beyond the limits of the platform. A straight-line transition is assumed between F and N. The pressure on the sheeting is then represented by $ABGNF$.

Some authors have proposed variations of the same general approach

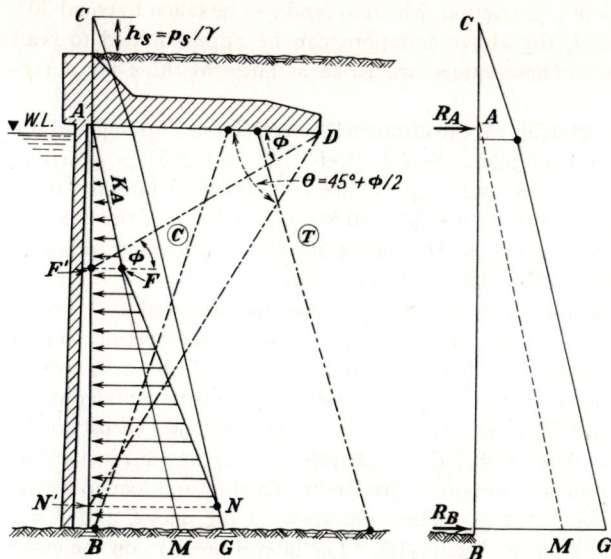

Fig. 14-37. Conservative conventional estimation of lateral pressures on sheeting (the screening effect of platform on sheeting is considered, but that of batter piles is ignored).

outlined above.   They will not be gone into further here since this approach is very conservative; it ignores the very real effect of the presence of the piles under the platform.

Model tests performed at the Franzius Institut, Hannover (Refs. 117; 325; and 367, figs. 5-65 to 5-67) showed that when the ratio $b/a = 0.5$, where b is the pile diameter and a is the center-to-center spacing of the piles,[†] the screening was almost complete so that the entire outside pressure was taken up by the piling under the platform.   In such cases a noncohesive soil between such piles and the sheeting will tend to act as if it were inside an infinitely long silo.

Because of friction along the vertical walls of a silo, a maximum lateral pressure p' is reached at a depth t and remains constant below that depth; any further increment of weight is supported by wall friction (see Art. 10-6). It can be shown that for an infinitely long silo (or trench)[†]

$$p' = \frac{\gamma f}{2 \tan \delta} \tag{14-31}$$

and

$$t = \frac{f}{2K_a \tan \delta} \tag{14-32}$$

[†] The symbols here conform with those in Fig. 14-25 and are different from those used in Ref. 367.

where δ is the angle of wall friction, which in sand can be taken to equal $30°$. Since $\tan 30° = 0.577$, the above equations can be approximated to read $p' = \gamma f$ and $t = 3b$. (These values are twice as large as those for a rectangular silo.)

As shown on Fig. 14-1(5), f is the distance between the sheet piling and the adjoining row of vertical piles. Streck (Refs. 117 and 325) proposed to design sheet piling to resist only the uniformly distributed lateral "silo" pressure p' from Eq. (14-31) when $b/a \geq 0.5$. When $b/a = 0$, the conventional earth-pressure diagram ABM (Fig. 14-38) and intermediate values of earth pressures for $0 < b/a \leq 0.5$ should be used.

Bending stresses in the outer row T of piles can be estimated as shown in Fig. 14-36. In this case there is no row of piles close to the sheeting, so that no silo action can develop. Therefore the sheeting should be designed for the pressure triangle ABM and otherwise handled in the same manner as the sheeting of anchored bulkheads (Art. 14-3C). The horizontal thrust on the platform should be determined, conservatively, as the upper reaction R'_a of a beam having a second support at dredge-line level R'_b and loaded by the full-pressure diagram $C'ABGD$. The axial loads on the piles C and T are then determined as stated in Art. 14-4B. The lateral pressure on the outer row of tension batter piles T can, however, be taken as the area $AFNN'$ of the pressure diagram. No active pressures are to be expected below the intersection of piles T with an imaginary slope at an angle of repose equal to the angle of internal friction ϕ. That slope surface is loaded by the weight

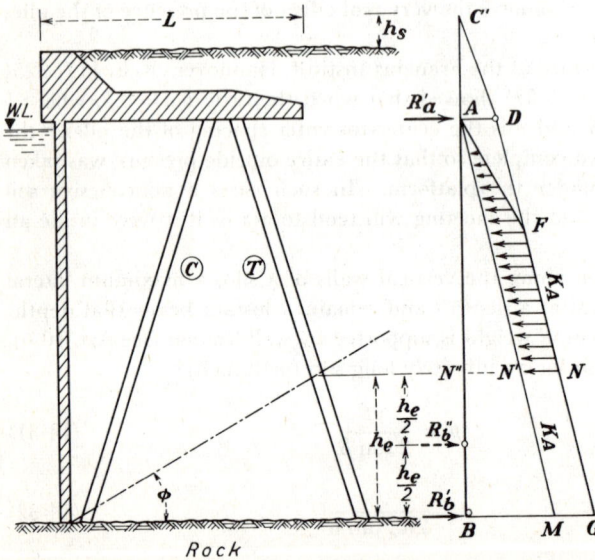

Fig. 14-38. Estimation of lateral pressures and bending moments in rear row of piles under a relieving platform. (*After Drouin and Paul, Ref. 88a.*)

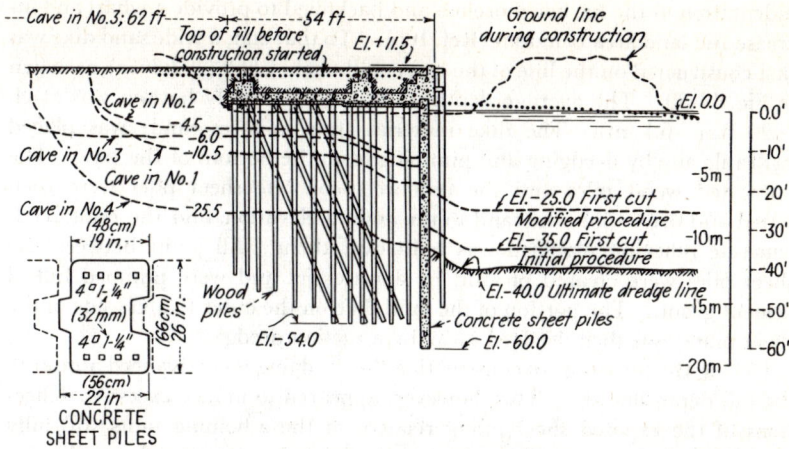

Fig. 14-39. Heavy relieving platform on wood piles with reinforced-concrete sheet-pile bulkhead of the sunk-wall type. Fine sand leaked through gaps between sheet piles, causing cave-ins, until repairs were made. (*After Gebhard, Ref. 105.*)

of the overlying soil. The soil below the slope surface will therefore offer passive resistance much more effectively than the free slope in front of sheeting on the land side of a relieving platform. However, just as in the case illustrated by Fig. 14-46, the pressures below the upper support R'_a can be reduced by the triangle ADF of an area equal to CAD. The triangle $AN'N''$ represents part of the reaction of the sheeting to pressures for which it is to be designed. This leaves the pressure area $AN'NF$ to be resisted by the T piles. The maximum pressure on each pile can be taken as twice its width times the unit pressure of Fig. 14-38.

For plastic clay soil the distance h_e in Fig. 14-38 from the surface of the rock or of firm soil below dredge-line level into which the piles penetrate can be roughly estimated from the charts in Fig. 7-6 by using the angle α for $\phi = 0$ of these charts instead of the angle ϕ of Fig. 14-38. If the strength of the clay above the dredge-line level is c and its value increases below that level, the chart of Fig. 7-6(I) can be used. For a platform of width L a stable slope corresponding to an angle $\alpha = \phi = 30°$, as drawn to scale in Fig. 14-38, will give a height $h_e = L \sin 30°$. For a 50-ft-wide (15.2-m) platform we then get $h_e = 25$ ft (7.6 m) and, from the chart, the corresponding minimum required cohesion $c = 500$ lb/ft² (2,445 kg$_f$/m²). If the actual strength is smaller, repeat the check for a smaller angle α.

The use of *reinforced-concrete sheet piles* presents special problems. Figure 14-39 is an example. It is a heavy relieving platform of the *sunk-wall* type; i.e., the piling was not backfilled but was driven (sunk) into existing soil, which was then dredged out on the water side. In the case illustrated by Fig. 14-39 a 3,000-ft (915-m) long quay wall had to be built across an indentation in the harbor shoreline and backfilled to provide a wharf and increase the land area behind it (Ref. 105).   To that end, a wide sand dike was first constructed on the line of the quay wall to el. +11 ft (+3.36 m), as shown in Fig. 14-39.   The average depth of the original sandy bottom was at el. −20 ft (−6.1 m).   The dike material (fine uniform sand) was placed hydraulically by dredging and pumping from the bottom of the bay.   The untreated wood piles and the reinforced-concrete sheet piles were then jetted and driven into the sand to the desired elevation, and the reinforced-concrete relieving platform was built over them.   All joints between the sheet piles were cleared of sand by a water jet and were pumped full of cement grout.   The portion of the sand dike on the outer (water) side of the sheet piling was then dredged away by a suction dredge.

During the first stage of construction the dredging was advanced almost to the full depth desired.   This, however, appeared to induce excessive deflections of the exposed sheet piling relative to the adjoining units still fully embedded in the sand.   The grout in the joints between the sheet piles was damaged thereby, so that the fine sand trickled out through the openings (see Fig. 14-40).   The resultant cave-ins behind the relieving platform, shown in Fig. 13-39, extended well beyond the usual natural 1 : 2 slope of such sand.   This may be attributed to the action of seepage forces induced by the suction of the dredge.   During the second stage of construction the procedure was changed.   Dredging was done in steps, and joints were inspected by divers and regrouted if necessary.   The suction cutter head of the dredge was kept at least 25 ft (7.6 m) away from the sheet piling.   No further trouble was encountered.   The sheet piling was somewhat over-designed (see 1st ed., Prob. 16-6, and compare with Prob. 16-7).

The loss of up to 8,000 yd³ (6.180 m³) of sand fill just in one largest single cave-in of Fig. 14-39 was due to a special type of localized quick condition which is provided by so-called *piping*, where a stream formed by a liquefied sand-water mixture moves through surrounding stable sand as if it were flowing through a pipe.   Figure 14-40 illustrates a laboratory demonstration of that effect in a seepage flume.   A temporary vertical partition was placed across the flume.   It had, at a quarter of its height above the bottom, a small 2-in. = 5-cm diameter) semicircular hole next to the plate-glass side of the flume.   The hole was plugged with a removable stopper, and the flume was filled with fine beach sand on one side of the partition.   Artificially colored black sand was placed in horizontal layers at 2-in. (5-cm) elevation intervals.   The two white arrows indicate the water level, which was the same on both sides of the partition.   When the stopper was removed and sand began to trickle out laterally through the hole, a column of land immediately above the hole appeared to be liquefied and was set into downward motion as if it were moving along a pipe.   A crater was formed at the surface.   Its slope corresponded to the natural angle of repose.   The sand rolled down along that slope toward the " pipe," which had almost

A

B

Fig. 14-40. Laboratory demonstration of the formation of a vertical "pipe" during the escape of submerged sand backfill through a small opening in a model sheet-pile retaining structure which simulated prototype conditions of Fig. 14-39.

vertical walls.   The lateral pressure exerted by the heavy fluid sand-water mixture must therefore have been sufficient to keep the surrounding sand in place by counterbalancing its active lateral pressure.   The latter, of course, must have been relatively small because of arching phenomena around the fluid "pipe," similar to those likely to occur around shafts.

No attempt was made to simulate the suction of the dredge, and the final natural slope in the model is therefore steeper than that of the prototype (Fig. 14-39).

A different kind of problem can be created by the *use of reinforced-concrete sheet piles in plastic clays susceptible to remolding*.   The nature of this problem will be outlined with reference to Fig. 14-41, which gives a cross section of a quay wall in the harbor of Santos, Brazil.   The precast reinforced-concrete sheet piles (row A) were 15.7 in. (40 cm) thick, and the individual piles were 14.8 in. (37.5 cm) square.   The strength of the clay increased with depth, as indicated in Fig. 14-41.

This appears to be the same clay layer described by Machado in connection with his settlement studies in the nearby city of Santos (Refs. 203 and 204).   The liquid limit ω_L of that layer varied from 80 to 130 percent; the plastic limit was $\omega_P = 40$ percent; the natural water content w_n varied from 60 to 80 percent; the modulus of volume change m_v varied from 0.09 to

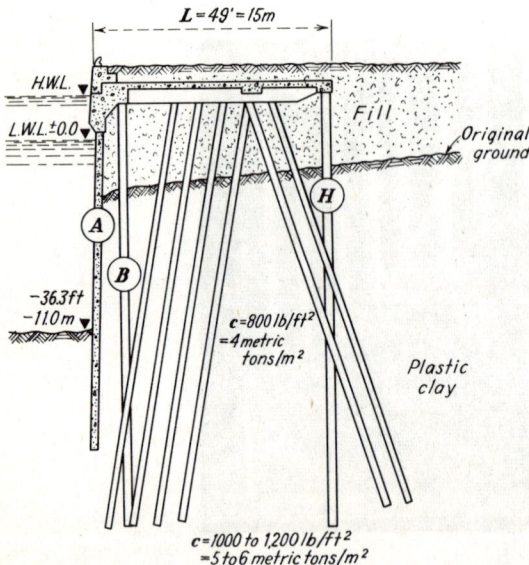

Fig. 14-41.   Cross section of a relieving platform in the harbor of Santos. Load tests demonstrated lower bearing capacity of friction piles in plastic clay of row B, near the massive sheeting A, compared with the piles of row H.   (*From report by Brazilian authorities.*)

0.12 cm²/kg$_f$, and the coefficient of consolidation c_v from 3.57 to 4.45 m²/year (1.00 to 1.25 × 10⁻³ cm²/sec).

The Brazilian authorities carried out an extensive series of some 80 field load tests on vertical production piles in rows B and H of a quay wall 1,180 ft (360 m) long shown in cross section by Fig. 14-41.   The design load was 60 metric tons per pile, and the desired factor of safety was 1.5; the test piles were supposed to carry 90 metric tons when tested 15 days after driving. Tests were made at times varying from 30 to 260 days after driving.   For both rows B and H the failure load was found to increase with time.

For the landside row H, which was the furthest from the massive sheeting (A), the desired load of 90 metric tons was reached after 30 days from the day of driving.   The failure load of 90 metric tons increased almost linearly with time to an additional 25 percent after 260 days, giving a factor of safety $F = 1.87$, which presumably reached a value of 2.00 a year after driving.

This was correctly attributed to a gradual regain of shearing strength by the remolded clay as it reconsolidated.

However, the piles in row B, which were most affected by remolding due to the proximity of the massive sheet-pile wall A, were found to have a factor of safety of only 0.95 at 30 days which increased to 1.40 after 260 days, i.e., by 48 percent.

Therefore in similar cases the use of steel Z sheet piling has advantages since it will minimize remolding, having a cross-sectional area 16 times smaller than the 15.7-in.-thick (40-cm) concrete sheet piles of Fig. 14-41. These massive sheet piles displace as much clay and hence account for as much remolding as all the rectangular solid piles under that platform, i.e., 3 percent for the sheet piles alone of the area of the platform in plan.   Further, the solid rectangular reinforced-concrete piles could be advantageously replaced by hollow concrete piles (see Art. 6-8), the soil having been continuously augered or jetted out from the interior of their hollow shaft as the driving progressed.

It is regrettable that no comprehensive instrumented control measurements of the actual performance of relieving platforms have so far been made anywhere, except for sheeting deflections.   The situation appears to be somewhat similar to the one which prevailed up to the 1950s in respect to anchored-bulkhead design (see Art. 14-3C) when the temperament of the designer governed the selection of the most "liberal" procedure, the Danish rules, or the more conservative ones.   It is probable that a similar comprehensive study of relieving-platform performance would have a similar result, namely, that the most "liberal" relevant design procedures do not provide the customarily required factors of safety but that some reductions are possible in the requirements of the more conservative ones, e.g., the design of the axial piling loads under the platform for the full lateral pressure $C'BG$ of Figs. 14-37 and 14-38.   It is not impossible that it might be reduced to

$C'N''N$ in all soils, or even to $ADNN''$ (Fig. 14-38) in plastic clay soils if uneven consolidation of the latter pulls the fill above the water level away from the platform in a manner similar to that observed on piled bridge abutments and described in Art. 10-9.

14-6. Some Construction-procedure Problems. Driving piles behind the sheeting for a relieving platform will naturally compact the fill and as a result create lateral compaction pressures against the sheeting (see Art. 10-1). However, the final nature of the *interaction between the sheet piling and the piles supporting the relieving platform* behind it will be strongly affected by the depth of subsequent dredging in front of the sheeting.

If the subsequent dredging is considerable (hd_1 in Fig. 14-42), the resulting outward lateral deflection of the sheeting will not only remove the existing lateral compaction pressures due to pile driving, but will mobilize the flexural resistance of the piles so that they will all act together with the sheeting in resisting active lateral earth pressures. This was indicated by measurements on a quay wall at Baltimore, where 40 ft (12.2 m) of the final 41-ft (12.5-m) water depth were dredged after completed construction of the platform (see Ref. 383, case *D*, also Ref. 385). The proportion of the total active lateral load carried by the steel sheeting and by the Monotube piles appeared approximately to correspond to their *EI* values.

When the subsequent dredging is partial (hd_2 in Fig. 14-42) the resulting small outward deflection of the sheeting may barely suffice to relieve the lateral compaction pressures of the preceding pile driving without bringing the flexural resistance of the piles into play. This was indicated by measurements on a pier at Galveston, where only 7 ft (2.12 m) of the 33-ft (10.1-m)

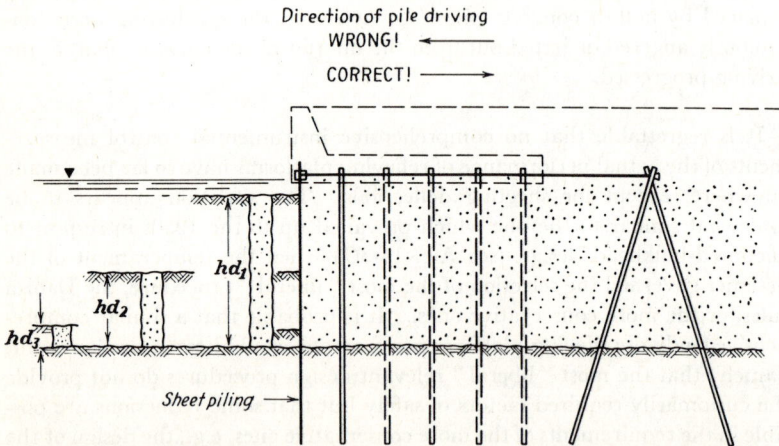

Direction of pile driving
WRONG! ←
CORRECT! →

Fig. 14-42. Effect on pressures against sheet piling under a relieving platform of directional sequence of pile driving and depth of subsequent dredging. (*From Tschebotarioff, Ref. 366.*)

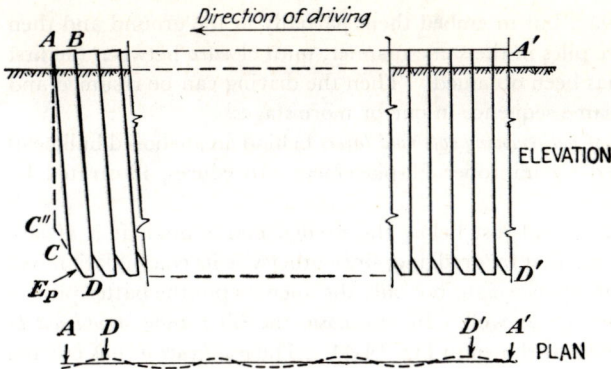

Fig. 14-43. Causes of some of the difficulties encountered when driving long, continuous walls of sheeting, especially when timber or reinforced-concrete sheet piles are used.

water depth were dredged after completed construction of the platform (see Ref. 383, case C, also Ref. 385).

It is therefore logical to assume that if later dredging is quite insignificant (hd_3 or less in Fig. 14-42), the compaction pressures of pile driving may not be fully relieved.

The *directional sequence of pile driving* may be very important.   In the case illustrated by Fig. 14-42 the piles were erroneously driven from the A-frame anchorage toward the sheeting, creating thereby a progressively increasing wedging of the sand between the piles and the sheeting.   This produced compaction pressures of such intensity that anchor-bolt connections at the sheeting failed.   The right way would be to start driving the piles near the sheeting first and continue landward.   Then the piles already in place would work together with the sheeting in resisting the compaction pressures due to subsequent pile driving.

A special problem arises when *driving long continuous walls of sheet piling*. As shown in Fig. 14-43, the top of the wall can be made to form a straight line at the soil surface by proper guiding of the individual piles there. However, all types of sheet piles inevitably deviate somewhat from a vertical plane as they are driven and encounter small stones or other obstacles which deflect them from their original direction.   Excavations frequently indicate that the lower portion of a sheet-pile wall follows an undulating line, as shown in plan by the broken line DD' in Fig. 14-43.   Since a straight line $A'A$ between two points is shorter than an undulating line $D'D$, the lower edge D of a pile does not reach a vertical line through its upper edge B, and after a while the piles begin to get more and more inclined, as shown by the pile $ABCD$ in Fig. 14-43.   The insertion of a specially made trapezoidal sheet pile $ABC''D$ may then become necessary to permit further driving. When sheet piling is to form a closed circuit it is advisable not to drive the first piles all the way, but to embed them partially in the ground and then drive the successive piles in the same manner, until closure between the first and the last pile has been obtained.   Then the driving can be resumed and completed in the same sequence in one or more stages.

The *consequences of not removing soft mud layers* behind an anchored bulkhead may be aggravated by improper fill-placement procedures, illustrated by Fig. 14-44.

If the soft layer at and just below the dredge line is mud, it is always advisable to remove it first by dredging, since otherwise its consolidation will cause the fill to load by its weight not only the anchors but the batter piles of the A-frame anchorage as well.   In any case, the fill *placing should not be done from the land side*, as shown in Fig. 14-44.   The *mud wave b* thus created would tend to push the A-frame anchorage over and buckle the slender anchor rods.   A case of this kind has occurred.   On the other hand, placing the fill from a barge, as shown in Fig. 14-44, will tend to induce the formation of a mud wave *a* which will push the A frame in the opposite direction, creating tension in the anchor rods.   At the same time, by displacing the mud next to the sheeting, it will create a sand dike there which will help to resist the anchor-rod tension and will have a generally beneficial later effect (see Art. 14-3*B*).

If a soft clay layer cannot be conveniently removed and one wishes to improve its properties (see Art. 5-2) by *surcharging*, this *should be done before the sheeting or anchor piles are driven*.   Otherwise they can be overstressed by the weight of the overlying soil plus surcharge as the underlying plastic clay consolidates, as shown in Fig. 14-45.   That sketch represents an actual case when several hundred feet of an anchored bulkhead tipped over during a postconstruction surcharging of the soil surface behind the bulkhead.   Here

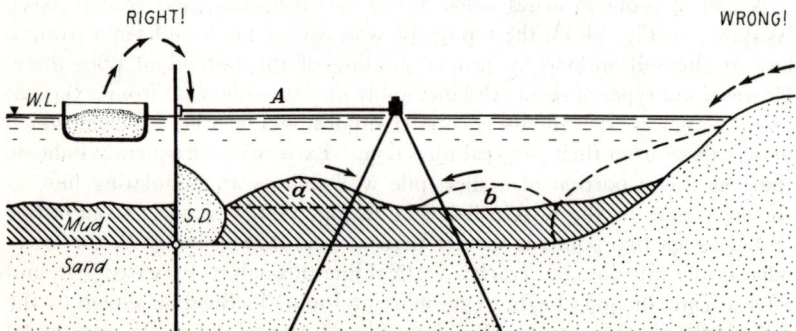

Fig. 14-44.   Right and wrong way to place sand backfill.   The "right" way will only offset some unfavorable consequences of not dredging out all the mud layer first.

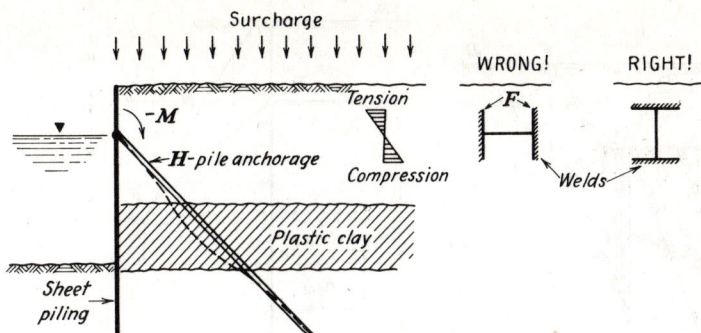

Fig. 14-45. Postconstruction surcharging of plastic clay layer and improper orientation of anchor-pile welded connection caused bulkhead collapse. (*From Tschebotarioff, Ref. 366.*)

things were aggravated by the orientation of the H-pile anchors as a result of which the bending moments of fixation $-M$ produced stress concentrations at the upper ends F of the vertical welds, progressively ripping them off completely (see also Ref. 311).

14-7. Wharf Platforms with Sheeting, If Any, on Land Side. This type of platform frequently permits greater depths of water than platforms with sheeting on the water side because the sheeting on the land side is of shorter span.

When checking the stability of some old existing piers at Hamburg, Germany, Ehlers (Ref. 92) found that the stresses in the timber sheet piling AB behind old existing massive relieving platforms, if computed on the basis of the Coulomb distribution of lateral earth pressures, reached values of 6,000 lb/in.^{2} (420 kg$_f$/cm^2), which were incompatible with stability.   Ehlers concluded that the stresses must be lower because of the formation of two planes of shear failure, AC and BD, instead of the one plane of failure BD assumed by the Coulomb theory [Fig. 14-46(I)].   As a result, sand arches may be formed between these two planes of failure, and part of the Coulomb pressure is thereby transferred from the sheet piling AB to the relieving platform above it.   In the light of our present knowledge, this concept appears sound, since the sheet piling of the type illustrated by Fig. 14-46(I) has practically immovable supports and a large part of the backfill soil above the upper abutment A would be in place before the full load comes to bear on it. Ehlers did not attempt to evaluate the change of lateral-earth-pressure distribution induced by this arching but suggested using higher design stresses in such cases.

As yet there are no experimental data available which would permit the exact computation of the reduction of lateral pressures on the sheet piling

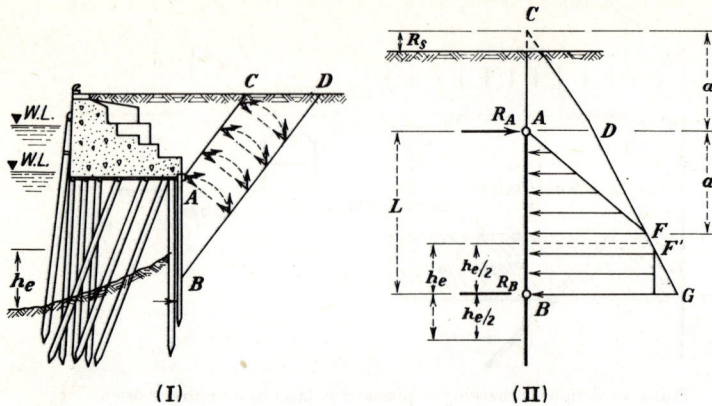

Fig. 14-46. (I) The concept of arching was used by Ehlers (Ref. 92) to explain the stability of old overstressed timber sheet piles behind relieving platforms in the Hamburg harbor. (II) A conservative estimation of pressure reductions on sheet piling.

under similar circumstances. Figure 14-46(II) illustrates a method for the rough estimation of such reduction. It is based on the fact that the frictional forces along a plane AC under the conditions of support shown in Fig. 14-46(I) are reversed as compared with the conventional Coulomb case (the pressure diagram $CABGD$ corresponds to the latter). Therefore [Fig. 14-46(II)], not only will the pressure triangle CAD above the upper support R_A of the sheeting not contribute to the lateral pressures against it, but a triangle ADF of equal size to CAD can be subtracted, as shown, from the lateral pressures below the upper support R_A. This procedure is believed to be conservative, since it ignores the possibility of additional reductions due to arching between the planes AC and BD, indicated in Fig. 14-46(I).

The lower point of support R_B and the point of contraflexure (hinge) of the sheeting can be taken opposite one-half of the height h_e of the slope. No increase of active lateral pressure need be considered below the point F' at the top of the slope. These procedures apply to a slope of sand, gravel, or stiff to medium clay. Otherwise the hinge of the sheeting should be assumed at the upper surface of the underlying firm soil layer.

The depth of embedment of the sheeting should be determined without making any allowance for the beneficial effects of wall friction, since the outward tilting of the platform may tend to pull the sheeting out of the ground.

Because of bottom currents and eddies the soil slope in front of the sheeting should be no steeper than 1 : 2.5. For clays of medium stiffness its structural stability should be checked as outlined above in Art. 14-5 with reference to Fig. 14-38.

Figures 14-47 to 14-50 illustrate a case where *considerable trouble resulted mainly because of a much too steep slope of the fill under and behind the pile-supported reinforced-concrete platform of a wharf.* Contributing causes were the layout of the batter piles and a high silt content of the hydraulic fill.

A 3,000-ft-long (915-m) new wharf consisted essentially of a 42-ft-wide (12.8-m) high-level reinforced-concrete platform supported by precast and prestressed 18-in.-square (46-cm) concrete piles. Under the concrete platform of the wharf a slope of 1.25 horizontal to 1 vertical was formed by a series of rock dikes used to retain a hydraulically placed sand backfill (see Fig. 14-47).

First, the muck bottom at the site of the wharf was dredged out to approximately el. ± 0.0, where a good natural sand bottom was located. Then a 12-ft-high (3.76-m) rock dike was placed approximately 12 ft (3.76 m) on the outboard side of the platform and hydraulically backfilled with sand dredged out from a borrow area in the vicinity. Nine rows of piles were then driven. The first eight rows formed bents spaced 20 ft (6.1 m) on centers, as shown in Fig. 14-48. In six of these rows the piles were vertical; in two rows D and E, they had a 3 : 1 batter and were oriented as shown in Fig. 14-48. The last row of piles, J, further inboard was vertical and, since they had to support shed columns, were more closely spaced. Expansion joints were provided every 300 ft (91.7 m).

After all the piles were driven behind rock dike 1, rock dike 2 was placed between the piles and was backfilled hydraulically. Then the same procedure was followed for rock dikes 3, 4, and 5.

The first movements, of the order of 2 in. (5 cm) transversely and about the same longitudinally, were observed well before construction was completed. The seaward movement increased to about 3.2 in. (8.1 cm) when the fill was

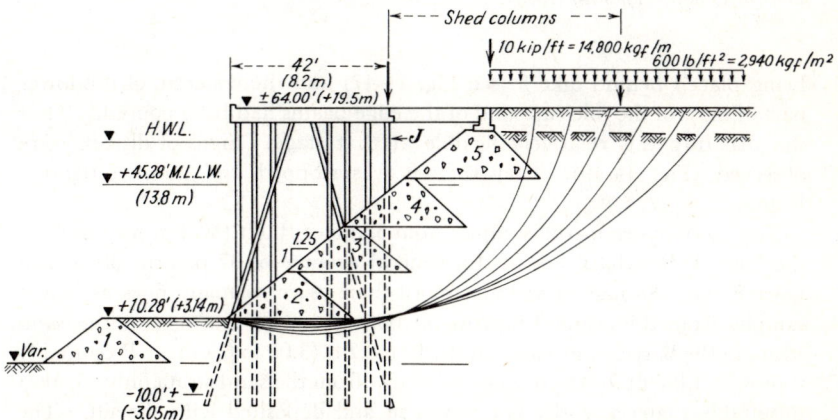

Fig. 14-47. Too steep slope of backfill caused movements which damaged platform (see Figs. 14-48 to 14-50). (*From Ref. 168.*)

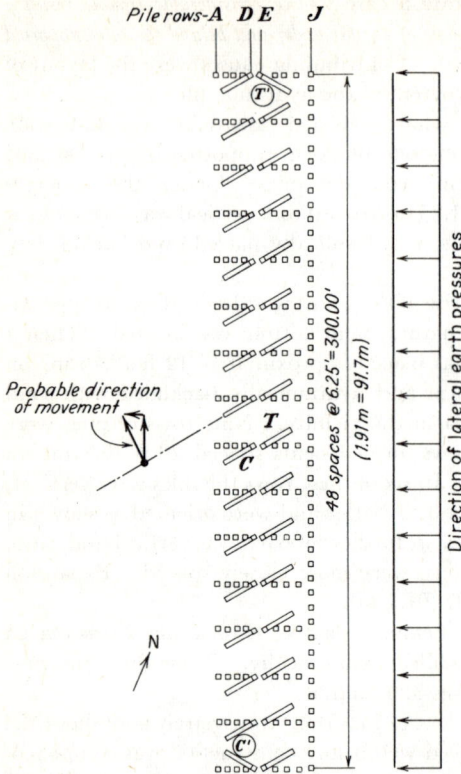

Fig. 14-48. Pile layout permitted longitudinal movements (see Figs. 14-47 to 14-50). *(From Ref. 168.)*

being placed behind dike 5 (see Fig. 14-47) and the concrete of the lower part of most of the pile caps and of the edge beams had been poured. Thus the structure was relatively flexible at that stage. Signs of distress were observed (Fig. 14-49). Construction was stopped and an investigation begun.

Testing of hydraulic-fill samples from 35 holes 100 ft (30.5 m) or less from the face of the wharf indicated a general average of 37 percent of the soil passing the 200-mesh sieve; i.e., more than twice as many fines as in the samples from the original borrow-pit borings. The thickness of the sand strata in the borrow pits varied from 10 to 22 ft (3.05 to 6.7 m). Presumably it proved difficult for the dredge to borrow from the sand strata only, so that unsuitable material easily got mixed in and deposited with the fill. The filling took place first behind the center of the wharf; 14-ft (4.26-m) tides resulted in currents of alternating direction in the channel, along one bank of which the wharf was built. Contrary to expectations, these currents did not carry all fines away but seemed to deposit most of them at the two ends of the wharf.

Two independent computerized Swedish circle (Art. 7-2) stability analyses were performed for the proposed final design loading. The six circles are shown on Fig. 14-47. A value of $\phi = 30°$ was used, which is the highest one can prudently assign to a clean but necessarily loosely deposited hydraulic sand fill. Tidal drawdown conditions were considered, but not a 5 percent of gravity earthquake force (see Art. 15-5) required by the design. The most unfavorable arc gave a factor of safety of only $F = 0.87$.

A similar analysis without any surcharge or column loads and for the actual maximum fill level at the time work was stopped (shown by a broken line on Fig. 14-47) gave a factor of safety $F = 1.02$ for $\phi = 30°$. Since the actual value of ϕ was bound to be smaller because of the high silt content in the fill, the actual factor of safety should be smaller than unity. Complete sliding failure was probably prevented only by the dowel action of the piles (see Art. 7-5).

The probable direction of the movement resulting from the one-directional orientation of most of the batter piles (as shown on Fig. 14-48) was confirmed by measurements of width changes in the nine expansion joints which progressively opened up at the south end of the wharf and closed toward the north end, reflecting thereby the cumulative effect of the longitudinal

Fig. 14-49. Cracks in pile-capping beam of a bent over a tension pile T (see Fig. 14-48). (*Photo by Tschebotarioff, from Ref. 168.*)

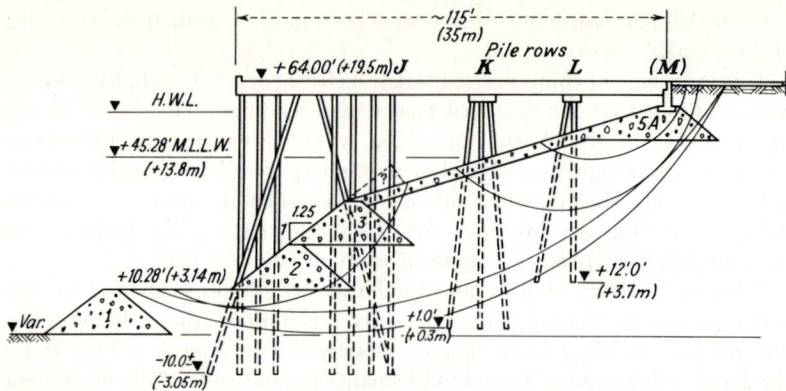

Fig. 14-50. Modification of original design (see Figs. 14-47 to 14-49).   (*From Ref. 168.*)

displacement component of the ten 300-ft-long (91.5-m) wharf sections. This longitudinal displacement component was bound to be largest at the center third of the wharf since the fill there was highest, at the level shown by a broken line in Fig. 14-47, dropping off from there by some 30 ft (9.1 m) toward the wharf ends.

A change of design, namely, a flattening of the original slope, was obviously needed. This could not be done under the platform since the rocks dumped between the pile bents were of a size which made it likely that they had wedged themselves between the piles. Attempts to remove these rocks might therefore damage the existing piles. Widening the platform toward the channel also was not feasible because piles for it could not be driven through the existing dike 1 (see Fig. 14-47). Therefore widening the platform and the related slope flattening had to be done on the land side, as shown in Fig. 14-50. Satisfactory factors of safety were obtained for the circles shown on that diagram.

Driving piles in the additional rows K and L served to compact the hydraulic fill left in place; the width of the platform was increased to 115 ft (35 m) from the original 42 ft (12.85 m), the deck being cast monolithically for each 300 by 115 ft (91.5 by 35 m) section in plan, thereby tying together the old and the new piling; the batter piles of the new row K—in addition to the transverse batter shown on Fig. 14-50—had a longitudinal batter as well, thereby providing resistance to longitudinal mooring forces in any direction.

Frequently the batter of piles in two directions from a single bent presents structural difficulties, requiring an additional special cap. Figures 14-51 and 14-52 illustrate the successful *three-dimensional design of the Jurong Wharf at Singapore*,† where the batter-pile layout and orientation prevented rotation or

† Owner: Economic Development Board of Singapore; engineers: J. H. Pomeroy & Co., Inc. (now Santa Fe–Pomeroy, Inc.), San Francisco; contractors: a joint venture: Hawaiian Dredging–Pomeroy–Gerwick (Ref. 329).

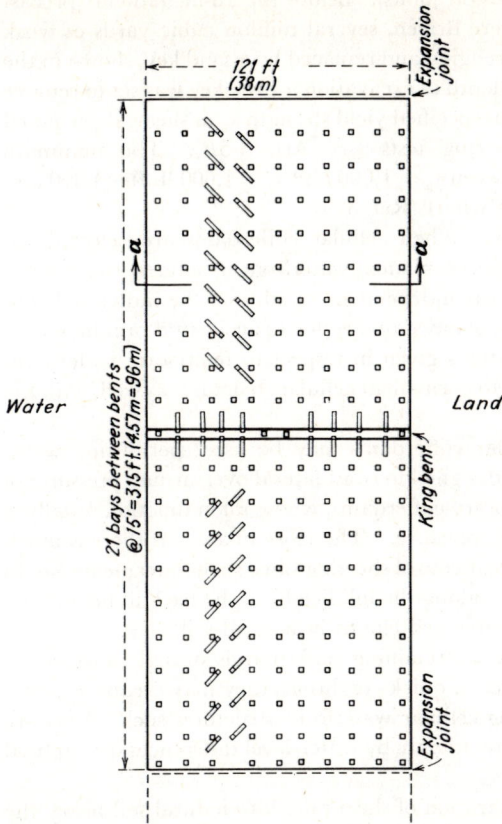

Fig. 14-51.   Successful pile layout for Jurong Wharf at Singapore; see text for credits.

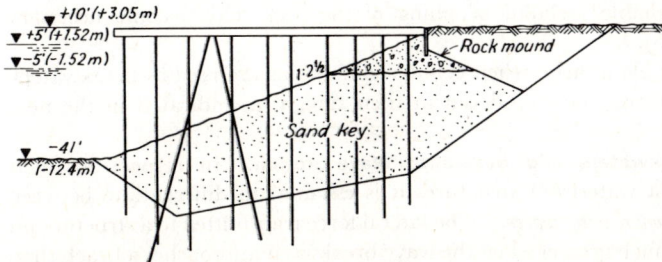

Fig. 14-52.   Cross section *aa* of Fig. 14-51.

displacement in any direction of the 315 by 121 ft (96 by 37 m) monolithic deck sections between expansion joints. Before the 18-in. (46-cm) precast prestressed concrete piles were driven, several million cubic yards of weak material were removed by dredging and replaced by a sand key, shown in the section in Fig. 14-52. The depth of excavation for the key was set to remove all clay weaker than a certain specified yield strength s_y in shear, determined by laboratory double-shear-ring tests (see Art. 3-5B). The minimum acceptable value was set between $s_y = 1,000$ and $s_y = 1,600$ lb/ft² (4,890 and 7,830 kg$_f$/m²) sections of the wharf (Ref. 329).

14-8. Cellular Cofferdams. When cellular cofferdams are selected for wharves, breakwaters, or other permanent waterfront structures, the circular type is preferred because of the independent stability of the individual cells and the resulting localization of any damage due to accidental ramming by a ship. The design considerations given in respect to temporary cofferdams by Arts. 12-4 and 12-5 apply to permanent cellular structures as well, with the following main differences.

Wharves for which cellular cofferdams may be used, permitting water depths of 50 ft (15.3 m), are designed to resist lateral overturning pressures of backfill, in contrast to temporary cofferdams, whose main function usually is to resist overturning by water pressure. Therefore in a wharf there is much less danger of pullout to the rear row of sheeting since such movements would be resisted by frictional forces along the full height of the backfill behind the cell and not just along its embedded length in natural soil.

Further, the design of a water-retaining cofferdam is strongly affected by seepage forces and the danger of quick conditions they may create, whereas in permanent earth-retaining cellular waterfront structures such effects are minimal since they can be caused only by water-level differences due to tidal lag (see Fig. 14-21).

For these reasons the penetration of sheet piles into natural soil below the dredge-line level on the land side of earth-retaining cells is frequently made somewhat shorter than that of sheet piles on the water side. The depth of sheet-pile penetration should satisfy overall stability considerations related to possible sliding along surfaces passing below the tips of the sheeting. When sheeting reaches to a sloping rock surface with little soil cover to provide a reliable toehold, benching of the rock may become necessary (see Art. 12-5).

Special problems arise when cellular cofferdams are used as breakwaters. Wave action must be considered in their design, as indicated in the next article.

14-9. Breakwaters and Seawalls; Wave Action. In respect to their action against waterfront structures it is essential to differentiate between *breaking and nonbreaking waves*. The lateral force transmitted to a structure hit by a wave is much greater when the wave breaks as it approaches a beach than when it does not break in deep water. "Deep" water in this sense means a water depth at the structure greater than about 1.5 times the maximum expected wave height H (Ref. 388).

For a given nonbreaking wavelength L and height H, diagrams indicating lateral-water-pressure differences against a wall in respect to still-water conditions and the height of the resulting *standing wave*, or "clapotis," have been developed on the basis of the Sainflou and Molitor methods (Ref. 259, art. 2.3; Ref. 388, art. 4.2). Similar diagrams based on Minikin's method for waves breaking at the structure are given in Ref. 388, art. 4.231; also diagrams for waves which had already broken before reaching the structure.

A further discussion of waves is beyond the scope of this book. The length, height, breaking point, and other essential characteristics of waves depend on many factors such as wind velocities, their directions and frequencies of occurrence, shoreline configuration, and depth and slope of beach in front of structure. Therefore the determination of the wave characteristics needed for the wave-pressure diagram against a structure should be left to specialists in this branch of oceanography.

Once a lateral-wave-pressure diagram has been drawn up, it can be used for the stability analysis of a breakwater or seawall in the same manner as described earlier in respect to earth pressures against other retaining structures.

A seawall is intended to protect the land behind it. Therefore it should be made high enough to prevent overtopping by waves or part thereof which might wash away its backfill and hence endanger its stability and effectiveness against flooding of areas to be protected.

Monolithic breakwaters should be built only when the underlying soil conditions are found to preclude the possibility of a shear failure or of excessive settlements (see Chap. 4). Otherwise rubble-mound breakwaters should be used. In cross section they are essentially small dams, and the stability of their slopes in respect to the strength of the underlying soil is analyzed in a similar manner (see Arts. 8-7 and 8-9).

If the underlying exposed natural soil is a sensitive clay, a sand blanket should be deposited first between it and any rock fill to distribute the weight of the latter. This prevents remolding of the clay by high contact pressures of individual rocks and the resulting increase of settlements which are reported (Ref. 344) to have been doubled in a case when the sand blanket was omitted.

The slopes of a rubble-mound breakwater should be protected by a layer of *armor* from erosion by wave action. The weight W of the individual stones selected for the outer layer of armor is related to the slope of the rubble mound and its design height and to the length of waves. Steeper slopes—not exceeding 1 on 1.2—result in heavier stones being needed if other conditions remain equal. This weight W often reaches values of 10 tons or more.

If the desired weight of outer armor stones cannot be economically obtained from quarries in the vicinity, the use of reinforced concrete blocks or patented interlocking armor units (tetrapods, tribars, or quadripods) can be considered.   They come in weights of up to 25 tons.

Below the layer of outer armor units of weight W usually comes a layer of stones weighing $W/10$ to $W/15$ and then a layer of $W/200$ stones to provide a graded filter effect, similar to that discussed in Art. 7-9 (for further details see Ref. 388, chaps. 4 and 5).

14-10. Dry Docks and River Locks.   The walls of some river locks are built as independent gravity retaining walls with no rigid structural connection to the lock floor.   Special measures are then needed to relieve uplift pressures against the floor when the lock is empty.

Dry docks and large river locks are usually built as U-shaped structures the reinforced concrete walls of which form one monolithic unit with the floor.   It is often impractical to design the floor to resist the bending stresses created by large *uplift pressures*.   A method to reduce such stresses consists in *anchoring the floor of the dock* to the underlying soil *by means of closely spaced piles*. This method is of advantage when the soil is soft so that piles would be needed anyway to support the weight of the floor when the dock is filled with water.   The same piles can then serve to resist tension when the dock is empty and to increase the weight of the floor which resists uplift by the weight of the soil around the piles.   The piles should then be spaced close enough for the negative friction of the soil against the pile, as determined by pulling tests, to be greater than the volume of the soil around each pile.

A special patented† type of dry-dock floor anchorage, illustrated by Fig.

† By E. Lackner.

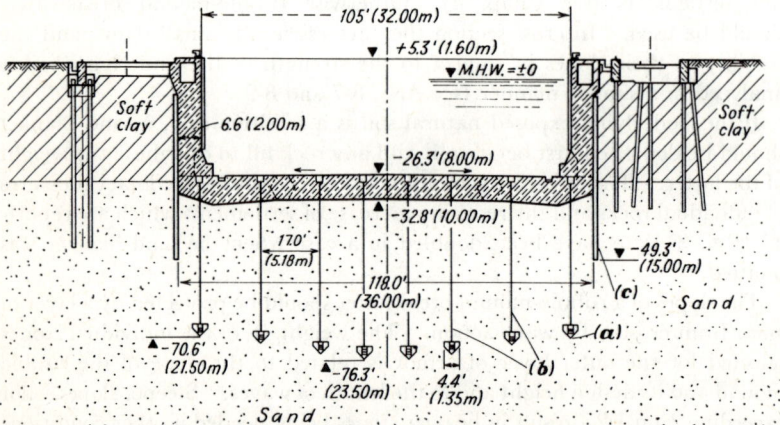

Fig. 14-53.   Section of dry dock in Emden.   When dock is empty floor uplift is resisted by prestressed cables (*b*) of anchor cones (*a*) sunk through sand by vibroflotation.   (*From Agatz and Lackner, Ref. 4.*)

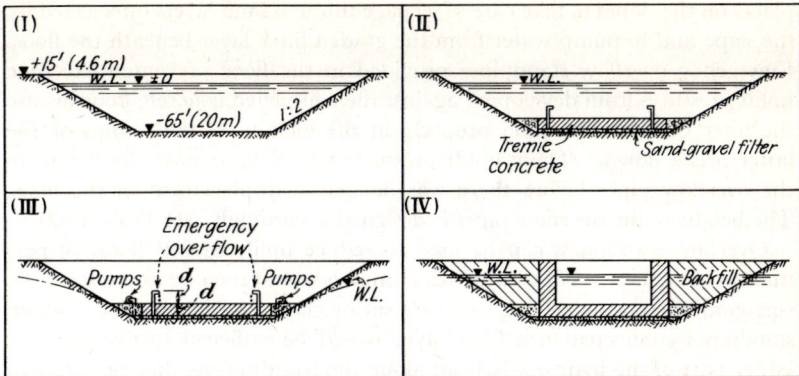

Fig. 14-54. Steps in the construction of a large U.S. Navy drydock. (I) Excavation by dredging. (II) Underwater concreting of floor by the tremie method. (III) Unwatering (note overflow standpipes, an emergency safety device against displacement of floor by hydrostatic uplift). (IV) Backfilling after walls were concreted in the dry.

14-53, was used in the North Sea harbor of Emden, Germany (Ref. 4). Steel sheeting c was driven around the outer perimeter of the dock and braced internally; the groundwater was lowered by means of deep wells, whereupon the excavation was performed; 496 reinforced-concrete *anchor cones*, with their cables attached, were then sunk by *vibroflotation* (Art. 5-3) down to the prescribed elevation, compacting thereby the entire originally loose sand deposit. At some locations, additional compaction by vibroflotation was done between the anchorages. The anchor cables received a seven-ply corrosion protection. After the reinforced-concrete floor was poured, each cable was prestressed by a 105-metric-ton load. The cable connections to the floor slab were designed to permit later access for checks of the prestress load. This ensured that the entire buoyed weight of the compacted sand mass above anchor-cone level continued to act as an integral part of the floor slab in resisting uplift pressures.

A different method of coping with deep excavations and uplift pressures is illustrated by Fig. 14-54, which refers to the construction of a U.S. Navy dry dock in Bayonne, New Jersey. The soil was mainly compact clay with some sand layers. First, suction dredges performed the 65-ft-deep (20-m) underwater excavation, as shown by Fig. 14-54(I). In the second stage [Fig. 14-54(II)] a *graded sand-gravel filter* (Art. 7-9) was placed over the dredged bottom; steel trusses were lowered into place by floating cranes to serve as reinforcement of the massive concrete floor; this was also done for the forms. Divers checked the adjustment. Concreting of the floor was done by the *tremie method* (see Art. 6-10 and Fig. 6-35). In the third stage [Fig. 14-54(III)] the excavation was unwatered after building a temporary cofferdam across the end of the excavation next to the free water. Well points were used in places on the slopes to take care of seepage through sand layers intersected by the slope and to pump water from the graded filter layer beneath the floor. Emergency overflow standpipes provided in the floor prevented excessive uplift pressures from developing against the completed concrete floor in case the filter ceases to function properly in the vicinity of the pumps or the latter break down.   These uplift pressures would be relieved by means of the overflow pipes before there was danger of displacement of the floor. The height of the overflow pipes is designed accordingly (see Prob. 12-2).

Overflow standpipes can be used to reduce uplift against floors of permanent structures.   No continuous pumping would then be necessary if the surrounding and underlying soil were silt or clay.   A slight trickle through standpipes connected to a filter layer would be sufficient to dissipate the larger part of the hydrostatic head along the length of the flow lines drawn in Fig. 12-3, in the same manner as shown for a sand soil in Probs. 12-2. If the trickle were stopped, full uplift pressure would develop with time.

Great care in designing and placing the graded filter for the uplift-pressure relief system is essential to prevent it from clogging, the consequences of which could be very serious.

An example of an elaborate pressure-relief system for a large U.S. Navy dry dock at Bremerton, Washington, is given in Ref. 415.

U-shaped monolithic locks without special floor anchorage or pressure relief systems are frequently analyzed for various possible assumptions of soil-reaction distribution against the floor—uniform, p; trapezoidal, with a zero reaction value at center and $2p$ at ends (after Engels); or concave parabola, simulated by stepped uniform reaction pressures equal to 0.75 times average value p for center half of lock floor base width and to $1.25p$ over the outer quarter widths (after Siemonsen).   Various combinations of these assumptions with possible water-level variations inside and outside the lock and lateral water and earth pressures are made.   The structural design of each lock floor or wall element should meet the most unfavorable bending and shear values given by any possible combination of loading conditions.

Attempts to use the subgrade-modulus approach for lock-floor designs cannot give reliable results.   In addition to the generally weak points of the method outlined in Art. 14-4C, the use of this method for U-shaped locks does not permit taking into account the interaction between the backfill and the walls of the structures.

In view of the many existing design uncertainties, the U.S. Army Corps of Engineers undertook an extensive experimental and analytical research program.   *The Port Allen Lock* on the lower Mississippi, built in 1957–1961, was instrumented to provide at different construction stages measured data on earth and water pressures against the base of the floor slab and the walls†

---

† Carlson soil-stress meters, strain meters, concrete stress meters, pore-pressure cells, resistance thermometers; U.S. Waterways Experimental Station earth-pressure cells; piezometers.

and on the stresses and strains within the floor and the walls.   Soil heave during excavation and later settlements and floor deflections were measured at different points of the lock.   Wall deflections were determined at various elevations by means of deflectometers running within pipes embedded in the concrete (Ref. 293).

Consistent results were obtained, although some were unusual.   For instance, when the lock was filled with water, its walls deflected inward but the lateral earth pressures against them increased.   An explanation for this was given in part of an extensive subsequent finite-element analysis of the measured data by Clough and Duncan (see Refs. 60 and 90).   As shown in Fig. 14-55, the soil-displacement vectors determined by them indicate a greater deflection of the floor slab at its center and hence a resulting inward tilt of the walls; at the same time the lateral and upward squeezing of the underlying silts, combined with the effect of some rise of the outside water level, caused a movement of the sand backfill toward the upper part of the wall.

This result could not have been checked by any other presently known procedure and is given here to illustrate the potentialities of the finite-element method (see Art. 1-11) as a valuable tool for design research.   The usual difficulty of choosing realistically correct values of soil parameters for the analysis was overcome here by extensive and careful soil testing and by the

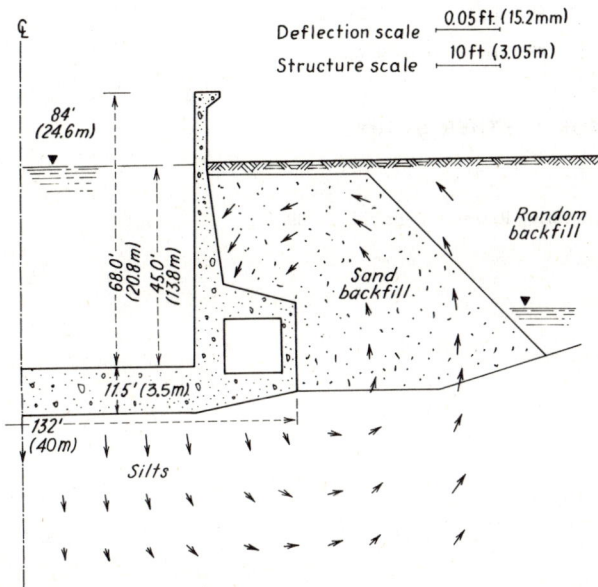

Fig. 14-55.   Example of finite-element-analysis results; soil-displacement vectors caused by filling the Port Allen Lock with water.   (*From Clough and Duncan, Refs. 60 and 90.*)

opportunity of checking these laboratory test values in a comparison between the computed and observed values of the heave of the bottom of the excavation. A refinement of the analytical techniques also became possible in the process of this comparison. Thus the soil-strength and deformation characteristics and the techniques applied to the final analysis of the soil-structure interaction had already been checked at the site.

Insofar as the analysis of the completed structure was concerned, good agreement was obtained between the calculated and observed values of lock settlements, structural deflections, and earth pressures on lock walls. However, the calculated and the observed values of soil-reaction pressures against the base of the floor slab were not in good agreement. Further detailed analytical comparisons led to the conclusion that the calculated soil reactions were more correct than those measured. In this connection it should be noted that these pressures were measured by single earth-pressure cells (see the relevant discussion in Art. 1-9).

REVIEW PROBLEM

14-1. Draw force diagrams and determine the tensile forces T and the compressive forces C and V required to balance a horizontal force $A_P = 25$ tons for the two types of anchorage, (B) and (C), shown in Fig. 14-24 if the batter of piles is 3 : 1.

Answer:

Case (B): $C = 39.5$ tons $T = 39.5$ tons

Case (C): $V = 75$ tons $T = 79$ tons

RECOMMENDED FOR FURTHER STUDY

EAU, Ref. 91.
Quinn, Ref. 259.
U.S. Army Coastal Engineering Research Center, Ref. 388.

CHAPTER 15

SOIL VIBRATIONS AND FOUNDATION DESIGN.
VIBRATORY PILE DRIVING

15-1. Soil Response to Vibrations and to Slow Repetitional Loading.
Both laboratory tests and field observations have shown that vibrations have
a much stronger effect on dry or submerged sands than they do on clays
or cohesive silts. Presumably this is because the cohesive bonds between
the particles of the clays and silts have a certain elasticity, permitting
repeated slight oscillating displacements of these particles in respect to each
other without a rupture of these bonds.   To a lesser extent this also holds for
moist sands, where capillary cohesive bonds are likely to act in a similar way.
But the shearing strength of dry or submerged sands of loose to medium
density depends solely on the frictional forces between the sand particles and
hence on the contact pressures between them.   Since the intensity of these
contact pressures is bound to fluctuate during vibrations, some slight slippage
between the sand grains will occur at each cycle.   The cumulative effect can
be considerable.   The application of these findings to soil compaction has
been outlined in Art. 5-3.

Particularly susceptible to vibrations are sands of uniform size and
rounded shape because angular protuberances create some interlocking of the
grains, which somewhat hinders their sliding on each other (Art. 3-5A).
This is illustrated by Fig. 15-1, which gives the results of a controlled-stress
load test on a very uniform dry Florida sand from Daytona Beach compacted
to medium density in a 6-in.-diameter (15.2-cm) CBR type mold.   First a
165-lb (75-kg$_f$) static load was applied in steps through a 2-in.-diameter

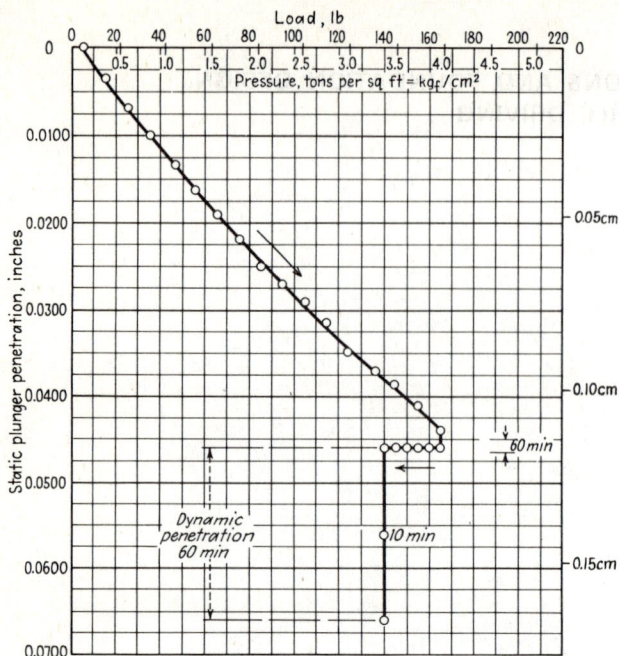

Fig. 15-1. A vibratory force equal to only 1.05 percent of the original static load produces after 10 min of vibration on uniform dry sand of medium density a plunger penetration (settlement) equal to 27 percent of the total static settlement.   (*After Tschebotarioff and McAlpin, Ref. 377.*)

(5-cm) plunger.   This load was maintained for 60 min and was then reduced to 140 lb (63.6 kg$_f$).   Thereupon a small vibrator was started.   It was of the type discussed in the next article with reference to Fig. 15-6 and was attached to the top of the plunger.   Its excenters were adjusted to produce a centrifugal vertical force equal to only 1.05 percent of the 140-lb (63.6-kg$_f$) static load at an operational speed of 1,500 rev/min (25 Hz = 25 cycles/sec).   This was well below the natural frequency of the system, which varied between 2,100 and 2,750 cycles/min (35 and 46 Hz), as determined experimentally by the procedure shown in Fig. 15-7.   Thus there was no magnification of the vibratory forces due to resonance.   Yet the vibratory force of only 1.05 percent of the static load produced a settlement of the plunger equal to 27 percent of the settlement under the static load.   Other similar comparisons indicated that for this "ball-bearing" type of Florida sand the effects of a vibratory force could be from 15 to 140 times greater than those of an equally large static force† (see Ref. 377).   For clays the

---

† This sand came from the site of the Daytona Beach automobile race track.   Thus the firm surface of that track is due not to the sand gradation but to the cementing action of salt from evaporated seawater brought up by capillarity.

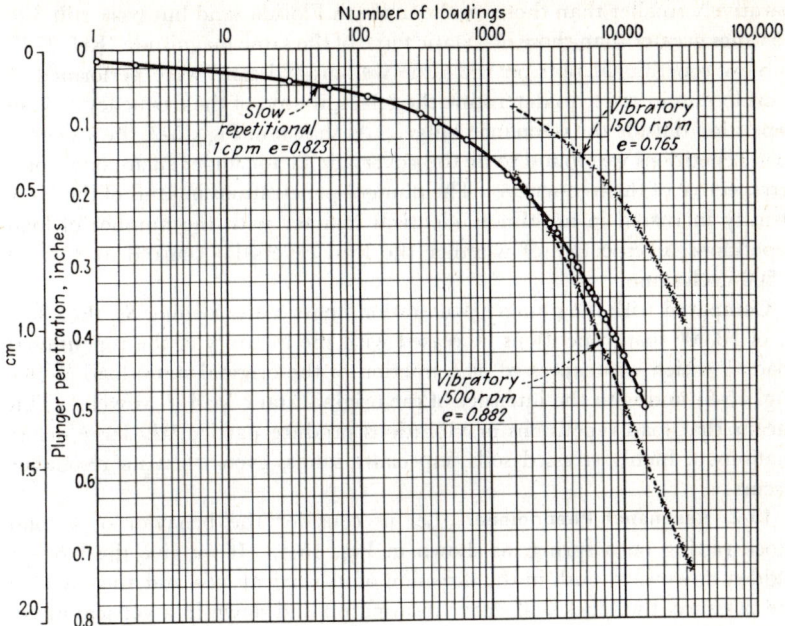

Fig. 15-2. Comparison of plunger penetrations into sand under the effect of vibratory and slow repetitional loading. (*After Tschebotarioff and McAlpin, Ref. 377.*)

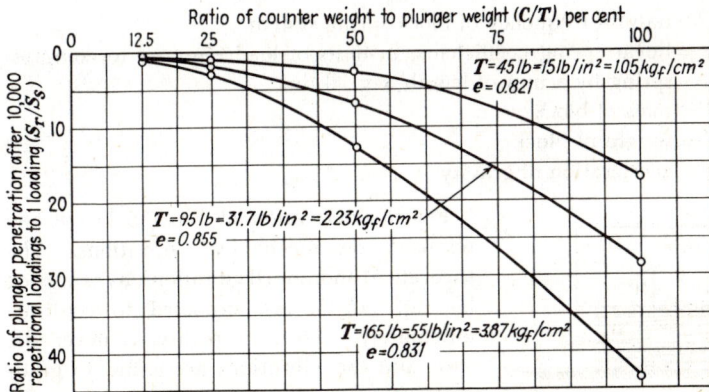

Fig. 15-3. The effect on plunger penetrations of slow repetitional loading increases with the intensities of the repetitional load and the original static load. (*After Tschebotarioff and McAlpin, Ref. 377.*)

vibratory and static load effects were about equal.   For well-graded sand of the type used for plaster work the effects of a vibratory force were comparatively smaller than those on the uniform Florida sand but were still 3 to 15 times greater than those of a static force of the same magnitude (Ref. 377).

Slow repetitional tests on the same well-graded sand were performed at 1 cycle/min in order to determine the effect, if any, of the frequency of load repetition outside the resonance range.   As shown in Fig. 15-2, the *number* of load repetitions was found to be the governing factor under such conditions, irrespective of the frequency.   The plunger penetrations in sand of the same density increased in an almost identical manner with the number of load repetitions, irrespective of whether the load reversals occurred at 1 or at 1,500 cycles/min.

Compared with the plunger penetration under static loading S_s, the effect S_r of 10,000 load repetitions increased with the intensity of the repetitional load C, which was expressed as a fraction of the original static load T (see Fig. 15-3) and with the intensity of the original static load T as well.   This means that load repetitions or vibrations produce particularly large deformations of highly stressed soils, especially sands, even when no resonance occurs.

15-2. Resonance Phenomena.   Let us consider the behavior of a solid block resting on a spring, as shown in Fig. 15-4.   If we give the block a sudden downward push in the direction of its vertical axis and then release the pressure, the block will start vibrating up and down in a vertical direction.   Assuming that no forces whatsoever oppose this *free vibration*, its theoretical *frequency*, i.e., the number of cycles of motion per unit of time, will be

$$f_n = \frac{1}{2\pi}\sqrt{\frac{k}{M}} = \frac{1}{2\pi}\sqrt{\frac{kg}{W}} \qquad (15\text{-}1)$$

where f_n = natural frequency of block-spring system
   k = linear spring coefficients, in units of load required to compress spring by a unit of length, e.g., lb/in.
   M = mass of block
   W = weight of block
   g = acceleration of gravity

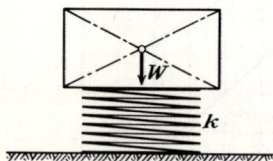

Fig. 15-4.   Sketch illustrating the terms of Eq. (15-1).

For the derivation of Eq. (15-1) see any textbook on mechanical vibrations.   The theoretical undamped vibrations, as expressed by Eq. (15-1), are supposed to continue indefinitely.   This, in reality, is never the case, and the vibrations are found to gradually decrease in amplitude, i.e., in the distance of their oscillatory motion, and to stop entirely after a while, unless the push which excited the vibrations in the first place is repeated periodically, i.e., unless we deal with *forced vibrations*. The frequency of such vibrations of decreasing amplitude, i.e., of *damped vibrations*, is

$$f_{nd} = \frac{1}{2\pi} \sqrt{\frac{k}{M} - \frac{c^2}{4M^2}}$$ (15-2)

where f_{nd} = natural frequency of damped vibration
   c = damping constant

The other symbols have the same significance as in Eq. (15-1). It will be noted from a comparison of Eqs. (15-1) and (15-2) that the presence of damping decreases somewhat the natural frequency of a vibrating body. To this day no reliable and practicable methods have been developed which would permit numerical determination of the damping constant c of soils. For that reason damping is usually neglected in the analysis of field experiments involving determination of the natural frequency of foundation-soil systems. These analyses use Eq. (15-1) as a starting point.

In the case of an actual foundation it is no longer possible to neglect the weight of the soil spring, as was done in the derivation of Eq. (15-1), where it was assumed that the weight of the spring is negligible in respect to the weight W of the block. The soil acts as a spring for the foundation and vibrates together with it, as shown in Fig. 15-5. Lorenz (Ref. 200), attempted to assign a definite value to the mass of the vibrating soil and, to that end, transformed Eq. (15-1) to read

$$f_n = \frac{1}{2\pi} \sqrt{\frac{k'Ag}{W_s + W_v}}$$ (15-3)

where A = contact area between base of foundation and soil
   $k' = k/A$ = dynamic modulus of soil reaction, or volume spring coefficient
   W_v = weight of machine and of its foundation
   W_s = weight of vibrating soil

Equation (15-3) is often quoted without any reservations, and Lorenz even attempted to use it to determine experimentally the actual value of W_s. To do this he had to assume that the coefficient k' represented a constant value which was independent of the contact area A. This assumption was incorrect, as shown in Art. 18-3 of the first edition.

A glance at Fig. 15-5 will show that the motions of the soil are more complex than the motion of the machine and foundation. The term W_s in Eq. (15-3) should therefore be considered as referring to what might be called an *equivalent weight* of soil, with no clearly defined physical boundaries.

Studies of the effect of forced vibrations on soils, including resonance phenomena, are frequently performed by means of a machine the action of

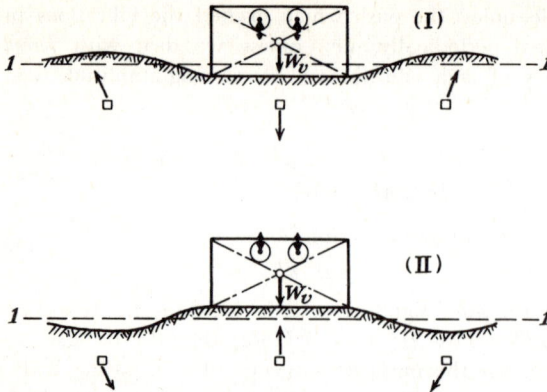

Fig. 15-5. The probable nature of the soil-surface deformations around a two-mass vibrator inducing vertical oscillations. (*After Crockett and Hammond, Ref. 70.*)

which is illustrated by Fig. 15-6.   It was adapted to this work in 1933 by the German Research Society for Soil Mechanics (DEGEBO).

The machine is sometimes referred to as a *two-mass oscillator*.   It has two shafts which are geared together and which rotate in opposite directions. Each shaft has an eccentric weight, shown black in Fig. 15-6, which is so mounted that the horizontal component of its centrifugal force cancels out the corresponding component of the eccentric weight on the other shaft of the machine, and vice versa.   Only the vertical component of the centrifugal forces remains; it varies according to a sinusoidal curve, as shown in Fig. 15-6, reaching a maximum downward value at stage b and a maximum upward value at stage d.   For constant values of the eccentric weights, their

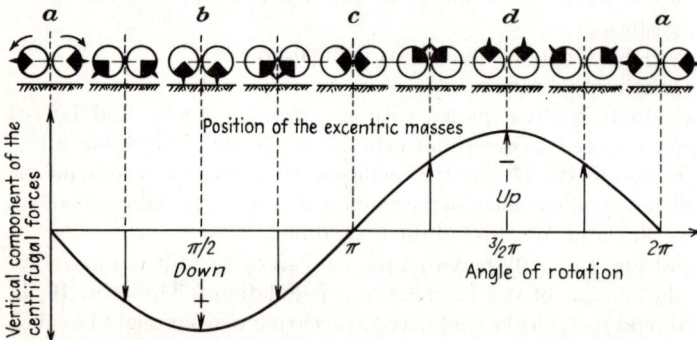

Fig. 15-6. Variation of the vertical component of the centrifugal force during one shaft revolution of the two-mass oscillator. (*After Hertwig, Fruh, and Lorenz, Ref. 127.*)

centrifugal forces increase with the square of the speed of rotation of the shafts. In some modern oscillator machines the unbalanced eccentric weight can be varied while the machine is in operation.

Figure 15-7 illustrates the DEGEBO-type procedure used to determine the natural frequency of a soil-vibrator system for the tests described in the preceding article and illustrated by Fig. 15-1. The vibrator is started at a low speed and allowed to run for 1 min. Then the speed is increased in increments after identical intervals of time. The settlement (penetration) of the plunger and the amplitude of vibration of the plunger are recorded at each stage and plotted as shown on Fig. 15-7. Although the vertical force continues to increase with the square of the vibrator velocity, the plunger penetrations decrease markedly after 2,100 cycles/min (35 Hz) and so do the amplitudes of vibration. This indicates that the natural frequency of the system has been passed at that speed since *resonance* has occurred. By *resonance* is meant the great increase in the amplitudes of oscillations and in the dynamic vibratory forces which *occurs when the operational speed of a*

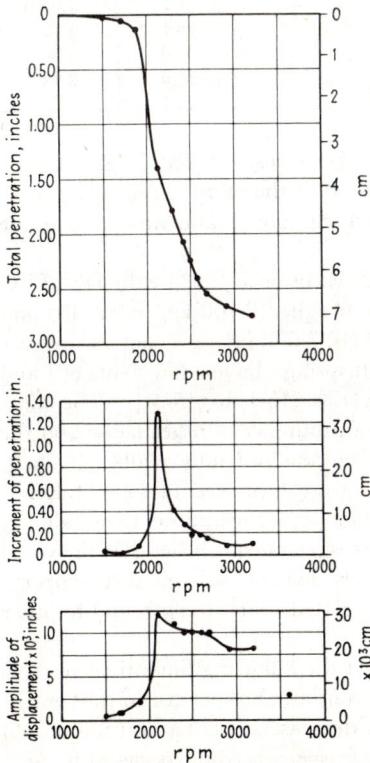

Fig. 15-7. Determination of resonance range of loaded 2-in.-diameter (5-cm) plunger on dense, dry, well-graded sand from the increment of penetration-vs.-velocity curve. (*After Tschebotarioff and McAlpin, Ref.* 377.)

TABLE 15-1.   Natural Frequencies of a DEGEBO Standard-type Vibrator on Different Kinds of Soils

Nature of soil	Natural frequencies f_{nd}	
	Hz (cycles/sec)	Cycles/min
6 ft of peat overlying sand	12.5	750
6-ft-thick old fill consisting of medium sand with remnants of peat	19.1	1,145
Gravelly sand with clay lenses..................................	19.4	1,165
Old slag fill well compacted by traffic........................	21.3	1,280
Very old, well-compacted fill of loamy sand...............	21.7	1,300
Tertiary clay, moist..	21.8	1,310
Lias clay, moist...	23.8	1,430
Very uniform yellow medium sand............................	24.1	1,445
Find sand with 30 percent medium sand.....................	24.2	1,455
Uniform coarse sand...	26.2	1,570
Nonuniform compacted sand...................................	26.7	1,600
Quite dry tertiary clay...	27.5	1,650
Compact clay..	28.1	1,685
Limestone, undisturbed rock...................................	30.0	1,800
Sandstone, undisturbed..	34.0	2,040

machine coincides with the natural frequency of the machine-soil system.   Knowledge of the factors affecting this natural frequency is therefore of primary importance for machine-foundation design, which should aim at avoiding the possibility of resonance.

Table 15-1 summarizes the results obtained prior to 1933 by the DEGEBO with their standard-type vibrator, which weighed 2,700 kg_f (6,000 lb) and had a contact area with the soil of 1.0 m^2 (10.7 ft²), giving a contact pressure of 0.28 ton/ft². Soft soils, similarly to soft springs, have a low value of k and k' and, hence, a low natural frequency f_{nd} [Eqs. (15-1) to (15-3)]. The effect of the contact area A with the soil and of a number of other factors on the natural frequency of a soil-vibrator system was not fully realized at first. The results of the early DEGEBO tests were reprinted in some English-language publications without any indications as to the limits of their validity. A consequence of this has been a widespread erroneous belief that the value of the natural frequency of a soil is a clearly defined basic physical property of a soil type, which can be numerically related to its strength and to other similar relevant engineering properties.

Later studies of the DEGEBO indicated the following limitations of their procedure. All other factors remaining constant, an increase in the centrifugal force of a vibrator brought about a decrease in its natural frequency. Thus a standard-type DEGEBO vibrator (see preceding paragraph) at a low centrifugal-force setting was found to have on a certain sand a natural frequency $f_{nd} = 1,600$ cycles/min.   A progressive increase in the centrifugal force progressively decreased this value on the same soil down to a minimum of $f_{nd} = 1,320$ cycles/min, i.e., by 17 percent.   Presumably greater exciting forces cause a larger equivalent weight of soil W_s to participate in the oscillations; according to Eq. (15-3), this would decrease the value of f_n (see Lorenz, Ref. 200, and Ref. 377).   Similarly, a decrease in the weight of the standard DEGEBO vibrator from 6,000 to 4,500 lb on the same soil, all other factors remaining unchanged, had a reverse effect.   At a low value of the centrifugal force the natural frequency f_{nd} was raised from 1,600 to 1,740 cycles/min and at a high centrifugal-force value from 1,320 to 1,380 cycles/min.

These facts, as well as others given in Art. 18-3 of the first edition, have shown that there is no such thing as a definite value for the natural frequency of a certain type of soil.   There are, however, certain *ranges* for such frequencies.   Thus natural frequency values published by Crockett and Hammond (Ref. 71), which were obtained by striking the ground with a heavy hammer and measuring ground vibrations by means of an oscillograph, fell within the same ranges as the values obtained by forced vibration and reported in Table 15-1.   Rocks had values exceeding 30 cycles/sec (1,800 cycles/min); peats and soft clays from 15 cycles per sec (900 cycles/min) down to 7.5 cycles/sec (450 cycles/min); sands and medium to stiff clays had intermediate values between these two extreme types of materials.   However, even if one employs the impact method to determine the natural frequency of a soil, one will find that different values may be obtained on the same site, depending on whether a new structure has been added or an old one removed close to the place of the test.

Therefore, instead of speaking about the natural frequency of a soil or of the ground, it is more rational to refer to the *natural frequency of a site* or of a *soil-foundation system*, where the terms "site" or "system" cover all characteristics which may affect the value of the natural frequency of a new foundation.   These are the nature of the soil and rock stratification and the depth and the properties of the successive layers; the presence next to the site of surcharges, such as buildings, other machines and foundations thereof, embankments, or cuts; the weight of the machine itself and of its foundations; the size of the contact area of the new foundation with the soil; the characteristics of the exciting forces; and other factors.

Very little precise information has been published concerning actual cases of resonance.   The writer observed a gas-compressor pumping station on the lower Mississippi where excessive vibrations due to resonance caused continuous breakage of pipe connections.   This can have serious consequences in a cold climate requiring enclosure of the machinery within a building sealed against the outside.   Barkan (Ref. 22) mentions a similar case of resonance when the resulting seepage of gas within a compressor house caused an explosion which blew it up.

Tschebotarioff and Ward (Ref. 381) attempted to correlate the few

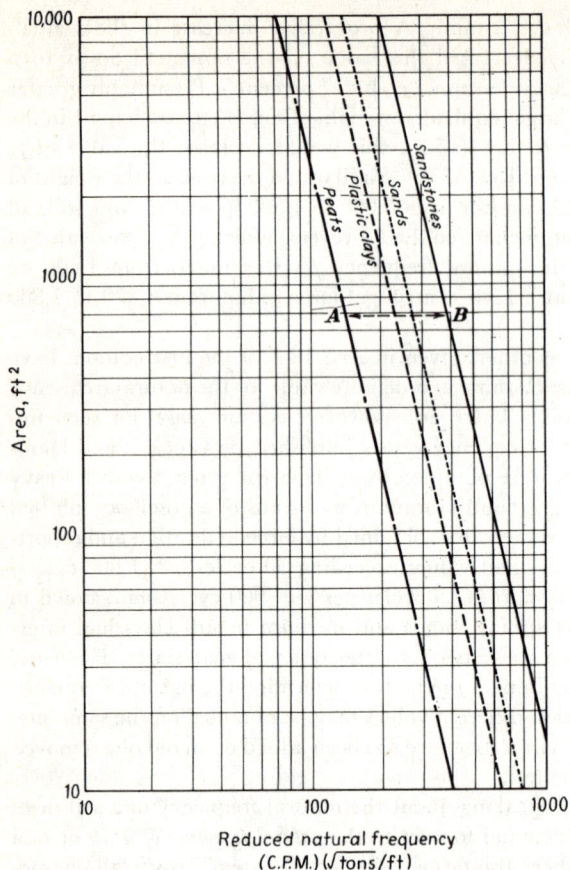

Fig. 15-8.   Cases of resonance have been reported in the belt AB.
(*From Tschebotarioff, Ref. 359.*)

data that were available by plotting the recorded natural frequencies f_{nd} against the contact area A of the foundation with the soil (see Fig. 15-8). The results showed considerable scattering, which could be attributed, in part, to different intensities of contact pressure p with the ground.   To eliminate this variable, Eq. (15-3) was transformed to read

$$f_n = \sqrt{\frac{A}{W_v}} \frac{1}{2\pi} \sqrt{\frac{k'g}{1 + W_s/W_v}} = \frac{1}{\sqrt{p}} f_{nr} \tag{15-4}$$

where p = unit average contact pressure between foundation and soil
   f_{nr} = reduced natural frequency = natural frequency at average unit
      pressure p on ground equal to unity
The other symbols have the same significance as in Eqs. (15-1) and (15-3).

When the reduced natural frequencies of known cases of resonance were plotted against the contact area between foundation and soil, they fell within a danger belt AB, shown in Fig. 15-8 (see Ref. 359). Most of the troublesome cases were caused by reciprocating engines operating at comparatively low speeds of 300 to 400 cycles/min (5 to 6.7 Hz).

By using the elastic half-space theory Richart, Hall, and Woods have shown (Ref. 265, pp. 338–340) that the lines for different types of soil given in Fig. 15-8 have a direct physical significance which is related to the values of the shear modulus G of these soils.

A direct method for the prediction of the natural frequency of a foundation, in the process of its design, was developed in 1948 by Barkan (Ref. 22) and will be outlined in the next article.

15-3. Foundation Design for Machines and Forge Hammers. A properly designed foundation for a machine must first meet the general requirements for all foundations (Art. 4-1). Then the first special step in the design of a machine foundation is to determine its dimensions in such a manner that the amplitude of its vibration will not exceed a specified tolerable value. Naturally, this includes the estimation of its natural frequency so that resonance can be avoided. The only method achieving this aim which is known to have been successfully tested in practice is the semiempirical procedure developed in the 1930s and 1940s by the Soil Dynamics Laboratory of the

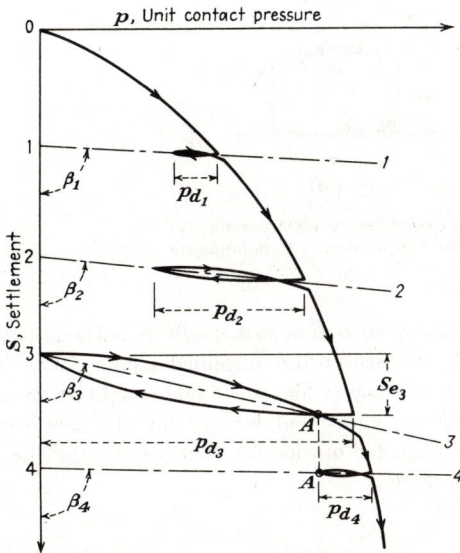

Fig. 15-9.   First step in the original attempts to estimate values of the dynamic modulus of soil reaction.

Institute of Foundations and Underground Structures in Moscow, headed by Dominik D. Barkan.

At the time the writer was preparing the first edition of the present book (1951) he was aware of only the preliminary work done there in the 1930s and critically discussed it as inadequate with reference to what is now Fig. 15-9.   However, on learning of Barkan's 1948 book on the subject, the writer was so impressed by its contents that he arranged for its translation into English (after updating by Barkan) and served as editor thereof (Ref. 22). Barkan's procedure will be illustrated here by a summary of the steps in its application to vertical and to rocking oscillations.

Vibratory or slow repetitional loads, depending on their direction and on the point of their application to a rigid body, can produce six types of motion thereof, in accordance with the six *degrees of freedom* of such a body in space. There can be three types of *translation*, i.e., displacements, namely, in the vertical direction and in two horizontal directions at right angles to each other.   Also, there can be three types of *rotation*, namely, around a vertical axis and around two horizontal axes at right angles to each other.

The treatment of translation in the two horizontal directions at right angles to each other is identical; so is the treatment of rotations around the two horizontal axes.   This leaves four basic types of machine-foundation movement for which analytical procedures have to be developed: vertical translation (Fig. 15-10A), horizontal translation, rotation around a horizontal axis (Fig. 15-10B), and rotation around a vertical axis.

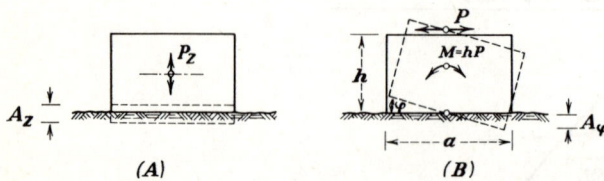

Fig. 15-10.   Sketch illustrating Barkan's equations for determination of vibration amplitudes: (A) uniform soil compression; (B) nonuniform soil compression (rocking).

The *analysis of vertical translations by the Barkan method* will be outlined first (see Fig. 15-10A).   This analysis is based on the simplified assumption that the machine-foundation-soil system behaves like the single weight W on a spring shown by Fig. 15-4.   This is equivalent to ignoring the damping effects of the soil, which can be neglected outside the resonance range; i.e., within the range of all practical designs.

Then one can rewrite Eq. (15-1)

$$f_{n'z}^2 = \frac{c_r}{m} = c_u A \frac{g}{W} \qquad (15\text{-}5)$$

where $f_{n'z}$ = undamped natural circular frequency of vertical vibrations, Hz = $2\pi/T_{nz}$

T_{nz} = period or time of one oscillation

c_r = coefficient of rigidity of soil base, kg_f/cm

m = mass of foundation and machine = W/g, $tons_f\text{-}sec^2/m$

W = weight of foundation and machine

g = acceleration of gravity

c_u = coefficient of elastic uniform compression of soil, kg_f/cm^3

A = horizontal contact area of foundation with soil, cm^2

From the theory of vibrations it follows that

$$A_z = \frac{P}{m(f_{nz}^2 - \omega^2)} \tag{15-6}$$

where A_z = amplitude of forced vertical vibrations

P = exciting force

ω = angular velocity of machine rotation = $2\pi N/60$, where N = number of oscillations per minute

The practical value of the Barkan method is due to the organized effort expended on the experimental determination of the actual values of the coefficient c_u for full-scale machine foundations on different types of soil. This was done as follows.

Initial values were obtained from the hysteresis loop of small-scale static loading and unloading tests, as shown in Fig. 15-9:

$$c_u = \frac{p_d}{S_e} \tag{15-7}$$

where p_d = alternating component of average contact pressure with soil due to repetitional (dynamic) forces

S_e = elastic rebound in a static-load test ($\approx$ elastic soil compression caused by $p_d \approx$ one-half of amplitude of vibration)

It can be seen from Fig. 15-9, however, that the value $c_u = \tan\beta$ will vary considerably with the intensity of the unloading increment p_d. The size of the loaded area A also is obviously of importance. A correction, based on the following equation of the theory of elasticity, was attempted to take care of this effect

$$c_u = 1.13 \frac{E}{1-\nu^2} \frac{1}{\sqrt{A}} \tag{15-8}$$

where E = Young modulus of soil

ν = Poisson ratio of soil

The speed of loading and unloading was also found to affect the results. Since it was impossible to do this at the speed of a machine, field load ests with vibrators of the type shown by Fig. 15-6 were undertaken. This

TABLE 15-2.   Recommended Design Values of the Coefficient of Elastic Uniform Compression c_u†

Soil-group category	Soil group	Permissible load on soil under action of static load only, kg_f/cm^2	Coefficient of elastic uniform compression c_u, kg_f/cm^2
I	Weak soils (clays and silty clays with sand, in a plastic state; clayey and silty sands; also soils of categories II and III with laminae of organic silt and of peat)	Up to 1.5	Up to 3
II	Soils of medium strength (clays and silty clays with sand, close to the plastic limit; sand)	1.5–3.5	3–5
III	Strong soils (clays and silty clays with sand, of hard consistency; gravels and gravelly sands; loess and loessial soils)	3.5–5	5–10
IV	Rocks	Greater than 5	Greater than 10

† From Barkan, Ref. 22.

provided further corrections to the coefficient c_u. Final corrections were obtained from measurements on operating full-scale machine foundations. The results are summarized by Table 15-2.

With these data it is possible to design a foundation which will not exceed a certain amplitude range of vibration. According to Barkan, maximum safe values are $A_z = 0.20$ to 0.25 mm $= 0.008$ to 0.010 in. This is a limit value which may not cause structural damage but nevertheless may create discomfort to personnel in the building (see the discussion of Fig. 15-11).

To permit the foundation design the engine manufacturer should supply design data about his machine such as the range of its operational speeds ω and the maximum possible unbalanced force P. It is obvious from Eq. (15-6) that, if ω coincides with the natural frequency $f_{n'z}$, the amplitude of vibration A_z would become theoretically infinite if there were no damping in the soil. Damping does set limits thereon, but damaging amplitudes of vibration may nevertheless result (see Fig. 15-14). If Eq. (15-5) gives a value of the natural frequency close to the value of ω, the foundation contact area A or its weight W should be altered to increase the difference between $f_{n'z}$ and ω until the amplitude of vibration A_z is reduced to an acceptable value.

A similar procedure was used by Barkan to analyze the *case of rocking oscillations*, which involve elastic nonuniform compression of the soil (see Fig. 15-10B). The basic equations of importance for such foundation designs are

$$f_{n'\varphi}^2 = \frac{c_\varphi I}{W_0} \tag{15-9}$$

$$A'_\varphi = \frac{a/2M}{W_0(f_{n'\varphi}^2 - \omega^2)} \tag{15-10}$$

where $f_{n'\varphi}$ = undamped natural circular frequency of rocking vibration

c_φ = coefficient of elastic nonuniform soil compression

I = moment of inertia of foundation area in contact with soil with respect to axis of rotation of foundation

W_0 = moment of inertia of mass of machine and foundation with respect to axis of rotation

A'_φ = amplitude of vibration

M = exciting moment = Ph

P = exciting force of reciprocal engine

ω = angular velocity of machine rotation $(2\pi N/60)$, where N = number of oscillations per minute

TABLE 15-3.   Values of the Coefficient of Elastic Nonuniform Compression c_φ for Different Soils and Sizes of Foundations†

Description of soil	Base contact area of foundation m^2	c_u, $\mathrm{kg_f/cm^3}$	c_φ, $\mathrm{kg_f/cm^3}$	$\dfrac{c_\varphi}{c_u}$
Saturated brown silty clays with some sand	2.0	4.40	12.0	2.73
	4.0	2.50	4.0	1.60
	8.0	2.05	3.0	1.46
Saturated gray soft silty clays with some sand	0.5	3.5	3.55	1.02
	1.0	2.52	3.61	1.44
	1.5	2.11	3.79	1.80
Loess at natural moisture content	0.81	14.2	25.0	1.76
	1.4	10.8	17.6	1.63
	2.0	10.2	15.5	1.51
	4.0	8.0	12.9	1.61
Saturated gray fine dense sands	4.0	7.5	14.5	1.92
	8.0	5.6	9.5	1.71
	15.0	4.0	9.2	2.30

† From Barkan, Ref. 22.

Equations (15-9) and (15-10) are rigorously correct.

The values of the coefficient c_φ (see Table 15-3) were established experimentally in a manner similar to that described above for the coefficient c_u.

To improve stability, it is obvious that the dimension h should be decreased and a should be increased as much as possible for all reciprocating engines mounted on the top of the block.

In his book (Ref. 22) Barkan outlines similar computation procedures for the treatment of cases of *horizontal oscillations* (elastic uniform shear of soil), *oscillations around a vertical axis* (elastic nonuniform shear of soil), and elastic resistance to vibratory loading of pile foundations.

Figure 15-11 illustrates a *case of excessive vibrations*.   One of two adjoining gas-compressor units vibrated excessively, producing complaints from personnel in the station building and even in neighboring small structures.   It will be termed unit 1.   Cracks had appeared in the basement wall of the lower-level generator room after several years of compressor operation. Both compressor engines were fixed to the top of separate massive concrete foundation blocks over a deep deposit of medium to dense sand of glacial origin.

A number of measurements at selected locations on the blocks and in the building were made by means of a portable three-component seismograph, which provides a photographic record on the same chart of simultaneous vertical, longitudinal, and transverse oscillations with a magnification of 50 (Ref. 368).   The measured values at three points of unit 1, when both units were operating, are shown by dashed lines in Fig. 15-11.   The resulting picture of rotational movements was also obtained for unit 2, except that there the vibration amplitudes were less than one-half of those shown for unit 1 on Fig. 15-11.   This was attributed to the absence of a basement next to unit 2, such as was present opposite unit 1.   The rule of thumb of static construction that it is safe to make cuts not encroaching on a 1 : 2 slope from the edge of a foundation obviously does not hold for dynamic conditions.

Chemical solidification of the sand under the edges of the foundation under unit 1 was then carried out by the Joosten process (Art. 5-6).   It greatly reduced the vibration amplitudes of unit 1, as shown in Fig. 15-11.   The theoretical value of the vertical amplitude of vibration at the edge of the foundation in unit 2 was computed by the Barkan method to be 0.0027 in. (0.07 mm) (see Prob. 15-1).   This was on the safe side but of the same order as the 0.0016 in. (0.05 mm) actually measured when the compressors of unit 2 were operating alone (Ref. 368).

An interesting point is that the measured frequencies of the foundation blocks were approximately 10 cycles/sec, i.e., 600 cycles/min, or twice operational speed of the compressors.

In recent years attempts have been made to handle the entire problem of machine-foundation-soil vibrations on a mathematically rigorous basis by treating the soil as an *elastic half-space*.   Progress has been made in this direction (see Refs. 265 and 209a).

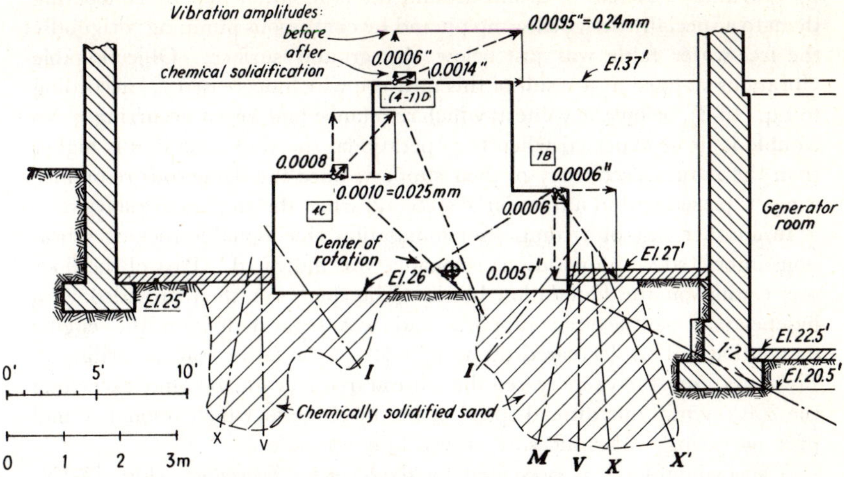

Fig. 15-11. Measured amplitudes of vibration for compressor unit 1 after grouting (solid lines) and amplitudes of vibration before grouting (dashed lines). Chemical solidification of the sand reduced movement to about one-seventh that which originally occurred. (*After Tschebotarioff, Ref. 368.*)

The following general *auxiliary design measures* should be borne in mind. Considerable rigidity of the machine foundation is essential, since a slight deflection of a few thousandths of an inch may cause bearing trouble, especially when several bearing supports are required. The possibility of warping of concrete slabs should be considered in this connection. Such warping may occur when the top surface of the slab dries out whereas the lower surface remains moist. Massive block-type construction is the best measure against warping of this type.

Objectionable vibrations of existing installations can often be traced to resonance, i.e., to the coincidence of the operational speed of the machines with the natural frequency of the soil-foundation system. Usually it is not possible to change the operational speed of a machine, and it therefore becomes necessary to change the natural frequency f_n of its support.

With reference to Eqs. (15-5) and (15-9), this can be done either by improving the properties of the soil, in a manner similar to that shown in Fig. 15-11, to increase the values of the coefficient c_u or c_φ, or by changing the weight W of the foundation and hence its mass m. This presents special problems and has limitations (see discussions in Ref. 359).

Cases are on record where this was successfully accomplished. In the case of the Mississippi pumping station referred to earlier in Art. 15-2 and in Figs. 18-15 and 18-16 of the first edition the effective weight W_v of the foundation was increased by some 7 percent by lowering the free-water table 2 to 3 ft (60 to 90 cm) along the depth of the mat. This was accomplished by providing a system of drains around the foundation mat by connecting them to a specially designed sump pit and by continuous pumping; originally the free-water table was just below the ground surface. Objectionable vibrations stopped as a result of this measure which decreased f_n, according to Eq. (15-3), below the value at which resonance had beeen occurring. No trouble is to be expected when the operational speed of machines is higher than the natural frequency of their support, since the dangerous resonance range is passed within a fraction of a second when the engines are started.

In another case of a compressor foundation objectionable rocking vibrations interfered with operation; resonance was indicated. Part of the floor was resting on the foundation block. The floor was then provided with independent cantilevered supports and was separated from the engine foundation. This decreased the weight W_v of the latter and, according to Eq. (15-3), must have increased the natural frequency f_n to values exceeding the 300 rev/min operational speed of the machine at which resonance had been occurring. This measure proved fully effective.

A special problem is presented by *forge-hammer foundations* (Fig. 15-12). The foundation must have a large mass to absorb the effects of the shock waves generated by hammer impacts and must be specially reinforced in critically stressed zones.

According to Andrews and Crockett (Ref. 8), the largest unit in operation when they wrote (1945) had a 25-ton hammer B (*tup*), and its foundation G weighed 3,000 tons. This gives a 1 : 120 ratio between the weights of the hammer itself and of its foundation. The frame A is usually connected to the steel anvil D on which rest the dies C. Oak-timber or plywood pads E

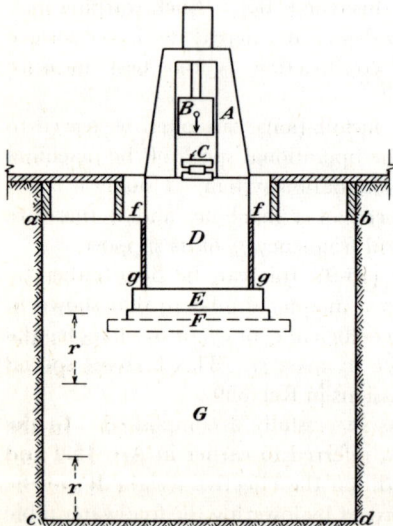

Fig. 15-12. A forge-hammer foundation. (*After Andrews and Crockett, Ref. 8.*)

support the anvil and are underlain by a grillage of steel I beams F, which are concreted together with the foundation block G; zones r in Fig. 15-12 are heavily reinforced.   Spring pads fg are placed between the anvil D and the foundation block G.   A number of design variations are possible (see Ref. 8).

15-4. Screening Vibrations.   The following simple *measures at the source of the vibrations* are helpful.   Foundations of machinery should be separated from the foundations and floors of the building itself.   Small foundations can be supported by springs.   According to Crockett and Hammond (Ref. 70), a machine weighing 110 tons was successfully mounted on compressed-air springs; laminated and helical springs have also been used for lighter machines.   This is an effective method of preventing the transmission of vibrations to adjoining structures through the ground.   Spring pads have been employed for the same purpose for heavier machines up to 700 tons, but they appear to be somewhat less effective.   Cork is a satisfactory spring-pad material only so long as it does not get wet and start rotting.   Asbestos fiber appears to be the most enduring of similar materials (see Ref. 68).

Trenches in the ground, whether open or filled with bentonitic slurry or similar damping materials, can be fully effective only under certain infrequent conditions.   Namely, the smallest dimension of the screen, i.e., the depth or length of the screening trench, must be not less than $0.3L$, where L is the length of the vibratory wave propagating through the soil (Barkan, Ref. 22).   A sheet-pile cutoff wall, or other such barrier, will act in a similar manner whether located close to the source of vibrations or in front of the structure to be protected.   Vibratory waves tend to flow under or around barriers, and if the latter are shallow or short, the protected zone in the shadow of the barrier becomes inadequately small.

With reference to Arts. 2-2 and 5-3, it will be noted that the velocity of wave propagation in a soil is a function of its density and will increase with it, varying from about $v_s = 490$ ft/sec (150 m/sec) for loose sands to $v_s = 1,540$ ft/sec (470 m/sec) for dense sands.   For rock it is at least $v_s = 6,000$ ft/sec (1,830 m/sec) and for water $v_w = 4,700$ ft/sec (1,430 m/sec).

Table 15-4 gives wavelengths for different frequencies and periods of oscillation at the source and wave velocities.   It follows that for a compressor engine running at 300 cycles/min on a sand of medium density the wave velocity would be 300 m/sec and the wavelength $L = 60\ m = 197$ ft.   Therefore, to be effective, a screening trench would have to be $0.3L = 59$ ft (18 m) deep, which makes it impractical.

Barkan concluded that it is impossible in practice effectively to screen waves propagating from low-frequency machines.   He illustrated his point by citing a number of such full-scale attempts which failed.

Elaborate model vibratory tests by Woods (Ref. 409), employing wave-length-scaling techniques by the use of high-frequency oscillators (200 to 350 Hz or cycles/sec), confirmed Barkan's conclusions.   A trench depth equal to

TABLE 15-4. Wavelengths for Different Wave Velocities, Periods of Waves, and Numbers of Oscillations of Source of Waves†

Number of oscillations of source, min^{-1}	Period of wave, sec	Wavelength, m, for velocity, m/sec, of:					Notes
		50.0	100	200	300	500	
50	1.2	60	120	240	360	600	Low-frequency
100	0.6	30	60	120	180	300	machines (diesels,
200	0.3	15	30	60	90	150	compressors, gas
300	0.2	10	20	40	60	100	motors, etc.)
500	0.12	6.00	12	24	36	60	
800	0.075	3.75	7.5	15	22.5	37.5	High-frequency
1,000	0.060	3.00	6.0	13	18.0	30.0	machines (mainly
1,200	0.050	2.50	5.0	10	15.0	25.0	turbodynamos and
1,500	0.040	2.0	4.0	8.0	12.0	20.0	forge hammers)

† After Barkan, Ref. 22.

$0.6L$ was needed to reduce the amplitude of vibrations within the screened zone to one-fourth that at the source.

15-5. Effect of Shocks Caused by Blasting or Earthquakes.   Blasting is frequently resorted to in all types of construction work involving excavations. The safe amount of explosives which can be used without damage to adjoining structures represents a problem of considerable interest both to construction contractors and to insurance companies.   A comprehensive study of the matter was carried out by the Liberty Mutual Insurance Co. (see Crandell, Ref. 69).

Experiments were performed over a number of years with charges of between 1 and 100 lb (0.45 and 45.4 kg$_f$) of dynamite, fired at distances of between 25 to 250 ft (7.6 to 76 m) from adjoining buildings.   An accelerograph was used to measure the frequencies f and the accelerations a of the vibrations induced in the ground by the blasting.   Seismographs were used to measure frequencies f and displacements D_1 of the vibrations.   It was found that damage to buildings could be related to the kinetic energy (KE) of the oscillating ground

$$\text{KE} = \frac{MV^2}{2} = \frac{W}{2g \times 4\pi^2}\frac{a^2}{f^2} \qquad (15\text{-}11)$$

$$\text{KE} = \frac{W}{2g \times 4\pi^2}16\pi^4 f^2 D_1{}^2 \qquad (15\text{-}12)$$

where KE = kinetic energy

M = mass of the vibrating soil

W = weight of the vibrating soil

g = acceleration of gravity, ft/sec^2

a = measured acceleration ft/sec^2

f = measured frequency of vibration, cycles/sec

D_1 = measured vibratory displacement of ground, ft

There was no way of determining either the mass M or the weight W of the vibrating soil. Therefore all observations were correlated with the so-called *energy ratio* (ER) of the vibrating ground

$$\text{ER} = \frac{a^2}{f^2} \qquad (15\text{-}13)$$

$$\text{ER} = 16\pi^4 f^2 D_1{}^2 \qquad (15\text{-}14)$$

The energy ratio ER could be determined experimentally from Eq. (15-13) if an accelerograph was employed for the field measurements and from Eq. (15-14) if a seismograph was used.

The results of the studies are summarized in Fig. 15-13. Normally built structures, not prestressed as a result of differential settlements, were not damaged if the energy ratio ER of the vibrations induced by the blast was smaller than 3; there was a considerable probability of damage if the energy ratio ER was greater than 6. For old buildings a lower safe value of ER =

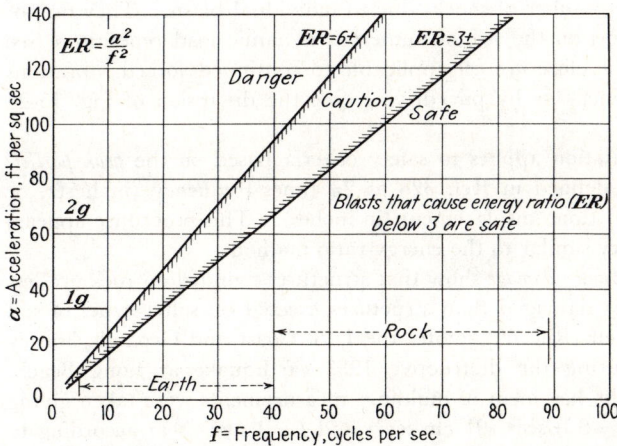

Fig. 15-13. Relationships between frequency and acceleration of shock waves through the ground, as caused by blasting, and established by field studies, which may be dangerous. doubtful, or safe for adjoining buildings. (*After Crandell, Ref. 69.*)

1.00 was recommended. The following relationship was established experimentally:

$$\text{ER} = \left(\frac{50}{D}\right)^2 C^2 K \qquad (15\text{-}15)$$

where ER = energy ratio [see Eqs. (15-13) and (15-14)]

D = distance from the center of the detonation, ft

C = amount of dynamite detonated at any instant, lb

K = constant depending on the ground conditions at site

The results of the above investigation (Ref. 69) can be applied in practice as follows. A few experimental blasts are made at the new site with small charges of known weight, and vibration measurements are performed. The energy ratio ER is computed from Eq. (15-13) or (15-14), depending on the type of instrument employed for the measurements. The value of ER is inserted in Eq. (15-15). Since C and D are known, the constant K characterizing the soil conditions of the site can be computed from Eq. (15-15). The same equation (15-15) can then be used to determine the weight of the maximum safe charge C, by setting ER = 3.

Crandell's paper (Ref. 69) mentions the following additional important facts. By exploding charges with millisecond delays, instead of instantaneously, the detrimentally effective energy transmitted through the ground was greatly reduced. *Human beings are much more sensitive to vibrations* than buildings, and an ER value of 0.6 had a severe effect on persons; advance warning of the coming blast decreased the severity of its effect.

It should be emphasized that the energy-ratio safety criteria are applicable only to a limited number of shocks due to individual blasts. They do not consider the effects on the soil of numerous dynamic load repetitions (see Fig. 15-2) and therefore are *not* applicable to continued forced vibrations caused by machinery or by pile driving (see the discussion of Fig. 15-25 which follows).

The same limitation applies to safety criteria based on the *peak particle velocity*, which is defined in Ref. 328 as 2π times frequency (in hertz, or cycles per second) times displacement (in inches). This procedure appears to give results very similar to the energy-ratio method.

Studies of *earthquake damage* show that structures founded on rock are less apt to be severely damaged than structures erected on softer types of soil deposits. Crandell (Ref. 69) quotes the U.S. Coast and Geodetic Survey measurements during the destructive 1933 earthquake at Long Beach, California. In the basement of buildings measurements were taken giving on an average $a = 3$ ft/sec² (91 cm/sec²) and $f = 1$ cycle/sec; according to Eq. (15-13) this gives a very high energy ratio of ER = 9. Thus accelerations which are a fraction of gravity g can cause severe damage on soft ground, where the frequency is extremely low, but this will not be the case on rocks which transmit vibrations at high frequencies (see Fig. 15-13).

Attempts have been made to provide flexible foundation connections between the superstructure and the ground, the idea being that the ground could then oscillate under the superstructure, which would remain stationary in space and would therefore be unaffected by the earthquake. A small experimental one-story reinforced-concrete house was built on a system of rollers which were placed in two layers at right angles to each other. This method can be applied only to very small and light structures, and even then it is so expensive that it is not likely to be adopted for general use.

Plans were also made to build multistoried houses as a rigid unit from the second story upward and to provide long unstiffened slender columns in the first story; only the partitioning of the first floor was then expected to be damaged by an earthquake. However, the consequences of a failure of this type of experiment would have been too disastrous, and the plans never materialized. The present general practice is to stiffen structures at all elevations.

If spread footings—with or without piles—are used instead of a mat in an earthquake region, then the individual footings should be connected to each other by reinforced-concrete struts and thus stiffened. An example of successful use of this procedure was provided by pile-supported floating foundations of aseismically designed tall buildings (up to 43 stories high), in Mexico City which did not suffer damage during a severe earthquake in 1957 (see Refs. 232 and 413).

Earthquakes frequently produce landslides and displace gravity retaining structures. The severity of an earthquake to be expected in an area is expressed for civil-engineering design purposes by the acceleration it is likely to induce, which usually is expressed as a fraction of the acceleration g of gravity; 10 percent, or $0.1g$, is not an infrequent value for which structural designs have to be made in earthquake-prone areas.

The stability of slopes can then be roughly checked by the procedure illustrated in Fig. 7-7 for static conditions. Earthquake shocks are frequently assumed to be directed upward under a 45° angle from the horizontal. Therefore, for an earthquake shock of $0.1g$, an upward force equal to 10 percent of the weight of a soil slice on Fig. 7-7, and an identical horizontal force, should be applied to the center of gravity of each soil slice, in addition to the static forces.

The increase of lateral earth pressures against a retaining structure during an earthquake can be estimated in a similar manner. Massive gravity retaining structures are most susceptible to damage since, in addition to an increase of earth pressure against them, they will be subjected to a horizontal force equal to 10 percent of their own weight (for an earthquake shock of $0.1g$) applied at the center of gravity of the structure. Further, any frictional resistance to sliding along their base, which is a function of their weight, will be reduced by the same amount.

Liquefaction phenomena, especially of loose saturated sands (Art. 8-4), introduce additional hazards and can make earthquakes even more dangerous. Studies of earthquake damage show that, in general, structures founded on rock are less apt to be severely damaged than structures erected on softer types of soil deposits. A discussion of the details of this entire complex subject is beyond the scope of this book.

15-6. Vibratory Pile Driving.   There are two main groups of vibratory pile drivers, the *subsonic* and the *sonic* types.   The latter are so named because their operational frequencies fall within the range of the frequencies of sound waves, the lower limit of which is approximately 40 Hz, or 2,400 cycles/min.

This means that sonic vibratory hammers operate at frequencies well in excess of the natural damped frequency f_{nd} of most sites as illustrated by Fig. 15-14.   The original diagram of Fig. 15-14 was taken from Ref. 22 and illustrates the theoretical effect of damping on the vibration amplitudes of a foundation close to its point of resonance, at which point the operational angular velocity ω equals the natural frequency $f_{n'z}$ [Eq. (15-5)], so that the ratio thereof is $\xi = \omega/f_{n'z} = 1.0$.   The resulting amplitudes of vibration A_z^* are expressed in Fig. 15-14 by the dynamic modulus of damped vibrations $\eta^* = A_z^*/A_{st}$, where A_{st} is the displacement of the foundation under an equivalent static load.   The reduced damping coefficient Δ is

$$\Delta = \frac{c}{f_{n'z}} \qquad (15\text{-}16)$$

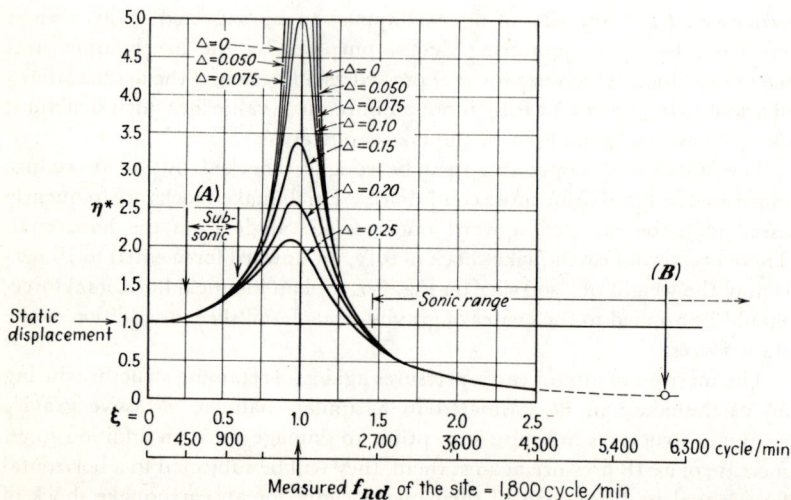

Fig. 15-14. Relationship between the dynamic modulus of damped vibrations η^* and the ratio ξ of actual to natural frequencies $\omega/f_{n'z}'$, for varying values of the reduced damping coefficient Δ. To the original diagram of Ref. 22 have been added arrows indicating operational speeds N of some vibratory drivers; (A) subsonic and (B) sonic (Bodine) for a site where $f_{nd} = 1,800$ cycles/min.

Fig. 15-15.   Freehand chalk vibrograms of an H-pile driven by a subsonic vibrator, obtained by procedure of Fig. 6-8.   (*Photo by Tschebotarioff.*)

where $c = \alpha/2m$ is the damping constant, the double value of which equals the coefficient of resistance α per unit of the foundation mass m.

To this original diagram the writer has added the scale of vibro-driver operational frequency N as a function ξ of the actually measured natural frequency $f_{nd} = 1,800$ cycles/min of the site illustrated by Fig. 15-25.

It will be seen from Fig. 15-14 that the dynamic displacement during one cycle of a sonic vibratory pile driver operating at 100 Hz = 6,000 cycles/min should be approximately one-tenth the dynamic displacement caused during one cycle of a subsonic vibratory pile driver operating at 10 Hz (=600 cycles/min). However, a large part of this apparent advantage will be offset by the fact that, in a unit of time, the sonic driver will have 10 times more load repetitions than the subsonic hammer and that the velocity of penetration into the ground of piles driven by both types of vibratory hammers appears to be approximately the same. This point will be discussed in greater detail in the next article with reference to Fig. 15-25.

The character of vibration of the pile itself is quite different for the two types of vibratory drivers. For subsonic vibrators the entire pile oscillates as one unit with the vibrator itself at amplitudes of about 1 in. Figure 15-15 shows an H-pile after driving by a subsonic vibrator. Horizontal chalk lines were first drawn on it at 1-in. (2.5-cm) intervals. Then, during driving, another freehand horizontal line was quickly drawn, producing a result similar to the one shown on Fig. 6-8, in this case a vibrogram. It can be seen that the double amplitude of vibration (peak-to-peak displacement) was close to 1 in. (2.5 cm).

By contrast, the *sonic* vibrators do not attempt to oscillate the pile as one

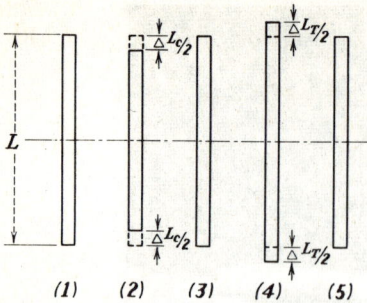

Fig. 15-16. Theoretical deformations of a pile due to a standing wave from a sonic vibrator.

unit but aim at creating a *standing wave* in it, the action of which is illustrated by Fig. 15-16.   With reference to Art. 6-3, the velocity a of a shock wave traveling along a pile is governed by the Young modulus and the unit weight of the pile material, as expressed by Eq. (6-10).   The time for a wave to travel along the length L of a pile and back is $t = 2L/a$.   Theoretically, a standing wave is created when the frequency of the successive compression waves transmitted by a sonic vibrator to the top of the pile is such that every new wave coincides with the reflected previous waves and adds its effect to theirs, thus creating a condition of resonance within the pile itself, the compression ΔL_c of which, stage 2, alternates with its extension ΔL_T, stage 4, as sketched on Fig. 15-16.

Whether this is actually achieved in practice and is as advantageous as sometimes claimed appears somewhat doubtful.   Theoretically, because of the resonance, a minimum amount of energy input is required to maintain a standing wave.   Yet sonic vibrators used in practice (Fig. 15-21) are provided with 600- to 1,000-hp engines to drive the same type of pile into the ground at approximately the same speed of penetration as was achieved at the same site by a much smaller subsonic vibrator (Fig. 15-18) with only 70-hp engines.

The writer observed both types of vibrators on the site of Fig. 15-25 drive 60-ft-long (18.3-m) H-piles in approximately 2 min through a sand deposit of medium density.   However, when the pile tip reached very dense layers characterized by an SPT value of approximately $N = 80$ blows/ft (standard penetration test; see Art. 2-4A), both types of vibrators had great difficulty in moving the pile at all to reach the prescribed elevation.   By contrast, single-acting impact hammers did so slowly but surely.   Apparently vibrations strongly decrease only the sliding and rolling components of the frictional resistance of sands (Art. 3-5A) and do not affect the component due to interlocking of the grains, which is likely to predominate in the shearing resistance of very dense sands.   On the other hand, the shocks transmitted by heavy impact hammers can crush the protruding corners of individual interlocking grains, thereby making further penetration of the pile into the ground possible.

All types of vibratory pile drivers are apt to stop pushing the pile down when it encounters some obstruction, such as a buried log, since they cannot smash through it.

The *weight of a vibratory pile driver*, whether subsonic or sonic, is of considerable importance since it supplements the effect of vibrations and helps force the pile into the ground while its shearing strength and frictional properties are reduced by the vibrations. The point is illustrated by Fig. 15-17, which gives the results of a relevant Soviet test (Ref. 160).

The practical use of subsonic vibratory pile drivers was first developed in the Soviet Union. A whole "stable" of such electrically driven vibrators was built there in the 1950s on the principles of Fig. 15-6 (see Ref. 160), many of them operating at low frequencies of 400 cycles/min. Lighter units were used for driving sheet piles and the heavier ones for driving piles of different types. The theory of operation and design of subsonic vibratory drivers was given in a book by Barkan published in 1959 in Russian and translated into French in 1963 (Ref. 23).

A French company ("P.T.C.") developed its own similar line of subsonic vibratory pile drivers and extractors which are available in the United States through the L. B. Foster Company.

Figure 15-18 shows a $2 \times 35 = 70$-hp Foster vibrator at the start of the drive of an H-pile. A remote-control hydraulic grip rigidly clamps the vibrator and the pile together. Figure 15-15 shows an H-pile after completed driving by this vibrator, and Fig. 15-23 shows it during completion of the driving.

Most Foster vibratory electric pile drivers operate at frequencies which can be varied between $N = 700$ cycles/min and $N = 1,020$ cycles/min and produce vibratory amplitudes between $\frac{1}{4}$ and 1.0 in. (6.3 and 25 mm). The lightest has $2 \times 17 = 34$ hp, weighs 5,500 lb (2,500 kg$_f$) suspended (11,100 lb = 5,000 kg$_f$ for shipping), is 57 in. (145 cm) long and 27 in. (69 cm) wide, and has an eccentric moment $W_e \times r = 650$ in.-lb (750 cm-kg$_f$), where W_e is the weight of the excenters and r their radius of rotation. The heaviest

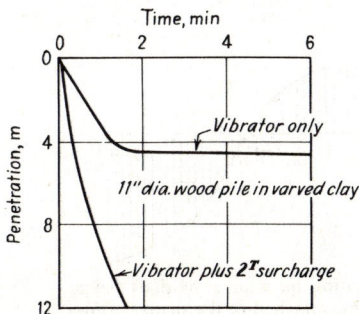

Fig. 15-17. Effect of surcharge on rate of vibrated pile penetration. (*From Ref. 160.*)

Fig. 15-18. A Foster $2 \times 35 = 70$-hp vibro-driver in action on an H-pile. (*Photo by Tschebotarioff.*)

Foster vibrator has $2 \times 75 = 150$ hp, weighs 15,500 lb (7,000 kg$_f$) suspended (28,500 lb = 13,000 kg$_f$ for shipping), is 128 in. (325 cm) long and 54 in. (137.5 cm) wide, and has an eccentric moment $W_e \times r = 3,470$ in.-lb (4,000 cm-kg$_f$).

Since the centrifugal force F_c of a rotating excentric mass is

$$F_c = mr\omega^2 = \frac{Wr}{g}\left(\frac{2\pi N}{60}\right)^2 \tag{15-17}$$

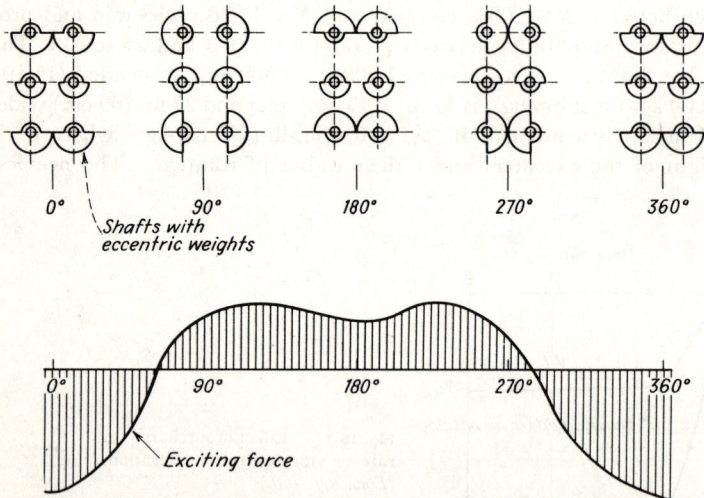

Fig. 15-19. Schematic diagram showing how exciting force of a six-shaft Soviet vibrator varies with position of the eccentric weights attached to the shafts. (*From Ref. 365.*)

Fig. 15-20.   Unit with two VP-160 Soviet vibrators for driving reinforced-concrete cylindrical-shell dolphins in Leningrad harbor.   (*Photo by Tschebotarioff, from Ref. 160.*)

this means, with reference to Fig. 15-6, that the exciting force of the Foster vibrators varies between approximately 9 tons for the lightest and 49 tons for the heaviest type at 1,000 cycles/min.   This is approximately the range of exciting forces of the original group of Soviet vibrators (Ref. 160).

The Foster vibrators are also used as extractors.   They are quite effective, since during extraction they do not have to meet the problem of high point resistance which, as explained above, is a weakness of all vibratory drivers.

One related successful Soviet development which does not seem to have been used as yet in countries of the West are heavy vibrators to drive precast reinforced-concrete cylinder shells for caissons of up to 18 ft (5.5 m) in diameter, groups of which are used to support bridge piers (see Figs. 15-19 and 15-20).   The shafts with smaller excenters rotate at twice the speed of the other shafts (Ref. 365).   The result, shown in Fig. 15-19, is that the overall downward exciting force is larger than the upward force and can reach 160 tons for one vibrator.   When two are mounted on a single unit, as shown in Fig. 15-20, the downward exciting force can reach 320 tons.   For an 18-ft-O.D. (5.5-m) cylinder shell, 10 cm (4 in.) thick, this gives an exciting downward pressure on the ground of 17.5 tons/ft².   The type of driver head shown in Fig. 15-20 permits the removal of soil from within the cylindrical shell during driving.

The method is widely used in the Soviet Union for the foundations of bridge piers on its many rivers with deep alluvial deposits.

Fig. 15-21.   A Bodine sonic vibrator, with two large power units attached to each side of it, completing the driving of an H-pile.   (*Photo by Tschebotarioff.*)

Figure 15-21 shows a Bodine sonic vibrator with two attached large power units on each side in the process of completing the driving of an H-pile at frequencies in excess of 100 cycles/sec = 6,000 cycles/min.   No details of the operating mechanism have been published.   A discussion of it is therefore not possible beyond the general review of its known performance as given in this and in the next articles.

The rate of penetration into the soil of a pile driven by a vibratory hammer can be used as an indication of its bearing capacity.

The New York City Building Code (Ref. 228, p. 119) requires that first comparison piles be driven by an impact hammer to the required design resistance.   Then "index" vibratory piles are to be driven to exactly the same depth of penetration within 4 to 6 ft (1.22 to 1.83 m) of the comparison piles and load-tested in the customary manner.

15-7. Effects of Pile Driving on Adjoining Structures.   These effects will be outlined with reference to an actual case for which the writer had the opportunity to serve as an observer and which is illustrated by Fig. 15-25. Some 3,000 H-piles, spaced approximately 3 ft (90 cm) on centers, had to be driven to support a heavy reinforced-concrete mat for a new high-rise building.   This was to be done from el. (2), the natural water level having been lowered to just below that elevation by pumping from sump pits.   The adjoining wall of an old six-story building was underpinned as shown.   The first H-piles were driven at the center of the lot by means of a heavy single-acting impact hammer.   Soil vibrations were registered by a seismograph at a distance of some 20 ft (6 m) from a driven pile and gave an energy-ratio value of approximately $ER = 0.01$.   The lowest safe value for blast effects (Art. 15-5) was $ER = 1.00$.   Thus a factor of safety of about 100 was present if the energy-ratio criteria, which were developed for blast control, were also applicable to the effects of pile driving.   That they were not was indicated by the over 1-ft (30-cm) settlement of the sand surface around the piles (see Fig. 15-22).

(A)

(B)

Fig. 15-22.   Sand surface next to 60-ft-long (18-m) H-pile P: (A) before being driven by single-acting impact hammer; (B) after driving. (*Photos by Tschebotarioff.*)

A subsonic vibrator was then tried to drive groups of H-piles against which the old six-story building could be braced. This was accomplished, the seismographs 20 ft (6 m) away recording values of approximately ER = 0.005, thus giving a factor of safety of about 200 according to the energy-ratio criteria for blasts. Nevertheless, some settlement of the sand surface did occur around the piles, although to a lesser degree than when an impact hammer was used.

Of interest was the appearance of the soil surface, which seemed to "boil" between the flanges of the H-pile, little spurts of a sand-water mixture continuously shooting up 1 in. (2.5 cm) or so into the air, presumably as a result of the densification of the sand lower down and the escape of excess water to the surface along "pipes" within the liquefied sand mass between the H-pile flanges (Fig. 15-23).

A sonic vibrator appears to have had a similar effect on the sand around the pile, as can be seen from Fig. 15-24. Direct comparisons with the subsonic vibrator, however, are not possible in this case since the latter was driven from el. (2) and the sonic vibrator from el. (1), after temporary backfilling, when no groundwater lowering was required. A seismograph 20 ft (6 m) away recorded an approximate value of ER = 0.001, thus giving a factor of safety of approximately 1,000 according to the energy-ratio criteria for blasting.

The natural frequency of the site (see Art. 15-2) appeared to be approxi-

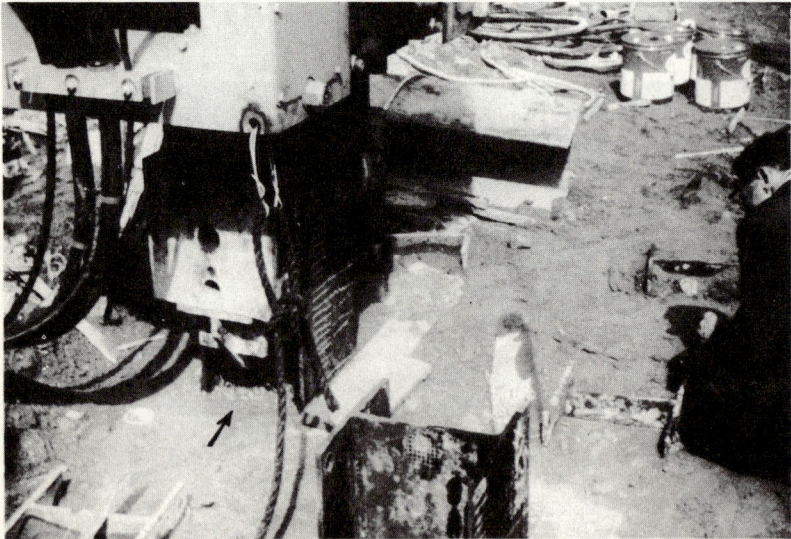

Fig. 15-23. Subsonic vibrator completing the driving of 60-ft-long (18-m) H-pile. Arrow points to "boiling" of sand-water mixture between the pile flanges. (*Photo by Tschebotarioff.*)

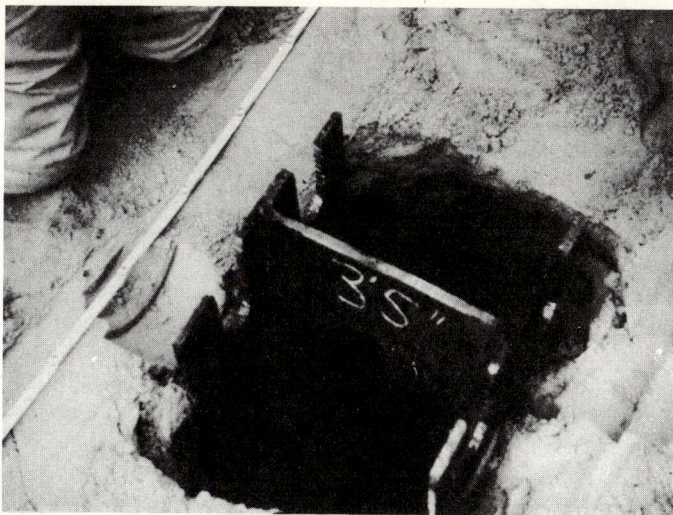

Fig. 15-24.   Sand surface around top of 60-ft-long (18-m) H-pile after driving by sonic vibrator from elevation several feet above natural water table. (*Photo by Tschebotarioff.*)

mately 1,800 cycles/min since it was at this value that the seismograph which was recording soil vibrations 20 ft (6 m) away from the pile suddenly registered a large increase of vibration amplitudes as the sonic vibrator was started up to reach 6,000 cycles/min and more.   These amplitudes immediately decreased as the 1,800 cycles/min frequency was passed.   The increase of vibration amplitudes lasted only a fraction of a second and therefore could not be harmful.

The sonic vibrator was then used to complete the installation of all H-piles.   It did this first alongside the adjoining six-story building, then proceeding away from it.   But before it could finish the job, the deformation picture shown on Fig. 15-25 developed.

The underpinning of the old wall next to the excavation for the new building was performed admirably.   By taking the precaution of leaving all the pretest jacks in place (see Fig. 6-31) over the underpinning piles and using them when needed, the wall above them (which fortunately was not weakened by windows) was maintained intact in its original position with less than 1 in. (2.5 cm) settlement.

The damage to the adjoining buildings resulted from unforeseen larger settlements well beyond the area underpinned.   These settlements were aggravated by the underdesigned spread footings of the old 16-story building. When one of them was exposed later, it was found that it transmitted 5 tons/ft^2 (5 kg$_f$/cm^2) pressure to the medium dense sand, or about twice as much as would be considered safe nowadays (see Art. 4-7).

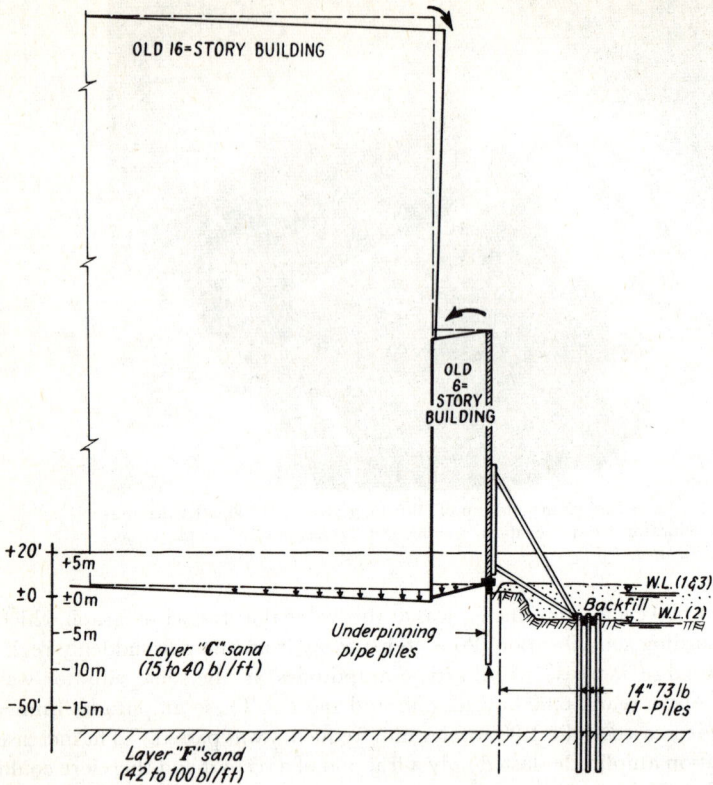

Fig. 15-25. Sketch of deformations in adjoining building induced by pile driving.

The two old buildings tilted toward each other and were so severely damaged as a result that they had to be demolished before sonic pile driving could be resumed.

The need to take into account the number of vibratory load repetitions, whether sonic or otherwise, is evident. However, there still are no precise criteria whatsoever which would permit a numerical forecast of how far the detrimental effects of vibrations induced by pile driving would have reached.

Theoretical or small-scale model studies cannot be expected to provide relevant solutions. Thus, this is an example of the type of full-scale measurements which are urgently needed to provide the civil engineering profession with requisite design tools but which can be successfully handled only by specialized research organizations (see Art. 1-10).

REVIEW PROBLEMS

15-1. Given the compressor unit 2, of the same dimensions as unit 1 shown in Fig. 15-11 except that there is no adjoining basement generator room. With reference to Fig. 15-10B: width $a = 17$ ft (5.2 m); height $h = 14$ ft (4.27 m); length $b = 19$ ft (5.8 m). The unbalanced force was estimated by mechanical engineers as $P = 8,300$ lb (3,770 kg$_f$). Operational speed of compressors $N = 300$ cycles/min. Determine the vertical amplitude of vibration A'_φ under edge point $1B$.

Answer:

$$M = 8,300 \times 14 = 116,000 \text{ ft-lb}$$

$$W_0 = 1.98 \times 10^5 \text{ lb}_f \times \sec^2 \times \text{ft} \quad [\text{Eq. (15-10)}]$$

$$\omega = \frac{2\pi N}{60} = 31.4$$

$$\omega^2 = 985$$

From Table 15-3:

$$c_\varphi = 9.0 \text{ kg}_f/\text{cm}^3 = 5.6 \times 10^5 \text{ lb/ft}^3$$

From Eq. (15-9):

$$f_n^2 = \frac{ba^3}{12} \frac{c_\varphi}{W_o} = 2.2 \times 10^{-4} \sec^{-2}$$

From Eq. (15-10):

$$A'_\varphi = \frac{8.5 \, M}{W_o(f_n \varphi^2 - \omega^2)} = 2.25 \times 10^{-4} \text{ ft}$$

$$= 27 \times 10^{-4} \text{ in.} = 0.0665 \text{ mm}$$

15-2. During the construction of some German superhighways the spacing of the transverse joints in the concrete pavement was alternated between 17 and 20 m (54.7 and 65.6 ft) for the purpose of preventing vibratory resonance in cars traveling at high speeds. The natural frequency of a car on rubber tires at normal air pressure varies between 2 and 3 cycles/sec. At what speed would a car with $f = 2$ cycles/sec have to travel in order to vibrate in resonance with bumps produced at every transverse joint uniformly spaced at $L = 19$ m?

Answer. $L = 19/0.305 = 62$ ft. The period of vibration of the car is $T = 1/f = \frac{1}{2} = 0.5$ sec. To be in resonance, the car would have to travel at a speed

$$v = \frac{L}{T} = \frac{62.5}{0.5} = 125 \text{ft/sec} = 125 \frac{60 \times 60}{5,280} = 85 \text{ mph}$$

$$= 85 \times \tfrac{8}{5} = 135 \text{ km/hr}$$

RECOMMENDED FOR FURTHER STUDY

Barkan, Ref. 22.
Richart, Hall, and Woods, Ref. 265.

REFERENCES

Some Abbreviations

AASHO American Association of State Highway Officials, Washington, D.C.

Am. Roadbuilders' Assoc. Tech. Bull. American Roadbuilders' Association Technical Bulletin, Washington, D.C.

CAA Tech. Dev. Civil Aeronautics Administration Technical Development, Indianapolis, Indiana.

Can. Geotech. J. Canadian Geotechnical Journal, published by the National Research Council, Ottawa.

Civil Eng. Civil Engineering, published by ASCE, New York.

Contrib. Soil Mech. Boston Soc. Civ. Eng. Contributions to Soil Mechanics of the Boston Society of Civil Engineers.

Eng. News. Rec. Engineering News-Record, published by McGraw-Hill, New York

Highway Res. Rec. Highway Research Record published by the Highway Research Board, Washington, D.C.

Highway Res. Board Spec. Rep. Highway Research Board Special Report, Washington, D.C.

J. Boston Soc. Civ. Eng. Journal of the Boston Society of Civil Engineers.

J. Inst. Civ. Eng. Journal of the Institution of Civil Engineers, London.

J. Soil Mech. Found. Div., ASCE Journal of the Soil Mechanics and Foundations Division, American Society of Civil Engineers, New York.

J. West. Soc. Eng. Journal of the Western Society of Engineers, Chicago.

Proc. ASCE Proceedings of the American Society of Civil Engineers, New York.

Proc. ASTM Proceedings of the American Society for Testing and Materials, Philadelphia.

Proc. Highway Res. Board	Proceedings of the Highway Research Board, Washington, D.C.
Proc. ASCE Spec. Conf. Perf. Earth & Earth Supp. Struct. Purdue Univ., 1972	Proceedings of the Specialty Conference on the Performance of Earth and of Earth Supported Structures, Soil Mechanics and Foundations Division, American Society of Civil Engineers, 1972, at Purdue University.
Proc. 5th Eur. Conf. Found. Eng., Madrid, 1972	Proceedings of the 5th European Conference on Soil Mechanics and Foundation Engineering, 1972, Madrid.
Proc. 1st Int. Conf. Soil Mech. Found. Eng., Cambridge, Mass., 1936	Proceedings of the International Conference on Soil Mechanics and Foundation Engineering, 1936, Harvard University, Cambridge, Mass.
Proc. 2nd Int. Conf. Soil Mech. Found. Eng., Rotterdam, 1948	Proceedings of the 2nd International Conference on Soil Mechanics and Foundation Engineering, 1948, Rotterdam.
Proc. 3d Int. Conf. Soil Mech. Found. Eng., Zurich, 1953	Proceedings of the 3rd International Conference on Soil Mechanics and Foundation Engineering, 1953, Zurich.
Proc. 4th Int. Conf. Soil Mech. Found. Eng., London, 1957	Proceedings of the 4th International Conference on Soil Mechanics and Foundation Engineering, 1957, London.
Proc. 5th Int. Conf. Soil Mech. Found. Eng., Paris, 1961	Proceedings of the 5th International Conference on Soil Mechanics and Foundation Engineering, 1961, Paris.
Proc. 6th Int. Conf. Soil Mech. Found. Eng., Montreal, 1965	Proceedings of the 6th International Conference on Soil Mechanics and Foundation Engineering, 1965, Montreal.
Proc. 7th Int. Conf. Soil Mech. Found. Eng., Mexico City, 1969	Proceedings of the 7th International Conference on Soil Mechanics and Foundation Engineering, Mexico City, 1969.
Proc. 3rd PanAm. Conf. Soil Mech. Found. Eng., Caracas, 1967	Proceedings of the Third PanAmerican Conference on Soil Mechanics and Foundation Engineering, 1967, Caracas.
Proc. 4th PanAm Conf. Soil Mech. Found. Eng., San Juan, 1971	Proceedings of the Fourth Pan-American Conference on Soil Mechanics and Foundation Engineering, 1971, San Juan, Puerto Rico.
Proc. Conf. Des. Install. Pile Found. Cell. Struct., Lehigh Univ., 1970	Proceedings of The Conference on Design and Installation of Pile Foundations and Cellular Structures, Lehigh University, 1970.
Struct. Eng.	The Structural Engineer, published by the Institution of Structural Engineers, London.
Trans. ASCE	Transactions of the American Society of Civil Engineers, New York.
U.S. Bur. Reclam.	United States Bureau of Reclamation, Denver, Colorado.
U.S. Eng. Dept.	United States Engineer Department, Department of the Army, Washington, D.C.
U.S. Waterw. Exp. Stn., Vicksburg, Miss.	United States Waterways Experimental Station, Vicksburg, Mississippi.

1. Abu-Wafa, Taher, and Aziz Hanna Labib: Aswan High Dam: Rockfill Built under Water, *Civ. Eng.*, August 1971, pp. 64–68.
2. Adams, J. I., and T. W. Klym: A Study of Anchorages for Transmission Tower Foundations, *Can. Geotech. J.*, vol. 9, no. 1 (February 1972).

3. Agatz, A., and E. Schultze: *Der Kampf des Ingenieurs gegen Erde und Wasser im Grundbau*, Springer, Berlin, 1936.

4. Agatz, A., and E. Lackner: Das Neue Trockendock der Nordseewerke Emden, *Hansa*, Hamburg, no. 50/51, 1954.

5. American Wood Preservers' Association: *Manual of Recommended Practice*, Washington. D.C. (revised periodically).

6. Ammann, O. H.: The Hell-Gate Bridge and Approaches of the New York Connecting Railroad over the East River in New York City, *Trans. ASCE*, 1918, pp. 852–1039.

7. Andrew, Charles E.: The Lake Washington Pontoon Bridge, *Civ. Eng.*, December 1939, pp. 703–706.

8. Andrews, Walter C., and J. H. A. Crockett: Large Hammers and Their Foundations, *Struct. Eng.*, October 1945, pp. 453–492.

9. Applegate, L. M.: *Cathodic Protection*, McGraw-Hill, New York, 1960.

10. D'Appolonia, David J., Elio D'Appolonia, and Richard F. Brissette: Settlement of Spread Footings on Sand, *J. Soil. Mech. Found. Div., ASCE*, May 1968.

11. D'Appolonia, D. J., R. V. Whitman, and E. D'Appolonia: Sand Compaction with Vibratory Rollers, *J. Soil Mech. Found. Div., ASCE*, SM1, January 1969, pp. 263–283.

12. Armento, W. J.: Performance of Bracing Systems in Subway Excavation, *Proc. Spec. Conf. Perf. Earth & Earth Supp. Struct., Purdue Univ., 1972.*

13. Armour Research Foundation: Evaluation of Steel H-beam Piling, *Final Report to U.S. Steel Corporation*, December 1954, Chicago, 186 pp.

13a. ASCE Committee on the Bearing Value of Pile Foundations: Pile-driving Formulas— Progress Report, *Proc. ASCE*, May 1941, pp. 853–866.

14. *ASCE Conference on Placement and Improvement of Soil to Support Structures, Cambridge, Mass., 1968*, 440 pp.

15. ASCE preprint volume of state-of-the-art papers presented at *1970 Specialty Conference on Lateral Stresses in the Ground and Design of Earth Retaining Structures, Cornell University*, 328 pp.

16. ASCE Research Committee: *Report on Research Needs in Soil Mechanics and Foundation Engineering*, undated, prepared in 1964–1966.

16a. *ASCE Specialty Conference on the Performance of Earth and Earth Supported Structures*, Purdue University, June 1972; Proceedings, 3 vol.; vol. 1 in 2 parts (1535 pp.); vol. 2 (154 pp.); Vol. 3 (in press)

17. ASTM: *Metric Practice Guide: A Guide to the Use of SI, the International System of Units*, ASTM Des. E-380-70, Philadelphia.

18. ASTM; *Annual Book of Standards;* pt. 11 (1971) includes the Standards of Committee D-18 on Soil and Rock for Engineering Purposes, Philadelphia.

19. Australian Commonwealth Scientific and Industrial Research Organization: *Moisture Equilibria and Moisture Changes beneath Covered Areas: A Symposium*, Butterworths, London, 1965, 278 pp.

20. Babitskaya, S. S., and V. D. Posdniakova: Concerning Soil Swelling Criteria (in Russian), *Proc. 3d All-Union Conf. Soil Mech. Found. Eng. Kiev, 1971*, pp. 152–154.

21. Baguelin, F., G. Goulet, and J. Jezequel: Étude expérimentale d'un pieu sollicité horizontalement, *Proc. 5th Eur. Conf. Soil Mech. Found. Eng., Madrid, 1972*, pp. 317–324.

22. Barkan, Dominik D.: *Dynamics of Bases and Foundations* (trans. from Russian), McGraw-Hill, New York, 1962, 433 pp.

23. Barkan, Dominik D.: *Méthodes de vibration dans la construction* (Vibration Methods in Construction Work), French trans. from Russian, Dunod, Paris, 1962, 302 pp.

24. Barron, Reginald A.: Consolidation of Fine-grained Soils by Drain Wells, *Trans. ASCE*, vol. 113, pp. 718–754 (1948).

25. Bazaraa, A. R. S.: *Use of Standard Penetration Test for Estimating Settlements of Shallow Foundations on Sand*, Ph.D. thesis, University of Illinois, 1967.

26. Bertram, G. E.: An Experimental Investigation of Protective Filters, *Harv. Univ. Grad. Sch. Eng. Pub. 267, Soil Mech. Ser. 7*, 1940.

27. Bertram, G. E.: Soil Tests for Military Construction, *Am. Roadbuilders' Assoc. Tech. Bull.* 107, 1946, 95 pp.

28. Beskow, Gunnar: *Soil Freezing and Frost Heaving* (trans. from Swedish by J. O. Osterberg), Northwestern University, Evanston, Ill., 1947, 147 pp.

29. Binger, Wilson V., and Thomas F. Thompson: Excavation Slopes: Panama Canal, *Trans. ASCE*, 1949, pp. 734–755.

29a. Bison Instruments Inc.: *Signal Enhancement Instruction Manual*, Seismograph Model 1570B, 3401 48th Ave. N. Minneapolis, Minn. 55429.

30. Bjerrum, L.: Norwegian Experiences with Steel Piles to Rock, *Geotechnique*, vol. 7, pp. 73–96 (1957).

31. Bjerrum, L., and K. H. Andersen: In-situ Measurement of Lateral Pressures in Clay, *Proc. 5th Eur. Conf. Soil Mech. Found. Eng. Madrid, 1972*, pp. 11–20.

31a. Bjerrum, L., C. J. F. Clausen, and J. M. Duncan: Earth Pressures on Flexible Structures, state-of-the art report, *5th Eur. Conf. Soil Mech. Found. Eng., Madrid, 1972*.

32. Blessey, Walter E.: Pile Foundation Loads and Deformations Mississippi River Deltaic Plain, *Proc. Conf. Des. Install. Pile Found. Cell. Struct., Lehigh Univ., 1970*, pp. 1–26.

33. Blum, H.: *Einspannungsverhältnisse bei Bohlwerken*, Ernst, Berlin, 1931.

34. *Bodenmechanik und neuzeitlicher Strassenbau*, symposium by 24 authors, Volk und Reich, Berlin, 1936, 108 pp.

35. Boussinesq, J.: *Applications des potentiels a l'étude de l'équilibre et du mouvement des solides élastiques*, Gauthier-Villars, Paris, 1885.

36. Bouyoucos, G. J.: *Mich. State Coll. Agric. Eng. Expt. Stn. Tech. Bull.* 22, 1915.

37. Bowles, Joseph E.: *Foundation Design and Analysis*, McGraw-Hill, New York, 1968, 657 pp.

38. Breth, H., and H. R. Wandschek: The Influence of Foundation Weights upon Earth Pressure Acting on Flexible Strutted Walls, *Proc. 5th Eur. Conf. Soil Mech. Found. Eng. Madrid, 1972*, pp. 251–258.

39. Briske, Rudolf, and Eugen Pirlet: Messungen über die Beanspruchung des Baugrubenverbaues der Kölner U-Bahn, *Bautechnik*, no. 9 (September 1968).

40. Brown, Philip P.: *A Critical Study of Existing Lateral Earth Pressure Theories, Including the Design of a Model Flexible Anchored Bulkhead for the Investigation of These Theories*, master's thesis, Princeton University, January, 1948.

41. Brown, Philip P.: Personal communication, July 2, 1971.

42. Bruggen, J. P. van: De Maastunnel te Rotterdam, *De Ingenieur*, 1941.

43. Brumund, William F., and Gerald A. Leonards: Subsidence of Sand due to Surface Vibration, *J. Soil Mech. Found. Div., ASCE*, SM1, January 1972, pp. 27–42.

44. Buchholz: Erdwiderstand auf Ankerplatten, *Jahrb. Hafenbautech. Ges.*, vol. 12 (1930/1931).

45. Building Research Advisory Board: *Proc. Permafrost Int. Conf., Nov. 1963, Natl. Acad. Sci., Publ.* 1287.

46. Caquot, Albert, and J. Kérisel: *Tables for the Calculation of Passive Pressure, Active Pressure and Bearing Capacity of Foundations* (trans. from French by Maurice A. Bec; rev. trans. by Ministry of Works, Chief Scientific Advisers' Division, London), Gauthier-Villars, Paris, 1948.

47. Carillo, Nabor: *The Subsidence of Mexico City and Texcoco Project* (in Spanish with parallel English translation; memorial volume), Mexico City, 1969, 328 pp.

48. Casagrande, Arthur: Characteristics of Cohesionless Soils Affecting the Stability of Slopes and Earth Fills, *Contrib. Soil Mech. Boston Soc. Civ. Eng.*, 1940, pp. 257–276 (also *J. Boston Soc. Civ. Eng.*, January 1936).

49. Casagrande, Arthur: Classification and Identification of Soils, *Trans. ASCE*, 1948, pp. 901–992.

50. Casagrande, Leo: Näherungsverfahren zur Ermittlung der Sickerung in geschütteten Dämmen auf undurchlässiger Sohle, *Bautechnik*, no. 15 (1934).

51. Casagrande, Leo: *The Application of Electro-osmosis to Practical Problems in Foundations and Earthworks*, Department of Scientific and Industrial Research, London, 1947, 16 pp.

52. Casagrande, Leo: Electro-osmosis in Soils, *Geotechnique*, London, vol. 1, no. 3, pp. 159–177 (June 1949).

53. Castro, Gonzalo: The Liquefaction of Sand, *Harv. Soil Mech. Ser.* 81, 1969, 112 pp.

54. CE Prof. Quits Teaching after 27 years: Protests Trends, *Eng. News Rec.*, July 30, 1964.

55. CE Education Needs Attention, letters by Rossiter L. White and Ross M. Lanius, Jr, *Eng. News. Rec.*, Sept. 3, 1964, p. 7.

56. Chadwick, W. L., and R. Howard Annin: Subsidence in Long Beach Harbor Area Requires Special Engineeering Construction, *Civ. Eng.*, June 1950, pp. 17–22.

57. Chellis, R. D.: Pile Foundations, chap. 7, pp. 633–768, in G. A. Leonard (ed.), *Foundation Engineering*, McGraw-Hill, New York. 1962.

58. Christie, I. F.: A Re-appraisal of Merchant's Contribution to the Theory of Consolidation, *Geotechnique*, vol. 14, pp. 309–320 (1964).

59. Clisby, M. Marrett, and Robert M. Mattox: *A Comparison of Single to Multiple Under Reamed Bored Piles*, paper presented to Highway Research Board, January 1971.

60. Clough, G. W., and J. M. Duncan: Finite Element Analyses of Port Allen and Old River Locks, *U.S. Waterw. Exp. Sta. Vicksburg, Miss., Contract Rept. S-69-6*, September 1969.

61. Colburn, R. T.: Discussion of Ref. 342, *Trans. ASCE*, 1945, pp. 1135–1145.

62. Committee on the Cause of the Failure of the South Fork Dam: Report, *Trans. ASCE*, vol. 24, pp. 431–460 (1891).

63. Converse, F. J.: *The Practical Use of Shear Test Data*, paper presented to 36th Annual Convention American Roadbuilders' Association, San Francisco, 1939.

64. Cooling, L. E., and W. H. Ward: Damage to Cold Stores Due to Heaving, *Proc. Inst. Refrig.*, London, 1944, pp. 31–47.

65. Cooling, L. E.: Development and Scope of Soil Mechanics, pp. 1–30, in *The Principles and Applications of Soil Mechanics*, Institute of Civil Engineers, London, 1944.

66. Costa Nunes, A. J. Da.: Discussion, *Proc. 6th Int. Conf. Soil Mech. Found. Eng.*, *Montreal, 1965*, vol. 3, pp. 526–527.

67. Coulomb, Charles Augustin: Essai sur une application des règles de maximis et minimis à quelques problèmes de statique relatifs à l'architecture, *Mem. Div. Savants, Acad. Sci.*, Paris, vol. 7 (1776).

68. Cox, Dennis: *Pilot Model Tests of Surface Earth Anchors*, master's thesis, Princeton University, 1955.

69. Crandell, F. J.: Ground Vibration Due to Blasting and Its Effect upon Structures, *J. Boston Soc. Civ. Eng.*, April 1949 (summary in *Eng. News. Rec.*, May 4, 1950).

70. Crockett, J. H. A., and R. E. R. Hammond: Reduction of Ground Vibrations into Structures, *Inst. Civ. Eng. Struct. Pap.* 18, London, 1947.

71. Crockett, J. H. A., and R. E. R. Hammond: The Dynamic Principles of Machine Foundations and Ground, *Inst. Mech. Eng.*, London, 1949.

72. Cuevas, Jose A., Lazarus White, and Karl Terzaghi: Discussion on the Movements within Foundation Pits during Excavation, *Proc. 1st Int. Conf. Soil Mech. Found. Eng.*, *Cambridge, Mass, 1936*, vol. 3, pp. 228–331.

73. Culp, M. M.: personal communications, 1971.

74. Cummings, A. E.: Dynamic Pile Driving Formulas, *Contrib. Soil Mech., Boston Soc. Civ. Eng.*, 1940 (also *J. Boston Soc. Civ. Eng.*, January 1940).

75. Cummings, E. M.: Cellular Cofferdams and Docks, *J. Waterw. Harbors Div.*, ASCE (WW3), *Pap.* 1366, September 1957.

76. Cunningham, J. A., Slurry Wall Performance, *Proc. ASCE Spec. Conf. Perf. Earth & Earth Supp. Struct. Purdue Univ.*, *1972*.

77. Cusens, A. R.: Civil Engineering: The University and the Profession, *Engineer*, London, February 18, 1966.

78. Dastidar, A. G.: *Pilot Tests to Determine the Effect of Piles in Resisting Shear Failures in Clay*, report on research performed at Princton University, March 1956.

79. Davis, Raymond E., and Alfred R. Bacher: California's Culvert Research Program: Description, Current Status and Observed Peripheral Pressures, *Highway Res. Rec.* 249, pp. 14–23, 1968.

80. Day, Walter C.: The Corps of Engineers Nuclear Construction Research Activities, *Highway Res. Rec.* 339, pp. 1–18, 1970.

81. De Beer, E., and M. Wallays: Application des drains Kjellman-Franki et de l'électroosmose, *La Technique des Travaux*, Mars-Avril 1965.

82. De Beer, E. E., and M. Wallays: Stabilization of a Slope in Schists by Means of Bored Piles Reinforced with Steel Beams, *Proc. 2d Congr. Rock Mech. Yugoslavia, 1970*, Pap. 7–13, vol. 3, pp. 361–369.

83. De Beer, E. E., and M. Wallays: Forces Induced in Piles by Unsymmetrical Surcharges on the Soil around the Piles, *Proc. 5th Eur. Conf. Soil Mech. Found. Eng., Madrid, 1972*, pp. 325–332.

84. Deen, Robert C.: Performance of a Reinforced Concrete Pipe Culvert under Rock Embankment, *Highway Res. Rec.* 262, pp. 14–28, 1969 (with discussion by M. G. Spangler).

85. Deere, D. U., and F. R. Patton: Slope Stability in Residual Soils (state-of-the-art paper), *Proc. PanAm. Conf. Soil Mech. Found. Eng., San Juan, P.R., June 1971*, vol. 1, pp. 87–170; published by ASCE, New York. (See also six related papers in vol. 2, pp. 105–178.)

86. Donnelly, C. William: River Yields to Below-sea-level Dock Construction, *Constr. Methods Equip.*, New York, March 1971.

87. Donovan, Neville C.: *The Dowel Action of Piles*, master's thesis, Princeton University, May 1956.

88. Dore, Stanley M.: Foundations and Embankments of Quabbin Dams, *Proc. 1st Int. Conf. Soil Mech. Found. Eng., Cambridge, Mass, 1936*, vol. 2, pp. 300–307.

88a. Drouin, Gaston, and Malcolm W. Paul; *Some Soil Reaction Considerations in the Design of Waterfront Structures*. Master's Thesis, Princeton University, 1958.

89. Duke, C. Martin: Field Study of a Sheet Pile Bulkhead, *Trans. ASCE*, 1953, pp. 1131–1156.

90. Duncan, James M., and G. Wayne Clough: Finite Element Analyses of Port Allen Lock, *J. Soil Mech. Found. Div. ASCE*, SM8, August 1971, pp. 1053–1068.

91. EAU: *Recommendations of the Committee for Waterfront Structures of the Society for Harbor Engineering and the German Society for Soil Mechanics and Foundation Engineering* [English trans. of 4th German ed. (1970)], Ernst, Berlin, 1971.

92. Ehlers, H.: *Beitrag zur statischen Berechnung von Spundwänden*, Hamburg, 1910.

93. Ehrenberg, J.: Das Ausfliessen einer Sandkippe in einer Braunkohlengrube, *Bautechnik*, no. 19 (1933).

94. Eide, Ove, and Ivar J. Johannessen: Measurements of Strut Loads in the Excavation for Oslo Technical School, *Proc. Bruss. Conf. Earth Pressure Probl., 1958*, vol. 2, pp. 82–98.

95. Engelund, Auker: A Special Foundation Method for Bridge Piers Adopted in Danish Fjords, *Proc. 1st Int. Conf. Soil Mech. Found. Eng., Cambridge, Mass., 1936*, vol. 1, pp. 291–294.

96. *The Evening News*, Newburgh, N.Y., Aug. 28, 1961.

97. Fellenius, W.: *Erdstatische Berechnungen*, Ernst, Berlin, 1927; 4th ed., 1948.

98. Forchheimer, Philip: Zur Grundwasserbewegung nach isothermischen Kurvenscharen, *Sitzungsber. K-K. Akad. der Wissenschaft.*, Vienna, vol. 126, no. 4, pp. 409–440 (1917).

99. Forehand, P. W., and L. J. Reese, Jr.: Prediction of Pile Capacity by the Wave Equation, *J. Soil Mech. Found. Div., ASCE*, SM2, March 1964, pp. 1–25.

100. Francis, A. J.: Analysis of Pile Groups with Flexural Resistance, *J. Soil Mech. Found. Div., ASCE*, May and November 1964, July 1965.

101. Franzius, O.: Versuche mit passivem Druck, *Bauingenieur*, Berlin, 1924, pp. 314–320.

102. Freyssinet, E.: *Une Révolution dans les techniques du beton*, Paris, 1939.

103. Frolov, A. F.: Nature of Loess Soil Collapse and Its Influence on the Value of Relative Collapsibility (in Russian), *Proc. 3d All-Union Conf. Soil Mech. Found. Eng., Kiev, 1971*, pp. 104–107.

104. Garrison Dam: A Symposium (Harris H. Burke, Investigation and Construction; S. Kenneth Lane, Evaluation of Test Results), *Trans. ASCE*, vol. 125, *Pap.* 3022 (1960) (also *J. Soil Mech. Found. Div. ASCE*, SM4, November 1957).

105. Gebhard, J. C.: Cave-ins of Sandy Backfills, *Proc. ASCE*, January 1948, pp. 84–93; also *Trans. ASCE*, 1949, pp. 490–499.

106. Gibbs, H. J., and W. G. Holtz: Research on Determining the Density of Sands by Spoon Penetration Testing, *Proc. 4th Int. Conf. Soil Mech. Found. Eng., London, 1957*, vol. 1, pp. 35–39.

107. Gilboy, Glennon: The Scientific Method in Earthwork, *Civ. Eng.*, December 1937, pp. 822–830.

108. Gill, T. C. (Senior Engineer, Moretrench Corporation): personal communication, Oct. 5, 1971.

109. Glanville, W. H., G. Grime, E. N. Fox, and W. W. Davies: An Investigation of the Stresses in Reinforced Concrete Piles during Driving, *Br. Build. Res. Board Tech. Pap.* 20, 1938.

109a. Goble, George G., Frederick K. Walker, and Frank Rausche: Pile Bearing Capacity—Prediction vs. Performance, *Proc. ASCE Spec. Conf. Perf. Earth & Earth Supp. Struct. Purdue Univ. 1972*, vol. 1, pp. 1243–1258.

110. Golder, Hugh Q.: Measurement of Pressure in Timbering of a Trench in Clay, *Proc. Int. Conf. Soil Mech. Found. Eng., Rotterdam, 1948*, vol. 2, pp. 76–81.

111. Golder, Hugh Q., James P. Gould, Gregory P. Tschebotarioff, and Stanley D. Wilson: Predicted Performance of Braced Excavation, *J. Soil Mech. Found. Div. ASCE*, SM3, May 1970, pp. 801–816.

112. GOSSTROY U.S.S.R. (State Committee on Construction in U.S.S.R.): *Construction Regulations*, SNiP-II-B.1-62 (in Russian), chap. 1, Bases and Foundations of Buildings and Structures: Design Norms, Moscow, 1964.

113. GOSSTROY U.S.S.R. (State Committee on Construction in U.S.S.R.): *Construction Regulations.*, SNiP-II-B.2-62 (in Russian), Chap. 2, Bases and Foundations of Buildings and Structures on Collapsible Soils: Design Norms, Moscow, 1964.

114. Groote, J. F.: The New Harbors of Aruba and Curaçao, *Dock Harbour Auth.*, June 1950. pp. 39–45.

115. Grouting, Symposium on: *J. Soil Mech. Found. Div., ASCE*, SM2, April 1961, pp. 1–149.

116. *Grouts and Drilling Muds in Engineering Practice, Symposium, 1963*, Butterworths, London, 236 pp.

117. *Grundbau-Taschenbuch*, vol. I, Ernst, Berlin, 1955.

118. Hall, Charles E.: Compacting a Dam Foundation by Blasting, *J. Soil Mech. Found. Div., ASCE*, SM3, June 1962, pp. 33–52.

119. Hanna, Thomas H.: The Bending of Long H-section Piles, *Can. Geotech. J.*, vol. 5, no. 3.

120. Hanna, W. S., Settlement Studies in Egypt, *Geotechnique*, London, vol. 3, no. 1, pp. 33–45 (June 1950).

121. Hanna, W. S., and Gregory Tschebotarioff: Settlement Observations of Buildings in Egypt, *Proc. 1st Int. Conf. Soil Mech. Found. Eng., Cambridge, Mass., 1936*, vol. 1, pp. 71–77.

122. Hansen, J. Brinch: *Earth Pressure Calculations*, Danish Geotechnical Press, Copenhagen, 1953.

123. Hansen, J. Brinch: The Stabilizing Effect of Piles in Clay, *CN-POST*, no. 3, Christiani & Nielsen, Copenhagen, n.d.

124. Hansen, J. Brinch: discussion, *Proc. Bruss. Conf. Earth Pressure Probl., 1958*, vol. 3, pp. 270–271.

125. Harroun, D. T.: Stability of Cohesive Earth Masses in Vertical Embankments, *Proc. Highway Res. Board*, 1940, pp. 751–756.

126. Heller, Robert A.: *Earth Resistance Computations (Effect of Wall Friction and Adhesion)*, master's thesis, Princeton University, 1954.

127. Hertwig, A., G. Fruh, and H. Lorenz: Determination by Means of Forced Vibrations of Soil Properties of Particular Importance for Construction Work (in German), *DEGEBO Pub.* 1, Berlin, 1933.

128. Heydenrych, Ron: The Carlton Center, *Arup J.* (published by Ove Arup & Partners, 13 Fitzroy St., London), vol. 5, no. 3 (September 1970).

129. Highway Research Board: Proceedings of International Conference on Effects of Temperature and Heat on Engineering Behavior of Soils, *Spec. Rep.* 103, Washington, D.C., 1969, 300 pp.

130. Highway Research Board: Pile Foundations, 12 reports, *Highway Res. Rec.* 333, Washington, D.C., 1970, 129 pp.

131. Hiley, A.: Pile Driving Calculations with Notes on Driving Forces and Ground Resistance, *Struct. Eng.*, vol. 3, pp. 246–259, 278–288 (1930).

132. Hinckley, H. V.: *Lessons from the Austin Dam Failures*, Oklahoma Engineering Society 1911. (On file at United Engineering Societies Library, New York.)

133. Hiriart, Fernando, and Marsal, Raul J.: The Subsidence of Mexico City, *Nabor Carillo Memorial Volume*, pp. 109–147, Mexico City, 1969.

134. Holtz, W. G., and H. J. Gibbs: Discussion of Ref. 10, *J. Soil Mech. Found. Div.*, *ASCE*, SM3, May 1969, pp. 900–905.

135. Holtz, Wesley G.: personal communication, October 1971.

136. Housel, W. S.: Earth Pressure on Tunnels, *Trans. ASCE*, 1943, pp. 1037–1058.

137. Housel, William S.: Checking up on Vertical Sand Drains (with discussion by L. A. Palmer), *Highway Res. Board Bull. 90*, Washington, D.C., 1954.

138. Hutchinson, J. N.: Settlements in Soft Clay around a Pumped Excavation in Oslo, *Proc. Eur. Conf. Soil Mech. Found. Eng., Wiesbaden, 1964* (also *Norw. Geotech. Inst., Publ. 58*, pp. 1–8, 1964).

139. Hvorslev, M. Juul.: *Subsurface Exploration and Sampling of Soils*, report on the joint research project of the ASCE; the Engineering Foundation, Harvard University; and the U.S. Waterways Experiment Station, Engineering Foundation, New York, 1949, 521 pp.

140. International Society for Soil Mechanics and Foundation Engineering: *Technical Terms, Symbols and Definitions* (in English, French, German, Swedish, Portuguese, Spanish, Italian, and Russian) 3d ed., Zurich, 1967, 183 pp.

141. Iowa Road Carved through Loess Bluffs, *Eng. News. Rec.*, April 29, 1940, pp. 277–279.

142. Ireland. H. O., O. Moretto, and M. Vargas: The Dynamic Penetration Test: A Standard That Is Not Standardized, *Geotechnique*, vol. 20, no. 2, pp. 185–192 (1970); discussions in vol. 20, no. 4, pp. 452–456 (1970); vol. 21, no. 2, p. 183 (1971).

143. Ishihara, Kenji, and Yoshichika Yuasa: Earth Pressure Measurements in Subway Construction, *Proc. 2d Asian Reg. Conf. Soil Mech. Found. Eng. Tokyo, 1963*, pp. 337–343.

144. Jaky, J.: The Coefficient of Earth Pressure at Rest, *J. Soc. Hung. Archit. Eng.*, Budapest, 1944, pp. 355–358.

145. Jamieson, J. A.: Grain Pressures in Deep Bins, *Eng. News.*, New York, 1904, pp. 236–243.

146. Jennings, J. E.: Foundations for Buildings in the Orange Free State Goldfields, *J. S. Afr. Inst. Eng.*, Pretoria, November 1950, March 1951.

147. Jennings, J. E., and J. E. Kerrich: The Heaving of Buildings and the Associated Economic Consequences with Particular Reference to the Orange Free State Goldfields. *Civ. Eng. S. Afr.*, vol. 4, no. 11, pp. 221–248 (November 1962), and vol. 5, no. 5, pp. 122–135 (May 1963).

148. Jennings, J. E.: personal communication, 1966.

148a. Johnson, A. W., and J. R. Sallberg: Factors That Influence Field Compaction of Soils, *Highway Res. Board Bull. 272*, 1960.

149. Johnson, Edmund G.: *The Effects of Restraining Boundaries on the Passive Resistance of Sand*, master's thesis, Princeton University, 1953.

150. Johnson, Sidney M.: Determining the Capacity of Bent Piles, *J. Soil. Mech. Found. Div.*, ASCE, SM6, vol. 88 (December 1962).

151. Johnson, Sidney M., and Thomas C. Kavanagh: *The Design of Foundations for Buildings*, McGraw-Hill, New York, 1968, 393 pp.

152. Johnson, Stanley J.: Precompression for Improving Foundation Soils, *J. Soil Mech. Found. Div.*, ASCE, SM1, January 1970, pp. 111–144.

153. Johnson, Stanley J.: Foundation Precompression with Vertical Sand Drains, *J. Soil Mech. Found. Div.*, ASCE, SM1, January 1970, pp. 145–175.

154. Jurgenson, Leo: The Application of Theories of Elasticity and Plasticity to Foundation Problems, *Contrib. Soil Mech. Boston Soc. Civ. Eng.*, 1940, pp. 148–183 (also *J. Boston Soc. Civ. Eng.*, July 1934).

155. Kapp, Martin S.: Discussion, Div. 5, *Proc. 4th Int. Conf. Soil Mech. Found. Eng., London, 1957*, vol. 3, p. 232.

156. Kapp, Martin S.: Slurry Trench Construction for Basement Wall of World Trade Center, *Civ. Eng.*, April 1969.

157. Kennedy, John F.: personal communications, 1970.

158. Kérisel, J.: General Report, Earth Pressure on Structures and Tunnels, *Proc. 4th Int. Conf. Soil Mech. Found. Eng., London, 1957*, vol. 2, pp. 457–462.

159. Kérisel, J., et al.: Mesures de poussée et de butée faites avec 42 paires de butons asservis, *Proc. 5th Eur. Conf. Soil Mech. Found. Eng., Madrid, 1972* (the complete report in French can be obtained from SEMALY, Grand Palais de la Foire, Quai Achille Lignon, 69, Lyon 6, France).

160. Kersten, Miles S., Gerald A. Leonards, T. William Lambe, John Lowe III, H. Bolton Seed, Gregory P. Tschebotarioff, and Willard J. Turnbull: Soil and Foundation Engineering in the Union of Soviet Socialist Republics, *Highway Res. Board Spec. Rep.* 60, Washington, D.C., 1960, 188 pp.

161. Kezdi, A.: Grundlagen einer allgemeiner Bodenphysik, *Ver. Dtsch. Ing. Z.*, 1966, no. 5.

162. Killer, J.: Fondations économiques des pylones de lignes aeriennes, *Proc. 3d Int. Conf. Soil Mech. Found. Eng., Zurich, 1953*, vol. 3, pp. 265–276.

163. Kim, J. B., R. J. Brungraber, and C. H. Kindig: Lateral Load Tests on Full-scale Pile Groups in Cohesive Soils, *Proc. ASCE Spec. Conf. Perf. Earth & Earth Supp. Struct., Purdue Univ., 1972.*

164. Kimball, William P.: Soil Mechanics in Foundation Engineering, *J. Eng. Inst. Can.*, March 1939.

165. King, Howard L.: Subaqueous Tunnel Construction, *Civ. Eng.*, March 1939.

166. King and Gavaris: *Report* on . . ., 1958.

167. King and Gavaris: *Report on the Stability of Fill Slopes at the . . . Warehouse.* Aug. 6, 1959.

168. King and Gavaris: *Report to . . . on Wharf Stability at . . .*, June 1961.

169. King and Gavaris: *Report to . . . on the Causes of the Cofferdam Failure at . . .*, May 1962.

170. King and Gavaris: Movement Towards Its Backfill of Pile Supported Bridge Abutment, *Res. Rep. N.J. State Dep. Trans.*, September 1970.

171. Klenner, C.: Versuche über die Verteilung des Erddruckes über die Wände ausgesteifter Baugruben, *Bautechnik*, no. 19, p. 316 (1941).

172. Koegler, F.: Baugrundprüfung im Bohrloch, *Bauingenieur*, Heft 19/20, fig. 7 (1933).

173. Koegler, F., and A. Scheidig: Druckverteilung im Baugrunde, *Bautechnik*, 1927–1929.

174. Koegler, F., and A. Scheidig: *Baugrund und Bauwerk*, Ernst, Berlin, 1938; 5th ed., 1948. 288 pp.

175. Krey, H.: *Erddruck, Erdwiderstand*, 5th ed., Ernst, Berlin, 1936, 340 pp.

175a. Krizek, J. R., R. A. Parmelee, J. N. Kay, and H. A. Elnaggar; Structural Analysis and Design of Pipe Culverts, *Nat. Coop. Res. Proj. Rep. 116*, Highway Research Board, Washington, D.C.

176. Kyle, John M.: The Use of Sand Drains under Buildings at Port Newark, *Proc. 3d Int. Conf. Soil Mech. Found. Eng., Zurich, 1953*, vol. 1, pp. 397–401.

177. Kyle, John M., and Martin S. Kapp: Sand Drain Applications by the Port of New York Authority, *ASCE Proc. Sep. no.* 456, June 1954.

178. Kyle, J. M., and Martin S. Kapp: A Flexible Bulkhead for New York Harbor, *Proc. 4th Int. Conf. Soil Mech. Found. Eng., London, 1957*, vol. 2, pp. 218–222.

179. Laboratoire Central des Ponts et Chaussées: *Essai pressiométrique normal*, Dunod, Paris, 1971, 52 pp.

180. Ladd, C. C., J. J. Rixner, and D. J. Gifford: Performance of Embankments with Sand Drains on High Sensitivity Clays, *Proc. ASCE Spec. Conf. Perf. Earth & Earth Supp. Struct., Purdue Univ., 1972.*

181. Lambe, T. William: Stress Path Method, *J. Soil Mech. Found. Div., ASCE*, SM6, November 1967, pp. 309–331.

182. Lambe, T. William, and Robert V. Whitman: *Soil Mechanics*, Wiley, New York, 1969, 551 pp.

183. Lambe, T. William, L. Anthony Wolfskill, and H. Wong: Measured Performance of Braced Excavation, *J. Soil Mech. Found. Div., ASCE*, SM3, May 1970, pp. 817–836.

184. Lambe, T. W., L. A. Wolfskill, and W. E. Jaworski: Performance of a Subway Excavation, *Proc. ASCE Spec. Conf. Perf. Earth & Earth Supp. Struct., Purdue Univ., 1972.*

185. Landau, Richard E.: Post Hole Digger Comes of Age in Sand Drain Work, *Contractors and Engineers*, April 1958, pp. 154–158.

186. Landau, Richard E.: Method of Installation as a Factor in Sand Drain Stability Design, *Highway Res. Rec.* 133, Washington, D.C., 1966, pp. 75–97.

187. Larson, M. L.: Predicted and Measured Forces on an Earth-retaining System, *Proc. Spec. Conf. Perf. Earth & Earth Supp. Struct., Purdue Univ., 1972.*

188. Laursen, Emmett M., and Arthur Toch: Scour around Bridge Piers and Abutments, *Iowa Highway Res. Board Bull.* 4, May 1956.

189. Le Fevre, E. W., and Phillip G. Manke: A Tentative Calibration Procedure for Nuclear Depth Moisture/Density Gages, *Highway Res. Rec.* 248, Washington, D.C., 1968, pp. 82–90.

190. Le Gorgeu, M. V.: La Reconstruction du quai d'accostage des ferry-boats au port de Dunkerque, *Haventechnik*, Antwerp, 1949.

191. Lehigh University: *Proceedings, Conference on Design and Installation of Pile Foundations and Cellular Structures, April 1970.*

192. Leonards, Gerald A.: *Foundation Engineering*, Engineering Properties of Soils, chap. 2, pp. 66–240, McGraw-Hill, 1962.

193. Leussink, H., and K. P. Wenz: Storage Yard Foundations on Soft Cohesive Soils, *Proc. 7th Int. Conf. Soil Mech. Found Eng., Mexico City, 1969*, vol. 2, pp. 149–155.

194. Litvinov, I. M.: *Basic Requirements for the Design and Performance of Thermic Soil Solidification* (in Russian), Gosstroyizdat Ukr. S.S.R., Kiev, 1959, 53 pp.

195. Litvinov, I. M.: A New Method for the Deep Compaction of Settling Loess Soils of Large Thickness, *Symposium on Site Investigation for Foundations, Roorkee, India, March 1967.*

196. Litvinov, I. M.: *Strengthening and Compaction in Depth of Collapsible Soils* (in Russian), Boudivilnik Publishers, Kiev, 1969, 184 pp.

197. Litvinov, I. M.: The Deep Compaction of Highly Compressible Loess (in English and German), *European Civil Engineering*, Bratislava-Praha-Wien, no. 1, pp. 1–8 (1971).

198. Lohmeyer: Discussion, *Trans. ASCE*, 1953, p. 776.

199. Loos, Wilhelm: Comparative Studies of the Effectiveness of Different Methods for Compacting Cohesionless Soils, *Proc. 1st Int. Conf. Soil Mech. Found. Eng., Cambridge, Mass., 1936,* vol. 3, pp. 174–179.

200. Lorenz, H.: New Results of Dynamic Investigations of Foundation Soils (in German), *Z. Ver. Deutsch. Ing.,* March 24, 1934.

201. Lyman, A. K. B.: Compaction of Cohesionless Foundation Soils by Explosives, *Trans. ASCE,* 1942, pp. 1330–1342.

202. McCammon, N. R., and H. Q. Golder: Some Loading Tests on Long Pipe Piles, *Geotechnique,* vol. 20, no. 2, pp. 171–184 (June, 1970), discussions in vol. 20, no. 4, pp. 459–460 (December 1970) and vol. 21, no. 2, pp. 175–180 (June 1971).

203. Machado, Jose: Estudo Comparativo de Recalques Calculados e Observados em Fundacões Diretas em Santos, *Anals do II Congresso Brazileiro de Mecanica dos Solos, 1958,* vol. 1, pp. 21–36.

204. Machado, J.: Settlements of Structures in the City of Santos, Brazil, *Proc. 5th Int. Conf. Soil Mech. Found. Eng., Paris, 1961,* vol. 1, pp. 719–725.

205. Mackenzie, Thomas R.: *Strength of Deadman Anchors in Clay,* master's thesis, Princeton University, 1955.

206. Mackey, R. D., and P. A. Mason: Pressure Distribution during Filling and Discharging a Silo, *Proc. 5th Eur. Conf. Soil Mech. Found. Eng., Madrid, 1972,* pp. 55–62.

207. Mackin, J. Hoover: A Geologic Interpretation of the Failure of the Cedar Reservoir, Washington, *Univ. Wash. Eng. Exp. Stn. Ser. Bull.* 107, March 1941.

208. Mansur, C. I., and R. I. Kaufman: Pile Tests, Low Sill Structure, Old River, La., *J. Soil Mech. Found. Div., ASCE,* SM4, October 1956, pp. 1079–1 to 1079-33.

209. Marche, René, and Yves LaCroix: Stabilité des culées de ponts établies sur des pieux traversant une couche molle, *Can. Geotech. J.,* vol. 9, no. 1 (January 1972); discussion by G. P. Tschebotarioff, vol. 9, no. 2 (May 1972).

209a. Margason, B. E., R. L. McNeill, and F. M. Babcock: Case Histories in Foundation Vibrations, *ASTM Spec. Tech. Pub. 450,* 1969, pp. 167–196.

210. Maslov, N. N.: Shear Strength of Clay under Conditions of Incomplete Consolidation (in French), *Proc. 5th Int. Conf. Soil Mech. Found. Eng., Paris, 1961,* vol. 1, pp. 243–248.

211. Maslov, N. N., and L. K. Karaulova: Problem of General Stability of Rigid Retaining Structures on Clay, *Proc. 5th Eur. Conf. Soil Mech. Found. Eng., Madrid, 1972,* pp. 173–180.

212. Mayer, Armand: Washboard Waves on Desert Roads, *Proc. Highway Res. Board,* 1947, pp. 472–479.

213. Merkin, Theodore A.: *Small-scale Model Tests of Dead-man Anchorages,* master's thesis, Princeton University, May 18, 1951.

214. Mexico 1969, *Spec. Sess.* 14 (Cast in Situ Diaphragm Walls) and 15 (Anchorages, Especially in Soft Ground), *7th Int. Conf. Soil Mech. Found. Eng., Mexico City, 1969,* 216 pp., Société de Diffusion des Techniques du Batiment et des Travaux Publics, Paris.

215. Meyerhof, George G.: Some Recent Research on the Bearing Capacity of Foundations, *Can. Geotech. J.,* vol. 1, no. 1 (September 1963).

216. Meyerhof, George G.: Shallow Foundations, *J. Soil Mech. Found. Div., ASCE,* March 1965.

217. Mohan, D., V. S. Aggarwal, and D. S. Tolia: The Correlation of Cone Size in the Dynamic Cone Penetration Test with the Standard Penetration Test, *Geotechnique,* vol. 20, no. 3, pp. 315–319 (1970), discussion in vol. 21, no. 2, pp. 184–190 (1971).

218. Montgomery, T. J.: Tunnelers Dig Past Heavy Structures, *Eng. News Rec.,* May 21, 1959.

219. Moorhouse, Douglas C., and Gerald L. Baker: Sand Densification by Heavy Vibratory Compactor, *J. Soil Mech. Found. Div., ASCE,* SM4, July 1969, pp. 985–994.

220. Moran, Proctor, Mueser, & Rutledge: Study of Deep Soil Stabilization by Vertical Sand Drains, *Bur. Yards Docks Rep. NOy-88812,* Department of the Navy, Washington, D.C., June 1958, 189 pp., 63 plates.

221. Moretrench Controls 54 Feet of Water in Fine, Running Sands, *Eng. News Rec.*, July 13, 1967.

222. Muhs, H.: Erddruckmessungen an einer 24 m. hohen starren Wand, *Bauplanung nud Bautechnik*, Berlin, vol. 1, no. 1, pp. 11–16 (July 1947).

223. Mustafayev, A. A., et al.: Pipe Filled Piles of Sea Oil Field Structures and Methods for Their Calculation for Lateral Forces, *Proc. 5th Eur. Conf. Soil Mech. Found. Eng., Madrid, 1972*, pp. 381–386.

224. National Bureau of Standards: *Corrosion of Steel Pilings in Soils, Monog.* 58, Oct. 24, 1962.

225. Navy, Department of the: Design Manual: Soil Mechanics, Foundations, and Earth Structures, NAVDOCKS DM-7.

226. New Jersey Turnpike Authority: Standard Specifications and Contract Documents for Sections 6 & 7, Contract No. 2, December 1949.

227. Newmark, Nathan M.: Influence Charts for the Computation of Stresses in Elastic Foundations, *Univ. Ill. Eng. Expt. Stn. Bull. Ser.* 338, 1942.

228. New York, City of: *Building Code*, December 1968, 413 pp.

229. Nicolet, Justin, and V. E. Gunlock: Construction of Chicago's First Subway: Structural Design and Construction of Tubes and Stations, *J. West. Soc. Eng.*, vol. 49, no. 2, pp. 111–131 (June 1944).

230. Nicu, N. D., D. R. Antes, and R. S. Kessler: Field Measurements on Instrumented Piles under an Overpass Abutment, *Highway Res. Rec.* 354, pp. 90–91, 1971.

231. Nixon, I. K.: Correspondence on $\phi = 0$ Analysis, *Geotechnique*, London, vol. 1, nos. 3 and 4, pp. 208, 272–276 (1949).

232. No Damage Occurred to Tallest Building, *Eng. News Rec.*, Aug. 15, 1957, pp. 44–46.

233. Nordlund, Reymond L., and Don U. Deere: Collapse of Fargo Grain Elevator, *J. Soil Mech. Found. Div., ASCE*, March 1970.

234. Nordlund, R. L.: Pressure Injected Footings, *Proc. Conf. Design Install. Pile Found. Cell. Struct., Lehigh Univ., 1970*, pp. 297–308.

235. Nordyke, Milo D., and Louis J. Circeo: Progress in Nuclear Excavation Technology, *Highway Res. Rec.* 107, pp. 54–65, Washington, 1966.

236. Northey, R. D.: Report on Specialty Session on Engineering Properties of Loess and Other Collapsible Soils, *Proc. 7th Int. Conf. Soil Mech. Found. Eng., Mexico, 1969*, vol. 3, pp. 445–452.

237. Ohde, J.: Zur Theorie des Erddruckes unter besonderer Berücksichtigung der Erddruckverteilung, *Bautechnik*, nos. 10/11, 13, 19, 25, 37, 42, 53/54 (1938).

238. Osterberg, J. O.: A Survey of the Frost Heaving Problem, *Civ. Eng.*, 1940, pp. 100–102.

238a. Osterberg, J. O.: New Piston Type Soil Sampler, *Eng. News. Rec.*, Apr. 24, 1952, pp. 77–78.

239. Ovesen, N. Krebs: Cellular Cofferdams: Calculation Methods and Model Tests, *Dan. Geotech. Inst. Bull.* 14, Copenhagen, 1962, 84 pp.

240. Palmer, L. A., and James B. Thompson: The Earth Pressure and Deflection along the Embedded Lengths of Piles Subjected to Lateral Thrust, *Proc. 2d Int. Conf. Soil Mech. Found Eng., Rotterdam, 1948*, vol. 5, pp. 156–161.

241. Parsons, James D.: Foundation Installation Requiring Recharging of Ground Water, *J. Constr. Div., ASCE*, September 1959.

242. Parsons, James, D., and Stanley D. Wilson: Safe Loads on Dog-leg Piles, *Trans. ASCE*, vol. 121, pp. 695-721, 1956.

243. Pawsey, S., and C. B. Brown: The Modification of the Pressures on Rigid Culverts with Fill Procedures, *Highway Res. Rec.* 249, pp. 37–43 (with Discussion by M. G. Spangler).

244. Peck, O. K., and Ralph B. Peck: Experience with Flexible Culverts through Railway Embankments, *Proc. 2d Int. Conf. Soil Mech. Found. Eng., Rotterdam, 1948*, vol. 2, pp. 95–99.

245. Peck, Ralph B.: Earth Pressure Measurements in Open Cuts, Chicago (Ill.) Subway, *Trans. ASCE*, 1943, pp. 1008–1036.

246. Peck, Ralph B.: Foundation Exploration: Denver Coliseum, *ASCE Proc. Sep. no. 326*, November 1953.

247. Peck, R. B., and F. G. Bryant: The Bearing Capacity Failure of the Transcona Elevator, *Geotechnique*, vol. 3, pp. 201–214 (1952–1953).

248. Peck, Ralph B., and Abdel Rahman S. Bazaraa: Discussion of Ref. 10, *J. Soil Mech. Found. Div.*, *ASCE*, SM3, May 1969, pp. 905–909.

249. Peck, Ralph B.: Deep Excavations and Tunneling in Soft Ground, *Proc. 7th Inst. Soil. Mech. Found. Eng.*, *Mexico City, 1969*, State of the Art Volume, pp. 225–290.

250. Petterson, K. E.: Kajraseti Goteborg des 5te Mars 1916, Tekniske Tidskrift, vol. 46, p. 289 (July 29, 1916).

251. Philbrick, Shailer S.: Design of Rock Slopes, *Highway Res. Rec.* 17, pp. 1–12, Washington, D.C. (1963).

252. Prandtl, L.: Eindringungsfestigkeit und Festigkeit von Schneiden, *Z. Angew. Math. Mech.*, vol. 1, no. 1, pp. 15–20 (1921).

253. Prentis, Edmund Astley, and Lazarus White: *Underpinning*, 2d ed., Columbia, New York, 1950.

254. Proctor, Carlton S.: The Foundations of the San Francisco–Oakland Bay Bridge, *Proc. 1st Int. Conf. Soil Mech. Found. Eng.*, *Cambridge, Mass., 1936*, vol. 3, pp. 183.

255. Proctor, Carlton S.: Bridge Foundations, *Publ. Int. Assoc. Bridge Struct. Eng.*, *Zurich*, vol. 5, pp. 261–273 (1938).

256. Proctor, Carlton S.: Cap Grouting to Stabilize Foundation on Cavernous Limestone, *Proc. 2d Int. Conf. Soil Mech. Found. Eng.*, *Rotterdam, 1948*, vol. 4, pp. 302–308.

257. Proctor, R. R.: Design and Construction of Rolled Earth Dams, *Eng. News Rec.*, Aug. 31; Sept. 7, 21, and 28, 1933; pp. 245–248, 286–289, 348–351, and 372–376.

258. Proctor, R. V., and Thomas White: *Rock Tunneling with Steel Supports*, Commercial Shearing & Stamping Co., Youngstown, Ohio, 1946 (contains five chapters by Karl Terzaghi on rock defects and loads on tunnel supports).

259. Quinn, Alonzo D.: *Design and Construction of Ports amd Marine Structures*, McGraw-Hill, New York, 1961, 531 pp.; 2d ed., 1972.

260. Rankine, W. J. M.: On the Stability of Loose Earth, *Trans. R. Soc. London*, vol. 147 (1857).

261. Rebuilding Marshall Creek Dam, *Eng. News Rec.*, 1939, pp. 23–25.

262. Record Slipformed Core Rises from a Tricky Excavation, *Eng. News. Rec.*, Dec. 3, 1970.

263. Résal, Jean: *La Poussée des terres*, Paris, 1910.

264. Reuss: *Mem. Imp. Russian Natural. Soc.*, Moscow, vol. 2, pp. 327–337 (1808).

265. Richart, Jr., F. E., J. R. Hall, Jr., and R. D. Woods: *Vibrations of Soils and Foundations*, Prentice-Hall, Englewood Cliffs, N.J., 1970, 414 pp.

266. Rimstad, I. A.: *Zur Bemessung des doppelten Spundbauwerkes*, Copenhagen, 1940, 117 pp.

267. Ritchie, Arthur M.: Evaluation of Rockfall and Its Control, *Highway Res. Rec.*, 17, 1963, pp. 13–28, Washington, D.C.

268. Rodio, M. G.: Les Affaissements de la gare transatlantique du Havre, *Centre d'etudes et de recherches géotechniques*, *Bull. 3*, Paris, 1935, 55 pp.

269. Rodio, M. G.: *Centre d'études et de recherches géotechniques*, *Bull.* Paris.

270. Romanov, D. A. (ed.): reports presented at *Seminar on Use of Pile Foundations in Industrial and Housing Construction* (in Russian), Boudivelnik Publishers, Kiev, 1970, 207 pp.

271. Rosenqvist, I. T.: *Subsoil Corrosion of Steel*, The Norwegian Academy of Technical Science, Trondheim, 1961, 93 pp.

272. Rowe, Peter W.: Anchored Sheet-pile Walls, *Proc. Inst. Civ. Eng.*, London, vol. 1, pt. 1, pp. 27–70, 616–619 (1952).

273. Rowe, Peter W.: A Theoretical and Experimental Analysis of Sheet Pile Walls, *Proc. Inst. Civ. Eng.*, January 1955, pp. 32–86.

274. Rowe, Peter W.: The Flexibility Characteristics of Sheet Pile Walls, *Struct. Eng.*, May 1955, pp. 150–158.

275. Rowe, Peter W.: Sheet Pile Walls in Clay, *Proc. Inst. Civ. Eng.*, vol. 7, pp. 629–654 (July 1957).

276. Rutgers University: *Engineering Soil Survey of New Jersey*, 22 reports, 1950–1957, joint project with New Jersey State Highway Department.

277. Rybakoff, V. I.: *Foundation Settlements of Structures* (in Russian), Moscow, 1937, 349 pp.

278. Sandick, R. A. van: Nog eens de Campanile di S. Marco te Venetie, *De Ingenieur*, The Hague, 1902.

278a. Sanglerat, G.: *The Penetrometer and Soil Exploration*, English trans. by G. Gendarme, Elsevier, Amsterdam, 1972, about 500 pp.

279. Scheer, Alfred C., and Gerald A. Willett, Jr.: Rebuilt Wolf Creek Culvert Behavior, *Highway Res. Rec.*, 262, pp. 1–13, 1969 (with discussion by M. G. Spangler).

280. Scheidig, Alfred: Das Bauwerk, *Baugrund und Bauwerk*, Berlin, 1937, nos. 5, 6, 8.

281. Schneebeli, G., and R. Cavaille-Coll: Contribution to the Stability Analysis of Double-wall Sheet Pile Cofferdams, *Proc. 4th Int. Conf. Soil Mech. Found. Eng., London, 1957*, vol. 2, pp. 233–238.

282. Schultze, E., and H. Knausenberger: Experience with Penetrometers, *Proc. 4th Int. Conf. Soil Mech. Found. Eng., London, 1957*, vol. 1, pp. 249–255.

283. Schultze, Edgar, and Heinz Muhs: *Bodenuntersuchingen für Ingenieur-Bauten*, Springer, Berlin, 1967, 722 pp.

284. Scott, Ronald F.: *Principles of Soil Mechanics*, Addison-Wesley, Reading, Mass., 1963, 550 pp.

285. Seed, H. Bolton, and Kenneth L. Lee: Liquefaction of Saturated Sand during Cyclic Loading, *J. Soil Mech. Found. Div.*, ASCE, SM6, November 1966, pp. 105–135.

286. Seed, H. Bolton and Izzat M. Idriss: Simplified Procedure for Evaluating Soil Liquefaction Potential, *J. Soil Mech. Found. Div.*, ASCE, SM9, vol. 97, pp. 1249–1292 (September 1971).

286a. Seed, H. B., R. J. Woodward, Jr., and R. Lundgren: Prediction of Swelling Potential for Compacted Clays, *J. Soil. Mech. Found. Div.*, ASCE, SM3, 1962, pp. 53–87.

286b. Selig, E. T.: Unified System for Compactor Performance Specification, 12-p. preprint of paper presented at September 1971 meeting of *Society of Automotive Engineers*, New York.

286c. Selig, Ernest T.: Subsurface Soil-Structure Interaction, A Synopsis, *Highway Res. Rec.*, in press.

287. Serota, Stanley, and Anil Jangle: A Direct Reading Pocket Shear Vane, *Civ. Eng.*, January 1972, pp. 73–74.

288. Steel Sheet Piling Cellular Cofferdams on Rock, *Tenn. Val. Auth. Tech. Monogr.* 75, vol. 1, Knoxville, Tenn., 1957.

289. Sherif, Mehmet A.: Flow and Fracture Properties of Seattle Clays, *Univ. Wash. Soil Eng. Rep.* 1, January 1965.

290. Sherif, Mehmet A.: Deformation and Flow Properties of Clay Soils from the Viewpoint of Modern Material Science, *Highway Res. Rec.* 119, Washington, D.C., 1966, pp. 24–49.

291. Sherif, Mehmet A.: Physical Properties of Seattle Freeway Soils, *Univ. Wash. Soil Mech. Res. Ser.* 2, September 1966.

291a. Sherif, Mehmet A., and Ming-Jiun-Wu: Summary and Practical Implications of University of Washington Soil Engineering Research (1965–1970), *Univ. Wash. Soil Eng. Res. Rep.* 7, Seattle, 1970.

292. Sherif, Mehmet A., and David E. Koch: Coefficient of Earth Pressure at Rest as Related to Soil Precompression Ratio and Liquid Limit, *Highway Res. Rec.* 323, Washington, D.C., 1970, pp. 39–48.

293. Sherman, Jr., W. C., and C. C. Trahan: Analysis of Data from Instrumentation Program, Port Allen Lock, *U.S. Waterw. Exp. Stn., Vicksburg, Miss., Tech. Rep.*, S-68-7.

294. Silver, Marshall L., and H. Bolton Seed: Volume Changes in Sand during Cyclic Loading, *J. Soil Mech. Found. Div.*, ASCE, SM9, vol. 97, pp. 1171–1182 (September 1971).

295. Singer, Max: *Der Baugrund*, Springer, Berlin, 1932, 393 pp.
296. Singstad, Ole: The Queens Midtown Tunnel, *Trans. ASCE*, 1944, pp. 679–762.
297. Skempton, A. W.: Discussion of Paper on Tunnel Linings, *J. Inst. Civ. Eng.*, vol. 20, p. 53 (1943).
298. Skempton, A. W.: Earth Pressure and the Stability of Slopes, *The Principles and Applications of Soil Mechanics, Institute of Civil Engineers*, 1946, pp. 31–611.
299. Skempton, A. W.: The Rate of Softening in Stiff Fissured Clays, with Special Reference to London Clay, *Proc. 2d Int. Conf. Soil Mech. Found. Eng., Rotterdam, 1948*, vol. 2, pp. 50–53.
300. Skempton, A. W.: Vane Tests in the Alluvial Plane of the River Forth near Grangemouth, *Geotechnique*, vol. 1, no. 2, pp. 111–124 (1948).
301. Skempton, A. W.: Long Term Stability of Clay Slopes, *Geotechnique*, vol. 14, pp. 77–102 (1964).
302. Skempton, A. W., and W. H. Ward: Investigations Concerning a Deep Cofferdam in the Thames Estuary Clay at Shellhaven, *Geotechnique*, September 1952, pp. 119–139.
303. Skempton, A. W., and J. Hutchinson: Stability of Natural Slopes and Embankment Foundations, *Proc. 7th Int. Conf. Soil Mech. Eng., Mexico City, 1969*, State of the Art Volume, pp. 291–340.
304. Smith, E. A. L.: Pile Driving Analysis by the Wave Equation, *Trans. ASCE*, vol. 127, pt. I, pp. 1145–1193 (1962).
305. Soil Conservation Service (U.S. Department of Agriculture): *Eng. Mem. 27* (Rev.) *Suppl. 6 Re: Earth Dams*, June 4, 1971.
306. *Soil Mechanics and Foundation Engineering*, a cover-to-cover translation from the Russian of the Moscow journal *Osnovaniya, Fundamenty i Mekhanika Gruntov*; six issues per year, listed each year as SM1 through SM6, Plenum Publishing Corporation, New York.
307. SoilTest, Inc.: *Catalogues*, Evanston, Illinois.
308. Sowada, Gerhard: Der Ruhedruckbeiwert, *Bergbautechnik*, no. 12, pp. 625–629 (December 1968).
309. Sowada, Gerhard: Zur Frage der Scherhaftfestigkeit bei Ruhedruckundersuchungen, *Wasserwirts. Wassertech.*, 1969, no. 5, pp. 174–176.
310. Sowers, George F.: Fill Settlement Despite Vertical Sand Drains, *J. Soil Mech. Found. Eng. Div., ASCE*, pt. 1, vol. 90, SM5 (September 1964).
311. Sowers, George B., and George F. Sowers: Failures of Bulkhead and Excavation Bracing, *Civ. Eng.*, January 1967.
312. Spangler, M. G.: Lateral Pressures on Retaining Walls Caused by Superimposed Loads, *Proc. Highway Res. Board*, vol. 18, pt. 2, pp. 57–65 (1938).
313. Spangler, M. G.: Underground Conduits: An Appraisal of Modern Research, *Trans. ASCE*, 1948, 316–374.
314. Spangler, M. G.: A Theory on Loads on Negative Projecting Conduits, *Proc. Highway Res. Board*, vol. 30, pp. 153–161 (1950).
315. Spangler, M. G.: *Soil Engineering*, 2d ed., International Textbook Company, Scranton, Pa., 1953.
316. Spangler, M. G.: A Practical Application of the Imperfect Ditch Method of Construction, *Proc. Highway Res. Board*, vol. 37, pp. 271–277 (1958).
317. Spangler, M. G.: The Case against the Ultimate Load Test for Reinforced Concrete Pipe, *Highway Res. Rec. 176*, 1967, pp. 35–42.
318. Special Committee on Earths and Foundations, Lazarus White, chairman: Report, *Proc. ASCE*, May 1933.
319. Spencer, Charles B.: Drilled in Caissons with Heavy H-Cores Carry 16-story Navy Warehouse, *Eng. News. Rec.*, September 25, 1941.
320. Spencer, Charles B.: Steel Braces Hold High Clay Bank in Albany, *Eng. News Rec.*, Mar. 2, 1950.

321. Spilker, A.: Mitteilung über die Messung der Kräfte in einer Baugrubenaussteifung, *Bautechnik*, 1937, no. 1, p. 16.

322. Stermac, A. G., M. Derata, and K. G. Selby: Unusual Movements of Bridge Abutments Supported on Endbearing Piles, *Can. Geotech. J.*, vol. 5, no. 2, pp. 69–79 (May 1968); discussions in vol. 5, pp. 253–255 (November 1968); vol. 6, pp. 215–219; 366–367 (1969).

323. Steuermann, M.: Wärmegänge der Kühlhausgründungen, *Bautechnik*, Aug. 28, 1936, pp. 547–548.

324. Stokes, W. Lee, and David J. Varnes: *Glossary of Selected Geologic Terms with Special Reference to Their Use in Engineering*, Colorado Scientific Society, Denver Public Library, Denver, Colorado.

325. Streck, Alfred: 23 Jahre Baugrundforschung, *Hannoverschen Versuchsanstalt für Grundbau und Wasserbau*, Technische Hochschule Hannover, 1950.

326. Stross, Walter: Weiderherstellung der Mohamed Aly Moschee in Cairo, *Beton und Eisen*, no. 22 (Nov. 20, 1936).

327. Swatek, E. P., Sherwin P. Asrow, and Arthur M. Seitz, Performance of Bracing for Deep Chicago Excavation, *Proc. ASCE Spec. Conf. Perf. Earth & Earth Supp. Struct., Purdue Univ., 1972*, vol. 1, pt. 2, pp. 1303–1322.

328. Swiss, John F.: Effects of Blasting Vibrations on Buildings and People, *Civ. Eng.*, July 1968, pp. 46–48.

329. Talbot, W. J. Jr. (Chief Engineer Santa Fe–Pomeroy, Inc., San Francisco): personal communication, 1971.

330. Taylor, Donald W.: Stability of Earth Slopes, *Contrib. Soil Mech., Boston Soc., Civ. Eng.*, 1940, pp. 337–386 (also *J. Boston Soc. Civ. Engr.*, July 1937).

331. Taylor, Donald W.: Abstracts of Selected Theses on Soil Mechanics, *MIT Dept. Civ. Eng., Publ. Ser. 79*, June 1941.

332. Taylor, Donald W.: *Fundamentals of Soil Mechanics*, Wiley, New York, 1948, 700 pp.

333. Tchekotillo, A.: Solving the Problem of "Nalyeds" in Permafrost Regions, *Eng. News Rec.*, Nov. 28, 1946.

334. Teng, Wayne C.: *Foundation Design*, Prentice-Hall, Englewood Cliffs, N.J., 1962, 466 pp.

335. Terzaghi, Karl: Large Retaining Wall Tests, *Eng. News. Rec.*, 1934, pp. 136, 259, 316, 403, 503.

336. Terzaghi, Karl: Stability of Slopes of Natural Clay, *Proc. 1st Int. Conf. Soil Mech. Found. Eng., Cambridge, Mass., 1936*, vol. 1, pp. 161–165.

337. Terzaghi, Karl: Settlement of Structures in Europe and Methods of Observation, *Trans. ASCE*, 1938, pp. 1432–1502.

338. Terzaghi, Karl: General Wedge Theory of Earth Pressure, *Trans. ASCE*, 1941, pp. 68–97.

339. Terzaghi, Karl: Shield Tunnels of the Chicago Subway, *J. Boston Soc. Civ. Engr.*, July 1942 (Also *Contrib. Soil Mech.*, 1941–1953.)

340. Terzaghi, Karl: Liner-plate Tunnels on the Chicago (Ill.) Subway, *Trans. ASCE*, 1943, pp. 970–1008, 1090–1097.

341. Terzaghi, Karl: *Theoretical Soil Mechanics*, Wiley, New York, 1943, 510 pp.

342. Terzaghi, Karl: Stability and Stiffness of Cellular Cofferdams—with Discussions, *Trans. ASCE*, 1945, pp. 1083–1202.

343. Terzaghi, Karl: Evaluation of Coefficients of Subgrade Reaction, *Geotechnique*, vol. 5, pp. 297–326 (December 1955).

344. Terzaghi, Karl, and Ralph B. Peck: *Soil Mechanics in Engineering Practice*, 2d ed., Wiley, New York, 1967 (1st ed., 1948).

345. Timmers, John H.: Load Study of Flexible Pipes under High Fills, *Highway Res. Rec.* 125, 1956, pp. 1–11 (with Discussion by M. G. Spangler).

346. Timoshenko, S.: *Theory of Elasticity*, McGraw-Hill, New York, 1934, 416 pp.

347. Todor, P. C., and William Gartner, Jr.: Evaluation of Direct Transmission-type Nuclear Density Gage for Measuring In-place Densities of Soils, *Highway Res. Rec. 107*, 1966, pp. 13–24.

348. Tomlinson, M. J.: The Adhesion of Piles Driven in Clay Soils, *Proc. 4th Int. Conf. Soil Mech. Found. Eng.*, *London, 1957*, vol. 2, pp. 66–71.

349. *Trenton Evening Times*, photograph, July 10, 1952.

350. Tschebotarioff, Gregory P.: Comparison between Consolidation, Elastic and Other Soil Properties Established from Laboratory Tests and from Observations of Structures in Egypt, *Proc. 1st Int. Conf. Soil Mech. Found Eng.*, *Cambridge, Mass., 1936*, vol. 1, pp. 33–36.

351. Tschebotarioff, Gregory P.: Relation between Observed Inequalities of Settlement of Buildings in Egypt and Theoretical Stress Distribution, Based on Boussinesq Formulas, *Proc. 1st Int. Conf. Soil Mech. Found. Eng.*, *Cambridge, Mass., 1936*, vol. 1, pp. 57–61.

352. Tschebotarioff, Gregory P.: Settlement Studies of Structures in Egypt, *Trans. ASCE*, 1940, pp. 919–972.

353. Tschebotarioff, Gregory P.: Discussion, *Proc. 2nd Int. Conf. Soil Mech. Found. Eng.*, *Rotterdam*, vol. 6, pp. 108–111, 1948.

354. Tschebotarioff, Gregory P.: Determination from Bending Strain Measurements of the Distribution of Lateral Earth Pressures against Model Flexible Bulkheads, *Geotechnique*, vol. 1, no. 2, pp. 98–111 (1948).

355. Tschebotarioff, Gregory P.: Large Scale Model Earth Pressure Tests on Flexible Bulkheads, *Proc. ASCE*, January 1948, pp. 9–48; also *Trans. ASCE*, 1949, pp. 415–455, 524–539.

356. Tschebotarioff, Gregory P.: Large Scale Earth Pressure Tests with Model Flexible Bulkheads, *Princeton Univ. Final Rept. Bur. Yards Docks, U.S. Navy*, January 1949, 272 pp.

357. Tschebotarioff, Gregory P.: Einfluss der "Gewölbebildung" auf die Erdruckverteilung (Influence of "arching" on earth pressure distribution), *Bautechnik-Archiv*, Heft 8, Berlin, 1952.

358. Tschebotarioff, Gregory P.: The Resistance to Lateral Loading of Single Piles and of Pile Groups, *ASTM Spec. Tech. Publ.* 154, 1953.

359. Tschebotarioff, Gregory P.: Performance Records of Engine Foundations, *ASTM Spec. Tech. Publ. 156*, 1953.

360. Tschebotarioff, Gregory P.: A Case of Structural Damages Sustained by One-storey Houses Founded on Swelling Clays, *Proc. 3d Int. Conf. Soil Mech. Found. Eng.*, *Zurich, 1953*, vol. 1, pp. 473–476.

361. Tschebotarioff, Gregory P.: Discussion of Ref. 89, *Trans. ASCE*, 1953, pp. 1157–1163.

362. Tschebotarioff, Gregory P.: Discussion of Terzaghi's paper "Anchored Bulkheads," *Trans. ASCE*, 1954, pp. 1287–1296.

363. Tschebotarioff, Gregory P.: Discussion of General Report on Earth Pressures, *Proc. 4th Int. Conf. Soil Mech. Found. Eng. & F.E.*, *London, 1957*, vol. 3, pp. 239–241.

364. Tschebotarioff, Gregory P.: Discussions, *Proc. Bruss. Conf. 58 Earth Press. Probl., 1958*, vol. 3, (a) pp. 229–233, (b) pp. 243–244, (c) pp. 264–268.

365. Tschebotarioff, Gregory P.: How Russians Drive Piles by Vibration, *Eng. News Rec.*, July 16, 1959.

366. Tschebotarioff, Gregory P.: Neuere Beobachtungen an Spundwand Uferbauten, *Int. Baugrundkursus, Aachen, 1961*, pp. 215–234.

367. Tschebotarioff, Gregory P.: Retaining Structures, chap. 5 in G. A. Leonards (ed.), *Foundation Engineering*, McGraw-Hill, New York, 1962.

368. Tschebotarioff, Gregory P.: Vibration Controlled by Chemical Grouting, *Civ. Eng.*, May 1964.

369. Tschebotarioff, Gregory P.: Design and Construction of Flexible Retaining Structures, *Lecture Series: Design of Structures to Resist Earth Pressures*, pp. 35–48, Chicago, 1964 (sponsored by Illinois Section ASCE and Civil Engineering Department Illinois Institute of Technology).

370. Tschebotarioff, Gregory P.: Training the Student to Face Engineering Problems, letter, *Civ. Eng.*, April 1965.

371. Tschebotarioff, Gregory P.: Analysis of a High Crib Wall Failure, *Proc. 6th Inst. Conf. Soil Mech. Found. Eng., Montreal, 1965*, vol. 2, pp. 414–416.

372. Tschebotarioff, Gregory P.: What Should the Goals of Engineering Education Be?, discussion at ASCE Conference, Denver, May 1966, *Civ. Eng.*, July 1966, pp. 48–49.

373. Tschebotarioff, Gregory P.: General Report, Div. 4, *Proc. 3d Pan-Am Conf. Soil Mech. Found. Eng., Caracas, 1967*, vol. 3, pp. 301–322.

374. Tschebotarioff, Gregory P.: Friction Piles and Prediction of Length and Bearing Capacity, *16th Ann. Conf. Soil Mech. Found. Eng., Univ. Minn.*, Apr. 11, 1968.

375. Tschebotarioff, Gregory P.: Bridge Abutments on Piles Driven through Plastic Clay, *Proc. Conf. Des. Install. Pile Found. Cell. Struct., Lehigh Univ.*, 1970.

376. Tschebotarioff, Gregory P.: Discussion of Ref. 230, *Highway Res. Rec. 354*, 1971, pp. 99–101.

377. Tschebotarioff, Gregory P., and George W. McAlpin: The Effect of Vibratory and Slow Repetitional Forces on the Bearing Properties of Soils, *CAA Tech. Dev. Rep.* 57, October 1947, 70 pp.

378. Tschebotarioff, Gregory P., and John R. Bayliss: The Determination of the Shearing Strength of Varved Clays and of Their Sensitivity to Remolding, *Proc. 2d Int. Conf. Soil Mech. Found. Eng., Rotterdam, 1948*, vol. 1, pp. 203–207.

379. Tschebotarioff, Gregory P., and Philip P. Brown: Lateral Earth Pressure as a Problem of Deformation or of Rupture, *Proc. 2d Int. Conf. Soil Mech. Found. Eng., Rotterdam, 1948*, vol. 2, pp. 81–86.

380. Tschebotarioff, Gregory P., and James R. Schuyler: Comparison of the Extent of Disturbance Produced by Driving Piles into Plastic Clay to the Disturbance Caused by an Unbalanced Excavation. *Proc. 2d Int. Conf. Soil Mech. Found. Eng., Rotterdam, 1948*, vol. 2, pp. 199–205.

381. Tschebotarioff, Gregory P., and Edward R. Ward: The Resonance of Machine Foundations and the Soil Coefficients Which Affect It, *Proc. 2d Int. Conf. Soil Mech. Found. Eng., Rotterdam, 1948*, vol. 1, pp. 309–313.

382. Tschebotarioff, Gregory P., and John D. Welch: Effect of Boundary Conditions on Lateral Earth Pressures, *Proc. 2d Int. Conf. Soil Mech. Found. Eng., Rotterdam, 1948*, vol. 3, pp. 308–313.

383. Tschebotarioff, Gregory P., and Edward R. Ward: Measurements with Wiegmann Inclinometer on Five Sheet Pile Bulkheads, *Proc. 4th Int. Conf. Soil Mech. Found. Eng., London, 1957*, vol. 2, pp. 248–255.

384. Tschebotarioff, Gregory P., Edward R. Ward, Elmo DiBiagio, and Jack Watkins: The Performance Check and the First Field Measurements with the Wiegmann Inclinometer, *Princeton Univ. Prog. Rep. Off. Nav. Res. Wash., D.C.*, Apr. 15, 1955, 55 pp.

385. Tschebotarioff, Gregory P., Edward R. Ward, Elmo DiBiagio, Jack Watkins, and David Perrine: Field Measurements with the Wiegmann Inclinometer in the harbors of Galveston, Philadelphia, Baltimore and Cleveland, *Princeton Univ. Rep. Off. Nav. Res. Wash., D.C.*, Aug. 1, 1956, 129 pp.

386. Tsytovich, N. A.: Bases and Foundations on Frozen Soil (trans. from Russian), *Highway Res. Board Spec. Rep.* 58, 1960, 93 pp.

387. Turnbull, W. J.: Utility of Loess as a Construction Material, *Proc. 2d Int. Conf. Soil Mech. Found. Eng., Rotterdam, 1948*, vol. 5, pp. 97–103.

388. U.S. Army Coastal Engineering Research Center: Shore Protection, Planning and Design, *Tech. Rep. 4*, 3d ed., 1966, 550 pp. (Superintendent of Documents, Washington, D.C., 204–2).

389. U.S. Steel Corporation: Steel H-Piles, *Catalogue* (n.d.), p. 38; Typical Driving and Test Data, 12 in. Steel H pile as Friction Pile, February 1959.

390. Vassilieff, B. D.: *Osnovanya i Fundamenti* (in Russian), Moscow, 1937, 582 pp.

391. Verdeyen, J., V. Roisin, and J. Nuyens, *La Mécanique des sols*, Dunod, Paris, 1968, 508 pp.

392. Vesic, Aleksandar S.: Load Transfer in Pile-soil Systems, *Proc. Conf. Des. Install. Pile Found. Cell. Struct., Lehigh Univ., 1970*, pp. 47–74.

393. Walker, F. C.: *Development of Earth Dam Design in the Bureau of Reclamation*, Commissioner's Office, Denver, Colorado, August 1958.

394. Walker, F. C., and W. G. Holtz: *Comparison between Laboratory Test Results and Behavior of Completed Embankments and Foundations*, paper presented at ASCE meeting, Los Angeles, May 1950.

395. Ward, William H.: The Effect of Vegetation on the Settlement of Structures, excerpt from *Proc. Conf. Biol. Civ. Eng.*, Institution of Civil Engineers, London, 1948.

396. Ward, William H., and E. C. Sewell: Protection of the Ground from Thermal Effects of Industrial Plant, *Geotechnique*, vol. 2, no. 1, pp. 64–81 (June 1950).

397. Water Removes Water from Deep Cut-and-cover Tunnel, *Eng. News Rec.*, Oct. 1, 1959.

398. Watkins, Jack: *Large Scale Triaxial Tests of the Cell Type on Clay*, master's thesis, Princeton University, 1955.

399. Weidlinger, Paul: personal communication, 1970.

400. White, Lazarus: *Report . . . on the Collapse of . . . Silos* (unpublished), 1940.

401. White, Lazarus, and Edmund Astley Prentis: *Cofferdams*, Columbia, New York, 2d ed., 1950.

402. Wild, Philip A.: *Design, Calibration and Use of a Medium-scale Earth Pressure Testing Machine for Evaluating the Effects of Restraining Boundaries*, master's thesis, Princeton University, 1952.

403. Wilson, Guthlac: The Calculation of the Bearing Capacity of Footings on Clay, *J. Inst. Civ. Engr.*, vol. 17, pp. 87–96 (1941).

404. Winkler, E.: *Neuere Theorie des Erddruckes*, Vienna, 1872.

405. Winterkorn, H. F.: Affinity of Hydrophilic Aggregate for Asphaltic Bitumen, *Ind. Eng. Chem.*, vol. 30, pp. 1362–1368 (1938).

406. Winterkorn, H. F.: The Condition of Water in Porous Systems, *Soil Sci.*, August 1943, pp. 109–115.

407. Winterkorn, Hans F.: Fundamental Similarities between Electro-osmotic and Thermo-osmotic Phenomena, *Proc. Highway Res. Board*, 1947, pp. 443–455.

408. Winterkorn, H. F.; and L. D. Baver: Sorption of Liquids by Soil Colloids, *Soil Sci.*, vol. 38, pp. 291–298 (1934); vol. 40, pp. 403–419 (1935).

409. Woods, Richard D.: Screening of Surface Waves in Soils, *J. Soil Mech. Found. Div.*, ASCE, SM4, vol. 94 (July 1968).

410. Wooltorton, D.: A Preliminary Investigation into the Subject of Foundations in the "Black Cotton" and "Kyatti" Soils of the Mandalay District, Burma, *Proc. 1st Int. Conf. Soil Mech. Found. Eng., Cambridge, Mass., 1936*, vol. 3, pp. 242–256.

411. Wright, Roy E.: Chemical Stabilization of Sand Speeds Driving of 10-ft. Tunnel, *Eng. News Rec.*, Aug. 4, 1949.

412. York, Donald L.: *Investigation of Lateral Earth Pressures at Rest*, master's thesis, Princeton University, 1957.

413. Zeevaert, Leonardo: Compensated Pile Foundation to Reduce the Settlements of a Building on the Highly Compressible Clay of Mexico City, *Proc. 4th Int. Conf. Soil Mech. Found. Eng., London, 1957*, vol. 2, pp. 81–86.

414. Zienkiewicz, O. C., and Y. K. Cheung: *The Finite Element Method in Structural and Continuum Mechanics*, McGraw-Hill, New York, 1967, 274 pp.

415. Zola, S. P., and P. M. Boothe: Design and Construction of Navy's Largest Drydock, *J. Waterw. Harbors Div.*, ASCE, March 1960, pp. 53–84.

416. Zurich, Organizing Committee of the 3rd International Conference on Soil Mechanics and Foundation Engineering: *Bull. 3*, August 1953.

NAME INDEX

SUBJECT INDEX

A

Aalborg pier, 517
Abutments of bridges (*see* Retaining walls, gravity)
Acker Drill Co., Inc., 24, 47, 48
Adobe, 63
Adsorbed moisture films, 57, 60, 61, 98
Air content, definition of, 67
Air-photo soil surveys, 20, 22
Airfield soil-classification system (*see* Unified system)
Alaska, 177
Albany clay, 79, 91, 301, 437
Allamuchy research project, 14, 247, 401–406
American Association of State Highway Officials (AASHO), 116, 117, 204, 212
   compaction test of, 204, 205
American Heritage Dictionary, xiii
American Institute of Steel Construction, 221
American National Standards for letter symbols, xvii
American Society of Civil Engineers (ASCE), xvii, 17, 245, 414, 428, 433, 457

American Society of Mechanical Engineers (ASME), xxvii
American Society for Testing Materials (ASTM), xxv, 62, 72, 74, 83, 113, 117, 126, 204, 212, 448
Anchorages:
   retaining structures of, 448–452, 536–542
   transmission towers of, 186
Angle:
   of friction, 97
   of obliquity, 97
   of repose, 99
Antiseepage collars, 338, 346, 347
Aqueduct, Croton, 21
Arching in soils, 395, 417, 418, 527, 528, 529, 530, 559, 560
Art in engineering, xiv
Atterberg limits, 72
Auger, screw-type, 24

B

Bar (*see* Metric units)
Barco rammer, 211
Base exchange, 60, 61